1006177057

The Business School for the World®

COMMITTED TO
IMPROVING THE STATE
OF THE WORLD

The Global Information Technology Report 2007–2008

Fostering Innovation through Networked Readiness

Soumitra Dutta, INSEAD
Irene Mia, World Economic Forum
Editors

The Global Information Technology Report 2007–2008 is a special project within the framework of the Global Competitiveness Network. *The Global Information Technology Report* is the result of a collaboration between the World Economic Forum and INSEAD.

Professor Klaus Schwab,
Executive Chairman, World Economic Forum

EDITORS

Soumitra Dutta, Roland Berger Professor of Business and Technology and Dean of External Relations, INSEAD

Irene Mia, Senior Economist, World Economic Forum

GLOBAL COMPETITIVENESS NETWORK

Fiona Paua, Head of Strategic Insight Teams

Jennifer Blanke, Senior Economist
Ciara Browne, Senior Community Manager
Agustina Ciocia, Coordinator
Margareta Drzeniek Hanouz, Senior Economist
Thierry Geiger, Economist
Pearl Samandari, Research Assistant
Eva Trujillo Herrera, Research Assistant

INFORMATION TECHNOLOGY AND TELECOMMUNICATIONS INDUSTRIES TEAM

Alex Wong, Head of Centre for Global Industries (Geneva)

Michelle Barrett, Coordinator
Sandra Bétemps, Senior Coordinator
Joanna Gordon, Global Leadership Fellow
Silvia von Gunten, Head of Telecommunications Industry
William Hoffman, Senior Community Manager
Simon Mulcahy, Head of Information Technology Industries
Ana Sepulveda, Global Leadership Fellow

A special thank you to Hope Steele for her superb editing work and Ha Nguyen for her excellent graphic design and layout.

The terms *country* and *nation* as used in this report do not in all cases refer to a territorial entity that is a state as understood by international law and practice. The terms cover well-defined, geographically self-contained economic areas that may not be states but for which statistical data are maintained on a separate and independent basis.

Copyright © 2008
by the World Economic Forum and INSEAD

All rights reserved. No reproduction, copy or transmission of this publication may be made without written permission.

No paragraph of this publication may be reproduced, copied or transmitted save with written permission or in accordance with the provisions of the Copyright, Designs and Patents Act 1988, or under the terms of any licence permitting limited copying issued by the Copyright Licensing Agency, 90 Tottenham Court Road, London W1T 4LP.

Any person who does any unauthorized act in relation to this publication may be liable to criminal prosecution and civil claims for damages.

The authors have asserted their rights to be identified as the authors of this work in accordance with the Copyright, Designs and Patents Act 1988.

First published 2008 by
PALGRAVE MACMILLAN
Houndmills, Basingstoke, Hampshire RG21 6XS and
175 Fifth Avenue, New York, N. Y. 10010
Companies and representatives throughout the world

PALGRAVE MACMILLAN is the global academic imprint of the Palgrave Macmillan division of St. Martin's Press, LLC and of Palgrave Macmillan Ltd. Macmillan® is a registered trademark in the United States, United Kingdom and other countries. Palgrave is a registered trademark in the European Union and other countries.

ISBN-13: 978-1-4039-9932-0
ISBN-10: 1-4039-9932-5

This book is printed on paper suitable for recycling and made from fully managed and sustained forest sources.

A catalogue record for this book is available from the British Library.
A catalog record for this book is available from the Library of Congress.

10 9 8 7 6 5 4 3 2 1
17 16 15 14 13 12 11 10 09 08

Printed and bound in Switzerland by
SRO-Kundig, Geneva

Contents

Preface v
Klaus Schwab (World Economic Forum)

Foreword vii
John Chambers (Cisco Systems, Inc.)

Executive Summary ix
Soumitra Dutta (INSEAD) and Irene Mia
(World Economic Forum)

The Networked Readiness Index Rankings xix

Part 1: Selected Issues of Networked Readiness 1

1.1 **Assessing the State of the World's Networked Readiness: Insight from the Networked Readiness Index 2007–2008** 3
Irene Mia (World Economic Forum) and Soumitra Dutta (INSEAD)

1.2 **The Emerging Nexus: Now Is the Time to Plot a Balanced Course that Delivers on the Promise of ICT** 23
Ewan Morrison, Robert Pepper, and Enrique J. Rueda-Sabater (Cisco Systems, Inc)

1.3 **The Missing Link: Why Does ICT Matter for Innovation? Exploring the Effect of Information and Communication Technologies on Innovation-Based Competitiveness** 39
Carlos A. Osorio-Urzúa (Adolfo Ibáñez School of Management; Berkman Center for Internet & Society at Harvard Law School)

1.4 **Innovation at the Speed of Life** 57
Matt Bross (BT Group)

1.5 **Unified Communications: Leading Advances in Global Decision Making and Economic Development** 67
Sandor Boyson (Robert H. Smith School of Business, University of Maryland, College Park) and David Boyer (Avaya)

1.6 **Building E-skills for the Information Age** 77
Bruno Lanvin (INSEAD, eLab) and Pamela S. Passman (Microsoft Corporation)

1.7 **Rethinking Regulation in Emerging Telecommunications Markets** 91
Scott C. Beardsley, Ilke Bigan, Luis Enriquez, Mehmet Guvendi, Can Kendi, Miguel Lucas, Oleg Timchenko, Sergio Sandoval, Ashish Sharma (McKinsey & Company, Inc.)

1.8 **Business Network Transformation: Rethinking Relationships in a Global Economy** 101
Henning Kagermann (SAP AG), Philip Lay, and Geoffrey Moore (TCG Advisors)

1.9 **The Participative Web: Innovation and Collaboration** 109
Sacha Wunsch-Vincent and Graham Vickery (OECD)

Part 2: Leveraging ICT and Innovation for Competitiveness: Selected Case Studies 119

2.1 **Singapore: Building an Intelligent Nation with ICT** 121
Ng Cher Keng, Ong Ling Lee, Tanya Tang (Infocomm Development Authority, Singapore) and Soumitra Dutta (INSEAD)

2.2 **Qatar: Leveraging Technology to Create a Knowledge-Based Economy in the Middle East** 133
Hessa Al-Jaber (ictQATAR) and Soumitra Dutta (INSEAD)

2.3 **Small- and Medium-Sized Enterprises Hold the Key to European Competitiveness: How to Help Them Innovate through ICT and E-business** 145
Dana Eleftheriadou (European Commission)

Part 3: Country/Economy Profiles 157

Country/Economy Profiles
How to Read the Country/Economy Profiles 159
List of Countries/Economies 161
Country/Economy Profiles 162

(Cont'd)

Part 4: Data Tables 289

Data Tables
How to Read the Data Tables 291
List of Data Tables 293
Data Tables 295

Technical Notes and Sources 375

About the Authors 379

List of Partner Institutes 385

Acknowledgment 391

Preface

KLAUS SCHWAB
Executive Chairman, World Economic Forum

Information and communication technologies (ICT) has played a central role in fostering innovation and development of societies and economies. Not only has ICT increased productivity significantly in a variety of ways and therefore driven sustainable growth, but it has also provided people all over the world with better opportunities to improve their life conditions and their businesses. The Internet has brought about a revolution in businesses, education provision, and ways of interacting on a global scale, by offering each one of us, in the developed and developing world, unprecedented access to information and knowledge. In addition, especially through the Web 2.0 technologies, it has made the world smaller, facilitating the development of virtual communities and social networks, and nurturing information and experience sharing among individuals separated by geography.

The advances enabled by telecommunications are just as impressive, with mobile telephony providing small businesses and farmers in remote communities with access to new markets and real-time information on commodities prices, or creating new forms of entrepreneurship among the poor, as in case of the Grameen phones in Bangladesh. Further, mobile telephony has radically changed communication patterns among individuals more generally, be they busy executives conducting business over the BlackBerry on their way to the airport, or teenagers exchanging SMS messages.

The extraordinary power of ICT to enable growth, reduce poverty, and improve citizens' lives has become increasingly clear to policymakers and civil society alike, and ICT promotion has gradually found a more privileged place in national competitiveness strategies and policy agendas. The example of countries such as Singapore, Estonia, and Israel has shown how ICT can be the enabler of a competitive transformation of the economy, allowing countries to leapfrog to more advanced stages of development as well as production and export structures.

At the World Economic Forum, we have long understood the importance of innovation and ICT for national competitiveness and have contributed, over the years, to raising public awareness on the subject through our research and activities, especially with the *Global Information Technology Report* (GITR) series, in partnership with INSEAD. The GITR series, published annually since 2001, lays out a broad framework—the Networked Readiness Index (NRI)—identifying the enabling factors for countries to leverage ICT developments, with a particular focus on the role of the three main social actors: individuals, businesses, and governments. The NRI provides a unique benchmarking instrument for economies to monitor their progress over time and vis-à-vis relevant comparators, and has turned into an authoritative platform for policymakers, business leaders, and other relevant stakeholders to discuss and elaborate national roadmaps toward increased networked readiness and competitiveness.

The Global Information Technology Report 2007–2008, the seventh in the series, includes the latest findings of our research, providing once again a comprehensive networked readiness snapshot of the world. In line with our continuing effort to expand the coverage of the *Report,* a record number of 127 economies has been assessed this year, accounting for more than 95 percent of the world's GDP. Also featured in the *Report* is an extensive section of data tables with global rankings covering nearly 70 indicators, together with a number of essays and case studies on notable trends and issues in networked readiness, and on national ICT development stories of particular interest.

We would like to express our gratitude to the eminent academics and practitioners who contributed insightful papers to this *Report,* casting light on important ICT developments and showcasing best practices and policies in ICT diffusion. We especially wish to thank the editors of the *Report,* Soumitra Dutta at INSEAD and Irene Mia at the World Economic Forum, for their energy and long-lasting dedication to the project. Appreciation also goes to Fiona Paua, who heads the Strategic Insights Teams, and the other members of the Global Competitiveness Network: Jennifer Blanke, Ciara Browne, Agustina Ciocia, Margareta Drzeniek Hanouz, Thierry Geiger, Pearl Samandari, and Eva Trujillo Herrera. Last but not least, we would like to commend our network of 142 Partner Institutes worldwide, without whose enthusiasm and hard work the annual administration of the Executive Opinion Survey and this *Report* would not be possible.

Foreword

JOHN CHAMBERS
Chairman and CEO, Cisco Systems, Inc.

The 2008 Annual Meeting of the World Economic Forum was focused on *The Power of Collaborative Innovation,* which crisply sums up what has been our focus for some time. I believe that our ability to successfully harness technical and human networks to help us collaborate—across geographical regions, cultures, and job roles—will unleash a new wave of social inclusion, productivity, and economic growth, the impact of which will rival or even dwarf what we experienced in the first phase of the Internet. It is no longer about one-to-one interactions, but rather about many-to-many. Societies and economies are rapidly changing; and the power of "us" has become far more important than the power of "you." If technology has the ability to help an individual doctor treat cancer more effectively, imagine the impact thousands of doctors collaborating globally could make on curing it.

I believe this second great phase of the Internet will be focused on empowering collaboration—groups of individuals working together toward a common goal. First developed and embraced by consumers, as they harnessed the Internet for innovative new activities such as social networking, this wave of collaborative technologies and behaviors is now moving into business and government. They are beginning to transform not only our social interactions, but also our business and political ones.

Here is just one example in the medical community. A Nobel Prize–winning doctor, Alfred Gilman, is leading a radical effort to build a "virtual cell" that would allow drug tests and experiments to be conducted online—virtually—from anywhere in the world. Instead of working within a small, closed group of researchers, he has opened his medical research up to hundreds of colleagues from around the world. This work has the potential to shorten the pre-clinical trial review process from years to months to even days, with the goal of bringing new life-saving drugs to market much faster than before. This is the power of collaboration—*the power of us.*

Harnessing this potential will require much more than technology changes—more than in the first phase of the Internet, this phase will require significant changes in human behavior. Business and government leaders will need to lead from a "collaboration and teamwork" mentality as opposed to the traditional "command and control" perspective. As we adopt this collaboration mentality in our personal lives, we are beginning to carry similar expectations into our work lives, fueling demand for collaborative technologies and behaviors at work. Encouraging this collaborative behavior will also require us to teach students and employees how to work well together and to make good collective decisions—and then reward them for reaching collective goals, not only individual ones.

We are at one of the great inflection points of our time. Our opportunity is to build a globally connected human network capable of working collectively to address the significant social, economic, and political issues of our time. As leaders, it is our responsibility to lead by collaborative example, encourage and reward these behaviors, and welcome the innovations that will enable a world that is more connected than ever before.

I believe the combination of education, innovative environment, supportive government, and broadband infrastructure are the ingredients for global competitiveness. And, in particular, education and the Internet are global equalizers for individuals. Thus it is our responsibility to work toward universal broadband access, so we can provide groups and individuals the necessary platform for collaborating effectively on a global basis. We are not limited by technology, but only by our own imagination and our willingness to adapt and embrace this exciting new era.

Cisco is pleased to sponsor the *Global Information Technology Report 2007–2008,* including the Networked Readiness Index. We hope these will provide greater insight into how we can get better connected and work together more collaboratively to address the great challenges and exciting opportunities we face as a global community.

Executive Summary

SOUMITRA DUTTA, INSEAD
IRENE MIA, World Economic Forum

The world is becoming more networked with the passing of each day. Not only are the number of interconnections amongst individuals, businesses, and governments increasing, but there is also increased recognition of connectivity as a key component of public infrastructure in general.[1] New definitions portray high bandwidth connectivity as a necessity, perhaps even a public utility on the order of drinking water. For instance, the Chicago Digital Access Alliance has promoted the notion of universal broadband access as a public right.[2] Similar statements by the European Commission present high bandwidth connectivity as a service of general economic interest.[3] Providers have also jumped on the bandwagon of broadband as a "universal service." For example, in October 2007, the UK Post Office launched a new service specifically designed to attract late adopters of broadband services.

Next-generation technologies such as WiFi and WiMAX are being adopted rapidly and are enhancing connectivity. WiFi has quickly evolved from a WLAN application, providing indoor, short-range wireless Internet access for mobile computers, to a broadband wireless service with many opportunities on a global scale. According to estimates provided by local authorities in North America, in a typical city, at least 45 percent of the municipal employees are mobile. Police, fire, public works, parks, and inspections departments are out daily and need to access information. Therefore, cities across the United States and Canada have been setting up networks to allow wireless connections.

Many developing countries are using WiMAX deployments to leapfrog past copper wire. By early 2007, Motorola and Wateen Telecom, a subsidiary of UAE-based Warid Telecom, had rolled out a WiMAX network in 17 major cities across Pakistan.[4] In India, WiMAX is publicized as 30 times faster than 3G mobile technology and 100 times faster than wireless data rates, and has been widely anticipated to cure the problems of rural connectivity. It has been promoted as the answer to India's last-mile connectivity issues, which have hampered Internet take-up in rural India. In the context of having to apportion chunks of finite spectrum, WiMAX is appealing because it holds the promise of increased sharing. Rural connectivity is promised as long as power supply is available, PCs are given, local languages are used in developing content, and people are provided with training in using PCs.[5]

The benefits of increased connectivity in areas such as better and more diverse access to information have been documented qualitatively in the literature. In large measure, they have contributed to digital literacy and fluency, as a platform for human capital growth that requires public investment.[6] There are other, less tangible but equally crucial benefits of increased connectivity: in a wider social context, connectivity has been recognized as having a positive impact on transparency, good governance, and democracy. There are also implications of increased connectivity that are currently in the process of being defined, particularly in areas such as urban systems, lifestyles, and quality of life. For example, according to a 2006 technology needs assessment and economic development impact study conducted in the United States for the city of Saint Paul, amidst intensifying global competition for talent, high bandwidth connectivity has the ability to enhance the city's appeal to the "creative class" of knowledge workers.[7]

Across the world, increased connectivity has also become a prominent factor in the discourse on strengthening and maintaining social cohesion. Narrowing the digital gap between urban and rural areas has been a priority for public sectors worldwide, regardless of their countries' overall information and communication technologies (ICT) maturity. This agenda has served to placate fears that the rapid advances in technology would benefit urban areas at the expense of those geographic segments that are already struggling with their distance from markets. Indeed, there has been differentiation in governments' perspectives on the benefits of connectivity proliferation along the lines of central, regional, and municipal government.

The Global Information Technology Report 2007–2008 is released at a time in which the importance of high-bandwidth connectivity for countries' competitiveness, sustained growth, and poverty reduction is widely recognized. Facilitating access and effective use of ICT has increasingly moved to the top of national agendas in most developed and developing economies, while more resources are invested in ICT infrastructure upgrading and development. The *Report* is the seventh of a series and builds on a long-term partnership between the World Economic Forum and INSEAD, aimed at furthering understanding of networked readiness and its main enablers.

The *Report* features four thematic parts. Part 1 includes the findings of the Networked Readiness Index (NRI) 2007–2008, together with a number of insightful essays on selected issues of networked readiness, with a specific focus on how it can foster innovation. Topics covered stretch from the link between innovation and ICT to recent trends in innovation (such as Unified Communications) and e-skills and telecommunications regulation in emerging markets.

Part 2 focuses on country/regional case studies showcasing best policies and practices in fostering networked readiness. This year, Singapore, Qatar, and EU cases are analyzed in depth.

Part 3 provides detailed profiles for each of the 127 economies covered in the *Report,* presenting a comprehensive snapshot of each economy's current networked readiness status and allowing for international and historical comparison on specific variables or components of the NRI.

Last but not least, Part 4 provides detailed data tables for each of the 68 variables composing the NRI this year, with global rankings.

Part 1: Selected Issues of Networked

Each year, *The Global Information Technology Report* includes a deep-dive analysis on issues with a particular relevance for countries' networked readiness, together with a report on the latest NRI findings. This year we examine the following specific areas: (1) the emerging nexus delivering the promises of ICT to developing countries; (2) the impact of ICT on innovation; (3) the new, current innovation modalities at the "speed of light"; (4) Unified Communications; (5) the development of e-skills for the information age; (6) regulations in emerging telecommunications markets; (7) business network transformation and their implications for the global economy; and (8) innovation and collaboration on the participative Web.

The Networked Readiness Index

Chapter 1.1, "Assessing the State of the World's Networked Readiness: Insight from the Networked Readiness Index 2007–2008," reports the latest results and findings of the NRI, the main outcome of a research project jointly conducted by the World Economic Forum and INSEAD since 2002. The NRI aims at measuring economies' capacity to fully leverage ICT for increased competitiveness and development, building on a mixture of hard data collected by well-respected international organizations, such as the International Telecommunication Union (ITU), the World Bank, and the United Nations, and survey data from the Executive Opinion Survey, conducted annually by the World Economic Forum in each of the economies included in the *Report*. The NRI 2007–2008 covers a record number of 127 developed and developing economies all over the world, accounting for over 95 percent of the world GDP.

The Networked Readiness Framework, underlying the NRI and unchanged since 2002, assesses:

- the presence of an ICT-friendly and conducive environment, by looking at a number of features of the broad business environment, some regulatory aspects, and the soft and hard infrastructure for ICT;

- the level of ICT readiness and preparation to use ICT of the three main national stakeholders—individuals, the business sector, and the government; and

- the actual use of ICT by the above three stakeholders.

The NRI rankings for 2007–2008 confirm Denmark as the most networked economy in the world for the second year consecutively, as a culmination of an upward trend observed since 2003. The other Nordic countries also continue to show their prowess in leveraging ICT for increased competitiveness, with Sweden, Finland, Iceland, and Norway at 2nd, 6th, 8th, and 10th position, respectively. Among the top 20, Switzerland is up two places, at 3rd position, continuing last year's notable upward trend, while the United States improves three ranks to 4th place. Korea, at 9th, realizes one of the most impressive improvements (10 places) from last year among the 127 economies covered by the *Report*. Other Asian economies featured in the top 20 are: Singapore (5th), Hong Kong (11th), Australia (14th), Taiwan (17th), and Japan (19th). With regard to the largest Asian emerging markets, India is down four places in a constant sample at position 50th, while China is improving five positions in a constant sample to 57th.

The networked readiness snapshot for Latin America and the Caribbean this year appears less positive than it did in 2006–07, with Mexico (58th), Brazil (59th), and Argentina (77th) all dropping a number of positions, and only four economies among the top 50: Chile (34th), Barbados (38th), new entrant Puerto Rico (39th), and Jamaica (46th).

Notwithstanding the important advances sub-Saharan Africa experienced in the last decade or so in ICT penetration, the large majority of the region continues to lag behind in the NRI ranking this year, with only South Africa (51st) and Mauritius (54th) featured in the first half of the rankings.

The picture for North Africa is more positive, with Egypt and Morocco posting an impressive 17-place (the highest in the sample) and 5-place improvement, respectively, in a constant sample, climbing to 63rd and 74th. Also most of the countries in the Middle East realized important advancements in the rankings, with Qatar (32nd), Bahrain (45th), and Jordan (47th) at the forefront, with a remarkable 4-, 6-, and 11-place rise, respectively, in a constant sample.

The chapter also features a trend analysis of the entire NRI time-series, identifying the countries and regions in the world that have progressed the most in the NRI rankings since 2001, proving themselves to be particularly dynamic in benefiting from ICT advances.

Mapping out a balanced path for developing countries in leveraging ICT

Establishing a pervasive and prosperous Internet culture is as much about creating the right business environment as it is about adopting the right technology. If governments—national, regional, and municipal—want to harness the potential of ICT, they must not only invest in ICT infrastructure and the capabilities to support it, but also be ready to modify their country's relevant institutional setting—or ICT ecosystem—to allow ICT to yield its transformative powers. In their paper "The Emerging Nexus: Now Is the Time to Plot a Balanced Course that Delivers on the Promise of ICT," authors Ewan Morrison, Robert Pepper, and Enrique J. Rueda-Sabater (all at Cisco Systems, Inc.) introduce a diagnostic framework reflecting those two dimensions along with a mapping tool employing NRI component indicators. The aim is to allow countries to gain insight into how to chart a balanced path between ICT infrastructure and ecosystem initiatives that serves their own mix of social inclusion and economic growth objectives.

The framework provides "map" coordinates that illustrate the best path forward to ensure that investment in infrastructure and capacity are matched with a good institutional ecosystem for ICT. Understanding a country's position with respect to these factors is, thus, a good basis for mapping out steps toward improved ICT adoption and IP network connectivity. The two dimensions in question are:

- *ICT ecosystem,* which refers to institutional factors that underpin entrepreneurial creativity, competitive dynamics for service provision, and fairness in the distribution of economic gains. These factors are hard to measure, but the most critical factors pertain to the legal framework around ICT deployment—in particular, the quality of ICT regulations, the ease of doing business in a country, and the existence of lively competition and innovation.

- *ICT infrastructure and capacity,* which refers to assets, such as networks and other telecommunications and connectivity infrastructure, as well as the existence of technical skills and systems capable of effectively managing the infrastructure.

The paper explains in detail how this diagnostic approach works, and provides the authors' insights after their initial efforts working with the framework.

Why does ICT matter for innovation?

In his paper "The Missing Link: Why Does ICT Matter for Innovation? Exploring the Effect of Information Technology on Innovation-Based Competitiveness," Adolfo Ibáñez University Professor Carlos A. Osorio-Urzúa explores the relevance of information and communication technologies for innovation from the perspective of how ICT fosters innovation. The relevance of this issue, explains the author, relies on the fact that most nations treat innovation and ICT policy as different areas of concern, missing opportunities for greater and deeper changes.

The paper explores the relationship between innovation and ICT by studying how a slightly adapted version of the innovation subpillar of the Global Competitiveness Index (GCI), featured in the World Economic Forum's *Global Competitiveness Report,* is related to the NRI, and how, particularly, the use of ICT relates to innovation. Results support the idea that the more intensive and sophisticated the use of ICT, the higher its impact on innovation, even considering important contextual factors such as intellectual property protection, availability of local venture capital, participation of exporting firms on the various stages of their industries' value chain, and per capita income level. Osorio-Urzúa argues, however, that the relevance of ICT use is different among high- and low-income nations, in line with the view that innovation processes require sophisticated ICT use. While the extent of business Internet use is the most relevant ICT factor related to innovation among high-income nations, low-income nations exhibit a more basic approach, showing that use of ICT by governments and generating access among the population are the most relevant needs that show a relationship with innovation. While high-income nations are in the stage of exploiting ICT for innovation, low-income nations are still building the basic infrastructure to enter that stage. However, the efforts of low-income nations toward fostering ICT access among the poor, mostly as a matter of democratization, can also serve to enhance innovation and be a source of equity and national competitiveness. The right policy to capitalize on this opportunity is to create instruments to incentive and foster grassroots innovation, concludes the author. National competitiveness is based not only on how the firms at the top of the pyramid perform, but also on the performance of those at the bottom. However, most innovation policies in developing nations are designed for globalized firms or sophisticated startups.

Innovation at the speed of life

In his paper "Innovation at the Speed of Life," Matt Bross (at BT Group) argues that the rapid advances in ICT have unleashed an explosion of innovation and creativity of such power and impact that it is been called the "Innovation Big Bang."

As a result, consumers now have a bewildering array of products and services they can choose from. And if they still cannot find what they want, they don't have to worry since innovations are being brought to market at an unprecedented rate. For every firm, the challenge is immense. To stay in the game, it must open its innovation process, enlisting the help of as many as it can, and not just those on its payroll.

However, the author believes, openness itself is not enough. Innovations must now be delivered at the speed of customers' personal and professional lives, eliminating the gap between what they are looking for and what they can have. Fortunately, an array of technology-enabled options is already available to help firms open their innovation processes and accelerate the delivery of ideas to market. With more yet to come, firms are now free to choose how open and agile an innovator they want to be. In this context, Bross notices that the world is full of people who are keen to offer their ideas, and firms need to become exceptional exploiters of this immense pool of talent if they are to survive. By creating opportunities for many more people to participate in the innovation process and share the wealth that is created, Bross believes open innovation will help overcome the digital divide.

Unified Communications

One of the traditional benchmarks of a nation's ability to foster economic growth and protect and enhance the well-being of its citizens has been good communications. As communications technology has advanced, nations need to reconsider what "good" communications is.

In their paper "Unified Communications: Leading Advances in Global Decision Making and Economic Development," Sandor Boyson (Robert H. Smith School of Business, University of Maryland, College Park) and David Boyer (Avaya) provide a compelling account of the development and diffusion of digital platforms that unify what have until now been separate communications channels, that is, Unified Communications (UC). Indeed, convergence has created a UC network, a revolutionary services platform capable of orchestrating processes and people on a scale never seen before. Unified Communications can bring people and their expertise into business and government processes as needed, through better communications.

The paper argues that we must go beyond the present framework of communications to Unified Communications–enabling social and business collaboration. *Unified Communications* can be defined as communications integrated to optimize business processes. The authors believe that nations urgently require a bold set of adjustments in public and private strategy to harness Unified Communications as a catalyst to new economic and social development. The key to national success will lie in mobilizing cross-boundary collaborations and partnerships cutting across government and industry borders to ensure the growth of the open standards, business process definitions and governance mechanisms that will be needed to propel Unified Communications forward. To attain success, a broad coalition of leaders must become energized by the potential of Unified Communications and committed to its rapid scale-up and diffusion across society.

Leaders should formulate and steer a multifaceted policy agenda to take advantage of Unified Communications' ability to improve public- and private-sector processes. With these policies in place, the authors are confident that nations will be ready to catch at its peak the next great technology-driven long wave of economic growth.

E-skills for the information age

As global competition becomes increasingly knowledge-intensive, many warning signs tell public and private decision makers that our economies may not be generating the appropriate volumes and levels of e-skills. "Building E-skills for the Information Age," by Bruno Lanvin (INSEAD, cLab) and Pamela S. Passman (Microsoft Corporation), addresses three main issues against the background of the parallel quest for innovation, competitiveness, and employability: (1) why (and how fast) the need for e-skills is growing; (2) how the supply of such skills is generated and is meeting current and foreseeable needs; and (3) what are some of the main priorities that governments and business should address to solve the upcoming "e-skills crunch."

Available evidence confirms that e-skills are pervasive and not limited to IT specialists; they are increasingly required in all sectors and at all levels of activity in which creativity, innovation, and interdisciplinary teamwork are required as tools for competitiveness. In both the private and public sectors, leaders need not only to be e-literate, but also to display and nurture the new qualities required by "e-leadership." Moreover, the authors argue, the emerging global knowledge economy will significantly increase the need for more e-skills at all levels (from unspecialized workers to corporate leaders), in all industries (not just the IT sector), and in the public sector. Finally, e-skills will be of central importance in determining workers' vertical and horizontal mobility, and hence the proper functioning of labor markets and adequate employability and inclusion levels. Faced with such needs, our economies fall short of providing the necessary volume and levels of e-skills required. The gap is growing between the ability of existing educational systems to provide e-skilled workers and managers on one hand, and the requirement of knowledge-intensive economies on the other. In a number of industries and regions, this gap is particularly acute, and calls for rapid adjustments in educational systems and improvements to the image of IT jobs. Urgent efforts are required in the legal and regulatory systems that underpin the well-functioning of labor markets.

From a policy point of view, addressing foreseeable e-skills shortages may yield significant side benefits. The authors believe that, with the right mix of strategies and policies and the proper dose of engagement from all major stakeholders, the current lack of e-skills may indeed prove a major opportunity to involve a larger share of the world population in creating, and in benefiting from, a truly inclusive information society.

Regulations in emerging telecommunication markets

In their paper "Rethinking Regulation in Emerging Telecommunications Markets," authors Scott C. Beardsley, Ilke Bigan, Luis Enriquez, Mehmet Guvendi, Can Kendi, Miguel Lucas, Oleg Timchenko, Sergio Sandoval, and Ashish Sharma (all at McKinsey & Company, Inc.) discuss the fundamental role of regulation in enabling the development of the telecommunications (telecom) industry in emerging markets. A sound regulatory framework, which takes into account specific local market characteristics, will be crucial not only for operators to capture new sources of growth and revenues, but also for governments to build an industry that is a fundamental enabler of economic development.

Designing such a regulatory framework, the authors argue, requires a deep understanding of the specific characteristics and needs of emerging telecom markets. Although they are far from homogeneous, emerging markets typically differ significantly from mature markets in several ways, among them the distribution of their populations, income levels, and industry structures. Developing countries that ignore their local characteristics and borrow regulatory frameworks from more developed countries will fail to create a vibrant sector that serves as engine for the economic development of the country.

The chapter proposes a simple segmentation with three types of emerging markets that have distinct starting points and characteristics. This assessment can be a useful first step toward prioritizing regulatory objectives, proposing adequate policies, and defining a vision for the future industry structure.

Business network transformation and the global economy

In their paper "Business Network Transformation: Rethinking Relationships in a Global Economy," Henning Kagermann (at SAP AG) and Philip Lay and Geoffrey Moore (both at TCG Advisors) examine how companies are gaining competitive advantage through networked business models by taking advantage of deregulation, access to global markets, and strategic use of technology. They argue that companies are focusing on their strengths and tapping into complementary sources of talent and ideas across the globe to defend themselves against commoditization and disruptive innovation. By working in global business networks, companies spend less on duplication and more on innovation, resulting in higher degrees of differentiation, greater customer willingness to pay a premium, and thus higher returns on invested capital.

Since innovation happens continuously in business networks, the authors believe that business executives need to shift their companies from "built-to-last" models and recast themselves as "built-to-adapt" organizations, ready to climb the value chain and take on new roles in the business networks. Under this pressure to transform, business leaders are being forced to re-examine long-held assumptions on strategy, structure, systems, and style to coordinate tasks and collaborate better with customers, partners, and even competitors. The paper addresses the right context in which to view this change in business climate, and it analyzes two modes in which business networks operate. It also discusses how business network dynamics evolve as markets emerge, scale, mature, and decline, as well as what core principles or practices can be used as guideposts in the foray out into this new territory of business networks. And, finally, implications of these networked business models for managing investment in ICT systems are explored.

Innovation on the participative Web

The paper "The Participative Web: Innovation and Collaboration," by Sacha Wunsch-Vincent and Graham Vickery (both at the OECD), describes the rapid growth of user-created content and its increasing role in worldwide communications, and draws out policy implications.

The authors notice that innovation in broadband applications and digital content is an important driver of the digital economy, building on the infrastructure push that has provided widespread high-speed network access. Indeed, the Internet has altered the nature and the economics of information production. Entry barriers for content creation and distribution have declined radically and encouraged broader participation in media production, increased user autonomy, increased diversity, and a shift away from simple passive consumption of broadcasting and other unidirectional models of mass distribution of content. Terms such as the *participative Web* describe an Internet increasingly influenced by intelligent Web services, based on new technologies enabling the user to be a growing contributor to developing, rating, collaborating, and distributing Internet content and developing and customizing Internet applications (user-created content).

The authors argue that the participative Web provides a testing ground for low-cost experimentation with implications for business, organizational and social change far beyond technology. New business and entrepreneurial activity is a major feature of the participative Web, and existing firms are under pressure to make their business models relevant to this new environment. Moreover, the participative Web harbors potential for educational, political, and social objectives.

The authors also highlight a number of business and policy issues to be addressed, such as rising copyright disputes among copyright holders, user-created content platforms, and users. User-created content platforms will also have to address privacy concerns of users and regulators as popular platforms may more and more be subject to "phishing" and other cyber-attacks, making user data vulnerable. Content quality, safety on the Internet, and possibly better self-governance of users will be issues with which to deal. Increased concentration among the user-created content platforms and the growing role of gatekeepers will be continuing business and policy issues.

Part 2: Leveraging ICT and Innovation for Competitiveness: Selected Case Studies
This year's *Report* presents three case studies related to innovation and networked readiness in Singapore, Qatar, and the European Union. It is hoped that these can provide important insight on best policies and practices in view of fully leveraging ICT and innovation for increased competitiveness.

Singapore, an intelligent nation
As a small island nation without natural resources except for its people, ICT is important to Singapore's growth and a key component of its economic infrastructure. In their paper "Singapore: Building an Intelligent Nation with ICT," authors Ng Cher Keng, Ong Ling Lee, Tanya Tang (all at the Infocomm Development Authority, Singapore), and Soumitra Dutta (INSEAD) relate the story of Singapore's ICT journey over the past 26 years, beginning with the introduction of the National Computerisation Plan in 1981 to equip the country with the then-new tools to increase productivity and economic competitiveness. As its computerization efforts bore fruit, the government's confidence in ICT as an economic enabler grew, along with the ambition to grow Singapore's ICT capabilities. From equipping the government, the relevant authorities went on to drive nationwide efforts to extend ICT capabilities to the enterprises and the population, wire up and connect the nation with high-speed broadband connectivity, and transform different economic sectors through the use of ICT. Starting from a very low base, Singapore is now host to a vibrant ICT industry and home to a technologically savvy population, argue the authors. This has, in part, been achieved through the formulation and implementation of six ICT master plans, each guided by a developmental theme relevant for the economy then. "An Intelligent Nation, a Global City, powered by ICT" is the vision of Singapore's latest ICT master plan, Intelligent Nation 2015 (or "iN2015" in short). The role of ICT, as a strategic enabler to enhance national competitiveness and as an industry in itself, underlies iN2015. By harnessing the power of ICT, Singapore aims to develop an inclusive digital society and ensure the continued growth and vitality of its economy.

Singapore's focus on linking ICT to strategic objectives combined with strong leadership from the very top of the government provides useful insights for other countries as they seek to leverage the potential of ICT for their own development and competitiveness. The paper also highlights two specific areas of ICT deployment where Singapore has achieved world-class excellence: e-government and e-education.

Creating a knowledge-based economy in Qatar
Qatar is one of the richest economies in the world, with a per capita income of over US$62,000 per person. Despite its enormous wealth, it has only recently started on its journey of modernization, with ICT seen as a key enabler. The aim, through ICT, is to create a core engine for a competitive economy, universalize access to social services, and create a knowledge-based society. In addition, ICT is seen as having a multiplier effect in all sectors, extending the reach of political reforms and helping Qatar to reach its goal of becoming a modern progressive nation. The first major step on this journey was accomplished when, by a Royal Decree in 2004, Qatar's Supreme Council of ICT (ictQATAR) was formed with a clear and authoritative mandate as both regulator and enabler of Qatar's ICT sector. ictQATAR has enthusiastically taken on the role of ICT champion for the entire country, and has consistently pushed for an integrated and holistic approach to ICT implementation. It has managed to win cooperation and support from other government agencies and departments.

The effect of the ICT focus is already being felt. In a commendable feat, Qatar is ranked 32nd in the NRI this year. With a full-fledged national ICT plan in place, initiatives are happening on many fronts: policy reforms; steps with regard to security concerns; ICT initiatives in health care, education, e-government, and infrastructure; and deregulation in the telecommunications industry. For Qatar, the journey in ICT has only started. But despite the relatively late start, the country has succeeded in making its mark on the world's networked readiness map.

In their paper "Qatar: Leveraging Technology to Create a Knowledge-Based Economy in the Middle East," Hessa Al-Jaber (at ictQATAR) and Soumitra Dutta (at INSEAD) present an overview of the transformation of Qatar into a knowledge economy and a flag-bearer of technology-driven excellence in the entire region. Besides outlining the key strategic initiatives in Qatar's ICT agenda, the paper also outlines the key implementation hurdles faced by Qatar, and identifies best practices and lessons from the country's transformation for other nations engaged in similar processes of change.

European SMEs and innovation through ICT
It is clearer than ever that ICT and e-business models are the most important drivers of innovation and competitiveness today. ICT has revolutionized the way business

is currently done and will continue to do so in the future. But ICT can induce substantially higher productivity gains only when accompanied by appropriate organizational changes, innovative e-business models and investment in skills. Nonetheless, the great potential of ICT-enabled innovations and reorganization of business models is still largely underexploited by European small- and medium sized enterprises (SMEs). Improving the integration and innovative use of ICT by European SMEs, has, therefore, been a major challenge for policymakers over the past years. In her paper "Small- and Medium-Sized Enterprises Hold the Key to European Competitiveness: How to Help Them Innovate through ICT and E-business," Dana Eleftheriadou, at the European Commission, provides a comprehensive overview of the Commission's most recent endeavor to improve the effectiveness of SME public policies promoting the innovative use of ICT and the exchange of good practices: the eBusiness Support Network for SMEs (eBSN). This is a "policy intelligence" initiative, which observes policy developments and identifies new trends. Through the eBSN, the author argues, we are witnessing the combination of three major trends: (1) the increasing economic importance of SMEs as key players in implementing the Lisbon Strategy for growth and jobs, as well as their increasing potential to act as global players in the emerging global economy; (2) the incontestable recognition of the merits of ICT and new e-business processes, as major enablers of innovation, productivity, and competitiveness growth; and (3) the strong engagement of governments to stimulate the uptake of ICT, e-business models, and modern management practices by their enterprises, in particular SMEs.

While analyzing in more depth the government engagement to promote e-business models, eBSN witnessed a policy shift from general ICT awareness raising, sponsoring, and co-financing ICT investments and Internet connectivity toward policy instruments that stimulate SMEs to explore the innovation potential of ICT and e-business. More recently, eBSN observed new policy developments, favoring the sectoral policy approach for e-business. Their aim is to support the participation of SMEs in global digital supply chains of specific business sectors. The current proliferation of such sector-specific initiatives among several EU countries needs efficient policy coordination in order to put them in perspective and valorize them at EU level.

Nonetheless, Eleftheriadou notes that the structural complexity of supply chains, particularly for companies dealing with different industry sectors (thus calling for cross-sectoral coordination), represents a major challenge to the sector-specific e-business initiatives. While the consideration of the sectoral characteristics of a value chain is absolutely critical, cross-sectoral requirements should also be identified and addressed, as a next step. Therefore, the harmonization of data exchange models and business processes across different business sectors will probably be one of the key ICT-related issues in the future, and will feature at the top of the e-business policy agenda in the years to come. As in other policy areas, the author calls for the European Union and Member States to join forces and coordinate relevant e-business policies to gear up European progress toward the Lisbon objectives.

Parts 3 and 4: Country/Economy Profiles and Data Presentation

Parts 3 and 4 include detailed profiles for each of the 127 economies covered in the *Report* and data tables for each of the 68 variables composing the NRI, with global rankings. Each part is preceded by a description of how to interpret the data provided. Technical notes and sources, included at the end of Part 4, provide details on the characteristics and sources of the individual hard variables included in the *Report*.

Notes

1 Broadband can be provided as a fixed line or as a wireless connection. DSL and Packet Cable are the most popular types of fixed broadband connectivity options. WLAN (802.11) GSM/GPRS are the more popular wireless broadband modes. WiMax is an emerging wireless mode for broadband.

2 CDAA 2007.

3 See http://ec.europa.eu/information_society/eeurope/2005/all_about/broadband/index_en.htm.

4 PriMetrica 2006.

5 Goliath 2006.

6 CDAA 2007.

7 St. Paul 2006.

References

CDAA (Chicago Digital Access Alliance). 2007. *Ten Principles for Digital Excellence.* February 28. Available at www.accesschicago.org/principles-for-digital-excellence.

Goliath. 2006. "WiMAX Will Connect Rural India." *M2 Presswire.* November 10. Available at http://goliath.ecnext.com/coms2/browse_R_M045.

PriMetrica. 2006. WiMAX Market Tracker. Network News: 2nd Quarter. TeleGeography, July 2006. Available at http://www.telegeography.com/products/wimax/index.php.

St. Paul, Minnesota, City of. 2006. Broadband Technology Needs Assessment and Economic Development Impact Study. Final Report. May. Available at www.stpaul.gov/depts/ot/BITS5-23.pdf.

The Networked Readiness Index Rankings

The Networked Readiness Index 2007–2008 rankings

2007–2008 rank	Country/ Economy	Score
1	Denmark	5.78
2	Sweden	5.72
3	Switzerland	5.53
4	United States	5.49
5	Singapore	5.49
6	Finland	5.47
7	Netherlands	5.44
8	Iceland	5.44
9	Korea, Rep.	5.43
10	Norway	5.38
11	Hong Kong SAR	5.31
12	United Kingdom	5.30
13	Canada	5.30
14	Australia	5.28
15	Austria	5.22
16	Germany	5.19
17	Taiwan, China	5.18
18	Israel	5.18
19	Japan	5.14
20	Estonia	5.12
21	France	5.11
22	New Zealand	5.02
23	Ireland	5.02
24	Luxembourg	4.94
25	Belgium	4.92
26	Malaysia	4.82
27	Malta	4.61
28	Portugal	4.60
29	United Arab Emirates	4.55
30	Slovenia	4.47
31	Spain	4.47
32	Qatar	4.42
33	Lithuania	4.41
34	Chile	4.35
35	Tunisia	4.33
36	Czech Republic	4.33
37	Hungary	4.28
38	Barbados	4.26
39	Puerto Rico	4.25
40	Thailand	4.25
41	Cyprus	4.23
42	Italy	4.21
43	Slovak Republic	4.17
44	Latvia	4.14
45	Bahrain	4.13
46	Jamaica	4.09
47	Jordan	4.08
48	Saudi Arabia	4.07
49	Croatia	4.06
50	India	4.06
51	South Africa	4.05
52	Kuwait	4.01
53	Oman	3.97
54	Mauritius	3.96
55	Turkey	3.96
56	Greece	3.94
57	China	3.90
58	Mexico	3.90
59	Brazil	3.87
60	Costa Rica	3.87
61	Romania	3.86
62	Poland	3.81
63	Egypt	3.74
64	Panama	3.74
65	Uruguay	3.72
66	El Salvador	3.72
67	Azerbaijan	3.72
68	Bulgaria	3.71
69	Colombia	3.71
70	Ukraine	3.69
71	Kazakhstan	3.68
72	Russian Federation	3.68
73	Vietnam	3.67
74	Morocco	3.67
75	Dominican Republic	3.66
76	Indonesia	3.60
77	Argentina	3.59
78	Botswana	3.59
79	Sri Lanka	3.58
80	Guatemala	3.58
81	Philippines	3.56
82	Trinidad and Tobago	3.55
83	Macedonia, FYR	3.49
84	Peru	3.46
85	Senegal	3.46
86	Venezuela	3.44
87	Mongolia	3.43
88	Algeria	3.38
89	Pakistan	3.37
90	Honduras	3.35
91	Georgia	3.34
92	Kenya	3.34
93	Namibia	3.33
94	Nigeria	3.32
95	Bosnia and Herzegovina	3.22
96	Moldova	3.21
97	Mauritania	3.21
98	Tajikistan	3.18
99	Mali	3.17
100	Tanzania	3.17
101	Gambia, The	3.17
102	Guyana	3.16
103	Burkina Faso	3.12
104	Madagascar	3.12
105	Libya	3.10
106	Armenia	3.10
107	Ecuador	3.09
108	Albania	3.06
109	Uganda	3.06
110	Syria	3.06
111	Bolivia	3.05
112	Zambia	3.02
113	Benin	3.01
114	Kyrgyz Republic	2.99
115	Cambodia	2.96
116	Nicaragua	2.95
117	Suriname	2.91
118	Cameroon	2.89
119	Nepal	2.88
120	Paraguay	2.87
121	Mozambique	2.82
122	Lesotho	2.79
123	Ethiopia	2.77
124	Bangladesh	2.65
125	Zimbabwe	2.50
126	Burundi	2.46
127	Chad	2.40

(Cont'd.)

Part 1

Selected Issues of Networked Readiness

CHAPTER 1.1

Assessing the State of the World's Networked Readiness: Insight from the Networked Readiness Index 2007–2008

IRENE MIA, World Economic Forum
SOUMITRA DUTTA, INSEAD

National competitiveness is a multifaceted phenomenon, driven by many diverse and interrelated factors. Among these, knowledge and the capacity to generate technology and/or absorb and adapt it to national needs have increasingly emerged as crucial elements. In particular, information and communication technologies (ICT) can significantly contribute to a country's overall competitiveness and sustained growth by impacting the efficiency of production processes across sectors and industries, accelerating the growth of knowledge-based services and industries, and empowering people to access to unprecedented sources of information and markets. Indeed, ICT has been found to have a noteworthy impact on economic performance,[1] and to account for a large part of total factor productivity increases that, in turn, have been associated with at least half of the growth in per capita income over the last 50 years.[2] Thus, it is not surprising to see many countries, even from developing regions, making significant investments in ICT.[3]

ICT has also radically transformed the way individuals live, work, and learn, improving lifestyles and creating social networks and virtual communities stretching across the globe and providing extraordinary opportunities of interaction.[4] For example, many organizations from the public and private sectors are reaping rich benefits from the use of broadband. The adoption of broadband to enable flexible work practices can enable significant financial benefits for multinational firms. For example, BT has approximately 8,500 workers who work flexibly via broadband from home. On average, they each save the company accommodation costs of approximately £6,000 per annum, they have an increased productivity rate averaging at 20 percent but recorded between 15 percent and 31 percent, they have on average only 3 days sick absence per annum against an industry average of 12 days. All of this adds up to an annual saving of in excess of £60 million per year.[5] The benefits of ICT and broadband also extend to small- and medium-sized enterprises (SMEs), for which faster access to online content and value-added applications improve the ability to drive productivity improvements.

Taking into account the centrality of innovation and technological readiness for national competitiveness, the World Economic Forum (the Forum) has undertaken, in cooperation with INSEAD since 2002, a research project aimed at identifying the factors enabling countries to fully leverage ICT in daily activities in order to effectively boost growth and prosperity. The main outcome of this project has been the *Global Information Technology Report* (GITR) series, published annually since 2001 and currently in its seventh edition.

The authors would like to thank Pearl Samandari and Thierry Geiger for their excellent research assistance for this chapter.

Figure 1: Networked readiness vs. GDP evolution

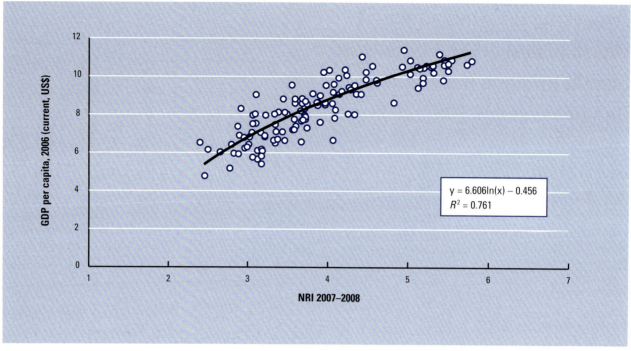

Source: IMF, *World Economic Outlook Database* (December 2007); NRI 2007–2008.

The Networked Readiness Index (NRI), featured in the GITR series, establishes an international framework by which the performance in networked readiness of a large number of economies can be assessed and benchmarked against one another and over time. In this way, relative competitive advantages and areas of weakness can be identified for each country, offering a unique platform to governments and civil society alike to prioritize policies and initiatives toward enhanced ICT penetration and leverage. At the same time, the NRI series, stretching back to 2001,[6] provides a invaluable instrument to monitor countries' progress over time.

Furthermore, over the years the GITR series has successfully contributed to raising general awareness of the close link existing between ICT prowess and continued growth and prosperity (see Figure 1), and has evolved into one of the world's most respected international assessments of countries' capacity to leverage technology for increased competitiveness.

Very much in line with past editions of the *Report*, the *GITR 2007–2008* aims at furthering the understanding of ICT-enabling factors and at benchmarking countries' networked readiness, extending its coverage to a record number of 127 developed and developing economies worldwide and accounting for more than 95 percent of the global GDP. The rest of this chapter will be devoted to present the findings of the NRI 2007–2008. After briefly outlining the Networked Readiness framework used in this 2007–08 edition, its theoretical underpinning, and its main components, an in-depth analysis of the results of the NRI 2007–2008 computation will be conducted, with a special focus on the top 10 countries by overall ranking and on the principal regional features. A trend analysis of the entire time-series will be also performed in order to identify the countries and regions in the world that have moved particularly fast in the NRI rankings from 2001, proving themselves to be particularly dynamic in benefiting from ICT advances.

The Networked Readiness Index 2007–2008: The framework and the methodology

The NRI 2007–2008 rests, as in previous years, on the Networked Readiness Framework developed by INSEAD in 2002.[7] The framework aims at assessing the different degrees to which countries around the world leverage ICT for enhanced growth and competitiveness and is based on the following three theoretical underpinnings:

1. *Environment is key:* An essential precondition for a country to benefit fully from the opportunities offered by ICT is the presence or establishment of an environment that is conducive to the development of ICT and is ICT friendly. In this sense, the appropriate business environment, regulatory framework, and infrastructure must be in place for a country's stakeholders to use and leverage ICT for development. ICT development does not happen in a vacuum, but requires an enabling environment.

Figure 2: ICT readiness and usage

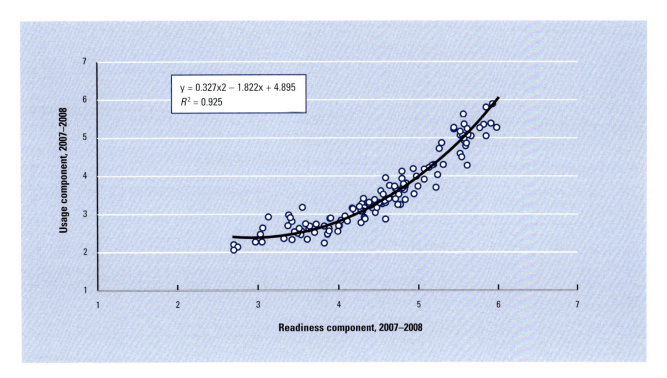

2. *Leveraging ICT depends on a multistakeholder effort:* The most successful networked economies show that ICT success is the result of the joint effort of multiple stakeholders—the government, businesses, and civil society. The government needs to take the lead in recognizing the importance of ICT penetration and innovation for overall competitiveness, by prioritizing it in its national agenda and facilitating the establishment of the necessary soft and hard infrastructure. However, this alone is not sufficient. The successful development experiences of Taiwan, Singapore, Israel, and Estonia emphasize the importance of involving the business sector and, more generally, mobilizing civil society from a very early stage in the implementation of the digital agenda.

3. *ICT readiness fosters ICT usage:* There is a strong correlation between the degree of preparedness and propensity to use ICT of the three main social actors mentioned above (government, businesses, and individuals) and their actual ICT usage, as displayed in Figure 2. The regression in Figure 2 not only demonstrates a very high value for R^2, but also shows that usage of ICT increases significantly as the readiness or preparedness to use ICT advances. Hence, a society that is well prepared and well disposed to use ICT will be more likely to successfully leverage the competitive and development potential of ICT.

Figure 3 provides a snapshot of the resulting networked readiness framework, with its three environment, readiness, and usage dimensions. While the environment component is broken down along market, regulatory, and infrastructure lines, the latter two include the readiness and usage of the three key stakeholder groups respectively—government, businesses, and individuals.

In line with the above, the NRI is composed of three subindexes, assessing respectively ICT environment, readiness, and usage, for a total of 9 pillars and 68 variables, as follows:

1. Environment subindex:
   — market environment
   — political and regulatory environment
   — infrastructure environment

2. Readiness subindex:
   — individual readiness
   — business readiness
   — government readiness

3. Usage subindex:
   — individual usage
   — business usage
   — government usage

All pillars are given the same weight in the calculation of the three subindexes, while the overall NRI is a simple average of the three subindexes; the underlying

Figure 3: The Networked Readiness Index 2007–2008: The framework

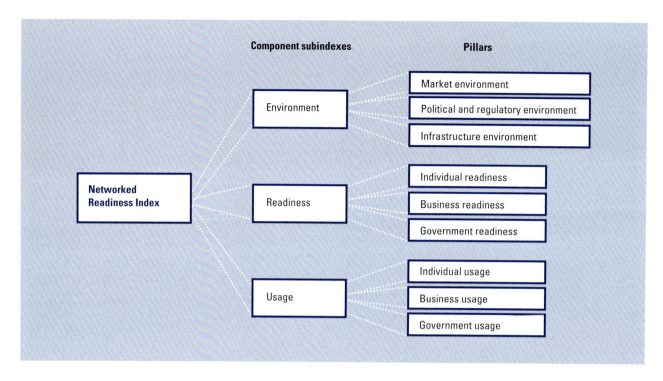

assumption is that all the Index components provide a similar contribution to the overall networked readiness of a country. Appendix A provides a more detailed description of the composition and computation of the NRI 2007–2008.

The different subindexes, pillars, and variables' scores offer important insights on the relative strengths and weakness of each economy in leveraging ICT, and can help governments to prioritize the areas in need of improvement in their national agendas.

Although the networked readiness framework remained constant after 2002–03, it is noteworthy that the number of variables included in the NRI has varied slightly from one year to the next. This has been made necessary by the rapid pace of innovation in the ICT sector and the need to ensure that the NRI is an updated and comprehensive instrument to gauge countries' networked readiness each year. This being said, the uniformity of the networked readiness framework guarantees an overall comparability of the NRI results over time.

Below is a brief description of each subindex and pillar composing the NRI.

Environment subindex

As stated earlier, governments, business communities, and individuals can fully leverage the competitive and development potential of ICT only if an appropriate environment is in place: the environment subindex aims at capturing the ICT conduciveness of the environment in a country by assessing a total of 30 variables related to the market environment, the general and ICT-specific regulatory framework, and the hard and soft (in terms of human resources) infrastructure for ICT development.

The *market environment pillar* (14 variables) gauges the friendliness of the business environment for ICT development, including aspects such as the presence of appropriate capital sources (notably venture capital), the degree of business sophistication (looking at cluster development and high-tech exports), and the innovation potential (measured by the number of utility patents), together with the ease of doing business (including the presence of red tape and fiscal charges), the freedom of exchanging information in the net (measured by the freedom of the press) and, for the first time this year, the extent of convergence of ITC industries and the related accessibility of digital content.

The *regulatory and political environment pillar* (9 variables), in turn, looks at the efficiency and transparency of the legal framework, taking into account such general aspects as the independence of the judiciary, the effectiveness of the law-making process, and the protection of the property rights, as well as ICT-specific elements such as the existence and development of appropriate legislation or the protection of intellectual property.

Last, the *infrastructure environment pillar* (7 variables) measures the degree of development of ICT-conducive soft as well as hard infrastructure. With regard to the former, quantitative aspects such as tertiary enrollment rates and, as of this year, education expenditure are blended with a qualitative assessment of the country's scientific research institutions and the availability of scientists and engineers. The dimension of hard infrastructure is measured by a range of variables including the number of telephone lines and electricity production.

Readiness subindex
Once an ICT-conducive environment is in place, ICT usage can develop and thrive if a country's principal stakeholder groups are sufficiently prepared, interested, and enabled to use technology. The readiness subindex (23 variables) examines whether the appropriate human skills for using ICT are in place, the degree of access and affordability of ICT for businesses and citizens, and the extent to which the government prioritizes ICT and uses it in its daily activities and organization.

Accordingly, the *individual readiness pillar* (9 variables) measures the disposition and preparedness of citizens to use ICT through a range of variables, including the quality of the educational system (with a focus on math and science education), the availability of Internet access in schools, residential telephone connection charges, broadband and telephone subscription charges, and the cost of mobile telephone calls.

The *business readiness pillar* (10 variables) gauges companies' preparedness to fully incorporate ICT in their operations and processes, including the extent of training of the labor force, companies' spending on research and development (R&D), the degree of collaboration between academia and the industry (this is, incidentally, a precondition for a cluster's successful operations), the quantity and quality of suppliers in the economy, and the affordability of ICT for business and the levels of ICT imports.

Last but not least, the *government readiness pillar* (4 variables) measures the degree to which ICT is prioritized in the government's agenda and to which there is a clear vision on how to promote its use and penetration.

Usage subindex
The usage subindex (15 variables) assesses the actual ICT usage by the three main stakeholders of the networked readiness framework, providing insight on the potential efficiency and productivity gains associated with the adoption of ICT.

The *individual usage pillar* (5 variables) gauges ITC penetration at the individual levels, notably for personal computer (PC) and the Internet.

The *business usage pillar* (5 variables) examines the extent to which businesses generate and absorb technology, looking at variables such as the prevalence of foreign licensing and the capacity for innovation, together with the availability and usage of fixed telephone lines for business and Internet usage by businesses in their transactions and operations.

The *government usage pillar* (5 variables) deals with the extent to which the government's vision for ICT has been implemented successfully (by assessing government's success in promoting ICT penetration and the development of e-government services and e-democracy), as well as the government's own ICT usage (by measuring the improvement of government productivity as a consequence of ICT introduction and use, and ICT pervasiveness in public offices).

Computation methodology and data
Along the lines of the past editions and the Forum's general competitiveness methodology, the NRI 2007–2008 builds on a mix of hard and survey data to capture, in the most complete possible manner, all the determinants of networked readiness. In particular, 27 variables out of 68 are hard, quantitative data, collected from respected international organizations such as the International Telecommunication Union (ITU), the World Bank, and the United Nations. The remaining 41 variables capture dimensions that are more qualitative in nature and come from the Executive Opinion Survey (Survey), conducted annually by the Forum in all the economies covered by this *Report*.[8] The Survey data allow the Index to factor into the model dimensions that are very relevant for a country's networked readiness, but for which no hard data are available from international sources. For example, a government's vision for ICT and the extent to which it prioritizes ICT are important drivers of overall networked readiness in an economy. No hard data are available on these aspects in international datasets. However, these questions are included in the Survey and the results are used for the computation of the NRI's government readiness pillar. Appendix B provides methodological notes on the combining of hard and Survey data.

The inclusion of new countries in the NRI every year is driven by the Survey coverage: Table 1 shows the evolution of the NRI and the Survey's coverage from the GITR series' inception. Of the 131 economies covered by the Survey in 2007, four—Montenegro, Serbia, Timor Leste, and Uzbekistan—could not be retained in the NRI computation because of the scarcity of reliable hard data. At the same time, eight new economies entered the NRI rankings for the first time this year, namely: The Gambia, Libya, Oman, Puerto Rico, Saudi Arabia, Senegal, Syria, and Tajikistan.[9]

Table 1: Evolution of the coverage of the Networked Readiness Index

Year	Number of economies
2001–02	72
2002–03	82
2003–04	102
2004–05	104
2005–06	115
2006–07	122
2007–08	127

As highlighted earlier, the variables included in the NRI may experience some variation over time, given the dynamism of the ICT sector. In order for the NRI to provide an updated snapshot of countries' networked readiness, those time-sensitive variables included in past editions but that have not been recently updated by relevant international institutions may need to be dropped by the NRI structure and calculation at any given year. With respect to last year, four new variables have been introduced in the current NRI computation,[10] either to complement, with hard data, qualitative variables already included in the past, or to capture new qualitative dimensions. The hard data variables introduced this year are total tax rate and education expenditure levels; newly included Survey data are the accessibility of digital content and the quantity of suppliers.

Particular care has been taken, as usual, to make certain that the total set of variables used for the NRI this year ensures broad comparability of the current results with those for previous years.

The NRI 2007–2008: Results and regional highlights

This section will reference the main findings of the NRI 2007–2008, with a particular emphasis on the top performers globally as well as on a number of selected economies per region. Tables 2 displays the NRI rankings and scores for 2007–08, with 2006–07 comparisons, while Tables 3 and 4 provide some insights on the most networked economies in the world, by looking respectively at the best performers per pillar in the current NRI calculation, and the evolution in the top 10 rankings since 2001–02. In turn, Tables 5, 6, and 7 show the rankings and scores for each of the three subindexes and nine pillars composing the NRI.

As highlighted by Table 2, Denmark and Sweden continue to lead the world in networked readiness. The two countries share a similar emphasis on education and innovation as well as a coherent vision of their respective governments on the importance of ICT for enhancing overall competitiveness.

Denmark, in particular, occupies the top position for the second year consecutively, culminating an upward trend observed since 2003–04 (see Table 4). Among the drivers of Denmark's success in networked readiness, one can mention the supportive ICT environment (ranked 2nd), characterized by one of the best regulatory frameworks (2nd) for doing business and for ICT. Denmark is ranked 1st in the world for the development of its ICT legislation and for the efficiency of its legal framework to settle disputes. Also the country is showing the rest of the world the way in ICT usage, boasting the highest Internet bandwidth (349 mb/s per 10,000 population) and the highest broadband Internet penetration rates (31.7 percent) in the sample, together with extensive e-commerce and e-business practices (7th for the extent of business Internet usage). The remarkable ICT penetration rates have much to do with the government's clear vision on the importance of ICT diffusion, its consistent prioritization of the ICT sector from a very early stage, and its capacity to mobilize civil society in this regard.[11] This is reflected in the 2nd place for government readiness, complemented by a 1st place for government usage, demonstrating an excellent degree of implementation of the digital agenda, notably for what concerns the availability of online services (3rd) and e-participation (3rd). Other elements explaining Denmark's ICT preeminence are its well-functioning and developed internal market, which provided the national ICT industry with a large number of consumers at its early stages; its top-notch educational system; and the Danish people's cultural openness and talent for developing, pioneering, and using new technologies and applications.

Besides Denmark, the other **Nordic countries** confirm their prowess in leveraging ICT for increased competitiveness, with Sweden, Finland, Iceland, and Norway all among the most networked economies in the world, at 2nd, 6th, 8th, and 10th position, respectively. It is worth noticing that their continuous focus on education and innovation and high levels of technological readiness also drive their performance in general competitiveness, as witnessed by the top ranks occupied by the latter in the Forum's Global Competitiveness Index.[12]

Switzerland is up two places, at 3rd position, continuing last year's impressive upward trend (i.e., four positions up from 2005–06 to 2006–07). It is worth noting that Switzerland's remarkable performance in networked readiness seems to be driven mainly by businesses and individuals (readiness ranks of 1st and 3rd, respectively, and usage ranks of 4th for both), rather than by the strength of the government's specific ICT strategy and vision, as evidenced by the rather low ranking in government readiness and usage (20th and 18th, respectively). This is unique among the most networked economies in the world, in which a strong government leadership has often been a common feature of success. Switzerland's rise in the rankings is driven by its strength in the overall environment subindex (ranked 6th) as well as a world-class educational system.

Singapore, down two positions at 5th place, displays the most ICT-conducive market and regulatory environment and among the highest levels of government readiness (1st in the sample) and usage (4th) in the world, representing a textbook case of how governments can promote ICT—and thus general competitiveness—with a comprehensive ICT strategy, a continued focus on education and innovation, and savvy public-private partnerships. The successful e-strategy adopted by the government in Singapore is detailed in Chapter 2.1, "Singapore: Building an Intelligent Nation with ICT," of this *Report*.

The **United States** improves three ranks to 4th place, continuing to benefit from one of the most efficient

Table 2: The Networked Readiness Index 2007–2008 and 2006–2007 comparison

Economy	NRI 2007–2008 Rank	NRI 2007–2008 Score	NRI 2007–2008 rank (among 2006 countries)	NRI 2006–2007 Rank	NRI 2006–2007 Score	Economy	NRI 2007–2008 Rank	NRI 2007–2008 Score	NRI 2007–2008 rank (among 2006 countries)	NRI 2006–2007 Rank	NRI 2006–2007 Score
Denmark	1	5.78	1	1	5.71	Uruguay	65	3.72	62	60	3.67
Sweden	2	5.72	2	2	5.66	El Salvador	66	3.72	63	61	3.66
Switzerland	3	5.53	3	5	5.58	Azerbaijan	67	3.72	64	71	3.53
United States	4	5.49	4	7	5.54	Bulgaria	68	3.71	65	72	3.53
Singapore	5	5.49	5	3	5.60	Colombia	69	3.71	66	64	3.59
Finland	6	5.47	6	4	5.59	Ukraine	70	3.69	67	75	3.46
Netherlands	7	5.44	7	6	5.54	Kazakhstan	71	3.68	68	73	3.52
Iceland	8	5.44	8	8	5.50	Russian Federation	72	3.68	69	70	3.54
Korea, Rep.	9	5.43	9	19	5.14	Vietnam	73	3.67	70	82	3.40
Norway	10	5.38	10	10	5.42	Morocco	74	3.67	71	76	3.45
Hong Kong SAR	11	5.31	11	12	5.35	Dominican Republic	75	3.66	72	66	3.56
United Kingdom	12	5.30	12	9	5.45	Indonesia	76	3.60	73	62	3.59
Canada	13	5.30	13	11	5.35	Argentina	77	3.59	74	63	3.59
Australia	14	5.28	14	15	5.24	Botswana	78	3.59	75	67	3.56
Austria	15	5.22	15	17	5.17	Sri Lanka	79	3.58	76	86	3.27
Germany	16	5.19	16	16	5.22	Guatemala	80	3.58	77	79	3.41
Taiwan, China	17	5.18	17	13	5.28	Philippines	81	3.56	78	69	3.55
Israel	18	5.18	18	18	5.14	Trinidad and Tobago	82	3.55	79	68	3.55
Japan	19	5.14	19	14	5.27	Macedonia, FYR	83	3.49	80	81	3.41
Estonia	20	5.12	20	20	5.02	Peru	84	3.46	81	78	3.43
France	21	5.11	21	23	4.99	Senegal	85	3.46	n/a	n/a	n/a
New Zealand	22	5.02	22	22	5.01	Venezuela	86	3.44	82	83	3.32
Ireland	23	5.02	23	21	5.01	Mongolia	87	3.43	83	90	3.18
Luxembourg	24	4.94	24	25	4.90	Algeria	88	3.38	84	80	3.41
Belgium	25	4.92	25	24	4.93	Pakistan	89	3.37	85	84	3.31
Malaysia	26	4.82	26	26	4.74	Honduras	90	3.35	86	94	3.09
Malta	27	4.61	27	27	4.52	Georgia	91	3.34	87	93	3.12
Portugal	28	4.60	28	28	4.48	Kenya	92	3.34	88	95	3.07
United Arab Emirates	29	4.55	29	29	4.42	Namibia	93	3.33	89	85	3.28
Slovenia	30	4.47	30	30	4.41	Nigeria	94	3.32	90	88	3.23
Spain	31	4.47	31	32	4.35	Bosnia and Herzegovina	95	3.22	91	89	3.20
Qatar	32	4.42	32	36	4.21	Moldova	96	3.21	92	92	3.13
Lithuania	33	4.41	33	39	4.18	Mauritania	97	3.21	93	87	3.25
Chile	34	4.35	34	31	4.36	Tajikistan	98	3.18	n/a	n/a	n/a
Tunisia	35	4.33	35	35	4.24	Mali	99	3.17	94	101	2.96
Czech Republic	36	4.33	36	34	4.28	Tanzania	100	3.17	95	91	3.13
Hungary	37	4.28	37	33	4.33	Gambia, The	101	3.17	n/a	n/a	n/a
Barbados	38	4.26	38	40	4.18	Guyana	102	3.16	96	98	3.01
Puerto Rico	39	4.25	n/a	n/a	n/a	Burkina Faso	103	3.12	97	99	2.97
Thailand	40	4.25	39	37	4.21	Madagascar	104	3.12	98	102	2.95
Cyprus	41	4.23	40	43	4.12	Libya	105	3.10	n/a	n/a	n/a
Italy	42	4.21	41	38	4.19	Armenia	106	3.10	99	96	3.07
Slovak Republic	43	4.17	42	41	4.15	Ecuador	107	3.09	100	97	3.05
Latvia	44	4.14	43	42	4.13	Albania	108	3.06	101	107	2.87
Bahrain	45	4.13	44	50	3.89	Uganda	109	3.06	102	100	2.97
Jamaica	46	4.09	45	45	4.05	Syria	110	3.06	n/a	n/a	n/a
Jordan	47	4.08	46	57	3.74	Bolivia	111	3.05	103	104	2.93
Saudi Arabia	48	4.07	n/a	n/a	n/a	Zambia	112	3.02	104	112	2.75
Croatia	49	4.06	47	46	4.00	Benin	113	3.01	105	109	2.83
India	50	4.06	48	44	4.06	Kyrgyz Republic	114	2.99	106	105	2.90
South Africa	51	4.05	49	47	4.00	Cambodia	115	2.96	107	106	2.88
Kuwait	52	4.01	50	54	3.80	Nicaragua	116	2.95	108	103	2.95
Oman	53	3.97	n/a	n/a	n/a	Suriname	117	2.91	109	110	2.82
Mauritius	54	3.96	51	51	3.87	Cameroon	118	2.89	110	113	2.74
Turkey	55	3.96	52	52	3.86	Nepal	119	2.88	111	108	2.83
Greece	56	3.94	53	48	3.98	Paraguay	120	2.87	112	114	2.69
China	57	3.90	54	59	3.68	Mozambique	121	2.82	113	115	2.64
Mexico	58	3.90	55	49	3.91	Lesotho	122	2.79	114	116	2.61
Brazil	59	3.87	56	53	3.84	Ethiopia	123	2.77	115	119	2.55
Costa Rica	60	3.87	57	56	3.77	Bangladesh	124	2.65	116	118	2.55
Romania	61	3.86	58	55	3.80	Zimbabwe	125	2.50	117	117	2.60
Poland	62	3.81	59	58	3.69	Burundi	126	2.46	118	121	2.40
Egypt	63	3.74	60	77	3.44	Chad	127	2.40	119	122	2.16
Panama	64	3.74	61	65	3.58						

(Cont'd.)

Table 3: Top performer on each pillar of the Networked Readiness Index 2007–2008

Country/Economy	Market environment	Regulatory environment	Infrastructure environment	Individual readiness	Business readiness	Government readiness	Individual usage	Business usage	Government usage
Singapore	1	1	26	2	12	1	18	15	4
Iceland	10	9	1	8	22	15	10	10	21
Finland	5	4	7	1	3	9	14	6	20
Switzerland	4	8	9	3	1	20	4	4	18
Netherlands	12	5	16	19	16	16	1	12	19
Sweden	9	11	3	9	10	4	3	1	6
Denmark	11	2	4	6	6	2	2	5	1

Table 4: Evolution of the Networked Readiness Index since 2001–02

Country/Economy	2001–02	2002–03	2003–04	2004–05	2005–06	2006–07	2007–08
(Number of economies)	72	82	102	104	115	122	127
Denmark	7	8	5	4	3	1	1
Sweden	4	4	4	6	8	2	2
Switzerland	16	13	7	9	9	5	3
United States	1	2	1	5	1	7	4
Singapore	8	3	2	1	2	3	5
Finland	3	1	3	3	5	4	6
Netherlands	6	11	13	16	12	6	7
Iceland	2	5	10	2	4	8	8
Korea, Rep.	20	14	20	24	14	19	9
Norway	5	17	8	13	13	10	10

market environments and ICT-related infrastructures in the world. In particular, the well-qualified and large pool of human resources (12th for availability of scientists and engineers), as well as the top-notch research institutions (ranked 2nd), provide an excellent infrastructure for innovation to flourish and for the development of the ICT industry. This has resulted in the country's undisputed role as the world's innovation powerhouse, witnessed by the 1st position obtained by the United States for the number of registered utility patents.

On a less positive note, some red tape and rigidities seem to hinder the US business environment, notably with respect to the burden of government regulation and the relatively high tax rates (67th). Moreover, the regulatory framework, assessed at 22nd, presents a number of relatively problematic features with respect to the independence of the judiciary (37th), the efficiency of the legal framework for disputes (30th), and protection of property rights (30th), among others.

Korea, at 9th place, realizes one of the most impressive improvements (10 places) from last year among the 127 economies covered by the *Report*. This reflects the country's comparative advantages in the quality of its higher educational system, availability of qualified labor force (13th for the availability of scientists and engineers), and leading research institutions (11th). This, combined with a very dynamic and sophisticated business sector,[13] has fostered remarkable degrees of innovation (as reflected in Korea's 8th place in the world for the number of registered utility patents) and the emergence of word-class multinationals, notably in the high-tech sector, whose exports amounted in 2005 to 25 percent of total exports (7th place overall). Last but not least, the coherent and continued role of the government in making ICT and, more generally, innovation a cornerstone of Korea's development strategy must be highlighted (3rd in government readiness), as well as its success in promoting ICT diffusion and in using ICT as an engine of increased productivity and efficiency (3rd in government usage).

A look at Tables 3 and 4 complements the observations just made on the most notable networked economies this year, by showing the top performer in each of the nine pillars composing the NRI, and the evolution of the top-10 ranked countries since 2001–02, respectively.

Table 3 highlights Singapore as the country topping the largest number of pillars, notably market environment, regulatory framework, and government readiness. Singapore's showing is even more impressive when compared with the top performers in the remaining pillars—each topping only one. This reflects Singapore's continuous advances in enhancing and fine-tuning the networked readiness enablers to increasingly leverage ICT for competitiveness.

Among the other pillars, Iceland displays the best ICT infrastructure in the sample, with notable marks registered for the number of telephone lines (3rd), secure Internet servers, and electricity production (both 1st out of 127 countries).

Two Nordic countries, Finland and Sweden, top the individual readiness and business usage pillars, respectively. While Finland displays the highest degree of individual readiness in the world, mainly in view of its top-class educational system (notably in math and science), Sweden's business sector appears to be the most effective in using ICT, thanks to the excellent innovation potential of its firms.

Switzerland is in turn the best performer in the business readiness pillar, scoring among the top countries in the world in most of the variables included in the pillar.

Last, the Netherlands ranks 1st for individual usage, and has Internet and PC penetration rates that are among the highest in the world.

Interestingly enough, Denmark—despite being ranked top country in the overall NRI—is outperforming the rest of the sample in only one pillar (government usage), but is consistent in being ranked among the best in the world in all three component subindexes—it is 1st, 2nd, and 2nd for the usage, environment, and readiness, respectively.

The rest of this section will be devoted to highlighting the main findings of the NRI 2007–2008 per region, namely Europe and North America, Asia and the Pacific, Latin America and the Caribbean, and sub-Saharan Africa and Middle East and North Africa (MENA).

Europe and North America

Europe remains an important player in networked readiness this year: indeed, not only Denmark tops the NRI rankings, but 10 other European countries are among the top 20, as follows: Sweden (2nd), Switzerland (3rd), Finland (6th), the Netherlands (7th), Iceland (8th), Norway (10h), the United Kingdom (12th), Austria (15th), Germany (16th), and Estonia (20th).

As shown in Table 4, the **Nordic countries** have featured consistently among the top 10 over the last seven years, with impressive ICT penetration and diffusion rates. The reasons for this remarkable performance have been detailed above and have much to do with a few common features: a continuous focus on education, which resulted in top-class national educational systems; a culture for innovation with an outstanding public and private disposition to create and adopt new technologies; and a business-friendly market and regulatory environment.

As in previous years, the networked readiness picture for the **EU15** is more mixed in nature.[14] The Nordic countries, the Netherlands, the United Kingdom, Germany, Austria, **France** (21st), **Ireland** (23rd), and **Belgium** (25th) present satisfactory levels of networked readiness and benefit from ICT advances. However, countries such as **Greece** (56th) and, to a lesser extent, **Italy** (42nd) continue to lag behind and even seem to be losing speed with respect to the 2006–07 rankings.

Among the **EU accession 12,**[15] countries such as **Estonia** (20th), **Slovenia** (30th), **Lithuania** (33rd), the **Czech Republic** (36th), and **Hungary** (37th) have made remarkable progress in networked readiness, as well as general competitiveness, over the last two decades. Among these countries, Estonia, the tiny homeland of Skype, has benefited from a savvy e-leadership from the government that fostered innovation and universal ICT access as a platform for improved competitiveness.[16] Another Baltic state, Lithuania, realizes one of the biggest improvements (six positions) in Europe from last year.

Poland (62nd) and **Bulgaria** (68th) struggle, even if it must be noted that the latter posted a very large improvement (seven positions in a constant sample)[17] from 2006–07, boosted by better levels of usage, especially from its citizens (46th vs. 53rd last year). Poland, in turn, continues to show notable weaknesses specifically in government readiness (96th) and usage (103rd), as well as in the regulatory environment (90th), indicating the unsatisfactory role of the government as an engine of ICT diffusion.

Turkey is broadly stable at 55th, with a rather even performance across the three NRI components and much room for improvement especially in the readiness subindex (61st), typically in the accessibility of ICT, the quality of education, and the government's vision and e-leadership in ICT diffusion.

Russia positions itself, largely unchanged, at 72nd place this year. Its networked readiness rests on the country's good-quality education and research institutions as well as on firms' innovative potential. Nevertheless, the poor quality of the market (88th) and regulatory (92nd) environments, coupled with a lack of focus on ICT in the government's agenda (as highlighted in the poor marks for government readiness and usage, at 89th and 101st, respectively), remain reasons for concern.

Within **North America,** the United States and **Canada** continue to feature, at 4th and 13th respectively, among the leading networked economies in the world. The United States' performance has already been analyzed early in this paper. With respect to Canada, the NRI points out the readiness component (20th) as an area in need of relative improvement, especially of the business sector (19th) and of the government (25th).

Table 5: Environment component subindex

ENVIRONMENT COMPONENT			Market environment		Political and regulatory environment		Infrastructure environment	
Rank	Country/Economy	Score	Rank	Score	Rank	Score	Rank	Score
1	Iceland	5.69	10	5.15	9	5.80	1	6.12
2	Denmark	5.51	11	5.14	2	5.96	4	5.44
3	Finland	5.50	5	5.45	4	5.89	7	5.17
4	Sweden	5.50	9	5.15	11	5.76	3	5.58
5	United States	5.46	3	5.49	22	5.29	2	5.60
6	Switzerland	5.43	4	5.49	8	5.80	9	5.02
7	Norway	5.30	19	4.89	13	5.73	6	5.29
8	Canada	5.30	16	5.08	19	5.42	5	5.40
9	Singapore	5.23	1	5.58	1	6.13	26	3.98
10	United Kingdom	5.22	13	5.12	12	5.73	11	4.80
11	Germany	5.17	17	5.01	3	5.93	14	4.57
12	Australia	5.17	21	4.80	7	5.84	10	4.86
13	Netherlands	5.14	12	5.13	5	5.86	16	4.43
14	New Zealand	5.07	27	4.64	15	5.53	8	5.03
15	Ireland	5.01	15	5.09	17	5.46	15	4.49
16	Hong Kong SAR	5.01	2	5.51	10	5.77	33	3.74
17	Korea, Rep.	4.99	7	5.18	20	5.37	17	4.42
18	Japan	4.97	14	5.12	14	5.55	21	4.24
19	Israel	4.97	8	5.18	25	5.06	13	4.66
20	Austria	4.96	22	4.78	6	5.84	20	4.25
21	Taiwan, China	4.84	6	5.36	42	4.42	12	4.72
22	France	4.83	25	4.68	16	5.46	18	4.35
23	Luxembourg	4.67	20	4.86	18	5.44	35	3.71
24	Estonia	4.66	23	4.78	24	5.18	24	4.02
25	Belgium	4.64	26	4.67	23	5.19	22	4.07
26	Malaysia	4.57	18	4.97	21	5.32	41	3.42
27	Barbados	4.36	59	3.91	27	4.89	19	4.27
28	Portugal	4.34	32	4.36	30	4.84	27	3.83
29	Malta	4.34	34	4.33	28	4.87	29	3.81
30	Cyprus	4.21	40	4.18	33	4.65	30	3.80
31	Puerto Rico	4.19	28	4.59	34	4.63	43	3.36
32	Hungary	4.18	38	4.27	40	4.46	28	3.83
33	Spain	4.15	43	4.13	36	4.54	31	3.79
34	Lithuania	4.12	47	4.10	37	4.50	32	3.75
35	Chile	4.10	30	4.43	31	4.71	50	3.16
36	Kuwait	4.09	29	4.46	51	4.22	37	3.60
37	Slovenia	4.07	58	3.93	48	4.26	23	4.03
38	Tunisia	4.07	41	4.16	29	4.84	47	3.22
39	United Arab Emirates	4.05	24	4.73	45	4.35	56	3.08
40	South Africa	4.05	35	4.28	26	5.00	66	2.86
41	Thailand	4.02	31	4.39	35	4.61	58	3.04
42	Czech Republic	4.01	46	4.12	54	4.19	34	3.72
43	Qatar	4.00	48	4.09	32	4.65	46	3.25
44	Latvia	4.00	45	4.12	43	4.40	40	3.47
45	Saudi Arabia	3.93	37	4.27	53	4.19	45	3.34
46	Greece	3.93	77	3.64	55	4.17	25	3.98
47	Slovak Republic	3.90	36	4.27	50	4.23	48	3.20
48	Mauritius	3.90	33	4.34	41	4.45	62	2.90
49	Jordan	3.85	54	4.00	38	4.49	57	3.06
50	Bahrain	3.80	42	4.15	57	4.16	54	3.09
51	Turkey	3.79	51	4.06	44	4.35	60	2.96
52	Croatia	3.73	61	3.87	63	3.97	44	3.36
53	Jamaica	3.73	39	4.19	52	4.20	73	2.80
54	India	3.73	49	4.09	47	4.26	71	2.82
55	Italy	3.72	71	3.74	75	3.79	36	3.63
56	Oman	3.72	44	4.12	46	4.30	76	2.73
57	Panama	3.62	50	4.07	66	3.94	69	2.83
58	Poland	3.61	74	3.72	90	3.58	38	3.54
59	Kazakhstan	3.58	72	3.74	67	3.92	55	3.09
60	Egypt	3.57	66	3.85	61	4.01	64	2.86
61	Costa Rica	3.57	70	3.78	71	3.80	52	3.13
62	Mexico	3.54	57	3.96	70	3.83	67	2.84
63	Romania	3.53	60	3.90	77	3.78	61	2.91
64	Russian Federation	3.53	88	3.52	92	3.54	39	3.53
65	Botswana	3.52	63	3.86	49	4.25	93	2.44
66	China	3.51	69	3.79	58	4.15	86	2.58
67	Morocco	3.50	65	3.85	65	3.95	78	2.70
68	Namibia	3.48	85	3.53	39	4.46	92	2.45
69	Uruguay	3.48	83	3.58	60	4.02	68	2.84
70	Ukraine	3.46	94	3.45	94	3.52	42	3.40
71	Bulgaria	3.43	82	3.59	89	3.58	53	3.13
72	Mongolia	3.37	95	3.44	97	3.51	51	3.16
73	Vietnam	3.37	80	3.60	59	4.03	91	2.46
74	Indonesia	3.36	52	4.03	81	3.68	99	2.35
75	Sri Lanka	3.36	64	3.85	72	3.80	95	2.41
76	Azerbaijan	3.34	81	3.60	74	3.79	83	2.62
77	Philippines	3.33	56	3.96	80	3.72	101	2.32
78	El Salvador	3.33	53	4.02	76	3.79	106	2.18
79	Georgia	3.32	68	3.83	91	3.56	85	2.58
80	Colombia	3.32	96	3.43	79	3.75	74	2.78
81	Trinidad and Tobago	3.31	67	3.84	108	3.26	70	2.83
82	Macedonia, FYR	3.27	93	3.46	101	3.39	59	2.97
83	Dominican Republic	3.27	62	3.86	68	3.85	108	2.09
84	Kenya	3.24	98	3.41	88	3.59	77	2.72
85	Mali	3.22	78	3.63	73	3.00	103	2.23
86	Brazil	3.22	116	3.12	86	3.64	63	2.89
87	Tanzania	3.19	90	3.51	62	3.99	110	2.06
88	Honduras	3.17	76	3.66	85	3.65	104	2.21
89	Moldova	3.17	114	3.16	82	3.66	79	2.70
90	Guatemala	3.17	55	3.98	95	3.52	115	2.02
91	Nigeria	3.15	73	3.72	78	3.76	120	1.98
92	Argentina	3.15	118	3.08	115	3.18	49	3.18
93	Uganda	3.14	101	3.30	87	3.59	88	2.52
94	Gambia, The	3.14	103	3.28	56	4.17	122	1.96
95	Burkina Faso	3.13	92	3.47	69	3.85	109	2.07
96	Tajikistan	3.11	121	2.97	64	3.95	97	2.40
97	Algeria	3.09	117	3.09	96	3.51	80	2.67
98	Peru	3.08	79	3.62	109	3.25	98	2.37
99	Zambia	3.07	87	3.52	83	3.66	113	2.04
100	Armenia	3.07	102	3.29	107	3.26	81	2.67
101	Pakistan	3.07	75	3.68	93	3.54	118	2.00
102	Lesotho	3.06	113	3.22	114	3.19	75	2.77
103	Senegal	3.04	84	3.58	110	3.25	102	2.30
104	Kyrgyz Republic	3.03	115	3.15	103	3.33	84	2.60
105	Syria	3.03	107	3.26	106	3.31	87	2.52
106	Madagascar	3.02	91	3.49	99	3.39	105	2.19
107	Guyana	2.99	112	3.24	112	3.22	89	2.51
108	Benin	2.97	109	3.25	84	3.66	117	2.01
109	Libya	2.97	123	2.77	102	3.33	72	2.81
110	Nepal	2.96	86	3.53	100	3.39	121	1.97
111	Bosnia and Herzegovina	2.95	104	3.28	116	3.13	94	2.44
112	Mauritania	2.90	108	3.26	98	3.43	116	2.01
113	Bolivia	2.88	120	2.99	120	3.02	82	2.63
114	Paraguay	2.87	89	3.51	125	2.77	100	2.34
115	Albania	2.87	106	3.26	111	3.24	107	2.10
116	Nicaragua	2.86	97	3.43	117	3.12	114	2.03
117	Venezuela	2.85	124	2.74	121	2.97	65	2.86
118	Ethiopia	2.80	105	3.27	113	3.20	124	1.94
119	Cambodia	2.79	99	3.39	105	3.31	127	1.66
120	Mozambique	2.77	111	3.24	104	3.33	126	1.73
121	Ecuador	2.76	110	3.24	119	3.04	119	1.99
122	Zimbabwe	2.72	125	2.71	122	2.96	90	2.50
123	Bangladesh	2.70	100	3.39	124	2.77	123	1.95
124	Cameroon	2.69	122	2.95	118	3.08	112	2.04
125	Suriname	2.68	119	3.04	127	2.61	96	2.41
126	Burundi	2.50	126	2.58	123	2.85	111	2.06
127	Chad	2.30	127	2.49	126	2.61	125	1.79

(Cont'd.)

Table 6: Readiness component subindex

Rank	Country/Economy	READINESS COMPONENT Score	Individual readiness Rank	Individual readiness Score	Business readiness Rank	Business readiness Score	Government readiness Rank	Government readiness Score
1	Singapore	5.98	2	6.52	12	5.52	1	5.89
2	Denmark	5.93	6	6.36	6	5.67	2	5.77
3	Korea, Rep.	5.91	7	6.36	11	5.62	3	5.76
4	Sweden	5.85	9	6.29	10	5.64	4	5.63
5	Finland	5.85	1	6.52	3	5.74	9	5.29
6	Switzerland	5.82	3	6.46	1	5.96	20	5.04
7	United States	5.77	14	6.17	4	5.72	5	5.41
8	Austria	5.66	10	6.28	5	5.71	23	4.98
9	Taiwan, China	5.62	12	6.27	17	5.40	11	5.20
10	Norway	5.61	17	6.14	20	5.34	6	5.37
11	Malaysia	5.61	22	6.10	18	5.38	7	5.36
12	Japan	5.60	27	6.01	9	5.64	14	5.14
13	Germany	5.59	21	6.10	2	5.83	27	4.85
14	Israel	5.57	18	6.12	13	5.52	17	5.08
15	Hong Kong SAR	5.57	4	6.42	21	5.24	19	5.05
16	France	5.57	15	6.17	15	5.47	18	5.06
17	Netherlands	5.56	19	6.11	16	5.45	16	5.12
18	Iceland	5.55	8	6.31	22	5.22	15	5.13
19	Ireland	5.54	16	6.15	8	5.66	28	4.80
20	Canada	5.52	11	6.27	19	5.35	25	4.95
21	United Kingdom	5.52	23	6.09	14	5.47	22	4.99
22	Belgium	5.52	5	6.37	7	5.66	35	4.52
23	Estonia	5.44	26	6.03	31	4.93	8	5.36
24	Australia	5.44	13	6.23	24	5.16	26	4.93
25	United Arab Emirates	5.31	33	5.90	37	4.80	10	5.23
26	Luxembourg	5.29	24	6.07	38	4.79	21	5.01
27	New Zealand	5.26	20	6.10	26	5.05	30	4.63
28	Qatar	5.24	28	5.99	41	4.78	24	4.96
29	Tunisia	5.22	25	6.05	32	4.90	29	4.69
30	Malta	5.19	30	5.98	49	4.45	13	5.14
31	Portugal	5.17	45	5.62	44	4.71	12	5.18
32	Slovenia	5.13	29	5.98	29	4.96	37	4.44
33	Czech Republic	5.07	31	5.95	25	5.08	49	4.18
34	Spain	5.07	36	5.73	27	5.01	36	4.46
35	Thailand	4.99	40	5.69	43	4.73	32	4.56
36	Chile	4.97	53	5.53	35	4.81	33	4.56
37	India	4.94	46	5.62	28	4.97	45	4.23
38	Lithuania	4.93	35	5.81	48	4.53	38	4.43
39	Hungary	4.84	42	5.67	47	4.61	44	4.26
40	Barbados	4.83	34	5.88	65	4.27	39	4.35
41	Oman	4.83	49	5.57	46	4.68	46	4.22
42	Croatia	4.82	44	5.65	45	4.70	54	4.11
43	Puerto Rico	4.82	60	5.39	23	5.17	72	3.90
44	Slovak Republic	4.81	39	5.69	42	4.74	62	4.01
45	Cyprus	4.80	32	5.94	60	4.33	52	4.13
46	Italy	4.79	47	5.61	39	4.78	64	3.98
47	Bahrain	4.79	41	5.67	79	4.12	31	4.57
48	Costa Rica	4.77	52	5.54	34	4.83	66	3.95
49	Saudi Arabia	4.75	71	5.13	40	4.78	40	4.34
50	Mauritius	4.74	54	5.51	57	4.36	41	4.34
51	South Africa	4.71	72	5.12	30	4.96	59	4.06
52	Jordan	4.71	55	5.47	77	4.13	34	4.53
53	Latvia	4.70	37	5.73	50	4.43	67	3.94
54	China	4.70	59	5.42	58	4.35	42	4.32
55	Brazil	4.64	77	5.07	36	4.81	61	4.04
56	Romania	4.63	43	5.66	61	4.32	69	3.92
57	Greece	4.59	50	5.56	63	4.29	70	3.92
58	Indonesia	4.59	38	5.71	33	4.86	111	3.20
59	Jamaica	4.59	65	5.26	54	4.38	55	4.11
60	Kuwait	4.58	48	5.57	53	4.38	80	3.79
61	Turkey	4.56	63	5.31	52	4.41	65	3.96
62	Azerbaijan	4.55	78	5.07	56	4.38	47	4.20
63	Mexico	4.53	67	5.20	64	4.27	53	4.12
64	Colombia	4.52	74	5.12	55	4.38	57	4.07
65	Poland	4.51	51	5.55	59	4.35	96	3.62
66	Vietnam	4.48	80	4.98	74	4.17	43	4.28
67	Russian Federation	4.46	56	5.45	69	4.23	89	3.70
68	El Salvador	4.45	70	5.14	78	4.13	56	4.09
69	Bulgaria	4.45	61	5.38	84	4.05	71	3.92
70	Egypt	4.42	83	4.89	73	4.19	48	4.19
71	Panama	4.42	64	5.29	71	4.20	82	3.78
72	Ukraine	4.40	58	5.42	80	4.09	91	3.69
73	Uruguay	4.38	73	5.12	82	4.08	68	3.92
74	Argentina	4.37	66	5.26	51	4.42	106	3.42
75	Macedonia, FYR	4.33	69	5.14	81	4.09	84	3.75
76	Morocco	4.32	79	5.04	76	4.14	79	3.79
77	Botswana	4.32	62	5.34	90	3.91	88	3.72
78	Kazakhstan	4.31	96	4.57	72	4.20	50	4.16
79	Dominican Republic	4.31	82	4.93	92	3.85	51	4.15
80	Sri Lanka	4.30	88	4.85	87	3.97	58	4.07
81	Guatemala	4.29	84	4.89	70	4.21	83	3.76
82	Trinidad and Tobago	4.28	57	5.42	99	3.67	86	3.73
83	Algeria	4.28	81	4.97	86	3.99	74	3.87
84	Venezuela	4.26	75	5.11	83	4.07	97	3.62
85	Peru	4.21	89	4.84	67	4.24	101	3.56
86	Senegal	4.18	94	4.62	75	4.15	81	3.78
87	Philippines	4.17	87	4.86	88	3.95	90	3.70
88	Mongolia	4.11	92	4.75	103	3.53	60	4.04
89	Pakistan	4.08	103	4.13	68	4.24	73	3.87
90	Honduras	4.03	95	4.61	89	3.93	102	3.55
91	Bosnia and Herzegovina	4.01	68	5.17	97	3.72	114	3.15
92	Georgia	4.00	76	5.09	109	3.44	104	3.47
93	Guyana	3.99	91	4.76	95	3.76	105	3.44
94	Nigeria	3.90	108	3.73	62	4.30	92	3.68
95	Kenya	3.89	107	3.73	66	4.25	93	3.68
96	Tajikistan	3.88	99	4.40	104	3.52	87	3.72
97	Ecuador	3.88	90	4.79	94	3.82	122	3.03
98	Libya	3.86	93	4.70	98	3.71	113	3.17
99	Albania	3.86	86	4.87	119	3.22	103	3.48
100	Namibia	3.82	98	4.41	91	3.87	112	3.17
101	Suriname	3.82	85	4.87	85	4.01	124	2.57
102	Moldova	3.72	102	4.14	107	3.46	100	3.56
103	Armenia	3.70	101	4.16	101	3.57	107	3.38
104	Madagascar	3.64	112	3.55	102	3.55	77	3.82
105	Bolivia	3.63	100	4.34	110	3.43	116	3.14
106	Kyrgyz Republic	3.61	97	4.42	115	3.32	119	3.08
107	Tanzania	3.59	114	3.31	100	3.65	78	3.80
108	Mauritania	3.55	117	3.16	105	3.49	63	3.99
109	Cambodia	3.54	110	3.66	114	3.33	94	3.64
110	Cameroon	3.53	109	3.70	93	3.82	120	3.08
111	Syria	3.51	111	3.62	117	3.28	95	3.63
112	Nicaragua	3.49	105	4.06	121	3.12	110	3.29
113	Zambia	3.45	106	3.94	113	3.35	121	3.06
114	Burkina Faso	3.42	120	2.99	96	3.72	99	3.57
115	Paraguay	3.42	104	4.10	116	3.29	123	2.86
116	Mali	3.40	118	3.07	118	3.28	75	3.85
117	Gambia, The	3.38	115	3.23	124	3.08	76	3.84
118	Benin	3.37	119	3.06	108	3.45	98	3.61
119	Nepal	3.32	113	3.52	112	3.36	118	3.08
120	Uganda	3.13	126	2.19	106	3.47	85	3.73
121	Mozambique	3.06	125	2.69	120	3.13	108	3.38
122	Lesotho	3.05	116	3.18	126	2.83	117	3.14
123	Ethiopia	3.03	124	2.69	123	3.09	109	3.32
124	Bangladesh	2.97	121	2.85	125	2.92	115	3.14
125	Chad	2.75	123	2.69	122	3.11	127	2.46
126	Zimbabwe	2.70	127	2.17	111	3.41	126	2.52
127	Burundi	2.70	122	2.74	127	2.81	125	2.54

(Cont'd.)

Table 7: Usage component subindex

USAGE COMPONENT			Individual usage		Business usage		Government usage	
Rank	Country/Economy	Score	Rank	Score	Rank	Score	Rank	Score
1	Denmark	5.89	2	5.71	5	5.96	1	5.99
2	Sweden	5.80	3	5.69	1	6.14	6	5.58
3	Netherlands	5.62	1	6.20	12	5.76	19	4.89
4	Korea, Rep.	5.38	15	4.30	7	5.87	3	5.96
5	Hong Kong SAR	5.36	5	5.04	19	5.51	7	5.54
6	Switzerland	5.35	4	5.14	4	6.00	18	4.90
7	Singapore	5.27	18	4.16	15	5.71	4	5.94
8	Estonia	5.27	11	4.56	23	5.29	2	5.96
9	United States	5.26	17	4.21	8	5.87	5	5.70
10	Norway	5.24	8	4.81	14	5.73	12	5.16
11	Australia	5.23	7	4.94	21	5.38	9	5.37
12	United Kingdom	5.17	6	5.01	11	5.76	22	4.73
13	Taiwan, China	5.08	19	4.15	17	5.67	8	5.42
14	Iceland	5.07	10	4.59	10	5.81	21	4.80
15	Canada	5.07	12	4.46	16	5.69	15	5.05
16	Finland	5.05	14	4.33	6	5.93	20	4.89
17	Austria	5.05	16	4.22	13	5.76	13	5.16
18	Israel	4.99	13	4.43	9	5.86	26	4.67
19	France	4.93	23	3.88	18	5.54	10	5.36
20	Luxembourg	4.87	9	4.72	27	5.18	25	4.70
21	Japan	4.86	22	4.02	3	6.03	31	4.52
22	Germany	4.79	21	4.06	2	6.06	38	4.26
23	New Zealand	4.72	24	3.86	24	5.26	14	5.05
24	Belgium	4.59	20	4.09	20	5.49	41	4.19
25	Ireland	4.50	26	3.67	28	5.12	24	4.71
26	Malta	4.30	39	2.77	37	4.91	11	5.22
27	United Arab Emirates	4.30	36	2.97	32	5.00	17	4.92
28	Malaysia	4.28	45	2.52	22	5.36	16	4.97
29	Portugal	4.28	33	3.02	29	5.10	23	4.71
30	Slovenia	4.22	27	3.56	34	4.94	42	4.16
31	Lithuania	4.19	30	3.25	42	4.81	32	4.51
32	Spain	4.18	29	3.43	40	4.83	37	4.27
33	Italy	4.12	25	3.68	45	4.68	47	4.00
34	Qatar	4.03	40	2.75	46	4.66	27	4.67
35	Chile	3.99	48	2.34	31	5.01	28	4.62
36	Jamaica	3.95	28	3.49	58	4.50	52	3.85
37	Czech Republic	3.91	31	3.20	25	5.23	92	3.29
38	Hungary	3.81	38	2.81	41	4.81	54	3.81
39	Bahrain	3.80	43	2.64	56	4.52	39	4.25
40	Slovak Republic	3.79	34	3.01	38	4.88	78	3.47
41	Brazil	3.75	64	1.84	36	4.91	33	4.51
42	Puerto Rico	3.75	52	2.15	30	5.02	45	4.07
43	Thailand	3.73	70	1.74	35	4.93	30	4.53
44	Latvia	3.73	35	2.98	55	4.52	61	3.68
45	Tunisia	3.70	66	1.80	33	4.97	35	4.33
46	Cyprus	3.69	37	2.86	54	4.54	63	3.66
47	Jordan	3.68	63	1.85	39	4.87	36	4.30
48	Croatia	3.64	41	2.69	52	4.56	62	3.67
49	Mexico	3.61	62	1.89	63	4.39	29	4.55
50	Barbados	3.60	32	3.12	66	4.33	87	3.36
51	India	3.53	109	1.20	26	5.18	40	4.21
52	Turkey	3.52	57	2.00	43	4.80	56	3.77
53	Saudi Arabia	3.52	56	2.02	49	4.59	51	3.95
54	China	3.50	80	1.60	59	4.47	34	4.45
55	Romania	3.41	44	2.58	80	4.11	73	3.55
56	Dominican Republic	3.41	72	1.74	62	4.41	44	4.08
57	South Africa	3.40	67	1.79	44	4.72	60	3.68
58	El Salvador	3.38	77	1.62	64	4.37	43	4.16
59	Oman	3.38	69	1.78	67	4.32	46	4.04
60	Kuwait	3.35	47	2.36	51	4.57	97	3.13
61	Uruguay	3.31	55	2.07	73	4.26	70	3.60
62	Greece	3.30	50	2.31	69	4.29	91	3.31
63	Poland	3.30	42	2.66	70	4.28	103	2.96
64	Colombia	3.29	65	1.81	74	4.23	53	3.84
65	Guatemala	3.27	81	1.59	47	4.61	69	3.61
66	Azerbaijan	3.27	90	1.45	65	4.36	48	3.99
67	Argentina	3.26	51	2.19	82	4.10	76	3.51
68	Bulgaria	3.25	46	2.52	97	3.80	82	3.44
69	Costa Rica	3.25	61	1.90	76	4.20	64	3.65
70	Mauritius	3.25	59	1.91	71	4.27	72	3.57
71	Ukraine	3.23	54	2.09	90	3.96	67	3.63
72	Egypt	3.22	94	1.35	57	4.52	55	3.79
73	Venezuela	3.20	60	1.90	83	4.10	71	3.59
74	Mauritania	3.18	98	1.32	72	4.27	50	3.95
75	Vietnam	3.17	92	1.40	79	4.13	49	3.99
76	Panama	3.17	85	1.57	53	4.55	84	3.39
77	Morocco	3.17	71	1.74	68	4.30	77	3.47
78	Philippines	3.16	88	1.52	60	4.45	75	3.51
79	Kazakhstan	3.14	76	1.67	86	4.05	58	3.70
80	Senegal	3.14	101	1.29	61	4.41	57	3.72
81	Sri Lanka	3.09	104	1.25	50	4.59	83	3.43
82	Peru	3.08	75	1.69	77	4.19	88	3.36
83	Trinidad and Tobago	3.08	49	2.34	89	4.00	106	2.89
84	Russian Federation	3.04	53	2.09	87	4.04	101	2.99
85	Gambia, The	2.98	103	1.25	85	4.06	65	3.64
86	Pakistan	2.95	102	1.27	75	4.21	85	3.38
87	Uganda	2.93	119	1.08	84	4.07	68	3.63
88	Botswana	2.92	87	1.52	96	3.81	80	3.44
89	Mali	2.91	118	1.08	91	3.95	59	3.69
90	Nigeria	2.90	107	1.23	81	4.10	86	3.37
91	Kenya	2.89	105	1.25	78	4.18	95	3.24
92	Macedonia, FYR	2.88	58	2.00	102	3.65	100	2.99
93	Indonesia	2.87	97	1.32	48	4.59	112	2.70
94	Honduras	2.84	100	1.30	94	3.87	89	3.34
95	Mongolia	2.82	91	1.41	105	3.58	79	3.47
96	Burkina Faso	2.81	121	1.06	98	3.74	66	3.64
97	Algeria	2.78	79	1.61	108	3.54	96	3.20
98	Tanzania	2.75	115	1.12	93	3.88	94	3.24
99	Moldova	2.74	83	1.58	104	3.59	99	3.06
100	Georgia	2.70	89	1.46	99	3.73	105	2.92
101	Bosnia and Herzegovina	2.70	68	1.79	100	3.69	116	2.61
102	Benin	2.70	110	1.19	113	3.39	74	3.51
103	Namibia	2.69	93	1.35	88	4.03	113	2.69
104	Madagascar	2.69	120	1.06	107	3.56	81	3.44
105	Mozambique	2.64	117	1.10	106	3.58	93	3.25
106	Syria	2.63	99	1.32	95	3.86	110	2.72
107	Ecuador	2.63	73	1.72	112	3.40	109	2.76
108	Bolivia	2.62	96	1.32	121	3.21	90	3.33
109	Cambodia	2.56	122	1.06	109	3.50	98	3.13
110	Tajikistan	2.56	125	1.03	101	3.67	102	2.98
111	Zambia	2.54	111	1.16	92	3.91	120	2.55
112	Armenia	2.52	106	1.24	103	3.62	111	2.70
113	Nicaragua	2.50	95	1.33	116	3.29	107	2.89
114	Guyana	2.50	78	1.62	119	3.23	114	2.65
115	Libya	2.48	84	1.58	117	3.28	117	2.57
116	Albania	2.47	82	1.59	118	3.27	119	2.56
117	Ethiopia	2.47	127	1.00	110	3.45	104	2.95
118	Cameroon	2.46	114	1.13	114	3.36	108	2.87
119	Nepal	2.36	124	1.03	111	3.44	115	2.62
120	Kyrgyz Republic	2.34	112	1.16	115	3.34	122	2.52
121	Paraguay	2.33	86	1.53	124	3.04	125	2.41
122	Lesotho	2.27	113	1.14	122	3.13	121	2.54
123	Bangladesh	2.27	116	1.11	120	3.22	124	2.47
124	Suriname	2.24	74	1.71	123	3.07	127	1.95
125	Burundi	2.20	126	1.01	125	3.02	118	2.57
126	Chad	2.14	123	1.03	127	2.88	123	2.50
127	Zimbabwe	2.06	108	1.22	126	2.95	126	2.02

(Cont'd.)

Asia and the Pacific

The networked readiness assessment for Asia and the Pacific, as a region, is once again extremely diverse, pointing to very different capacities for leveraging ICT advances. While six Asian and Pacific economies are ranked in the top 20—namely **Singapore** (5th), **Korea** (9th), **Hong Kong** (11th), **Australia** (14th), **Taiwan** (17th), and **Japan** (19th)—countries such as **Cambodia** (115th), **Nepal** (119th), and **Bangladesh** (124th) continue to fall toward the end of the NRI rankings, displaying serious shortcomings in their networked readiness enablers.

Comments about the performances of Singapore and Korea have been made in earlier sections of this chapter. **Hong Kong,** broadly stable from last year, continues to benefit from high levels of ICT usage (5th overall), especially for citizens (5th) and the government (7th), and one the most ICT-friendly market environment in the world (2nd).

Taiwan, although losing some ground this year (four places),[18] is still ranked at a satisfactory 17th place overall, showing its resilience as one of the world's largest ICT exporters and producers (1st for the high-tech exports as a percentage of total exports) and a leading innovator (3rd for the number of registered utility patents). Taiwan's development story is textbook example of how a resource-poor rural economy can transform itself in the short span of three decades thanks to coherent e-leadership from the government in fostering ICT penetration, innovation, and education.[19]

Japan is down five positions at 19th, mainly because of deterioration in the market environment conditions (from 7th in 2006–07 to 14th this year) and in the individual readiness pillar (from 14th last year to 27th this year). In particular, the fall in the market environment can be explained, among other elements, by the inclusion of new hard data capturing the tax rate, for which the country ranks a dismal 91st. Nevertheless, the country benefits from a sophisticated and innovative business sector, displaying high ranks in readiness (9th) and usage (3rd). The government has also played a major role in promoting ICT diffusion (15th in the government prioritization of ICT variable), by constantly prioritizing the latter in the national strategy and adopting a comprehensive digital agenda from an early stage.[20]

India, at 50th, loses four positions in a constant sample from 2006–07. Although the country scores well for the sophistication of its business environment, availability of qualified labor force (an impressive 4th place for the availability scientists and engineers), and innovation potential, the poor state of the ICT infrastructure (71st) and the extremely low levels of ICT penetration among individuals (109th for individual usage) present severe obstacles for the country to fully use and leverage ICT in its economic and social activities.

China is up five positions in a constant sample at 57th,[21] presenting similar weaknesses as India, notably in its underdeveloped ICT infrastructure (86th) and scarce individual usage (80th). On a more positive note, ICT penetration seems to occupy a rather central position in the government agenda (42nd for government readiness). Moreover, the government's ICT strategy appears to have already borne some fruit in the form of ICT promotion, e-government services, and the government's productivity and efficiency improvements (34th for government usage).

Azerbaijan, at 67th, retains its predominance in Central Asia; it is followed closely by **Kazakhstan,** up five places from last year in a constant sample to 71st place. Notwithstanding this improvement, Kazakhstan continues to present a number of weaknesses, especially in individual readiness (96th) and usage (76th) and in business usage (86th).

Tajikistan re-enters the rankings at 98th this year.

Latin America and the Caribbean

The networked readiness snapshot offered by the NRI 2007–2008 for Latin America and the Caribbean appears less positive than last year, when a generalized upward trend was observed. This highlights the dynamism of the ICT sector, and the importance of economies making continuous progress in ICT diffusion, as well as innovation adoption, to maintain their competitive advantages.

At 34th (down three positions from 2006–07), **Chile** is again leading the region in networked readiness, with a relatively homogeneous performance across the three NRI subindexes, boosted by a strong focus of the government on ICT penetration and by the early adoption of a comprehensive digital agenda. This agenda has resulted in the establishment of world-class e-government services (ranked 12th) and in sophisticated e-commerce practices.[22]

Among the regional top performers this year, a handful of Caribbean economies—**Barbados** (38th), new entrant **Puerto Rico** (39th), and **Jamaica** (46th)—seem to be benefiting from ICT advances. Barbados is an interesting case of networked readiness driven mainly by its citizens (34th and 32nd for individual readiness and usage respectively) and by an ICT-conducive regulatory framework (27th) and infrastructure (19th). The relative degree of prioritization of ICT in the government agenda has failed so far to translate into higher levels of government usage (87th).

Mexico and **Brazil** drop a few places each this year, to 58th and 59th place, respectively. In both cases, the fall in ranking does not correspond to a dramatic fall in the absolute performance of the country vis-à-vis last year,[23] but rather to the fact other countries have progressed more rapidly. Although the two countries have realized significant progress in business as well as government readiness and usage, and they both show a high degree of ICT prioritization in their national agendas, their overregulated market environments, the poor quality of their educational systems, and low R&D

investments remain serious hindrances to achieving higher levels of networked readiness.

In the middle of the rankings, **Panama,** at 64th, is up four positions in a constant sample, while **Colombia,** at 69th, is down two positions in a constant sample. **Argentina** is down to 77th place, experiencing a fall of 11 rankings in a constant sample. A note of caution must be introduced here, since the country's absolute score is unchanged from last year. Nevertheless, the poor assessment of the market (118th) and regulatory (115th) environments in the country, as well as the perceived lack of focus on ICT penetration in the government agenda (106th), are all important shortcomings that need to be addressed as priorities by the new administration.

Peru (84th) and **Venezuela** (86th) follow, while **Bolivia** (111th), **Nicaragua** (116th), and **Paraguay** (120th) continue to lag behind the rest of the region, and most of the world, in networked readiness.

Sub-Saharan Africa and MENA

Despite the outstanding advances in ICT penetration that **sub-Saharan Africa** experienced in the last decade or so, which led the region to narrow the telecommunications access gap from 10 percent of the global average in 1991 to 19 percent in 2004,[24] the large majority of the region continues to lag in the global rankings of the NRI. Only **South Africa** (51st) and **Mauritius** (54th) feature in the first half of the rankings this year. In particular, South Africa, down two positions in a constant sample from 2006–07, continues to rest its ICT prowess on its conducive ICT market (35th) and regulatory (26th) environments and on a sophisticated business sector that has taken the lead in ICT penetration and usage, as confirmed by the good marks registered in business readiness (30th) and usage (44th).

Botswana, one of the traditional ICT champions in the region, is down eight positions in a constant sample to a disappointing 78th place. Again, in line with the earlier comments about Argentina, this drop in rankings should be taken with caution since it corresponds to an actually small 0.03 improvement in the absolute score from last year. **Senegal** enters the rankings this year at 85th position, just above **Kenya** (92nd), **Nigeria** (94th), and **Mauritania** (97th).

As in the past, the bottom ranks of the NRI 2007–2008 are occupied by sub-Saharan countries, notably **Cameroon** (118th), **Mozambique** (121st), **Lesotho** (122nd), **Ethiopia** (123rd), **Zimbabwe** (125th), **Burundi** (126th), and **Chad** (127th), highlighting once again the magnitude of the challenges involved for the region to benefit from the development and competitive potential of ICT. A lack of extensive and well-functioning infrastructure, overregulated and inefficient business environments, and poor governance and educational standards are all important hindrances in these countries.

The assessment given by the NRI 2007–2008 for **North Africa** is more positive, with **Egypt** and **Morocco** posting an impressive 17-place (the highest in the sample) and 5-place improvement, respectively, in a constant sample, and climbing to 63rd and 74th; only **Algeria** (at 88th) lost some ground. Egypt has advanced notably in the environment component (from 74th in 2006–07 to 60th this year), especially in the regulatory environment (from 77th to 61st this year), as well as in government readiness (from 81st to 48th this year), pointing to an increased emphasis on ICT penetration in the national development strategy.

The top performer in North Africa, **Tunisia,** is stable at 35th place. Its performance is boosted by an ICT-friendly regulatory environment (29th), a significant degree of preparedness and inclination to use ICT by all social actors (29th), and satisfactory usage levels by the business sector (33rd) and the government (35th). The satisfactory marks obtained in government readiness and usage point to the importance accorded to ICT in the national agenda, and to the successes realized by the government in ICT promotion and diffusion.

Last but not least, the networked readiness picture for the **Middle East** this year is very encouraging, with significant progress in ICT spearheaded by the Gulf States. Indeed, the latter are increasingly emphasizing the role of ICT for national development, both as a key infrastructure and as a promising sector in view of diversifying their economies away from oil.

Most of the countries in the region posted important improvements in the rankings, with **Qatar** (32nd), **Bahrain** (45th), and **Jordan** (47st) being at the forefront, with a remarkable 4-, 6-, and 11-place rise, respectively, in a constant sample. Qatar's promising government's e-strategy and initiatives are the subject of Chapter 2.2, "Qatar: Leveraging Technology to Create a Knowledge-Based Economy in the Middle East," in this *Report*. Also **Kuwait** (52nd) climbed four positions in a constant sample from last year.

Israel, unchanged at 18th place, continues to lead the Middle East in networked readiness, displaying outstanding levels of technological sophistication and innovation, world-class research institutions and educational system, and excellent ICT penetration. The country represents another success story of a resource-poor economy turned into an ICT powerhouse in the short span of three decades, thanks to visionary e-leadership from the government and its highly educated and entrepreneurial citizens.[25]

The **United Arab Emirates (UAE),** unchanged from last year at 29th place, continues to lead the Gulf States in networked readiness, owing to a leading government role in ICT promotion as witnessed by the excellent marks the country obtains in government readiness (10th) and usage (17th). Dubai's e-Government Initiative, initiated in 2000 and fostering ICT implementation in the UAE, has been recognized as a success story by practitioners and is an integral part of Dubai Vision 2010, which aims to establish Dubai as a knowledge-based economy by leveraging tourism, ICT, media, trade, and services.

One must also note that of the four newly included countries from the region this year, **Saudi Arabia** and **Oman** enter the rankings in fairly high positions: they are 48th and 53rd, respectively, while **Libya** (105th) and **Syria** (110th) seem to have still a long way to go to catch up the rest of the region in networked readiness.

More details on the performance of countries from the Middle East are presented in the following section.

Some historical trends on networked readiness: The most dynamic countries from 2001 to 2007

A unique feature of the NRI is that it has been computed for the last seven years and hence provides a rich source of longitudinal data about the evolution of countries in networked readiness. As the number of countries has increased from 72 in the first year (2001–02) to 127 this year, we have performed an analysis of the movement of countries across the years based upon deciles. Countries included in the NRI rankings each year have been assigned a decile score and we have analyzed the variations in their decile scores over the last seven years.

Table 8 presents a summary of the countries that have moved up in their decile score by more than two ranks over the last seven years. Note that this table does not list countries that were already in the highest decile groups in 2001–02 and have stayed stable in that decile group (this would typically include countries from developed regions such as North America and Western Europe). As evident from Table 8, three BRIC countries —**China, India,** and **Russia**—have made important upward movements in their networked readiness over the last seven years. The advances made by India and China, in particular, are very impressive; this is line with the progress observed in both countries, especially in the domain of ICT services and goods, respectively. India has occupied a prime position in global ICT services, with exports totaling around $60 billion and the emergence of global players in the sector such as Infosys and Wipro. China has also emerged rapidly as the biggest exporter of ICT goods in the world, eclipsing the United States and Europe, driven by its growing domestic market and its success in global manufacturing.

Lithuania, too—influenced by the successes of neighboring Estonia and Finland—has made important progress in networked readiness. Also of note are the important steps taken forward by other emerging economies such as **Vietnam** and **Ukraine,** as well as Jordan and Egypt in the Middle East. As GDP evolution shows a good correlation with networked readiness (Figure 1), the future development prospects of these economies look good.

Table 9 presents a historical analysis of the evolution of networked readiness across different regions of the world.[26] The advanced economies of the world show little movement, as noted earlier. Several parts of the

Table 8: Variations in decile ranks of countries from 2001–02 to 2007–08

Country/Economy	Earliest	Latest	Difference
China	9	5	4
Egypt	8	5	3
Guatemala	10	7	3
India	8	4	4
Jamaica	8	4	4
Jordan	7	4	3
Lithuania	6	3	3
Romania	9	5	4
Russian Federation	9	6	3
Ukraine	9	6	3
Vietnam	10	6	4

Table 9: Variations in decile ranks of regions from 2001–02 to 2007–08

Region	Earliest	Latest	Difference
Advanced economies	2	2	0
Africa	8.5	8	0.5
Central and Eastern Europe	5.5	4	1.5
Commonwealth of Independent States and Mongolia	9	7.5	1.5
Developing Asia	8	6.5	1.5
Middle East	7.5	4.5	3
Western Hemisphere	7	6.5	0.5

world—such as Central and Eastern Europe and Developing Asia—have made good progress over the last seven years. The progress of Central and Eastern Europe has been influenced by the ongoing expansion of the European Union. As countries in this region join the European Union, they are required to make deep changes in their market and policy environments and also get support for improving their infrastructures. In the Developing Asia region, China, India, and Vietnam are clearly the drivers of progress and improvement.

However, the **Middle East** stands out as having made the largest progress in networked readiness over the last seven years, improving as a region across three decile groups. During the past six years, the region recorded the largest growth in Internet users among the major world areas as the number of Middle Eastern citizens accessing the Web soared by more than 600 percent, three times the world's average increase. Some Gulf countries, such as the UAE, stand out in their efforts to promote and leverage ICT. Since 2000, UAE policymakers have promoted building the Emirates into information-rich societies. The UAE has also launched several technology-intensive innovation initiatives, such as Dubai Media City (DMC), launched in November 2000; next to DMC are Dubai Internet City (DIC) and Knowledge Village (KV). The major goal of the multi-billion dollar DMC, DIC, and KV complex is to create a cluster of innovation comprising educators, incubators, logistic companies, multimedia businesses, telecommunications companies, remote service providers, software developers, and venture capitalists in one place. Dubai Internet City is the region's first technology innovation zone and is viewed by decision makers in the UAE as an economic driver not only to Dubai's economy, but to the country's as a whole. Today, hundreds of high-tech firms are housed in the DIC. The DMC houses more than 550 media companies, including global giants, along with regional companies and new startups. Companies in this high-tech corridor employ more than 7,000 knowledge workers from all around the world.

Similar examples of ICT excellence can be found in other countries in the Middle East, including the richer Gulf States (see Chapter 2.2 on Qatar in this *Report*), as well as less rich economies such as Jordan and Egypt. Jordan has championed innovation in its educational system through the use of ICT. Through the Jordan Education Initiative (JEI), the country's main objectives are to enable its students to compete globally in the knowledge economy, to train teachers and administrators to use technology in the classroom, and to guide students through critical thinking and analysis. Today, the JEI is being replicated in Rajasthan, India (launched in November 2005); the Palestinian Territories; Bahrain; and, most recently, Egypt (launched in May 2006), as well as other countries.

Of great concern is the relative stagnation of **African countries** at the bottom of the decile rankings. Though some African countries in North Africa, such as Tunisia, are performing well and others such as Egypt and Morocco are improving their positions, the continent as a whole (with the exception of South Africa) is not succeeding in keeping up with the rapid pace of change in ICT in other regions of the world. Note that the stagnation in the decile rankings for African countries does not indicate that they have not made progress in leveraging ICT. Many are heavily investing in ICT and have a clear digital strategy in place, as is the case of Ethiopia, previously highlighted. However, the progress being made is slower in relative terms than the progress being made by other regions of the world.

Conclusions

More important than rising Internet access or ringing mobile phones is awareness among public and private stakeholders and decision makers that it is no longer possible to relegate ICT policies to an administrative sideshow. A country's ICT capabilities can profoundly affect its capacity to innovate and its global competitiveness, as well as improve the socioeconomic prospects of its less-advantaged citizens. Senior-level attention to ICT as a key enabler of innovation has been expressed in different ways in different countries, but a fundamental and salutary change is that these issues now rank as top agenda items.

Efforts such as the Networked Readiness Framework and the NRI serve as important tools for leaders from the public and private sectors to use in enhancing their understanding of the links between ICT investment and improvements in competitiveness and development. They also serve to provide an objective basis for comparing the achievements of specific countries or regions in networked readiness and in identifying best practices. Although the limitations of the NRI and its underlying data have to be noted, the *Global Information Technology Report* series over the last seven years provides a valuable repository of longitudinal data on networked readiness. Case studies included in the various *Global Information Technology Reports* complement the empirical data with qualitative analyses of specific best practices.

Notes

1 See Kusakabe and Moffatt 2004.

2 See Trajtenberg 2006.

3 A notable example in this area is Ethiopia, whose government is investing 10 percent of the country's GDP into modern ICT over the next five years. This investment is justified, Ethiopian officials believe, if they are to make investments in education, agriculture, health care, and the economy pay off. To make dreams come true, Ethiopia is looking to Cisco to help build one of the most sophisticated IP networks in all of Africa. Ultimately, Ethiopia hopes to provide 450 secondary schools with email and Internet connectivity, and connect 600 local administrations with 11 regional government offices and the federal government. Also, Ethiopia aims at rolling out broadband to some 16,000 villages across the country—enough so that every citizen will be within five kilometers from an access point. For further information, see http://emergingtimes.typepad.com/bestoftimes/country_transformation/index.html.

4 See Farnsworth et al. 2007.

5 BSG 2004.

6 A note of caution must be introduced when comparing the last six years of NRI results with the one featured in the very first edition of the *Report* in 2001–02. Since the NRI framework, in its current form, was developed by INSEAD in 2002, it is not strictly comparable to the one used in the first edition. For more information on the 2001–02 theoretical framework, see Kirkman et al. 2002.

7 For further details on the networked readiness framework and its theoretical conception, see Dutta and Jain 2003.

8 For a more in depth analysis of the Survey's process and methodology, see Browne and Geiger 2007.

9 Tajikistan, in particular, was included in the Survey and in the NRI computation for the first time in 2005–06, but could not be included in the *Report* last year because of the many missing hard data points.

10 Until the 2005–06 GITR edition, factor analytical techniques were used to select the variables used to compute the NRI from a larger set of possible variables. Although this was a technically rigorous approach, it reduced the ability to easily explain the underlying logic for including specific variables and to make strict comparisons over time. As a consequence, starting from 2006–07, expert opinion has played a predominant role in selecting the variables, obviously with the benefit of previous experience in identifying appropriate variables for computing the NRI,

thus aligning the NRI's to the Forum's general competitiveness methodology. In this sense, the treatment of missing variables has also changed: whereas until 2005–06, those were estimated using analytical techniques such as regression and clustering, beginning in 2006–07 they are indicated with "n/a" and not taken in consideration in the calculation of the specific pillar to which they belong. Moreover, the scale used to compute the NRI and the variables that compose it has been aligned to the Forum's (increasing) 1–7 scale, changing with respect to the scale used previously for a couple of years (i.e., positive and negative scores around a standardized mean of 0). For more detailed information on the old computation methodology and on the changes introduced in 2006–07, see Dutta and Jain 2006 and Mia and Dutta 2007.

11. An important element of the government far-sightedness in promoting ICT diffusion has been the early liberalization of the telecommunications sector in 1996, well ahead most of the European Union. Incidentally, this also greatly contributed to the development of a world-class local high-tech industry, whose exports accounted in 2005 for 9.38 percent of total exports, representing 25th place in the sample.

12. See Sala-i-Martin et al. 2007.

13. Indeed, Korea displays one of the most developed cluster system in the world (3rd), characterized by an important degree of cooperation between academia and industry (5th) and by companies investing heavily in R&D (6th) and with a high innovation potential (7th).

14. Countries in the EU15 are Austria, Belgium, Denmark, Finland, France, Germany, Greece, Ireland, Italy, Luxembourg, the Netherlands, Portugal, Spain, Sweden, and the United Kingdom.

15. The 12 EU accession countries are Bulgaria, Cyprus, the Czech Republic, Estonia, Hungary, Latvia, Lithuania, Malta, Poland, Romania, Slovakia, and Slovenia.

16. For a full analysis of Estonia's ICT development story, see Dutta 2007.

17. By referring to a country's performance in a "constant sample," we mean its ranking with respect to the same countries included in the GITR 2006–2007—that is, excluding the ones covered for the first time this year.

18. In particular, the regulatory environment seems to have experienced some deterioration from last year (from 31st in 2006–07 to 42nd this year), as well as individual readiness (which dropped from 7th to 12th), notably with respect to some elements of ICT accessibility, for which Taiwan does not seem to have progressed as rapidly as other economies.

19. For a more detailed analysis of Taiwan's story, see Dahl and Lopez-Claros 2006.

20. See Shimizu et al. 2007.

21. As in previous years, one must keep in mind that India and China show both large regional disparities in general competitiveness as well as in the extent of ICT penetration and usage; disparities which tend to be partially hidden by the overall national NRI assessment.

22. For a full account of Chile's digital agenda, see Alvarez Voullième et al. 2005.

23. In this sense, Mexico and Brazil's respective 6- and 3-place drops in a constant sample correspond to a minor negative delta of 0.01 for Mexico and to a modest positive delta of 0.03 for Brazil in the respective scores.

24. Haacker 2007. The author also points out how the number of mobile telephone subscribers has grown at an impressive 91 percent annual average rate, while the total telephone subscribers has grown at a rate of 21 percent from 1991 to 2004 and at 31 percent from 1999 to 2004.

25. For a full account of Israel's inspiring development story, see Lopez-Claros and Mia 2006.

26. The classification of countries by the International Monetary Fund (IMF) has been used as a basis for assigning countries to specific regions.

References

Álvarez Voullième, C., C. Capdevila de la Cerda, F. Flores Labra, A. Foxley Rioseco and A. Navarro Haeussler. 2005. "Information and Communication Technologies in Chile: Past Efforts, Future Challenges." *The Global Information Technology Report 2005–2006*. Hampshire: Palgrave Macmillan. 71–88.

Browne, C. and T. Geiger. 2007. "The Executive Opinion Survey: The Voice from the Business Community." *The Global Competitiveness Report 2007–2008*. Hampshire: Palgrave McMillan. 85–96.

BSG (Broadband Stakeholder Group). 2004. "Impact of Broadband-Enabled ICT, Content, Applications and Services on the UK Economy and Society to 2010." *BSG Briefing Paper* 27. September. Available at http://www.broadbanduk.org/component/option,com_docman/task,doc_view/gid,111/.

Dahl, A. and A. Lopez-Claros. 2006. "The Impact of Information and Communication Technologies on the Economic Competitiveness and Social Development of Taiwan." *The Global Information Technology Report 2005–2006*. Hampshire: Palgrave Macmillan. 107–18.

Dutta S. 2007. "Estonia: A Sustainable Success in Networked Readiness?" *The Global Information Technology Report 2006-2007*. Hampshire: Palgrave McMillan. 81–90.

Dutta, S., A. de Meyer, A. Jain, and G. Richter. 2006. *The Information Society in an Enlarged Europe*. Berlin: Springer-Verlag.

Dutta, S. and A. Jain. 2003. "The Networked Readiness of Nations." *The Global Information Technology Report 2002–2003*. New York: Oxford University Press. 2–25.

———. 2006. "Networked Readiness and the Benchmarking of ICT Competitiveness." *The Global Information Technology Report 2005–2006*. Hampshire: Palgrave Macmillan. 3–24.

Dutta, S., B. Lanvin, and F. Paua, eds. 2003. *The Global Information Technology Report 2002–2003: Readiness for the Networked World*. New York: Oxford University Press.

Dutta, S. and A. Lopez-Claros, eds. 2005. *The Global Information Technology Report 2004–2005: Efficiency in an Increasingly Connected World*. Hampshire: Palgrave Macmillan.

Dutta, S., F. Paua, and B. Lanvin, eds. 2004. *The Global Information Technology Report 2003–2004: Towards an Equitable Information Society*. New York: Oxford University Press.

Dutta, S., A. Lopez-Claros, and I. Mia, eds. 2006. *The Global Information Technology Report 2005–2006: Leveraging ICT for Development*. Hampshire: Palgrave Macmillan.

Farnsworth R., L. Gibbons, T. Lewis and M. Powell. 2007. "Networks Changing the Way We Work, Live, Play, and Learn." *The Global Information Technology Report 2006–2007*. Hampshire: Palgrave McMillan. 23–38.

Haacker M. 2007. "Access to Communications Services in Sub-Saharan Africa." *The Global Information Technology Report 2006–2007*. Hampshire: Palgrave McMillan. 91–106

IMF (International Monetary Fund). 2007. *World Economic Outlook Database,* December 2007. Washington, DC: International Monetary Fund.

Kirkman, G., P. Cornelius, J. Sachs, and K. Schwab, eds. 2002. *The Global Information Technology Report 2001–2002: Readiness for the Networked World*. New York: Oxford University Press.

Kusakabe M. and P. Moffatt. 2004. *Information and Communication Technology, Policy Reform and Rural Communication Infrastructure*. London: European Bank of Reconstruction and Development.

Lopez-Claros, A., L. Altinger, J. Blanke, M. Drzeniek, and I. Mia. 2006 "Assessing Latin American Competitiveness: Challenges and Opportunities." *The Latin America Competitiveness Review 2006*. Geneva: World Economic Forum. 1–36.

Lopez-Claros, A. and I. Mia. 2006. "Israel: Factor in the Emergence of an ICT Powerhouse." *The Global Information Technology Report 2005–2006*. Hampshire: Palgrave Macmillan. 89–105.

Mia, I. and S. Dutta. 2007. "Connecting the World to the Networked Economy: A Progress Report Based on the Findings of the Networked Readiness Index 2006-2007. "*The Global Information Technology Report 2006–2007*. Hampshire: Palgrave McMillan. 3–21.

Sala-i-Martin X., J. Blanke, M. Drneziek Hanouz, T. Geiger, I. Mia and F. Paua. 2007. "The Global Competitiveness Index: Measuring the Productive Potential of Nations." *The Global Competitiveness Report 2007–2008*. Hampshire: Palgrave McMillan. 3–50.

Shimizu H., K. Ogawa, and K. Fujinuma. 2007. "Information and Communication Technologies Policy in Japan: Meeting the Challenges Ahead." *The Global Information Technology Report 2006–2007*. Hampshire: Palgrave McMillan. 107–16.

Trajtenberg, M. 2006. "Innovation Policy for Development: An Overview." Foerder Institute for Economic Research, WP 6-06, July.

Appendix A: Technical composition and computation of the Networked Readiness Index 2007–2008

The Networked Readiness Index 2007–2008 separates environmental factors from ICT readiness and usage, and is composed of three subindexes. Each subindex is further divided into three pillars. The 68 ICT-related variables used in the computation of the NRI are then distributed among the nine pillars.

NETWORKED READINESS INDEX

Networked Readiness
Index = 1/3 Environment component subindex
+ 1/3 Readiness component subindex
+ 1/3 Usage component subindex

Environment subindex

Environment subindex = 1/3 Market environment
+ 1/3 Political and regulatory environment
+ 1/3 Infrastructure environment

1st pillar: Market environment
- 1.01 Venture capital availability
- 1.02 Financial market sophistication
- 1.03 Availability of latest technologies
- 1.04 State of cluster development
- 1.05 Utility patents (hard data)
- 1.06 High-tech exports (hard data)
- 1.07 Burden of government regulation
- 1.08 Extent and effect of taxation
- 1.09 Total tax rate (hard data)
- 1.10 Time required to start a business (hard data)
- 1.11 Number of procedures required to start a business (hard data)
- 1.12 Intensity of local competition
- 1.13 Freedom of the press
- 1.14 Accessibility of digital content

2nd pillar: Political and regulatory environment
- 2.01 Effectiveness of law-making bodies
- 2.02 Laws relating to ICT
- 2.03 Judicial independence
- 2.04 Intellectual property protection
- 2.05 Efficiency of legal framework for disputes
- 2.06 Property rights
- 2.07 Quality of competition in the ISP sector
- 2.08 Number of procedures to enforce a contract (hard data)
- 2.09 Time to enforce a contract (hard data)

3rd pillar: Infrastructure environment
- 3.01 Telephone lines (hard data)
- 3.02 Secure Internet servers (hard data)
- 3.03 Electricity production (hard data)
- 3.04 Availability of scientists and engineers
- 3.05 Quality of scientific research institutions
- 3.06 Tertiary enrollment (hard data)
- 3.07 Education expenditure (hard data)

Readiness subindex

Readiness = 1/3 Individual readiness
+ 1/3 Business readiness
+ 1/3 Government readiness

4th pillar: Individual readiness
- 4.01 Quality of math and science education
- 4.02 Quality of the educational system
- 4.03 Internet access in schools
- 4.04 Buyer sophistication
- 4.05 Residential telephone connection charge (hard data)
- 4.06 Residential monthly telephone subscription (hard data)
- 4.07 High-speed monthly broadband subscription (hard data)
- 4.08 Lowest cost of broadband (hard data)
- 4.09 Cost of mobile telephone call (hard data)

5th pillar: Business readiness
- 5.01 Extent of staff training
- 5.02 Local availability of specialized research and training services
- 5.03 Quality of management schools
- 5.04 Company spending on R&D
- 5.05 University-industry research collaboration
- 5.06 Business telephone connection charge (hard data)
- 5.07 Business monthly telephone subscription (hard data)
- 5.08 Local supplier quality
- 5.09 Local supplier quantity
- 5.10 Computer, communications, and other services imports (hard data)

6th pillar: Government readiness
- 6.01 Government prioritization of ICT
- 6.02 Government procurement of advanced technology products
- 6.03 Importance of ICT to government vision of the future
- 6.04 E-Government Readiness Index (hard data)

Usage subindex

Usage = 1/3 Individual usage
+ 1/3 Business usage
+ 1/3 Government usage

7th pillar: Individual usage
- 7.01 Mobile telephone subscribers (hard data)
- 7.02 Personal computers (hard data)
- 7.03 Broadband Internet subscribers (hard data)
- 7.04 Internet users (hard data)
- 7.05 Internet bandwidth (hard data)

8th pillar: Business usage
- 8.01 Prevalence of foreign technology licensing
- 8.02 Firm-level technology absorption
- 8.03 Capacity for innovation
- 8.04 Availability of new telephone lines
- 8.05 Extent of business Internet use

9th pillar: Government usage
- 9.01 Government success in ICT promotion
- 9.02 Availability of government online services
- 9.03 ICT use and government efficiency
- 9.04 Presence of ICT in government offices
- 9.05 E-Participation Index (hard data)

Appendix B: Methodological notes

Combining hard data and Survey data

The responses to the Executive Opinion Survey (Survey) constitute the "Survey data." Responses to the Survey range from 1 to 7.

The hard data were collected from various sources, as described in the Technical Notes and Sources at the end of the *Report*. All of the data used in the calculation of the NRI can be found in the Data Tables section of the *Report*. The standard formula for converting each hard data variable to the 1-to-7 scale is:

$$6 \times \frac{(\text{country value} - \text{sample minimum})}{(\text{sample maximum} - \text{sample minimum})} + 1$$

The sample minimum and sample maximum are the lowest and highest values of the overall sample, respectively. For some variables, a higher value indicates a worse outcome (e.g., higher mobile phone subscription costs are worse than lower costs). In this case, we "reverse" the series by subtracting the normalized variable from 8. In some instances, adjustments were made to account for extreme outliers in the data.

CHAPTER 1.2

The Emerging Nexus: Now Is the Time to Plot a Balanced Course that Delivers on the Promise of ICT and Networks

EWAN MORRISON, Cisco Systems, Inc.
ROBERT PEPPER, Cisco Systems, Inc.
ENRIQUE J. RUEDA-SABATER, Cisco Systems, Inc.

Establishing a pervasive and prosperous Internet culture is as much about creating the right business environment as it is about adopting the right technology. If governments—national, regional, and municipal—want to harness the potential of information and communication technologies (ICT), they must not only invest in *ICT infrastructure* and the capabilities to support it, but also be ready to modify their country's relevant institutional setting—or *ICT ecosystem*—to allow ICT to yield its transformative powers. Using a diagnostic framework reflecting those two dimensions and a mapping tool that employs Networked Readiness Index (NRI) component indicators, countries can gain insight into how to chart a balanced path between ICT infrastructure and ecosystem initiatives that serves their own mix of social inclusion and economic growth objectives.

A diagnostic approach

It would be a gross understatement to say that emerging countries are in the midst of an economic and technological transition. What we are seeing is the largest global economic revolution in over a century, one fueled in part by the introduction and use of ICT.

The opportunities presenting themselves to emerging economies right now, with the introduction of ICT, are unprecedented. These opportunities, if maximized, may well represent the best hope for economic transformation. The Internet Protocol (IP) network platform is at the heart of this shift. The ability of emerging countries to capitalize on these opportunities depends on how well they build *and exploit* their networks' capabilities. In other words, the technology without the appropriate supporting legal and regulatory climate, or vice versa, will result in less-than-ideal results—and both are needed in order for countries to capture the promise of ICT.

Some countries in the emerging world are just starting with basic broadband build-out, connecting citizens and businesses. Others are moving into the next phase, using the power of the network to meet or surpass the developed world in the adoption of mobile and advanced technologies. Although they may be emerging today, the strongest countries will be transformed tomorrow. Those that understand the power of technology and act on that understanding will get there first.

As countries develop strategies to move toward universal access to broadband, a useful preliminary exercise is to put common enablers in perspective and to diagnose possible deficiencies. It is also important to keep in mind that, while a sound ICT infrastructure is needed for broadband connectivity, it is not sufficient to ensure economic benefits. The benefits of connectivity will ensue only if the conditions are right for extensive adoption of the technology *and* its applications. Hence, in considering possible actions toward universal connectivity, it is important to think of enablers common to two major objectives of most economies: growth and productivity on one hand, and social inclusion on the other.

In order to help emerging countries better understand and act on the available opportunities, we have developed a diagnostic basis for reviewing a country's current position relative to best-practice ICT environments. This framework can then provide the coordinates for a map that illustrates the best path forward to ensure that investment in infrastructure and capacity are matched with a good institutional ecosystem for ICT. Understanding where a country's position is with respect to these factors is, thus, a good basis for mapping out steps toward improved ICT adoption and IP network connectivity. The two dimensions in question are:

- *The ICT ecosystem,* which refers to institutional factors that underpin entrepreneurial creativity, competitive dynamics for service provision, and fairness in the distribution of economic gains. These factors are hard to measure, but the most critical pertain to the legal framework relating to ICT deployment—in particular, the quality of ICT regulations, the ease of doing business in a country, and the existence of lively competition and innovation.

- *ICT infrastructure and capacity,* which refers to assets, such as networks and other telecommunications and connectivity infrastructure, as well as the existence of technical skills and systems capable of effectively managing the infrastructure.

The main implication of this framework is that the further away from optimal infrastructure and ecosystem a country remains, the more likely it is to miss the opportunities offered by ICT, the faster it will fall behind in global competitiveness, and the more reduced its ability to reach growth and social inclusion objectives becomes. A balance between a positive ICT ecosystem and widespread deployment of ICT infrastructure and capacity will maximize the likelihood of success.

A narrow focus on the "hard assets" of ICT is not sufficient. Governments, businesses, nongovernmental organizations (NGOs), and other organizations interested in creating a sustainable ICT environment must also promote and invest in ICT ecosystems: those business, legal, and cultural rules and regulations that foster investment in and adoption of technology solutions. Ecosystems include institutional factors that encourage a friendly climate for business and investment, ensure competition at various levels of service provision, create the potential for public-private partnerships, and promote general policies supporting innovation and entrepreneurship to meet the needs of a country's citizens and businesses.

Indeed, it will be argued in this chapter that a country's position along these two ICT investment dimensions—ecosystems and infrastructure—provides an excellent diagnostic of the current state of its technological transformation toward increased connectivity.

A true emergence

A major geo-economic trend is underway: emerging countries today account for almost 30 percent of global GDP (nominal terms); over the next three years, global GDP is projected to grow by over $5 trillion in real terms. Emerging countries are expected to generate nearly two-thirds of this incremental GDP.[1] And, as this *Report* is published, a major milestone is being crossed—more Internet users live in emerging than in developed countries (Figure 1).[2]

It is doubtful this trend will reverse anytime soon. Emerging nations account for the bulk of mineral reserves, more than 80 percent or the world's population, and virtually all the growth in global population. But it is not population or mineral wealth that is driving the sea change. It is the unleashing of enterprise creativity, combined with high rates of investment, which explain much of this remarkable transition from slow growth to hyper-growth.

It could be argued that the rapid growth in many emerging economies has resulted from major injections of labor and capital into productive activities. To sustain the growth and become truly global, these countries will have to increase productivity faster, and this is where ICT comes as an important enabler. Most of the productivity-inducing ICT developments (notably IP networks) are too new for definitive quantitative analysis, but there are plenty of indications of their value to productivity. Viviane Reding, the European Commissioner for Information Society and Media, was recently quoted as saying "We know that ICT accounts for half of the productivity growth in modern economies."[3] The World Economic Forum has also noted a strong correlation between its Global Competitiveness and Network Readiness Indexes.

The experience of the United States provides a significant reference point. Academic research has highlighted the important role played by information technology (IT) in the American economic growth resurgence during the decade between 1995 and 2005 and, more recently, the promising impact of broadband. Both increased investment in technology and improvements in productivity were central factors—with IT-producing and IT-using industries (which account for less than 30 percent of GDP) contributing more than half of the growth in that period.[4] As for broadband specifically, there is a positive effect on output, but also—more surprisingly—on employment.[5]

There are many other indications of the potential "growth dividend" from ICT adoption—the best documented in connection with the spread of mobiles phones across the world (in developed and developing countries alike).[6] In some emerging countries, such as

Figure 1: Internet users in emerging markets vs. users in developed economies, 2000–10

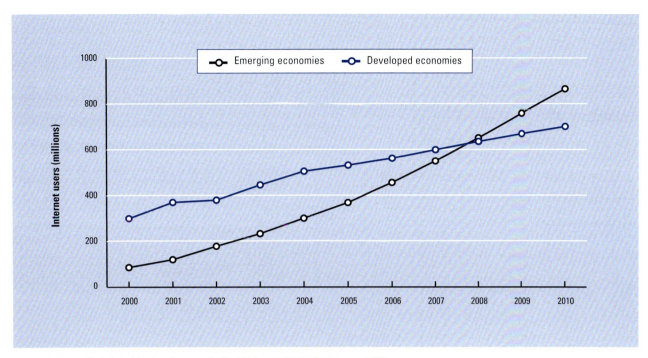

Source: Authors' calculations, based on data compiled by EIU, Internet World Statistics, and BMI.

Korea, Rep. (Korea) and Estonia, the adoption of ICT is already playing a major role in economic transformation. In other countries, such as India, it has opened up new areas of economic growth.

But even while new leaders are taking their place at the global economic table, many emerging countries are just at the beginning of their ICT development and deployment. There is a window of opportunity for these nations to better position themselves and gain maximum benefit from the current era of networked globalization.

The opportunity is more accessible than ever, thanks to technological advances (such as wireless and other low-cost forms of connectivity) and to a decline in the prices of many components and devices necessary for connectivity—such as computer equipment, whose prices experienced an eightfold decline in less than two decades (see Figure 2).[7] These price drops were particularly pronounced in the late 1990s, as the decline in the cost of semiconductors accelerated. The crucial question is whether most of the factors behind these price drops have already run their course.

The threat of being left behind is also a major concern. National, regional, and municipal governments must think about becoming ICT enablers so that creative private enterprise and community partners can deploy solutions that are sustainable, profitable, and equitable.

The speed at which technology is evolving means that the current opportunity to bolster competitiveness through ICT adoption is not one with a long time frame. As countries race to move to the next phase of development and become more globally competitive, ICT will continue to be a significant contributor. The overwhelming majority of the increase in the number of personal computers (PCs) in use is now taking place in emerging nations (Brazil, China, India, Russia alone are on track to add about one billion PCs over the next decade—compared with one billion currently in use worldwide).[8] Already emerging countries are home to nearly 60 percent of the global wireless market, and will be responsible for 87 percent of the 1.5 billion new wireless connections expected between now and 2010.[9]

Like electricity, roads, and water systems in earlier stages of development, high-speed broadband connectivity is quickly becoming a necessary infrastructure for economic growth and competitiveness, and for government contributions to the welfare and empowerment of their citizens. Many emerging countries are making ubiquitous access to high-speed connectivity a major priority. In practice, this does not assume that everyone in a country will have PCs connected to the Internet or telephone—but the goal should be to provide all citizens and businesses with the ability to tap Internet potential toward enhanced standards of living and productivity.

The move to embrace ICT is fueled not only by businesses, academics, and governments that recognize the potential benefits, but increasingly by individuals and communities in emerging countries. They are keenly aware of ICT potential in general, and of IP networks in particular, to enable access to information, new

Figure 2: Price index for computers and computer equipment, 1990–2006

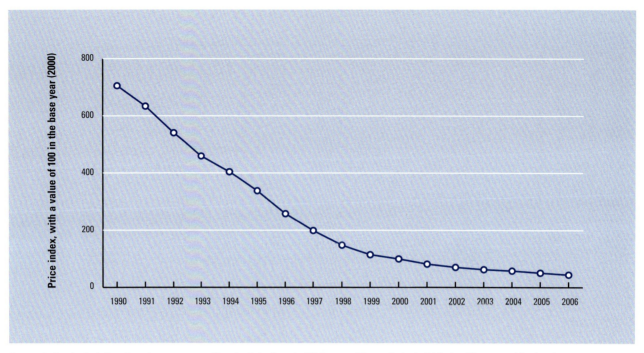

Source: Authors' calculations, based on constant-quality price index from the US Bureau of Economic Analysis' National Income and Product Accounts.

educational opportunities, a greater public voice, and economic opportunities.

Some examples:

- In India, 2.8 million rural farmers are using locally manufactured public Internet kiosks called *e-Choupals* to check fair market prices for their crops.

- In South Africa, 14 million adults without bank accounts now have access to point-of-sale facilities that provide a secure way to save and make financial transactions at an average cost that is 30–60 percent lower than previous entry-level accounts in the banking sector.

- In Bangladesh, where rural electricity service is erratic, solar-powered cell phones financed by micro-loans have found their way into the hands of thousands of women who sell telephone services to villagers.

- In Morocco, rural villagers are getting health-care services, many for the first time, via video links with doctors hundreds of kilometers away.[10]

There is a perfect storm brewing in the emerging world: globalization is making people aware of the new opportunities to better their lives; governments are increasingly sensitive to the transformative power of ICT; and hardware, software, and applications are becoming more affordable and more easily deployable—from the most populated cities to the remotest regions. Research in large cities in emerging countries suggests near-universal awareness of the potential of Internet across age and income groups (Box 1). But we also know that access to PCs, high-speed connections, bandwidth, and applications in most emerging countries are well below the levels required to take advantage of IP connectivity.

What is the appropriate role of government?

The role of government is a central question because, more than any other entities, governments can either largely enable or inhibit ICT development.

As we witness the creative and varied ways emerging economies are putting ICT to use, the benefits of IP connectivity fall into two basic categories:

- *Economic growth:* Potential benefits include productivity gains (e.g., through reduced transaction costs; scalability; and fast, reliable information flows) and the enabling of innovation (through online collaboration tools and new ways to market goods and services). These are the same ICT productivity gains that have benefited developed economies over the last two decades and are accelerating their impact as they expand from large enterprises to smaller businesses, as well as to government and nonprofit organizations.

- *Social inclusion:* This benefit pertains to extending the potential of networks across society to dramatically improve the access of people and communities to education resources, health-service providers, government assistance, and market information. Network connectivity also opens communication channels with the potential to empower individuals to exercise their rights as citizens and become active participants in political processes and social dynamics (including entertainment).

As convergence around IP networks gains momentum over the next decade, the potential benefits increase —and so do the stakes. Emerging economies that make significant progress during this window of opportunity have a chance to accelerate growth and close the gap with—or even leapfrog—countries that are currently more advanced. On the other hand, laggards will be left further and further behind in terms of national competitiveness, productivity, and standards of living and care for their citizens.

A diagnosis for adoption

Ensuring that the fundamentals are right for ICT development is the crucial criteria for the pursuit of universal connectivity and the benefits it brings—there is no substitute.

The best place to begin is with an understanding of a nation's current position, an understanding that can be achieved with the infrastructure/ecosystem mapping that we propose (Figure 3).

This two-dimensional approach is tantamount to a diagnostic tool and, as detailed below, can help chart a high-level course on the path toward improvements that governments can set in motion to capitalize on the promise of technology to improve access to education and government and health services, as well as fuel economic growth, competitiveness, and innovation. These prescriptive options, which governments have at their disposal, represent a broad menu of sorts from which they can select solutions to match their particular goals and the availability of resources.

Although such diagnostic exercise is useful even at a conceptual level, it is particularly valuable in order to map where countries stand relative to each other in our two ICT coordinates. This can be done by building on

---

Box 1: Internet use and demand in emerging market cities

A 2007 survey conducted by Illuminas Global LLC with citizens and businesses in 24 emerging market cities confirms that there is widespread awareness of the benefits to be derived from access to the Internet. Despite differences in population size, citizens' awareness of the benefits of Internet services access in mid-size cities is nearly as high as awareness levels in the largest cities. Among businesses, Internet use is nearly universal across all the countries surveyed with a very few exceptions (businesses surveyed without current access tend to be smaller in size).

The survey has covered cities across Argentina, Brazil, Mexico, Poland, Russia, and South Africa with populations ranging from just under half a million to over 20 million inhabitants; it consisted of interviews with a total of 6,000 citizens and 1,800 businesses. The research identified considerable unmet demand for various types of Internet-based services across all countries and cities.

Comparing **citizens** who use the Internet regularly (on a daily basis) with infrequent users and those who are currently not Internet users, it is striking that most share a high opinion of the role of the Internet in improving peoples' lives, the importance of PC skills, and the potential for high levels of interest in using Internet-based services in the future. The exception are citizens who indicate no interest in using the Internet—typically older and less educated, as well as those showing other indications of lower socioeconomic levels.

Across all types of Internet users (and those who are not current Internet users), there is a clear expectation that governments should make available more information and services online and, more generally, that they should do more to make Internet access easier.

Even though Internet users generally have also access to mobile phones, only a small minority consider them to be a sufficient way of accessing the Internet.

Businesses interviewed share with citizens high expectations regarding the role of governments to facilitate access to Internet-based services. Among businesses, Internet usage is widespread; however, in many cases not all employees have access to an Internet-connected PC or have Internet access only through a shared PC. Businesses attribute to the Internet significant improvements in their business environment and more generally in their national economy. While many are already using the Internet to connect with customers, partners, and banks, they envisage expanded use in those areas and in others—notably e-commerce and transactions with governments.

Figure 3: A two-dimensional approach to ICT development

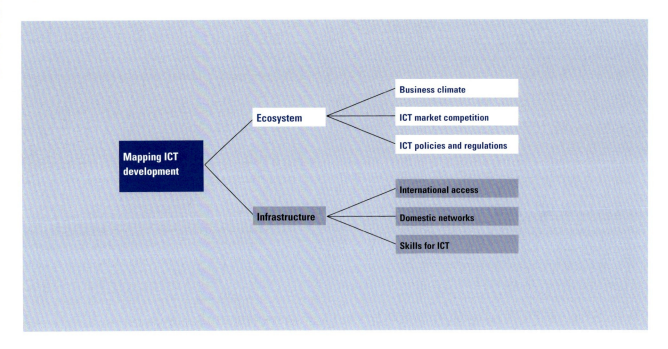

Figure 4: An ICT mapping tool from NRI component indicators

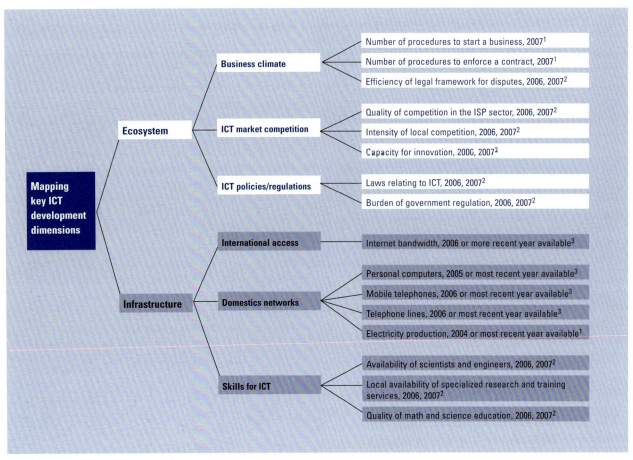

[1] World Bank 2007; [2] World Economic Forum, Executive Opinion Survey, 2006, 2007; [3] ITU 2006 or most recent year available.

the NRI—the components of which provide sound indicators both for mapping the position of specific countries and for documenting the impact on connectivity that different positions have. The diagram in Figure 4 details how we have drawn from the NRI components to construct our ICT development map. Behind the *ecosystem* dimension there are eight NRI component indicators, and behind the *infrastructure* dimension there are another eight.[11] Although the choice of specific indicators reflects a pragmatic approach to available information, we believe that the NRI component indicators provide a good basis for documenting the logic behind each dimension and a good measure of quantification.

The ICT ecosystem dimension is composed of the following elements:

- **Business climate:** Although this institutional component is not ICT-specific, it is important to ensure that entrepreneurial creativity and private-sector investment respond to demand for services. Of these services, ICT-related ones are increasingly important. In addition, providing the right package of connectivity, service, and applications to varied needs requires a lively small- and medium-sized business (SMB) community around ICT. Three indicators look at various aspects of the business climate that will make that possible—or hinder it:

  — *Procedure and ease of starting a business:* In the United Kingdom, it can take as little as 24 hours to set up a business. In many emerging nations, the process can take up to several months.

  — *Procedures to enforce a contract:* Investors and business people must feel confident that a legal system will back them in the case of a contractual dispute.

  — *Efficiency and efficacy of the legal framework:* How well does a country's legal system provide for the settlement of disputes and for challenging government actions? A wait of months or years for a legal ruling is tantamount to none at all.

- **ICT market competition:** It is clear that, in the fluid environment of technological advance and demand progression in ICT, healthy competition is one of the best means of ensuring efficient response to opportunities. Although there are no direct measures for this component, three NRI indicators provide solid insights into it:

  — *Quality of competition in the ISP sector:* One crucial distinction emerging from experience across countries and sectors with regard to government intervention is that infrastructure-type public investment (capital expenditure) can play an enabling role, while attempts to directly subsidize usage (operational or current expenditure) hinder the long-run sustainability of adoption.

  — *Intensity of local competition:* Competition fosters greater responsiveness to needs while monopolist environments keep connectivity costs artificially high, thereby discouraging use.

  — *Capacity for innovation:* Business, legal, and cultural institutions foster innovation, and this is reflected in the innovativeness of enterprises in a country.

- **ICT policies and regulations:** A sound regulatory environment is indicative of a healthy relationship between governments and businesses, while the quality of ICT-specific laws indicates the extent to which a country has kept up with the changing regulatory needs of the sector. Both of these aspects are covered by NRI indicators:

  — *Laws relating to ICT:* Typically, most people's first connections to the Internet have been through dial-up telephone lines and, hence, broadband regulations in many countries have tended to be an offshoot of voice telephony regulations. The impact of broadband, as well as the technology and fluidity of the applications, demand a different approach. Regulatory treatment works best when it treats connectivity as basic infrastructure, rather than as service provision. Countries with high marks on this indicator often have laws and regulations that promote the separation of services (content, applications) from connectivity.

  — *Burden of government regulation:* How difficult is it to comply with administrative requirements? Prohibitive tariffs, along with red tape, act as an obstacle to business in general and repress ICT adoption, connectivity, and technology usage in particular.

The ICT infrastructure dimension is composed of:

- **International access:** This indicator measures bandwidth and reflects the existence of fiber and other links with sufficient bandwidth at reasonable prices that permit extensive connectivity to the global Internet and with other countries and regions.

- **Domestic networks:** These networks offer good insight into the development of the ICT infrastructure. Although there is no single complete measure, four NRI indicators provide solid information on this key feature.

    — *Personal computers:* PCs play a critical role in increasing effective demand for connectivity. As the number of Internet users in emerging countries increases, often there are many Internet users per PC terminal—which limits broad and regular connectivity.

    — *Mobile telephone penetration:* Lively mobile-service provision is likely to be a good platform on which to expand options for connectivity.

    — *Telephone-line penetration: Telephone lines are* often the first, and sometimes only, way of introducing connectivity (DSL). Countries with extensive fixed-line networks have had a head start toward connectivity.

    — *Electricity production:* You cannot turn on a modem if you don't have electricity, and this is a reliable indicator of fundamental infrastructure constraints.

- **Skills for ICT:** Although not considered part of narrower definitions of infrastructure, we see ICT-relevant skills as an important component of the infrastructural capacity of a country. Three NRI indicators provide insights into this component:

    — *Availability of scientists and engineers:* This is an important factor behind the ability of domestic enterprises to adopt technology and innovate appropriately.

    — *Local availability of specialized research and training services:* Quality training programs are an important enabler of investment (domestic and foreign alike).

    — *Quality of math and science education:* This serves as a further indicator of a country's ability to keep its skill base up to date in ICT-relevant areas.

The "diagonal" solution

It is with these two dimensions in mind that we undertook the diagnostic mapping of connectivity using data compiled for the NRI from the indicators mentioned above.

We combined the component indicators of the NRI behind each of the two dimensions, discussed above, to classify each country along four simple categories (poor, moderate, good, and excellent), placing countries relative to each other along the two dimensions.

These categories are then used to "map" into one of sixteen possible ICT development positions. Of these, only ten are meaningful positions (not surprisingly, there are no countries to be found with both "excellent" infrastructure and "poor" ecosystems—or vice versa). The thresholds for the four categories reflect logical breaks in the distribution of countries along each axis, rather than evenly spread groupings. The thresholds are unavoidably arbitrary and simply designed as a sorting device that is then validated by looking at differences across countries in the different categories.

The two-dimensional map places countries in context (not only in relation to emerging markets and regional neighbors, but also in relation to developed nations). The absolute position on this ICT map offers insights into areas in which improvements may have the greatest impact, while the relative position of a country points to more advanced countries that can be sources of best-practice action plans.

We first carried out a detailed analysis and tested the model with indicators from the NRI from the *Global Information Technology Report 2006–2007*. We were then able to validate and update the analysis with the latest NRI data, from the current *Report*. The analysis described reflects these latest NRI data.

We explore the results of this analysis below, but it is worth noting two points up front:

- The thresholds between the "moderate" and "good" categories are the most significant—more significant than those separating "poor" and "moderate" or "good" and "excellent."

- For the overwhelming majority of countries, the message is that the greatest pay-off will come from balanced improvements to both the ecosystem and infrastructure dimensions, moving along a *diagonal* path (though for a few outliers, moving to remedy imbalances means that they may be able to gain significantly from more vertical or horizontal paths).

A gridless map summarizes the implications, while a series of matrixes shows how countries are distributed among the 10 active combinations of categories, differences in the aggregate NRI, and in specific indicators of progress with connectivity. Dots in the map (Figure 5) show the position of all the countries covered by the NRI.

As the map shows, there are great differences from countries positioned in the bottom left and countries in the upper right. This *upward diagonal* charts a course from low broadband penetration and high connectivity costs to just the opposite—high broadband penetration and low connectivity costs. A country's positioning in the

Figure 5: Country positions and implications

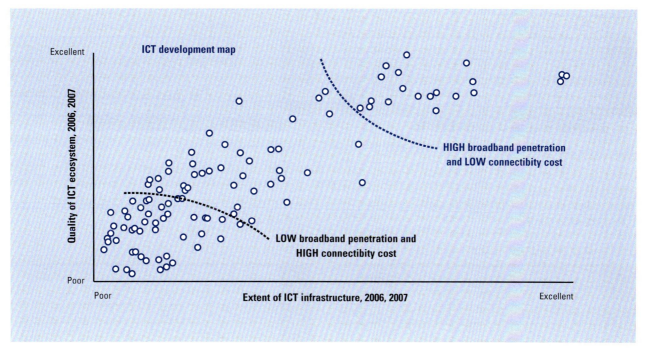

Source: Authors' calculations.

ICT development map will provide a good indication of its relative deficiencies, and also allows for the identification of countries that provide relevant reference points and have achieved a better position.

Only 30 countries of the 107 for which data have been compiled are in "good/excellent" territory (Table 1), where connectivity is best and the positive impact of ICT in productivity is greatest. Most but not all are very high income countries, and they all share a few common traits that confirm the importance of different factors that result in high networked readiness levels. These will be examined below, but can be sorted into four groups: strategic investment, competition among technologies and services, evolved regulation reflecting ICT platform convergence, and a lively SMB community with technical expertise in computers and networking.

On the other hand, 58 countries are in poor/moderate territory where significant deficiencies limit their ICT development. Without decisive actions, these countries run the risk of being left further and further behind, as other countries turn their adoption of technology and their network connectivity into greater competitiveness.

Overall, NRI scores are a strong indicator of the benefits that countries are poised to derive from ICT. Although the compressed scale (1 to 7 and, in practice, ranging from about 3 to 6) can minimize them, differences are very significant. One point apart in the NRI actually implies very different network readiness levels and positioning for countries. The average NRI of intersection categories from the ICT map (Table 2) not only shows significant differences but also points to the value of "diagonal" improvements that balance the infrastructure and ecosystem dimensions.

On the basis of this categorization of countries, and still using NRI components (but only those not included as a component of the infrastructure and ecosystem dimensions), it is possible to then see the implications of the different ICT development positions. We illustrate those here, first by looking at broadband penetration as a proxy for productivity-inducing features (Table 3), and then at the cost of broadband subscriptions as indicative of the hurdles faced by network connectivity (Table 4).

Broadband penetration and costs are strongly inversely correlated and equally powerful indicators of the value of balanced ICT development. A poor positioning in the ICT development map means that people in that country have much less access to connectivity, and if they do have connectivity, they pay a lot more for it. Again (particularly until a country gets into "good/excellent" territory), the greatest improvements come from moving diagonally across categories.

Isn't it all about money, though?

A fair reaction to this analysis would be: interesting model, but it probably just hides the fact that wealthier countries have better connectivity and their markets drive prices down through economies of scale. Undoubtedly, income levels play a role (per capita GDP is certainly higher for countries in the upper right than

Table 1: Number of countries in each intersection category

Ecosystem \ Infrastructure	Poor	Moderate	Good	Excellent	
	—	—	9	11	Excellent
	—	6	9	1	Good
	13	19	13	—	Moderate
	17	9	—	—	Poor

Table 2: Average 2007–08 NRI of countries in each intersection category

Ecosystem \ Infrastructure	Poor	Moderate	Good	Excellent	
	—	—	5.26	5.42	Excellent
	—	4.22	4.77	4.92	Good
	3.35	3.76	4.11	—	Moderate
	3.02	3.41	—	—	Poor

Table 3: Average broadband penetration, 2006 (subscribers per 100 inhabitants)

Ecosystem \ Infrastructure	Poor	Moderate	Good	Excellent	
	—	—	20	25	Excellent
	—	2	14	19	Good
	<1	1	7	—	Moderate
	<1	1	—	—	Poor

Table 4: Average cost of broadband subscriptions, 2006 (US$ per month)

Ecosystem \ Infrastructure	Poor	Moderate	Good	Excellent	
	—	—	50.0	52.8	Excellent
	—	67.4	81.0	51.2	Good
	380.8	185.1	88.6	—	Moderate
	931.2	906.3	—	—	Poor

in the lower left). But econometric analyses show that income alone does not explain the full range of differences in connectivity across countries, while the quality of ICT laws is a very significant factor—both on its own and in combination with income levels (as illustrated in Figure 6).[12]

In a regression for the 127 countries covered by the NRI, income levels alone explain between half and two-thirds of the variability in Internet usage and broadband penetration (as suggested by the resulting R^2 value). An important component of the ecosystem dimension—the quality of the legal/regulatory environment for ICT—alone accounts for even more of the variability. Only when both variables are used together in a multiple regression does the proportion of the variation that they explain jump above 80 percent.

Similarly, analyses of broadband penetration in Europe (where income differentials are much narrower than they are globally) show that the bulk of the variability can be attributed to diversity in the technology platforms available for connectivity, closely related to another of the components of the ICT ecosystem—competition. This is cause for optimism: connectivity is not purely subject to economic determinism.

Through well-designed improvements in its ICT ecosystem, alongside judicious investments in infrastructure, a country (or region or city) can achieve significant ICT development—potentially allowing relatively low income countries to enhance productivity and better compete globally through ICT adoption and network connectivity.

Using ICT to reach economic and social objectives

The diagnostic model that we have designed using NRI component indicators provides a good basis for assessing a country's starting position. The hope is that governments can use the orientation while charting a course for improving ICT penetration—IP networking, in particular—to enhance productivity, promote economic growth, and extend social inclusion. Looking at fast-developing best practices from leading countries in this regard, one can also start sketching out some prescriptive options that governments and other country leaders might consider.

We underscored at the outset the important threshold that we are now crossing: more Internet users are now in emerging than advanced countries. Let us keep in mind that other thresholds need to be crossed: density of PCs (that will affect frequency of use of IP networks) and pervasive broadband (that will permit the connection speeds and the bandwidth required for productivity enhancement and other demanding applications in areas such as health care and education).

Figure 6: ICT laws vs. broadband penetration

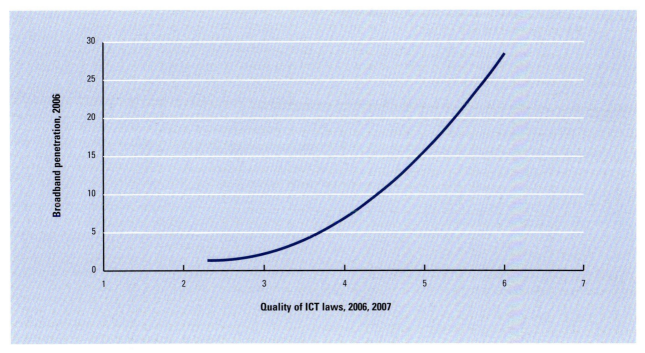

Source: Authors' calculations.
Note: Regression controlling for income levels.

We now focus on broadband as shorthand, or a proxy, for progress in this regard. There are three aspects to keep in mind when exploring prescriptive options:

1. *Universal access* implies both depth and breadth of a robust national ICT infrastructure that enables broadband connectivity, including a countrywide digital high-speed, expandable-capacity backbone. Desirable characteristics include:

   — multiple broadband access technology platforms;

   — speed capable of supporting rich media applications and advanced services (at least 2 mb downstream, 1 mb upstream); and

   — wide availability of affordable broadband access devices such as PCs or PDAs.

2. *Affordability* is crucial—not just for social purposes, but also to ensure that demand reaches the critical mass required for powerful network effects to be triggered:

   — Competition is the best route to affordability in many market segments, while government incentives and support may be needed for segments that are harder to reach (for geographical or economic reasons).

   — Multiplicity of options, including payment for services rather than for access and different payment plans, provides opportunities to a wider range of participants.

3. *Value applications and services* increase the value of the network platform. These include:

   — a broad range of local broadband content, applications, and services on an individual and industrial cluster basis; and

   — ICT skill development—for business and individuals (including ICT training for older generations).

Framework for success

The question is which policies governments and their partners can implement in order to achieve these conditions. How can governments translate these broad objectives into action? What are the key ingredients for success?

- *Regulation:* Countries that have made great strides in broadband connectivity have seen their regulatory framework evolving from one designed for a telecommunications monopoly to one that recognizes IP convergence and promotes competition. The old-style telecommunications regulation was focused on voice and reflected a very different cost structure in the industry—applying it to broadband creates distortions and even risks that generate perverse incentives.

- *Investment:* Strategic investment (similar to trunk roads or interstate highways) may be required to establish a national foundation on which private investment and local initiatives can build. Investment is best leveraged when focused on creating a sustainable investment dynamic, *not* serving as a subsidy for retail connectivity.

- *Competition:* Successful countries have found ways to promote diversity in platform technologies and service provision that are specific to their circumstances. This is the most powerful means for expanding the reach of networks, promoting usage, and ensuring affordability.

- *SMBs:* IP networks, by their nature, are best utilized when the national ICT sector consists of dynamic structures—and networks. The range of service demands and useful applications that can now be made available to businesses and households is best fulfilled by entrepreneurial SMBs in an environment in which ICT-related entrepreneurship can thrive.

Thinking in the regulatory arena is too often limited by the legacy of the telephone industry and the regulatory environment that has historically surrounded it. In virtually every country around the globe, the traditional telephone industry was organized around five central concepts: (1) the primary service is voice; (2) the minute is the metric for pricing, billing, and regulation; (3) location of the user is important; (4) costs and, therefore, price are sensitive to the duration of the call; and (5) the network is distance sensitive, leading to distance-sensitive prices. These conditions, along with the heavy capital expenditures needed to deploy a telephone network, led to a heavily regulated market and, hence, a monopolistic environment. This has kept the cost of telephone service prohibitively high in many countries and has squelched the competition that might drive prices down and thereby increase usage.

None of these five assumptions applies to broadband. New broadband IP networks are distance, duration, and location insensitive, making billing increments based upon minutes of little value at best, and counterproductive at worst. Voice is but one application in a plethora of applications available to the end user. Traditional voice-based telephone companies are joined by providers from the ICT world in which competition can be fierce, innovation occurs at a rapid pace, and precipitous drops in price are an everyday occurrence.

The only similarity between the telephone and broadband networks is the capital expenditure needed to create the basic physical transmission network. Broadband networks still require digging ditches and hanging wires, and these civil-engineering costs can be calculated at a fairly constant rate (though the advent of spectrum-based radio networking promises to drastically reduce even these costs).

Regulatory change—then what?
Regulatory change is likely to be a necessary step in many countries, as noted above, but it is also not likely to be sufficient—particularly when we take into account the stakes involved in catching (or missing!) the powerful ICT wave-in-the-making. Thankfully, governments still can draw from an extensive toolkit to promote broadband penetration. They can bridge gaps quickly with a menu of innovative financial, physical, and legal incentives for users and suppliers.

Here is an approach that looks at the gaps that governments should consider breaking along the traditional lines of supply and demand:

Supply-side incentives tend to work best in rural areas where extending broadband service is expensive and low population density reduces the likelihood of a profitable return. Governments can reduce deployment costs by coordinating infrastructure deployment.

- *Coordinate infrastructure design and implementation:* It is much cheaper to lay cable alongside roads as they are being built than to return later, dig a ditch, and lay cable. Even if roads are being built with no network in the near term, they can be designed with empty ducts beneath or easily assessable trenches so cable and fiber can be added later at a fraction of the cost. In Paris, network cables travel inside sewers. Infrastructure coordination is an effective strategy for municipal and regional governments, since there is no need for a federal decree to make coordination happen.

- *Take advantage of existing infrastructure and assets:* Existing government and educational buildings and facilities can be used as tower sites facilitating radio-based network deployment. Governments can introduce incentives to promote the use of existing utility poles and structures for broadband cable. Leveraging assets already in place can drive great value.

- *Reduce the cost of capital:* Before even considering subsidies of any kind, governments can reduce the cost of capital for private investors by issuing low-interest loans or bonds or by providing loan guarantees. Governments can also structure service agreements as a customer by "frontloading" payments that will provide needed early cash flow for new network operators. Furthermore, they can select from the traditional list of well-documented and successful financial mechanisms designed to reduce or share risk and attract vendors to otherwise unprofitable or marginal projects.

- *Use government buying power:* In many countries, governments are the largest buyers of IT services. They can aggregate or unbundle services. They can bring broadband expansion projects to the table during negotiations, tying less desirable projects to more profitable projects.

- *Allocate new and existing radio spectrum wavelengths:* Television's migration from analog to digital transmission is opening up a broad swath of the radio spectrum that is ideal for wireless broadband networks. As part of their spectrum management authority, governments can ensure that reclaimed spectrum is made available to network providers, particularly at frequencies best suited to deliver signal over the rugged terrain and topography of many emerging countries. Wireless broadband will never be as fast as fiber, but the limitations are more than made up for by its reach and affordability. In many parts of the world, wireless may be the only way to introduce broadband, and it is the same type of "leapfrogging technology" that has made mobile phones more popular globally today than the fixed-line phones that reigned supreme for more than a century.

- *Balance competition:* Simply put, monopolies innovate less and invest less than competitors in a competitive market. A balanced competitive environment will consider the needs and investments already made by incumbent players, yet provide incentives for newcomers. Competition does not work if regulation becomes confiscatory for incumbents or prohibitive for competitors. The mobile-telephone market again is an excellent example of this principle. At first, mobile phones were seen as a niche market and therefore flew "under the radar" of regulatory bodies. This "freedom" allowed competition to flourish and, as a result, a rapid investment and deployment of the mobile marketplace was observed. The mobile experience demonstrates the benefits of competition; it promotes innovation and expands markets rapidly while providing healthy profit margins for providers. Those countries ranking high on the NRI tend to have the healthiest competitive environments of all.

Demand-side incentives target the end user, many of whom have rarely or never used a computer or Internet connection. Very low income levels are obviously the great enemy of demand, but there are still several powerful tools and incentives available to promote demand.

- *Remove or reduce regulations that suppress demand:* Regulations that favor monopolies or inhibit innovation keep prices artificially high. In many countries, Voice over IP (VoIP), for example, is illegal for little reason other than to protect traditional revenue streams for the telecommunications incumbent. This strategy is counterproductive to the growth of an emerging economy and the economic and cultural goals, set forth at the beginning of this chapter. Combining old regulation with new "under-the-radar" deregulation can have paradoxical effect. In Korea, for instance, the high per-minute price of traditional dial-up telephone connections to Internet service helped drive users to flat-rate broadband service.

- *Build desirable demand-creating applications:* Why should users even care to have broadband access? They will care more if they can go online to access government, education, and health-care services, or to access potential jobs and sources of income. Governments can promote demand by building applications that meet the needs of the people, and encouraging the private sector to develop other demand-creating applications such as local-language Web content.

- *Improve PC penetration:* There is a strong correlation in the literature between PC penetration and broadband use. In many ways, attempting to promote broadband with a low PC-to-citizen ratio is putting the proverbial cart before the horse. Governments can provide PCs at very low or subsidized cost, or at a low lease fee. In Korea, citizens can lease PCs for a very low price from the post office, removing cost as a barrier to adoption in low-income families. Egypt recently began a program that allows residents of low-income households to buy PCs over time with no or little money up front. The households have a low monthly fee added to their telephone bill. As of this writing, some 155,000 households were online as a result of this program. PC penetration dramatically expands the addressable market.

- *Make the Internet available in public settings:* Many citizens in developing countries experience the Internet for the first time in a school, library, government building, Internet café, or solar-powered village kiosk. By helping to promote Internet access in public places, governments can increase demand simply by demonstrating the power of the technology.

- *Assist in pre-commercial R&D:* Genius resides everywhere. One of the best ways to leverage a small investment is to finance early trials of solution-based research. There are academics and entrepreneurs in every country who just may have the solution specific to their country or perhaps to the world. Big ideas can come from the humblest of places, and investing in innovation is a sure way to make it happen.

Once broadband penetration reaches approximately 30–35 percent of the population, even more incentives become available—most notably, advertising. With a critical mass of users, service and content providers can start subsidizing the cost of delivery with revenue from advertising; this is quickly becoming the preferred method of revenue creation in developed countries.

Cities: Best point of entry for broadband penetration?

Although extending connectivity to all parts of a country at once is a noble objective, for many emerging markets this may not be achievable from the start. A more viable approach may be to focus on cities first—indeed, progress in cities is likely to create a stronger foundation from which to expand the reach of networks, especially as developing countries become increasingly urbanized.

Cities tend to have a critical mass of both household and business demand that makes more ventures commercially viable. They often have better execution capabilities for whatever government support is needed and will offer more partnership possibilities—at least initially—on both connectivity and applications.

City inhabitants in emerging countries are fully aware of the potential benefits of network connectivity and are willing to pay for the value the network represents, according to recent research (see Box 1). The opportunity exists for developing nations to use not only their most populated cities, but also more remote regional centers in rural areas, as focal points from which the benefits of network connectivity can emanate.

Conclusions

Emerging nations are at a critical juncture. Technology is now available to help to transform their economies quickly and efficiently. But the transformation will occur only if governments understand that an investment in ICT infrastructure must be matched by a concerted effort to change the legal, regulatory, business, and cultural ecosystems with the aim of promoting and sustaining broadband penetration.

The diagnostic tool detailed in this chapter is a good place to start. It can help countries compare and contrast themselves with one other in the journey toward networked readiness. The tool is an early indicator of what successful countries are doing right and, hence, a source of ideas on how developing countries can best seize the moment to improve education, government, and health services; raise income levels and GDP; and enjoy the many business and social benefits of a connected world.

Notes

1. Authors' calculations, based on nominal GDP data and real growth projections from the IMF's *World Economic Outlook*, October 2007, as updated in January 2008. For these calculations, we use—as for other calculations in this chapter—a broad definition of *emerging economies* (all economies except the United States and Canada, the EU15, Japan, Australia, New Zealand, Korea, and Singapore).
2. Authors' calculations based on data compiled by EIU, Internet World Statistics, and BMI.
3. Reding 2005.
4. Jorgenson et al. 2005.
5. Crandall et al. 2007.
6. See, for instance, work by Waverman et al. 2005.
7. Based on constant-quality price index from the US Bureau of Economic Analysis' National Income and Product Accounts.
8. Forrester Research 2007.
9. Standard & Poor's 2007.
10. These examples are from Mohiuddin and Hutto 2006.
11. Please note that these indicators overlap with but are not the same as those that make up the NRI's infrastructure pillar.
12. The slope in the graph and the R^2 referred to in the following paragraph reflect the results of Cisco regression analyses using 2006 per capita GDP and the ICT laws measure used in the NRI 2007–2008.

References

Crandall, R., W. Lehr, and R. Litan. 2007. "The Effects of Broadband Deployment on Output and Employment." *Issues in Economic Policy,* June. Available at http://www.brookings.edu/reports/2007/06labor_crandall.aspx.

Forrester Research. 2007. "Worldwide PC Adoption Forecast, 2007 to 2015." June 11.

ITU (International Telecommunication Union). 2007. *World Telecommunication Indicators 2007.*

IMF (International Monetary Fund). 2007. *World Economic Outlook,* October. Washington, DC: International Monetary Fund. Available at http://www.imf.org/external/pubs/ft/weo/2007/02/index.htm.

———. 2008. *World Economic Outlook,* January 2008 Update. Washington, DC: International Monetary Fund. Available at http://www.imf.org/external/pubs/ft/weo/2008/update/01/index.htm.

Jorgenson, D. W., M. S. Ho, and K. J. Stiroh. 2005. *Productivity, Volume 3: Information Technology and the American Growth Resurgence.* Cambridge, MA: MIT Press.

Mohiuddin, S. and J. Hutto. 2006. "Connecting the Poor." PPI Policy Brief. Washington, DC: Progressive Policy Institute. Available at http://www.ppionline.org/documents/Connecting_the_Poor_030106.pdf.

Reding, V. 2005. "How to Make Europe's Information Society Competitive." Speech to eEurope Advisory Group, Brussels, February 22. Available at http://europa.eu/rapid/pressReleasesAction.do?reference=SPEECH/05/107&type=HTML&aged=0&language=EN&guiLanguage=en.

Roeller, L.-H. and L. and Waverman. 2001. "Telecommunications Infrastructure and Economic Development: A Simultaneous Approach." *American Economic Review* 91(4): 909–23.

Standard & Poor's. 2007. *Telecommunications: Wireless Industry Survey.*

Waverman, L., M. Meschi, and M. Fuss. 2005. "The Impact of Telecoms on Economic Growth in Developing Countries." 2005. Vodafone Policy Paper Series 2. Available at http://web.si.umich.edu/tprc/papers/2005/450/L%20Waverman-%20Telecoms%20Growth%20in%20Dev.%20Countries.pdf.

US Department of Commerce, Bureau of Economic Analysis. Available at www.bea.gov/national/nipaweb.

World Bank. 2006. *2006 Information and Communications for Development: Global Trends and Policies.* Washington, DC: World Bank.

———. 2007. *Doing Business 2008: Comparing Regulation in 178 Economies.* Washington, DC: World Bank.

World Economic Forum. 2006; 2007. Executive Opinion Survey.

CHAPTER 1.3

The Missing Link: Why Does ICT Matter for Innovation? Exploring the Effect of Information and Communication Technologies on Innovation-Based Competitiveness

CARLOS A. OSORIO-URZÚA, Adolfo Ibáñez School of Management and the Berkman Center for Internet & Society at Harvard Law School

In May 2003, in his paper "IT Doesn't Matter," Nicholas G. Carr argued that as information and communication technologies (ICT) become ubiquitous among firms, they no longer matter as strategic differentiators.[1] His point was that improvements in the management of information can be copied, resulting in little or no gain in competitive advantage.

In this chapter, we argue that ICT does matter. Furthermore, we argue that IT does matter for innovation, which is undeniably the source of today's and tomorrow's competitive advantage.

The relationship between ICT and productivity was elusive for a long time.[2] In the same way, the relationship between ICT and innovation might not seem direct. ICT is changing the speed and economics of innovation by (1) decreasing the costs of experimentation and prototyping; (2) increasing the rate of failure and speeding the discovery of sub-optimal alternatives by speeding design-test cycles;(3) allowing better acquisition, management, and analysis of information; and (4) empowering customers to become innovators and firms to benefit from the innovations created by their customer base.

In this paper we explore the effects of these changes among nations by studying, first, the relationship between the Networked Readiness Index (NRI) and a slightly modified version of the innovation subpillar of the Global Competitiveness Index featured in the World Economic Forum's *Global Competitiveness Report* series;[3] and, second, the relationship among relevant variables of ICT use on innovation.

The chapter starts with a brief explanation of firms' competencies for innovation, and a look at how information technologies can help to enhance the innovativeness of companies. Then we make the connection with how and why, at an aggregated level, nations with the highest NRI ranks are those characterized by innovation-based economic growth. This helps to explain the high correlation between the Global Competitiveness Index and the NRI.[4]

The chapter concludes that ICT does indeed matter... a lot. The more intense and sophisticated the use of ICT by a nation's people and firms, the higher the likelihood that ICT will enhance the effectiveness of innovation processes. Innovation processes are methods that, when followed, help companies to innovate in a predictable and consistent way. As a consequence, innovation results more from firms' abilities rather than from lucky strikes. The more innovative the firms will be, the more likely that a nation's competitiveness will be based on innovation.

The relevance of the innovation process

How can the intensive and sophisticated use of ICT by firms contribute to building competitiveness based on innovation for a nation? Answering this question requires some understanding about innovation processes, some core competencies for innovation, and the role of ICT. This is because, although it is a national goal, innovation happens at the firm level.

Innovation can be fostered or hindered by what happens outside the firm. The availability of venture capital and skilled labor, sound labor regulations, and a culture that values learning from failures are among the contextual factors that can affect firms' performance in innovation. Many nations are now working to improve those factors by increasing public spending in innovation, reforming national innovation systems, restructuring their capital markets, and creating bodies for long-term planning, designing their innovation policies, and so on. Despite the relevance of these efforts, their impact might be limited by the capabilities of firms based in a nation, their knowledge, and practices for innovation.

Achieving higher levels of innovativeness—more and better innovation—and enhancing innovation-based competitive advantage require changing and aligning processes, culture, organization, and management of firms. Information technologies can help in at least two of these dimensions: the processes and management of innovation. In this context, important research developments support the fact that firms can learn to innovate better and faster through innovation processes.[5] In short, innovation processes allow firms to innovate more frequently and with better effect in consistent and predictable ways. One example of a firm that sells a high-throughput innovation process is IDEO, a Silicon Valley design firm that creates more than 90 new products and services each year for clients as varied as Apple, Prada, and the American Cancer Society, among others.

These types of processes could be understood as the journey for searching and testing the information about the best solution for a problem (the market pull approach) or the best market areas for a new solution (the technology push approach). The acquisition, analysis, and management of the right information are critical tasks and, because information is the commodity for ICT, the latter becomes critical as well.

There are five core competencies for achieving higher levels of innovation:

1. learning to identify sources of innovation;
2. developing creativity capacity;
3. developing exploration capacity;
4. learning how to fail as soon, as much, and as cheaply as possible; and
5. improving capacity for execution and implementation.[6]

ICT is enhancing for all of the above core competencies, and can help firms to identify sources of innovation better and faster. As a result, firms can determine the best innovation locus by focusing on latent needs that have not been adequately fulfilled, and identifying areas of need that have been overlooked or solutions that do not work sufficiently well.[7] ICT is particularly useful for searching, mining, analyzing, and discovering patterns from information. Additionally, ubiquitous technologies such as video and photo cameras, mobile phones, and voice recorders can become powerful tools when used in sophisticated ways for ethnographic analysis to discover and research need areas. If necessity is the mother of invention, then ICT can be thought as an aunt.

Developing creative capacity can be understood as thinking outside the box and learning to perceive reality in a different way.[8] Market information is everywhere and, although competing firms in a global economy *see* the same reality, each one *perceives* it in different ways. The important issue is learning how to perceive reality in a different way, and learning how to take advantage of the new perception to create competitive advantage. For instance, Gastón García, founder of the Chilean firm Reth!nk, has reinvented the business of exporting grapes by discovering a method for keeping them alive after harvesting. Instead of focusing on the traditional industry approach of keeping safe a harvested fruit that is dying, the company focused on how to avoid the death of the fruit. By natural methods, they developed a method for teasing out the grapes and *making them behave as though they had never been separated* from the vine.

ICT can also foster the innovative process by enhancing firms' exploration capacities, helping them to *fail* as much, as soon, and as cheaply as possible. In this context, failure is a desired and expected result from the process and should be understood as information that tells the firm what might not work. This is achieved through cycles of prototyping and testing. Failing is part of a learning process. The sooner a firm knows what might not work, the more it can focus on those alternatives that can lead to success; it can also avoid investing in less favorable options. As Edison did with the light bulb, and as clearly stated by Thomke and Schrage,[9] firms that learn to unlock the power of experimentation can innovate better and faster, and ICT can enable such experimentation.

ICT is at the core of speeding innovation by enhancing exploration capacity through simulation and prototyping. The electronic spreadsheet, for example, made possible inexpensive financial simulation and helped innovation in new services; real option analysis has helped to better invest in new technologies. Rapid prototyping has streamlined innovation in new products and is becoming less expensive every year—so inexpensive that MIT professor Neil Gershenfeld's Fab Labs are bringing the power of prototyping to rural schools in developing nations.[10] Gene sequencing and computational chemistry have become critical in biotechnology, by providing high-throughput solutions for screening and synthesis of samples.

Besides the previous competencies, enhancing execution and implementation capacities can further minimizing a firm's performance gap in innovation. A firm's ability to obtain payback from innovation is heavily based on its capacity to take its innovations to the market and continuously manage their life cycle, both of which require high levels of workflow and network coordination, managerial systems, lean production and thinking, and managing knowledge and information.

All this can be better achieved when powered by ICT, which plays a critical role in enhancing these competencies by decreasing costs and times for prototyping, feedback, access to market information, shortening time to market, and increasing flexibility in product development, among other benefits.

Does ICT matter for innovation?

Nicholas Carr stated that, from a strategic standpoint, "IT doesn't matter" that ICT, although relevant as a national goal, is "no longer a source of advantage at the firm level."[11] However, research in recent years has shown that information technologies are of strategic importance for what has been called the "new generation innovation process": processes for innovation that are supported by technologies that help to improve and increase the capacity to acquire, transfer, transform, and control the information necessary for innovating faster and better.[12]

Differences in the intensity and sophistication of ICT use are reflected in firms' creation of differentiated value. *Intensity in the use of ICT* refers to how much the technologies are used, while *sophistication* refers to the characteristics, complexity, and superior performance achieved by their use. This is why off-the-shelf solutions might not necessarily be a good option for the innovation-driven firm, but only for the factor- and efficiency-driven company. When companies consider ICT as a commodity, their competitors can also have access to that commodity—this is a problem in developing nations common even among the leading firms. Firms that invest time and resources in developing their own solutions can create competitive advantages based on knowledge. In the presence of an adequate intellectual property regime, these firms can protect their knowledge so it cannot be easily appropriated or copied by their competitors and, as result, create value from market rents.

At the firm level, the intensity and sophistication of business applications for innovation vary across solutions for designing, manufacturing, and coordinating the development of new products and services. Dodgson et al. argue that, after adopting ICT for innovation, firms have been able to enhance project quality and increase profitability, product flexibility, and market share while reducing rejection and set-up times, time-to-market, and labor requirements, among others.[13] This happens at the firm level.

Based on the previous discussion, we explore the relevance of ICT on innovation at a national level in the next sections. This relevance, however, needs to be understood in the context of other important environmental factors (such as venture capital availability, intellectual property protection, the breadth of the value chain, and so on). Is ICT more or less relevant when considered in the context of these previous factors? Can government ICT policies have an impact on innovation? We analyze these questions in the rest of the chapter.

Networked readiness and innovation

The role of ICT in innovation needs to be understood in the context of other relevant factors. For simplification and consistency purposes, we will use a modified version of the innovation pillar from the World Economic Forum's Global Competitiveness Index 2007–2008 as a measure of a nation's innovativeness. The modified version of this pillar, here named the *innovation factor*, results from the aggregation of seven variables:[14]

1. a country's *capacity for innovation* that measures whether firms obtain technology from licensing or imitating foreign companies, or by conducting formal research to develop their own;

2. the *quality of scientific research institutions* with respect to the best institutions in their field worldwide;

3. *companies' spending on R&D* relative to international peers;

4. *university-industry research collaboration;*

5. the extent to which *government procurement of advanced technology products* is based on price or on technical performance and innovativeness;

6. local *availability of scientists and engineers;* and

7. the *number of utility patents* granted during 2006 per million population.

We use the NRI 2007–2008 and its subindexes for a first analysis of the relevance of ICT for innovation. Based on this, we follow with a second analysis focused on specific variables taken from the usage component subindex.

The innovation factor can be seen as a proxy for how much a nation's economy is based on innovation. It focuses on both resources for and outcomes from innovation. The scores for the innovation factor are between 1 and 7, where 1 is the lowest and 7 the highest possible score. As shown in Table 1, the variations from low- to high-income nations are important: the average innovation factor score for low-income nations is 2.96 (medium low), while for high-income nations the average is 4.25 (medium high).

Table 1: Summary statistics

Dimension	Variable	Mean (standard deviation) All countries	Mean (standard deviation) Low-income countries*	Mean (standard deviation) High-income countries*	Description
Innovation	Innovation factor	3.42 (.90)	2.96 (.45)	4.25 (.92)	Innovation factor adapted from the innovation pillar of the *Global Competitiveness Index 2007–2008*
Readiness	NRI	3.94 (.85)	3.42 (.48)	4.83 (.59)	Networked Readiness Index 2007–2008
	Environment	3.76 (.83)	3.26 (.40)	4.63 (.64)	Environment component subindex 2007–2008
	Readiness	4.50 (.82)	4.04 (.62)	5.30 (.45)	Readiness component subindex 2007–2008
	Usage	3.55 (.97)	2.97 (.48)	4.56 (.74)	Usage component subindex 2007–2008
Variables from usage component subindex	Extent of business Internet use	4.02 (.96)	3.52 (.60)	4.94 (.80)	Firms' use of the Internet for buying and selling goods and for interacting with customers and suppliers (Survey, 2006, 2007)
	Government strategy for ICT	4.01 (.85)	3.73 (.76)	4.52 (.78)	Government strategy for utilizing ICT for improving the country's overall competitiveness (Survey, 2006, 2007)
	Broadband penetration	5.46 (7.72)	.77 (1.23)	13.00 (7.78)	Internet broadband subscribers per 100 inhabitants, International Telecommunication Union, *World Telecommunication Indicators 2007*
Contextual variables	Venture capital availability	3.27 (.90)	2.79 (.57)	4.15 (.72)	Ease of finding venture capital by entrepreneurs for financing innovative but risky projects (Survey, 2006, 2007)
	Intellectual property protection	3.80 (1.21)	3.12 (.70)	5.05 (.95)	Strength of intellectual property protection in the country (Survey 2006, 2007)
	Breadth of the value c Chain	3.79 (1.06)	3.26 (.62)	4.78 (.98)	Presence of exporting companies in various links of the value chain (Survey, 2006, 2007)
	GDP per capita (US$)	13,952.67 (12,599.1)	5,680.0 (3,862.3)	29,151.1 (8,024.5)	GDP per capita (PPP), IMF *World Economic Outlook,* April and September 2007 editions
	Number of observations	122	79	43	

Source: Author's calculations, based on data from different sources as indicated in the table.
Note: *Low-income countries* are defined as those with a GDP per capita (PPP) ≤ US$15,000; *high-income countries* are defined as those with GDP per capita (PPP) > US$15,000. *Survey* refers to the World Economic Forum's Executive Opinion Survey.

The differences between low- and high-income nations are also present for the NRI and its subcomponents. The NRI score is 3.42 for low-income nations and 4.83 for higher-income ones, with 3.26 for low- and 4.63 for higher-income countries in the environment subindex; 4.04 and 5.30 for the readiness component subindex; and 2.97 and 4.56 for the usage component subindex.

However, the relation between the innovation factor and the NRI partial regression analysis shows that, controlling for the effect of GDP per capita (PPP), higher levels of networked readiness are associated with a higher innovation, as measured by the innovation factor (see Figure 1). We include the effect of national income—GDP per capita (PPP)—to consider to some extent the fact that, at an aggregated level, firms in richer nations will devote more and better resources for innovation. In spite of the importance of economic resources, our results show that performance in the NRI is strongly correlated with performance in the innovation factor ($R^2 = 0.8161$).

The NRI is formed by three component subindexes (environment, readiness, and usage). Studying the relevance of ICT to the innovation factor requires excluding variables that are included in both the NRI and innovation factor. The number of utility patents, availability of scientists and engineers, and quality of research institutions are also included in the environment component subindex, and company spending on R&D, university-industry collaboration, and government procurement of advanced technology products are included in the readiness component subindex. Finally, the usage component subindex includes the variable capacity for innovation.

However, based on what discussed in the previous section, one thing that really makes a difference for innovation is the use of ICT. Thus, later in this chapter we further our analysis using three usage variables for individuals, businesses, and government.

As shown in Figure 2, the relationship between the usage component subindex and the innovation factor is strong and significant. Results show that a score difference of 1.0 points in the usage component is associated with a difference of 0.79 score points in the innovation factor.

Figure 1: Networked Readiness Index vs. innovation factor

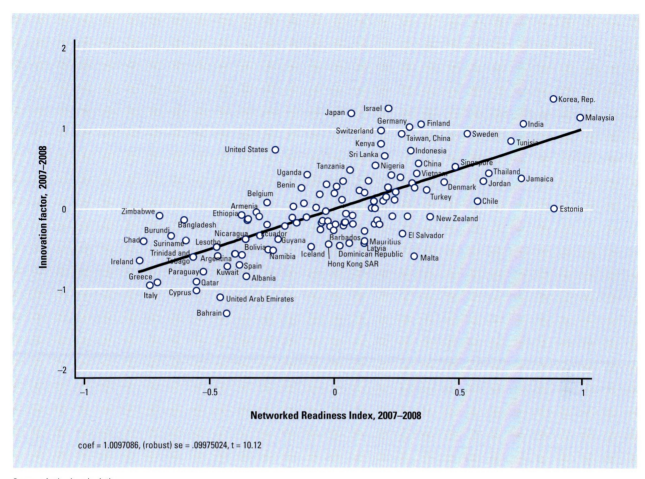

Source: Author's calculations.
Note: Partial regression, controlling for GDP per capita (PPP).

Some nations stand out among the overperformers in innovation, given their income level and NRI: Japan, Israel, Korea, Rep. (Korea), Malaysia, India, and, to a lesser extent, the United States and Costa Rica. Underperforming nations include Bahrain, Cyprus, Italy, the United Arab Emirates, Malta, and Estonia.

As expected, this relationship differs for low- and high-income nations. Among low-income nations, the relationship between the usage component and the innovation factor is relatively small; this may result from the fact that ICT usage is less sophisticated in lower-income than in higher- income nations. Instead of a difference of 0.79, a score increase of 1.0 points in low-income countries is associated with a score increase of 0.75 points in the innovation factor, and with a R^2 value of 0.5886.

Malaysia and India are two nations that show an above-average performance in this relationship, given their income level. Albania, Paraguay, Bolivia, Bahrain, El Salvador, and Mauritania are among those that are below what we could expect. In the case of high-income nations, the relationship between usage and innovation is stronger. A score increase of 1.0 points in the usage component is associated with a score increase of 0.85 points in the innovation factor but, additionally, the goodness of fit is also higher (0.7105). Korea, Japan, Israel, Germany, Finland, China, and Taiwan exhibit a relationship between usage and innovation above average for their usage and income level. In the group of nations that perform below expectations, given their usage and income level, we find Estonia, Hong Kong, Iceland, the Netherlands, and Malta.

These results are preliminary, but show the relationship between the use of ICT and innovation. A closer look at the usage component subindex, however, allows us to gain a better understanding on whether its composing pillars (individual, business, and government usage) are associated with innovation.

Based on our discussion about the role of the innovation processes, individual usage and business usage should exhibit a stronger relationship with innovation than government usage. Analysis, not included in this chapter, illustrates this point. Individual and business usage are positively associated with innovation based on

Figure 2: Usage component subindex vs. innovation factor

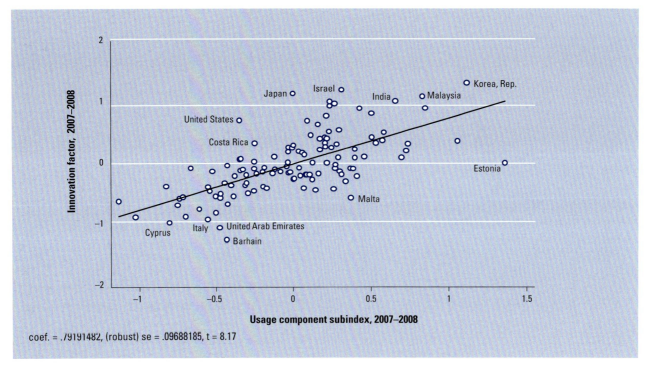

Source: Author's calculations.
Note: Partial regression, controlling for GDP per capita (PPP).

the role of ICT for speeding and improving the innovation process, shortening time-to-market, and enhancing flexibility of new product and service development.

Testing the relationship between the government usage pillar and the innovation factor, when also controlling for individual usage, business usage, and GDP per capita (PPP), shows that—not surprisingly—government usage of ICT is not associated with innovation. This could result from various reasons but, mainly, it is because government usage considers the use of ICT by the central administration, which is not generally a generator of innovations. There are exceptions, such as ChileCompra, the Chilean online government procurement system, which has received awards from the United Nations, the American States Organization, and the Asia-Pacific Economic Cooperation, among others.

The previous analysis of the relationship between the NRI and the innovation factor as well as between the usage component subindex and its three pillars (individual, business, and government usage) illustrates where the relationship between ICT and innovation might come from. We extend our understanding about this issue below to establish a clearer relationship between ICT and innovation.

ICT in the context of innovation

In this section we choose one variable from each pillar and further our analysis. The variables are: (1) broadband Internet subscribers (from the individual usage pillar), (2) the extent of business Internet use (from the business usage pillar), and (3) government strategy for ICT (from the government usage pillar).

The extent of business Internet use serves as a proxy for the intensity and sophistication of use of ICT-based solutions for supporting internal processes of firms (technology strategy, operations management, logistics, etc.),[15] and particularly for testing whether there is any relationship with innovation. Based on the summary statistics in Table 1, the data tell us that the extent of business Internet use in our sample is medium (with a score of 4.02), but the differences between low- and high-income countries are clear: low-income nations score 3.52, while high-income nations score 4.94.

The second ICT-related usage variable is the government ICT strategy for improving the nation's competitiveness. If ICT does matter for innovation, then ICT policy should play a role and we would expect to see some relationship between this policy and the innovation factor. On average, the quality of ICT policy is medium (with a score of 4.01), but, again, the differences between low- and high-income nations are clear: a score of 3.73 (medium-low) versus a score of 4.52 (medium-high), respectively.

The last variable we consider here is broadband penetration, from the individual usage pillar, as a proxy for ICT use by individuals. As the sophistication of ICT-based solutions for supporting innovation increases, the demand for bandwidth also increases. Some examples of such solutions and processes are computer-aided design (CAD) and transmission of CAD files, distant and rapid prototyping, video conferencing, Just-in-Time logistics and delivery systems, remote high-speed machining, and so on. Also, the difference between low- and high-income nations is worrisome: low-income nations exhibit an average of 0.77 broadband subscribers per 100 inhabitants, while high-income nations show 13 subscribers per 100 inhabitants.

Analyzing the relationship between the use of ICT and innovation additionally requires taking into account some contextual variables that are important for innovation. This is relevant because we need to understand whether ICT loses significance when accounting for the possible effect of such contextual variables. The contextual variables included in our analysis are intellectual property protection, availability of venture capital, the breadth of the value chain, and national income per capita. The reasons for choosing them are explained below.

Good schemes for intellectual property protection are relevant because they help the innovator to reap appropriate returns from the innovative activity. On average, as shown in Table 1, while the strength of intellectual property regimes in the whole sample scores a little lower than the medium (3.8), the difference between the average score for low- and high-income nations is clear (3.12 versus 5.05). In other words, high-income countries exhibit stronger intellectual property protection than low-income nations. Innovation is a risky process, where innovators need to manage relatively high levels of uncertainty and ambiguity in order to succeed; these are additional reasons for intellectual property protection.

Funding innovative activities may be a further problem. Considering that funding by traditional financial players is not commonly available for this type of projects, the availability of local venture capital firms is relevant for our analysis. A local and sophisticated venture capital industry provides entrepreneurs with the necessary funds for financing innovation. On average, it is relatively difficult for firms to find venture capital for innovative projects (with an average score of 3.27, in a 1-to-7 scale, in Table 1). There are important differences in access to venture capital between low- and high-income nations (with average scores of 2.79 and 4.15, respectively). That is, firms in high-income nations have more opportunities to succeed, because they can tap into a more sophisticated and better developed local venture capital industry.

Additionally, innovation is a social phenomenon heavily based on networks—a topic that has been discussed by various authors.[16] Based on their research, we know that nations with exporting firms present along the various segments of the value chain (product design, marketing, etc.) have more and better access to market information and the resources from their networks, are more likely to identify sources of innovation, and are better positioned to innovate. Again, the difference between low- and high-income nations is relevant: low-income nations show an average score of 3.26 (medium-low), while high-income countries exhibit an average score of 4.78 (medium-high).

Finally, the difference in GDP per capita between low- and high-income nations is also relevant, as shown in Table 2. Those nations with an innovation factor score higher than 4.0 exhibited an average GDP per capita (PPP) of US$35,949 in 2006, while those with an innovation score below 4.0 showed an average value of US$9,229 (and the correlation between income per capita and innovation displays an R^2 value of 0.7609, with a significance level of 1 percent).

Income per capita is associated with disparities in various areas (education and infrastructure, among others). Including GDP per capita (PPP) in our analysis helps to capture some of these differences and to control for the possible effect being a rich nation might have on being a more innovative nation.

Looking at these ICT-related variables from the perspective of the variables included in the context of innovation, three questions arise:

1. Is the use of ICT by firms relevant for innovation when considered within the innovation context?

2. Do (and can) government ICT policies have an impact on innovation?

3. Does broadband matter in a special way?

We believe there are positive answers to these questions, and explore them in the following section with respect to the whole sample and the differential relationship that might exist between low- and high-income nations.

The relevance of ICT for innovation

Exploring the relevance of ICT for innovation has taken us from understanding the innovation process and role of information technologies at the firm level to testing whether the relevance of ICT for innovation can be perceived at the national level, based on answers provided by firms to the World Economic Forum's Executive Opinion Survey (Survey) and hard data from various sources. In this section, we explore whether—considering the effect of the contextual variables—ICT does indeed matter for innovation. We do this by performing multivariate regression analysis for testing whether the three ICT-related variables do matter in the context of innovation, and including brief cases to illustrate how ICT has been used to create innovation-based value.

The extent of business Internet use
Results from our analysis show that the extent of business Internet use by firms is positively associated with

Table 2: The innovation factor and GDP per capita (PPP), 2006

Economy	Innovation factor	GDP per capita (PPP, US$)	Economy	Innovation factor	GDP per capita (PPP, US$)	Economy	Innovation factor	GDP per capita (PPP, US$)
United States	5.77	43,259	Chile	3.48	12,889	Bulgaria	2.96	9,751
Switzerland	5.74	37,301	Kenya	3.47	1,300	Algeria	2.95	7,849
Finland	5.67	34,458	Italy	3.45	30,824	Burkina Faso	2.94	1,377
Japan	5.64	32,531	Lithuania	3.45	16,134	Argentina	2.91	15,884
Israel	5.57	30,789	Croatia	3.43	13,875	Macedonia, FYR	2.88	7,871
Sweden	5.53	34,375	Slovak Republic	3.42	17,596	Armenia	2.87	5,501
Germany	5.46	30,942	United Arab Emirates	3.37	31,240	Mongolia	2.86	2,306
Korea, Rep.	5.36	24,074	Azerbaijan	3.36	6,159	Botswana	2.85	14,153
Taiwan, China	5.24	30,449	Turkey	3.36	8,906	Tajikistan	2.82	1,452
Denmark	5.11	36,734	Jordan	3.34	5,378	Bahrain	2.81	24,354
Singapore	5.08	32,996	Barbados	3.32	18,828	Venezuela	2.79	7,103
Canada	4.90	35,474	Russian Federation	3.31	12,122	Peru	2.78	6,535
Netherlands	4.88	34,959	Poland	3.28	14,724	Honduras	2.75	3,133
United Kingdom	4.79	35,481	Jamaica	3.27	4,438	Gambia	2.74	2,080
Austria	4.76	36,308	Cyprus	3.25	28,020	Cambodia	2.69	3,103
Belgium	4.74	35,062	Morocco	3.25	4,728	Cameroon	2.68	2,430
France	4.69	31,873	Malta	3.24	20,318	Dominican Republic	2.67	8,508
Norway	4.60	43,925	Greece	3.23	26,079	Zimbabwe	2.67	2,182
Ireland	4.54	44,454	Nigeria	3.22	1,353	El Salvador	2.66	5,517
Iceland	4.52	40,573	Ukraine	3.22	7,744	Namibia	2.66	8,215
Malaysia	4.50	12,130	Vietnam	3.22	3,330	Georgia	2.65	3,556
Australia	4.41	33,341	Egypt	3.17	4,626	Moldova	2.62	2,272
Hong Kong SAR	4.34	37,057	Kuwait	3.16	22,013	Ethiopia	2.61	989
Luxembourg	4.18	74,250	Pakistan	3.15	2,624	Suriname	2.58	7,218
New Zealand	4.09	25,810	Tanzania	3.15	785	Zambia	2.58	1,081
Tunisia	4.02	8,957	Colombia	3.11	8,174	Bangladesh	2.56	2,288
Czech Republic	3.95	23,190	Mexico	3.11	10,817	Ecuador	2.56	4,826
India	3.90	3,715	Kazakhstan	3.10	9,485	Mauritania	2.56	2,307
Estonia	3.75	18,842	Uganda	3.10	1,623	Mozambique	2.56	1,488
Slovenia	3.75	23,921	Romania	3.09	9,887	Bosnia and Herzegovina	2.53	6,653
Portugal	3.71	22,807	Latvia	3.08	15,515	Kyrgyz Republic	2.53	2,112
South Africa	3.71	12,740	Serbia and Montenegro	3.08	6,850	Guyana	2.49	5,260
Costa Rica	3.62	11,611	Philippines	3.03	5,469	Nepal	2.49	1,596
Thailand	3.62	9,219	Mauritius	3.01	12,713	Nicaragua	2.48	4,058
Hungary	3.61	19,514	Uruguay	3.01	10,648	Lesotho	2.31	2,928
China	3.60	7,543	Guatemala	3.00	4,711	Burundi	2.29	666
Spain	3.58	27,994	Trinidad and Tobago	3.00	17,428	Chad	2.28	1,640
Sri Lanka	3.58	4,987	Madagascar	2.99	952	Bolivia	2.25	2,974
Indonesia	3.56	4,256	Mali	2.98	1,194	Timor-Leste	2.17	1,753
Qatar	3.54	30,772	Benin	2.97	1,232	Paraguay	2.11	4,954
Brazil	3.50	9,006	Panama	2.97	8,349	Albania	2.10	5,795

Source: World Economic Forum, 2007; International Monetary Fund, 2007.

innovation when controlling for the availability of local venture capital, the strength of intellectual property protection, the breadth of the value chain of exporting firms, GDP per capita, broadband penetration, and government strategy for ICT (see Figure 3). Results show that, everything else being equal, nations where firms make intensive and sophisticated use of ICT exhibit higher innovation scores than nations with firms that make a less intensive and sophisticated use of it.

Indeed, a score increase of 1.0 points in the extent of business Internet use is associated with a score increase of 0.28 points in the overall innovation factor. In practical terms, this would mean that a country such as Slovenia, which scored 3.75 on the innovation factor, would have had an innovation score of 4.03 if the Internet use by firms had been 5.58 instead of 4.58, all else being equal.

Here, we define the overperforming nations as those that, for their level of extent of business Internet use and relative to other variables, exhibit a superior innovation factor. Among all nations, outstanding overperformers in Figure 3 are Algeria, Brazil, the Czech Republic, Finland, Israel, Japan, Mongolia, Russia, Taiwan, and the United States. The underperformers include Bahrain, Estonia, Guatemala, Hong Kong, Italy, Malta, Mauritius, Panama, and Spain. Here we consider the position of nations relative to others in the context of the variables included in the analysis.

Why would this happen? This indicator assesses whether firms in a country make extensive use of the Internet for electronic commerce and for interacting with customers and suppliers. From the perspective of innovation, the most interesting dimension is not electronic commerce but the ways in which firms can

Figure 3: Extent of business Internet use vs. the innovation factor

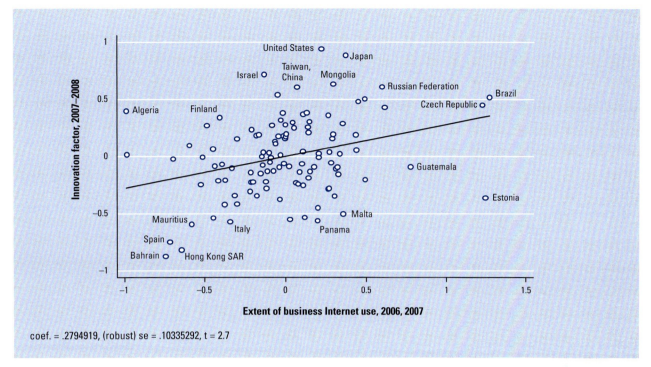

coef. = .2794919, (robust) se = .10335292, t = 2.7

Source: Author's calculations.
Note: Partial regression, controlling for venture capital availability, intellectual property protection, breadth of the value chain, GDP per capita, broadband penetration, and government strategy for ICT.

interact with their networks of clients, customers, providers, partners, and competitors in order to solve problems, discover new ones, and be empowered to become innovators.

Extensive work, based on theories of lead-user innovation and Web 2.0, is being developed in order to use Internet-based tools for increasing the speed and effectiveness while decreasing the cost of innovating in new products and services. These developments, along with the new methods of cognition, coordination, and cooperation illustrated by Surowiecki,[17] have gone beyond using the Internet for participatory lead-user innovation and created new techniques for innovation, such as brainsourcing, as proposed by Joyce.[18] *Brainsourcing* can be defined as active brainstorming where geographically dispersed participants not only give ideas, but also become active participants and designers in the innovation process. These techniques, however, are new and sophisticated and, from the perspective of the usage of ICT, one would expect to see a higher impact among firms in high-income nations than in low-income ones.

Testing the same hypothesis for both sets of nations, we found that the variable extent of business Internet use is significant only at a 20 percent confidence level for low-income nations and the magnitude of the relation is small (a 0.12 increase in the innovation factor with a 1.0 increase in the extent of business Internet use; see Figure 4). This can be explained by two factors. First, it is common practice among firms in developing nations to look for technology that has already been developed, and transfer it once it has been tested elsewhere. Second, with few exceptions—including the retail and financial sectors—technology-based business models in developing nations rely more on investing in hardware infrastructure than on developing new software applications. Among low-income nations, the most notable overperformers are Algeria, Brazil, Costa Rica, Kenya, Mongolia, and Russia. The clearest underperforming nations include El Salvador, Guatemala, Honduras, Mauritius, Panama, and Paraguay.

Among high-income nations, however, this relationship is higher and statistically more significant. A score increase of 1.0 points in the extent of business Internet use among high-income nations is associated with a score increase of 0.53 on the innovation factor (see Figure 5). This can be explained by the fact that, in the developed world, firms have long realized that sustained competitive advantages are built on diversified and novel ways of creating value for the market and returns for companies. In the case of Siemens, for instance, more than 70 percent of its revenues come from products with less than five years in the marketplace.[19] In contrast, most firms in developing nations continue to focus their efforts toward efficiency and productivity growth on technology transfer and exploitation of their most successful business areas, without explicit consideration for the exploration of new revenue sources.

Figure 4: Extent of business Internet use vs. innovation factor for low-income nations

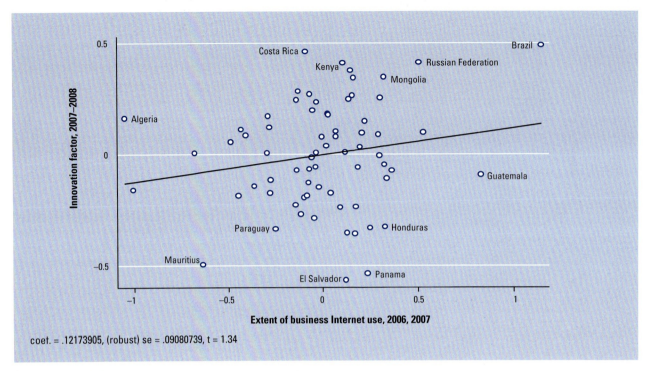

coef. = .12173905, (robust) se = .09080739, t = 1.34

Source: Author's calculations.
Note: Partial regression, controlling for venture capital availability, intellectual property protection, breadth of the value chain, GDP per capita, broadband penetration, and government strategy for ICT.

Figure 5: Extent of business Internet use vs. innovation factor for high-income nations

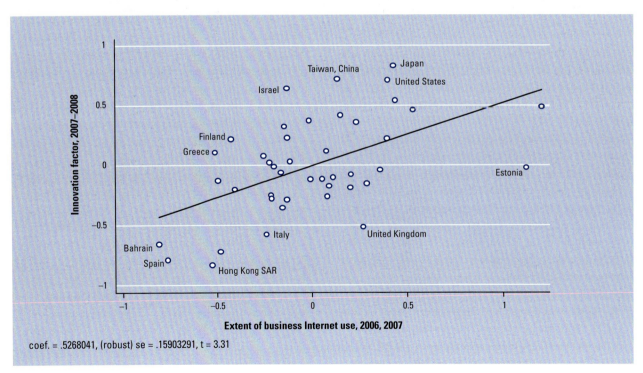

coef. = .5268041, (robust) se = .15903291, t = 3.31

Source: Author's calculations.
Note: Partial regression, controlling for venture capital availability, intellectual property protection, breadth of the value chain, GDP per capita, broadband penetration, and government strategy for ICT.

For high-income nations, the overperformers shown in Figure 5 are those characterized by high levels of innovativeness, among which: Japan, the United States, Taiwan, Israel, and Greece. The underperforming countries include Bahrain, Estonia, the United Kingdom, Hong Kong, Italy, and Spain.

As result, this difference among high- and low-income nations might not necessarily be the result only of different income levels or environment's different innovation conduciveness, but also of a focus on creating sustained competitive advantages based on the novel use of available technologies.

Government strategy for ICT
The second question was whether the government strategy for ICT was likely to have a significant impact on innovation, when accounting for the effect of availability of local venture capital, the strength of intellectual property protection, the breadth of the value chain of exporting firms, GDP per capita, extent of business Internet use, and broadband penetration.

If ICT does matter, given that many governments have been active in promoting ICT to enhance their nation's competitiveness, we could expect to see some relationship between government strategy for ICT and the innovation factor. There are, however, important subtleties and—given the differences in the timing, sophistication, and implementation of ICT strategies between high- and low-income nations—the overall relationship between government strategy for ICT and the innovation factor might be unclear.

Indeed, results in Figure 6 show that, considering the whole sample, government strategy for ICT exhibits no statistically significant relationship with the innovation factor. Breaking down the sample among high- and low-income nations, however, illustrates the previous points about the difference in relative importance for innovation between high- and low-income countries.

Regardless of the lack of statistical significance, Figure 6 allows us to identify those nations well above and below average. In this context, Germany, Israel, Japan, Mongolia, Switzerland, Taiwan, and the United

---

Box 1: ICT-enabled customer innovation

Innovation in ICT is done not only by software firms, but also by firms in industries as varied as food, manufacturing, and sports, among others. ICT-enabled innovation in these and other sectors has been well documented. To put it simply, Trek's Project One allows customers to build their own bicycles. NikeiD allows customers to design and customize their own sports shoe and gear.

Thomke and von Hippel discuss how various companies are using ICT to go beyond listening to their customers to discover what they want. Instead they are allowing those customers to be active participants in designing their own products, thus allowing a better transfer of information.[1] In the food industry, a particularly interesting development has been the application of ICT for bringing objectivity to the subjective matter of defining taste and smell.

Bush Boake Allen (BBA), acquired by International Flavors and Fragrances in 2000, was in the food industry, producing flavors for food companies such as Cargill and Nestle. BBA faced a problem. According to Thomke and von Hippel, there were numerous iterations before a client was satisfied with a new flavor, but BBA generated revenues only after a client was fully satisfied and made an order for the new flavor. According to their research, customers only accepted 15 percent of flavors for evaluation, and only 5 to 10 percent reached the market.

BBA addressed this problem by creating a toolkit that allowed customers to translate the highly subjective attributes of flavors to chemical formulation. Unlike the specifications for a personal computer, the request for a specialty flavor requires various iterations until finding the "right" flavor and the customer is satisfied. Each iteration could take up to three to four weeks—including designing custom flavors and making samples by BBA, and then receiving feedback after the client had run taste tests, analyzed results, and generated feedback.

The toolkit combined simulation and rapid prototyping for less expensive and faster development of new specialty flavors. Using an Internet platform integrated with a database of flavors and a rapid prototyping machine, customers could create samples over the Internet that were fabricated in real time and later sent back to them. This started a trial-and-error process where the cycle for designing, fabricating, and testing of new flavors was in customers' hands rather than in BBA's. The toolkit allows clients to tinker with their prototypes and become the designers. After the toolkit was operative, all the stages of the new process were in customers' hands, iteration time was reduced by 75 percent, and market size increased since the firm could now lower its sales threshold and receive orders from smaller customers.

As pointed out by von Hippel in an earlier work, by using these ICT-based toolkits for innovation companies can innovate faster, and be much more effective than using the traditional manufacturing-based tools.[2] Companies can turn customers into innovators by developing ICT-based toolkits, but they will also require changing their managerial mindset in order to empower their customer base with the knowledge, expertise and tools necessary to make them active functional sources of innovation.

Notes
1 See Thomke and von Hippel 2002.
2 See von Hippel 2001.

Figure 6: Government ICT strategy vs. the innovation factor

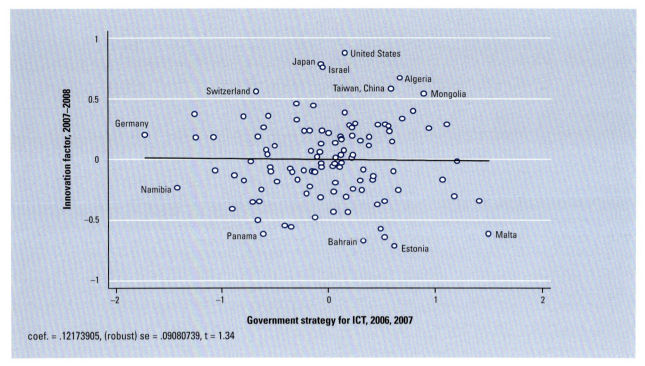

Source: Author's calculations.
Note: Partial regression, controlling for venture capital availability, intellectual property protection, breadth of the value chain, GDP per capita, broadband penetration, and extent of business Internet use.

States are the most notable overperformers, while Bahrain, Estonia, Malta, Namibia, and Panama are underperforming.

Most high-income nations developed their ICT long-term strategies a long time ago and now have shifted focus toward innovation policy. Additionally, the most relevant problems for using ICT in high-income nations have shifted from building infrastructure in the early 1990s and privacy and security in the early 2000s, to the current time where the social network has met the Internet to create Web 2.0. Time has passed, and the impact of ICT policy in developed nations has already been felt, while in low-income nations part of its promise is yet to be fulfilled. As a result, the relevance of government ICT strategies in high-income nations might not be as significant as innovation policy and the effect of firms' sophistication in the use of ICT for innovation.

Low-income developing nations, however, are still in the process of creating sound, well-financed, and sustainable long-term ICT strategies, mostly focusing on infrastructure, advancing access to ICT and the creation of basic efficiency-enhancing solutions. From this perspective, and based on the fact that most firms in developing nations are not highly sophisticated Internet users, we might expect to see a higher relevance of government ICT strategies than is the case in high-income nations.

Our results confirm this view. The relationship between government strategy for ICT and the innovation factor is significant among low-income nations (see Figure 7). According to our analysis, a difference in 1.0 score point in government strategy for ICT is associated with an increase of almost 0.14 score points in the innovation factor.

The notable overperforming nations in Figure 7 are Algeria, China, Costa Rica, Indonesia, Kenya, Malaysia, Mongolia, Russia, Suriname, and Zimbabwe. The underperforming countries include Chile, El Salvador, Honduras, Mauritius, Namibia, and Panama. It is worrisome to notice that most of these underperformers are in Latin American.

Among high-income nations, however, the significance of this relationship is lost (see Figure 8). There are some reasons for this. One possible reason is the increasing shift in focus from long-term ICT strategies to long-term innovation strategies—possibly this might have a more relevant effect on innovation. Another explanation can be found in timing and maturity. High-income nations developed their ICT strategies more than a decade ago and, as result, these strategies might have already had most of their impact on the productive sector.

Regardless of the lack of significance of the results for high-income nations, the notable overperformers in government strategy for ICT are clear: Israel, Japan, Taiwan, Singapore, and Switzerland. The underperformers include the United Kingdom, Estonia, Hong Kong,

Figure 7: Government ICT strategy vs. the innovation factor for low-income nations

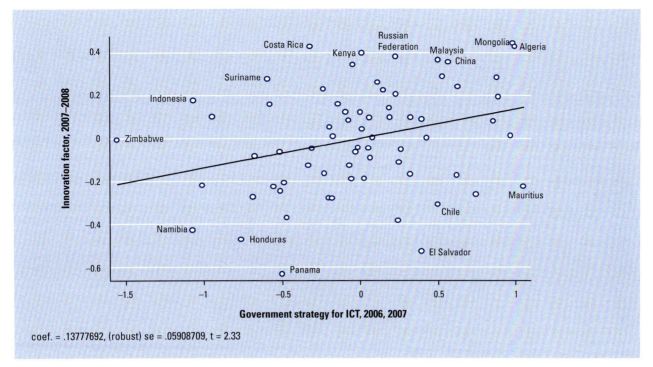

Source: Author's calculations.
Note: Partial regression, controlling for venture capital availability, intellectual property protection, breadth of the value chain, GDP per capita, broadband penetration, and extent of business Internet use.

Figure 8: Government ICT strategy vs. the innovation factor for high-income nations

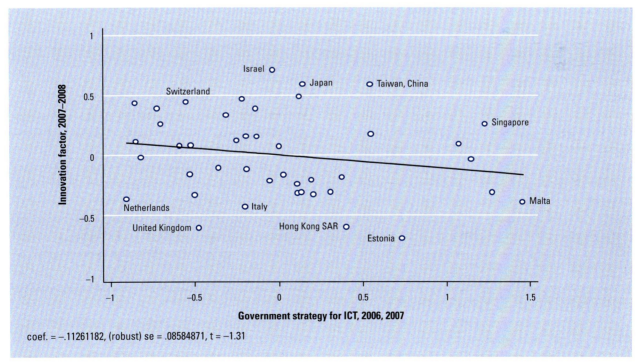

Source: Author's calculations.
Note: Partial regression, controlling for venture capital availability, intellectual property protection, breadth of the value chain, GDP per capita, broadband penetration, and extent of business Internet use.

Figure 9: Broadband penetration vs. the innovation factor

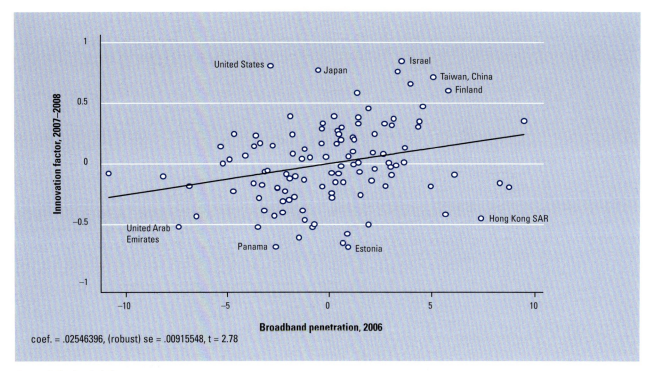

Source: Author's calculations.
Note: Partial regression, controlling for venture capital availability, intellectual property protection, breadth of the value chain, GDP per capita, extent of business Internet use, and government strategy for ICT.

Italy, Malta, and the Netherlands. Hong Kong, the United Kingdom, and Estonia are the three lowest-performing nations in the innovation factor.

The relevance of high-speed Internet access
As previously mentioned, we have used the penetration of high-speed Internet access as a proxy for individual use of ICT. Now, more than ever, the intensity and sophistication of the use of ICT is strongly dependent on the availability of broadband. Various studies have shown the relationship between economic development and broadband availability.[20]

The penetration and use of high-speed Internet also appears to be relevant for innovation. As shown in Figure 9, a score difference of 1.0 points in broadband subscription rate is associated with a small, but significant, difference of almost 0.03 score points in the innovation factor. Some of the reasons were discussed above: broadband is becoming increasingly relevant for applications supporting collaborative and distributed innovative work.

Based on their broadband penetration, and everything else being equal, the overperforming nations are the United States, Japan, Israel, Taiwan, and Finland. Among underperformers we find Estonia, Panama, Hong Kong, and the United Arab Emirates. There are, however, some issues to take into account when following the analysis. Broadband Internet is an important policy issue around the world. However, on average, low-income nations exhibit 17 times fewer broadband subscribers than high-income countries (0.77 versus 13.00 per 100 inhabitants, respectively). One could argue that, when broken down by income level, broadband availability might not appear to be relevant to either group for at least two reasons: (1) there is not enough broadband adoption among low-income nations to establish a relationship with innovation, and (2) there is too much variation even among high income nations to explain a relationship by separating nations by groups. This might result from the fact that broadband is not yet as ubiquitous as one would want.

Breaking down the sample between low- and high-income nations shows, indeed, little relationship between broadband and innovation in our sample (see Figures 10 and 11). Besides the reasons mentioned above, there are two additional reasons why this might happen.

First, average broadband penetration among low-income nations is very low, and unlikely to have shown relevant aggregated results. In the case of high-income nations, where high-speed Internet access is more and better used, broadband penetration is highly correlated with the extent of business Internet use (0.7807), almost exactly doubling the same correlation for low-income nations (0.4136).[21]

Thus, broadband availability is a problem in both low- and high-income nations. The difference might lie in the way in which it is used. Although in low-income nations there is lack of broadband availability, the problem is aggravated by solutions and business models that make

Figure 10: Broadband penetration vs. the innovation factor for low-income nations

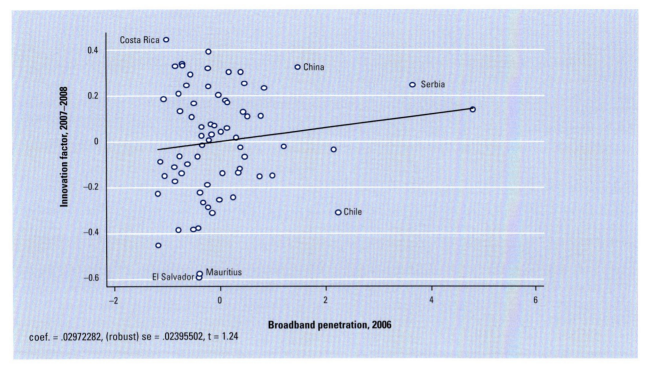

Source: Author's calculations.
Note: Partial regression, controlling for venture capital availability, intellectual property protection, breadth of the value chain, GDP per capita, extent of business Internet use, and government strategy for ICT.

Figure 11: Broadband penetration vs. the innovation factor for high-income nations

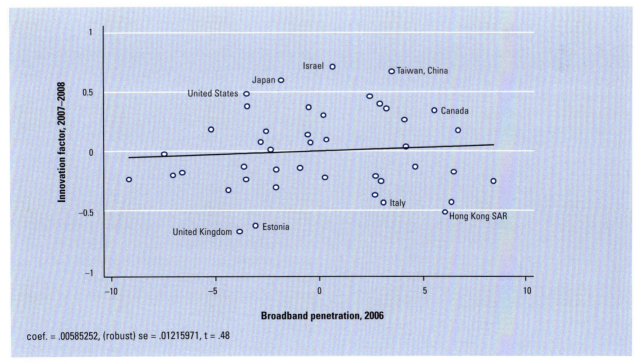

Source: Author's calculations.
Note: Partial regression, controlling for venture capital availability, intellectual property protection, breadth of the value chain, GDP per capita, extent of business Internet use, and government strategy for ICT.

> **Box 2: Grassroots ICT-based innovation**
>
> The lack of data about use of ICT at firm level does not account for the fact that that ICT is not necessarily associated with broadband but with more basic technologies, especially in developing nations. This fact intersects with another: there are billions of people and micro firms who, based on their income level, are not included in the target market of multinationals.
>
> Since C. K. Prahalad wrote *The Fortune at the Bottom of the Pyramid,* many companies and nations have started looking at how they could harvest the bottom of the pyramid. The following case helps to illustrate the potential of ICT for creating value and increasing the competitiveness of firms at the bottom of the pyramid, as well as for discovering holes in ICT policy.
>
> Veronica Oliva and her husband Hugo Reyes lived for years in Isla Negra, a small town in the Chilean Pacific shore. After the birth of their first son, Vicente, Veronica and Hugo were looking for better opportunities for making a living. Thus, they moved to Llo-Lleo, another small coastal town and, after a year, they moved again to Chile's capital, Santiago, in search for a better life.
>
> Once in Santiago, Veronica took over a small convenience store previously owned by her brother. The store is located in Lo Hermida, a poor neighborhood of the also-poor municipality of Peñalolén. Neither Veronica nor Hugo knew how to manage a store, allocate inventory, or manage accounts receivable. Hugo, however, knew a little about computers. With the pressing need for solving this problem, and earning their living, Hugo created a simple software solution through various iterations with Veronica, who was managing the store.
>
> The final version, "El Vichito," named after their son's nickname, is unsophisticated by the standards of all major software companies, but highly effective for the low-end market where the big software companies do not look for potential customers. Nowadays, the orders from other convenience store owners around Santiago are pouring in, exceeding Veronica and Hugo's wildest expectations. They have started to sell the software and train other convenience store owners. Their convenience store has a spin-off: a grassroots software development company.[1]
>
> Usually, micro enterprises such as Veronica and Hugo's are thought to be lacking the necessary sophistication for using ICT, and are the target for public policies to facilitate access to ICT. This case, however, is an example of what policymakers might be overlooking: sources of low-end disruption. Anil Gupta, from the Indian Institute of Management in Ahmedabad and the founder of the Honey Bee Network, has extensively studied and documented cases like this in rural India.
>
> **Note**
> 1 Based on the author's current research on grassroots and lead-user innovation.

limited use of its potential. In high-income nations, broadband deployment is not pervasive, but people and firms make a more intensive and sophisticated use of it.

At a global level, higher individual use of ICT—as measured by broadband penetration—seems to be associated with high levels of innovation. Not everyone, however, has high-speed Internet access, and not all broadband services are equal. While in countries such as Korea, broadband services might be of high quality, in others such as Chile or Bermuda, one can still find services where the "band is not broad enough" to run applications common in developed nations.

Conclusions

The objective of this chapter is to explore the reasons why ICT does matter for innovation. We have offered a first attempt to answer this question by studying the relationship between the NRI and the innovation factor, adapted from the innovation pillar of the Global Competitiveness Index. We found that, after controlling for the effect of being a rich nation—measured by a high level of GDP per capita (PPP)—there is a close relationship between the NRI and the innovation factor. Everything else being equal, nations that score high on NRI also score high on the innovation factor. In other words, nations more prepared and that make a more intensive use of ICT also exhibit a higher potential for innovation-based competitiveness.

We then focused our attention on the NRI's usage component subindex because, with one exception, the variables included in the innovation factor were also included in the environment and readiness components of the NRI. There was also a more profound reason: analyzing the relationship between ICT and innovation needs to be based on ICT usage. Our analysis found that, both individual usage and business usage of ICT are indeed closely related to innovation, when controlling for the effect of GDP per capita (PPP). The relevance of this result relies on a basic fact: innovation is done at the firm and people levels, and so it is the intensive and sophisticated use of ICT that can foster and accelerate the innovation process, and also help to innovate better.

We extended then our analysis and included three variables critical to usage—extent of business Internet use, broadband penetration, and government strategy for ICT—one for each pillar of the usage component subindex. At this point, we also accounted for the relevance of important contextual variables often cited and used in innovation policymaking: intellectual property protection, availability of local venture capital, participation of exporting firms in the various stages of their industries' value chain, and per capita income level. In all cases, our results tend to confirm the hypothesis that ICT does matter for innovation, but they matter in different ways for high- and low-income nations.

Among high-income nations, the extent of business Internet use is the most relevant ICT-related factor for innovation, and the most relevant players are firms. There is enough evidence that firms in developed nations use ICT to foster their innovation processes by enhancing the acquisition of more and better market data, improving prototyping and test cycles, increasing the power of their networks in order to leverage the resources of their ecosystem, and boosting their capabilities for learning before doing by embracing failure through experimentation. These practices, while common among some large and global firms from developing nations, are still in their infancy among most companies in low-income nations.

Among low-income nations, however, the most relevant factor seems to be how governments design, develop, and implement their long-term strategies for ICT. Interestingly, many governments manage both ICT and innovation policies as separate and distinct matters. Chile, for example, often cited as a good example, has little linkages and coordination between its ICT and innovation policies. Higher levels of integration and coordination could significantly enhance the effectiveness of both ICT and innovation policies in developing nations.

Innovation needs a basic context to flourish, and this context includes aspects such as adequate schemes for intellectual property protection, local sources for financing innovation, and firms that have valuable global business relations through their value chain. Besides, policymakers should pay attention to the aspects detailed below.

First, the extent to which nations can leverage the power of ICT will be closely related to the level of absorption of these technologies by the production sector and individuals. However, it is not only the technology that matters, because the levels of intensity and sophistication in its use are closely associated with organizational practices, capabilities, and capital.[22] From this perspective, ICT and innovation policies need to include investing in such capabilities in order to allow higher productive impact and the flourishing of innovation-based competitiveness.

Second, firms will be able to adopt and create new technologies, and generate the required new organizational practices and capabilities, only in the context of sound and well-financed government strategies for using ICT as a foundation for long-term competitiveness. This should not be an effort focused solely on generating access to ICT, isolated from innovation policy. Instead, ICT strategy should be focused on enhancing intensity and sophistication in the use of ICT, and coordinated with innovation policy, with the objective of enhancing the competitiveness of firms.

Third, low-income nations have seen fostering access to ICT among the poor mostly as a matter of democratization. Here we argue that it is, more importantly, also a matter of equity and national competitiveness. It has been established that grassroots innovation leads to higher equity, increases the wealth of grassroots innovators, and also enhances the competitiveness of the areas where they are located. The Honey Bee Network—the grassroots innovation network founded by Professor Anil Gupta from the Indian Institute of Management in Ahmedabad—can provide many examples. National competitiveness is based not only on how the firms at the top of the pyramid perform, but also on the performance of those at the bottom. However, most innovation policies are designed for globalized firms or sophisticated startups. Harvesting the innovation of tomorrow requires a more balanced approach that includes identifying, helping, and financing grassroots innovation today.

Finally, it has been clear for a long time that broadband is not only necessary, but a key future asset for a more intensive and sophisticated use of ICT. If there is a policy matter related to access that needs to be addressed, this is it. Quoting David D. Clark, from MIT Computer Sciences and Artificial Intelligence Laboratory, a good definition of *broadband* for this purpose is "future proofing."[23] In this context, what does *future proofing* mean? The increasing relevance of ICT for innovation, and the growth of practices based on Web 2.0, have made high-speed Internet access an important requirement for innovation. Collaborative and distributed innovation practices are increasingly based on some relevant bandwidth-intensive applications. As such, instead of being measured in megabytes per second, the need to understand broadband as future proofing is that, given its relevance for innovation, bandwidth should not become an obstacle for advancing and reinventing the future.

Notes

1. Carr 2003.
2. Jorgenson 2004.
3. See World Economic Forum 2007.
4. Mia and Dutta 2007.
5. See Cooper 1986; Osorio 2007; and Thornke 2001.
6. Osorio 2007.
7. This approach is based on the seminal work done by von Hippel 1988, 2002; von Hippel and Sonnack 1999.
8. See de Brandandere 2006.
9. See Thomke 2003; Schrager 2000.
10. Gershenfeld 2005.
11. See comment on Nicholas Carr's website: http://www.nicholasgcarr.com/articles/matter.html.
12. See Dodgson et al. 2007; Osorio 2007.
13. Dodgson et al. 2007.

14 The innovation pillar also includes a measure for intellectual property protection, which in this paper we consider to be more of a contextual variable for enabling innovation. For this purpose, we have recalculated an innovation factor that includes all the innovation pillar's variables, with the exception of intellectual property protection.

15 Various authors have discussed the relevance of IT for internal business efficiency and operations, in terms of the type of solutions used by firms. See Brynjolfsson et al. 2002; Forman et al. 2003; and Forman et al. 2005.

16 See Burt 1987; Chesbrough 2003; de Bresson and Amesse 1991; Lutje and Herstatt 2004; and von Hippel 1988.

17 See Surowiecki 2004.

18 See http://www.consciencedesign.ca/blog/.

19 Personal communication with Juan Ricardo Rothe, General Manager, Siemens Chile.

20 See Brough 2003; Crandall and Jackson 2001; and Lehr et al. 2006.

21 The pair-wise correlation between broadband penetration and extent of business Internet use among high-income nations is 0.79, while it is almost 0.41 for low-income countries.

22 For more about this, see Brynjolfsson et al 2002.

23 See NRC 2002.

References

Brough, W. T. 2003. *State Economies Can Benefit from Broadband Deployment*. Washington, DC: CSE Freedom Works Foundation. Available at http://www.cse.org/reports/Broadband_Study.pdf.

Brynjolfsson, E., L. Hitt, and S. Yang, S. 2002. "Intangible Assets: Computers and Organizational Capital." *Brookings Papers on Economic Activity* 2002 (1): 137–45.

Burt, R. 1987. "Social Contagion and Innovation: Cohesion versus Structural Equivalence." *American Journal of Sociology* 92 (6): 1287–1335.

Carr, N. 2003. "IT Doesn't Matter." *Harvard Business Review* May: 5–17.

Chesbrough, H. 2003. *Open Innovation*. Boston, MA: Harvard Business School Press.

Cooper, R. 1986. *Winning at New Products*. Reading, MA: Addison Wesley.

Crandall, R. and C. Jackson. 2001. The $500 Billion Opportunity: The Potential Economic Benefit of Widespread Diffusion of Broadband Internet Access. Mimeo. Washington, DC: Criterion Economics.

de Brandandere, L. 2006. "Perception and Creativity." Working paper. The Boston Consulting Group.

de Bresson, C. and D. Amesse. 1991. "Networks of Innovators: A Review and Introduction to the Issue." *Research Policy* 20 (5): 363–79.

Dodgson, M., D. Gann, and A. Salter. 2002. "The Intensification of Innovation." *International Journal of Innovation Management* 6 (1): 53–83.

Forman, C., A. Goldfarb, and S. Greenstein. 2003. "The Geographic Dispersion of Commercial Internet Use." *Rethinking Rights and Regulations: Institutional Responses to New Communication Technologies*, ed. L. F. Cranor and S. S. Wildman. Cambridge, MA: MIT Press. 113–45.

———. 2005. "Geographic Location and the Diffusion of Internet Technology." *Electronic Commerce Research and Applications* 4: 1–113.

Gershenfeld, N. 2005. *Fab: The Coming Revolution on Your Desktop—From Personal Computers to Personal Fabrication*. New York: Basic Books.

IMF (International Monetary Fund). 2007. *World Economic Outlook Database*. April and September 2007. Washington, DC: International Monetary Fund.

Jorgenson, D. 2004. "Information Technology and the U.S. Economy." Updated. Harvard Institute of Economic Research Working Paper No. 1911. Dept. of Economics, Harvard University.

Lehr, W., S. E. Gillett, C. Osorio, and M. Sirbu. 2006. "Measuring Broadband's Economic Impact." Report prepared for the U.S. Department of Commerce, Economic Development Administration. Cambridge, MA: Massachusetts Institute of Technology's Communications Futures Program.

Lutje, C. and C. Herstatt. 2004. "The Lead User Method: An Outline of Empirical Findings and Issues for Future Research." *R&D Management* 34 (5): 553–68.

Mia, I. and S. Dutta. 2007. "Connecting the World to the Networked Economy: A Progress Report Based on the Findings of the Networked Readiness Index 2006–2007." *The Global Information Technology Report 2006–2007*. Hampshire: Palgrave Macmillan. 3–21.

NRC (National Research Council). 2002. *Broadband: Bringing Home the Bits*. Washington, DC: National Research Council, National Academy Press.

Osorio, C. 2007. "Competencies for Innovation." AISM Working Paper No. 50. Santiago, Chile: Adolfo Ibañez School of Management.

Prahalad, C. K. 2005. *The Fortune at the Bottom of the Pyramid*. Upper Saddle River, NJ, Wharton School Publishing,

Schrager, M. 2000. *Serious Play: How the World's Best Companies Simulate to Innovate*. Cambridge, MA: Harvard University Press.

Surowiecki, J. 2004. *The Wisdom of Crowds: Why the Many Are Smarter Than the Few and How Collective Wisdom Shapes Business, Economies, Societies and Nations*. Boston, MA: Little-Brown.

Thomke, S. 2001. "Enlightened Experimentation: The New Imperative for Innovation." *Harvard Business Review* 79 (2): 67–75.

Thomke, S. and E. von Hippel. 2002. "Customers as Innovators: A New Way to Create Value. *Harvard Business Review* April 1.

von Hippel, E. 1988. *The Sources of Innovation*. New York, NY: Oxford University Press.

———. 2001. "Perspectives: User Toolkits for Innovation." *Journal of Product Innovation Management* 18 (4): 247–57.

———. 2002. "Horizontal Innovation Networks—by and for Users." MIT School of Management Working Paper No. 4366-02, June. Available at http://web.mit.edu/evhippel/www/papers/UserInnovNetworksMgtSci.pdf (accessed November 1, 2007).

von Hippel, E. and M. Sonnack. 1999. *Breakthroughs to Order at 3M via Lead User Innovations*. Available at http://web.mit.edu/evhippel/www/papers/3M%20Breakthrough%20Art.pdf (accessed November 2 2007).

World Economic Forum. 2007. *The Global Competitiveness Report 2007–2008*. Basingstoke, UK and New York: Palgrave MacMillan.

CHAPTER 1.4

Innovation at the Speed of Life

MATT BROSS, BT Group

If you feel the world is spinning faster these days, you certainly are not alone. The pace of change is accelerating all the time.

Even in the world's wealthiest countries, it was at least 50 years before the majority of homes were receiving electricity from a main power line.[1] When broadband came along, similar levels of take up were achieved in some countries in less than a decade.[2]

But even these rates of adoption pale into insignificance compared with those for the latest online services. In Korea, Rep., for instance, the Cyworld social networking site counted "almost every Korean in their 20s" among its subscribers by 2005, according to its founder, Yoo Hyun-oh. This astounding achievement took little more than five years.[3]

It is the same story all over the world. Once they have captured the public's imagination, innovations spread like wildfire. It's dizzying, and so too is the rate at which new ideas are reaching market. And innovation is no longer just about new technology. Indeed, innovations in the way firms do business can have a bigger impact on their success than new technology alone.

Whatever its focus, however, innovation is essentially a chain reaction. From the beginning of time, every advance the human race has made has inspired others.

Consider the telecommunications industry, for instance. Oersted's discovery that a wire carrying a current could deflect a magnetized compass needle led to the invention of the electric telegraph. The telegraph led to the phone, which made it much easier for a head office to coordinate the efforts of teams in different factories and offices. In doing so, it paved the way for the multinational, multisite organizations we are familiar with today. It's the same today, but globalization and technology have come together to accelerate every step of the process, stimulating the creation of new ideas and speeding them on their way to market. The ideas then trigger a new cycle of innovation—one that may well progress at an even faster rate.

The result is an explosion of creativity that shows no sign of coming to an end—the Innovation Big Bang, a unique event in human history.[4]

The Innovation Big Bang

The past decade has seen tremendous progress in many different areas of information and communication technologies (ICT). The increases in the power of microprocessors, the capacities of disc drives, and the bandwidths of data networks are examples. In each case, performance has advanced at an exponential rate, making a whole lot more possible.

Now imagine each direction of progress as a vector whose length defines what is possible. Imagine further that the set of vectors is arranged as the radii of a sphere of possibilities. This is where the combined impact of all the separate advances becomes obvious. If each radius were to grow by a factor of 10, the sphere that defines what is possible would grow by 100,000 percent!

Depending on how you look at it, this explosion of possibilities presents the world's corporations with one of two things: a major headache or a tremendous opportunity.

Traditionally, firms depended on their in-house research and development (R&D) departments for new ideas and to drive those selected for deployment through to market. Often, these departments were shrouded in secrecy. To maintain the corporation's competitive advantage, ideas had to be kept confidential until they were adequately protected by intellectual property rights, or until products or services were launched. Strict "need to know" policies operated within firms and few outsiders ever got involved. Those who did were required to sign comprehensive nondisclosure agreements up front.

One result of this approach was that the pace of innovation was limited. With fixed team sizes and budgets, only a certain number of ideas could be worked on at any one time. Inevitably, this favored larger firms that could afford to spend more on R&D.

Another—and perhaps more troubling—result was that firms could find it difficult to think "out of the box." Closed communities tend to focus in on themselves, sometimes even developing their own languages to describe technologies or ways of working. This further isolates them from the world at large.

Those managing internal R&D teams can also face a conflict of interest. The budgets on which they depend may come from those whose views and policies need to be challenged. Under those circumstances, it should be no surprise to find in-house researchers who are reluctant to challenge established wisdom, even when that is the right thing to do. Instead, they water their ideas down or hold them back to avoid upset.

These are not new issues, of course. Where they've existed, they have always hampered creativity and weakened competitiveness. Historically, though, the consequences have not been that severe. Research by McKinsey in the 1980s, for example, found that companies that were three to six months late to market could see their profits reduced by between 10 and 33 percent. Although clearly a cause for concern, there was no suggestion that the delays might bring firms to their knees.

The Big Bang has changed all this forever. As far as innovation is concerned, the room for poor performance is already small, and it's vanishing fast. Firms that have too few of the right ideas will soon find business ebbing away. So too will businesses that are slow to turn their ideas into marketable products and services.

The photography industry has provided a graphic example of the consequences. There, makers of film were surprised how quickly digital cameras sold, and how soon people took to swapping photos online. They were not prepared for the new era, so their sales plummeted. Only swift and radical change prevented the firms' collapse.

Innovation at the speed of life
The experience of the photography industry also highlights the opportunity the Big Bang has created. If you have a winning idea and can get it to customers quickly enough, the market could well be yours for the taking —even if it's dominated by firms from a completely different industry than your own.

The problem, unfortunately, is that any lead might be short lived. New ideas can come from anywhere at any time—that is, after all, how you "stole" the market in the first place. Add to that the fact that it is getting easier and easier for firms to clone their competitors' products, and it is clear that having one or a few winning ideas is going to be far from good enough. To take and hold the initiative, you need a pipeline that can pour innovations onto the market at what, by yesterday's standards, would be a blistering pace. You may only have a few weeks', or perhaps a few days', head start on your competitors, so there is no chance at all to stand still.

The ideal would be to be able to innovate at the speed of life—that is, to be so at one with your customers' thinking that you consistently deliver the new products and services they are looking for at just the moment they need them, and ensure there never is a gap between what they ask for and what you offer. And what matters is the speed at which customers are able to improve their personal and professional lives, not the speed at which new technologies become available. As far as customers are concerned, genuine innovation happens only when their daily lives actually get better or their firms achieve greater success as a result.

This is an ideal, of course—a level of performance a business can approach but will never reach. But it is impossible for firms even to get close if they use traditional methods of innovation. To aspire to match the speed of their customers' lives, firms must innovate the way they innovate.

Open innovation
Now that the innovation genie is out of the bottle, firms have little alternative but to change their approach. Those who get it right will reap big returns. According to Arthur D. Little, "Top innovators have 2.5 times more sales and get more than 10 times higher returns from their innovation investments."[5]

But how exactly can firms transform their innovation processes to deliver the throughput they will need in the future?

The answer varies from industry to industry, and from business to business. Central to the success of many firms to date, however, has been the concept of open innovation.

In open innovation, firms invite people from outside their traditional R&D teams to take part in the innovation process. They may be people working in other parts of the company—in sales, marketing, or customer support, for example. They could be university researchers and academics, business partners or suppliers. They could even include the firm's customers and the public at large.

Equally, adopters of open innovation recognize that there are more ways of getting returns on their innovation investment than turning them into products and services or using them to improve their own efficiency. Ideas that are good but don't have a role in their own business can be licensed to other firms, used as the basis of spin-out companies, and so on.

Businesses have been doing such things for many years, of course. Suggestion schemes are hardly new, and firms often trade intellectual property or work together to exploit new opportunities. But it wasn't until Henry Chesbrough established an intellectual framework that brought the elements of the approach together that open innovation attracted significant attention.

Chesbrough is now executive director of the Center for Open Innovation at the University of California at Berkeley, a part of the university's Haas School of Business. While studying Xerox's failure to reap the benefits of ideas pioneered at its Palo Alto Research Center (XEROX PARC), he recognized that this had not been the failure of management that many had suggested. Rather, it was the result of the company's use of the traditional, closed approach to innovation. Like others, Chesbrough noted, "it sought to discover new breakthroughs; develop them into products; build the products in its factories; and distribute, finance and service those products—all within the four walls of the company."[6]

In contrast, open innovation engages a much broader community in the creation and development of ideas, and exploits many more routes to get innovations to market and generate returns.

As Joel West, associate professor at San José State University's College of Business, has noted: "Open innovation means treating innovation like anything else—something that can be bought and sold on the open market, not just produced and used within the boundaries of the firm."[7]

At first sight, this definition looks simply to bring together all the different forms of relationship corporate R&D departments have developed and used to advantage over the years and put them on a more formal footing.

In doing so, however, open innovation has opened the minds of executives all over the world to the possibilities. Why limit suggestion schemes to your employees when you could ask your customers for ideas as well? Why cling to intellectual property you don't have a use for when others could be making money from it and giving you a share of their profits? Once you recognize that innovation is a commodity you can trade, there are all sorts of options to explore.

The question, of course, is whether the business case holds up. Is there money to be made from open innovation?

This is where the move online has had a huge impact. The Internet makes it easy to involve many, many more people in the innovation process—not just business partners and universities, but people companies don't know and have never met. Crucially, it allows this to be done at an acceptable cost. It is this that has taken open innovation that vital stage forward—from being just an idea to being an idea whose time has come.

Toronto-based mining company Goldcorp Inc. provides a dramatic example of what has become possible. Chairman and CEO Rob McEwen was frustrated by the failure of his in-house geologists to find significant new deposits of gold on the firm's 55,000 acre stake in Red Lake, Ontario. The answer, he decided, was to see if anyone else in the world could do better.

To do this, Goldcorp had to take the radical step of making confidential geological data available to outside "prospectors." When the Goldcorp Challenge was launched in 2000, more than 1,400 corporations, consultants, agencies, and universities from 50 countries downloaded it to begin their virtual exploration.

The Challenge's judges were astonished by the creativity of the entries. The winners—Fractal Graphics of Perth, Australia—had worked with Taylor Wall & Associates from Queensland to build a 3-D computer model of the mine and identify probable deposits. The innovative approach worked: by 2002, Goldcorp had drilled four of the winner's five top targets and had struck gold every time.[8]

Others who have benefited by adopting open innovation include the food company Kraft; oil, gas, and chemicals business Shell;[9] aircraft maker Boeing;[10] car maker BMW; electronics giant Philips;[11] and ICT companies such as BT.[12]

BMW is one of many companies to post challenges on its website, enlisting the help of customers and others in coming up with solutions. It received thousands of responses after making a toolset available that allowed customers to design features for cars of the future. Some of those ideas have since been implemented.[13]

Another company to take this approach is Kraft. Its "Innovate with Kraft" website openly welcomes ideas from the public, offering rewards up to US$5,000 for those selected. The first product to reach market as a result of the scheme combined a block of Parmesan cheese with a disposable plastic cheese grater. The idea was submitted to the American firm by a small grocery store in Italy. Open innovation also led Kraft to launch the first-ever microwaveable hot dog and bun.[14]

As Kraft's example demonstrates, open innovation is not just about making big advances. Small ones can just as easily create good revenues and competitive advantage. Nor is open innovation restricted to the areas typically associated with corporate R&D departments—new technologies and their application, for example. Firms can apply the approach right across their activities, from technological innovation to the delivery of customer service.

And customer service is one of a broad range of areas in which telecommunications company BT has been using open innovation to drive itself forward. The company designed its My Customer program to focus its employees' attention on the importance of customer service and make it clear that everyone in the company has a vital role to play—not just those who work at the customer interface. Each year, a tournament called the Challenge Cup is organized to encourage people from diverse backgrounds to come together and generate ideas that will deliver improvements. In 2006, more than 2,500 people from every part of the company took part in the 319 teams that submitted entries.

Like the other forward-looking companies that have adopted open innovation, BT has been delighted with the results. In addition to achieving advances that have improved customer satisfaction, it has brought many new products and services to market. And to take things further, it has launched a software development kit that puts the opportunity to innovate directly in developers' hands, which has been downloaded more than 3,000 times so far.[15] Taken together, innovations brought in from suppliers, partners, and academia contributed around £500 million in potential new product and service revenues between 2002 and 2006.[16]

Little wonder, then, that few regard open innovation as hype. A 2006 survey by the Research & Technology Executive Council found that three-quarters of respondents felt expectations of the approach were realistic or too low.[17]

ICT: Fueling open innovation

A feature of open innovation—especially when it is enabled by advanced ICT—is that it has changed how the innovation process works. Ideas no longer flow step by step from research through development and engineering to delivery. In open innovation, the process is generally much more iterative, with users and/or customers being involved at as early a stage as possible so their views can help shape the eventual solution.

Research conducted by Mark Dodgson, David Gann, and Ammon Salter of Imperial College, London, suggests that open innovation involves three overlapping activities. They call them "Think," "Play," and "Do."[18] *Think* is the creative process—the activity that generates ideas and finds answers to problems. *Play* involves the use of rapid prototyping and similar techniques to get feedback from users and/or customers very early in the process. And *Do* is about making the innovation real—building the version that will be taken to market.

Whether or not you agree with their analysis, it is clear that ICT is playing a central role in broadening participation in the innovation process and accelerating each of the activities involved.

Enabling participation

Something that great innovators have in common is their breadth of knowledge. Because their thinking is not constrained by the artificial boundaries that define subjects such as physics, chemistry, biology, engineering, or the social sciences, they can draw on their understanding of one area to create advances in another.

The same is true of other, perhaps less prominent, people. Studies of scientists and engineers, for instance, have shown that those with access to the widest variety of information are the most creative.[19] This stands to reason: if innovation is a chain reaction, the more ideas someone is exposed to, the more he or she is likely to generate.

In this context, the World Wide Web has had a major impact in enabling many more people to access information and encounter ideas. Knowledge that was once locked up in the libraries of corporate R&D departments is now either freely or readily available to anyone who can get online, regardless of their location and, to an increasing degree, their economic circumstances. As the report produced after the 2005 UN World Summit on the Information Society in Vienna observed: "ICTs triggered the Information Revolution, dissolving the boundaries of material media and setting free human inspiration from most restrictions in form and content."[20]

Other features of modern ICT that have broadened participation in the innovation process are its escalating performance and rapidly reducing cost. When Bill Hewlett and Dave Packard decided to go into the electronics business in 1939, they needed a garage to house the equipment needed to design and test their first product. Now you don't even need that—powerful PCs and global networks serve as a global platform for innovation that is available wherever you happen to be.

In a growing number of cases, products no longer have to be built until the very last minute. Computer models can be built and simulations can be conducted to evaluate the product's likely performance. And there is no need to worry if you need access to an expensive item such as a supercomputer. Increasingly, you can "timeshare" such things over the Internet. People can use Sun's Grid Compute Utility for as little as US$1 per central processing unit (CPU) hour, for example. At that rate, a calculation that needed to use 1,000 CPUs for one minute would cost only US$17.[21]

Life-sciences company Applied Biosystems is among those to have used Sun's facility to accelerate its innovation process. By being able to access a much more powerful computing facility than it could afford to maintain itself, it was able to develop millions of new genomic assays—tools researchers use to characterize variations in human DNA—in a matter of days rather than months.[22]

Dassault, a French aircraft manufacturer, is another striking example. To accelerate the development of its Falcon 7X business jet, Dassault teamed up with IBM to create a virtual development platform that would allow the 27 partners involved in the project to work on the design of the prototype simultaneously and share information in real time. Assembly time and tooling costs were both cut by half as a result of eliminating physical prototypes.[23]

Enabling collaboration

Innovation rarely happens in a vacuum, of course. It is a social activity—even within corporate R&D departments, people like to "bounce ideas off one another," get together to "kick the tires" of their ideas, and so on.

Such interactions are routine when people are located together. But as firms use open innovation to involve more and more people in their innovation process, the likelihood that the people who need to exchange their ideas, work on designs, and so on will be located in the same premises is reducing fast. Chances are they will be on different sides of the world.

Technologies that make it possible for people to collaborate at a distance are therefore of prime importance. Significant among these are audio, video, and Web-based conferencing services; unified collaboration tools that bring such services together with email, instant messaging, and office automation applications; and wikis and other shared online workspaces.

The impact of wikis and other Web 2.0 technologies that facilitate collaboration has been dramatic. As Peter Gloor and Scott Cooper of MIT's Sloan School of Management have noted, they enable collaborations of a scale and pace far beyond what we have seen before. These "unleash tremendous creativity, spurring exciting and valuable innovations" that extend "from the realm of idea generation and product development to the very essence of doing business."[24]

An example of the result is *Wikipedia*—the collective work of more than 100,000 volunteers. By September 2007, their efforts had resulted in some 8,700,000 articles in more than 250 languages.[25] True, the accuracy of some of its content is questionable. As a result of one mischievous posting, several British newspapers and TV channels wrongly reported the achievements of a prominent composer who died in 2007. But a study commissioned by the journal *Nature* in 2005 found broadly comparable numbers of errors in both *Wikipedia* and the online version of the world-renowned *Encyclopaedia Britannica*. Checking their entries on 50 different topics, it found 162 errors in *Wikipedia* and 123 in the *Encyclopaedia Britannica*.[26]

Creating marketplaces for ideas

The Web has also been used to create marketplaces for ideas.

InnoCentive, for example, is an online forum that gives the world's scientists the chance to earn big money by solving complex challenges posed by companies such as Dow AgroSciences, Eli Lilly and Company, and Procter & Gamble. Most challenges attract an award of between US$10,000 and US$100,000, but one—for a device that can measure the progress of motor neuron disease—is being advertised at US$1 million. Set up in 2001, the site now claims to allow companies to connect with "a global network of more than 125,000 of the world's brightest minds."[27] Similar marketplaces are operated by NineSigma and the InnovationXchange.

Yet2.com operates in a different arena. It was set up to help firms create new revenue streams by licensing intellectual property that is underused or no longer key to their own businesses. Licensees benefit by getting access to tried and tested ideas—many created by the world's leading corporate R&D departments—without having to develop them themselves.

In addition to these examples, numerous companies operate their own "shops" for ideas, often with the aim of involving their customers in the innovation process. The websites used by BMW and Kraft were discussed earlier, for example. BT's website provides another example. In November 2007, it offered developers the chance to win £1,000 by creating an application for Wi-Fi-enabled smartphones based on the Symbian operating system. Applications were required to make use of the phone's Wi-Fi connection.[28]

Accelerating testing, production, and delivery

BT is also one of a growing number of companies to use its website to obtain early feedback from customers on the ideas it has under development. One service that has been on trial recently on the BT.com Beta site is BT BizBox. Developed in partnership with Tierlinear Web Applications, it provides a fully integrated suite of Web-based business productivity tools. The service offers customer and contact management tools, timesheets, calendaring and scheduling tools, and a document management system.[29]

Vodafone's Betavine website serves a similar purpose. Managed by the company's corporate R&D group, it allows Vodafone to assess the likely interest in its ideas and gain feedback on the usability and performance of alpha-stage and beta-stage prototypes.

Intel's CoolSW (cool software) website operates in a somewhat different way. Recognizing that professional pundits often get it wrong when it comes to identifying the software applications that will be biggest commercial successes in the future, the CoolSW encourages independent developers to post details of the new software available for trial. Visitors to the site are then asked to vote for their favorites. Developers gain from the feedback, while Intel gets the chance to learn about new independent software suppliers and identify promising entrepreneurs.[30]

In a very different area, book publisher Simon & Schuster has partnered with Media Predict, a company that operates a website that uses prediction markets to identify work worthy of investment and development. In Simon & Schuster's Project Publish literary contest, players were given fantasy money they could use to buy futures contracts in various projects. As in a real-world market, prices associated with the book proposals that were posted rose and fell depending on how well users thought the works would perform. This helped the publisher identify the proposals it should take forward.[31]

Such open feedback is becoming increasingly essential to open innovation. The process is harsh—a case of kill or cure—but it does identify winners quickly and drive rapid progress. By making software available through its beta test site, Internet giant Google was able to take its Google Maps application from trial to launch in just eight months.[32]

This highlights another of the benefits that ICT is delivering: reducing the costs and timescales associated with engineering new products and services and readying them for sale. A number of organizations are making it easy for people to use their applications and data as the basis of new developments, for example. Among these is the British Broadcasting Corporation (BBC), whose Backstage network allows developers to make use of the corporation's content in their prototypes.[33]

Mashups—Web applications that combine data from more than one source into a single integrated tool—are another example of how developers can get ideas to market quickly by piggy-backing on existing innovations. *Wikipedia* cites as an example the use of cartographic data from Google Maps to add location information to real-estate data from free-ads website Craigslist, thereby creating a new and distinct Web service that was not originally envisaged by either source.

Elsewhere, software companies now have the option to reduce the need for up-front investment in computing infrastructure by renting capacity in an operator's data center, while sites such as YouTube give new talent the same chance to access global audiences as established film makers and TV companies.

Open innovation: The cutting edge
Taken together, the current applications of ICT in open innovation are having a significant impact in broadening the world's innovation pipeline, accelerating the pace of innovation and giving many more innovators a chance of success.

But these are early days. Some of the approaches and applications of ICT discussed are still in their infancy, while others are far from reaching the end of their life-cycle. A great deal of progress is yet to come.

The dawn of the innovation prospector
Some progress will be achieved by increasing still further the numbers of people able to participate in the innovation process in one way or another.

Firms that adopt open innovation will, in effect become innovation prospectors.

To ensure that they can supply their customers in the future, prospectors working for oil companies and mining businesses are constantly searching for new deposits. Those who are first to identify, say, a new oil field stand to make the biggest gains. Similarly, firms that adopt open innovation are constantly looking for new sources of ideas and innovations they can tap. Communities with different backgrounds and cultures have different experiences to draw on and look at problems in very different ways, for example. The ideas they come up with often have the edge firms are looking for.

The younger generation is an obvious example. "Generation Y"—people born between 1975 and 2000—grew up in the information age. Technology is an integral part of their lives, not the adjunct to it that it is for older generations. They are quick to adopt innovations, and they do so in imaginative—and sometimes unexpected—ways. Text messaging was originally promoted as a way for secretaries to keep their bosses up to date, for example. Some do that, but it was Generation Y that took to texting in a big way and has driven the development of advanced text messaging services.

Unsurprisingly, innovative firms have been quick to engage with these young adults and tap their brains for winning ideas. Microsoft is an example. Now in its sixth year, the company's Imagine Cup is the world's largest technology competition for students. Each year, students are asked to form teams to come up with novel solutions to a particular global issue—the competitions in 2006 and 2007 focused on health care and education, for instance—and thousands of entries are received. Those selected as winners go on to take part in the Innovation Accelerator—an intensive two-week program where students get help in turning their ideas into reality from some of the best minds at Microsoft and BT, co-sponsors of the program.[34]

No doubt Generation Z—those born between 2001 and 2021—will prove to be an equally productive source of new ideas. But the younger generations of developed societies are only some of the new sources of innovation that can be tapped. There are many living in the developing countries who will be able to make just as valuable a contribution to advancing the state of the art.

The Economist noted recently that many in China and India use their mobile handsets as their primary interface to the Internet. Their requirements may therefore be very different from those of Western users, most of whom use computers at home or work.[35] It also noted that villagers in Africa and Bangladesh have gone straight from having no phones to having mobile phones, making a big jump up the technology ladder. Such a "democratisation [of innovation] releases the untapped ingenuity of people everywhere and that could help solve some of the world's weightiest problems," it said.[36]

It is certainly the case that the unique challenges faced by the world's developing countries have inspired those from the developed world to come up with innovative solutions. Lifelines India, for example, supports the UN's Millennium Development Goal of helping developing countries become part of the digital society. The Internet has yet to reach the more remote areas of India, depriving those who live there of access to agricultural and veterinary advice and other information that would enrich their lives. LifeLines enables them to get answers to their questions using the few landline phones that are available in local kiosks.[37]

Another project in India is I-Shakti. Supported by Unilever, it has helped women to set up information kiosks to give those living in their villages access to information for education and business purposes.[38]

Similar services operate in Africa. Sponsored by the International Institute for Communication and Development, the IKON Telemedicine Project allows people living in remote areas to get medical advice over their mobile phones. It also allows doctors in regional hospitals to get advice from senior colleagues working in cities.[39]

Another advance inspired by the problems of the developing countries is the XO—a laptop computer for use by students that costs around US$100. Developed by the One Laptop per Child (OLPC) initiative, the XO employs several radical innovations to keep costs down and address the realities of life in disadvantaged communities. One is a novel user interface called Sugar. According to IEEE Spectrum, the OLPC team abandoned the desktop metaphor, reasoning that it is both outdated and irrelevant in societies where desks are scarce. Instead, Sugar displays a world of collaborators, clustered around icons representing work in progress.[40]

Once the communities the XO is designed to serve are online, open innovation will have many more minds it can tap—those of people whose imagination is "uncontaminated" by the ideas and solutions of the past, but who have a real thirst to advance in the future.

No doubt innovation prospectors will pursue these communities as sources of ideas and feedback as they emerge, but in doing so they should not overlook the potential of underdeveloped communities closer to home. YourEncore, for example, has built a network of retired scientists and engineers that can provide firms with the proven experience they need to accelerate their pace of innovation. It claims to be "uniquely positioned to help clients recover lost knowledge and to enable them to make remarkable connections to solve challenging problems using expertise from a variety of industries."[41]

Achieving innovation at the speed of life

Another area in which significant progress can be expected is in reducing the time it takes to get innovations to market—matching the "innovation at the speed of life" goal discussed earlier.

Bottlenecks and other problems have to be eliminated from every step—especially those that isolate people involved in the innovation process from the point of customer contact. Whether it is a clever innovation that is poorly productized, a clever product that is poorly delivered to market, or a well-delivered product from a company that cannot scale up in line with its success in the market, failures severely damage a firm's success and limit its chances of capitalizing on innovative thinking.

This is one reason why agile development methods are attracting so much interest from the software community. According to the Agile Alliance, a global organization with almost 4,000 members, "agile approaches to software development ... deliver value to organizations and end users faster and with higher quality."[42] They do this by changing the entire product development process, from the identification and evaluation of new opportunities to the development and delivery of those with the best chance of success. Software developers, business specialists, marketers, and others work together throughout, focusing the full breadth of their expertise on the project such that a better result is achieved and it's achieved much more quickly.

The need for greater agility also explains the growing enthusiasm among larger firms for making resources they would once have guarded jealously available to small businesses and other innovative third parties.

Amazon and BT are among the firms that have followed the trend set by Microsoft and others to offer access to the capabilities that underpin their businesses online through software development kits (SDKs). Amazon's e-commerce service allows developers to build novel applications that they can use to make money selling Amazon products,[43] while BT's SDK allows developers to incorporate the company's phone and messaging services in their applications.[44] BT's SDK also provides functions that developers can call on to authenticate the identities of users and manage their access rights.

Building leadership skills

Of course, open innovation demands more than new technology alone. As essential to its success will be the development of a range of new management and leadership skills.

Many of today's executives began their careers working in firms where departmental boundaries were set in stone and collaboration—even among colleagues working in different parts of a business—was difficult, if not actively discouraged. Competition was encouraged at all levels. Many companies operated internal marketplaces, for example, and the door was firmly closed between "us"—the company—and anybody outside, be they customers, suppliers, or competitors.

This couldn't be further removed from the world we live in today. Managers often have to lead teams where they are not the "boss" in the traditional sense, and they may not "own" the budget or the other resources they need to get the job done. Leaders have to be effective at harnessing the rich diversity that people from different cultures and backgrounds bring to a business, especially when it comes to understanding and responding to the needs of customers in different parts of the world.

Open innovation pushes these skills to the limit. Those who manage the process will have to be good at marshalling the efforts of vast numbers of innovators, with many of whom they won't communicate directly or ever meet. They will need to know how to sort through many thousands of ideas and responses. And excellent negotiation skills will be essential—for example, to agree on the financial and commercial basis on which ideas can be used. Human challenges such as these are likely to be among the most difficult to solve.

Conclusion

There is no doubt that open innovation is the way of the future.

Looking back, it's clear how easy it is for firms to lose the initiative and sink without trace. Of the companies included in the Fortune 100 when it was first published in 1917, 61 no longer exist. Of those that remain, only 18 make the list today—and only 2 of those have performed better than the average over the past 90 years.

And it is a similar story on the other side of the Atlantic. Only 24 of the companies listed when the FTSE 100 Index was established in 1984 remain in the list today.

The Innovation Big Bang increases the stakes. To ensure that their competitiveness is sustainable and differentiable in the long term, firms must now look well beyond the limits of their own R&D departments and indeed their own payrolls. The world is full of people who are keen to offer their ideas, and firms will need to become exceptional exploiters of this immense pool of talent if they are to survive.

For those used to relying on their own resources, it is a tremendous change—both in approach and in outlook. But it is a change that offers big benefits, and not just to firms themselves. By creating opportunities for many more people to participate in the innovation process and share the wealth that is created, open innovation will help overcome the digital divide.

Notes

1. The first electricity networks in the United Kingdom date from around 1880 (see http://en.wikipedia.org/wiki/Electrical_power_industry). Thirty-three percent of homes had electricity in 1931 and 67 percent in 1939 (see http://homepage.ntlworld.com/paul.linnell/sso/ssointroduction.html).

2. UK Office of National Statistics, 2007, quoted in http://www.tech.co.uk/computing/Internet-and-broadband/news/51-per-cent-of-uk-homes-have-broadband?articleid=717937052; "Broadband Markets: Europe, Asia and North America," IDATE, December 2003, http://www.idate.fr/fic/news_telech/117/IDATE_News_291VA.pdf.

3. Cameron 2005.

4. IEC 2007.

5. Arthur D. Little 2005.

6. Chesbrough 2005.

7. West 2007.

8. Australian Government 2001; Tischler 2002.

9. See Shell Chemicals 2003.

10. Business Innovation Insider 2006a.

11. Philips Research 2004.

12. BT 2006.

13. Gloor and Cooper 2007.

14. Business Innovation Insider 2006b.

15. BT, "Web21C SDK," http://web21c.bt.com/.

16. Radjou 2006.

17. Research & Technology Executive Council survey, "A Crowding Market for Externally-Sourced Technology," January 2007.

18. Dodgson et al. 2005.

19. Kasperson 1978.

20. UN 2005.

21. See Sun Microsystems, "Sun Utility Computing," http://www.sun.com/service/sungrid/index.jsp. Data accurate as of November 1, 2007.

22. See Sun Microsystems, "Sun Helps Genomics R & D Group in Leading Life Sciences Company Get Critical Research Tools to Market in Record Time," http://www.sun.com/customers/service/applied_biosystems.xml.

23. See IBM 2006.

24. Gloor and Cooper 2007.

25. See http://en.wikipedia.org/wiki/Wikipedia:About.

26. Giles 2005.

27. See the InnoCentive website, http://www.innocentive.com.

28. See BT, "Wi-Fi Developer Challenge," http://www.groupbt.com/Innovation.

29. BT BizBox, http://www.btbizbox.com/about/.

30. Intel Corporation, CoolSW website, http://coolsw.intel.com.

31. See Simon & Schuster 2007.

32. Musser et al. 2006.

33. See BBC Backstage website, http://backstage.bbc.co.uk

34. See Microsoft, "The Imagine Cup," http://www.microsoft.com/about/inventors.mspx.

35. *The Economist* 2007a.

36. *The Economist* 2007b.

37. See BT, "Lifelines India," available at http://www.btplc.com/Societyandenvironment/Videoandaudioclips/LifelinesIndia.htm.

38. I-Shakti website, http://www.hllshakti.com/sbcms/temp1.asp?pid=46802251

39. Wray and Mayet 2007.

40. See Perry 2007.

41. YourEncore website, http://www.yourencore.com.

42. The Agile Alliance website, http://www.agilealliance.org.

43 Amazon Web Services website, http://aws.amazon.com.

44 BT, "Web21C SDK," available at http://web21c.bt.com/.

References

Arthur D. Little. 2005. Innovation Excellence Survey.

Australian Government, Department of Communications, Information Technology and the Arts. 2001. Media release, "Australian Company Wins International IT Competition," April. Available at http://www.dcita.gov.au/Article/0,,0_4-2_4008-4_15633,00.html.

Business Innovation Insider. 2006a. "Boeing and the Art of Global Collaboration." April. Available at http://www.businessinnovation-insider.com/2006/04/boeing_and_the_art_of_global_c.php.

———. 2006b. "Open Innovation at Kraft." June. Available at http://www.businessinnovationinsider.com/2006/06/open_innovation_at_kraft.php.

BT. 2006. "Embracing Open Innovation." Available at http://www.networked.bt.com/pdfs/Embracing_open_innovation.pdf.

———. "Lifelines India." Available at http://www.btplc.com/Societyandenvironment/Videoandaudioclips/LifelinesIndia.htm.

———. "Web21C SDK." Available at http://web21c.bt.com/.

Cameron, D. 2005. "Koreans Cybertrip to a Tailor-Made World." *The Age*, May 9. Available at http://www.theage.com.au/articles/2005/05/06/1115092684512.html.

Chesbrough, H. W. 2003. *Open Innovation: The New Imperative for Creating and Profiting from Technology.* Boston: Harvard Business School Press.

Dodgson, M., D. Gann, and A. Salter. 2005. *Think, Play, Do: Technology, Innovation, and Organization.* Oxford: Oxford University Press.

The Economist. 2007a. Special Report on Innovation, "Can Dinosaurs Dance?" October: 8.

———. 2007b. Special Report on Innovation, "Something New Under the Sun." October 4.

Giles, J. 2005. "Internet Encyclopaedias Go Head to Head." *Nature*, December. Available at http://www.nature.com/nature/journal/v438/n7070/full/438900a.html.

Gloor, P. A. and S. M. Cooper. 2007. "The New Principles of a Swarm Business." *MIT Sloan Management Review*, Spring. Available at http://sloanreview.mit.edu/smr/issue/2007/spring/12/.

IBM. 2006. "Dassault Aviation Revolutionizes Aircraft Development with the Virtual Platform and PLM." Available at ftp://ftp.software.ibm.com/software/solutions/pdfs/ODB-0147-00.pdf.

IEC (International Engineering Consortium). 2007. "IEC and BT Discuss Innovation 'Big Bang.'" July. Available at http://www.iec.org/about/071207_big_bang.html.

Kasperson, C. J. 1978. "An Analysis of the Relationship Between Information Sources and Creativity in Scientists and Engineers." *Human Communication Research* 4 (2): 113–19.

Musser, J. with T. O'Reilly and the O'Reilly Radar Team. 2006. *Web 2.0 Principles and Practices*. O'Reilly Radar Report. November. Sebastopol, CA: O'Reilly Media, Inc.

Perry, T. S. 2007. "The Laptop Crusade." *IEEE Spectrum*. April. Available at http://www.spectrum.ieee.org/apr07/4985.

Philips Research. 2004. "Open Innovation." *Password Magazine*. July. Available at http://www.research.philips.com/password/archive/19/index.html.

Radjou, N. 2006. "Transforming R&D Culture." Forrester Research Inc., March 20.

Shell Chemicals. 2003. "GameChanger Case Study." Available at http://www.shellchemicals.com/magazine/1,1098,894-article_id=146,00.html.

Simon & Schuster. 2007. "Touchstone Imprint of Simon & Schuster Teams With New Website Media Predict for its Project Publish Literary Contest." May. Available at http://www.simonsays.com/content/feature.cfm?sid=33&feature_id=5903.

Sun Microsystems. "Sun Helps Genomics R & D Group in Leading Life Sciences Company Get Critical Research Tools to Market in Record Time." Available at http://www.sun.com/customers/service/applied_biosystems.xml

Tischler, L. "He Struck Gold on the Net (Really)." *Fast Company Magazine*. May. Available at http://www.fastcompany.com/magazine/59/mcewen.html.

UN (United Nations). 2005. UN World Summit on the Information Society, "Towards a Global Cooperation for Quality Content in the Information Society." Available at http://www.wsa-conference.org/data/viennaconclusions_051104.pdf.

West, J. 2007. "What Is Open Innovation?" August 28. Available at http://blog.openinnovation.net/.

Wikipedia. "Wikipedia: About." For current statistics, go to http://en.wikipedia.org/wiki/Wikipedia:About.

Wray, R. and F. Mayet. 2007. "Upwardly Mobile Africa: Key to Development Lies in Their Hands." *The Guardian*. October 29: 27.

CHAPTER 1.5

Unified Communications: Leading Advances in Global Decision Making and Economic Development

SANDOR BOYSON, Robert H. Smith School of Business University of Maryland, College Park

DAVID BOYER, Avaya

One of the traditional benchmarks of a nation's ability to foster economic growth and protect and enhance the well-being of its citizen has been good communications. As communications technology has rapidly advanced, delivering capabilities that break down more barriers of place and time, nations need to reconsider what "good" communications is.

More than ever, developed and developing nations need to implement a communications strategy that uses these advances so that their citizens and businesses can be more integrated into the global community, and government and industry can provide an array of advanced services to all sectors.

Unified Communications–led development: A new national readiness and economic catalyst model

Among the latest communications advances is the development and diffusion of digital platforms that unify what have until now been separate communications channels. The ability to simultaneously manage data, video, and voice traffic, from the network and user's perspective, has led to another breakthrough and surge in momentum in what has been an ongoing 200-year-old communications revolution.

This channel convergence, which is called *Unified Communications,* should attract the attention of industry leaders and policymakers. Industry and policy analysts have mainly been focusing on the installation of converged network infrastructure such as Voice over Internet Protocol (VoIP). Only very recently, attention has begun to shift to network applications software and to the design of unified infrastructure management services such as Service-Oriented Architecture (SOA) to enable the consumer to have a single sign-on to a portal for VoIP telephony, advanced electronic messaging, and "presence" information.

This convergence has created a Unified Communications (UC) network—a revolutionary services platform capable of orchestrating processes and people on a scale never seen before. Unified Communications represents a step-change in technological capability and will truly marry human intelligence with network intelligence.

Unlike previous technological waves, this one will not seek to automate humans out of the process but rather to engage people in a richer and more meaningful process of decision-making.

By bringing people and their expertise into business and government processes as needed, through better communication, nations and industries will communications-enable the business process.

The authors would like to thank Skip Cohen, Education & Local Government Sector, Avaya; and Padma Subramanian, Senior Product Manager Communications-Enabled Business Process, Avaya, for their support, guidance, and insights.

Table 1: The communications revolution: Three waves of innovation

Key wave feature	Technical innovations	Impact dimensions
1st wave (1830–1930): **Individual channel development** (Channel diversity) Channel infrastructures separately developed and installed	• Telegraphy • Telephony • Radio • Television • Video	Diminished distance: The far is made near. Compression of space and time through instantaneous data, voice, and image transmission. Widespread coordination of dispersed business assets is made possible for first time. Penetration of media into consumer households.
2nd wave (1950–2007): **Channel convergence** **Unified Communications** Analog channels digitizing, moving onto a single digital platform	• Internet Protocol Networks • Integrated digital voice/video/data platform • High touch tele-presence systems	Single network management cost-efficiencies. Blended realities and cross-media hybrids (i.e., click-to-call from a television set). User emotional resonance and rich collaboration.
3rd wave (2007–?): **Cross-channel services orchestration** **Advanced Unified Communications** Network intelligence enables end-to-end business and social process management (e.g., choreographies)	• Dynamic middleware/business rules-engines • Workflow automation • Highly distributed business intelligence software architectures • Intelligent presence and availability	Always on, persistent "presence portals" unite globally dispersed network participants. Instant multi-channel communications and rich real-time data-sharing enable compression of decision and action cycles. CEBP (communications-enabled business processes): Mass synchronization of people, processes and things within and across business value chains and social network ecosystems.

Source: Boyson and Boyer, 2006.

This paper argues that we must go beyond the present framework of communications to a wider concept: social and business collaborations enabled by Unified Communications. These collaborations represent a third wave of the communications revolution, as shown in Table 1.

Communications-enabling national development: The historical context

Before we discuss how the third communications wave can advance global decision-making and economic development, we have to examine the impact of the previous communications waves. As Beniger said in his book *The Control Revolution*:

> Beginning most notably in the United States in the late nineteenth century, the Control Revolution was certainly a dramatic if not abrupt discontinuity in technological advance. Indeed, even the word "revolution" seems barely adequate to describe the development, within the span of a single lifetime, of virtually all of the basic communications technologies still in use a century later: photography and telegraphy (1830s); rotary power printing (1840s); the typewriter (1860s); transatlantic cable (1866); telephone (1876); motion pictures (1894); wireless telegraphy (1895); magnetic tape recording (1899); radio (1906) and television (1923).[1]

These communications advances converged to drive economic and social development, first in the United States and then in other countries. Telegraph and telephone networks, laid down beside railroad beds, were the vanguard communications technologies that enabled a revolution in business management. As it seemed to Knowles in 1922:

> It is now possible to control world-wide interests as one great business undertaking. The result is the formation of combinations that make for efficiency in production. Businesses of this magnitude, national and international in scope, could not be carried on without daily correspondence to keep the whole in touch. They are therefore dependent for their existence on telegraphs and telephones.[2]

The benefits of the communications revolution quickly scaled from business transformation to economy-wide transformation. By the 1970s, we witnessed the emergence of an information sector in the advanced economies dominated by the media of communications and information services. By 1977, Porat and Rubin had produced a nine-volume study for the US Department of Commerce showing that this information sector accounted for 46.2 percent of gross national product (GNP).[3]

Communications technology was also a driving force in developing economies. In Puerto Rico, the information sector grew from 25.6 percent of GNP in 1972 to 53.6 percent in 1987. An important element in the rapid growth of this sector was the telecommunications industry, whose sales exploded from $70.2 million to $554.9 million in the same period.[4]

Such communications technology diffusion has already resulted in significant impacts on economic development across many nations. Recent cross-country empirical research has attempted to estimate the importance of communications to national development. This research is summarized in Box 1.

Throughout its history, communications has consistently demonstrated its power to energize national economic and social development. Unified Communications is the latest example of this power. With people being accessible via mobile and IP communications even in the remotest parts of the globe, an unprecedented opportunity exists to use this new access in ways that can exponentially increase development impacts.

Today's third communications wave

Now let us focus on better defining and understanding the current communications wave: Unified Communications. At its most basic level, *Unified Communications* can be defined as communications integrated to optimize business processes: "UC integrates real-time and non-real time communications with business processes and requirements based on presence capabilities, presenting a consistent unified user interface and experience across multiple devices and media types."[5]

Beyond the basic general definition above, there are three critical technology areas that dominate discussions about the definition of Unified Communications: presence, service-oriented architectures, and communications-enabled business processes.

Presence: The first key theme in defining Unified Communications

The theme of presence is critical to understanding Unified Communications. By *presence,* we mean the always-on stream of information about a network user that captures location, preferred mode of communication (mobile phone, PC, etc.), and availability of the user and uses that information to provide reliable network messaging and conferencing capabilities. Presence is a state characterized by the existence of an active device through which a user can directly communicate or through which the user's presence can be detected. The state is specific to a particular communication service (email, instant messaging) or presence detection service (video/audio detection, Bluetooth network, heat sensors, etc.). The presence service keeps track of what devices, applications, and services a user has available, as well as

Box 1: Impacts of communications development

- It was found that when countries have one more telephone per 100 people than the average number of telephones expected at their given income level, they receive 0.3 cents per $100 of gross domestic product (GDP) more foreign investment than countries with an average number of telephones.[1]

- A study of factories in rural Bangladesh found that the introduction of a telephone line reduced the amount of management travel, thus cutting associated travel costs (gasoline, salaries, etc.) by a factor 13 times the cost of installing the line.[2]

- Studies in Colombia and the Philippines have shown that the ratio of productivity gains arising through the use of the telephone service exceeds the annual cost of providing service by at least 20:1 for businesses.[3]

- The introduction of telephones in rural Thailand allowed farmers to regularly check prices in Bangkok, which significantly increased profits. One village chief reported that farmers' income in his village where a telephone was installed doubled.[4]

- In Uganda's rural areas, solar-powered computers and wireless telephone systems let villagers track produce prices on the Web to better time visits to market towns, and let local doctors send out emails in advance of births to trigger shipment to their clinics of Nevirapine, a drug to kill HIV in newborns. Currently, Uganda is making a $1.7 billion investment in optical fiber, associated data centers, and technology parks.[5]

Notes
1 Reynolds et al. 2001.
2 ITU 1998.
3 World Bank 1994.
4 ITU 1998.
5 New Vision website 2007.

Figure 1: Penetration of telephone integration with instant messaging (2006–09)

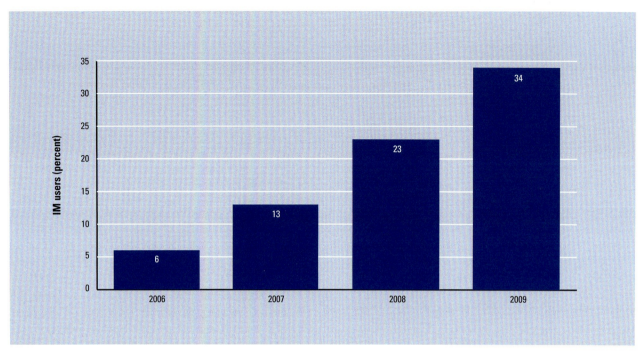

Source: Wainhouse Research, 2006.

determining a user's availability for a communications process with different users and applications.

Presence: The dial-tone for the 21st century

As Wainhouse Research observed, the convergence of data and communications leads to a presence dial tone with the ability to click-to-communicate across vast networks.[6] Current dial tone just tells us if a telephone is functioning. The next step will be for the caller to have presence information before placing a call. You will know that the person is available before actually placing the call, sending an email, and so on. Yet presence information does not actually replace dial tone. It does provide knowledge before actually placing the call through, rather than just dialing and hoping for the best. A more intelligent dial tone might go beyond presence to an enabling dial tone. The system might check a user's calendar and see that the user is hosting a meeting "in five minutes," so—even though the user is currently present—it may not be the best time to make that call. Intelligent dial tone can determine whether now is a good time to call.

Presence is predicted to play a significant role in the growth of UC markets, as shown in Figure 1.

We are beginning to see mass applications of presence. Large communications carriers in the United States are already offering products and services related to constant mobile phone presence tracking. Nextel's Loopt service sends you an alert when a friend is near. Verizon's Chaperone service sets up a "geo-fence" around a child and sends an automatic text message alert to a parent if their child, with a phone in hand, strays outside the fenced area.[7]

Service-Oriented Architecture: A second key theme

Another major theme of Unified Communications is that of an overall SOA approach. This is an open standards approach based on XML and Simple Object Access Protocol. These open standards enable data and communications networks to integrate into a common system architecture, a "true shared services design."[8]

SOA brings together disparate voice, video, and data services into a unified platform. Legacy and new services are available through a common standard service interface. The result can be a seamless user experience across all enterprise communications solutions regardless of the protocols supported by the underlying services.

The UC network's transformational potential is defined by its pervasiveness and ease of access over myriad devices. The network will keep users connected across multiple channels (phone, email, texting, etc.) and deploy enhanced 911 (E911) location services to constantly monitor and maintain a user's presence. In addition, the UC network's set of customizable and embedded business rules can bring together globally dispersed teams of people, providing real-time process alerts; multi-channel, real-time communications and decision data; and execution triggers.

New opportunities for economic and social development will open up as the advanced UC network becomes increasingly accessible to citizens around the world through devices of every kind.

We are convinced that decision makers in government and industry must increasingly heed the clear call to action, and design and launch strategies to harness the power of the UC network to help drive growth and prosperity across enterprise and sector boundaries.

Communications-enabled business processes: A third key theme

Communications-enabled business processes (CEBP) mobilizes communications and collaboration to improve business processes, real-time communication, conferencing and notifications, and escalation of events.

A 2007 Lippis report on CEBP states that:

> CEBP injects communications into business process in order to reduce human and system delay, hoping to speed workflow and increase the response of an organization to business events. In addition to workflow delay reduction, inter-industry collaboration will also play a role in CEBP adoption. For example, manufacturing, retail and transportation logistics have linked value chains and/or value networks. CEBP solutions implemented across multiple enterprises hope to improve the value chain for corporations, their partners and suppliers enabling quicker response to market demands and needs.
>
> Will CEBP have a large or small impact on corporate productivity and the global economy? Can CEBP be a change agent for the global economy by increasing productivity at either the same level as the internet did in the mid- to late-1990s? While it is too early to predict the magnitude of CEBP's contribution, it is a change agent. Business and IT leaders need to experience CEBP as it delivers on its promise of new types of applications and capabilities which use their converged network investments. CEBP is gaining business value through the integration of a converged network, information infrastructure, event driven processes, and SOA programming. If the industry can get CEBP right so that it's relatively easy to deploy and gain its value, then CEBP could be the next productivity growth change agent.[9]

IDC estimates the overall UC market, based on the innovations described above, will grow from $4.8 billion in 2007 to $17.5 billion by 2011, signaling its strong diffusion momentum.[10]

To summarize: presence, SOA, and CEBP are key elements of the UC infrastructure and create advanced value-added services. Taken together, these innovations enable end-to-end global services orchestration supporting business enterprises, public organizations, individual consumers, and diverse collaborations between them.

Unified Communications–enabled services orchestration

Unified Communications has generated a fundamentally new set of services orchestration possibilities. End-to-end automated business processes and network-embedded business rules to support those processes are being developed. RosettaNet calls these process flows "choreographies":

> We see choreographies all the time on the Web. They include those used in Internet credit card purchase transactions, including issuing the request to buy, verifying the credit card, confirming the purchase, contracting shipping facilities, and shipping product. The transaction is not completed until all of the above steps have been completed, perhaps over an extended period of time. One of the most complex early choreographies came from the travel industry, where a single transaction may be composed of airline, car rental, hotel, and other bookings that occur across multiple industries and organizations.[11]

Compared with these early examples, Unified Communications–enabled choreographies present great advances in orchestrating end-to-end business processes and people in real time. They open up the possibilities for an unprecedented scale of coordinated actions in business, government, and society. These choreographies become "activation energies" that bring together widely distributed organizations, groups, and individuals toward well-defined ends. They allow new ways to solve problems and new types of solutions not seen before. Current real-world examples of these choreographed services are shown in Table 2.

These real-world examples highlight the power of integrating communications into work flows across organizations and sectors to improve end-to-end processes.

For almost a decade, the Netcentricity Lab of the Robert H. Smith School of Business, University of Maryland, College Park, has been working on an extended research project with Avaya to explore these Unified Communications–enabled choreographies. We generated a series of UC case scenarios and prototyped choreographies to address the requirements of key users. We will present two of these scenarios to illustrate how these emerging technologies solve problems.

Scenario 1: Preventing adverse drug events in hospitals

Adverse drug events (ADEs) are a significant source of medical errors. There are an estimated 98,000 deaths per year in the United States due to medical errors. An ADE, on average, costs a hospital $4,700.

Radio frequency ID (RFID) tags on drug vials and on patients and their caregivers can be used to detect presence and authenticate people's identities, as well as to identify the drugs to be administered to a patient.

Table 2: Unified Communications–enabled services orchestration

Sector	Orchestration description	Benefits
Manufacturing	Events and exceptions management: notifications of inventory stock-outs and machinery or system failures to supervisory management or external service providers. Instantaneous conferencing in of problem-solving expertise regardless of location.	Exponential acceleration of speed of operational response and escalation of problem troubleshooting and resolution.
Banking	Mobile currency traders get alerts on mobile phones based on currency fluctuation levels. Bank customers calling into a branch and selecting an option on an interactive voice response system get routed to a mobile specialist who can help with a specific product or issue.	High reward "nano-second opportunism." Service cycle time/customer satisfaction benefits.
Petroleum	Pipeline sensors enable remote diagnostics and monitoring based on pre-established rules. Data trigger defined levels of troubleshooting and service activities, and alert and activate a network of technicians.	Avoid supply disruption and ensure business continuity.
Government disaster response	Satellite/sensor monitoring of wildfire hot spots, hurricane paths and undersea seismic activity or tsunami threats generate alerts to emergency authorities and first responders that guide evacuation and mitigation activities; and send reverse 911 messages to individual, household and business wired and wireless telephones.	Community disaster prevention and mitigation.
Health services	A mobile phone with an array of embedded sensors is used by a housebound person. The phone sensors monitor the person's vital signs and beam a results profile to an on-call physician's assistant.	Real-time sense and respond health services.
Military	Fighter aircraft engine sensors send pressure/temperature data to a contractor's servers for real time data mining. An anomaly is detected, indicating a part is about to fail. A replacement part is pulled from a warehouse and is delivered to the base where the plane will land to be available for the flight line mechanic to install.	Anticipatory logistics built upon extended supply chain business ecosystems operating in real time

Source: Boyson and Boyer, 2006.

We built a prototype that uses an Internet-connected drug-dispensing cart from Mobile Aspects Inc., which has an embedded RFID reader that can scan the drug vials about to be administered and check them against a drug interaction table hosted on an external website. If an interaction problem is identified, the UC choreography:

- notifies the attending physician and remote out-of-hospital specialists and updates their schedules appropriately, notifying necessary administrators, patients, and colleagues of the schedule changes. If the attending physicians are scheduled for surgery in the next half hour, or if they just finished a procedure and need a break, the system notifies backup physicians instead of the attending ones. The users' current state and real availability are determined, rather than including them on the call because their basic presence data indicate they are unavailable;

- conferences the hospital employees together to determine actions;

- supplies patient history and ADE details to conference participants via a Web portal; and

- arranges a follow-up doctor visit to monitor the actions taken during the call. The doctors' schedules are updated appropriately and they and their administrators are notified of the changes.

This solution integrates communications into enterprise applications and processes and orchestrates new high-value health services. This process flow is shown in Figure 2.

Scenario 2: Sensing and responding to tsunamis

The Indian Ocean tsunami that killed 300,000 people in December 2004, the deadliest tsunami ever recorded, spurred the development and growth of what has come to be called "event-driven science." In the aftermath of the disaster, the US National Science Foundation funded more than 20 scientific reconnaissance teams supported by the San Diego Supercomputer Center-based

Figure 2: Integrating communications into health-care applications and processes

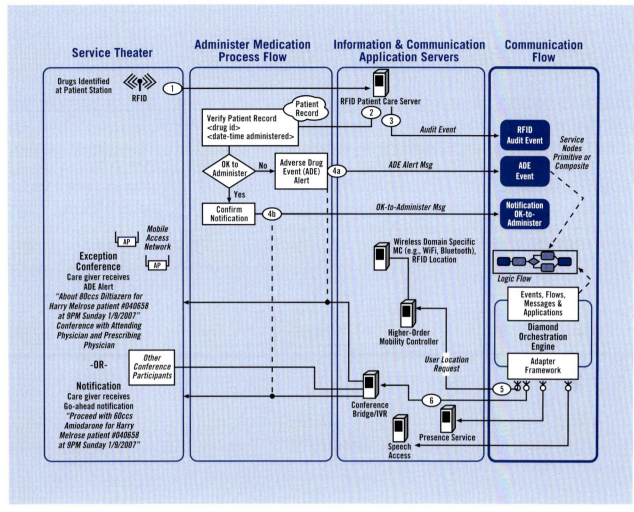

Source: Avaya.

Network for Earthquake Engineering Simulation Cyber-Infrastructure Center to work in Asia, gathering data to validate models of tsunami behavior.[12]

In October 2006, a system of event-driven sensors was used by California Institute of Technology seismologists to record and track seismic waves on an on-demand supercomputer. Within 30 minutes, scientists were able to issue guidance to the media and the public.[13]

Real-time access to supercomputers tied to communications could be transformational in enabling real-time alerts in a disaster event. Hosted on on-demand supercomputers, tsunami models could be refined by incorporating real-time data from undersea sensors to forecast effects. The architecture of such a solution was devised during our research and is shown in Figure 3. An ocean buoy equipped with seismic motion detection sensors detects the intensity of seismic activity, then triggers and relays alerts via satellite to a presence server.

This presence server contains all the location information about emergency task forces and key decision makers within the area of impact. The presence server will need to have access to enterprise and public data. The experts list will include local registered experts and experts who are traveling in the area (the expert's enterprise may share the location of its experts in case of an emergency, or this information may be tracked by a public system), as well as experts who are not in the area but who are well known internationally for specific expertise. Notifications are sent out simultaneously to all of them, activating a mass mobilization, evacuation, and mitigation effort. The presence server, built on an open SOA platform, could also initiate reverse 911 calls to households and businesses in the affected area, as well as sending out information to local participants in social networking sites (e.g., Facebook) and to local websites sponsored by providers such as Yahoo or Google. This process is shown in Figure 4.

These UC case studies in life-and-death situations provide a glimpse of its awesome power and potential to impact society.

Figure 3: Solutions to providing real-time alerts in a disaster

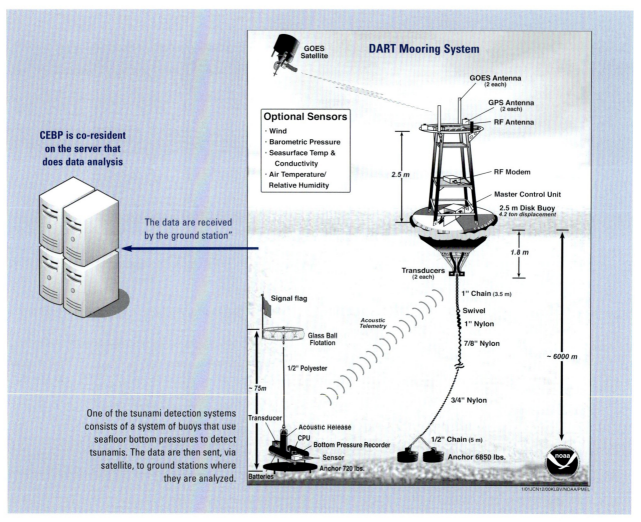

Source: Avaya.

Figure 4: Unified Communications in tsunami response

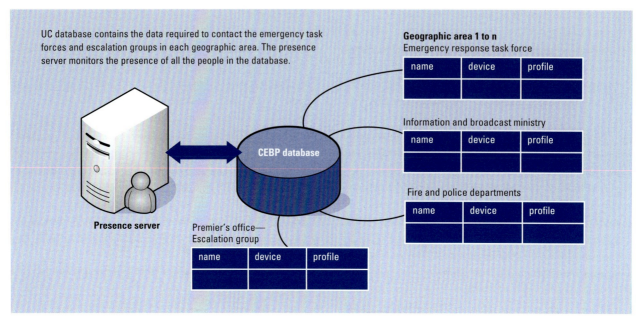

Source: Avaya

Mobilizing Unified Communications–led development: A call to action

Today, nations urgently require a bold set of adjustments in public and private strategy to harness Unified Communications as a catalyst for new economic and social development.

The key to national success will lie in mobilizing cross-boundary collaborations and partnerships cutting across government and industry borders to ensure the growth of the open standards, business process definitions, and governance mechanisms that will be needed to propel Unified Communications forward.

To attain success, a broad coalition of leaders must become energized by the potential of Unified Communications and committed to its rapid scale-up and diffusion across society. These leaders will likely fall into two major categories of influence:

- *The strategy executives:* These are the national leaders who are influential in steering the economy, the government, and civil society toward greater use of Unified Communications. Their influence spans the whole web of national investment in infrastructure, human capital, and venture capital. They will shape the regulatory policies that govern Unified Communications within and across local borders.

- *The managing executives:* These are the leaders who must translate policies into critical project portfolios and are responsible for the design, implementation, and effectiveness of large UC systems. Their influence spans across technology strategy and planning, systems lifecycle management, business process integration, quality management, and information security.[14]

These leaders will need to form a national UC vision and leadership group responsible for formulating and steering a multifaceted policy agenda with the following objectives:

- creating increasingly competitive cross-channel telecommunications and enterprise applications markets that can deliver UC services at the lowest possible price for the broadest possible penetration of Unified Communications into society;

- mobilizing formal business value networks—much as the United States' RosettaNet or Singapore's TradeNet did in a previous technology era— that can bring together affiliated companies to collaborate on UC rule-sets and end-to-end choreographies;

- nurturing a better trained and compensated specialized technical elite in business and government to manage increasingly complex, boundary-spanning UC networks that cut across enterprise and telecommunications applications;

- inculcating a network-centric collaboration ethos and associated business practices in organizations at every level of society and, through better training, speed up UC adoption; and

- expanding educational incentives to study Unified Communications, speeding up national and regional curriculum changes to produce UC leaders and managers, and spurring seed funds for UC-related business startups to quicken and sustain the rise of a new "network generation"—the young people raised on the multimedia Web—who will be the vanguard users of Unified Communications.

With these policies in place to promote Unified Communications, nations will be ready to catch the next great technology-driven long wave of economic growth at its peak.

Notes

1 Beniger 1986, p. 7.

2 Knowles 1922, p. 210.

3 Porat and Rubin 1977.

4 Boyson 1993.

5 See http:// www.unifiedcommunicationscon.com/2007/boston/web/index.htm.

6 See http://www.wainhouse.com/.

7 *Washington Post* 2007.

8 *Business Communications Review* 2007.

9 Schwarts 2007.

10 IDC 2007.

11 Drummond 2000, p. 1.

12 Berman 2005.

13 San Diego Supercomputer Center, available at www.sdsc.edu/news/invision.html.

14 Hanna and Boyson 1993.

References

Beniger, J. 1986. *The Control Revolution*. Cambridge, MA: Harvard University Press.

Berman, F. 2005. *Envision*. San Diego Supercomputer Center, Fall. Available at www.sdsc.edu/news/invision.html.

Boyson, S. 1993. "Technological Change & Development: The Case of Puerto Rico." *Technological Transformation in the Third World*, Vol.111: *Latin America*. S. Patel, ed. Aldershot, UK: Avebury Press, United Nations University/World Institute of Development Economics Research.

Boyson, S. and D. Boyer. 2006. "Communications-Enabling the Supply Chain." Presentation to World Bank E-Leadership Seminar, Robert H. Smith School of Business University of Maryland, College Park, June.

Business Communications Review. 2007. "SOA and Enterprise Voice Communications." August: p. 8.

Drummond, R. 2000. "XML: The Only Chance for a Worldwide Standard." *e-Business Advisor Magazine.* April. Available at http://e-businessadvisor.com/.

Grace, J., C. Kenny, and C. Z-W. Qiang. 2004. "Information and Communication Technologies and Broad-Based Development: A Partial Review of the Evidence." Working Paper No. 12. Washington, DC: IBRD/World Bank.

Hanna, N. and S. Boyson. 1996. "Information Technology and the East Asian Miracle." Discussion Paper No. 326. Washington, DC: World Bank.

IDC. 2007. *IDC's Definition of the Unified Communications Ecosystem.* Report, January. Available at 2007 Product Code IDC00166.

ITU (International Telecommunication Union). 1998. "Rural Telecommunications–Lessons Learned." Paper presented at the World Telecommunication Development Conference (WTDC-98), Valletta, Malta. March 23–April 1.

Knowles, L. C. A. 1922. *The Industrial & Commercial Revolutions in Great Britain During the Nineteenth Century.* London: George Rutledge & Sons.

The New Vision. 2007. "Uganda to Benefit from $1.7b ICT Project." October 17. Available at www.newvision.co.ug/D/8/220/592483.

Porat, Marc U. and M. R. Rubin. 1977. *The Information Economy.* Washington, DC: Government Printing Office.

PRNewswire. 2007. "Pulvermedia Announces the Unified Communications Conference in Boston, October 30–31, 2007." August 13. PRNewswire. Available at http://sev.prnewswire.com/computer-electronics/20070813/LAM01413082007-1.html.

Reynolds, T., C. Kenny, and C. Qiang. 2001. "Networking and FDI." Mimeo. Washington, DC: World Bank.

San Diego Supercomputer Center. Available at www.sdsc.edu/news/invision.html.

Schwartz, N. 2007. *Lippis Report* Issue 86: Communications-Enabled Business Processes (CEBP): An Outlook. July 16. Available at http://lippisreport.com/2007/07/16/lippis-report-issue-86-communications-enabled-business-processes-cebp-an-outlook/.

World Bank. 1994. "Infrastructure for Development (Initial Lessons Learned About Private Sector Participation in Telecentre Development, National Telephone Cooperative Association." *World Development Report 1994.* Available at http://www.ntca.org/content documents/telecentredev.pdf.

Wainhouse Research. Available at http://www.wainhouse.com/.

Washington Post. 2007. November 23, p. A35.

CHAPTER 1.6

Building E-skills for the Information Age

BRUNO LANVIN, INSEAD, eLab
PAMELA S. PASSMAN, Microsoft Corporation

In the current global competition for talents, which skills will be sought, and which will need to be kept at home? How will skills evolve? Can they be built and developed? These are some of the questions confronting businesses and governments in all parts of the world. The private sector is naturally concerned about its ability to create and maintain competitive advantage around an appropriate skill-mix across its human resources. Governments also look at these questions as priorities, both from the point of view of adapting national education and innovation policies to the requirements and challenges of global competition, and from that of employment creation and inclusion.

Since global competition is becoming increasingly knowledge-centric, skills related to the specific requirements of information intensive societies (e-skills) are becoming increasingly strategic. This chapter aims at raising three main sets of questions regarding e-skills:

1. Why (and how fast) is the need for e-skills growing?

2. How is the supply of such skills generated, and is it meeting current and foreseeable needs?

3. What are some of the main priorities that governments and business should address to solve the upcoming expected "e-skills crunch"?

These three topics will be addressed against the background (largely illustrated in the European context) of the necessity for businesses and governments to simultaneously pursue three major and interdependent objectives. These objectives constitute the "ICE triangle" of Innovation, Competitiveness, and Employability:

- *Innovation:* As product cycles keep shortening and technology becomes easier to spread, share, and replicate, no competitive advantage can be maintained without the continuous injection of innovation, both at product and process levels. Increasingly, financial innovation (including private-public partnerships) and social innovation (such as Web 2.0 style and multistakeholder partnerships) will combine to make this environment even more dynamic.

- *Competitiveness:* Over the last few decades, information and communication technologies (ICT) has emerged as a central contributor to growth in the global economy; however, it is now widely recognized that technology and infrastructure are not sufficient, and that, without the necessary human capital, benefits of the information revolution will

---

Background research for this chapter was produced by Martin Kralik, Director of INSEAD, eLab, in Abu Dhabi. Additional policy and programs material, and valuable comments on an earlier version, were received from Elena Bonfiglioli, Director, Corporate Citizenship, Microsoft, EMEA. Their contributions are gratefully acknowledged.

not be totally generated nor collected. In the growing "global search for talents," national educational systems and labor markets compete with one another and create new imperatives for individuals, businesses, and governments.

- *Employability:* As a majority of nations has come to embrace the principles of the market economy, the creation of sufficient jobs and an appropriate volume of skills has become a common concern. At the same time, globalization has been accompanied by the creation of new exclusion mechanisms, which need to be addressed before they become a serious hindrance to growth. Information technology (IT) and e-skills also have a critical role to play here, since (1) e-skills become a requirement not only to enter the workplace, but also to benefit from upward and horizontal mobility once employed; and (2) "e-inclusion" can be a powerful principle that can be used to build higher levels of competitiveness while fighting inequalities.

The worldwide demand for e-skills is growing

To identify, and possibly quantify, current and expected needs in e-skills, one needs to define them as precisely as possible. Yet any definition of e-skills is rapidly challenged by the expanding scope and purpose of such skills, because the rapid mutation of our societies from industrial and service economies to knowledge and experience societies makes these skills both more pervasive and more encompassing.

Knowledge economies require an increasing range of skills and e-skills. Leadership itself (in both private and public organizations) has to be redefined to better fit the need to set up and manage multicultural teams working across many different time zones, in increasingly flat organizations. Moreover, in recent years, the logic of globalization has placed innovation at the top of the agenda for businesses and government alike. Because innovation starts with people, the level of e-skills that resides within the workforce has become crucial. Research shows that, increasingly, e-skills are the entry ticket to better jobs and to employment in general.[1] Correspondingly, they have become a key not only to digital but also to social inclusion.

Defining e-skills

Existing literature broadly defines *e-skills* as ICT-related skills. The 2004 European e-Skills Forum put forward definitions for three different types of skills:

1. *ICT user skills*, required for effective application of ICT systems and devices by the individual;

2. *ICT practitioner skills*, required for researching, developing and designing, managing, producing, consulting, marketing and selling, integrating, installing and administrating, maintaining, supporting, and servicing ICT systems; and

3. *e-business skills*, needed to exploit opportunities provided by ICT, notably the Internet, to ensure more efficient and effective performance of different types of organizations, to explore possibilities for new ways of conducting business and organizational processes, and to establish new businesses.[2]

In nearly all contexts, e-skills are treated as a component of a broader strategy toward building the knowledge economy (e-economy) by fostering competitiveness, growth, employment, education and lifelong training, and social inclusion. Alongside industrial policy, small and medium-sized enterprise (SME) policy, and innovation priorities, the European Council has recognized e-skills strategy as one of the fundamental pillars of the Lisbon strategy, aimed at positioning the European Union as the world's most competitive economic zone.[3]

Knowledge economies require a broad range of e-skills

An increasing number of nations are competing to establish themselves as the world's leading knowledge economies. Across the globe, knowledge cities are being built from scratch (as in Saudi Arabia), or are vying to be recognized as "knowledge hubs."[4] In Europe, the 2000 Lisbon Agenda challenged the European Union to become "the most competitive and dynamic knowledge-based economy in the world, capable of sustainable economic growth with more and better jobs, and greater social cohesion" by 2010.[5]

It is now widely recognized that such knowledge-based strategies have to grant stronger priority to the generation of skills in general, and e-skills in particular. For example, according to the declaration issued by the European e-Skills 2006 Conference in Thessaloniki, Greece, "the success of the Lisbon strategy, the competitiveness of European industry and social cohesion are dependent on the effective use of ICT and the knowledge, skills, competencies and inventiveness of the European workforce and its ICT practitioners."[6]

However, addressing e-skills in the context of a knowledge agenda entails a significant broadening of the definition provided above. The kind of skills needed include not only computer skills and the ability to master and combine IT skills, but also a more generic set of competencies relating to the ability to communicate across cultural and institutional boundaries, to work in teams (often remotely), and, more generally, to create and share knowledge.

It is around this broader definition that longer-term knowledge strategies (such as the European Union's Lisbon Agenda) have identified e-skills as central for boosting innovation, productivity and employability, and responding to global challenges. The European Council has gone even further by insisting on the social dimension of such challenges, and has committed to an integrated approach to e-skills that emphasizes social cohesion, gender issues (including encouraging women to choose ICT careers), e-inclusion, and the promotion of new ICT professions and skills. In November 2007, the Council welcomed the Commission's proposal to establish a long-term e-skills agenda in response to the need to address e-skills as a way of contributing to the development of an economy based on knowledge-intensive products and services and a more inclusive society (see Box 1). It emphasized the need to rapidly implement such an agenda, to improve cooperation and mobilization of all stakeholders, and to adopt best strategies and practices in order to better face global competitive challenges.

In Europe particularly, but also globally, industry has played a key leadership role alongside public authorities to foster the development of new skills and training for the knowledge economy and to make people ready for the workplace of the 21st century. The private sector has been working side by side with EU institutions and national governments to facilitate diagnostics, raise awareness, and build action plans in the area of e-skills. As a leader in the field, Microsoft, for example, has been actively contributing to several successful multistakeholder partnerships (MSPs) such as the European

Box 1: European authorities make e-skills a priority

The e-skills topic and discussion have been present in the EU agenda and in its discussions with industry and other stakeholders since October 2002 with the European e-Skills Summit organized in cooperation with the Danish Presidency, the Council Conclusions adopted in December 2002, and the establishment of the European e-Skills Forum in 2003 by the European Commission. In 2006 and 2007 the debate has gained new momentum, and industry has provided input and concrete recommendations to the process, in particular regarding e-skills.

Those five years of work and cooperation culminated in the European Commission's Policy Communication of November 2007 on "E-skills for the 21st Century: Fostering Competitiveness, Growth and Jobs." The three main priorities emerging from that Communication are:

1. the imperative of adopting a regional EU long-term e-skills agenda to promote competitiveness, employability and workforce development, reduce e-skills gaps, and be in a better position to address global competitive challenges;

2. the need to improve cooperation between the public and private sectors on a long-term basis, in order to ensure a seamless framework linking basic e-skills training, vocational and higher education, and professional development; and

3. the necessity for industry and policymakers to promote the professionalism, the image, and the attractiveness of ICT jobs and careers and to foster better work, employment conditions, and perspectives.

Also in November 2007, on the occasion of its Competitiveness Council, the European Council further enhanced the importance of e-skills by:

- inviting the Commission, Member States, and stakeholders to proceed with the five action lines at the European level as presented in the Communication, with a view to complete them by 2010, while ensuring that any new proposals are consistent with existing initiatives and that Member States' responsibility for their education and training systems is respected;

- supporting the Commission's intention to continue to:
  1. provide a platform for the exchange of best practices,
  2. promote a regular dialogue on e-skills, and
  3. develop a European e-Competence Framework in cooperation with Member States and stakeholders;

- inviting the Member States to:
  1. further develop their long-term e-skills strategies, taking into account the key components and action lines proposed by the Commission, where appropriate;
  2. include e-skills strategy in their national reform programs, in the context of their lifelong learning and skills policies; and
  3. take into account SMEs' specificities in this field and the importance of ICT diffusion for their competitiveness;

- encouraging the industry, social partners, and education providers, including academia, to mobilize themselves, putting emphasis on social responsibility, to take initiatives contributing to the implementation of the long-term e-skills strategy;

- welcoming the Commission's intention to organize a conference in 2008 to report on progress made, present the results of the actions, and discuss the way forward, in view of releasing a report in 2010 to the Council and the European Parliament based on the results of an independent evaluation and the assessment of the stakeholders; and

- committing to continue and broaden the debate on these issues in order to achieve an integrated approach in which social cohesion, gender issues, such as encouraging women to choose ICT careers, e-inclusion, and promoting new ICT professions and skills can be fully discussed.

Source: Based on extracts from the European Council, 2007 (available at http://www.consilium.europa.eu/ueDocs/cms_Data/docs/pressData/en/intm/97225.pdf).

Alliance on Skills for Employability,[7] and the e-Skills Industry Leadership Board (see Box 5), in combination with its worldwide "Unlimited Potential initiative."[8]

The innovation imperative and the global sourcing of talents

Because the emergence of knowledge economies requires talents to be sourced globally, e-skills and e-leadership skills are in particularly high demand.

E-skills for innovation

For many years, innovation has been the preserve of the developed world. European, US, and Japanese companies focused their high-end activities on their home markets. In other markets, innovation was largely incremental and limited to adapting products to meet local requirements. But recently, the logic of innovation and research and development (R&D) internationalization has been changing. As companies have fanned out across the globe to access the potential of new markets, the footprints of their innovation and R&D activities have become more international and/or dispersed in character.[9]

In particular, the rate of innovation internationalization has increased in sync with the rapid economic emergence of India and China over the past five years. In tandem with these changes, companies worldwide have had to recognize and respond to an increasing global dispersion of knowledge and talent. Building and sustaining a strong pipeline of internal as well as external talent, across all levels of innovation, R&D, and management, is imperative for the 21st-century organization.[10]

E-skills for leadership

To drive multicultural (and often geographically dispersed) teams, and to attract talents from afar, new qualities are required from leaders in industry and government. Moreover, since such teams have to be managed in ways that will stimulate their creativity and enhance their ability to innovate, traditional top-down organizational models are not the most efficient. A thorough knowledge of technology will not be the main characteristic of the "e-leaders" required by knowledge economies; on the contrary, a deep understanding of the organizational, political, and social impact of global information networks will be a critical quality of this digital leadership. E-leaders will also be expected to understand the pervasive application of technology to organizational processes and to turn innovation into productivity gain.[11]

In parallel, efforts to redefine the roles, profiles, and functions of the chief information officer (CIO), whose role is becoming increasingly strategic and less technology-specific, have already been in place for some time. A leader in this area has been IBM and its recently established Center for CIO Leadership. As part of the opening of the Center, IBM launched the global 2007 CIO Leadership Survey. The Survey (which is in the process of being extended to another group of 500 CIOs across the Asia-Pacific region) reveals that CIOs are increasingly becoming trusted members of the executive business team. Eighty percent of CIOs responded that they are a valued member of the senior leadership team, with 69 percent indicating significant involvement in strategic decision-making. Further, organizations whose CIOs have high levels of strategic involvement demonstrate higher levels of business model and product and service innovation, as well as shared, centralized IT services.[12]

Interim conclusions 1

From the definitions and observations above, three initial conclusions can be drawn:

1. E-skills are pervasive, and not limited to IT specialists; they are increasingly required in all sectors and at all levels of activity in which creativity, innovation, and interdisciplinary teamwork are required as tools for competitiveness; in both the private and public sectors, leaders need to be not only e-literate, but also to display and grow the new qualities required by e-leadership.

2. The emerging global knowledge economy will significantly increase the need for more e-skills at all levels (from unspecialized workers to corporate leaders), in all industries (not just the ICT sector), and in the public sector.

3. E-skills will be of central importance to determine workers' vertical and horizontal mobility, and hence well-functioning labor markets and adequate employability and inclusion levels.

Such conclusions can be represented in the supply/demand diagram presented in Figure 1.

When considering the general picture of the expected uses of e-skills on one hand, and of their possible sources (internal and external) on the other hand, one is faced with a set of additional issues. Such issues relate in particular to the educational system, the image of IT jobs, the determinants of employability on national labor markets, and the role of external supplies of e-skills. These issues will be addressed in the next section of this chapter.

Why e-skills are in insufficient supply

When a society's development requires new skills, it naturally tends to turn to its educational system first, in order to generate the profiles and capacities it needs for the jobs it will create. However, when socioeconomic change accelerates, educational systems prove comparatively slow to react and adapt: typically, changes made in the primary/secondary educational systems will make their effect felt on job markets only 10 to 20 years later; for tertiary education, the lag is about 5 to 10 years.

Box 2: The new international distribution of talents

Produced in association with BT, the Global Innovation Index (GII) model was developed at INSEAD as a formal model to help show the degree to which individual nations and regions currently respond to the challenge of innovation. It is intended not only to serve as a means for determining a country's relative response capacity, but also to provide a clearer picture of its strengths and deficiencies with respect to innovation-related policies and practices. One of the central hypotheses of the GII model is that response readiness is directly linked to a country's ability to adopt, and benefit from, leading-edge technologies, expanded human capacities, better organizational and operational capability, and improved institutional performance. The eight innovation "pillars" in the GII framework are grouped in two separate categories: "inputs"—factors that underpin innovative capacity such as institutions and policies, human capacity, infrastructure, technological sophistication, and business markets and capital; and "outputs"—the benefits that a nation derives from the inputs in terms of knowledge creation, competitiveness, and wealth generation.

In the GII 2007, the United States was ranked top on both input and output. Relative to other countries, it clearly has both a better environment for innovation and is more effective at exploiting it. But the United States also faces question marks, both at home and abroad. Central to its leading position has been the magnetism it has traditionally exerted, building constantly on its human capital. Until now, the United States has managed to make up for the shortcomings of its primary and secondary education by attracting talent from overseas. Now it faces the need to produce more scientists and engineers from within.

Some emerging markets have walked in the United States' footsteps in attracting ICT talent from overseas. For example, the United Arab Emirates, 14th in the global list, has benefited from policies explicitly designed and implemented to attract skilled workers and technology-intensive companies.

There was a clear gap in the GII ranking between the emerging Asian powerhouses of India and China (23rd and 29th, respectively) on the one hand, and the other BRIC economies of Brazil (40th) and Russia (54th) on the other. All of them fared better on the output than input measures: India ranked 7th on outputs and China 9th, both hoisted by good competitiveness and respectable knowledge scores.

European markets have done well in the overall GII ranking, with Germany, the United Kingdom, and France ranked 2nd, 3rd, and 5th, respectively. But in the area of human capacity, among large European economies only France made it into the top 10. Overall, these countries performed better on the output side of the rankings than on the inputs. By contrast, the Nordic economies did relatively better on inputs than outputs, and scored high on human capacity.

Source: Dutta and Caulkin, 2007.

Figure 1: Elements of the supply and demand equation for e-skills

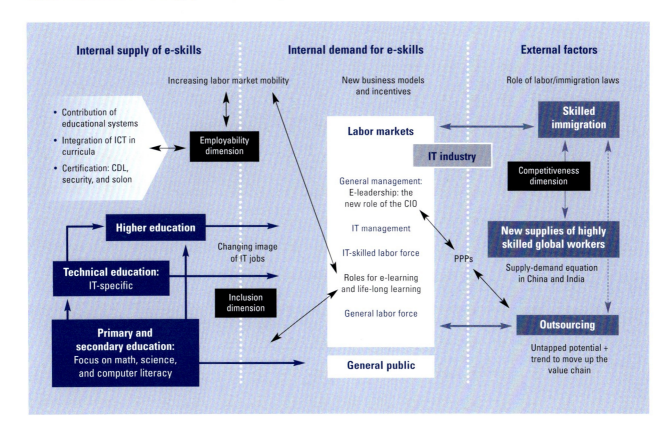

It is therefore not surprising, given the pace at which information societies have been reinventing themselves over the last two decades, that educational systems should still be producing much fewer e-skilled workers than needed. However, the current e-skills gap raises at least three questions, namely (1) how much of the current needs for e-skills can be satisfied by existing educational and training systems; (2) what can be done to improve the image of IT jobs in mature economies; and (3) how much can be done to improve overall employability through the development of e-skills.

Reasons and ways to improve educational systems

In most mature economies, concerns have been growing steadily about the ability of national educational systems to provide the e-skills needed by the growing share of knowledge activities in both production and consumption.

In the European Union, for example, statistics show:

- There is an ongoing decline in the number of students starting ICT courses.

- The demand for e-skills is growing while supply is declining.

- More than one-third of Europeans have no basic ICT skills.[13]

- The gender issue still remains, as less than 20 percent of ICT practitioners in the European Union are women.[14]

The shortage of qualified ICT professionals, however, has been felt not only in the developed markets of North America and Europe, but also in the Middle East, Russia, and, increasingly, India and China—markets once regarded as near-infinite sources of engineering talent. India's National Association of Software and Services Companies (NASSCOM) forecasts a shortage of 500,000 professional employees in the technology sector by 2010. Although the country continues to produce nearly 400,000 engineers a year, a recent NASSCOM survey found only one in four engineering graduates to be employable. The rest were deficient in the required technical skills, fluency in English, or ability to work in a team or deliver basic oral presentations.[15]

In China, a 2007 McKinsey study reported that fewer than 10 percent of Chinese job candidates, on average, would be suitable for work in a foreign company in nine core positions, including engineers, finance workers, accountants, quantitative analysts, life science researchers, medical doctors, and support staff. This is mostly because of their limited experience in projects and teamwork. Projecting these estimates onto China's 1.6 million entry-level engineers suggests that the country's pool of young engineers considered suitable for work in multinationals is just 160,000—no bigger than the United Kingdom's.[16]

Hence, one can consider the situation to be one of global inadequacy between the volume and nature of e-skills required by the global knowledge economy on one hand, and the ability of existing educational systems to generate them on the other hand.

Referring to Figure 1, several levels of education need to be considered to address this global inadequacy. At the primary or basic educational level, computer literacy has become a requirement of the same importance as reading, writing, and arithmetic. Yet this additional challenge is emerging at a time when the average level

---

Box 3: What is happening to mathematics and science?

The 2006 OECD's Programme for International Student Assessment (PISA) survey of 15-year-olds in major industrialized countries focused on science and also assessed mathematics and reading. Relevance to lifelong learning has been one of the hallmarks of the PISA surveys, which are conducted once in every three years.

Developed jointly by OECD member countries through the OECD's Directorate for Education, PISA aims at measuring how far students approaching the end of compulsory education have acquired some of the knowledge and skills essential for full participation in the knowledge society. PISA is an important part of the work of the Directorate for Education, which collects data and provides comparative indicators of education systems in OECD member and partner countries.

In addition to monitoring student performance in the three main subject areas of reading, mathematics and science, PISA seeks to deepen policy insights, among other things, by making use of computer-based assessments—not only to measure ICT literacy skills but also to allow for a wider range of dynamic and interactive tasks and to explore more efficient ways of carrying out the main tests of student knowledge and skills in reading, mathematics, and science.

In 2006, the following economies scored above the OECD average of 500 score points: Finland (the highest-performing country on the PISA 2006 science scale), Canada, Japan, New Zealand, Hong Kong, Estonia, Australia, the Netherlands, Korea, Rep., Germany, the United Kingdom, the Czech Republic, Switzerland, Austria, Belgium, Ireland, Liechtenstein, Slovenia, and Macao.

Nine of these economies also ranked among the top 15 in the Networked Readiness Index (NRI) 2007–2008, thus illustrating that building sustainable networked readiness on the national level requires consistently strong investment in education, particularly with an emphasis on science and mathematics, as well as their application in problem-solving. This confirms that emerging economies are moving up the scale of scientific education, relative to many mature economies in Europe and the United States.

Source: OECD, 2007.

of basic education in mathematics and science seems to be deteriorating, especially in some mature industrial economies (see Box 3).

It is clear that improving the quality and extent of citizen's basic education in mathematics and science will be only one of the many ingredients necessary to generate the required levels of e-skills in the coming years. One should not expect the educational system to provide all such needed ingredients. For example, instilling the necessary qualities to make an entire society more innovative will require more than good education (see Box 4).

Furthermore, and because of the rapidly changing IT landscape, it is clear that the set of e-skills taught and learned today through the formal educational system are already out of date when today's students reach the labor market. For e-skills to be forward-looking, open ended, entrepreneurial, and flexible enough to follow the innovation trends in the industry, the formal educational system needs the complement of a just-in-time

Box 4: Is innovation linked to education?

Drawing on the World Bank's Knowledge Assessment Methodology (KAM), the Knowledge Economy Index (KEI) provides an interesting way to further explore the correlation between quality of education and ability to innovate. The picture it offers is fully consistent with the one provided by the Global Innovation Index (GII) approach (see Box 2).

A quick comparison of the KEI's top-performing countries' relative innovation and education rankings illustrates that, although good-quality educational systems are typically a key building block in vibrant national innovation landscapes, the two indicators do not always evolve hand in hand (see the figure below). On the far side of the spectrum, Switzerland came out on top in the innovation ranking in 2007, but only 34th in the education ranking. On the other hand, Australia, despite claiming the number 5 spot for the quality of its educational system, ranked only 19th in the innovation subindex.

This shows that strong educational systems are not necessarily equated with strong innovation output, and vice versa. Other factors are also critical—for example, the structure of the GDP mix, the availability of venture capital, and the presence of R&D and innovation clusters. In addition, changes in methodologies and curricula, particularly if implemented at the primary level, may not yield visible results for another 10 to 20 years.

Nonetheless, the rankings show a strong correlation between societies' networked readiness (as measured by the NRI) and their cumulative strengths in education and innovation (as quantified using World Bank's KAM/KEI): nine of the KEI top 15 countries also appear in the NRI 2007–2008 top 15. The individual countries' relative weaknesses on either the education or innovation fronts have demonstrably hampered their response readiness to capitalize on the opportunities that are inherent in the knowledge economy vision.

Source: Knowledge Assessment Methodology, World Bank, 2007.
Note: The KEI description of the knowledge economy relies on four pillars, namely (1) Economic Incentive and Institutional Regime (EIR), (2) Education and Training, (3) Innovation and Technological Adoption, and (4) ICT Infrastructure. See www.worldbank.org/kam.

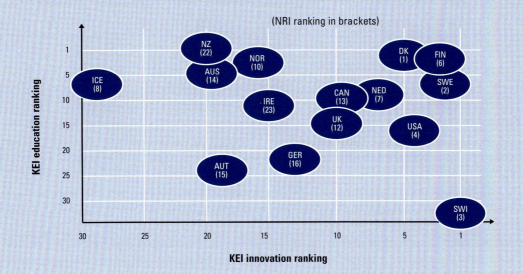

Figure 1: Innovation and education in the world's top 15 knowledge economies

Source: Knowledge Assessment Methodology, World Bank, 2007; World Economic Forum, NRI 2007–2008.

delivery system of e-skills through vocational training and lifelong learning.

Beyond formal education and training: Improving the image of IT jobs

The lack of appropriate education and training in schools and universities—still insufficiently complemented by professional lifelong training—is not the only reason why e-skills needs are not being satisfied by the educational systems. In many cases (especially in mature industrial economies), IT training is attracting diminishing numbers of students. One of the main reasons for this surprising situation is to be found in the image of IT and IT-related jobs. Significantly damaged by the burst of the dot.com bubble in 2000–01, this image has further deteriorated by at least two convergent phenomena:

1. A large number of IT jobs are currently provided (at least at entry level) by the "programming factories" or "IT departments" of large companies, in which students feel that little room is left for creativity and inventiveness;[17] the growing outsourcing of such jobs is also adding to their image of low-quality qualification.

2. Many "success stories" of leaders of IT companies have been described by the media (and often by themselves) as "college drop-outs" or "garage entrepreneurs," or even "hackers," before being recognized as their industry champions; to some extent, they are, in the eyes of the younger generation, an incarnation of an education counterculture.

Even the Internet, which was developed by college graduates with PhDs in some of the best universities in the world, is often perceived as the outcome of such a counterculture. The same applies to other spheres such as open source, social networking (Web 2.0 style), or even massive multiplayer videogames.

This situation has been compounded by the pursuance of die-hard gender stereotypes, which have surprisingly proved tougher to eradicate in IT than in most other—more traditional—sectors of our economies. Attracting more girls toward scientific studies and IT specializations will be part of the rebuilding of e-skills' image.

In some countries, efforts have recently been made to initiate such rebuilding. In France, for example, Pasc@line,[18] a multistakeholder association, has been created for this purpose. Citing a "growing and irrational lack of appetite for scientific education," the association stresses the paradox that currently exists between the diminishing number of students attracted by IT learning tracks on one hand, and the unmet needs of enterprises for IT-skilled jobs on the other hand. To address this paradox, it brings together educational institutions, business, and trade unions to assess why IT jobs are not attracting more young people and to change the image of such jobs through various campaigns of information across French schools and universities.

More partnerships of this kind, involving schools, universities, potential suppliers of IT jobs, and relevant public authorities will be needed to create a more faithful and realistic image of IT jobs, and to generate the necessary renewed interest to acquire e-skills among the younger generation.

The Holy Grail of employability

In and by itself, the development of higher levels and volumes of e-skills will not suffice to address the needs of knowledge economies for higher levels of employment and innovation. It may lead to further social and economic tensions if this development is not accompanied by a genuine effort to heighten the degree of employability of people with such skills. Several elements need further consideration in this respect, including (1) the limited efficiency of labor markets, especially in mature economies; (2) the positive and negative effects of an important pool of e-skills in emerging countries; (3) the (surprising) self-diminished ability of some large economies to take advantage of such a pool; and (4) the (less surprising) diminished interest of emerging economies to export such skills. All four of these factors have a direct impact on the e-skills/employability equation worldwide, particularly in the regions were such skills are in growing need, such as Europe.

Internal factors: A complex mesh of brakes and incentives
For many years, analysts have stressed the positive role that flexibility in labor markets can play to achieve higher rates of employment. In sectors characterized by high rates of technological innovation, such flexibility seems to be even more desirable, since (1) it will allow highly skilled workers to spread innovation across firms and sectors, (2) it will contribute to generate the multidisciplinary approaches required to nurture innovation, (3) it will make IT jobs more attractive to younger people, and (4) it will allow industry and potential employers to be more open to recruiting e-skilled workers in sectors considered as higher risk.

But most national economies are still fighting to find a balance between the interests or positions of various stakeholders with regard to labor market flexibility, employment security, and labor market security.[19] This often results in complex sets of laws and regulations, which tend to diminish each other's impact.

External factors: Stabilizers or amplifiers?
Information-intensive activities (such as system maintenance and call centers, as well as the handling of accounting or financial data) have been among the main beneficiaries of the recent wave of outsourcing.

Offshoring (or nearshoring) have been a major vehicle and tool of the rapid globalization of information services generally.

However, over the last decade, the scarcity of e-skills in advanced economies has increased the volume of labor migration from emerging countries with high levels of education (e.g., India) to more mature markets (e.g., the United States and Europe, but also Canada, Australia, and New Zealand). To some extent, this ability to rely on external providers of e-skills has diluted concerns about domestic e-skills imbalances in mature economies.

The pressure is now coming back with a vengeance, however, as some countries have tightened their visa policies for students and workers (e.g., the United States after September 2001), while some of the major sources of e-skilled workers (such as India) have become major consumers of such skills themselves, leaving less room and less incentive for such workers to migrate.

Less appetite in mature economies to attract e-skills from abroad?
In the United States, the reform of the country's immigration policy is stalled. Visa restrictions and stringent security measures that came into effect following the events of September 2001, have further dampened the enthusiasm of young ICT and science talent from overseas to pursue their academic and professional goals in the United States. Similarly, international consultancies and policy think tanks have pointed to the unwillingness of some European countries to tap talent from emerging economies. In fact, as of end 2007, the European Union has yet to allow free movement of labor among its own 25 Member States—a fundamental part of any "single market."

Skilled migration remains a controversial topic in the European Union. Calls for reforming immigration policies to make it easier for ICT and science talent to live and work in host countries are mixed with perceptions of "the offshore and nearshore invasion" as a demotivating factor in e-skills adoption.[20] According to a recent INSEAD study, what may be missing from the current e-skills formula in the European Union is a "culture of diversity, optimism and meritocracy, in which individual background is much less important than the desire to succeed."[21] As a sign, however, that European authorities have taken the measure of the growing competition for talents, the European Commission is proposing to create a European Blue Card offering a single admission procedure rather than 27 different ones. Once they have worked for two years in an EU country, highly qualified workers and their families will be able to move for professional purposes to another EU country. President Barroso recently stated that highly skilled people from all over the world are welcome in the European Union, saying "Labour migration into Europe boosts our competitiveness and therefore our economic growth. It also helps tackle demographic problems resulting from our ageing population."[22]

Evolving options for offshoring white-collar work; growing middle-class consumer bases in China, India, and Eastern Europe; political considerations; and laws and regulations at home and abroad are creating a multilayered and constantly changing challenge for transnational organizations.

Greater ability for emerging economies to retain e-skills?
Social considerations aside, the world is changing such that highly skilled and sophisticated workers, although they are in short supply, are now found worldwide, and are subject to global sourcing. The strategy for multinational organizations is to leverage the global talent pool wherever it exists. Nonetheless, there are limits that result from national labor laws, particularly if the effect is a lack of mobility and relative openness of the local labor market. Many emerging markets have been hot on the heels of developed nations in creating a competitive landscape for building management talent. India, for instance, has ranked highly in recent surveys on global talent, thanks to its rapid demographic growth, the mobility of its workforce, and its healthy labor market flexibility.

Interim conclusions 2
From the data available on both the supply side and demand side of e-skills worldwide, the following call for priority attention from public and private decision makers emerges:

1. The gap is growing between the ability of existing educational systems to provide e-skilled workers and managers on one hand, and the requirement of knowledge-intensive economies on the other hand; this gap is growing worldwide, and will be felt in a more acute fashion in the industries and regions in which significant investment has been made over the last decade to develop IT productions and knowledge-intensive societies.

2. For such industries and regions, adjustments are urgently needed to adapt educational systems (not only in schools and universities, but also through distance learning and lifelong education) to address medium-term e-skills needs; efforts to improve the image and career prospects of IT jobs—especially among the female part of the population—will be required to enhance the impact of such adjustments.

3. In the shorter run, legal and regulatory systems will have a crucial role to play to improve the functioning of labor markets, including through allowing greater upward and horizontal mobility

for e-skilled workers; industries and regions with the more urgent needs will have to consider ways to improve their access to foreign e-skills and talents, for which competition will become more and more intense in the next few years.

What can be done: The need for e-skills strategies
Based on the analysis carried out in the previous two sections, and considering the goal is to achieve the simultaneous pursuit (and attainment) of innovation, competitiveness, and employability, one can consider six sets of requirements to do so.

- *Skills:* Skills are a centerpiece to the whole edifice, because they are a necessary condition for making the best of available technologies and (more importantly) for re-inventing them on a daily basis to bring them closer to the needs of ordinary citizens; in that context, key e-skills should include (1) users' skills, (2) practitioners' skills, (3) e-business skills, and (4) e-leadership skills.

- *Knowledge:* Because it is broader than skills, the knowledge required to develop vibrant information societies has to pervade all of the channels by which individuals and communities exchange, share, and transmit knowledge. However, educational systems will retain a prominent responsibility in such a task, and will have to adapt to upcoming challenges by (1) reinforcing the quality and amount of mathematics and science in primary and secondary curricula; (2) updating tertiary and specialized education by making it more adaptable to tomorrow's technological changes, and linking it to other "generic" skills in management, business, economics, and human resources, for example; and (3) developing the ability of communities, businesses, and organizations in general to build the "institutional memory" without which knowledge grows and dies with individuals.

- *Agility:* Individuals and organizations will need to replicate the faculty of educational systems to "teach how to learn" rather than to transmit "established/textbook knowledge"; in a world in which technology changes on a daily basis, and where new business models and social structures emerge continuously, skills need to be updated and enriched at the same pace. Learning has become a lifelong experience, for which employers need to make room and investments (and for which e-learning provides a tool of growing importance because its content can be updated continuously, and delivered anywhere and everywhere). Such "learning agility" will become a central part of nations' ability to mobilize and adapt rapidly to multiple and mostly unanticipated changes. In such a context, specific attention will need to be devoted to smaller structures such as SMEs, which will act as a major provider of jobs and innovation in networked societies. Last but not least, agility will need to be nurtured through cross-societal networks (linking business, academia, public authorities, and local and cross-border communities) to shorten and accelerate innovation cycles; in this latter context, the existence of widely spread and dynamic venture capital cultures will prove increasingly vital.

- *Technology:* A more detrimental mistake for knowledge societies would be to regard technology as an end in itself. The social value of IT investment should be the main criterion in determining the amount of public resources going to information infrastructure, for example. When such provision falls under the responsibility of private players, a strong, transparent, and balanced regulatory framework should allow competition to benefit all citizens while maintaining industry's interest for further investing in technological innovation and deployment. Sufficient evidence is available today to accept as a valid working hypothesis that better and more widespread information infrastructure (including broadband) will bring significant benefits to all parts of human societies, including in developing countries.[23] Last but not least, as technological innovation accelerates and becomes more expensive at the same time, fewer and fewer players will be in a position to "reinvent the wheel": keeping an eye on existing best solutions and practices will become strategically important, and the opportunities attached to foreign licensing and, more generally, openness to ideas and tools invented abroad will be granted increasing attention worldwide.

- *E-inclusion:* It is hence of the utmost importance for such societies to establish efficient safeguards against the new exclusion mechanisms that IT could generate: equal access to e-skills should be a core principle in this regard. It would be equally important that specific mechanisms and tools be established to enhance employability through IT. Portals of different kinds can greatly help increase the fluidity of labor markets. Enterprises and public institutions also have to contribute by encouraging upward and horizontal mobility of e-skilled workers within and across organizations. Flexibility is now widely recognized as a key factor to enable labor markets to generate more jobs; in the case of IT-related jobs, such flexibility will need to be increased and extended internationally if some of the most urgent e-skills deficits (e.g., in Western Europe) are to be successfully addressed in the near future.

Figure 2: A possible multistakeholder approach for e-skills

SKILLS
- ICT users skills
- ICT practitioners skills
- e-business skills
- e-leadership skills

KNOWLEDGE
- basic math & science knowledge
- higher (tertiary) education knowledge
- institutional memory

AGILITY
- ability to update skills continuously (e-learning and lifelong learning)
- ability to mobilize light structures rapidly (SMEs)
- ability to accelerate innovation cycle (venture capital, links business-academia)

TECHNOLOGY
- availability of a critical level of information infrastructure (including broadband)
- ability of the network to update itself (regulatory/competition environment)
- readiness to adopt/adapt best practices (foreign licensing, for example)

E-INCLUSION
- safeguards against exclusion mechanisms due to IT
- specific mechanisms/tools to enhance employability through IT
- sufficient labor market flexibility to benefit from increased labor mobility due to IT

STRATEGY
- existence of an e-society vision, shared by all stakeholders
- promotion of IT jobs (education, image, leadership)
- shared commitment across stakeholders to promote a competitive and inclusive e-society

Socioeconomic impact of multistakeholder partnership

INNOVATION
COMPETITIVENESS
EMPLOYABILITY

Feedback from markets to stakeholders

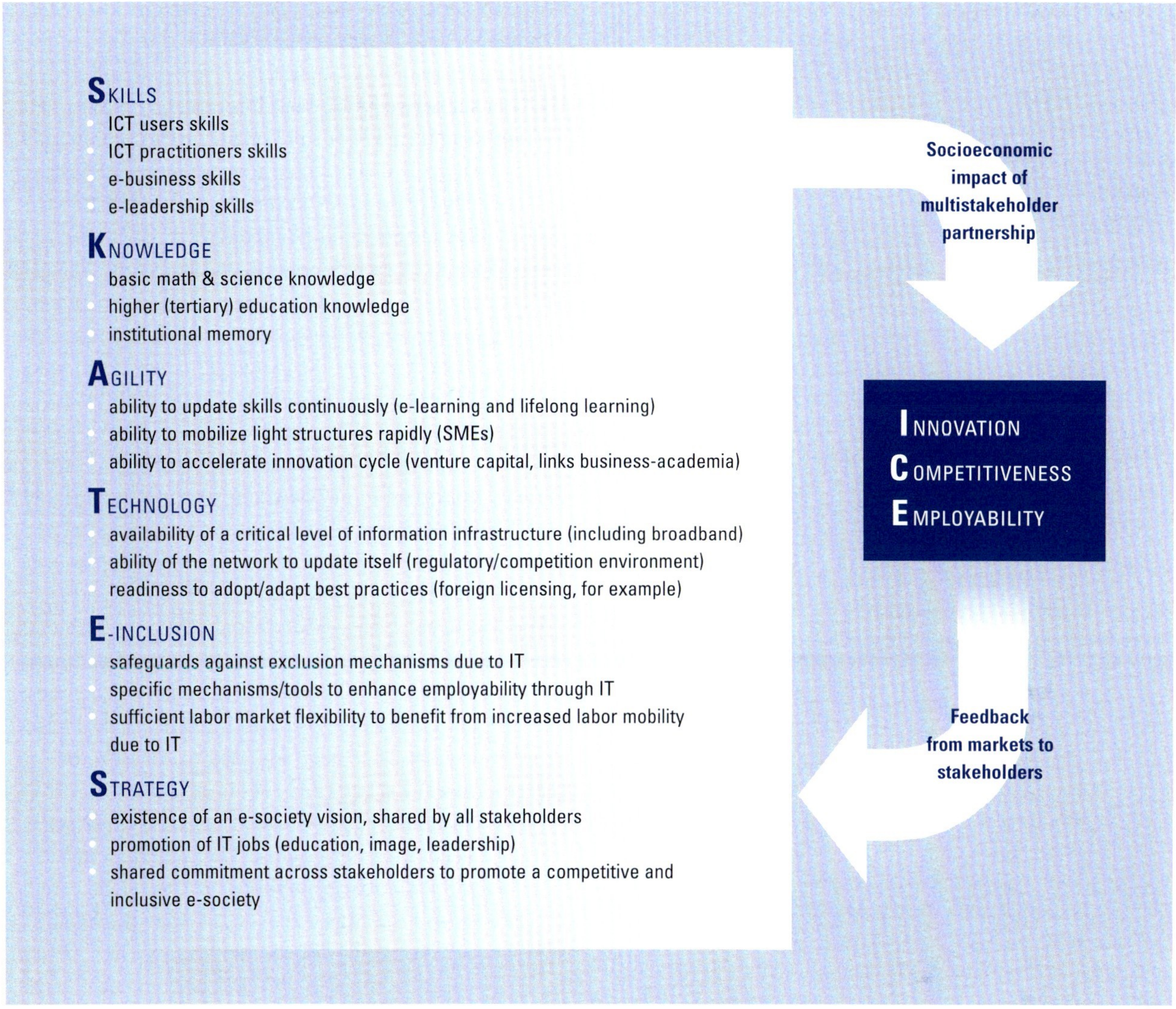

- *Strategy:* Because all five of the preceding requirements are intertwined across multiple levels of our societies, they cannot be met in the absence of a coherent and encompassing vision, shared by all stakeholders. Such a vision needs to include not only the obvious components of a viable socioeconomic strategy (such as guidelines and principles of a legal, regulatory, or fiscal nature), but also the ingredients that will make it attractive and compelling for all of its members. This is why promoting a new image of IT jobs, for example, or fighting gender stereotypes or other exclusion mechanisms that may surround them, is so strategically important. The ability to communicate such a vision and to implement such a strategy will require strong and determined leadership, and an ability for such leadership to engage all major stakeholders behind a set of shared objectives to build the innovative, competitive, and inclusive society required by the time.

Those six requirements are summarized in the diagram in Figure 2.

A possible multistakeholder approach for e-skills

In such a model, the mobilization of all categories of stakeholders around a set of common objectives is a key condition to the harmonious development of knowledge societies. This, however, is unlikely to happen as a result of a national decree or of an international conference.

Someone needs to take the lead (and the risks), and show the way. In different parts of the world, initiatives that offer more than a glimmer of hope have started to coalesce. In the European Union, for example, the private sector has been working side by side with EU institutions and national governments to facilitate diagnostics, raise awareness, and formulate concrete action plans to mobilize all available forces in favor of a rapid development of e-skills. As a result, the European Alliance on Skills for Employability (see Box 5) was created.

> **Box 5: A role for the private sector? The e-Skills Industry Leadership alliance**
>
> The e-Skills Industry Leadership Board (e-Skills ILB) was founded on June 7, 2007, by a group of prominent players in the ICT and knowledge field, including Cisco, Hewlett-Packard, Oracle, Microsoft, and Siemens. The e-Skills ILB defines its mission as "to lead the ICT sector's contribution to the development and implementation of a long-term e-skills and digital literacy agenda in Europe." It was then formally welcomed and endorsed by the Vice President of the European Commission and Commissioner for Enterprise and Industry, Günter Verheugen, as well as in the European Commission Communication on e-skills of September 2007.
>
> The e-Skills ILB proposes to move from policy recommendations to action and engagement by ICT industry stakeholders, and to partnership at the highest level, with the European Union's institutions and with educational institutions in EU Member States.
>
> It is committed to leading the ICT sector's contribution for the development and implementation of a long-term e-skills and digital literacy agenda in Europe. To do so, its Board will provide leadership, coordinate industry advice, and pool resources and expertise in support of EU and Member States policies and actions promoting ICT practitioner, user, and e-business skills and digital literacy, as well as the wider set of skills needed for innovation and employability in the 21st-century knowledge-based economy. In particular, the e-Skills ILB Board is committed to contributing to the implementation of the EU ICT Taskforce recommendations and of the European Commission policy Communication and actions on e-Skills and e-Inclusion, building upon previous initiatives on e-skills over the past five years such as the European e-Skills Forum, the Career Space initiative, the e-Skills competencies Consortium, and the European Alliance on Skills for Employability.
>
> Areas of initial focus of the e-Skills ILB's work will include:
>
> - motivating and empowering future generations with e-skills;
> - promoting ICT practitioner learning, education, competencies, and training;
> - boosting the employability and productivity of the workforce with ICT user skills, including the deployment of multistakeholder partnerships; and
> - providing foresight and support for future skills needed in a changing environment with emerging technologies and new business models.
>
> The e-Skills ILB welcomes additional members from among ICT industry stakeholders that share the same objectives and are able to contribute resources and expertise in support of European e-skills policies.
>
> Source: ILB, 2007.
> Note: Excerpts are from the ILB Declaration of June 7, 2007, endorsed by the Council of European Professional Informatics Societies (CEPIS), Cisco Systems, Comptea, the ECDL Foundation, Econet, Eito, Exin, the Global Knowledge Network, Hewlett-Packard, the INLEA.

Conclusion

In the chain of value and benefits that is currently being built across the socioeconomic fabric of our knowledge societies, e-skills largely remain a missing link. E-skills need to be learned and better distributed across all layers of societies and all parts of the world. If not, we cannot hope to reap the full benefits of the efforts and investment made over the last few decades to develop our collective capacity to gather, master, and share information seamlessly and globally.

However, what at first sight appears to be a challenge for the emerging global knowledge economy may be a blessing in disguise. With the right mix of strategies and policies, and the proper dose of engagement from all major stakeholders, the current lack of e-skills may indeed prove a fantastic opportunity to involve a larger share of the world population in the creation of, and benefits from, a truly inclusive information society.

The challenge is clear, visible, and measurable.[24] Addressing it will require a genuine partnership among all major stakeholders of knowledge societies: governments, businesses, and academia are all important building blocks to contribute to the common edifice. Among those, the IT industry has important stakes to consider and unique responsibilities to assume. Recent examples show that efforts have been initiated to mobilize the multistakeholder partnership required, and that the business community has not shied away from playing a leading role, both as a thought leader and as an investor in education and capacity building.

It is now to be hoped that, faced with the historic and exciting possibility of becoming innovative, competitive, and inclusive societies, we shall collectively engage in making it happen, in our respective spheres of activity and influence, because we all have a responsibility to do so.

Notes

1 IDC 2007.

2 See Frinking et al. 2005.

3 European Commission 2006.

4 A recent report by the European Union (*State of European Cities*, 2007b) quotes the following cities as "knowledge hubs": London, Hamburg, Frankfurt, Munich, Copenhagen, Barcelona, Helsinki, Lyon, Dublin, Milan, Amsterdam and Stockholm. The authors of the report define such knowledge hubs as "key players in the global economy," positioned above the national urban hierarchy and in the forefront of international industry, business and financial services based on high levels of talent and well connected to the world. The report underlines that "their GDP levels are 65% above the EU average, and almost 40% above the national average. Furthermore, their annual growth rates have been high—which means that they continue to forge ahead within their national contexts. Employment rates in knowledge hubs are high (68%), approaching the 70% target set by the Lisbon Agenda. Furthermore, elderly people tend to remain longer in employment than in virtually any other city-type. Finally, average unemployment rates are just 6.5%, and trending downward."

5 The European Union's Lisbon Agenda was adopted by the European Council in 2000 as an action and development plan to address stagnating productivity and low economic growth in EU's major member countries. The Agenda's proponents have maintained that "the promotion of growth and employment in Europe is the next great European project" (see in particular Kok 2004).

6 European Commission and Cedefop 2006, preamble, p. 1 (see http://eskills.cedefop.europa.eu/conference2006/Thessaloniki_Declaration_2006.pdf).

7 The European Alliance on Skills for Employability was created at the Microsoft Government Leaders' Forum in January 2006 with the endorsement of the European Commission President Barroso. The Employability Alliance is a reference example of multistakeholder partnerships at European level and recently received the EU CSR Laboratory Award. The Alliance aims to provide 20 million people with e-skills training and technology opportunities for the 21st-century workplace and information society by the end of 2010. Alliance partners adopt a value chain approach and better coordinate industry and community investment, services and other offerings, and dialogue and engagement with NGOs and public authorities. This enhances the positive impact of ICT literacy and professional training on employability prospects of the young, the disabled, older workers, and other unemployed or underemployed people throughout the European Union. This effort was spearheaded by Microsoft, Cisco, Randstad, State Street, FiT, and CompTIA, and to date it operates in five European countries. For more information see http://www.e-scc.org/alliance/default.aspx.

8 Microsoft's Unlimited Potential (UP) global initiative (http://www.microsoft.com/unlimitedpotential/default.mspx), aims to provide the next billion people with the benefits of relevant, accessible, and affordable technologies. Through innovative solutions and local partnerships that are transforming education, fostering local innovation, and enabling jobs and opportunities, this initiative promotes a continuous cycle of sustained social and economic growth as well as the provision of e-skills training and educational opportunities for the most disadvantaged.

9 Doz et al. 2006.

10 In recent years, innovation has been the highest-ranking priority of businesses and governments seeking to acquire or regain competitive advantages. Overall, large emerging countries such as India and China seem to have made spectacular progress on that front, as underlined by several recent studies and indicators, such as the World Business/INSEAD Global Innovation Index (GII) of 2007 (See Box 2). See also the Aho Report, "Creating an Innovative Europe," produced for the European Commission in January 2006, available at http://ec.europa.eu/invest-in-research/pdf/download_en/aho_report.pdf.

11 Liebenau 2007.

12 See http://www.cioleadershipcenter.com

13 Eurostat 2006.

14 Verheugen 2007.

15 Sengupta 2006.

16 McKinsey 2007.

17 Peynot 2007.

18 http://www.assopascaline.fr/. "Pascaline" was the name given to the first calculating machine, created by Blaise Pascal in 1642. The name was chosen to illustrate the power of cooperation between thinkers (academia) and doers (industry).

19 Rodgers 2007.

20 Peynot 2007.

21 Dutta and Caulkin 2007.

22 European Union 2007b, available at http://www.delchn.cec.eu.int/index.php?item=news_view&nid=79.

23 In November 2007, the World Bank announced a doubling of its commitment in Africa's broadband infrastructure development in the next five years by investing $1 billion in broadband infrastructure development (http://www.infoworld.com/article/07/11/02/World-Bank-$1-billion-to-spur-Africa-IT_1.html). See also World Bank In press.

24 Existing indexes and benchmarking instruments are lacking the necessary focus on e-skills, but work has been initiated to address this lacuna. Through a Microsoft-INSEAD partnership, a new e-skills index is being built, which should allow more precise analyses in the future.

References

Accenture. 2007, *Skills for the Future*. A report produced for the Lisbon Council (EU). Available at https://www.accenture.com/NR/rdonlyres/2EE74933-2694-4FDD-A53C-EED8E6E5ECBA/0/SkillsfortheFuture.pdf.

Ambrosini V., E. Bonfiglioli, and L. Moire. 2006. "Developing the Wider Role of Business in Society: The Experience of Microsoft in Developing Training and Supporting Employability." *European Journal of Corporate Governance*, Special Issue on Corporate Governance. 6 (4): 401–08.

Carr, N. 2004. *Does IT Matter? Information Technology and the Corrosion of Competitive Advantage*. Boston: Harvard Business School Publishing.

———. 2008. *The Big Switch: Rewiring the World, from Edison to Google*. New York and London: W. W. Norton.

Chaisson J. and A. Schweyer. 2004. "Global Talent Management: Fostering Global Workforce Practices That Are Scalable, Sustainable and Ethical." A Human Capital Institute Position Paper sponsored by Taleo. June. Available at www.research2recruit.com/documents/Global%20Talent%20Management.pdf.

Council of the European Union. 2007. "Integrated Council Conclusions on Competitiveness." 2832nd Competitiveness (Internal market, Industry and Research) Council meeting. Brussels, November 22 and 23. Available at http://www.consilium.europa.eu/ueDocs/cms_Data/docs/pressData/en/intm/97225.pdf.

Demunter, C. 2006. "How Skilled Are Europeans in Using Computers and the Internet?" *Statistics in Focus* 17 (2006). Eurostat: European Communities. Available at http://epp.eurostat.ec.europa.eu/cache/ITY_OFFPUB/KS-NP-06-017/EN/KS-NP-06-017-EN.PDF.

Doz Y.L., K. Wilson, G. Altman, S. Veldhoen, and T. Goldbrunner. 2006. "Innovation: Is Global the Way Forward?" A joint study by Booz Allen Hamilton and INSEAD. INSEAD and Booz Allen Hamilton. Available at http://www.boozallen.com/media/file/Innovation_Is_Global_The_Way_Forward_v2.pdf.

Dutta S. and S. Caulkin. 2007. "The World's Top Innovators." *World Business* 17 (January). Available at www.worldbusinesslive.com/article/625441/the-worlds-top-innovators.

European Commission. 2006. "Creating an Innovative Europe" ("Aho Report"). Report of the Independent Expert Group on R&D and Innovation appointed following the Hampton Court Summit and chaired by Mr Esko Aho. Available at http://ec.europa.eu/invest-in-research/action/2006_ahogroup_en.htm

European Commission and Cedefop. 2006. European e-Skills Conference:Towards a Long-Term e-Skills Strategy. Thessaloniki, Greece, October 5–6, 2006. Available at http://eskills.cedefop.europa.eu/conference2006/Thessaloniki_Declaration_2006.pdf.

European Union 2007a. Delegation of the European Commission to China. Press release. October 23. Available at http://www.delchn.cec.eu.int/index.php?item=news_view&nid=79.

———. 2007b. State of European Cities: Adding Value to the European Urbank Audit, Study contracted by the European Commission, prepared by ECOTECH Research and Consulting Ltd, with NordRegio and Eurofutures. Available at http://ec.europa.eu/regional_policy/sources/docgener/studies/pdf/urban/stateofcities_2007.pdf.

Eurostat. 2006. "How Skilled Are Europeans in Using Computers and the Internet?" *Eurostat* 17 (2006). Available at http://epp.eurostat.ec.europa.eu/cache/ITY_OFFPUB/KS-NP-06-017/EN/KS-NP-06-017-EN.PDF.

Frinking E., A. Ligtvoet, P. Lundin, and W. Oortwijn. 2005. "The Supply and Demand of e-Skills in Europe." Prepared for the European Commission and the European e-Skills Forum. September. Available at http://ec.europa.eu/enterprise/ict/policy/doc/eskills-2005-10-11.rand.pdf.

IDC. 2007. "E-Skills and Employability in Europe." Study commissioned by Microsoft and released in January 2007, covering 10 European countries and 6,000 employers. Available at http://download.microsoft.com/download/f/2/b/f2bcdab3-433b-4109-8d4e-410230c47c37/IDC-White-Paper-ESkills.pdf

ILB (Industry Leadership Board). 2007. The e-Skills Industry Leadership Board. Available at www.e-skills-ilb.org.

Kok, W. 2004. "Report on Progress Achieved in Implementing the EU's Lisbon Agenda, 2004." Available at http://ec.europa.eu/growthandjobs/pdf/kok_report_en.pdf.

Lanvin, B. 2005. "The Elusive Quest for E-Leadership." *E-Development: From Excitement to Efficiency*, ed. R. Schware. Washington, DC: World Bank.

———. 2007. "E-Readiness in Nordic Countries: How Long Will the Stars Keep Shining?" Report sponsored by CISCO. December.

Lanvin, B. and A. Lewin. 2006. "The Next Frontier of E-Government: Local Governments May Hold the Keys to Global Competition." *Global Information Technology Report 2006–2007*. Hampshire: Palgrave Macmillan. 51–63.

Liebenau, J. 2007. "Innovation Trends: Prioritising Emerging Technologies Shaping the UK to 2017." Economics Occasional Papers No. 8. London: UK Department of Trade and Industry,

McKinsey. 2007. "China's Looming Talent Shortage." *McKinsey Quarterly*. Abstract available at www.mckinseyquarterly.com/Public_Sector/Chinas_looming_talent_shortage_1685_abstract.

OECD (Organisation for Economic Co-operation and Development). 2007. Programme for International Student Assessment. Available at www.pisa.oecd.org.

Peynot, R. 2007. "Major European Economies' IT Graduate Deficit." A Forrester Research report prepared for Strategy Professionals, October 15.

Rodgers, G. 2007. "Labour Market Flexibility and Decent Work." DESA Working Paper No. 47 ST/ESA/2007/DWP/47. New York: The United Nations. Available at http://www.un.org/esa/desa/papers/2007/wp47_2007.pdf.

Sengupta, S. 2006. "Skills Gap Hurts Technology Boom in India." *The New York Times*. October 17.

Verheugen, G. 2007. "Vice-President of the European Commission Responsible for Enterprise and Industry." Speech/07/373, delivered at the E-Skills Industry Leadership Board Launch Event. Brussels, June 7.

World Bank. 2007. Knowledge Assessment Methodology (KAM). Available at www.worldbank.org/kam.

———. In press. "Impact of Broadband on Development." *Information and Communications for Development – 2009*. Washington, DC: World Bank.

World Economic Forum/INSEAD. 2001–2007. *Global Information Technology Report*. Available at www.insead.edu/v1/gitr/main/home.cfm.

CHAPTER 1.7

Rethinking Regulation in Emerging Telecommunications Markets

SCOTT BEARDSLEY, McKinsey & Company Inc., Belgium
ILKE BIGAN, McKinsey & Company Inc., Turkey
LUIS ENRIQUEZ, McKinsey & Company Inc., Belgium
MEHMET GUVENDI, McKinsey & Company Inc., Turkey
CAN KENDI, McKinsey & Company Inc., Turkey
MIGUEL LUCAS, McKinsey & Company Inc., Portugal
OLEG TIMCHENKO, McKinsey & Company Inc., Russia
SERGIO SANDOVAL, McKinsey & Company Inc., Belgium
ASHISH SHARMA, McKinsey & Company Inc., Singapore

Telefonica will invest between Euro 14 and 16 billion in Latin America through 2010, or half of its planned total investment for this period....Telefonica is facing an improved regulatory framework in Latin America, which will contribute to promoting investment for this period.

—*Cesar Alierta, CEO, Telefonica,* Total Telecom, *November 23, 2007*

We are saying that there is plenty of growth in a lot of places, and we are going to go after that growth, whether it is India, Turkey, Romania, South Africa, or China for that matter.

—*Arun Sarin, CEO, Vodafone,* Financial Times, *November 18, 2007*

We will seek growth where it is higher, notably in Africa, the Middle East and South East Asia.

—*Didier Lombard, CEO, France Telecom,* Les Echos, *September 7, 2007*

These statements reflect a shift in the telecommunications (telecom) industry. As mature markets lose momentum, top executives in the industry are now turning to emerging economies as a source of growth and profits.

The sense of urgency among telecom executives is shared by governments that realize the importance of this industry for the economic development of their countries. McKinsey, for example, valued the direct and indirect impact of the mobile industry on the Chinese economy at around US$108 billion, or 5 percent of GDP, in 2005.[1] These figures are even more impressive when considering that mobile penetration in China was only 28 percent that year—a number that compares with the Organisation for Economic Co-operation and Development (OECD) average of 90 percent. Increasing penetration levels help improve productivity and supports economic development in general by facilitating, among other things, innovation and trade. Developing the telecom industry in emerging markets is therefore an imperative both for the operators in the sector and the governments of these countries.

Operators and governments alike will have to overcome many challenges in order to bring telecommunications to the vast majority of the population in emerging markets. These challenges include, for instance, picking technologies that are appropriate for the economic conditions in a specific country in a way that

---

Thanks to Christoph Pennings at McKinsey & Company for researching the facts supporting the findings of this chapter. The views expressed in this article correspond to those of the authors and not those of McKinsey and Company.

Figure 1: Revenue growth in emerging markets vis-à-vis mature markets

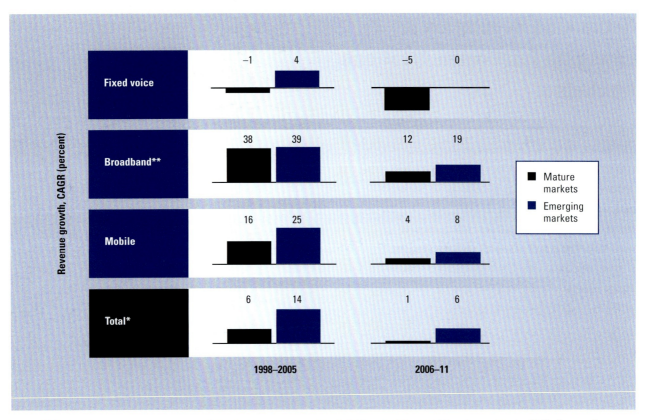

Source: ITU, *World Telecommunication Indicators 2006*; OECD *Communications Outlook 2007*; Pyramid Research, *Fixed Forecast Packs, Mobile Forecast Packs 2007*; Yankee Group, *Global Forecast 2007*; Analysys Research, *Country Market Data 2007*; IDC, *Worldwide Telecommunications Black Book 2007*; Ovum, *Fixed Voice Services 2007*; McKinsey analysis.
* Includes broadband for 2003–11; **Broadband figures correspond to 2003–05 and 2006–11.

---

they will foster the creation of adequate and innovative services.

However, the most important challenge might be to create a regulatory framework that can support the development of the industry into a vibrant, competitive sector that attracts investment and benefits consumers. Addressing this challenge is very difficult and depends on the specific characteristics and starting point of each country. It is clear to us that this challenge cannot be met by copying regulatory frameworks that were tailored to suit markets with completely different characteristics than those in emerging economies. On the contrary, such an approach can result in many undesired outcomes.

In this paper we illustrate the hazards of applying borrowed regulatory frameworks without taking into account the unique characteristics of emerging telecom markets. We also argue that getting it right depends heavily on balancing the tradeoffs that exist between the regulatory objectives of creating competition, improving penetration, and attracting investment. These objectives, and the appropriate regulatory tools, differ according to the maturity of a given telecom market.

Emerging markets: The key to telecom industry growth and profit

Slow revenue growth and intense competition in mature markets are prompting an increasing number of global telecom companies to look to emerging markets as the key to future success.

Mature markets such as the United States, Japan, and Western Europe are showing signs of weakness. As Figure 1 illustrates, their total industry revenues grew by 6 percent a year between 1998 and 2005, fueled mainly by strong growth in broadband and mobile services, but they are forecast to grow at just 1 percent rates from 2006 to 2011. Such a slow rate implies negative growth when taking into account that average inflation is forecast at 2.2 percent a year.

The decelerating revenue growth in mature markets is partly explained by the objectives of deregulation in these areas. When it started, most mature telecom markets had a monopolistic industry structure with high prices, low levels of innovation, and poor service.

One of the main objectives of deregulation was to bring greater benefits to consumers by creating an environment that supported price reductions and the introduction of new and innovative services. This was mostly

Figure 2: Decrease in price in mature telecom markets

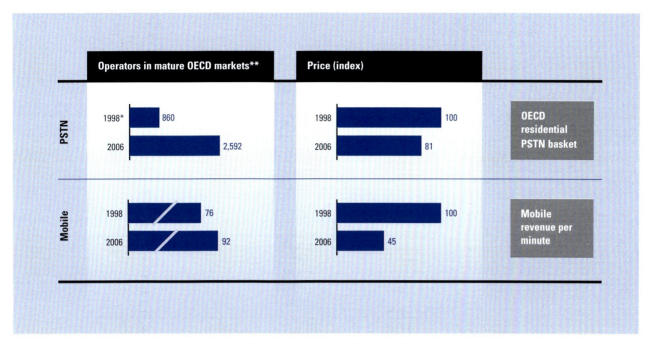

Source: OECD, *Communications Outlook 2001, 2007*; Informa, *World Cellular Information System (WICS+)*; European Commission, *Telecoms Price Developments 1998–2006*, 2006; Merrill Lynch, *Wireless Matrix 2005*, 2007; McKinsey analysis.
Note: PSTN = Public switched telephone network; *National calls only; **Australia, Belgium, Canada, Denmark, Finland, France, Greece, Germany, Iceland, Ireland, Italy, Japan, Korea, Rep., Luxembourg, Netherlands, New Zealand, Norway, Portugal, Spain, Sweden, Switzerland, United Kingdom, and the United States.

achieved by changing the industry landscape and creating more competition by lowering entry barriers for new players, which were granted access to incumbent's networks, and by easing licensing requirements for some voice services.

Lowering the barriers to entry eventually led to an increase in the number of operators in these markets. Figure 2 shows that, in the fixed line business alone, the number of competitors in mature OECD markets (excluding middle-income countries such as the Czech Republic, Hungary, Mexico, Poland, and Turkey) rose from around 850 in 1998 to approximately 2,600 in 2006. The mobile business has followed a similar path, with the number of operators growing from 76 in 1998 to 92 in 2006.

The increasing number of operators has brought considerable pressure on prices. The prices of fixed and mobile calls have gone down by 3 and 10 percent a year, respectively, since 1998.

While mature telecom markets are grinding to a halt, the outlook is bright for emerging markets, where total revenue growth is forecast to grow by 6 percent from 2006 to 2011, with particularly high growth rates in the mobile and broadband businesses of 8 and 19 percent, respectively. These markets will not only grow six times faster, but some of them boast profitability levels that are the envy of any telecom CEO in a mature market. In Russia, for instance, the mobile industry enjoyed on average an operating margin of 49 percent over the last two years, far above the average 33 percent earned by operators in the European Union.[2]

To capture the opportunity of much higher revenue growth, many large players from mature and emerging markets have gone on acquisition sprees. As shown in Figure 3, operators such as Telefonica, Telmex, and Vodaphone have acquired mobile operators in South America. Others, such as Telenor, China Mobile Limited, and Etisalat have been very active in buying mobile operators in regions such as Eastern and Central Europe, the Middle East, and Asia.

Emerging markets opportunity: Tradeoffs between sector sustainability and competition

Amid the enthusiasm, international and local telecom players, as well as governments and regulators, should keep in mind that unleashing the full potential of telecommunications in emerging markets will largely hinge on the regulatory framework that is put in place for each country. Indeed, the slowdown in mature markets illustrates the difficult tradeoffs between nurturing the sustainability of the sector and achieving lower prices in the short term.

Some countries in the Middle East and Africa started to reform their telecom sector only a year or two ago. Table 1 shows that even in countries where the reform process commenced earlier—such as India, the Philippines, and Thailand—it was launched 10 years after reforms began in the United States and the United

Figure 3: Increase in emerging market telecom acquisitions (1996–2006)

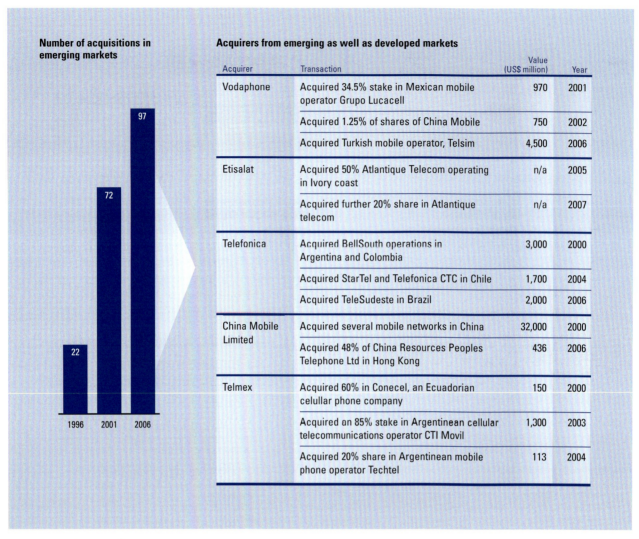

Source: Dealogic; Business Monitor International.

Kingdom. In most of these countries, the magnitude and implications of sector reform are posing significant challenges to regulatory authorities, most of which have recently been established.

The most pressing challenge these regulators face is how to create incentives for the massive investment required while bringing appropriate competition to the industry and driving ambitious penetration targets at the same time.[3] Investment is critical because it is the foundation of all the positive economic benefits of a modern information and communication technologies (ICT) sector that will support economic development through both direct effects, such as generating employment and contributing taxes, and indirect effects, such as increasing the productivity of the economy by reducing transaction costs. Competition, in turn, typically has the most immediately noticeable impact on prices; if they fall too low, they affect the overall viability of the industry and hence reduces the incentive to invest.

Emerging telecom markets face the challenge of closing a wide investment gap with mature markets. As can be seen in Figure 4, an emerging country with a population of 55 million needs to spend an additional US$4 billion a year on public telecom investment to reach the average investment levels in the OECD.

Emerging telecom markets differ from mature telecom markets

The first step toward designing a balanced regulatory framework is to gain a deeper understanding of the specific characteristics and needs of emerging telecom markets. Although they are far from homogeneous, emerging markets typically differ significantly from mature markets in several ways, among them the distribution of their population, income levels, and industry structures.

Table 1: Liberalization phase of selected emerging markets

Region	Country	Start of fixed-line liberalization	Establishment of National Regulatory Authority (NRA)
Asia	India	1994	1997
	Philippines	1993	1979
	Thailand	1992	2004
	Turkey	2003	2000
Middle East	United Arab Emirates	2005	2004
	Qatar	2007	2004
	Saudi Arabia	2007	2002
Latin America	Argentina	1999	1990
	Peru	1998	1994
Africa	Algeria	2005	2000
	Morocco	2005	1997
	South Africa	2005	2000
Eastern Europe	Russian Federation	2006	2000
	Bulgaria	2003	1998
	Czech Republic	2001	2000
	Romania	2002	2002
Western Europe	United Kingdom	1984	1984
North America	United States	1984*	1934

Source: International Telecommunication Union-D, *Regulatory Knowledge Centre;* World Trade Organization, UNESCAP, *Telecommunications in Indonesia and Its commitment in WTO,* 2003; Business Monitor International, *Intelligence Reports 2007;* Hot Telecom, *Country Profile Saudi Arabia,* 2007.
* Creation of Regional Bell Operating Companies

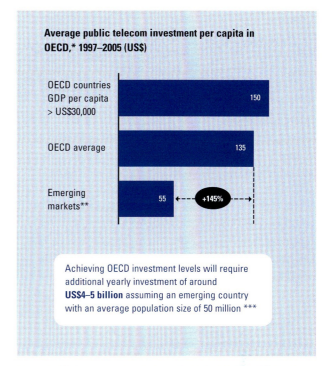

Figure 4: Estimated investment in infrastructure for emerging markets

Source: OECD, *Communications Outlook* 1999, 2001, 2003, 2005, 2007; Authors' analysis.
Note: * Includes expenditures in fixed and mobile telecommunications equipment, buildings, land, and nontangibles such as computer software; ** Czech Republic, Hungary, Mexico, Poland, and Turkey; *** US$70 multiplied by ~55 million people. Average population in emerging countries is assumed to be the average population of Czech Republic, Hungary, Mexico, Poland, and Turkey.

Emerging markets: Uneven population spread and higher rural population

Emerging countries, especially in Asia and Africa, are marked by a higher percentage of rural population and larger land areas than developed Europe, in particular. However, this masks areas of high urban concentrations such as Bangkok, Johannesburg, Karachi, and Mumbai that exceed most cities of the developed world in size. This creates a substantial challenge for the regulators who need to stimulate investment and ensure penetration not only on big cities, but also in rural areas.

Emerging markets: High-income pockets in a landscape of generally low-revenue customers

This uneven distribution leads to an even more concentrated revenue pattern than is found in mature markets. An extremely low portion of customers accounts for a disproportionate share of revenues and profits. The average Gini coefficient (a measure of income distribution) is 41 for developing countries and 30 for developed OECD countries—a lower Gini coefficient indicates more equal income distribution.

The combination of uneven population spread and low overall income mixed with pockets of extremely concentrated economic centers with relatively high income levels such as Bangkok, Istanbul, Karachi, Mexico City, Mumbai, and São Paulo makes liberalization a challenging task for regulators in emerging markets. Unless regulation takes these factors into account, new players will naturally enter only select areas and cherry-pick lucrative segments characterized by a high concentration of high-income customers. This will most likely result in a very small segment of the population enjoying the benefits of the free market in the form of competition and low prices while a large portion of the population remains either underserved or not served at all. The duality sharpens if prices fall too rapidly in these high-competition islands, with the result that players potentially do not have adequate resources to invest in expanding their reach within the country.

Emerging markets: Lower fixed-line penetration and infrastructure quality

The fixed-line penetration in emerging markets is substantially lower than in mature markets because of low historical investment levels. Universal service obligations usually were not enough to bring coverage to all rural and poor areas of these countries. Moreover, the existing fixed-line infrastructure is generally old and of low quality as a result of underinvestment in the networks, which makes it difficult to deliver broadband without making substantial new investment. In some extreme cases, such as Malaysia, fixed-line penetration has even stagnated or declined marginally. Thus regulators in emerging markets should be even more pressed than their colleagues in mature markets to stimulate infrastructure investment in order to increase the quality of their telecom networks.

Emerging markets: Thriving mobile sectors

Mobile telephony is already a success story in the majority of these markets, characterized by fast growth and high levels of mobile penetration. Even countries such India and Pakistan, where penetration is comparatively low, have seen extremely rapid growth in the mobile sector, currently accounting for 60 and 47 percent of industry revenues in emerging and mature markets, respectively. Given the predominance of mobile telephony in the emerging world, its regulators should consider policy tradeoffs across the whole industry, and treat mobile operators in the same way they would treat wireline incumbents.

Emerging markets: Less independent and sophisticated regulators

Implementing a liberalization process takes a lot of time and resources. In Germany, for example, the 1997 European Regulatory Framework Directive took many years to implement and required 21 consultations and public hearings with stakeholders. Sixteen consultation results were published, and the regulator received almost 140 responses from stakeholders to review. The US Federal Communications Commission has around 2,000 employees and is requesting an annual budget for 2008 of US$315 million.[4] Regulators of this size and budget are difficult to match in emerging countries with limited human and financial resources.

Emerging market regulators also tend to be less independent than their counterparts in mature markets. In Russia, for example, the Ministry of Information Technology and Communications acts as the regulator while it is also one of the three government bodies managing a controlling stake in the incumbent operator. Understandably, it is harder for regulators whose jobs involve juggling multiple and contradicting objectives to always make the right decisions.

It is clear that emerging markets are fundamentally different from mature markets. However, regulators often disregard these differences when defining policy objectives and deciding which regulatory tools and remedies to use in the industry. Moreover, with the aim of achieving faster sector development, they often try to copy and even accelerate the liberalization processes applied in mature markets.

The specific regulatory needs of emerging markets

Evidence suggests that a regulatory toolkit borrowed from more mature markets can hurt the development of the sector. Regulators tempted to use such an approach should examine very closely the development needs of their telecom sectors and assess whether they would be served or not served by this approach.

In Turkey, for instance, regulators attempted to fast forward competition by reducing fixed interconnection rates to Western European levels only 15 months after competition was introduced for long-distance call services. This development did not occur until 4 to 5 years after liberalization in most European countries, as shown in Figure 5. Moreover, Turkey's fixed-line incumbent was unable to raise its fixed access fees and so compensate for lower interconnection rates. The incumbent's and other players' revenues from long-distance services eventually eroded as a result of sharp price declines (around 70 percent in both domestic and long distance calls). This limited the resources available for investment in the industry.

Another interesting case example is the Philippines, where a universal service obligation was imposed on new license holders without taking into account some local market characteristics that, in turn, led to over investment in the sector. In 1993, the National Telecommunication Commission (NTC) created the Service Areas Scheme (SAS), which allowed network operators to cross-subsidize the provision of telecom services to underserved areas, with funds transferred from other more profitable areas such as international and mobile telephony. The SAS segmented the country into 11 areas and required each holder of a new international gateway license (IGL) or a new mobile license to install a minimum of 300,000 and 400,000 fixed lines, respectively, within a given area.[5] The main regulatory objective of the NTC was to achieve a 10 percent fixed-line penetration by 2000.

Despite a good start where the IGL and the mobile revenues were successfully funding the installation of fixed lines, in January 2002 the NTC suspended the SAS regime. Several factors contributed to its failure. First, some operators underestimated the costs of building their new networks in such a geographically disperse country and found it difficult to obtain the resources required to finance them. This situation got even worse when the Asian economic crisis struck in 1997. Second, operators faced large levels of fraud in the mobile market (SIM card cloning) and the proliferation of the unregulated international call-back system that significantly undermined the revenues from mobile and international calls. Third, new operators found very difficult to negotiate viable interconnection agreements that confined their networks to the local communities, as it was not easy to connect to the national network. Finally, the success of the mobile sector attracted fixed-line subscribers

Figure 5: Fixed interconnection rates: Turkey vs. European countries

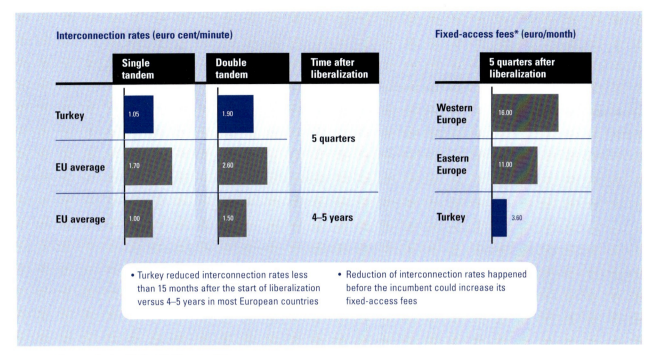

Source: Telecom Authority of Turkey; McKinsey analysis.
* Fixed fee for residential subscribers as of September 2005, including taxes.

to a service that was cheaper, more convenient, and with national coverage leaving little appetite in consumers to own a fixed line.

The failure of the SAS regime—only 2.85 million fixed lines actually in service out of a total of 4.3 million lines installed by the end of 2007—was due, among other things, to a misunderstanding of the specific characteristics of the telecom market in the Philippines. Authorities and operators alike believed in the need to deploy fixed telecom services in a universal way, even when the per-capita income levels of the country were extremely low and the success of the mobile industry was already on the horizon. This misunderstanding led operators to over invest valuable resources in networks that had no economic viability.

Many more examples of premature moves that could destroy value can be added to the list, threatening the bright outlook for the industry's growth and prosperity in emerging economies. The main cause of this "misregulation" is the failure to recognize the unique starting position of these markets and the failure to link regulation to country-specific development objectives.

The importance of objectives' definition and of the right sequence

As noted, regulators face major tradeoffs between regulatory objectives such as driving penetration and promoting competition and investment. It is critical that they define their priorities for each stage in the development of their telecom market. Regulatory objectives are mostly sequential and depend on the state of the market. The first objective is investment in infrastructure, which will drive penetration; only then should the objective become to foster service-based competition.

A good example is telecom regulation in Europe, where fixed-line services are heavily regulated to stimulate competition and mobile services have, until recently, been largely unregulated. This made sense because the continent's regulation developed at a time when fixed-line penetration was, on average, 49 percent for European (OECD) nations, while mobile was at a very nascent stage. To help mobile penetration grow, European regulators made a fixed-to-mobile call noticeably more expensive than a call from a mobile to a fixed phone by mandating a higher proportion of the interconnect charge to be passed from the fixed operator to the mobile. In addition, fixed operators were mandated to meet universal service obligations, while these rules where much more flexible for mobile companies.

In emerging markets, however, fixed penetration was only 15 percent when mobile was introduced. This creates a different regulatory paradigm and suggests that fixed services should be less exposed to competition and burdened by social obligations if companies in the fixed sector are to be able to invest in broadband infrastructure.

Because of the faster growth and significantly better time to market for mobile in terms of prices and ubiquity, and compounded by the regulatory tilt described above, the fixed sector in many emerging telecom markets is

Figure 6: Achieving national ICT objectives in emerging markets: The importance of wireline

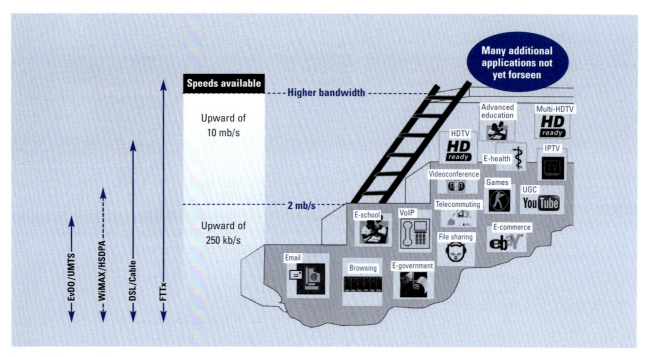

Source: McKinsey analysis.
Note: Compression technologies may reduce the quantum of bandwidth required.

now more limited in coverage as well as less economically viable at a time when national objectives require it to be most vibrant. Wireline is central to achieving future national ICT objectives, which revolve around broadband (Figure 6). While initially expensive and time-consuming to roll out, wireline represents the most future-proof path toward building high bandwidth and scaleable broadband infrastructure for a nation.

Emerging market regulators should consider who the true holders of significant market power in their markets are. Traditionally, in regions such as Europe, where fixed penetration was high, incumbent operators were thought to have significant market power over services such as the local voice market. In emerging markets, where mobile services often have deeper penetration, mobile operators are the ones most likely to hold significant market power in the market for local calls.

Emerging markets regulatory solutions for coverage, quality, and affordability

In order to create optimal solutions, regulators in emerging economies need to begin by assessing the current state of their telecom market. Figure 7 shows three types of emerging markets with distinct starting points and characteristics. This assessment can be a useful first step toward prioritizing objectives and defining a vision for the future industry structure.

Group 1: Underpenetrated and low-income emerging markets

This group of countries is characterized by a GDP per capita (PPP) below $5,000 and low fixed and mobile service penetration. Policy objectives in these countries should focus on providing incentives for potential stakeholders (for example, incumbents, cable operators, mobile operators, and new players entering the market) to make the necessary investment. Incentives should be geared toward stimulating provision of universal voice access. This should be driven mainly by increasing mobile penetration, and should be secured by universal coverage obligations.

Once voice access starts reaching levels close to 50 percent, as seen in countries like Pakistan and Morocco, policymakers can also focus on fixed networks in order to promote broadband penetration. This investment should initially target deployment in key cities that are the centers of economic activity.

Promoting lower prices by increasing competition and imposing tight regulation on operators should be a secondary objective for Group 1 countries. This means that features that promote lower prices, such as number portability and reduction of interconnection rates, may potentially be deferred to a stage when mobile penetration has reached the targeted levels.

Group 2: Transition economies with high mobile penetration

Countries in this group have a GDP per capita (PPP) of $5,000 to 20,000 with a moderately high mobile penetration. Their policy objectives should mainly be

Figure 7: Country clusters in emerging markets

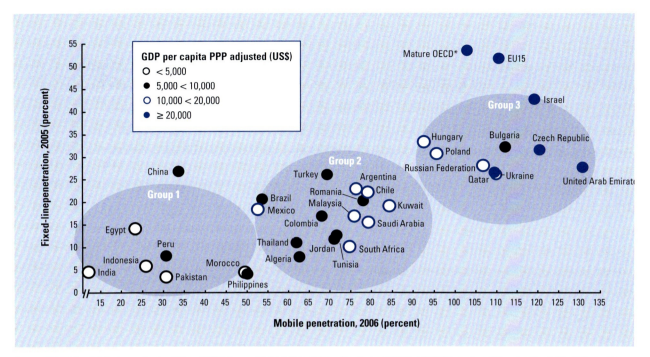

Source: International Telecommunication Union, 2006; Informa, *World Cellular Information System (WICS+)*, 2007; International Monetary Fund, *World Economic Outlook Database 2007*.
*OECD countries except the Czech Republic, Hungary, Mexico, Poland, and Turkey.

driven by an increase of broadband penetration and should also plant the first seeds of regulatory measures to increase the level of competition in the mobile sector.

Regulators can promote broadband penetration by encouraging investment in fixed networks, particularly the provision of fiber broadband in select areas, through a combination of financial and regulatory incentives. This could take the form of tax breaks and other investment incentives, as well as promoting nontraditional entrants to start offering fixed broadband services. For instance, cable companies and mobile operators in some countries have a reach far exceeding those of traditional fixed-line telecom companies. India is a Group 1 nation, but cable companies there already reach more than 70 million households and offer the best chance of rapidly increasing broadband penetration.

On the mobile side, the rapidly maturing levels of penetration would allow regulators the luxury of encouraging competition in the sector by introducing new policies on features such as mobile number portability. On the other hand, given the continued need for investment to increase the capacity and quality of the network, it will be too early for regulators to consider a more aggressive value shift from operators to consumers by introducing measures such as providing open access to virtual network operators.

Group 3: Mobile leaders with high income per capita

Countries in this group are characterized by very high mobile penetration and moderately high fixed penetration rates. Most have GDP levels of around $20,000 per capita (PPP) or higher. Policy objectives should be centered on increasing broadband penetration while establishing fair competition between mobile and fixed operators to promote lower prices and fast adaptation of new services. These countries are basically at a stage similar to the mature markets in Europe, where it is appropriate to drive competition to stimulate lower prices and new services.

Regulators in Group 3 countries should aim for rapid expansion in broadband services, particularly high-speed broadband through fiber-optic lines. This could be promoted by simply correcting some of the existing regulatory provisions to offer a more even playing field for the fixed-line sector, given the investment levels required for provisioning high-speed broadband and the marginal business case this normally represents. Direct or indirect financial support for the rollout of such networks may also be necessary. Possible measures include investment incentives for infrastructure deployment in certain areas, shifting significant market power regulation from the fixed to the mobile sector in recognition of its greater reach, as well as allowing the adoption of new technologies in the fixed sector such as Internet Protocol (IP) telephony as a way of reducing costs.

Objectives for policymakers and regulators in an emerging market will always include some of the following: attract investors, build the infrastructure, reduce prices, introduce new services, and improve quality. However, the combination and prioritization of objectives will differ from market to market based on a particular market's stage of development, as defined mainly by income and penetration levels. The challenge for regulators will be to define the center of gravity for their combination of objectives, and to design the right policies to achieve them.

Notes

1 McKinsey & Company 2006.

2 This is the simple average for mobile operators in Germany, the United Kingdom, Italy, and France.

3 This classic regulatory tradeoff is also present in mature markets. However, the sense of urgency to attain the desired levels of investment, competition, and penetration is much higher in developing markets because they are in an earlier economic and industrial stage.

4 US Federal Communications Commission, "FY 2008 Budget Estimates Submitted to Congress." February 2007.

5 Some licensees got both a mobile and an IGL, which meant an obligation to install 700,000 lines within a selected area.

References

Analysys Research. 2007. *Country Market Data & Forecasts*. Available at http://research.analysys.com/default.asp.

European Commission. 2006. "Report on Telecoms Price Developments from 1998 to 2006." December. Available at http://ec.europa.eu/information_society/policy/ecomm/library/ext_studies/index_en.htm#2006.

IDC. 2007. "Worldwide Telecommunication Black Book, Version 1, 2007." April. Available at www.idc.com.

Informa. 2007. *World Cellular Information System+*. Available at www.informatm.com (accessed October 2007).

IMF (International Monetary Fund). 2007. *World Economic Outlook Database*. October. Available at http://www.imf.org/external/ns/cs.aspx?id=28.

ITI (International Telecoms Intelligence). 2006. "Thailand Telecoms Market Report." July. Available at http://www.businessmonitor.com/.

———. 2007a. "Philippines Telecoms Market Report." August. Available at: http://www.businessmonitor.com/.

———. 2007b. "Zain Company Report." June. Available at http://www.businessmonitor.com/.

ITU (International Telecommunication Union). 2007a. *ITU World Telecommunication Indicators 2006*.

———. 2007b. ITU ICT Eye, Regulatory Knowledge Centre. Available at http://www.itu.int/ITU-D/ICTEYE/Regulators/Regulators.aspx.

McKinsey & Company. 2006. "Wireless Unbound." White paper, December.

OECD (Organisation for Economic Co-operation and Development). 2001. *OECD Communications Outlook*. Paris: OECD. Available at http://www.oecdbookshop.org/oecd/display.asp?sf1=identifiers&st1=932001021P1.

———. 2007. *OECD Communications Outlook*. Paris: OECD. Available at http://www.oecd.org/document/17/0,3343,en_2649_201185_38876369_1_1_1_1,00.html.

Ovum. 2007. "WirelineStrategy@Ovum, Fixed Voice Forecast." Data forecast, August. Available at www.Ovum.com.

Pyramid Research. 2007a. "Africa and Middle East Fixed Forecast Pack." Data forecast, September. Available at www.pyramidresearch.com.

———. 2007b. "Africa and Middle East Mobile Forecast Pack." Data forecast, September. Available at www.pyramidresearch.com.

———. 2007c. "Central and Eastern Europe Fixed Forecast Pack." Data forecast, September. Available at www.pyramidresearch.com.

———. 2007d. "Central and Eastern Europe Mobile Forecast Pack" Data forecast, September. Available at www.pyramidresearch.com.

———. 2007e. "Japan Mobile Forecast Pack" Data forecast, September. Available at www.pyramidresearch.com.

———. 2007f. "Latin America Fixed Forecast Pack." Data forecast, September. Available at www.pyramidresearch.com.

———. 2007g. "Latin America Mobile Forecast Pack." Data forecast, September. Available at www.pyramidresearch.com.

———. 2007h. "North America Fixed Forecast Pack." Data forecast, June. Available at www.pyramidresearch.com.

———. 2007i. "Western Europe Fixed Forecast Pack." Data forecast, June. Available at www.pyramidresearch.com.

———. 2007j. "Western Europe Mobile Forecast Pack." Data forecast, September. Available at www.pyramidresearch.com.

Wellenius, B. and J. Galarza. 2005. "Telecomunications and the WTO: The Case of Mexico." Presentation, April. World Bank.

Wellenius B., J. Galarza, and B. Guermazi, 2005. "Telecomunications and the WTO: The Case of Mexico." *Policy Research Working Paper* No. 3759. Washington, DC: World Bank.

WTO (World Trade Organization). "Highlights of the Basic Telecommunication Commitments and Exemptions." Available at http://www.wto.org/english/tratop_e/serv_e/telecom_e/telecom_highllghts_commit_exempt_e.htm (accessed October 2007).

Yankee Group. 2007a. "Global Consumer Forecast." Data forecast, April. Available at www.yankeegroup.com.

———. 2007b. "Global Enterprise Forecast." Data forecast. Available at www.yankeegroup.com.

CHAPTER 1.8

Business Network Transformation: Rethinking Relationships in a Global Economy

HENNING KAGERMANN, SAP AG
PHILIP LAY, TCG Advisors
GEOFFREY MOORE, TCG Advisors

The global economy is reshaping relationships among companies in new and not always comfortable ways. Leveraging unprecedented opportunities in communication and collaboration, companies are gaining competitive advantage through networked business models, tapping into talent across the globe to defend themselves against commoditization and disruptive innovation. Such rapidly changing market dynamics are stressing established companies' investment in rigid "built-to-last" systems and processes. The new era instead calls for fluid, "built-to-adapt" networks in which each company focuses on its differentiation and relies increasingly on its partners, suppliers, and customers to supply the rest.

Such business networks have come to the fore in the past decade or so as the power of customers and consumers has increased relative to the manufacturers and retailers that serve them. These networks enable these companies to deliver faster innovation to customers at lower costs by sharing investment, assets, and ideas. New market opportunities are unlocked by combining the products and services of the business network participants in creative ways and leveraging each other's market access and infrastructure on a global basis. Table 1 shows the nature of transformation that businesses are undergoing today.

Table 1: Business transformation for competitive advantage

Issue	"Built-to-last" global companies	"Built-to-adapt" business networks
Competitive advantage	Efficiency, stability, and reach	Differentiation, adaptability, and speed
Mode of operation	Command and control	Connect and collaborate
Source of innovation	Internal R&D	Co-innovation
Focus of attention	Supply	Demand
Organizing paradigm	Value chain	Alliance

Under the pressure of this ongoing transformation, business leaders are being forced to reexamine long-held assumptions about strategy, structure, systems, and style. Among the questions raised are the following:

- What is the right context in which to view this change in business climate? Is it a cyclical change or a secular one? Is it fad or fate?

This paper is based on field research including interviews conducted with executives in leading companies from over 20 different industries and business networks. The research was conducted between September and December, 2007, by TCG Advisors, an advisory firm based in San Bruno, California, in collaboration with SAP AG.

- Do business network dynamics evolve as markets emerge, scale, mature, and decline, or does one size fit all?

- What core principles or practices can be used as guideposts as we foray out into this new territory?

- What implications do these networked business models have for managing investment in information and communication technologies (ICT) systems?

In our view, the forces at play here are tectonic. For the most part, they will move businesses slowly but inexorably out of their comfort zones. That suggests there is time to plan and make considered moves. But occasionally the business landscape is shaken by quakes of great magnitude, out of which new power structures emerge in remarkably short order—as we have seen in the current century in financial services, telecommunications, and media. Overall, we believe a planned approach is best for most businesses, but we do not think it wise to use planning as an excuse for stalling.

The great disaggregation: A secular change
In the past 30 years or so, sector after sector of the global economy has migrated away from the vertically integrated enterprise toward an increasingly disaggregated model of specialized enterprises interoperating to create end-to-end deliverables. The clearest example of this has been in the computer industry, where in the 1960s and 1970s all the great computer companies—IBM, Hitachi, Fujitsu, ICL, and Siemens, as well as the "BUNCH" (Burroughs, Univac, NCR, Control Data, and Honeywell) —supplied a complete array of hardware, software, and services built atop proprietary and closely held technology. The model was carried over into the first generation of minicomputers—Wang, Digital Equipment Corporation, Data General, Prime, and the like—all proprietary systems, albeit ones increasingly struggling to shoulder the enormous research and development (R&D) expense of going it alone.

Two technologies radically changed this landscape: the relational database and the personal computer. They led a disaggregation of enterprise computing into a host of specialized companies in microprocessors, operating systems, databases, storage, networks, computers, and application software, all linked by a set of standardized interfaces. This, in turn, allowed innovation to evolve independently at each layer, the sum of which vastly exceeded the progress that any one company could have made. The net outcome of all this process is the massive amounts of wealth creation that has taken place across the globe, not to mention the fact that the mobile phone you carry with you outperforms the most expensive supercomputer available a scant two decades prior. Clearly this is a fundamental change.

At various times, the disaggregation model has played out in many other industries as well, albeit not always quite so dramatically. The vertically integrated film studios of the 1930s and 1940s have long since disaggregated into a collaborative network of producers, directors, writers, actors, artisans, distributors, and agents, all bound by a raft of lawyers (and a market with an insatiable appetite for digital fantasies). The semiconductor industry went "fabless" 20 years ago, separating chip designers from chip producers, while at the same time spinning out specialized roles for wafer suppliers, mask makers, equipment providers, and CAD software vendors. The automotive industry has migrated to a tiered system of suppliers, out-tasking virtually every subsystem that makes up a car except for the engine (and that will be next, given the enormous R&D expenses entailed by hybrid and all-electric drive systems). The aerospace industry is following in similar fashion, and even pharmaceuticals—one of the last bastions of the closely held end-to-end enterprise—has been driven to disaggregate the roles of upstream R&D, now increasingly outsourced, from downstream sales and marketing, still closely held.

Four forces have driven all these acts of disaggregation:

1. *ICT proliferation,* which enables work to be rapidly transferred back and forth at scale between geographically separated specialists;

2. *deregulation,* which leads to the opening up of previously protected markets;

3. *globalization,* which leads to the entry of low-cost competitors into these markets; and

4. *commoditization,* which leads to market expansion and increased consumption but at the same time to heavily challenged profit margins.

We can summarize the impact of these forces in the following single observation: specialization to create sustainable competitive advantage is the force driving business network transformation in the current era.

Such specialization, in turn, raises new challenges and critical questions for companies engaged in these business network transformations:

- How to orchestrate one's business network partners as "one company" to deliver reliably on business commitments?

- How to manage risk and compliance exposure across the entire business network?

- Who will own the customer relationship, and how to capture value in a distributed ownership?

These are the questions we seek to address in this article.

Business network transformation: An evolutionary model

Business networks arise at two stages in the evolution of a market or a product. In the *emergent* stage, *collaborative business networks* enable companies to explore and develop an emerging opportunity. Such a challenge is highly complex and largely undefined, so the emphasis is on communication, interaction, iteration, fast failure, and faster recovery, all trending toward delivering a complete solution to an end customer. In these networks there is typically a ringleader who has a vision for what is possible and rallies the other parties to pursue it. We call such entities the *orchestrators* because they must lead through influence rather than enforce their will through power. The other members of the network are included not only for their specialized expertise but also for their ability to team well with others in relationships that are not explicitly defined. This in turn implies relationships of trust built on a spirit of joint venturing to create new products and markets, the unifying principle being that the new market will reward all in reasonable terms.

Examples of collaborative business networks in emergent markets abound in the high-tech sector, because each new technology requires communal support if it is to proliferate. Whether it be the developer ecosystem needed to support a software platform, the co-design efforts that unite handset manufacturers with mobile operators, the chip design efforts that go into a new game machine, or the standards efforts that lead to a new network protocol, the requirement is always the same: potential rivals must overcome their natural defensiveness to collaborate toward creating a future market in which they will subsequently compete with one another.

In other sectors, where technologies come and go at a more steadied pace, the driver for next-generation collaborations can be the desire to adapt global products to developing economies, the opportunity to introduce new financial mechanisms such as mobile banking or micro-loans, or the political intent to develop a new industry. Whatever the driver, success depends on an orchestrator with a vision being able to recruit an ecosystem of once-and-future competitors to lay down their arms and work together for a common good.

Those arms will be taken up once more as the market's evolutionary state transitions from emergent to *scaling*. In order for any process or offer to scale, it must be transformed from custom creation to repeatable production. This is true whether the end product be a consumer packaged good or a transcontinental airliner, although the higher the volume of the output, the more important standardization becomes. Now the network must operate under a new social contract, one which puts a high value on efficiency.

We call these efficiency-focused networks *coordinated business networks,* and they are driven not by personal relationships of trust but rather by transactions specified by contract. As such networks ramp to maturity, their operations become increasingly driven by a *concentrator,* a member of the network who has gained greater bargaining power than the others and who drives the performance of the whole to its own greater benefit. In a sector that is supply-constrained, this will be the resource owner or the manufacturer. In a sector that is demand-constrained, it will be the end customers or consumers, or the sales channel that controls access to them. In either case, the network as a whole has become highly transactional in its relationships and becomes increasingly dependent on information technologies (IT) to manage and monitor its end-to-end operations.

As product and service categories pass through their life cycles, the relative role of the business network oscillates between collaboration and coordination, the former focused on enabling new and emerging markets, the latter on scaling mature ones. At the same time, however, the more complex the offering, the greater the affinity will be to extend the collaborative model indefinitely, and the need to master complexity trumping the need for transactional efficiency. Conversely, the more mass-market the offering, the greater the attraction will be toward the profit-generating coordinated model, and the greater the impatience to exit the money-losing collaborative phase that must precede it.

The foregoing distinctions are captured in Table 2.

Table 2: Business networks: Collaborative vs. coordinated

Issue	Collaborative business networks	Coordinated business networks
Phase of maturity	Emerging	Scaling and mature
Best fit	Complex systems	Volume operations
Focus	Relationships	Transactions
Performance	Adaptability	Efficiency
Engagement model	Alliance	Contract

Note that the values of coordinated business networks are essentially identical to those of a traditional vertically integrated enterprise operating in a mature market. In today's outsourcing-oriented economy, however, the lowest transaction costs are many times found *outside* the firm. The goal of participating in a coordinated network is to avail oneself of these economies while meeting or exceeding the reliability of a single end-to-end provider. We are taking a familiar model and simply disaggregating it, letting each company leave behind non-core tasks to focus on its own core, the goal being for all to generate greater differentiation and therefore higher returns on invested capital.

By contrast, collaborative business networks are driven by a different imperative. They seek to bring about something never before accomplished: either the completion of a program or project that transcends the capabilities of established offerings, or the incubation of a market that requires orchestrating the involvement of many different participants. In both cases, the goal is to tap into sources of funds that are not available to coordinated networks. The prize is gross margins that are much higher, since there are as yet no more efficient alternatives in the market. Over time, however, if the need is sufficiently broad and perennial, the transactional model will find its way into the market, and the balance of power will shift back to the coordinated network.

In light of these interactions, it behooves us all to understand how each network operates, what practices will enable companies to be most successful, and, in particular, what investment in IT and communications systems will yield the most benefit. That is the focus of the rest of this chapter.

Coordinated business networks: Competing in a commoditizing world

Coordinated networks are the norm for virtually all of the consumer sector and much of the enterprise sector as well. The rise of contract manufacturing—be it in retail, consumer electronics, home furnishings, industrial components, or the like—has disaggregated the value chain in industry after industry, creating separate vendor roles for design, sourcing and assembly, transportation and logistics, marketing, retail distribution, and post-sales customer support. The extraordinary success of this model, in turn, has given rise to a second follow-on wave of outsourcing to offload non-core *service processes*, including in-house business processes such as accounts payable, claims processing, benefits administration, and compliance reporting.

The net impact of these changes has been the radical commoditization of an enormous number of work processes. This in turn has destabilized long-standing business models by eliminating the market inefficiencies upon which their traditional value-creating roles depended. The resulting social turmoil has been great. While public policy can, and in our view should, *modulate* the onset of this onslaught of commoditization, no one believes it can *stop* it. And indeed, in the long term its benefits outweigh its pains, for it enables greater and greater value creation from a given level of asset deployment. But what about right now? What can leaders of businesses in higher-cost developed economies do to sustain the margins needed for life in their societies?

The response most ready to hand is to consolidate a large number of competing enterprises into a few major ones in order to gain bargaining power over the other members in a commoditizing value chain. This leads to a business network structure driven largely by a handful of *concentrators* who do their best to dictate terms to the other participants. The market shares of these companies give them the power to drive pricing discounts and special terms that add extra points of margin to their bottom line. Everyone else in the chain must hustle to keep their place in line, continuously innovating to meet the next "unreasonable" demand from the concentrator, the alternative being to lose out on so much volume they cannot sustain the total overhead of their operation. They have, in effect, become commoditized.

To get out from under this burden of commoditization one must reengineer one's role in the business network, or, if necessary, reengineer the network itself, in order to get access to more lucrative opportunities. This has been exemplified by the evolution of both the contract manufacturing industry in China and the contract services industry in India. Both began by taking whatever work the developed economies wanted to shed—typically low-margin, highly standardized labor-intensive tasks where the wage rate arbitrage made for a good deal on both ends. Under the pressure of success, both nations' economies then began to migrate upstream in the value chain, to seek to perform more complex higher-value work, taking non-core but resource-consuming tasks off their outsourcing customers' plates. There is still considerable more headroom to exploit on this journey, and thus the economies of Asia are booming.

Where does that leave those living and working in Europe, Japan, and the United States? These regions enjoy high-wealth populations with strong traditions of domestic consumption, and developed economy enterprises have a natural customer-intimacy advantage when marketing into their home base. Moreover, many of the latter's established brands are highly attractive to emerging markets in Asia, Central Europe, Latin America, and Africa. The global supply chain can flow in both directions, in other words, provided developed-economy enterprises are able to clear the productivity hurdles necessary to operate at very different price points.

Toward this end, one of the traditional competitive advantages many developed economy enterprises continue to enjoy by comparison with their developing-economy counterparts is experience and sophistication in the use and deployment of IT systems. To date, developed-economy enterprises' investment in IT has focused primarily on improving *internal productivity*, but as the consumer becomes more empowered, and suppliers become more distributed, future returns are increasingly going to come from getting better *visibility, control, and process productivity across the business network*. To compete going forward they must radically improve their ability to manage processes end to end, orchestrating not just the upstream supply chains, where considerable progress has been made in the past decade, but also the downstream demand chains, which even to this day typically operate largely in the dark.

In an era where brand was king and supply was scarce, such downstream opacity mattered little. Customers would wait for what enterprises had. But that is hardly the case in today's consumer-driven world. Fashion and other trend-driven businesses, in particular, demand faster and faster response times to hits, ensuring that stock-outs do not truncate the ability to capitalize on big winners when they come. Detecting these hits—transmitting accurate demand signals with shorter forecasting time frames—requires more extensive use of IT analytics fed by more up-to-date information and integration of processes across a business network. Moreover, to achieve the necessary productivity gains in inventory turns and reduced returns, execution-oriented transaction-processing systems must be reconfigured to act directly upon the insights of these analytics, adjusting commitments in near real time.

Key to the success of this model is the ability to have a *lingua franca* for the business network, an open but common vocabulary that all business network participants share on process and data definitions. Companies operating in coordinated business networks must deploy an end-to-end business process platform and a layer of next-generation applications designed from the ground up as inter-enterprise applications on top of that platform. These "composite applications," as they are sometimes called, provide visibility, control, and productivity improvements at key junctures in the business network. They focus on the edge, keeping things from falling through the cracks, just as the underlying internal enterprise resource planning (ERP) systems focus on the core, keeping mainstream operations moving.

Investments such as these are incremental to the massive IT upgrades driven by the Year 2000 effect. They tap directly into these existing systems of record—no rip and replace, no rewriting of that which is already written—to extract and re-contextualize the data those systems already hold. They are not disruptive.

Nonetheless, two things are still holding back this much-needed transition to next-generation capability:

1. At the line-of-business level, leaders are taking the limitations of their current IT systems for granted. Instead of driving for next-generation investment to address inter-enterprise issues at the wellhead, they consume their budgets using people and spreadsheets to firefight the downstream problems.

2. At the IT level, architects and systems owners continue to take the enterprise boundary for granted. Instead of embracing the challenges of operating across a global business network, they continue to push internal productivity projects whose return on investment is demonstrable but, sadly, increasingly irrelevant.

To move forward in this area of coordinated business networks, both the line-of-business leaders and the IT function must carve out a new space for inter-enterprise space collaboration and populate it with a new generation of composite applications. But unlike previous times, they must do so in collaboration with the other major players in their network. Collaboration does not come naturally to these networks, and progress is easily stalled. But stalling equates to continued deterioration of profit margins—the advance of commoditization is inexorable, there are no time-outs. So it behooves all such leaders to brush up their understanding of how best to operate in a collaborative business network.

Collaborative business networks: Tapping into new sources of wealth

In contrast to the high-volume orientation of coordinated business networks and their corresponding investment in transaction management, collaborative networks focus on high-complexity challenges that require investing in relationship management. Their focus is wide ranging, from the making of a movie to the development of a next-generation airliner, the initial private offering (IPO) of a new company, the commercialization of a novel therapy, or the industrialization of an entire country. Whether it be the capital markets, the public works sector, industrial manufacturing, the energy industry, enterprise software, or consulting services, the focus is on leveraging a wide range of technologies and expertise to tackle a novel set of challenges, collaboratively creating not only new products or services but also whole new systems and categories that simply did not exist before.

The range of these projects—the risks they entail, the capital they require, and the talent they must access—cannot be encompassed by the efforts of any single enterprise. In effect, the need to operate as a collaborative business network is built into the very structure of the problems these companies must address. And such collaborative networks have been in existence for centuries, typically brokered by a handful of highly respected enterprises and a remarkably small number of well-connected, highly effective individuals. The personal relationships these individuals develop and maintain are the backbone of the collaborative network, creating a fabric of mutual understanding, respect, and trust that enables extraordinary risks to be assessed and absorbed. The challenge is how this model can be reengineered to operate more effectively and efficiently at a global scale.

As we have already noted, the forcing function that drives enterprises to reframe their established practices is the deregulation, globalization, and commoditization of the world economy. As these forces continue to put pressure on the price margins of developed economies, enterprises are forced more and more to push beyond the boundaries of existing categories to develop new venues for wealth creation.

Consider three areas that are the focus of much reengineering at present:

1. *Research and development:* Traditionally treated as a closely held function, today more and more corporations are sharing R&D efforts across enterprise boundaries, be it the collaborative "connect and develop" R&D practices of a Procter & Gamble and BASF, the shared R&D ecosystem of biotech and the pharmaceutical industry, the joint ventures in the automotive industry to develop hybrid engine technology, or the next-generation military systems development in the defense arena.

2. *New market development:* Inherent in the capitalist economic model is the perennial need and expectation to develop new markets. Whether it is redesigning an existing product to go into a new market (as many consumer packaged goods firms are doing today to tap into the "bottom of the pyramid" opportunities in developing economies), or creating a new customer base for an unprecedented technology (as Apple and others are doing for digital music and media), or spawning an ecosystem of partners to expand demand for an existing platform (as SAP AG and others seek to do in enterprise software), the need everywhere is to collaborate in order to succeed. In the world of complex systems, what markets need is never what any single company can supply.

3. *Business model innovation:* As industries, sectors, and economies continue to mutate and evolve, legacy business models eventually lose ground in the competition to create value. At the same time, new market inefficiencies create opportunities for alternative business models to capitalize on latent demand. Whether it be the trading ecosystem of eBay, the rise of micro-credit in developing economies, the innovative use of mobile phones as pay-per-use business terminals in these same economies, enterprises are continually discovering and deploying novel mechanisms to capitalize on next-generation opportunities.

Given these examples of efforts already under way, what is the real challenge here? Simply put, we need more—*much more*—of this kind of collaborative innovation to fend off the commoditizing forces of globalization. The bottleneck is that the collaborative business networks needed to discover and capitalize on emerging market opportunities take too long to form, are too hard to scale, and are too susceptible to atrophy and decay. The choke point lies at the very heart of the model: its inherent reliance on personal relationships and close communication to iterate through cycle after cycle of approximation until a viable solution is found. Who has not experienced the joys of this process in a conference room at a whiteboard with a small group of engaged colleagues? Who has not experienced the frustrations of trying to operate that same process on a global scale?

Once again it behooves enterprises in developed economies to better leverage their existing investments in IT infrastructure. In this instance, however, the focus should not be on computing but rather communications systems. The rise of the Internet has led to a global restructuring of communications infrastructure such that all forms of communication—voice, video, data, or mobile—now run (or will do so shortly) over the Internet Protocol. This may be the single greatest technologically led transformation in human history. Not surprisingly, it is taking us all a bit of time to get our heads around it. But the sooner we reorient our thinking, the sooner we can leverage the new media to dramatically rescale our collaborative business networks.

The opportunities to supplement the current infrastructure of telephony and email are manifold. They include Unified Communications, telepresence, Web conferencing, instant messaging, chat, webcams, wikis, portals, dashboards, online workspaces, and social networking. All these technologies extend the reach of collaborative business networks, putting a company's best and brightest in touch with their peers in other companies and on other continents. Kids are using most of these tools already. Employees have them at home as well. Why do companies persist in making them less productive when they come to work?

Simply put, investing in upgrading communications infrastructure is thus the number one opportunity to improve and scale collaborative business networks in the current era. That said, we must heed the thinking of the American philosopher, Henry David Thoreau, who once observed the following about a communications revolution in his century:

> Our inventions are wont to be . . . improved means to an unimproved end. . . . We are in great haste to construct a magnetic telegraph from Maine to Texas; but Maine and Texas, it may be, have nothing important to communicate.[1]

To yield attractive returns, collaborations must be focused on the critical opportunities that truly matter. That does require some help from computing. Human beings are good at recognizing patterns once they are brought into view, but seeing them in the first place, particularly across a vast range of data, can be an enormous challenge. We are all familiar with the data overload of modern life, but that pales when compared with the data overload of modern businesses or governments, particularly when those data span multiple enterprises within a global network.

At such scale, only IT systems can operate with sufficient scope and precision to address the pattern-detection problem. The good news is that the cost of the required supercomputing has plummeted so fast and so far that now data mining across literally trillions of data records is a practical undertaking for any major enterprise. And the data warehouses and analytic software necessary to ferret out the signals amidst all this noise are also ready to hand. The need now is simply to invest.

But what are we investing in? The answer is *metadata*. And that is something that we are going to have to get a lot smarter about.

The rise of metadata and what it means

Metadata are data about data. They are the material of pattern detection, whether that be in the operations of a supply chain, the management of a data network, the movement of a ticker tape, or the behavior of a set of consumers. In coordinated networks, metadata are critical to maintain the visibility and control needed for process management and optimization. They are fundamentally an operational tool focused on productivity improvement. In collaborative networks, metadata are more of a discovery tool that helps direct future investment, whether that be in R&D, marketing, or mergers and acquisitions. In both cases metadata represent a powerful lens through which businesses can reevaluate their current resource deployment and reengineer their future asset allocation.

However, it is this very power that also makes metadata problematic. The risk of constructing or publishing metadata is that it exposes inefficiencies that can be exploited by others, especially in absence of proper security or relationships of trust. Often in such cases, the party exploited is the one that helped supply the data in the first place. Thus there is widespread fear that sharing metadata is likely to have unintended consequences, as the following examples will illustrate:

- patient sensitivity about insurers getting their personal health data,
- retailers not wanting to report out point-of-sale purchase data to product vendors,
- mobile operators wanting to control access to user location data,
- intelligence agencies classifying their metadata as "Top Secret,"
- algorithmic traders seeking to disguise their operations to evade metadata detection,
- consumers wanting to control access to their purchase histories, and
- Internet users' desire to periodically delete their browsing histories.

Now no one denies that metadata are needed to create next-generation innovations. The issue is, under what rules of engagement? This is a work in progress, to be sure, but there are some provisional rules emerging from successful collaborations, of which the following are a sample:

- Governance of metadata needs to be explicit and transparent to all parties involved.

- Private use of companies' own metadata for the purposes of improving their own performance, or those of their partners, has always been and continues to be acceptable. (Arguably that is what the proponents of Sarbanes Oxley—the US federal law of 2002 intended to ensure access to appropriate financial and accounting disclosure information—thought they were about.)

- Public-service uses of metadata are provisionally acceptable provided they are monitored and controlled. This includes fraud detection, traffic management, epidemic disease control, antiterrorist surveillance, and the like.

- Patented metadata are legal but socially concerning, particularly around information on the human genome and comparable global information sources. One can expect legislative controls in this arena at some point in the future.

- Consumer privacy is a deep-seated right, and metadata must not be collected without permission. The gray line here is between opt-in and opt-out methods of securing that permission, with the latter clearly being the high ground.

- Institutionalized sources of metadata are highly valued. This includes financial metadata providers such as Reuters, retail metadata providers such as Nielsens and IRI, and World Wide Web metadata providers such as Google. Positioning as a metadata hub is highly desirable but also jealously guarded against, as it confers enormous economic power to the enterprise in question.

One of the most difficult aspects of metadata is that it exposes inefficiencies, a situation in which someone's ox is all too likely to get gored. This challenge can be overcome to some extent through collaboration toward a common goal as opposed to exploiting the information on a win-lose basis. In coordinated business networks with strong concentrators, however, it is far more common to use metadata to exploit weaker members in the ecosystem to extract greater and greater concessions from them. This results in dysfunctional dynamics that undermine the effectiveness, efficiency, and ultimately the security and reliability of these networks.

In collaborative networks, a similar selfish behavior also generates a backlash. This was a lesson first learned by innumerable dot-coms whose business plans had them setting up digital fronts to reengineer any number of inefficient supply chains. They were shocked to learn that the members of the current community did not want to collaborate in their own demise. Similarly, pharmaceutical companies resist the deployment of diagnostics that may limit the prescription of their drugs, health-care providers resist being measured by patient outcomes, and school systems resist publicized test results. Why would we think they would not?

Metadata, nonetheless, are far too valuable to neglect simply because their politics and governance are so hard to navigate. We need instead to develop a set of ethics and norms to guide their collection and deployment so that we can use them to continue to drive global economic expansion. We believe that task is best left to industry, but we have no doubt that if industry fails to step up, governments will fill the vacuum. Unfortunately, legislation in areas such as this has typically proven inflexible, obstructive, and riddled with unintended consequences. It would be far better if industry were to take this matter in hand itself, and now.

Conclusion

The ability to operate effectively in business networks, be they coordinated or collaborative, is critical to sustaining competitive advantage in a commoditizing global economy. By focusing on their unique core capabilities, business network participants spend less on duplication and more on innovation, resulting in higher degrees of differentiation, greater customer willingness to pay a premium, and thus higher returns on invested capital. Next-generation ICT systems allow these business networks to operate at global scale, but investment in them has been allowed to lag. As a result, enterprises in the developed economies are falling behind the curve, especially in comparison with their Asian counterparts. By focusing on the specifics of the type of network that is most important to their companies, and in particular on the type of metadata that will most greatly enhance their competitive advantage, business and IT leaders can radically improve these outcomes by making measured incremental investment that augments their existing infrastructure.

Note

1 Thoreau 1966 (originally published 1854), chapter 1, p. 67.

References

TCG Advisors, in collaboration with SAP AG. 2007. Research conducted between September and December. The website of TCG Advisors is available at http://www.tcg-advisors.com; the website of SAP AG is available at http://www.sap.com.

Thoreau, H. D. 1966. *Walden: or, Life in the Woods*. C. Merton Babcock, ed. and Aldren Watson, ill. (1966). New York: Peter Pauper Press. Originally published 1854, Boston: Ticknor and Fields.

CHAPTER 1.9

The Participative Web: Innovation and Collaboration

SACHA WUNSCH-VINCENT, OECD
GRAHAM VICKERY, OECD

Innovation in broadband applications and digital content is an important driver of the digital economy, building on the infrastructure push that has provided widespread high-speed network access. This chapter analyzes developments in user-created content and impacts on Internet-based collaboration, business models, and policy.[1]

Toward a participative Web

The Internet has altered the nature and the economics of information production.[2] Entry barriers for content creation and distribution have declined radically, encouraging broader participation in media production, increased user autonomy, increased diversity of both content and users, and a shift away from simple passive consumption of broadcasting and other unidirectional models of mass distribution of content.

Terms such as *the participative Web* describe an Internet increasingly influenced by intelligent Web services, based on new technologies enabling the user to increasingly contribute to developing, rating, collaborating, and distributing Internet content and developing and customizing Internet applications. The OECD defines *user-created content (UCC)* as content that (1) is made publicly available over the Internet, (2) reflects a "certain amount of creative effort," and (3) is "created outside of professional routines and practices."[3] With lower access barriers, increased demand for content downstream, and lower entry barriers in upstream supply, the creation of cultural content and identification of new creators could potentially be enhanced.

Table 1 provides an overview of UCC platforms. Due to strong "network effects," only a handful of UCC platforms receive most user visits and engagement.

The participative Web provides a testing ground for low-cost experimentation with implications for business, and for organizational and social change far beyond technology. New businesses and entrepreneurial activity are a major feature of the participative Web, and existing businesses are under pressure to make their business models relevant to this new environment.

Market development

Rapid growth in participation in social networking, content sharing, and blog sites, along with the advancement of collaboratively developed platforms and news aggregators, is taking place. There has been a rapid expansion of UCC platforms offering users the possibility to upload and display content. Video sites and social networking sites, for instance, are becoming the most popular websites, ranking among the top 50 most visited websites in most OECD countries and among the 10 fastest-growing sites in terms of usage.

Participative websites have benefited from an ever-bigger and more experienced broadband user base, more widely available software (e.g., music mixing or blogging

Table 1: Platforms for user-created content

Type of platform	Examples
Blogs	• Blogs such as BoingBoing, Engadget, Ohmy News • Blogs on sites such as LiveJournal, Windows Live Spaces, Cyworld, Skyrock
Wikis and other text-based collaboration formats	• Sites such as Wikipedia • Sites providing wikis, such as PBWiki, Google Docs
Sites allowing feedback on written works	• Sites such as FanFiction.Net, SocialText
Group-based aggregation	• Sites where users contribute links and rate them, such as Digg, reddit • Sites where users post tagged bookmarks, such as del.icio.us
Podcasting	• Sites such as iTunes, FeedBurner (Google), WinAmp, @Podder
Social network sites	• Sites such as MySpace, Mixi, Facebook, Hi5, Bebo, Orkut, Cyworld, Imeem, ASmallWorld
Virtual worlds	• Sites such as Second Life, Active Worlds, Entropia Universe, Dotsoul Cyberpark
Video content or filesharing sites	• Sites such as YouTube, DailyMotion, GyaO, Crackle

Source: OECD.

software), technologies for interactive Web applications (e.g., Ajax, RSS), consumer electronic apparatus producing digital content, demographic factors, and new ways of monetizing UCC (see Box 1 for a list of drivers). Institutional and legal developments have also acted as drivers—including flexible licensing and copyright schemes and end-user licensing agreements granting copyright for UCC (e.g., in the 3D virtual world, Second Life). Hundreds of millions of pieces of content on the Internet are under various Creative Commons licenses.[4]

Overall, little official statistical information on UCC exists. However, available data show that broadband users produce and share content at a high rate, and point to evolving intergenerational and gender differences in Web media usage.[5]

In Japan, there were 8 million estimated bloggers and 35 million estimated blog readers (about 41 percent of Japanese Internet users) by end of March 2007—that is, roughly one out of five readers were creating blogs themselves.[6] There were an estimated 10 million Japanese users of social networking services (SNS) (about 12 percent of Japanese Internet users). In Korea, Rep. (Korea), roughly 16 million, or close to half of all Korean Internet users, read blogs or visited minihompys (i.e., mini homepages) in 2007 (Figure 1). Also about 8 million Koreans owned a minihomepage (about a fourth of all Korean Internet users), and around 40 percent of Korean Internet users used online communities.[7]

In the United States, 29 percent of Internet users read blogs and 12 percent of Internet users had created their own blog in 2007; the latter share comes close to 30 percent for teenagers between 12 and 17; and 17 percent of all Americans used online material in their own online creations.[8] In the European Union, in 2007 16 percent of all Internet users reported having created Web pages.[9]

Depending on the UCC type and the OECD country, the number of creators is often relatively small compared with those simply viewing content, especially for blogs and online videos. In the case of Wikipedia, for example, in 2006 about 4 percent of all contributors made the majority of contributions.[10] This does not apply as much for SNS where most users create some form of content.

Age remains a determinant for active contribution. Older teens are the most active users of social networking services in the United States: 55 percent of American adolescents between 12 and 17 years have created personal online profiles on sites such as Facebook or MySpace.[11] But in countries such as Korea, with a longer tradition of UCC, older age groups (including over-40-year-olds) are increasingly involved, and users between 20 and 29 years are the most active.[12]

Gender is another determinant of online activity. In many OECD countries, lower shares of females actively contribute, for example by putting up a webpage or a blog (see Figure 2). In contrast, in the United States 70 percent of all girls aged 15 to 17 years are reported to have used an online social network compared with 54 percent of boys; and girls constitute nearly 60 percent of webpage creators amongst teenagers aged 12 to 17.[13] In Japan, the 20-to-30 age group of women are also more active than men in finding friends online,[14] and blogging activity is high for Asian women.[15]

Box 1: Drivers of user-created content

Technological drivers
- Increased broadband availability
- Increased hard drive capacity and processing speeds coupled with lower costs
- Decrease in cost and increase in quality of consumer technology devices for audio, photo, and video
- Availability of technologies to create, distribute, and share content
- Development of simpler software tools for creating, editing, and remixing
- Rise of nonprofessional and professional UCC sites as outlets

Social drivers
- Shift to younger age groups ("digital natives") with substantial ICT skills, willingness to engage online (i.e., sharing content, recommending and rating content, etc.), who are less hesitant to reveal personal information online
- Desire to create and express oneself and search for more interactivity than on traditional media platforms such as TV
- Development of communities and collaborative projects
- Spread of social drivers to older age groups and for societal functions (social engagement, politics, and education)

Economic drivers
- Lower costs and increased availability of tools for the creation of UCC (e.g., for creating, editing, hosting content) and lower entry barriers
- Lower cost of broadband Internet connections for providers and users
- Increased commercial interest in user-created content and "long tail" economics (including mobile operators, telecommunication service providers, traditional media publishers, and search engines)
- Increased possibilities to finance UCC-related ventures and sites through venture capital and other investment vehicles
- Greater availability of advertising and new business models to monetize content

Institutional and legal drivers
- Rise of schemes that provide more flexible access to creative works and the right to create derivative works—(e.g., flexible licensing and copyright schemes such as the Creative Commons license)
- Rise of end-user licensing agreements that grant copyright to users for their content

Figure 1: Blog readers, bloggers, and minihompy owners in Korea, 2007

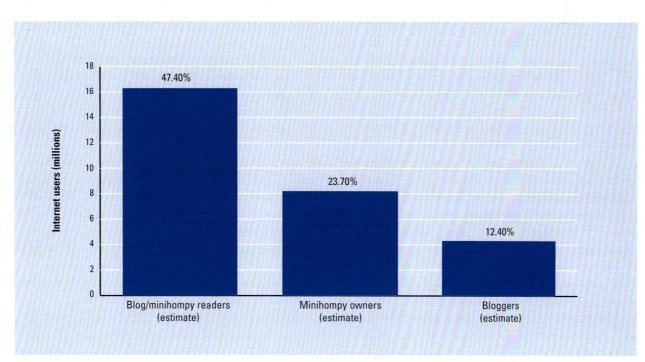

Source: Calculations based on NIDA 2007a, 2007b.
Note: A *minihompy* is a user profile page on popular social networking platforms such as Cyworld.

Figure 2: Share of adult female webpage creators in Europe, OECD Members and selected countries, 2007

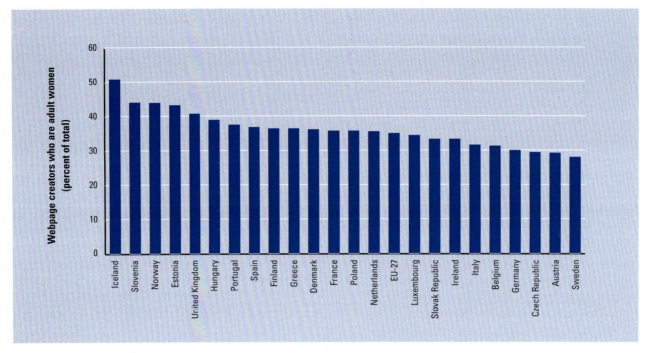

Source: OECD calculations based on data from Eurostat, "Community survey on ICT usage in Households and by Individuals." See OECD, 2007g, for more on ICT gender issues.

Emerging value chains

The traditional media-publishing value chain involves selecting, developing, and distributing the creator's work, often at high cost. Technical and content quality is maintained by traditional media "gatekeepers." In the UCC value chain, users create content for or on UCC platforms using content creation devices (e.g., digital cameras, microphones), software (video editing tools), the UCC platforms themselves, and an Internet access provider to create and post content (Figure 3). Users can often derive a higher value from such content as it may be more personalized and can be selected by users themselves.

Users become the gatekeepers and select which content works and which does not, through recommending and rating (i.e., another form of advertising), possibly leading some creators to recognition and fame that would not have been possible via traditional media publishers. The time taken for content to be created and distributed is greatly reduced compared with the traditional value chain, which can impact the type and quality of content in multiple ways.

New forms of governance of Internet and user activities are emerging on the participative Web (i.e., organizational structures such as peer review and rating to evaluate user activities and raise quality such as on Wikipedia). It is still not clear whether these will converge to one model or if a multiplicity of governance forms will persist.

New economic incentives and online business models

Initially, most UCC was not linked to expectations of remuneration or profit. Motivating factors included connecting with peers; self-expression; and achieving fame, notoriety, or prestige. But investment in participative Web services is growing strongly, as witnessed by acquisitions of major UCC platforms by established commercial firms (MySpace acquired by News Corporation, Flickr by Yahoo!, YouTube by Google). Also UCC sites are of increasing interest for investors and businesses, and venture capital funding of Web 2.0 businesses has increased significantly.

UCC platforms are increasingly attracting the attention of the advertising industry, search engine operators, and media firms who own UCC platforms or who select content from these platforms for distribution over traditional media publishing channels. A new set of economic incentives is emerging for these actors that creates pressure for innovation and reorganization of existing business models (see Table 2 for economic opportunities and challenges). ICT goods and services providers have seen positive economic impacts from this phenomenon as users purchase goods and services such as digital cameras, editing software, faster broadband subscriptions.

Most business models are still in flux, and revenue generation for content creators or firms is only beginning. There are essentially six approaches to monetize UCC described below; combinations of these approaches are illustrated in three cases in Table 3. Some of the

Figure 3: Internet value chain for user-created content

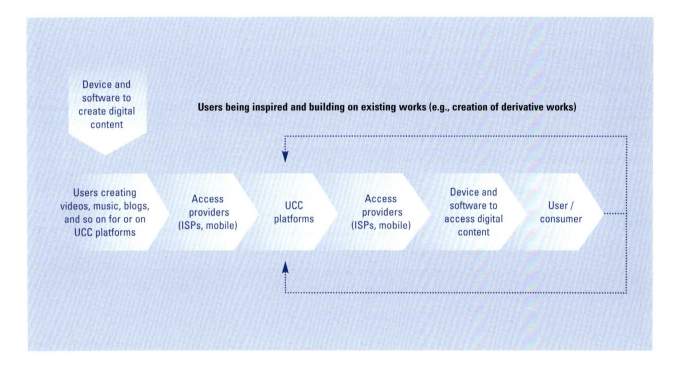

Table 2: Economic incentives and benefits for different UCC value chain participants

UCC participant	Incentive/ benefit
Consumer electronics and ICT goods content	• Selling hardware with new functionality and interoperability for users to create and access.
Software producers	• Providing ICT services and software for creating, hosting, and delivering of UCC.
ISPs and Web portals	• ISPs: using UCC to attract customers and build a user base for premium Internet services. • Web portals: aiming to attract traffic, build Internet audiences and advertising revenues (and avoid losing traffic to UCC-related sites).
UCC platforms and sites	• Attracting traffic, building Internet audiences and subscription and advertising revenues; increasing attractiveness for potential acquisition.
Creators and users	• Creators: Noncommercial incentives—entertaining or informing other users, for recognition or fame; commercial incentives—generating revenue through donations, sale of content, or sharing revenue from advertisement-based models. • Other users: free access to content that is entertaining, educational (e.g., on purchasing decisions, or advice).
Traditional media	• Participating in UCC online revenues (essentially through advertising-based business models); promoting own content to UCC audiences; broadcasting or hosting UCC to retain audience and advertisers and to prevent disintermediation.
Professional content creators	• Reinventing business models to compete with free Web content (e.g., photographs, images).
Search engines	• Using UCC audiences to attract advertising revenues while improving searchability.
Web services that benefit from UCC	• Using UCC to build more attractive websites and customer services and information (e.g., a travel agency or hotel chain that encourages users to post pictures and share appreciations).
Advertising	• Benefiting from increased online advertising directed at communities on UCC platforms; using UCC content in advertising campaigns.
Marketing and brands	• Expanding customer loyalty through promoting brands on social networking sites or through advertising to UCC communities.

Source: OECD.

models include remunerating creators, either by sharing revenues or by direct payments from other users. Very few UCC platforms currently generate significant revenues, and online advertising is seen as the main source in the future.

- **Voluntary donations:** Content creators make the content freely available but solicit donations from users (online by credit card or via PayPal). Blogging and citizen journalism sites such as Global Voices Online are supported by bloggers who provide content for free; operating expenses are funded by grants from foundations or in some cases news companies as well as user donations.

- **Charging viewers:** *Pay-per-item model*—Users make per-item (micro) payments to UCC platforms or creators to access individual pieces of content. *Subscription model*—Consumers subscribe to services. Users usually pay a subscription for both enhanced hosting services and access to other users' content. Paying a subscription to simply access other users' content is rarely used. In two-tiered subscription services, a user can opt for a "basic" account free of charge or for a paid "pro" account with advanced features.

- **Advertising-based models ("monetizing the audience") and marketing:** Advertising is generally seen as a promising source of revenue, and some UCC sites are distributing revenues among those creating or owning the content.[16] "Branded channels" have been launched on UCC platforms with content from a special brand or media publisher. Virtual worlds allow firms to create and display advertisements. Established brands have also begun experimenting with new ways to integrate UCC into their advertisements (e.g., a beauty product manufacturer encouraging users to create their own commercials). Yet it is currently unclear whether users will appreciate increased advertisements and commercialization. Some video-sharing platforms are also scaling back UCC in favor of traditional professional content, potentially changing the original nature and attractiveness of these platforms.

- **Licensing content and technology to third parties:** Increasingly, UCC is being used on other platforms, and licensing content to third parties (e.g., TV stations) may be a source of revenue. Users may agree to license the site to use their content without payment, sometimes reserving the right to commercially exploit the work, but a revenue-sharing model between content creators and the UCC site may apply. Mobile carriers as well as TV stations are increasingly acquiring licenses to distribute UCC and technologies that enable sharing of content.

- **Selling goods and services to the community:** Successful UCC sites are likely to have a large user base because of network effects. This can be monetized by selling items and services directly to users or developing transactions amongst them (e.g., sale of avatars, virtual accessories, or virtual land). UCC sites can also cooperate with third parties to allow them to sell directly to users while taking a share of the revenue. Under the term *social commerce*, Japanese social networking sites, for instance, allow users to rate and review books, DVDs, games, electronics, and other items and to purchase these.

- **Selling user data:** Other business models may involve the sale of mostly anonymous information about users to market research and other firms.

Beyond such user-created platforms, the participative Web will have profound impacts on business organization and innovation cycles. These platforms potentially reduce costs of collaboration and increase possibilities for greater productive use of external knowledge, skills, and sources of value. Individuals and consumers can co-create services, products, or information, and businesses use online communities to help solve research and development problems and to innovate. More impacts on businesses are to be expected from the internal or external use of participative Web technologies for their operations (e.g., wikis and blogs for internal knowledge management).

Business and policy challenges

A number of business, social, and regulatory challenges related to the participative Web are emerging.[17]

Fostering the economic and social potential of the participative Web

Apart from recent commercial development, the production and consumption of UCC has been accompanied by social and behavioral changes through increased participation. The participative Web has an impact on a much wider sphere than markets and commercial development alone and is helping to change government, politics, and civic life and to provide the ability for mass collaboration and communal activity. Given that it is user-driven and that many national/regional sites exist, the participative Web can encourage multilingualism and greater development of local cultural content and information. UCC is also a form of personal expression and speech for critical, political, and social ends. In education, platforms tend to be collaborative, encouraging the sharing of knowledge and "peer production."

Fostering more broad-based participation will be a continuing challenge. A greater gap between digitally literate users and others may accentuate social fragmentation and intergenerational differences. Moreover, most

Table 3: UCC platform business models: Citizen journalism and photos

Business model and example	Method of revenue generation
Citizen journalism: AgoraVox (France)	AgoraVox is a European site supporting "citizen journalism" based on voluntary in-kind contributions. Users submit news articles on a voluntary basis, and this content is moderated by the small AgoraVox staff and volunteers. Readers also provide feedback on the reliability of the information. AgoraVox aims to generate revenues through online advertising. Similar citizen journalism sites such as OhmyNews in Korea remunerate their writers. OhmyNews redistributes advertising revenues to writers for highly rated articles. Readers also directly remunerate citizen journalists through a micro-payment system.
Video: MyVideo (Germany)	The online video sharing site MyVideo derives its revenues mostly from advertising and from licensing its content to third parties. ProSiebenSat1 Media, Germany's largest commercial TV company, completed its purchase of MyVideo.de in 2007. The objective is to secure a share of Internet advertising, to cross-promote content (UCC content on TV, and TV content on UCC platforms), and to identify interesting content for traditional media publishing (e.g., talent search show). Video sites such as YouTube have also started licensing content to telecommunication service providers.
Photo: Flickr (United States)	Flickr is funded from advertising and subscriptions. A free account provides the possibility of hosting a certain number of photos. Advertising is displayed while searching or viewing photos. This revenue is not shared with users. A subscription "pro" account for US$24.95 per year offers unlimited storage, upload, bandwidth, permanent archiving, and an ad-free service. Flickr is part of Yahoo! and enhances membership and traffic to other Yahoo! sites. Similar photo sites, such as KodakGallery, are owned by photography firms. Users can create free accounts and revenues are generated through various photo services (e.g., purchase of prints).

Source: OECD, based on company information and press reports.

users consume UCC and, so far, only a limited number of young, early adopters actively and consistently contribute.

Improving access and the infrastructure

Broadband policies to ensure (regional) coverage and equal access to infrastructure and applications on fair terms and at competitive prices to all communities, irrespective of location, are general policy aims, as is a regulatory environment that encourages investment and competition in communication networks and technologies. One key technical challenge for the evolution of UCC is the low consumer availability of symmetrical networks. The majority of Internet connections are Asymmetric Digital Subscriber Line (ADSL) and cable services, with the volume of data flow greater in one direction than the other. This current infrastructure is not conducive to participation and more symmetrical user behavior. The deployment of new distribution technologies such as optical fiber (as in Japan and Korea, but also increasingly in Europe and the United States) is one solution to this problem.

Developing competitive, nondiscriminatory policy frameworks

To encourage further experimentation and competition in value chains and business models, it is essential to maintain and further develop competitive, nondiscriminatory policy frameworks and a pro-innovation business environment. Very strong network effects, potential for lock-in, and high switching costs have to be taken into account when making competition-related assessments of UCC services that have a critical mass of users. However, new forms of digital content innovations are often based less on traditional scale advantages and large initial capital investments and more on decentralized creativity, organizational innovation, and new business models for content production and diffusion.[18] These factors favor new entrants, particularly for new platform aggregation models, where content owners had no legacy advantages.

Intellectual property rights and user-created content

Copyright issues may emerge when users create content by using—in part or in full—pieces of others' work without authorization, or where the use does not fall within an exception and limitation. Examples that entail replicating or transforming certain works are the use of particular characters in writing fan fiction; using certain images while blogging; creating lip-synching videos with samples of existing songs; and the creation of UCC videos while using copyrighted characters, texts, or video images.

Depending on country-specific legislation, "fair use" and "fair dealing" principles and/or specific statutory exceptions allow courts to avoid the rigid application of the copyright statute's exclusive rights when, on occasion, it would discourage creativity and oppose the public interest in or wide dissemination of knowledge through copyrighted works. Under these circumstances, portions of works can be used without permission and without payment if their use is within one of the copyright exceptions and limitations. But there remains legal uncertainty on the side of the creator of the original work as well as with the creator of the derivate work.

Copyright issues also arise when users post unaltered third-party content on UCC platforms without authorization (e.g., uploading parts of popular TV series without the explicit consent of the content owner). The essential question is whether online intermediaries are treated as electronic publishers, and thus liable for content on their servers. In their copyright or e-commerce laws, many OECD countries have addressed the liability of ISPs and other information intermediaries who simply deliver content by creating liability exceptions (e.g., "safe harbor" under the US Digital Millennium Copyright Act).[19] This is an exemption from secondary liability, but it requires the online service providers to remove infringing materials upon notice. No general monitoring obligation is imposed on the service provider.[20] Most UCC platforms state clearly that they are not assuming editorial responsibility for the content posted (see Table 4).

Activities that involve the modification of transmitted information do not qualify for this exemption, and hosting services providers are encouraged to act expeditiously to remove or to disable access to the information concerned upon obtaining actual knowledge or awareness of illegal activities.[21] Under the principle of contributory liability, it may be that such online intermediaries are found liable to induce, cause, or materially contribute to the infringing conduct of their users. This holds particularly in cases where UCC platforms have knowledge of the infringing activity (i.e., "willful infringement"), when they do not simply host but edit or categorize the content (which is mostly the case), when they induce users to post unauthorized content (compare the US Supreme Court Ruling vis-à-vis the Grokster case),[22] or when they derive revenues (e.g., advertising-related revenues) from unauthorized postings.[23]

It is an ongoing discussion if and how Internet intermediaries should be made more responsible for copyright infringement on their networks and whether liability exceptions should be revisited—potentially involving the requirement of Internet intermediaries to "filter" or "inspect" content transiting over their networks. Care must be taken to ensure that new initiatives promote investment and innovation, and that privacy rights of users are respected. Often legitimate intellectual property rights challenges will be resolved through appropriate business agreements among rights holders, UCC platforms, and other associated entities. The developments in this transitional phase may have to be awaited before initiating legislative changes.

Information and content quality

UCC is produced in a nonprofessional context outside of traditional media oversight and often without any financial remuneration, and this can have implications for the "quality" of material being posted, admitting that the concept of quality is hard to define and has both subjective and contextual aspects.

In the case of blogs, commentary, and other UCC forms that refer to facts and figures, the accuracy of content and acknowledgment of sources may not be guaranteed. The availability of large amounts of information (some accurate and some not) shifts the responsibility to users to assess information found on UCC sites. Younger users especially will have to develop the skills to differentiate between incorrect and correct information.

Many UCC platforms and communities have adopted community standards and associated rules to reduce the incidence of inappropriate content and actions (see Table 4). These include, for example, rules on tolerance, on harassment, on assault in virtual worlds (e.g., shooting, pushing, etc.), on privacy and the prevention of disclosure of information, on indecency, and on undesired advertising content. If not respected, the service provider reserves the right to take actions against the user (e.g., temporary or permanent suspension of accounts).

Technological and self-regulatory solutions may help to limit access to such content. Age-rating systems or age limits are seen as important to ensure protection of minors, but these rating systems need to be clear and increasingly internationally recognized and adhered to in order to be meaningful. Filtering software and other parental controls may also provide solutions.

Privacy and identity theft

Concerns have been raised about users increasingly posting increasing amounts of information online about their identities, their own lives, and those of others.[24] Users post photos and videos, publicly accessible profiles on social networking sites, and online journals with intimate details of their lives on blogs and sites. Although such sites offer privacy settings to limit the availability of this information to personal contacts or friends, many users choose to make their information publicly available. SNS sites are reported to have been used to phish for users' personal information through spam campaigns. Individuals have used UCC platforms to expose content about somebody else (i.e., including posting online videos or other content without the consent of the persons involved) or creating accounts on behalf of another person with false information or content. Identity thieves can also track down information to mimic someone else's identity.

Most commonly used UCC platforms have adopted privacy principles. In principle, information that is not displayed publicly is protected and not sold to third

Table 4: Content and conduct provisions in terms of service of UCC sites

Content regulation and editorial responsibility	• Most sites specify that users are solely responsible for the content that they publish or display on the website or transmit to other members. The sites specify that they have no obligation to modify or remove any inappropriate member content, and no responsibility for the conduct of the member submitting any such content. • The sites reserve the right to review and delete or remove any member content that does not correspond to defined standards. • Some sites use age and content ratings or have designated areas for content that is rated mature.
Community standards	• Most sites have community standards on intolerance (derogatory or demeaning language as to race, ethnicity, gender, religion, or sexual orientation), harassment, assault, the disclosure of information on third parties and other users (e.g., posting conversations), indecency, and so on.
Actions to enforce standards	• Sites specify penalties when users infringe community standards. These penalties range from warnings and suspensions to banishment from the service. The creation of alternative accounts to circumvent these rules is tracked.

Source: OECD, based on a review of the terms of service of a sample of 15 widely used English-speaking UCC sites.

parties (Box 2). In the case of a merger or acquisition by a third party, however, this information is an asset that is acquired, and could potentially be misused. There may also be cases of data leakages, although so far little is known about any such cases that may have occurred via UCC sites.

> **Box 2: Privacy provisions in terms of service of UCC sites**
>
> • Most of the sites collect personal information relevant to the service, stating that this is to provide the user with a customized and efficient experience. This information is protected and not sold to third parties.
> • Sometimes personal information uploaded on SNS sites is provided to advertisers (sometimes delivered directly) and other parties in a personally identifiable manner and aggregate usage information in a non–personally identifiable manner, to present more targeted advertising to members.
> • Most sites reserve the right to transfer personal information in the event of a transfer of ownership or sale of assets.
> • Sites specify that personal information may be released for law enforcement purposes.
>
> Source: OECD, based on a review of the terms of service and the privacy policies of a sample of 15 widely used English-speaking UCC sites.

Conclusions

The popularity of UCC is likely to continue to grow, and new drivers will further increase UCC use and creation including:

- the increasing use of mobile phones and higher mobile uplink data transmission speeds to watch, capture, and contribute mobile UCC in order to advance development of other consumer devices allowing easier content upload;

- new types of UCC around more interactive social networks, video-sharing sites, and new types of virtual worlds that connect users in more immersive ways;

- new types of software and services enabling the creation of content, including social networking applications and personal profiles/digital identities working across separate UCC platforms; and

- economic incentives for users to create their own content, for instance by offering a share of revenues generated through sales, advertising, or licensing to traditional media outlets.

There are, however, a number of issues to be addressed. Copyright infringement often involves disputes among copyright holders, UCC platforms, and users. UCC platforms will also have to address privacy concerns of users and regulators, as popular platforms may increasingly be subject to phishing and other cyber-attacks, making user data vulnerable. Content quality, safety on the Internet, and possibly better self-governance of users will be issues to be addressed. Increased concentration among the UCC platforms and the growing role of gatekeepers will be continuing business and policy issues.

The impacts of UCC are wider than commercial applications, and despite increased attention given to business ventures and commercial innovation, harnessing the participative Web's potential for educational, political, and social objectives will have major impacts.

Notes

1. OECD work on digital content is available at www.oecd.org/sti/digitalcontent and is summarized in the *OECD Information Technology Outlook 2008*. This chapter also draws on the results of the OECD-Italy conference on "The Future Digital Economy: Digital Content Creation, Distribution and Access" (see http://www.oecd.org/sti/digitalcontent/conference) and the "OECD-Canada Technology Foresight Forum on the Participative Web: Strategies and Policies for the Future" (see www.oecd.org/futureinternet/participativeweb).

2. OECD 2006a, 2008b.

3. See OECD 2007 for more definitional details and shortcomings.

4. These pieces of content were counted using the number of "linkbacks" to these licenses on the Internet, as tracked by Google.

5. National statistical offices have only started to include such issues in surveys. Examples include the "Communications Usage Trend Survey for Households," Ministry of Internal Affairs and Communications (MIC), Japan; the "Survey on the Computer and Internet Use," National Internet Development Agency of Korea (NIDA); the "Community survey on ICT usage in Households and by Individuals," Eurostat.

6. See MIC 2007.

7. See NIDA 2007a.

8. November 2007; data made available by John B. Horrigan (Pew Internet & American Life Project, 2007b).

9. Eurostat survey "Community survey on ICT usage in Households and by Individuals."

10. OECD, based on Wikipedia at http://stats.wikimedia.org/EN/ (accessed August 4, 2007).

11. See Pew 2007a, 2007b.

12. NIDA 2007a, 2007b.

13. Pew 2007a, 2007b.

14. MIC 2005.

15. Xinhua-PRNewswire 2006.

16. OECD 2008a.

17. See OECD 2006b, 2007 and the OECD-Canada Technology Foresight Forum on the Participative Web: Strategies and Policies for the Future (at note 1).

18. OECD 2006b.

19. Section 512(c) of the US Digital Millennium Copyright Act.

20. See, for example, the EU Electronic Commerce Directive 2000/31/EC, "EU Directive on Electronic Commerce," Article 15.

21. For example, the "EU Directive on Electronic Commerce," Recitals 40 and 46.

22. US Supreme Court Decision in *Metro-Goldwyn-Mayer Studios, Inc. v. Grokster, Ltd.* 545 U.S. 913 (2005).

23. See WIPO 2005.

24. See www.oecd.org/sti/security-privacy for OECD work on privacy and ICT security.

References

MIC (Ministry of Internal Affairs and Communications of Japan). 2005. "Analysis on Current Status of and Forecast on Blogs/SNSs." Available at http://www.soumu.go.jp/joho_tsusin/eng/Releases/Telecommunications/pdf/news050517_2_1.pdf.

———. 2007. "White Paper on Information and Communications in Japan." Available at http://www.johotsusintokei.soumu.go.jp/whitepaper/eng/WP2007/2007-index.html.

NIDA (National Internet Development Agency of Korea). 2007a. "Survey on the Computer and Internet Usage." February. Available at http://isis.nida.or.kr/eng/.

———. 2007b. "2007 Korea Internet White Paper." Available at http://www.nida.or.kr/english/.

OECD (Organisation for Economic Co-operation and Development). 2006a. *OECD Information Technology Outlook 2006*. Paris: OECD.

———. 2006b. "Digital Broadband Content: Digital Content Strategies and Policies." Report presented to the Working Party on the Information Economy, unclassified. DSTI/ICCP/IE(2005)3/FINAL. Available at http://www.oecd.org/dataoecd/54/36/36854975.pdf.

———. 2007. *Participative Web and User-Created Content: Web 2.0, Wikis, and Social Networking*. Paris: OECD.

———. 2008a. "Digital Broadband Content: Online Advertising." Unclassified paper prepared for the Working Party on the Information Economy, DSTI/ICCP/IE(2007)1/FINAL.

———. 2008b. *OECD Information Technology Outlook 2008*. Paris: OECD.

Pew/Internet. 2007a. "Social Networking Websites and Teens: An Overview." Pew Internet & American Life Project, 1 July. Available at http://www.pewinternet.org/PPF/r/198/report_display.asp.

———. 2007b. "Teens and Social Media." Pew Internet & American Life Project, 19 December. Available at http://www.pewinternet.org/PPF/r/230/report_display.asp.

WIPO (World Intellectual Property Organization). 2005. "Online Intermediaries and Liability for Copyright Infringement." Presentation prepared by L. Edwards and C. Waelde for the WIPO Seminar on Copyright and Internet Intermediaries, Geneva, 18 April.

Xinhua-PRNewswire. 2006. Microsoft Windows Live survey: "Blogging Phenomenon Sweeps Asia." November 28. Available at http://www.prnewswire.com/cgi-bin/stories.pl?ACCT=104&STORY=/www/story/11-28-2006/0004480819&EDATE.

Part 2

Leveraging ICT and Innovation for Competitiveness: Selected Case Studies

CHAPTER 2.1

Singapore: Building an Intelligent Nation with ICT

NG CHER KENG, Infocomm Development Authority, Singapore
ONG LING LEE, Infocomm Development Authority, Singapore
TANYA TANG, Infocomm Development Authority, Singapore
SOUMITRA DUTTA, INSEAD

When Singapore took its first steps in information and communication technologies (ICT) in 1981, it did so with just two mainframe computers, 850 computer professionals, and a strong dose of faith. The starting aim was straightforward: to equip the young nation with the then new tools to increase productivity, thereby increasing Singapore's economic competitiveness. This was how the first IT master plan—the Civil Service Computerisation Programme (CSCP)—came about. The National Computer Board (NCB) was then set up to implement the plan.

As the efforts bore their fruit, the government's confidence in ICT as an economic enabler grew, along with its ambition to grow Singapore's ICT capabilities. From equipping the government, the NCB and its successor, the Infocomm Development Authority (IDA), went on to drive nationwide efforts to extend ICT capabilities to the country's enterprises and population, wire up and connect the nation with high-speed broadband connectivity, and transform different economic sectors through the use of ICT.

Many determined steps and 26 years later, Singapore today counts ICT as a key component of its economic infrastructure. The nation is now host to a vibrant ICT industry and home to a technologically savvy population. Singapore is also well regarded as a global leader in e-government, as evidenced by its top ranks in several e-government league tables and in the Networked Readiness Index's components on government readiness and usage (for which Singapore is ranked 1st and 4th, respectively, in 2007–08).[1] From very humble roots, Singapore has rapidly developed into a global leader in the world of ICT.

In 2006, the ICT industry saw double-digit growth and generated S$45 billion in revenue (see Figure 1). Beyond that, ICT has become an integral part of Singaporeans' lives. Mobile phone penetration exceeds 100 percent; almost 8 in 10 households have access to computers at home, and more than 7 in 10 households have broadband access and many of those are at higher broadband speeds (see Figure 2).

As a small island nation without natural resources except for its people, ICT is important to Singapore's growth. In today's increasingly interconnected world, ICT provides the necessary bridge for Singapore to reach the global markets beyond its shores. Since the establishment of the CSCP in 1981, the government has formulated and implemented six ICT master plans, each guided by a developmental theme relevant for the economy (see Table 1).

As a relatively mature economy today, always pushing the technology frontier, the constant challenge for Singapore is to find new development and growth models. The latest ICT master plan, Intelligent Nation 2015 (or "iN2015"), launched in June 2006, will further support the country's transformation into a knowledge-based economy with innovation-led growth. As more

Figure 1: ICT industry revenue, 2002–06

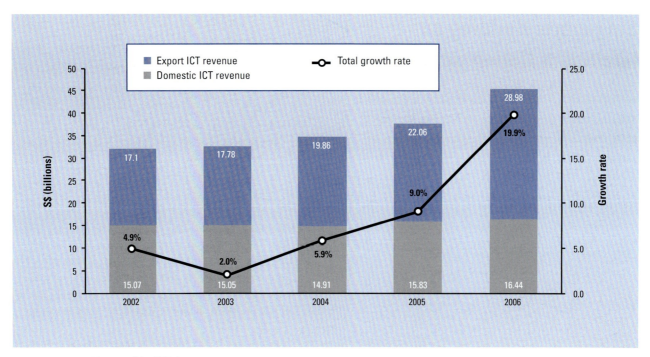

Source: IDA's Annual Surveys of the ICT industry.

Figure 2: Residential broadband subscriptions by speed, 2005–07

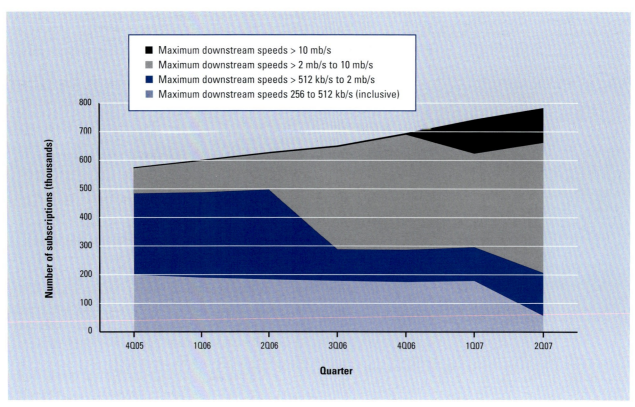

Source: IDA.

Table 1: Singapore's six ICT master plans

The period the master plan covers	National ICT master plan (theme)	E-government master plan	Purpose and focus
2006–15 2006–10	iN2015 (Creation)	iGov2010	iN2015 is Singapore's latest 10-year ICT master plan, which has a vision to develop "An Intelligent Nation, a Global City, powered by Infocomm" through the following four strategic thrusts: 1. Spearhead the transformation of key economic sectors, government, and society through more sophisticated and innovative use of ICT. 2. Establish an ultra-high speed, pervasive, intelligent, and trusted ICT infrastructure. 3. Develop a globally competitive ICT industry. 4. Develop an ICT-savvy and globally competitive workforce.
2003–06	Connected Singapore (Connectedness)	e-Government Action Plan II	Connected Singapore was formulated following the dot-com bust, in recognition of the need for Singapore to develop new sources of growth, including new areas involving creative inputs such as design and the arts. The vision for Connected Singapore was "Unleashing potential, realising possibilities, through Infocomm" by strengthening the foundational blocks of capability development, technology planning, and a conducive business environment.
2000–03	Infocomm 21 (Convergence)	e-Government Action Plan	Spurred by the convergence of telecommunications and IT, the Infocomm 21 blueprint was launched in 2000 to develop Singapore into a global ICT capital with a thriving and prosperous e-economy and an ICT-savvy e-society. Apart from its broad strategic thrust of "dot-comming" the public, people, and private sectors, the master plan also sought to establish Singapore as a premier ICT hub and ICT talent capital, and to create a pro-business and pro-consumer environment conducive to fostering the development and growth of the new economy.
1992–99	IT2000 (Connectivity and content)	Civil Service Computerisation Programme	The IT2000 master plan aimed to position Singapore as a global IT hub. Building on the National IT Plan, the expanded focus included improving the quality of life in Singapore, boosting the economy, linking communities locally and globally, and enhancing the potential of Singaporeans. In the public sector, greater emphasis was placed on the integration of computing resources through consolidation of computing facilities in a data center and through a civil service–wide network. The Internet was introduced as a new delivery channel providing both information and transaction-based services to the public. The Ge-BIZ portal on the e-government site was the world's first Internet-based government procurement system.
1986–91	The National IT Plan (Communications)	Civil Service Computerisation Programme	As Singapore's ICT strategies matured, the focus shifted to the provision of one-stop services through cross-agency linkages. The enhanced inter-agency communications resulted in the creation of three Data Hubs: Land, People, and Establishment. An increasing number of public services were developed in the direction of the "One-Stop, Non-Stop" strategy. The use of IT in automating and integrating traditional manual processes via networks culminated in the set-up of TradeNet, LawNet, and MediNet for the trade and logistics, legal, and medical communities, respectively.
1980–85	The National Computerisation Plan (Computerization)	Civil Service Computerisation Programme	One of the key objectives of the National Computerisation Plan was to embark on a Civil Service Computerisation Programme (CSCP) to computerize the major functions in every government ministry. Directed at improving public administration through the effective use of IT, the effort focused on automating traditional work functions, reducing paperwork and escalating the deployment of ICT in the public service. This "start small, scale fast" approach became a catalyst for the widespread acceptance of ICT. The other objectives of the plan were to facilitate the development and growth of the local ICT industry and to develop a pool of ICT manpower to meet the future needs of the industry.

Source: IDA.

countries leverage ICT for growth, it is hoped that successful implementation of iN2015 will help Singapore compete and stay relevant in the global digital economy. In the words of Dr Lee Boon Yang, Minister for Information, Communications and the Arts: "We envisage Infocomm becoming even more accessible to everyone —to work, live, learn and play with. Indeed, by developing an inclusive digital society, we will ensure continued growth and vitality of our knowledge-based digital economy. This master plan—Intelligent Nation 2015, or iN2015—has been drawn up with precisely this vision in mind."[2]

The purpose of this chapter is to provide the reader with an overview of the evolution of thinking in Singapore on the use of ICT for competitiveness. Singapore's focus on linking ICT to strategic objectives combined with strong leadership from the very top of the government provides useful insights for other countries as they seek to leverage the potential of ICT for their own development and competitiveness. Singapore has also achieved world-class excellence in specific areas of ICT deployment. Two such areas of excellence—e-government and e-education—are highlighted in this chapter. Finally, the chapter covers some lessons from the last two decades of ICT progress in Singapore and also outlines some of the challenges ahead in sustaining its position of global leadership.

ICT started small

After Singapore separated from Malaysia in 1965, it found itself alone, with a small and poorly educated population, few natural resources, and an economy that largely depended on entrepôt trade. With such difficult conditions surrounding the small domestic market, Singapore's economic strategy of import substitution then was not sustainable.

Early days of independence (1965 to late 1970s)
Compounded by the lack of trained manpower and capital to develop and grow domestic enterprises, Singapore turned to an export-oriented growth strategy, with foreign direct investment (FDI) seen as the means to generate the much-needed exports. To attract FDI, the government put in place measures to enhance the investment climate, including a variety of tax concessions and fiscal incentives that helped to create a low-cost and labor-intensive manufacturing sector and alleviated the unemployment situation.

With booming world trade and investment flows, American and European firms seeking sites for offshore assembly plants began to see Singapore as a viable manufacturing venue because of its low labor costs and tariffs. Multinational companies such as SGS, Texas Instruments, and Thomson eventually chose to set up their transistor assembly plants in Singapore, producing components that were mostly shipped back to their parent companies in the United States. As low-tech assembly work took off, capital-intensive industries also grew—Singapore soon became the largest petroleum refining center in Asia. By the late 1970s, there were several global petroleum companies—including Shell and British Petroleum—that had based their refinery operations in the island nation.

However, the disruptive effects of two oil shocks in 1973 and 1979 plunged the economy into recession. To make matters worse, Singapore's cost advantage in manufacturing was being eroded. Although the high unemployment rate of the 1960s had disappeared, real wages grew faster than labor productivity in Singapore, with countries such as Malaysia and Thailand emerging as competing FDI destinations with favorable offers of low-cost labor. In the face of stiffening cost competition, the Singapore government knew that the "low-wage, low-cost manufacturing" formula had to make way for higher-value manufacturing. In the words of Singapore's Permanent Secretary for the Information, Communications and Arts Ministry, Dr Tan Chin Nam: "It was recognised that we had to move from labour-intensive to capital-intensive, mechanisation and automation, and therefore higher wages. We cannot survive on cheap labour. Computerisation was to help us reduce manpower."[3]

Computerization was slowly gaining traction as a means to greater productivity and economic transformation. While the government was unsure about IT's full potential, they were willing to explore further and go beyond the two mainframes housed in two government agencies.

Beginnings of computerization (1981–85)
In 1980, the government set up a committee for national computerization to explore the potential of this new high-tech tool. Following their study, Singapore's first IT master plan came to be. The committee proposed a five-year "National Computerisation Plan" to look into three areas: the computerization of the civil service, the development of Singapore's computer industry, and growing a pool of computer professionals. The National Computer Board (NCB) was set up in 1981 to drive this plan.

One of NCB's first projects was to lead the Civil Service Computerisation Programme (CSCP) (see Table 1). By 1985, computer systems and software had been installed and shown to be able to enhance the government's overall efficiency and productivity.

Connecting the dots (1986–91)
In 1985, Singapore found itself mired in a severe global recession. Low oil prices worldwide affected its shipbuilding facilities, which made up 25 percent of its manufacturing sector. The rapid decline in the US growth rate, from 8 percent in 1984 to 2.3 percent in 1985, further hurt Singapore's export-led growth strategy. The computer peripherals and electronics sector in particular—a major part of Singapore's trade with the United States—faced temporary over-capacity and a slump of its own. Closer to home, low and falling commodity prices severely reduced the export earnings of the Association of Southeast Asian Nations (ASEAN), which in turn slowed the growth of those nations and, consequently, Singapore's trade and tourism with them.

Without doubt, Singapore needed to find new areas for growth and development. One critical challenge it faced had to do with its declining competitiveness as wage costs rocketed. In the five years after a wage increase policy was introduced in 1979,[4] labor costs had risen twice as fast as productivity. Beyond that, investment was not going into productive machinery or equipment but was being channeled into construction projects, where supply eventually outstripped demand in the slowing economy.[5]

Around this time, a national Economic Committee was established to review the weaknesses in Singapore's economy.[6] From this period of national economic restructuring, the next five-year National IT Plan (see Table 1) was launched in 1986. This plan was a response to the slowing manufacturing industry. Its two primary objectives were to develop a strong export-oriented IT industry and to exploit IT to improve productivity and competitiveness in every sector of the economy.

As part of the efforts to remodel the Singapore economy, the National IT Plan looked at how the different computer systems in the private and public sectors could be linked to boost productivity. To illustrate this idea of a network of computers, the TradeNet system for the trade and the logistics industry was introduced in 1989 (see Box 1). With IT enabling simpler and speedy processes, Singapore's status as a choice port of call was enhanced.

Box 1: Networked computers: TradeNet and TradeXchange

TradeNet
TradeNet is the world's first nationwide electronic trade network that integrates import, export, and transshipment documentation processing procedures. Introduced in 1989, the platform slashed the cost and turnaround time for the preparation, submission, and processing of trade and shipping documents from two days to 15 minutes. Less than three years after its launch, estimated savings from TradeNet amounted to some S$1.6 billion a year. A Web-based TradeNet was launched in 1998 with the advent of the Internet. Since 1989, the processing time has been reduced from 15 minutes to less than a minute, and the 3 to 35 sets of documents required for trade declarations was reduced to just one. Freight forwarders have estimated that they save 20 to 35 percent of the cost of handling trade documentation.

TradeXchange
Further enhancements made to this electronic platform led to TradeXchange. Launched in October 2007, TradeXchange is the latest national IT platform for the trade and logistics community. This neutral and secure trade platform offers a single electronic window for integrated workflow, submissions, and enquiries to the sea ports, airports, maritime authorities, and customs and controlling agencies. Users can also enjoy end-to-end services, such as e-procurement and freight management, offered by value-added service providers.

The next lap (1992–99)

In November 1991, under Prime Minister Mr Goh Chok Tong's leadership, a new national development plan, The Next Lap, was launched. The third IT master plan—Intelligent Island 2000 (IT2000) (see Table 1)—was launched with a vision to transform Singapore into an intelligent island and a global IT hub. The need for more research and development (R&D) work became apparent during this period as Singapore realized that such higher value-added activities could contribute to its economic competitiveness. In the same year, the government set up the National Science & Technology Board to drive this area.[7]

This R&D spirit was evident in IT2000, which sought ways to enable everyone to access IT and its related services. IT2000 unveiled a vision of a national information infrastructure (NII), which was to interconnect computers in virtually every home, office, school, and factory. The infrastructure would enable knowledge and information-intensive services to be provided from anywhere. What was unexpected, however, was the rise of the Internet in 1994. When IT2000 was launched in 1992, the Internet was virtually unheard of. The nationwide photovideotext service, called Teleview, was introduced in 1990.[8] It was to be the platform for IT2000 to deliver its NII vision, with its informational and transactional capabilities. The experiment was short-lived once the Internet took off in 1994. As the local precursor to the Internet, however, Teleview served to raise the awareness and value of being able to access information virtually anywhere. It enabled the government to recognize early enough the importance of broadband access. In June 1998, it embarked on the "SingaporeONE (One Network for Everyone)" program, which sought to put in place a nationwide broadband network.

SingaporeONE foresaw the importance of the broadband era and its transformational impact on the economy, and on the way people "live, work and play." However, the challenges were enormous, especially for the industry to handle alone. With only 10,000 broadband subscribers in the first year of its launch, high infrastructure costs, and the lack of compelling broadband content, the program needed a strong impetus. The government decided to take the necessary steps to attract investment for a pervasive and high-quality infrastructure. Only with that in place could the industry have a "product" with which to develop a broadband market. To further expedite the market's development, the government brought forward the full liberalization of the telecommunications market in April 2000. The regulatory framework for the liberalized telecommunications market called for open access terms for broadband interconnection. It also facilitated competition development, which led to eventual price drops in broadband access. By early 2001, more than 100,000 subscribers were on SingaporeONE. Prices have remained competitive and access speeds continue to climb. With increasing speed and affordability, more than 70 percent of households had broadband subscriptions by July 2007, and there has been a growing take-up of higher-speed access plans (see Figure 2).

In mid-1997, a major financial crisis swept across Asia. The drastic devaluation of the Thai baht ignited a currency crash that hit Asian economies including Korea, Rep. (Korea), Indonesia, Malaysia, and the Philippines. Given Singapore's reliance on the Southeast Asian hinterland, its export markets across Asia shrank as much as 30 percent, triggering a 0.7 percent contraction of its economy in the latter half of 1998. The unemployment rate also more than doubled from end-1997 to end-1998.

The situation prompted the government to review Singapore's economic model. Although its financial system survived the financial crisis, the primary concern for the government thereafter was the threat of economic stagnation. An Economic Review Committee was convened to review Singapore's development strategy. One of the recommendations of the committee was to diversify Singapore's economy, to reduce its reliance on manufacturing and finance. Thus it proposed new clusters to grow, such as private banking, pharmaceuticals, and new areas of manufacturing, while revamping established areas such as trading, logistics, ICT, and tourism. Such diversification and specialization aimed to inject dynamism and responsiveness into Singapore's economy, to ensure its continued growth and relevance in the world economy.

Changing with the times (2000–06)

Given the late-1990s trend of convergence in telecommunications, computers, and content, the NCB was merged with the Telecommunication Authority of Singapore, the telecommunication regulator, in 1999 to form the Infocomm Development Authority (IDA).

The objective then was to have a single agency responsible for the planning, policy formulation, regulation, and industry development of the IT and telecommunication sectors. At this time, confidence in the ICT sector was high. Going electronic or "e" was the buzzword. When the next ICT master plan, "Infocomm21" (see Table 1), was launched in 2000, its vision was to develop a thriving e-economy and a pervasive and ICT-savvy e-society. This was also the era of putting the "dot-com" in as many spheres of life as possible. The public and private sectors and civil society started putting as many services as possible online, and companies were encouraged to go into e-commerce.

With the onset of the dot-com bust in 2002, the outlook for ICT became more subdued. Infocomm21 was reviewed, and a new chapter of ICT development began. "Connected Singapore" (see Table 1), introduced in 2003, was the result of a revisioning exercise of Infocomm21 to fine-tune the plan following the dot-com bust. During this time the government held its ICT budget steady, helping to inject confidence into the ICT industry.

Present

In June 2006, the Intelligent Nation 2015 (iN2015, pronounced "in-twenty-fifteen") master plan was unveiled. Input from the private and public sectors was sought in the formulation of this sixth ICT master plan that will enhance Singapore's overall competitiveness in the next decade. Some 600 business leaders and senior executives were involved, from conceptualization to inception of iN2015. The result was a comprehensive master plan emphasizing the creation and usage of innovative ICT applications in seven key economic sectors (including the new growth area of digital media), as a means to boost the country's overall competitiveness. This in turn called for strengthening the building blocks of a digital economy: ICT infrastructure, workforce, and local ICT enterprises. In infrastructure, one key component of iN2015 focuses on putting in place an ultra-high-speed broadband network of the future, along with wireless access everywhere so that businesses and individuals can always stay connected to the global information grid.

iN2015's workforce development efforts include developing, attracting, and retaining ICT talent in Singapore. One area of focus is to groom a pool of globally competitive ICT professionals who can combine breadth of technology know-how with a good understanding of the business sectors so as to be able to propose ICT solutions that met real business needs and could transform these sectors. Beyond developing ICT professionals, iN2015 also seeks to raise the level of ICT skills of the general workforce so that they too can innovatively harness ICT to improve overall business productivity and competitiveness.

The importance of nurturing a vibrant ICT ecosystem comprising promising ICT local enterprises, leading multinational corporations, and innovative ICT technopreneurs and startups is also recognized, by including programs to boost the capabilities of the local ICT enterprises, grow ICT exports, and establish a brand identity. Infocomm Singapore, developed to serve as a unified brand for Made-by-Singapore ICT products and solutions, was launched in early 2007 to help local ICT enterprises gain mindshare in the highly competitive global ICT market. A virtual storefront in the form of an industry portal, which provides a one-stop directory listing and capabilities' maps of local companies, has also been set up for companies to profile their offerings.

As the ICT environment is fast-changing, iN2015 is intended to be a living and evolving master plan that will be further reviewed, taking into account the technological and local and global market developments and feedback from the industry, to ensure its continued relevance.

Singapore's e-government experience

E-government master plans were largely formulated in tandem with Singapore's national ICT master plans. While the themes of the national ICT master plans were aimed at transforming the industry and society, the various e-government ICT master plans focused on setting out the key thrusts and strategies for transforming the government sector (Table 1).

Civil Service Computerisation Programme (1980–99)

Computerization of the civil service was one of three focus areas in the first National Computerisation Plan. Armed with the understanding of the needs of various ministries, the CSCP was launched with a view to increase efficiency in the public sector. One notable aspect of the CSCP was the automation of the government's internal operations, which in turn helped to cut down paperwork significantly. In this regard, by 1985, 59 applications systems had been introduced in government departments. The number of computer professionals in Singapore grew almost five times, from 850 in 1980 to some 4,000 by 1985. The number of mainframe and minicomputer installations also grew from 350 in 1982 to more than 2,000 in 1985.

The focus then evolved as the National IT Plan (1985–91) came about. This plan sought to transfer the new knowledge and expertise from the civil service to the private sector. By the early 1990s, the emphasis shifted toward the consolidation of computing resources, aligned with the IT2000 plan (1992–1999) to transform Singapore into an "intelligent island." The late 1990s saw the convergence of ICT and the rise of the Internet, which transformed the concept of service delivery. This paved the way for the launch of Singapore's e-Government Action Plan I.

Many government agencies have also leveraged ICT, not just to enhance productivity and efficiency in their operations but also to solve common urban growth problems and catalyze sectoral transformation (see Box 2).

e-Government Action Plan I (2000–03)

The e-Government Action Plan I (eGAP I) was launched in 2000, just as other countries were beginning to explore how governments can be organized to deliver e-services to people, businesses, and organizations. The three-year S$1.5 billion plan focused on creating a platform for all public agencies to work together for an efficient deployment of e-government services in Singapore. The intent was to put as many government services online as possible. eGAP I was also the first official government master plan that bore the "e" prefix, signaling the country's move into the e-generation.

From eGAP I, SingPass (Singapore personal access), a nationwide personal authentication framework for e-services, emerged. SingPass, introduced in 2003, allowed each Singapore resident to perform e-government transactions using a common user identity.[9] To date,

---

Box 2. Singapore's e-services

Singapore's ICT strategies have not been limited to enhancing government and business efficiency alone. IT solutions have also been devised and deployed to solve common urban growth problems (such as traffic congestion) and to catalyze sectoral transformation.

Electronic Library Management System

In 1995, the newly formed National Library Board (NLB) set high targets to double annual book loans and triple the number of visitors by 2003. With the existing manual system, however, an increase in load would have increased queuing time to over an hour. The NLB found a solution in radio-frequency identification (RFID) tags, a technology that was still very new when the first prototype RFID check-in and check-out system was deployed in 1998. Today, all public libraries in Singapore have installed the Electronic Library Management System (ELiMS). Borrowing queues have disappeared while loans and visitor numbers have significantly increased. Developing and deploying ELiMS saved the NLB about S$50 million a year, and made it unnecessary to hire extra staff to keep library queues below 5 minutes. ELiMS, the world's first, was patented in July 1999. Over the last 10 years, libraries in Macao, Korea, Australia, and New Zealand have implemented similar systems.

Electronic Road Pricing system

The Electronic Road Pricing (ERP) system, introduced in 1998, is an example of how technology was brought in to solve the perennial problem of traffic congestion. Road users, under this concept of "pay per use" for roads, paid more to use popular roads during peak hours. The ERP system was the first of its kind in the world, using RFID technology to detect and deduct from the pre-paid toll card in every vehicle. Prior to this, enforcement officers had to stand at gantries to look for cars that did not have the toll label displayed. Such ICT-enabled traffic management system, pioneered in Singapore, has since found its place in other metropolitan areas. For instance, the London Congestion Charge, introduced in February 2003, came about after British officials visited Singapore to study its road pricing system and used it as a reference for the London system.

Infocomm@SeaPort

Jointly managed by the IDA and the Maritime and Port Authority (MPA), the Infocomm@SeaPort program launched in September 2007 seeks to significantly enhance the capabilities and efficiencies of Singapore's ports and improve the port community infrastructure. One of the first projects is WISEPORT (WIreless-broadband-access for SEaPort), a mobile wireless broadband network within 15 kilometers from Singapore's southern coastline providing low cost, high bandwidth, and secure access. By 2008, all ships in Singapore can have access to mobile wireless broadband, allowing real-time and data-intensive communication between the ships and their customers and business partners. Activities that could previously be done only onshore can now be performed offshore as well, from regulatory filings to broadband communications and real-time access to navigational data.

some 1,600 e-government services have been rolled out. More than 98 percent of government services are now "always-on" and available to Singaporeans online via the e-citizen portal (www.ecitizen.gov.sg).

eGAP II (2003–06)

The success of eGAP I set the stage for a second program, eGAP II, in 2003. With the majority of government services already online, eGAP II looked into improving the quality of such services. The aim was to bring e-government services to an even higher and more responsive level for closer citizen-government interaction by making services more user-friendly. With a fresh budget of S$1.3 billion, eGAP II aimed to develop Singapore into a leading e-government to better serve the nation in the digital economy.

With eGAP II, 15 cross-agency integrated e-services were also introduced, including:

- a one-stop government bills payment center to enable customers to make online payments for bills and fines;

- a one-stop job portal for online application for all government jobs; and

- EnterpriseOne Portal to provide businesses with relevant government information and services.

The annual e-government customer perception survey conducted in February 2007 showed that 89 percent of Singaporeans who needed to transact business with the Singapore government did so through electronic means, either on their own or with help, at least once in the past 12 months. And for those who did, almost 9 in 10 were satisfied with the service.

iGov2010 (2006–10)

The third e-government plan, iGov2010, was launched in June 2006 and is a key component of iN2015. iGov2010 is a longer-term program with a budget of S$2 billion. With government services well established online, the focus for iGov2010 is to integrate the government internally, including the integration of processes, systems, and information. The ultimate aim is to have "one view of our customer" so as to be able to serve the public and businesses more holistically. The guiding principle here is to "start with the user in mind"; this means putting oneself in the user's shoes in order to anticipate what he needs when he transacts business with the government. To realize this aim, four strategic thrusts have been identified:

- Make government e-services more user-friendly so that more people will know how to use it.

- Give government websites a "cooler" image; this includes packing in videos and interactive content for public sector portals.

- Integrate the back-end processes such as human resources and finance to improve business operations and to streamline common functions. This would also entail giving out one identification number—that is, a Unique Establishment Identifier (UEI)—for all companies to identify themselves across public agencies.

- Award more public-sector ICT projects based on a "build-operate-maintain" business model. Vendors would be paid according to the number of people using the system. The first such project would be the standard operating environment (SOE) to provide a common desktop and networking platform for some 60,000 civil servants.[10]

Seven years after launching the first e-government plan, the way public services are delivered has been transformed. Where it used to be paper forms, lines, and service during office hours only, citizens and businesses alike can now transact online for almost any public service anytime. To facilitate the sharing of Singapore's e-government experience with foreign nations, the e-Government Leadership Centre was set up in 2006 at the National University of Singapore (NUS) together with the Institute of Systems Science (ISS) and the Lee Kuan Yew School of Public Policy.

Singapore's education experience

Education is of high importance to the Singapore government. Recognizing how ICT can help improve the quality of education, the government has systematically introduced ICT technologies in the education sector since the 1990s.[11]

Ministry of Education's IT master plans (1997–2002, 2002–08)

The Masterplan for IT in Education was launched in 1997 with the goal of equipping schools with personal computers and computer networks, training teachers in IT and its use in teaching and preparing lessons, and changing mindsets for the way IT was used in the schools' instructional programs. Some goals achieved under this first plan were:

- training of in-service teachers from primary and secondary schools in the relevant IT skills and integrating IT into the curriculum;

- providing a central clearing-house service to source, review, and recommend software titles and Internet sites for schools; and

- converting existing classrooms into computer laboratories and IT learning resource corners.

More than 70 percent of the pupils surveyed at all levels agreed that the use of IT increases their knowledge, and more than 80 percent of the pupils surveyed at all levels agreed that the use of IT makes lessons interesting.[12]

With the foundation laid, the Masterplan II for ICT in Education (mp2) was implemented in July 2002. It continued to provide the overall direction on how schools can harness the possibilities offered by ICT for learning. The approach is to integrate key education components such as curriculum, assessment, instruction, professional development, and pupil learning using IT, with the focus on interaction among these components. Key priorities include the setting of baseline ICT standards for pupils' learning experiences to ensure that all schools achieve at least a rudimentary level of ICT use; supporting schools that are ready to achieve higher levels of ICT use in education, so that those schools can introduce more recognition schemes; and conducting further research on developing and prototyping pedagogical models.

Also in line with mp2 is the FutureSchools@Singapore effort, one of the education initiatives under iN2015. This effort aims to harness ICT effectively for engaged learning and to keep Singapore's education system and programs relevant in preparing students for the future. The emphasis will be on leveraging state-of-art technologies and innovative school designs to enable innovative curricula, pedagogies, and assessment programs for engaged learning and efficient administrative practices. ICT tools such as immersive virtual environments and educational games will be used to enhance learning. In addition, the schools will undertake studies on the impact of ICT use on students' cognitive, emotional, and social development. The learning points, ideas, programs, and technologies from these studies will then be shared with other schools.

The first phase of FutureSchools@Singapore involving five schools was announced in May 2007. These schools will push for innovative transformation of the education experience in Singapore, and lead the way for other schools in providing possible models for the seamless and pervasive integration of ICT into the curriculum for engaged learning in schools. Early response is favorable, as evidenced by the large number of applications of parents for their children to attend the first two primary schools under this program in August 2007.

Learning points from the ICT journey so far

As Singapore continues its journey and prepares itself for the future, there are some learning points to share:

- *Importance of political will and support*
Projects under the first master plan were able to take off quickly because of the government's belief in and commitment to computerization. The setting up of a central committee to manage resources and push for computerization was also useful. It created the NCB and paved the way for the concept of a central government Chief Information Officer, a function still filled by the IDA.

    Strong political will and support continue today, where large amounts of funding and resources are committed for ICT development. The country's top political leaders not only make public statements about the importance of ICT for Singapore, they also chair national-level committees to drive countrywide ICT projects. Singapore's Minister Mentor Lee Kuan Yew has said "The key is to get your people so completely familiar [with IT] as they grow up so that it becomes part of their nature. Countries with that capability will do better than those without."[13]

- *Close alignment with the larger national plans*
The national ICT master plans are formulated in such a way that they are closely aligned with the needs of the economy and society, and are in step with the general developments and trends of ICT around the world. In turn, the e-government ICT master plans were developed and implemented in tandem in order to complement and build upon the national ICT master plans.

    In close alignment with national interests and clear goals in mind, there is direction and focus for different government ministries and agencies to work together to achieve the desired outcomes. For instance, the success of TradeNet was the result of high-level multi-agency cooperation amongst 20 different government agencies involved in the processing of trade documents, working together to streamline their requirements.

- *Need for good governance*
The government considered that having a plan to computerize was not enough; there has to be a central agency to implement the plan and be accountable for the outcome. Having a central agency will also give the necessary organizational impetus to get the plan going. The NCB was set up for this purpose. With convergence of IT and telecommunications, two agencies were merged to become the single agency with responsibility for these sectors.

    The approach of setting up committees consisting of industry leaders and government officers is an integral part of Singapore's policy formulation process. This approach—of a public-private-people partnership—has been particularly important in the formulation and implementation of the subsequent master plans as their scope was increasingly extended to cover the wider economy.

- *Preparing the workforce and people*
Soon after Singapore embarked on its first computerization plan, it found that skilled workers were not readily available to support its efforts. As there were not enough computer science graduates at that time, an in-house training program was quickly drawn up by the NCB to convert young graduates from other disciplines into computer professionals. The local workforce shortfall was also supplemented with experienced professionals from abroad. That early episode of insufficient workforce has since served as a cautionary tale for Singapore, so that the country now always ensures that talent development remains a priority.

User training is just as important. The government was also certain that knowledge of ICT and its benefits should not be the preserve of a few tech-trained professionals. It realized that an IT-savvy population would complete the virtuous cycle of ICT innovation and usage. Programs were thus created to enable users: for instance, students and non-IT workers both needed to understand the value of new technology and its adoption.

- *Constant review and renewal*
The process of constant review and renewal is a fundamental part of the workings of the Singapore government. Plans are implemented in accordance with the strategic direction set; the progress and milestones reached are monitored and reviewed for further improvements where necessary, taking into account external developments and changes. Preparation for the next ICT master plan usually begins well before the present one is due to complete. An example is Connected Singapore, the ICT master plan covering the period 2003–2006. Work for the next master plan (iN2015) started in early 2005. At that time, ICT had increasingly become a national priority for many countries, with many launching extensive ICT master plans. iN2015 was the culmination of a year-long preparatory work with the public and private sectors.

Getting ready for the next wave

The importance of ICT—both as a strategic enabler to enhance the competitiveness of Singapore's economy and as an industry in itself—is clear. There are tremendous opportunities for ICT-enabled growth in the global economy. There are also strong challenges. Today, an increasing number of countries recognize the importance of ICT and are leveraging it to boost their economic might. Many developing economies are fast catching up on the provision of quality infrastructures. The pressure on Singapore to remain attractive and competitive as a business and commercial hub is mounting. In particular, Singapore faces strong challenges in maintaining its efficiency premium.

Looking ahead, the future of the global economy will be driven by ideas and talent. To keep pace, and to exploit such opportunities for growth, Singapore is stepping up its drive for innovation and R&D. In addition to launching the S$7.5 billion Science & Technology 2010 Plan, the government set up the National Research Foundation in January 2006. The Foundation comes with an assured funding of S$5 billion for the next five years, to turn R&D into a significant driver for the Singapore economy. Among the Foundation's three areas of strategic focus,[14] the Interactive & Digital Media one is especially important as Singapore seeks avenues to strengthen its ICT capabilities. It will benefit not only the ICT and media sectors, but also other areas such as education and health care. In those sectors, ICT can be integrated holistically to create new and creative products and services in a fast-changing world.

The Singapore government will also continue to invest in its economic infrastructure, and is taking concrete steps to upgrade its network infrastructure to meet the demands of tomorrow. A key initiative under iN2015 is the development and deployment of a Next Generation National Infocomm Infrastructure network, including a new ultra-high-speed network linking every home and office, and a wireless broadband network that allows Singaporeans to stay connected even while on the go. This infrastructure and the various sectoral ICT-enabled transformation initiatives under iN2015 are preparing Singapore for the future.

Indeed, as Singapore enters a new phase of development in the digital age, new strategies are being explored, reviewed, and deployed. Innovation-driven growth strategies will come to the fore and inspire new engines of growth. When one recalls that Singapore's achievements to date were sparked by just two mainframe computers and a leap of faith 26 years ago, the possibilities and opportunities for the country in harnessing the power of ICT will likely be exciting and limitless.

Notes

1 Singapore was ranked first in Accenture's 2007 study on "Leadership in Customer Service" and second in Brown University's Global e-Government 2007.

2 Minister's Foreword in the report by the iN2015 Steering Committee, IDA 2006.

3 Interviews in Reutens 2006, p. 12.

4 The wage increase policy was introduced with the aim of forcing the technology employed in Singapore's factories to shift up-market. The logic was that employers would no longer find it as profitable to produce low-wage, low-value products and so switch to the manufacture of higher-wage, higher-value products. A key element of the policy was a belief that manufacturers would not relocate all operations to other lower-cost countries, but would recognize enough value in Singapore's infrastructure, labor force, and pro-business government to stay in the country. Total impact on wages ranged between 14 and 20 percent.

5 Investment in productive machinery or equipment actually declined when measured as a proportion of GDP.

6 The Economic Committee was appointed by the Singapore government in 1985 to examine the longer-term problems and prospects of the national economy, identify new growth areas, and define new strategies for promoting growth. The Committee found that the recession could not be brushed aside as a cyclical difficulty that would eventually disappear by itself. Instead, the country had to change its policies and identify new growth areas, not only to overcome the recession, but also to set the correct direction for the longer term growth of Singapore.

7 The National Science & Technology Board was renamed the Agency for Science, Technology and Research in 2002 with the new mission to foster world-class scientific research and talent for a vibrant knowledge-based Singapore.

8 Teleview is often compared with an online videotext service in France called Minitel that was launched in 1982 by France Telecom. Minitel users could make online purchases and train reservations, check stock prices, search the telephone directory, and chat in a way similar to Internet chatting today.

9 By the time eGAP II was unveiled, there were over 7.9 million SingPass transactions annually from a user base of more than 800,000 SingPass holders.

10 The SOE project aims to standardize the desktop, messaging, and network environment for the public sector. When implemented, it will establish a robust and agile government ICT infrastructure. Operational efficiency should also be enhanced as agencies will share a common infrastructure, enabling them to work seamlessly as One Government. The estimated value of this tender is S$1.5 billion.

11 There are approximately 26,400 teachers and 532,000 students in 355 primary and secondary schools, junior colleges, and centralized institutes in Singapore. Another 130,000 learners attend full-time programs in 12 post-secondary educational institutes. There are three government-funded universities in Singapore: the National University of Singapore, Nanyang Technological University, and Singapore Management University. See MOE 2005.

12 See MOE; the numbers are from 2005.

13 Minister Mentor's speech at the second Russia-Singapore Forum, March 6, 2007.

14 The other two areas of focus are Environmental & Water Technologies and Biomedical Sciences.

References

Accenture. 2007. *2007 Leadership in Customer Service: Delivering on the Promise. Government Executive Series.* Available at http://nstore.accenture.com/acn_com/PDF/2007LCSDelivPromiseFinal.pdf.

Brown University. 2007. *Global e-Government 2007.* Report. Providence, RI: Brown University. Available at http://www.insidepolitics.org/egovt07int.pdf.

Channel NewsAsia. 2003. Final Economic Review Committee Report and Recommendations. Press release; "New Challenges, Fresh Goals: Towards a Dynamic Global City." February 6. Available at www.mti.gov.sg.

IDA (Infocomm Development Authority). Available at http//www.ida.gov.sg.

———. 2006. "Foreword." Report by the iN2015 Steering Committee. Singapore: IDA. Available at http//www.ida.gov.sg.

MOE (Ministry of Education). IT in Education Masterplans. Available at http://www.moe.gov.sg/edumall/mp2/mp2.htm.

———. 2001. *The Evaluation of Implementation of Masterplan for IT in Education Report (MPITE Evaluation Report) 2001.* Singapore: MOE.

MTI (Ministry of Trade and Industry). Science and Technology Plan 2010. Available at http://app.mti.gov.sg/default.asp?id=148&articleID=2461.

———. "The Singapore Economy: New Directions." Report of the Economic Committee. Available at http://app.mti.gov.sg/data/pages/885/doc/econ.pdf.

———. "Singapore's Overall Economic History." Available at http://app.mti.gov.sg/default.asp?id=545.

National Library Website: http://infopedia.nlb.gov.sg/articles/SIP_263_2005-01-13.html.

Reutens, L. 2006. *The Big Switch.* Book in set of four books *Innovationation: 25 Years of Infocomm in Singapore.* Singapore: IDA.

Singapore e-government plans. Available at http://www.igov.gov.sg/Strategic_Plans/?indexar=2.

The Straits Times. 2007. "Asian Financial Crisis: 10 Years On: The Day the Economies Went into Meltdown." July 1.

CHAPTER 2.2

Qatar: Leveraging Technology to Create a Knowledge-Based Economy in the Middle East

HESSA AL-JABER, ictQATAR

SOUMITRA DUTTA, INSEAD

> Our mission is to create an advanced information and communication technologies (ICT) community where the community at large can use ICT to improve the quality of their lives and actively contribute to the social and economic development of Qatar.
>
> —The Heir Apparent His Highness Sheikh Tamim Bin Hamad Al-Thani, Chairman, ictQATAR, Inaugural Launch Speech, May 2005

A revolution is slowly transforming Qatar's small, vibrant economy of less than a million people. ICT is propelling the country to greater progress and prosperity. And although Qatar has been a late entrant here, having made its first serious moves only in 2005, its leadership is convinced that ICT can bring far-reaching changes. That has been the cornerstone of Qatar's unfolding technology revolution.

These changes have been dovetailed with ongoing economic reforms. The aim is, through ICT, to create a core engine for a competitive economy, universalize access to social services, and create a knowledge-based online society. There are also hopes that ICT will have a technology multiplier effect in all sectors, extend the reach of political reforms, and help Qatar become a fully developed nation.

The effect of changes is already being felt. In a commendable feat, Qatar is ranked 32nd in the 2007–2008 Networked Readiness Index (NRI). With a full-fledged national plan in place, initiatives are taking place on many fronts: policy reforms; steps with regard to security concerns; ICT initiatives in health care, education, e-government, and infrastructure; and deregulation in the telecommunications sector. Qatar also boasts some of the highest penetration rates in telecommunications (both fixed line and mobile) and Internet in the region (see Figure 1).

Typically, with a small population and high per capita income at over US$62,000, many of these changes would be easy to make. But several challenges and roadblocks have had to be overcome over the last few years, including an acute shortage of trained workers, social norms and misconceptions about technology, and inter-ministerial and agency coordination issues. However, these have not proven serious deterrents. Ultimately, strong leadership and courage of conviction are pushing the nation further up the technology roadmap.

The purpose of this chapter is to present an overview of Qatar's transformation into a knowledge economy and a flag-bearer of technology-driven excellence in the entire region. The following section provides a broad overview of the vision and the framework of

---

The authors gratefully acknowledge the help of George Sakaria and Martin Kralik in the preparation of this chapter.

Figure 1: Fixed line, mobile, and Internet penetration rates, 2006 (percent)

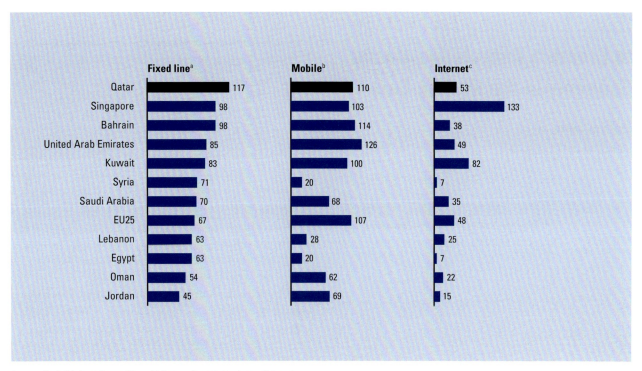

Source: Arab Advisors Group, Pyramid Research, operators' annual reports.
a *Fixed line penetration* is the total fixed residential lines divided by the number of households.
b *Mobile penetration* is the total reported mobile lines divided by population.
c *Internet penetration* is the total Internet accounts (dial up and broadband) divided by the number of households.

ICT-enabled change in Qatar. Next, key strategic initiatives in Qatar's ICT agenda are described, including efforts in e-education, cyber-security, e-government, and e-health. The following sections outline the key implementation hurdles faced by Qatar and identify best practices and lessons for other nations engaged in similar processes of change. The concluding section lists some future directions in the country's transformation into a competitive knowledge economy of the 21st century.

A national vision and framework

ICT is slated to create the core engine of an information-based economy, universalize access to social services, and create a knowledge-based online society. Building technology literacy and capability among the people of Qatar will be crucial in view of overcoming the country's shortage of skilled manpower. In addition, technology is envisaged to produce transformational effects across all sectors of the national economy, facilitate ongoing social and political reforms, and firmly establish Qatar as a developed nation.

Therefore, its ICT strategy and master plan is in tandem with the National Vision of Qatar, which seeks to adhere to principles of equality, democracy, and human development. While guided by international best practices, however, the strategy is tailored to the country's unique circumstances and requirements. The underlying philosophy is that technology and infrastructure should not be ends by themselves, but rather should be facilitators for economic and social gains.

The first major step on this journey was accomplished when, by a Royal Decree in 2004, Qatar established the Supreme Council of ICT (ictQATAR) with a mandate as both regulator and enabler of the ICT sector. In May 2005, its vision and mission was unveiled, and thereafter ictQATAR embarked on its plan of fulfilling the key objectives of the country's ICT strategy. Guided by a clear, authoritative mandate, ictQATAR serves as regulator and champion of the ICT sector. Its strength in leading, supporting, and coordinating ICT efforts is rooted in three design characteristics that are important to establishing a robust ICT implementation organization:

- ictQATAR has strong political champions. As ICT tends to involve launching programs across multiple sectors and working through multiple ministries, resistance to change can be high and clear leadership is essential to revamping departmental power bases and entrenched bureaucracy. Because of this resistance, an ICT organization requires the backing of senior political leadership to visibly champion ICT and to give the implementation organization real authority to make change happen. Sheikh Tammim Bin Hamad Al Thani, the Heir Apparent of Qatar and a strong advocate of ICT in the nation, is the Chairman of ictQATAR.

Figure 2: Qatar's long-term vision, socioeconomic development targets, and sector-specific initiatives as the basis for ICT strategy and master plan

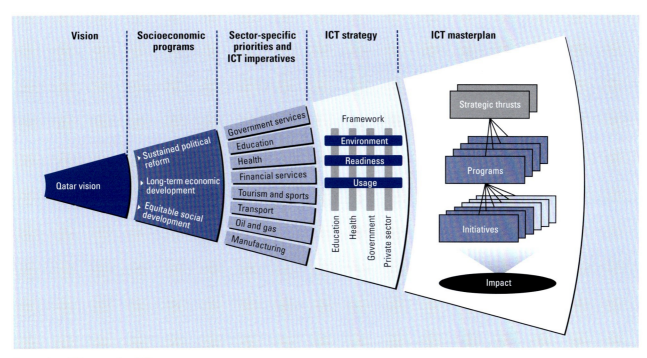

Source: Qatar ICT master plan, 2005.

- ictQATAR is a single entity with multiple stakeholders. Its effectiveness springs from its ability to achieve coherent policy development and implementation with involvement of key ICT stakeholders. ictQATAR has relied on collaboration with various government bodies that recognize the effectiveness of ICT programs to better serve their constituents and employees.

- ictQATAR has an independent budget. ICT efforts require sizeable financial investment and an ongoing commitment of resources to promote usage and adoption. In return for its independent budget for programs, ictQATAR has clear performance metrics so policymakers can measure what gains and successes are achieved for their substantial investment.

Figure 2 illustrates the integrated approach adopted by Qatar to achieve its long-term vision. Each of the components plays a complementary and indispensable role. From the start, ictQATAR began engaging in a focused dialogue with institutions in the public and private sectors that have direct input, contribution, and influence on the development of ICT in Qatar.

Qatar's ICT plan extends beyond the projected upgrading of the sector's physical infrastructure into nine national programs. It was understood that upgrading this infrastructure, although critical to success, is ineffective unless citizens and businesses have access and incentive to utilize it. Therefore, the country built its ICT national programs on the environment, readiness, and usage (ERU) framework.[1] The elements of this framework range from setting the *right environment* (through establishing conducive market conditions, appropriate policies, essential infrastructure) and *increasing readiness* of citizens, businesses, and government (by building awareness, trust, skills, and access), to providing the applications that will *drive adoption and increase usage* (e.g., applications and content for specific sectors such as e-health and e-education).

Figures 3 and 4 provide details on the key components of Qatar's master plan for ICT-enabled change. The national plans (see Figure 3) include: developing state-of-the-art infrastructure; innovation and capability-building; developing the necessary regulatory and legal framework; ensuring information safety and security; having an inclusive society; and focusing on information technology in the areas of education, health, government, and business. With this framework in place, and to achieve its broad objectives, ictQATAR has set in process a series of change initiatives as described in the following section.

Figure 4 presents a summary of the key aspects considered within the overall framework for deciding Qatar's ICT strategy. The top row captures elements of the different subdimensions of the environment for ICT in the state of Qatar—market, political, and infrastructure. The next two rows identify elements of the readiness and the adoption of ICT by the three main actors in the economy—citizens, businesses, and the government. The

Figure 3: Nine programs in the ictQATAR master plan

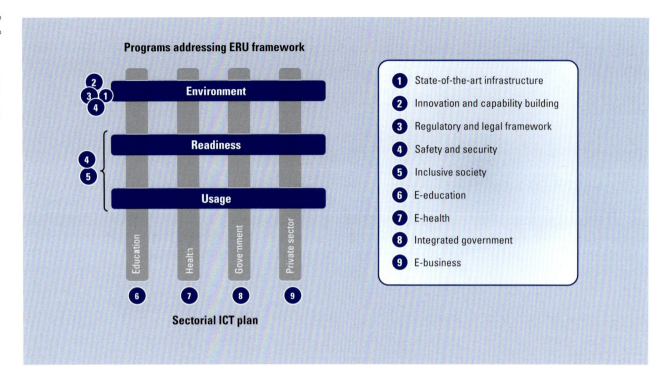

last row lists aspects of the impact of the adoption of ICT on the above three actors. Cumulatively, Figure 4 captures all key aspects of ICT readiness, adoption, and impact in Qatar.

Key initiatives

ictQatar introduced key initiatives addressing all three elements of the ERU framework: environment, readiness, and usage. Several of the most crucial are discussed in this section.

Telecommunications liberalization
ictQATAR moved almost immediately to liberalize the telecommunications sector. Developing and implementing a transparent process to open the market to competition was seen as critical for providing better value for consumers and for the rapid development of advanced products and services needed to support a growing, diverse economy. Three main objectives have driven Qatar's telecommunications liberalization:

- to foster an efficient telecommunications sector to benefit society,
- to create a showcase for successful sector reform, and
- to provide a sustainable business environment.

The process of telecommunications liberalization has been divided into two phases: first, World Trade Organization–mandated telecommunications services and infrastructure deregulation; and second, deregulation in areas such as e-commerce and e-legislation. The Telecommunications Law of 2006 enhanced existing laws and gave the regulatory body within ictQATAR the ability to issue licenses and to sanction additional spectrum. The Regulatory Authority was also given powers in competition analysis, the power to declare the incumbent provider, Qatar Telecom (Qtel), to be dominant, and the power to choose a second operator in the mobile and fixed-line segments of the market.

Because the size of the national market in the foreseeable future is unlikely to sustain more than two fixed and mobile infrastructure networks, ictQATAR began the liberalization process by offering one additional mobile license and one additional fixed license to new operators to compete with Qtel. The awarding of these licenses includes the possibility that an alternative infrastructure to Qtel's will be created. ictQATAR intends to review the market development of the sector by 2010. The review will include an assessment of the number of operators the market can sustain, as well as technological developments such as Mobile WiMAX and 4G, among others.

In addition to licensing, ictQATAR is developing a full regulatory framework that will include dominance designation and conditions, interconnection and access rules, tariff policy, spectrum and number policies, con-

Figure 4: Environment, readiness, and usage in the framework of ICT foundational requirements

ENVIRONMENT

Market
- Educational infrastructure
- Level of IT skills
- Supporting industries
- Climate for innovation
- Cost of access

Political
- Level of political leadership
- Enabling nature of legal and regulatory environment for e-readiness

Infrastructural
- Infrastructure availability
- Infrastructure quality

READINESS

Citizen
- Measures of barriers to uptake (awareness, trust, skills, cost)
- Penetration of access devices

Business
- Measures of barriers to uptake (awareness, trust, skills, cost)
- Penetration of access devices

Government
- Awareness, leadership, strategies
- Level of coordination
- Systems readiness, back office integration, standardization

UPTAKE AND USE

Citizen
- Level of basic use
- Ubiquity/fairness of adoption
- Sophistication of use

Business
- Level of basic use (including publication)
- Ubiquity/fairness of adoption
- Sophistication of use

Government
- Level of basic use (including publication)
- Sophistication of use

IMPACT

Citizen
- Impact on commerce/spending
- Impact on behavior
- Impact on service offering
- Impact on working practices
- Impact on costs/efficiency

Business
- Impact on commerce/spending
- Impact on service offering: additional/enhanced services
- Impact on working practices
- Impact on costs/efficiency

Government
- Impact on commerce/spending
- Impact on working practices
- Impact on costs/efficiency

---

sumer protection, and dispute resolution. Other areas that will come under its focus will be electronic transactions legislation, the application of UNCITRAL principles, domain name procedures, and e-government processes.

Integrated e-government

Qatar's e-government journey began in 2003. The first-generation e-government program produced a variety of online services, including issuance of entry visas, birth certificates, and health cards; renewal of driving licenses; Islamic charity payments; and payments of traffic fines and utility bills. The program was a frontrunner among the Gulf States in the use of smart cards for authentication. The e-government organization was integrated into ictQATAR in 2005, along with many valuable lessons learned for the way forward (see the last two sections of this chapter on "Overcoming implementation challenges" and "Emerging best practices" for more details on the lessons learned).

Box 1: Qatar's telecommunications transformation: Major milestones

- 1987: Establishment of the Qatar Public Telecommunications Corporation
- 1998: Qatar Public Telecommunications Corporation rechristened Qatar Telecom (Qtel)
- 2002: Establishment of the Information Technology and Communications Committee
- 2004: The formation of the Supreme Council for Information Technology (ictQATAR)
- 2006: Promulgation of the Telecommunications Law providing the regulator the power to issue new licenses
- 2007: Vodafone Consortium selected as a second mobile operator in Qatar and process started for second Fixed Line Operator

A nationwide effort is now underway to use ICT to make government work even better for residents, citizens, and visitors. Qatar is committed to a customer-focused approach to running the government in all areas. Across ministries, councils, and authorities, the second-generation e-government initiative will result in an integrated, state-of-the-art government with reduced redundancies, increased transparency, and heightened efficiency.

Qatar's plan to connect people with the government will include a high level of readiness for ICT capabilities in public administration and e-government information and services to make life easier. A comprehensive reference model for ICT architecture and standards is ready to roll out across all government agencies—a significant step toward government-wide integration of ICT systems. And the government is launching Hukoomi, a one-stop portal for government information and services, including preexisting e-services and recently implemented e-services for the issuance of exit permits and business commercial registration. Hukoomi is a historic milestone —the first time ever that more than 50 entities across the government have come together online. Hukoomi will help businesses improve productivity and compete in the marketplace, and will improve convenience and satisfaction in the daily lives of everyone in the country.

The initial impact of these services has been very positive. Besides order-of-magnitude improvements in turnaround time for the issuance of permits and licenses, businesses and the public at large welcome the change in government interactions from one of unclear rules and indefinite waiting to one that is transparent and process-driven right from the first click.

Similar gains in efficiency and transparency are expected with the implementation of e-procurement, an initiative that will speed up excessive procurement cycles across all industries. And existing administrative processes, such as setting up a new business—which currently requires an array of approvals from different agencies— will be greatly streamlined and simplified via an online one-stop gateway. Behind the scenes, experts are busily designing a secure information superhighway that will interconnect all government entities and enable them to operate as one ecosystem, collaborating seamlessly in the delivery of public services. Riding on the information superhighway will be many shared capabilities, including a government data center and a government-wide human resources and finance resource planning system.

An innovative series of state-of-the-art e-government programs will be implemented over the next three years. The government has already short-listed 52 initiatives that include hundreds of online services to benefit citizens and households as well as businesses and government employees. Sixteen initiatives are currently in progress, and another 12 will be launched in the coming months.

On the ICT infrastructure development level, the implementation of new e-services has been supported by two strategic initiatives: the Broadband for All program and the establishing of a Government Data Center (GDC). The Broadband for All initiative has been rolled out in tandem with the Universal Access Fund. Its charter also envisaged the creation of wireless neighborhoods covered by high-speed wireless Internet access. The setting up of the GDC aims to provide a variety of core hosting and value-added services. These include knowledge management, data storage, and centralized data management services, as well as retrieval of business, personal education, and entertainment-related information.

Enterprise development and small- and medium-sized enterprises

Qatar has a well-developed ICT strategy to benefit small and medium-sized enterprises (SMEs). The plan was developed following exhaustive analysis of market conditions and valuable interaction with stakeholders across the business landscape. The initial focus of this strategy is on heightened awareness and education about the added value of ICT to SMEs. Following this education process is the provision of business resources, ICT applications, and SME development activities.

In the business sector, the new Enterprise Development work program includes 21 projects. These will be executed in two phases, which are to be completed by the end of 2010. The Business Resource program aims at improving enterprise ICT readiness through the promotion of a readily available ecosystem of business support services (accounting, consulting, IT-integration, and legal services) at subsidized rates. The Business Application program has identified specific applications that can serve as "lighthouse" projects. These have encompassed a whole spectrum of activities, including those targeting the more intangible business segments such as national heritage. The e-Souq, for example, aims to combine the national heritage of Qatar with a modern application of e-business—that is, an online presence of a sample of shops with the option to buy online.

Another linchpin of the Enterprise Development program, particularly during its first phase, is the SME e-Business Pilot. As part of this program, a pilot group of SMEs will be selected and guided through an 18-month program that has been designed to increase the participants' e-maturity. This will be achieved through training, joint provision of ICT-related services with a cluster of partner companies (e.g., IT-consulting and auditing), and the presence of seasoned IT coaches. The program's objective is to demonstrate tangible ICT benefits, address the prevalent concerns of business owners and managers, and use the experience to build sustainable support structures for SMEs. Crucially, this will foster the adoption of ICT in the business community, build internal knowledge on ICT-related issues in the SME sector, and feed a broad awareness campaign in the next phases of development.

E-health

The health-care sector has seen a concerted effort by the government to build not only state-of-the-art infrastructure but also strong institutions and frameworks that will act as catalysts in bringing the benefits of e-services in this vital sector to all segments of the Qatari society.

The key stakeholders in formulating a comprehensive national e-health strategy have included ictQATAR, Hamad Medical Corporation, and the National Health Authority. Work has already started in developing and promoting e-health cards. The electronic health record will provide patients and clinicians invaluable and rapid access to medical information. Clinicians will have rapid access to their patients' medical histories. They will receive test results in hours rather than days. Integrated and secure information systems will allow patients to schedule appointments, coordinate multiple caregivers, and consult with their health-care team—at any hour, from anywhere.

Subsequently, the focus will shift to providing online health-care services and information. Improvements in the health-care sector are augmented through organizational revamps. As e-health matures in the country, efforts are also made to beef up the online security and privacy of patients. Programs have also been put in place to share diagnostic files among various institutions.

E-education

Integral to Qatar's National Vision is the government's commitment to building a world-class educational system. Education is at the heart of the country's drive to improve economic competitiveness and quality of life for all those in Qatar. The e-education objective is to support an individualized and flexible learning environment through technology. A technology-rich learning community is envisaged, where parents, students, and teachers have timely access to information, where teacher-student communication transcends time and geography, and where research and development are seamlessly integrated. Classrooms will be transformed into global learning centers, linking homes, schools, and society, so education truly happens anywhere, anytime.

E-learning is not limited to those of school age. ictQATAR connects adults to career-enhancing opportunities through technology, preparing them to enter the workplace, change careers, or deepen levels of expertise. ictQATAR is partnering with Qatar's Institute of Administration Development to offer 4,000 business and IT courses for government workers. Through a single e-learning portal, busy adults can access course materials in Arabic, English, or French anytime, day or night. All courses are accredited by internationally renowned institutes.

The most advanced ICT efforts can be found in the primary and secondary education sector. In partnership with the Supreme Education Council, the chief education policymaking body in Qatar, initiatives are in place to significantly expand infrastructure and e-education projects that support improved teaching and learning. Projects include:

- Knowledge Net, a portal that allows for three-way communication between parents, students and teachers. Knowledge Net has been rolled out in 12 schools and will be scaled up substantially.

- E-Schoolbag, which holds Tablet PCs programmed with science, math, and English content benchmarked to national curriculum standards.

- Global Gateway, a collaboration with the British Council, which creates a platform for teachers to interact with their counterparts around the world to share experiences and ideas.

- Model e-school, which brings world standard ICT best practices for education to a few select schools that can serve to stimulate the adoption of similar practices in other schools.

By 2010, Qatari Independent Schools—government-funded schools created to promote creativity and critical thinking—will be competently using ICT to enhance learning and improve student outcomes.

Strengthening cyber security

For Qatar, information security and the safety of young and adult Internet users is an absolute priority. To safeguard users as well as industry and government information and systems, in 2005 ictQATAR forged a partnership with Carnegie Mellon's Software Engineering Institute (CERT Coordination Center) to establish the Qatar Computer Emergency Response Team (Q-CERT). Working with public and private institutions, as well as the general public, Q-CERT raises awareness of cyber-security issues. Goals for the first three years have included the following:

- building incident response capability,

- creating a watch capability to monitor developments in this field, and

- working with critical organizations to establish and improve risk management practices.

Since Q-CERT is not an outsourcing provider, the idea is not for companies to simply hand over their security programs to a third party. Depending on ministry and organization needs, Q-CERT supports entities in security activities by promoting international standards and marshalling international support as necessary. Q-CERT's team of 30 professionals works with private- and public-sector organizations to build world-class information security capabilities and manage cyber-security risks. Q-CERT protects electronic data from unauthorized access, disclosure, destruction, or modification.

Since information security problems are not limited by national boundaries, Q-CERT is a member of the global Forum of Incident Response and Security Teams (FIRST). This organization fosters regional ties to security partners around the world in order to share up-to-date information about threats and vulnerabilities.

It is imperative that children are aware of cyber threats that could damage their PCs or expose sensitive information. ictQATAR is working with the Supreme Education Council to make sure parents and students in kindergarten through high school understand the need for security and cyber ethics.

Q-CERT's mandate does not end in educating companies and citizens: one of its many tasks focused on safe sharing of data between actors in finance and in the banking sector. In addition, it has been entrusted with creating a system to recover information that is required in prosecuting legal offences. The long-term goal is to build a regional center of excellence for information security.

Overcoming implementation challenges
Inevitably, the journey toward Qatar's ICT transformation has not been without challenges and roadblocks. In large measure, the story of Qatar's ICT success to date has been one of recognizing and facing those challenges. These constraints are far from trivial: they include a lack of key stakeholder capabilities and readiness, a lack of ICT skills and capabilities, and unique cultural and social norms that are not necessarily welcoming to change. Any of these challenges could have derailed Qatar's ICT agenda. As the country's experience in the past few years has demonstrated, leadership, courage, and conviction are required to overcome these obstacles.

Despite the significant contributions of ictQATAR, one of the implementation challenges revolves around its multiple roles as a regulator, champion, sponsor, and owner of specific IT programs. Although in theory there should be no conflict, implementation can become less seamless, with conflicts of interest between departments sometimes bubbling to the surface. In addition, where ictQATAR has acted as a sponsor, it has often been in the capacity of an incubator that sets up a project and then entrusts a government agency with running it. On occasion, this has raised the question of sustainability. The involvement of external consultants has further complicated the issue. Also, in many segments, the market is not big enough to warrant large investment from the private sector, which in bigger countries might be shouldered by the municipal government, for instance.

Stakeholder resistance, capability, and readiness
ICT programs tend to be applied across multiple sectors, and success depends on the capabilities and readiness of stakeholders to implement initiatives related to their own sector or specific organization. Moreover, resistance to change can be high if the stakeholder's capabilities are not addressed. For effective ICT delivery, ictQATAR is implementing ICT policies and initiatives with the involvement of key stakeholders and is making stakeholder capability-building a priority.

- *Formal approaches:* Many agencies engaged in reform do not possess the necessary skills, tools, or processes to effectively manage the change ICT enablement brings. Across all levels of management in agencies, understanding of ICT strategies, planning, and implementation—and even of benefits realization—is in most cases insufficient. This is evidenced in agencies' reluctance to engage early with ictQATAR on common initiatives designed to improve services. ictQATAR addresses this challenge in the ICT master plan by including stakeholder capability building in initiatives. At the strategic level, ictQATAR has developed joint working groups among stakeholders facilitated by experts to achieve common strategies and objectives. IT executive training and development programs are available to stakeholders to increase their ICT knowledge. A flexible engagement model for ictQATAR and its stakeholders takes into consideration varying levels of capability and readiness. In several instances, ictQATAR leads implementation along with the stakeholder as internal capabilities are grown.

- *Informal approaches:* Until recently, intermediary organizations seldom existed, as Qataris and residents did not enjoy full freedom of association. That changed when a Royal Decree granted the right of association, encouraging formation of social organizations. With this entirely new option for collaboration, ictQATAR intends to build functioning groups of stakeholders through active engagement with decision makers. The concept of professional networking will be used to kick-start collaboration. For example, a project manager might start inviting "interested parties" to topic-oriented lunch talks, exploring their shared interest for an ICT-specific topic.[2] A "lunch circle" built around an increasingly familiar "friends of ICT-topic X" could easily form the basis for a pilot program of ictQATAR in a specific area.

Lack of human capital
A deterrent to greater technology absorption has been a shortage of ICT-skilled workers at all levels. Although the country is not alone—indeed, the region and the

world face similar shortages—the problem is more pronounced in Qatar because of the following:

- the small size of the local population;
- Qatar's position as a relative latecomer in the technology revolution;
- the relatively low ICT-education levels in some segments of the population; and
- the economic boom created in the oil and gas sectors, which attracts talent.

Lack of ICT capability to drive implementation as well as ongoing support poses a real threat to achieving high-quality, timely outcomes. At the technology skills level, the shortage of local staff is being felt acutely, especially in areas such as IT project management, business process management, and outsourced management. The government and private industry have therefore focused on the large expatriate population. This has created some challenges, as the expatriate workforce may not be fully attuned to the culture, psyche, and aspirations of the local population. It also brings into question the sustainability of some projects.

ictQATAR and its stakeholders have recognized this challenge and have implemented capacity-building initiatives across the government and other sectors. Initiatives range from promoting basic IT literacy skills and application usage and support training, to professional development and training for IT decision makers in government and business. ictQATAR has been developing its own internal capabilities to support these initiatives by having key resource specialists work alongside its own staff. A knowledge transfer requirement for each engagement is formally written into agreements, and creative recruitment methods are used to ensure that suitable experts are onboard in a timely way.

The government recognizes the need to continue building homegrown capacities in education, research, and innovation. It has brought in the Supreme Council of Education, the Ministry of Education, Education City, and Qatar University, which are reforming the education sector to develop local talent in the long term. The private sector and various government agencies have been informing educational institutions of their long-term needs with a view to developing local courses that will meet these requirements.

Mindset and cultural issues

As in other societies undergoing a technology-fueled transformation, the mindset and attitudes of Qatari families, institutions, bureaucracy, and other societal structures require dramatic change so that people can access technology and think differently and creatively. Although such change will take time, Qatar's strategy to date has been to inform and engage all stakeholders.

For example, e-education programs cannot force teachers to adopt technology in the classroom. Instead, the program fosters champions and visionaries who have an impact on students and serve as role models for other teachers.

In Qatari society, the issue of inappropriate content on the Internet is a huge barrier to wholesale adoption of the technology. Some parents resist children's Internet use, and a wide technological divide exists between children and their parents. Although parents can protect their children physically from negative influences, they feel vulnerable when it comes to the Internet. So, although many e-education initiatives are technologically and pedagogically effective, children may not enroll because of parental anxiety. To offset these barriers to successful adoption of technology, Qatar offers parents and teachers training and e-security programs.

When a rare misuse or lapse occurs in the security platform of business operations, mistrust of technology and e-operations results. It is against this backdrop that Q-CERT operates. Workshops are conducted to improve e-security and specific programs are available for top management executives, parents, and businesses.

Although the government runs broad public awareness programs, the older generation is also learning from the younger one. For example, today the Holy Qur'an is available on the Internet. The fact that children and parents can read and study their religion electronically demonstrates how technology can strengthen families. Readings from the Qur'an are even heard through computer loudspeakers in many households. This could not have been imagined by the older generation.

Emerging best practices

No project can be successful without the leadership and vision to take it forward. That has been a key factor contributing to the success of ICT in Qatar. The vision comes from the firm belief that ICT will significantly impact Qataris' quality of life. With Qatar's economy leaping to double-digit growth figures over the last five years, the country's leadership has not taken their eyes off ICT.

A tool for development

The success of ICT is increasingly seen as a tool for development and, therefore, a way to gain a buy-in into society. This has been done irrespective of geographic location, age, or ability. ictQATAR's main stakeholders have been not only the government and ministries, critical-sector organizations, and businesses, but also the entire population—regardless of age, gender, occupation, and economic background. When comprehensive ICT transformation got underway three years ago, the government's perspective was that children should be afforded the same capability that ICT has given to the new generation across the world.

The e-education program in particular has not lost sight of traditionally underserved segments, such as students with special needs. In fact, by 2008–09, there will be technologies in place for the visually impaired, the hearing impaired, and those with learning difficulties. Increasingly, despite some resistance and reservations from parents, the beneficial usages of Internet and technology for families and society as a whole are helping in the spread of technology usage. A nationwide awareness campaign, "The Promise of e," uses advertising, stakeholder outreach, and media to showcase how technology brings benefits to families, businesses, classrooms, and social interactions—every aspect of life.

A local touch

From the outset, ICT strategy has internalized a strong Qatarization component. ictQATAR has made a long-term commitment for capacity building in local ICT talent and for lessening the current dependency on the expatriate workforce. A cadre of young engineers that is gradually taking shape will ensure the sustainability of the country's ICT master plan in the long term. Programs such as the Awareness/Community/Environment (ACE) one contain a mix of long-ranging lobbying initiatives. One of these aims at overcoming the prevalent ICT skill shortage through legal provisions. There are plans to shift from nationality-based immigration laws to skill-based ones. Focused awareness campaigns will also be in place; for example, a campaign to foster e-banking services by businesses collaborating with commercial banks.

ICT implementations to date have recognized and respected the unique aspects of the Qatari society, such as the absence of crime, the overall trusting and hospitable nature of local people's interactions, and the resulting anxiety that the introduction of technology can engender among citizens who have been proud and protective of their way of life.

A focus on implementation

A reason for the success of these programs is that ICT implementation has been done in an integrated manner across the country. While there is one nodal agency, ictQATAR, to broadly oversee the technology reform movement, champions are spread across government, society, and business to facilitate and ensure implementation. Strong institutional frameworks, coupled with a drive to build pilot projects and centers of excellence, have dominated ICT implementation in the past few years. The e-government initiatives described above have presented the people with a new face of the government.

Success and continuity of programs are ensured through phased implementation. In the early days, mindful of its status as a relatively late entrant to the global ICT game, Qatar started introducing large numbers of programs very rapidly. But it quickly realized that speed of implementation alone would be of little help in truly advancing ICT. Instead, it understood the need to focus on a smaller number of deliverable projects. Pilot initiatives have been started, particularly in the e-education program area, and their readiness is now starting to be measured, using an e-maturity model. That way, it becomes easier to evaluate and decide which initiatives should be fully implemented.

The government has also internalized the importance of metrics in gauging ICT progress, and realized that these metrics themselves need time to mature. For example, moving 200 schools under the e-education umbrella is a sizeable challenge. To that end, six pilot schools were first selected, and their readiness is now starting to be measured, using an e-maturity model. That way, it becomes easier to find out where they stand in the implementation process.

Open to learning

Qatar has been mindful of its status as a small, open economy. With an open mind, its leadership has studied the experience of many other countries in carrying out its ICT transformation. Many of the top echelons of Qatar's leadership have studied overseas and travel abroad often. The leadership is realizing how IT is transforming countries such as India, Singapore, and China, and how IT can therefore transform Qatar too. The notion that "the world is flat" has influenced Qatari leadership. Lessons from India have been particularly useful, especially the examples of cities such as Bangalore, companies such as Wipro and Infosys, and educational institutions such as the Indian Institute of Technology. The long-term goal is to become a regional center of excellence for information technology and the knowledge economy. As of late, there has been close and intensifying cooperation with Singapore's Infocomm Development Authority (IDA). At the same time, many of Qatar's ICT programs have been tailored specifically for Qatar, taking into account the unique national model and circumstances. While looking at best practices from Singapore and Korea, Rep., ictQATAR also realized that these can, at best, be reference points. For detailed planning and implementation, it would have to be creative in designing for the specific needs of Qatar's local communities.

Conclusion

> All these far-reaching benefits will lead to reinforcing Qatar as a progressive nation. Already rich in culture and resources, it is now trying to take full advantage of the most sophisticated and advanced technologies the world has to offer. These technologies will enrich the lives of its citizens through daily delivery of greater knowledge and enhanced social services and the creation of a powerfully-connected and effective community.[3]

For Qatar, the journey has only started. But despite its relatively late start, the country has succeeded in making its mark on the world's networked readiness map. Crucially, the lessons learned by Qatar since it has embarked on an ICT-driven transformation hold promise for other nations who have recognized the power of ICT to disseminate knowledge, spur development, and strengthen business competitiveness in the 21st century.

What then are some of the important lessons from Qatar's unfolding story? The biggest by far is that political and national leadership will make a crucial difference to the success or failure of these reforms. It is not that other nations don't have similar ambitions. It is also not that Qatar has not faced serious challenges in this journey. The difference is that despite challenges, setbacks, roadblocks, and limitations, the country has been able to forge ahead with single-minded devotion, conviction, and courage.

In addition, the country's ambitious knowledge agenda has been complemented with liberal doses of financial support and infused with the concept of developing a unique Qatari ICT adoption model. The latter has been particularly useful in securing a sense of ownership from the community at large. Despite pockets of resistance to making ICT all-pervading within a short time frame, a wide spectrum of local communities has been successfully engaged in the transformation project.

ictQATAR is the enthusiastic champion of ICT for the entire country, and has consistently pushed for an integrated and holistic approach to ICT implementation. It has managed to win cooperation and support from other government agencies and departments. It recognized early the importance of setting up pilot projects, testing and measuring their effectiveness, and from there proceeding to enlarge their scope.

A willingness to make mid-course corrections, along with widespread awareness campaigns, the national economy's global aspirations, and the recognition of the crucial role of education have all added momentum to the process of making ICT a part of the national agenda.

This has been Qatar's recent approach, and it has contributed in no small way in making the nation move forward. With all this and a can-do spirit, the small nation of Qatar has been able to make a big mark in ICT implementation and development and be a model for other countries in the region and around the world.

Notes

1 The ERU framework is inspired by the Networked Readiness Framework featured in the *Report*.

2 The integration of sector-specific agenda-setters and power-brokers will be especially important in this context.

3 The Heir Apparent His Highness Sheikh Tamim Bin Hamad Al-Thani, Chairman, ictQATAR, Inaugural Launch Speech, May 2005.

References

Dutta, S., A. De Meyer, A. Jain, and G. Richter. 2006. *The Information Society in an Enlarged Europe*. Berlin: Springer-Verlag.

Dutta, S., A. Lopez-Claros, and I. Mia, eds. 2006. *The Global Information Technology Report 2005–2006: Leveraging ICT for Development*. Hampshire: Palgrave Macmillan

Dutta, S. and I. Mia, eds. *The Global Information Technology Report 2006–2007: Connecting to the Networked Economy*. Hampshire: Palgrave Macmillan.

Friedman, T. L. 2005. *The World Is Flat: A Brief History of the Twenty-First Century*. New York: Farrar, Straus and Giroux.

ictQatar. 2005. The National ICT Masterplan 2005–2008, ictQATAR.

Sheikh Tamim Bin Hamad Al-Thani, Heir Apparent, Chairman, ictQATAR. 2005. Inaugural Launch Speech, May.

CHAPTER 2.3

Small- and Medium-Sized Enterprises Hold the Key to European Competitiveness: How to Help Them Innovate through ICT and E-business

DANA ELEFTHERIADOU, European Commission

The most important driver of innovation and competitiveness today is information and communication technologies (ICT). There is, by now, compelling evidence for the positive correlation between ICT and productivity growth. It is also well recognized that the issue is much broader than increasing investments in ICT: indeed, the latter can induce higher productivity growth only when accompanied by appropriate organizational changes, innovative e-business models,[1] and investment in skills. Those are key factors to firms' global competitiveness, particularly for small- and medium-sized enterprises (SMEs). Firms should not only be investing larger amounts in ICT equipment and infrastructure but, more importantly, should be investing in smarter ways to use ICT. Enterprises should not hesitate to reflect deeply about their current way of doing business and how to innovate by adopting new management practices, taking full advantage of the tremendous potential of ICT.

This need is pressing, especially for European SMEs, which make up a large part of Europe's economy: there are some 23 million of them in the European Union (EU), providing around 75 million jobs and accounting for 99 percent of all enterprises. SMEs are a key part of European industry, not least because they contribute up to 80 percent of employment in some industrial sectors, such as textiles, construction, or furniture. SMEs are a major source of entrepreneurial skills, innovation, and creativity, and they contribute to economic and social cohesion. More recently, SMEs have been emerging as global players by participating in global production and supply chains.

Nonetheless, SMEs are the firms that suffer the most from their limited possibilities to fully exploit the ICT potential. Recent surveys indicate that their uptake of ICT remains too low. SMEs often lack the managerial understanding, the knowledge, and the skills required to fully grasp the potential of ICT as a major enabler of organizational innovation and structural reforms. It becomes obvious that in this challenging race of competitiveness and excellence, where new technologies and innovation play a central role, European SMEs cannot afford to be left behind. For this reason, more and more governments around the world have been seeking opportunities to promote ICT and e-business models as a way of enhancing the competitiveness of their SMEs. In response, the European Commission and EU Member States established the eBSN (e-Business Support Network for SMEs) as an e-business policy coordination platform to exchange ideas on how to stimulate and support small businesses in their attempt to exploit ICT.[2] The goal of the eBSN is to improve the effectiveness of public SME policies promoting the innovative use of ICT and the exchange of good practices. It brings together decision makers in the field of e-business to share information and to discuss strategic policy directions.

Through the eBSN, we are witnessing the combination of three major trends:

1. the increasing economic importance of SMEs as key players in implementing the European Union's Lisbon Strategy for growth and jobs, as well as their growing potential to act as global players in the emerging global economy;

2. the incontestable recognition of the merits of ICT and new e-business processes as major enablers of innovation, productivity, and competitiveness growth; and

3. the strong engagement of governments to stimulate the uptake of ICT, e-business models, and modern management practices by their enterprises, particularly SMEs.

This paper will provide evidence of these three trends and will further elaborate on them from the point of view of policymakers, by addressing the following issues:

- the potential of ICT and e-business as enablers of more growth and jobs in an increasingly global economy;

- the role, if any, of public policies in promoting the innovative use of ICT by local SMEs;

- identification of examples of e-business policies that can be identified as good practices that are the new policy trends in this area; and

- the next steps in the policy agenda with regard to the promotion of e-business practices among SMEs.

EU and US productivity trends

Since the mid-1990s, productivity has been growing faster in the United States than in Europe. Productivity growth in the United States has accelerated in the last decade, from an average of 1.6 percent per year from 1980 to 1994 to 2.7 percent since then, while in Europe it has declined from 2.3 percent per year to 1.4 percent. So the United States experienced a structural shift upward in productivity growth, mostly as a result of ICT, while EU countries, a structural shift downward.[3]

Comparing the period after 1995 with the early 1990s, about half of 56 US industries saw productivity acceleration, compared with only about 20 percent of industries in the European Union. Much of the growth acceleration in the United States was driven by ICT-producing sectors and service sectors, especially wholesale and retail trade, banking, and other financial services. As a result, the labor productivity growth in the European Union has decreased to 92 percent of the US level in 2002, down from 96 percent in 1995.[4]

However, it seems that the renewed Lisbon Strategy for more growth and jobs is now bearing fruit. Despite current concerns, performance has improved: the labor productivity gap between Europe and the United States shrank in 2006. The European Union's real gross domestic product (GDP) grew by 3.0 percent in 2006—the highest growth rate since 2000. Almost 6.5 million extra jobs have been created there in the last two years, and 8 million are expected to be created over the period 2007–09. Lisbon reforms have undoubtedly reinforced the growth potential of the EU economy.

However, there is no room for complacency. Analysis shows that there is still a gap in total factor productivity, the portion of productivity growth generated by intangible factors such as technical progress or organizational innovation.[5] The evidence strongly suggests that the key factor in engineering such a productivity turnaround will be the ubiquitous use of ICT throughout the European economy and society.

ICT, innovation, and productivity

ICT is the biggest driver of innovation, productivity, and competitiveness in our days. It has opened enormous possibilities for innovation, right across the economy, by enabling not only technological innovation but also innovation in business models. ICT can revolutionize business processes and organizations, make them more efficient, and boost overall competitiveness. ICT impact is pervasive, for it is being used in virtually every sector of the economy—from farming and manufacturing to services and the government sector.

There now is compelling evidence that ICT was the greatest contributor to the astounding US productivity growth of the last decade. In a conclusive review of more than 50 studies, researchers found that "the productivity paradox as first formulated has been effectively refuted. At both the firm and the country level, greater investment in ICT is associated with greater productivity growth."[6]

In this sense, ICT was responsible for two-thirds of total factor growth in US productivity between 1995 and 2002 and for virtually all of the growth in US labor productivity.[7] Data since the 1980s show that ICT investment in the European Union has been consistently lower than in the United States. Comparative figures for 2004, for instance, show ICT investment in the United States running at 4.1 percent of GDP, with the European Union averaging less than 2.5 percent. And ICT investment produces growth: 0.8 percent of the 3.4 percent GDP growth in the United States is attributed to ICT capital growth. ICT capital contribution to overall economic growth in EU15 amounted to 0.5 percent of a much more modest GDP growth of 2.1 percent.

Comparing the three most technologically developed areas, in 2005, IT spending per capita in Europe was about half that of the United States and Japan (respectively, 634 euros, 1,118 euros, and 999 euros). IT spending on GDP for the same year was considerably lower in Europe, reaching 2.76 percent of GDP, as compared with 3.47 percent in Japan and 3.28 percent in the United States. And the picture is quite heterogeneous among the EU countries. The European country with the highest IT spending on GDP is Sweden (3.85 percent), while Greece is the one with the lowest (1.12 percent). The United Kingdom, France, and Germany perform better than the European mean (3.57 percent, 3.11 percent, and 2.93 percent, respectively), while Italy and Spain are in the last five positions of the ranking with less than half percentage of the other three leading countries.[8]

This gap in ICT investment really matters. A number of relevant analyses and studies corroborate that ICT capital produces greater productivity gains than other capital investments: "Accelerated investment in IT generated increases in productivity more than three times greater than would be the case if it were other kinds of capital investment."[9] "Money spent on computing technology delivers gains in worker productivity that are three to five times those of other investments."[10] "ICT capital showed five to eight times higher return on investment than non-ICT capital."[11]

It is not simply the underinvestment in ICT that matters, however. Not only is ICT investment in the European Union (as a share of GDP) only half the level achieved in the United States, but that investment is also seriously underexploited. Productivity growth in the United States has been mostly driven by the ICT-using sectors, while these sectors in Europe have not been in a position to capitalize on their investment. According to recent studies,[12] the overall contribution to labor productivity growth from ICT investments and from technical progress in the production of ICT goods and services accounted for about 40 percent of EU labor productivity growth over the second half of the 1990s, compared with 60 percent in the United States.

A possible reason for the above is that investment in ICT brings about higher productivity growth only when accompanied by appropriate organizational changes, innovative e-business models, and investment in skills. Those are key factors of firms' global competitiveness, in particular SMEs. Firms that invest significantly in ICT and at the same time organize the digital transformation of their business practices outperform their competitors. "Firms do not simply plug in computers or telecommunications equipment and achieve service quality or efficiency gains. Instead they go through a process of organizational redesign and make substantial changes to their service or output mix."[13]

This line of thought increasingly becomes the mainstream: 97 percent of business executives believe technology alone would not raise productivity in their firm to the highest level achievable, but that it must be accompanied by organizational changes.[14] A survey of European executives shows that most executives thought ICT had a beneficial impact, not on productivity only (55 percent) but also on work organization (61 percent), product quality (38 percent), and customer service (52 percent). Dutch firms that invested more in ICT not only enjoyed faster productivity growth but also produced more innovations.[15] In the European Union, 32 percent of companies reported innovations, with ICT enabling half of the product innovations and 75 percent of the process innovations.[16] These secondary effects prompt firms to make more significant productivity gains than they would achieve simply by using ICT to make an individual process more efficient. Such organizational and process changes, however, require the ability and agility to innovate. They require deeply reviewing and completely reforming one's business strategy and can, hence, be destructive, time-consuming, and costly in a first phase. As suggested by the significant EU-US gap in the total factor productivity growth (0.46 percent versus 0.8 percent annual growth, in the period 1995–2001),[17] European firms have been slower in making the process and organizational changes that would allow them to achieve the full benefits of ICT. Changes in total factor productivity are one measure of such business reengineering and organizational benefits.

Europe needs to devise policies to boost the total factor productivity growth, such as initiatives designed to foster technological progress, innovation, and the use of ICT, thus spurring the digital transformation.

Helping SMEs succeed in the age of globalization

In parallel, globalization has moved in recent years to the heart of the EU policy agenda. The Lisbon Strategy is the natural basis for building the European response to globalization, and the European Union is already achieving notable successes in shaping globalization.[18] The statement of President José Manuel Barroso stresses the high political attention on this matter: "The EU's raison d'être for the 21st century is crystal clear: to equip Europe for a globalized world. In order to do so, we must invest in people, in growth and jobs. . . . European leaders now need to maintain the vision and redouble their ambition."[19]

Naturally, globalization has raised new expectations about how public authorities should help citizens and enterprises to acclimatize and succeed in a constantly changing environment. Particular attention is paid to European SMEs, which make up a large part of the European economy, as explained above. SMEs are a major source of entrepreneurial skills and contribute to economic and social cohesion. Most important, SMEs hold the key to innovation, mostly because of their lean and flexible structure, which allow them to take risks more easily and adapt more quickly in changing conditions. Moreover, the emerging role of SMEs as global players, through their participation in global production and supply chains, is of particular interest. Nonetheless, SMEs suffer the most from their limited possibilities to fully exploit the ICT potential. They often lack the managerial understanding of ICT as well as the required skills. But ICT holds a tremendous potential for SMEs in particular, as an enabler not only of technological innovation, but also innovation in business models, business networking, knowledge transfer, and access to international markets.

For all these reasons, SMEs have been put high on the agenda of the Lisbon Strategy. The goal is to fully unlock the growth and jobs potential of SMEs and make full use of their innovative capacities. In this context, the European Commission, in collaboration with SMEs and their representatives, will design a "Small Business Act" for Europe by the end of 2008, with a view to making a wide range of proposals to support SMEs succeed in an increasingly globalized world.

The e-business solutions market for SMEs

ICT adoption by SMEs follows different patterns and different drivers than it does for large enterprises. While the main drivers for e-business adoption for SMEs is competitive advantage and market share, large firms are more focused on understanding supplier expectations and competitors' behavior, as well as customers' expectations. This implies that SMEs need specific e-business solutions and services, which respond to their particular needs. The question faced by SMEs for quite some years has been whether there are readily available, affordable, and user-friendly e-business solutions and services in the market, specifically addressing their needs. The evidence seems to be encouraging. Analysis of current market trends shows that the SME segment is increasingly gaining importance for e-business solution providers.[20] The SME segment is vast and has high growth potential, currently growing faster than the enterprise one.

At first, some ICT vendors tried a one-size-fits-all solution, instead of looking at SMEs' real requirements. The analysis shows that ICT suppliers quickly realized the complexity of the SME segment. They recognized that meeting SMEs' demand does not simply require a re-scaling and functionality reduction of applications and packages, but much more: it requires a new comprehensive approach, providing adequate and cost-effective solutions, developing specific technological support, and adjusting marketing and networking strategies. Specializations of products and solutions, integrations of functionalities and channels, and reorganization of strategies and internal structures are being adapted to the particular characteristics of SMEs. Mainstream supply side trends show that large software companies such as Oracle and SAP are getting it right by specifically developing offerings for the SME segment. Other suppliers, such as Microsoft and IBM, increasingly organize themselves to provide comprehensive integrated technological services.

Recognizing the specific needs of SMEs not only in terms of products, but also in terms of sales and marketing approach, ICT suppliers are increasingly adjusting their strategies. A key factor is the proximity and the possibility of reaching the largest number of SMEs. Typically, the large IT suppliers operate through two different, but not alternative, marketing channels, the first based on the physical proximity of resellers and partners, the second relying on Web solutions.

Historically, covering the SME e-business segment has been based on a partnership between large players and their network of resellers, ensuring a broad geographical coverage and adequate knowledge of SME requirements and their effective support. On the other hand, the whole IT sector, and in particular the SME segment, is moving toward a "software as a service" (SAAS) approach—that is, providing and managing software solutions as services over the Web. SAAS vendors are increasingly focusing on how their solutions help customers streamline business processes, providing best practice guidelines for business process improvement, pre-built integration solutions, and comprehensive business ecosystems to facilitate community relationships. According to the target segments, they are developing tailor-made marketing channels as well as pricing solutions.

The competition for the SME segment takes place at different levels. It involves the incumbent multinationals and their resellers and partners, but also the local small suppliers. This competition has positive impact on the market by ensuring the effective matching between the supply and the enterprises' needs, and making the ICT solutions affordable also for the smallest firms. And ensuring appropriate ICT products and services supply for SMEs surely represents a strong driver for their e-business transformation.

E-business policy actions: Drawing the strands together

Member States and the Commission alike have recognized the challenge to reinforce ICT and e-business uptake by SMEs and have devised policies in this direction. It is clear that the coordination of Member States' policies may bring benefits that are substantially superior to those derived from acting alone.[21] While countries can learn from each other, joint efforts and coordination can stimulate the drive to act. Most importantly, international spillover effects from national and regional policy initiatives, as well as coordinated implementation, may create benefits that would be absent had such policy initiatives been pursued unilaterally. For instance, roughly half of the potential increase of GDP generated by Member States' achievement of their research and development (R&D) targets would result from cross-border knowledge spillovers. And additional benefits accrue from complementarities between policies.

This is why the Commission and the Member States have established the eBSN for SMEs, with the goal of improving the effectiveness of public SME policies. It is a tool to make existing e-business policies more effective and involves over 200 public policies or private-public partnerships from 30 European countries. The eBSN supports policy analysis and benchmarking, shapes policy trends, generates synergies between national policies, and inspires new e-business policies by the exchange of good practices.

The eBSN is steered by the eBSN Steering Group, composed of representatives of the Member States, the Candidate and European Economic Area countries, and international organizations' experts. The Steering Group convenes twice a year. Moreover, the eBSN members organize two to three thematic workshops per year, usually hosted by the members (i.e., public authorities, often the Presidencies) with the support of the European Commission, on themes that are agreed upon by the eBSN Steering Group. The eBSN workshops provide the opportunity for all interested members to meet and exchange experiences and views on various e-business-related policy issues.

E-business policies for SMEs: Observations and trends

The eBSN is a "policy intelligence" initiative, which follows policy developments and identifies new policy trends. Since its establishment in 2003, it has been analyzing the evolution of e-business policies and shaping policy action at the European level when applicable. According to eBSN observations, e-business policies for SMEs have evolved through three major phases:

The **first phase** of e-business policy initiatives was mostly aimed at general ICT awareness raising as well as at sponsoring, and co-financing basic ICT investments and Internet connectivity. These policy initiatives were often devised in response to market speculations on the "new economy" hype, and were often on a rather ad-hoc basis. Many of these e-business measures were characterized by a lack of founded rationale or of documented analysis of the particular needs of local SMEs, as well as of concrete and measurable targets. Once the hype subsided, and in the aftermath of the "e-economy bubble" burst, many governments started reconsidering and reviewing their measures in order to achieve broader impact, and to make a difference for SMEs. In this context, it became apparent that any public policy action should have been based on a sound assessment of the real needs of local SMEs and designed to respond to those specific needs. Indeed, the *e-Business w@tch* confirmed that basic ICT infrastructure and access to the Internet were no longer considered major barriers to e-business uptake in Europe. The Internet has significantly decreased the gap between SMEs and large companies in terms of knowledge and market trends. More than 9 out of 10 SMEs with a computer had Internet access in 2005, as did more than 50 percent of those with a bandwidth of at least 200 kb/s. Naturally, the e-business needs of SMEs are changing over time, and policy initiatives should adapt accordingly to remain focused and effective.

This first phase process led to the **second phase** of e-business policies, namely policy instruments stimulating SMEs to explore the innovation potential of ICT and e-business. Although measures promoting online access and general awareness about the potential of ICT will continue to be valid, in particular at local and regional levels, more and more e-business policies are addressing the specific needs of SMEs by providing them with hands-on assistance by specialized e-business experts. The main policy concept is to have independent e-business consultants take a close look at the business processes of an enterprise in order to figure out what sort of organizational innovations could be introduced to eliminate inefficiencies and improve productivity through ICT systems (see Box 1). Practically all countries in Europe have endorsed this trend, and lots of initiatives of this type have been launched at national, regional, and local levels.

These second-wave e-business initiatives have provided very concrete and practical assistance to individual firms and helped to initiate the digital transformation of many enterprises that would not otherwise have done so. According to an impact assessment analysis of a number of e-business policies of that period,[22] the major achievements of these measures were:

- *Increase in e-business awareness and ICT literacy*
  All the analyzed policy initiatives have improved the degree of awareness and ICT literacy among the targeted SMEs. The adoption of basic infrastructure, moreover, has led the involved businesses to a stage of e-readiness, meaning that in principle these firms are now ready to face the decisions to go or not to go online, and if they decide to go online, to what extent. Another outcome is a better understanding of ICT services available in the market and the possibility of being more independent from service providers.

- *Entrepreneurial e-business understanding*
  Companies involved confirm that the policy initiatives have effectively helped them to improve managerial understanding of e-business opportunities and to think about possible next steps to be taken, as well as to make business processes more efficient and thus to prepare them for future business challenges.

> **Box 1: Policy example: The eAskel program's expert service, Finland**
>
> The eAskel program is one of the "branded expert services" offered to businesses via the Finnish Employment and Economic Development Centres. eAskel has been implemented as a public private partnership (PPP): the services are provided to SMEs by private-sector consultants, but are subsidized by the public sector. The aim of the program is the long-term, business-oriented development of the use of ICT by SMEs. It aims to make the use of information technology and networks part of a firm's planning and development of business activities, develop the working methods and processes of businesses, develop long-term planning for IT investment, and find solutions giving a competitive advantage and benefiting business activity.
>
> The services offered by the program consist in a 3.5-day consultancy (extendable to a maximum of 8.5 days) assisting the SME management in the development of a strategic plan for the implementation of e-business to support its business strategy. The process starts with an analysis of the firm's current situation and its overall business targets. This leads to the consideration and definition of the best ICT development strategies, and finally to the development of an action plan to implement the strategy. A formal deliverable in the program is a consultant report with recommendations and an action plan on ICT implementation—that is, a practical roadmap on how to internally reorganize business processes in order to take full advantage of ICT. The implementation of the action plan has to be carried out by the company on its own.
>
> As a result of the eAskel program, the management of a firm is better prepared to direct the development of an ICT strategy.
>
> Key lessons learned are the following: any ICT concept for a small company can be developed only from a sound analysis of the general business context and objectives; the firm's management must be involved; and the selection of high-quality, independent consultants are a critical issue for the overall quality of the service.
>
> Source: Databank et al., 2006.

- *Competitive advantage from improved relations with business partners*

    A very important effect of e-business concerns a firm's relations with business partners, both suppliers and customers. This relationship may take place with different degrees of sophistication; however, even the adoption of basic solutions can bring relevant competitive and organization advantages, including the possibility of reaching new customers. It can be argued that the capability to cooperate online with more advanced business partners reinforces the competitive positioning of micro and small SMEs. Whenever companies with a leading role in their supply chain adopt new working modalities, it is crucial that their business partners comply with them in order to stay competitive and not be excluded from further development of the sector value chain.

While fully recognizing the merits of such policy schemes, the continuous challenge of policymakers is to keep up with new developments and the new opportunities created, and to adapt to new realities. The assessment of these second-phase e-business policy initiatives, in combination with the changing environment, raised further reflection on how to enhance their scope and impact on the European economy, at both micro- and macroeconomic levels. Some Member States have then realized that the potential impact of their policy actions on the SME market would be much bigger if policies shift their target from individual firms to entire industrial or services sectors.

This, in turn, resulted in the **third phase**—namely, the sector-specific e-business policies for SMEs. These policies focus more on encouraging market forces to hasten the pace of ICT-enabled change in specific business sectors and less on incentives to use certain technology products or help particular companies. The aim of such policy initiatives is to support the participation of SMEs in global digital supply chains.

In fact, there is enormous value locked up in the value chain of firms and entire sectors. This is mostly the result of an apparent lack of quality and timely, structured information, as well as inefficiencies resulting from disjointed and manual paper-based processes. Large companies are increasingly streamlining and integrating their business processes. Smaller firms in lower tiers of the supply chain—often of more than one industry or services segment—risk elimination if they cannot comply with their customers' technical requirements. In order to maintain their business partners, smaller firms have to conform to different data processing architectures, ICT solutions, and standards for each of their major customers, resulting in complex ICT systems that are costly, time consuming, user-unfriendly, and inefficient. The direct result is a competitiveness deficit, which is, in turn, transferable to the whole value network, with negative effects for regional or national economies.

According to a recent study,[23] a wide range of e-business policies at European, national, and regional levels are increasingly deployed with the aim of counteracting this digital divide by creating a win–win situation for all players and positive overall effects. In recent years, several EU Member States—including France, Germany, Italy, Portugal, and Spain—have launched initiatives to promote e-business exchanges within and between sectors.

Several of these initiatives aim at harmonizing data exchanges between players in different segments of a sector's supply chain. If more companies can exchange data electronically based on agreed standards and processes, buyers and sellers will both benefit (see Box 2).

Significant challenges, requiring time and adequate resources, need to be addressed in this context: initiatives typically have a larger scale than earlier awareness-raising policies. Excellent project management involving stakeholders that are broadly accepted by the target groups is a critical success factor.

Developing an effective e-business policy initiative requires an in-depth understanding of the business culture and commitment that only the particular business sectors can provide. This is crucial to be able to make the necessary transformations of business practices. A sectoral focus helps to create critical mass: single firms are very limited in their ability to innovate without the cooperation and alignment of the entire industry or service sector.

Many sector-specific initiatives involve extended cross-border pilot projects, where business models and applications are tested in real life conditions to demonstrate the real benefits of e-business (see Box 3).

Certain sectoral policies also highlighted the combination of top-down and bottom-up approaches, with central management controlling regional or local deployment. Central coordination increases the efficiency of the action, avoids duplication of efforts, facilitates collaboration with international stakeholders (e.g., in standardization), and increases the possibility of replicating the initiative. At the same time, bottom-up regional implementation ensures close links with target beneficiaries and the provision of services tailored to customers' needs (Box 4).

There is probably no better inducement to ICT investment among SMEs than the demonstration of concrete, well-documented, and plausible success stories from peers. Initiatives that monitored and assessed the outcome of their activities can provide convincing evidence of effects that are largely positive. In almost every case, e-business can be regarded as an ICT-enabled process innovation. Understanding one's business processes, spotting inefficiencies, and improving them (be it to save costs or to improve service quality) is therefore the key underlying issue in most such initiatives.

In this sense, investments in ICT-enabled process innovation must increasingly be justified by demonstrable payback within acceptable timeframes. In the absence of clear metrics to assess performance improvement,

---

Box 2: Policy example: The TIC-PME 2010 action plan, France

The TIC-PME 2010 action plan launched by the French Ministry of the Economy, Finance and Enterprises aims at the integration of SMEs in industrial supply chains, which are typically dominated by large enterprises. The plan supports projects in selected sectors of the French economy, focusing on harmonizing data and exchange models within and between sectors, based on global technical standards such as ebXML and GS1.

The policy initiative has three main objectives:

- support the implementation and use of common ICT tools in companies belonging to the same sector in order to create "digital supply chains";
- improve interoperability across different sectors among the tools developed; and
- provide local technical assistance to SMEs, supporting organizational changes and helping them to integrate ICT into their internal processes and data exchange with suppliers and customers.

Emphasis was placed on appointing project leaders who were representative and recognized by all sectors participating in a project. The harmonization of data exchange models requires consensus among all players in a value chain, including prime contractors, original equipment manufacturers, and subcontractors.

Major expected outcomes are the definition of models of data exchanges within the value chain and the harmonization of business processes within the sectors addressed. This should make it possible to specify a stable architecture for data processing and exchange.

It is expected that 20,000–30,000 SMEs will be interconnected by 2008. The objective is to have 100,000 by 2010. If this can be achieved, and once the architectures have been standardized, it should be easier to define a software solution that matches SMEs' needs and requirements. For SMEs, the risks linked to ICT investments will become more acceptable because they can be anticipated.

The main innovative aspect of this plan can be found in its cross-sectoral approach. The optimization of customer and supplier relationships takes into consideration the wider eco-system of companies: many firms have relationships with several economic actors. Tier-n subcontractors in particular typically deal with firms from different sectors. The purpose of the cross-sectoral approach of this initiative is to relieve these companies of the requirement to adopt different architectures when processing data from different customers.

Source: Empirica et al., 2007.
Note: TIC is the French acronym for ICT; PME the French acronym for SME.

investment in this critical component of innovation will be lagging, leading to a clear competitiveness deficit. A good practice element is therefore to assess or even measure the return-on-investment, with documentation of project results, which can then be used as showcases. Several initiatives reported that showcasing effects are even more pronounced if delivered in a peer-to-peer context (see Box 5).

Most of these measures are quite recent and still ongoing, and therefore an ex-post impact assessment is not feasible at this stage. Nonetheless, a recent study has identified some interesting best practice elements in designing and deploying sector-specific policies, that are worth citing in this context:[24]

- *Effective and dedicated management is critical.* The involvement of numerous stakeholders causes organizational problems and imposes the need for consistent highlighting of the win-win outcome for the participants over and above any individual and conflicting interests. Effective marketing of the policy is key in order to become known and accepted by the relevant business sector.

- *Partnership with strong sectoral industry associations is key for industry outreach.* Sectoral associations have a key role to play in setting priorities, establishing communications channels, endorsing the findings, and further promoting the initiative.

- *Live pilot projects* are an excellent way to show real benefits of e-business for a particular business sector. This is often more convincing than research results.

- *Support of ICT industry is crucial.* The creation of broad partnerships between business sectors and ICT providers ensures that the technology developed is the most suitable for the particular sectors' needs.

In parallel, the current proliferation of such sector-specific initiatives necessitates efficient policy coordination in order to put these policy initiatives in a perspective and valorize them at the EU level. This is the reason for which the Commission plans to support, under the eBSN umbrella, a series of targeted actions of European scope, with the aim of harmonizing business processes and data exchange architectures and standards, at a European and/or international level (see Box 6).

Besides the relevant strengths of the sector-specific approach though, the study on "Sectoral E-Business Policies in Support of SMEs" identifies also specific challenges, in particular the typically cross-sectoral characteristics of value chains, referenced in the next section.

New challenges and future policy trends: Cross-sectoral cross-border e-business processes

A challenge of the sector-specific e-business initiatives is the structural complexity of supply chains, particularly for companies dealing with different industry sectors. This requires a cross-sectoral approach and coordination, particularly if different systems or standards are used in the sectors concerned. The most innovative policies recognize the need for a cross-sectoral approach. While the consideration of sectoral characteristics of the value chain (e.g., types of exchanges, players involved, and standards used) in e-business networking initiatives is absolutely critical, cross-sectoral requirements should be identified and addressed as a next step.

Many national and regional e-business policies have been dealing with the promotion of such horizontal e-business processes; examples are e-ordering, e-invoicing, dispatch advice, e-payment, and so on. The first such initiative, identified through the eBSN, followed a pilot approach aiming at engaging as many SMEs as possible in experimenting and realizing the concrete financial benefits of using such structured electronic data exchanges (see Box 7).

Other countries, such as Sweden, Denmark, Slovenia, Austria, and Italy, have taken initiatives similar to the Finnish e-invoicing described in Box 7. The legal environment of different countries is critical in encouraging or impeding the broad diffusion of e-invoices. Certainly, the public sector has an important role to play and high-level policy commitment is key for the promotion of e-invoicing. For example, Denmark has been the first

---

Box 3: Policy example: The Construction IT Alliance eXchange (CITAX), Ireland

CITAX, set up in July 2006, aimed to facilitate more efficient business transactions between companies in the Irish construction sector. Its objective was to standardize exchange practices among all players in construction projects—architects, designers, manufacturers, and suppliers of building materials as well as IT providers—and to deploy readily available ICT tools.

Its innovative strength lay in its implementation being based on five separate but collaborative modules (design, trading, electronic tendering, project collaboration, and computer-aided measurement). Each module focused on analyzing existing business processes and operational boundaries, highlighting inefficiencies in those processes, calculating the associated costs, reaffirming the inefficiencies in current processes, and demonstrating—through a live pilot project—the benefits to be obtained in a new environment.

Source: Empirica et al., 2007.

Box 4: Policy example: Digital districts in the textile and clothing sector, Italy

The digital districts in the textile and clothing sector (DDTA) initiative is part of the framework program for the development of the information society in southern Italy. Its main objective is to increase the competitiveness of the Italian textile and clothing districts through the adoption and usage of standard low-risk open solutions, requiring limited investments, in value-chain operations.

The initiative combines central management with local and regional implementation. At the central level, activities are carried out in standardization, definition, and validation of ICT solutions for the sector. Local implementation is essential to respond to local needs and to bring services close to the target beneficiaries. DDTA activities are carried out at the central and regional levels.

Action lines at the central level:

- Definition and diffusion of interoperability standards, selected from existing standards and national or international good practice. The new standards will be tested at the regional level through the district service centers (DSCs).
- Pilot projects for the validation of ICT solutions for the textile/clothing (T/C) sector, including the development of open-source tools and methods conforming to standards.

Action lines at the regional level:

- Setting up of DSCs: five DSCs have been established in the regional districts, and they are expected to provide assistance, service, and applications suiting the specific and differentiated needs of the participating SMEs within a district.
- Provision of training and services to T/C SMEs in the implementation phase.

The innovative approach of DDTA lies in its organizational model combining top-down and bottom-up approaches. This model is based on the central (government) coordination of activities implemented at regional district level. Central coordination allows increased efficiency and facilitates collaboration with international stakeholders, for example, in the field of standardization.

The bottom-up approach of regional implementation assures a close link with SMEs in the T/C sector. All activities, from the development of open-source applications to service and training provision, are tailored to their specific needs and the cultural and organizational circumstances of the sector and the regions.

Source: Empirica et al., 2007.

Box 5: Policy example: Supply chain logistics metrics, Canada

This project was initiated by Industry Canada (IC) in October 2005 with the goal of identifying key performance indicators for six key industrial sectors for the Canadian economy and establishing a benchmarking method for assessing supply-chain efficiency.

The objective was to develop a hands-on tool for Canadian firms to benchmark themselves vis-à-vis their supply-chain partners, competitors, and sectors both within Canada and with US firms and sectors. For each of the six key sectors, an individual supply-chain report was written, containing an economic model of the sector's supply chain based on key performance indicators. These reports were reviewed and adapted to the practical needs of the industry and subsequently presented at various industry forums and delivered electronically through IC and partner websites. The next phase in the project was the development of the assessment tool.

50,000 SMEs have downloaded the tool and/or received the reports through their key associations. There are at least 10 channel masters (i.e., large firms that set the terms and conditions for all members of their supply chains, including, at times, forcing the adoption of new technologies and processes) implementing performance measurement in supply-chain management with their Canadian and US suppliers.

Several large firms have adopted this system successfully, and have subsequently extended it to their external supply chains. Canada's two largest industry associations became active partners, promoting this initiative strongly to their members.

The assessment tool and the benchmarking data and analysis at the micro level have enabled executives responsible for supply-chain logistics management within Canadian firms to develop sound business cases to support the required internal investments for improving important business practices. The data analysis, identification of trends, and benchmarking enabled firms to assess relative improvement and to set investment priorities.

The development of a supply-chain perspective on an individual basis enables firms within the sector to see the wider picture over several years. In addition, each subsector has characteristics and nuances that must be addressed in detail to supply the data for building the internal rationale justifying investment.

Source: Empirica et al., 2007.

> **Box 6: The European Commission response: Harmonizing e-business processes and data exchanges for SMEs in the textile/clothing and footwear sectors in the European Single Market**
>
> The European Commission launched a pilot action with the aim of harmonizing business processes and data exchange architectures and standards, at European and/or international level, within the textile/clothing and footwear industries—both sectors of crucial economic importance for Europe. This initiative started in January 2008 and will last two years. Those two sectors have the potential to benefit significantly from the integration of ICT and e-business solutions and standards in their value networks. Important standardization work has already been agreed upon and approved through the European Standardization Organisations (ESOs). However, the uptake and application of these standards remain unexploited, mostly because of the lack of human and financial resources and skills by most enterprises in the sectors.
>
> The objective of this European action is to complete a reference architecture of business processes and data exchange standards, building on existing standardization achievements and joining them in a seamless architecture at the European or international level. Its ultimate objective is to create a favorable environment that would stimulate and enable the participation of SMEs in the value chains of those two highly SME-based sectors in Europe.
>
> The reference architectures will be based on existing standardization achievements, as well as on new technical specifications and processes, to be developed under the current project, where gaps exist. Moreover, reference architectures should be developed in a harmonized way across sectors, in order to deal with intersectoral transactions, while taking in full account the specific needs of the sectoral supply chain networks. To demonstrate the feasibility and test the aforementioned reference architecture for standardized electronic B2B transactions in the aforementioned sectors, a number of sectoral and intersectoral cross-border pilots or prototypes will be set up at local and cross-border levels. Awareness and dissemination of the results is foreseen through the involvement of sectoral associations and multiplier organizations and should take place at local and regional levels.
>
> The involvement of key stakeholders (representatives of the relevant sectors—both large firms and SMEs along the entire value chains, along with experts of the standardization community) in the project will ensure its acceptance by the relevant industries, as well as its effective implementation even after the end of the pilot action. The involvement of the ESOs at a certain stage of the project is crucial in order to (1) ensure a clear, public, and transparent procedure that allows building wide consensus among the industry players; (2) officially approve; and (3) further maintain and broadly disseminate the results after the end of the project.
>
> Source: European Commission, DG Enterprise and Industry.

EU country to legally enforce the use of e-invoices for all transactions with public administration, since the 1st of February, 2005.

Another key issue of such policy initiatives has been how to ensure interoperability among the plethora of different e-invoicing standards and applications. The technical aspects and challenges should not be underestimated, as it is a rather new application not yet widely used. This issue becomes even more important when e-invoicing is considered on a European, cross-border scale. Interoperability of standards on a cross-border basis is a key challenge to be addressed (see Box 8).

The emerging role of cross-sectoral e-business processes suggests that, in order to be more efficient, sector-specific initiatives should operate in two layers, with intrasectoral dimension and cross-sector nodes. In this context, the cross-sectoral, cross-border harmonization of data exchange models and business processes will probably be one of the key ICT-related issues in the future, and will feature at the top of the policy agenda in the years to come.

Conclusions

ICT and e-business models have a key role to play in stimulating innovation and increasing productivity and competitiveness. Nonetheless, the great potential of ICT-enabled innovations and reorganization of business models is still largely underexploited by European SMEs. Improving the integration and innovative use of ICT by European SMEs, has, therefore, been a major challenge for EU policymakers. In response to this challenge, European countries have been devising targeted e-business policies over the past years.

Similarly with other policy fields, it is obvious that the European Union can achieve its objectives for a more dynamic and e-business friendly environment only by joining forces and coordinating efforts. The coordination of Member States' policies stimulates action and substantially enhances their impact. This is the major goal of the eBSN: to learn from one another and re-enforce synergies and coordination between e-business policy initiatives all over Europe. eBSN has been instrumental in spreading knowledge from national and regional e-business policy experiences, lessons to be learned, and best government practices. It keeps on analyzing policy trends, benchmarking, identifying inefficiencies, facilitating policy synergies, and shaping policy orientations.

However, although policy coordination at the EU level is crucial and increases the efficiency of individual initiatives, a regional or local deployment ensures close links with the targeted SMEs, better understanding of their real needs, and, therefore, more tailored services. In conclusion, EU, national, and regional e-business measures need to work together to gear up visible European action toward the Lisbon objectives.

Box 7: Policy example: E-invoicing initiative in South Karelia, Finland

The e-invoicing initiative in South Karelia was launched in the beginning of 2004 by a number of regional stakeholders under the coordination of Kareltek Technology Centre in Lappeenranta, Finland (www.kareltek.fi), as part of a long-term regional e-business development policy. The policy focuses on assisting South Karelian SMEs in adopting e-invoicing. This application is seen as a relatively easy-to-realize opportunity for SMEs to save costs. In the long run, the initiative aims at making regional businesses increasingly networked. E-invoicing is regarded as the "killer application" that will raise demand for further, more advanced e-business applications.

An innovative feature of this policy is that large companies as well as the public sector of the region are involved as "e-pioneers," facilitating the diffusion of technology to smaller companies. The participating e-pioneers have agreed to contact their regional suppliers, mostly SMEs, and ask them to send their invoices electronically. Thus existing market pressure, enhanced by the e-pioneers, works as the main catalyst for e-invoicing adoption among regional SMEs. However, pressure is coupled with positive incentives. In this regard, funds for training staff in the use of the respective applications were provided. However, it soon turned out that the key challenge of the program was the lack of interoperability among the technical and contractual infrastructures that proved not ready for such a wide adoption of e-invoicing by SMEs.

This did not, however, discourage the project implementers. They launched a long and tiresome process of encouraging the e-invoicing infrastructure and service operators to agree on concrete steps to improve the interoperability of e-invoice transmission between themselves, through the adoption of common standards. For e-invoicing transactions to work properly, a great deal of pioneering work was necessary to develop this infrastructure. Once the main obstacles had been removed, the initiative moved on to its actual purpose: e-invoicing adoption in SMEs. Here, two forms of support are offered to the SME that opt for either simple e-invoicing using its bank's Internet applications, or integrating the e-invoicing application into the IT systems of the company.

The impact of this initiative is expected to be very concrete. Electronic processing is believed to halve the average total cost of processing an invoice, from about 40 euros to 20 euros. It is estimated that there are about 5.2 million invoices sent annually in South Karelia. With an e-invoicing penetration of 50 percent, annual savings would add up to about 52 million euros for the regional economy. Finally, by making processes more efficient, e-invoicing will have a positive impact on the overall firms' productivity.

Source: Databank et al., 2006.

Box 8: Policy example: Harmonizing cross-sectoral business processes in Europe: E-invoicing, European Union

The generating of remittances and processing invoices, including reconciling related payments, is central to any value chain. Therefore it is clear that improving invoicing performance will have benefits for a vast number of trading entities.

Invoicing, as a process, is central to the cash flow and liquidity of any trading organization, where even small improvements in efficiency can have tremendous commercial value. Examples of that value are improved working capital, reduced gearing, and better liquidity. E-invoicing links the internal processes of enterprises to the payment systems.

In particular, the SME sector, which to a large extent still employs manual, paper-based processes, will benefit from dematerialization of the invoice and automation of internal processes. Linking these organizations electronically within their respective value chains would contribute enormously to individual efficiency improvements and to that of European supply chains as a whole, which in turn will help drive the Lisbon Agenda.

Streamlining the flow of information in any value chain will reduce inefficiencies, improve certainty, and reduce cost. As Europe moves to adopt the Single Euro Payments Area (SEPA), it is logical that this is linked to the business processes that necessitate a vast majority of business-to-business and business-to-government payments.

By a decision on October 31, 2007, the Commission established the Expert Group on e-Invoicing. Its tasks will be to identify shortcomings in the regulatory framework for e-invoicing at Union and Member State levels, as well as identifying e-invoicing business requirements and data elements. Also it is tasked with proposing responsibilities to be assigned to standardization bodies and a time schedule for the execution of specific work—the European e-Invoicing Framework, to be completed by the end of 2009—and solutions supporting the provision of e-invoicing services in an open and interoperable manner across Europe.

Source: European Commission, available at http://ec.europa.eu/enterprise/ict/policy/standards/einvoicing_en.htm.

Notes

1 *E-business* is the digitization of all business processes (both intra and inter-firm) over computer mediated networks (OECD).

2 See http://ec.europa.eu/enterprise/e-bsn/index_en.html.

3 Atkinson 2007b.

4 European Commission 2003b.

5 European Commission 2007b.

6 Dedrick et al. 2003.

7 OECD 2004.

8 *E-business W@tch* 2006.

9 Gilchrist et al. 2001.

10 Atkinson 2007a.

11 Atkinson 2007a.

12 European Commission 2003a.

13 Bresnahan et al. 2000.

14 Violino 2004.

15 Van Leeuwen and van der Wiel 2004.

16 *E-business W@tch* 2006.

17 Mason et al. 2004.

18 European Commission 2007c.

19 Press release by President Barroso (see European Commission 2007b).

20 Fraunhofer IAO and FORMIT 2008.

21 European Commission 2007a.

22 Databank et al. 2006.

23 Empirica et al. 2007.

24 Empirica et al. 2007.

References

Atkinson, R. D. 2007a. "Digital Prosperity: Understanding the Economic Benefits of the Information Technology Revolution," Report, March. The Information Technology and Innovation Foundation, Available at http://www.itif.org/files/digital_prosperity.pdf.

———. 2007b. "Boosting European Prosperity through the widespread use of ICT." Report, November. The Information Technology and Innovation Foundation. Available at http://www.itif.org/files/EuropeanProductivity.pdf.

Bresnahan, T. F., E. Brynjolfsson, and L. M. Hitt. 2002. "Information Technology, Workplace Organization, and the Demand for Skilled Labor: Firm-Level Evidence," February, *Quarterly Journal of Economics* 117 (1): 339–76.

Databank, Empiria GmbH, and IDATE. 2006. *Assessment of the Impacts of Regional & National EBusiness Policies*, Study done for the European Commission. Available at http://ec.europa.eu/enterprise/e-bsn/publicationsandstudies/index_en.html.

Dedrick, J., V. Gurbaxani, and K. L. Kraemer. 2003. "Information Technology and Economic Performance: A Critical Review of the Empirical Evidence." *ACM Computing Surveys* 35 (1): 1–28.

E-Business W@tch. 2006. Chart Report. Available at http://www.ebusiness-watch.org.

Empiria GmbH, Databank, and IDATE. 2007. *Sectoral E-Business Policies in Support of SMEs: Innovative Approaches, Good Practices and Lessons to Be Learned*. Study done for the European Commission. Available at http://ec.europa.eu/enterprise/e-bsn/publicationsandstudies/documents/pdf/ebizpolicies_benchmarking_report.pdf.

———. ICT standardisation. Available at http://ec.europa.eu/enterprise/ict/policy/standards/einvoicing_en.htm.

———. 2003a. *European Economy: 2003 Review*. Available at http://ec.europa.eu/economy_finance/publications/publication7694_en.pdf.

———. 2003b. *EU Productivity and Competitiveness: An Industry Perspective: Can Europe Resume the Catching Up Process?* Mary O'Mahony and Bart van Ark, eds., Enterprise Publications. Luxembourg: European Communities. Available at http://ec.europa.eu/enterprise/enterprise_policy/competitiveness/doc/eu_competitiveness_a_sectoral_perspective.pdf.

———. 2007a. Communication from the Commission: "Raising Productivity Growth: Key Messages from the European Competitiveness Report," October 31. Available at http://ec.europa.eu/enterprise/enterprise_policy/competitiveness/doc/compet_report_2007/comprep_2007_com_666.pdf.

———. 2007b. President Barroso, Press release, October 3. Available at http://europa.eu/rapid/pressReleasesAction.do?reference=IP/07/1433&format=HTML&aged=0&language=EN&guiLanguage=en.

———. 2007c. Communication from the Commission: "The European Interest: Succeeding in the Age of Globalisation," October 3. Available at http://ec.europa.eu/commission_barroso/president/pdf/COM2007_581_en.pdf

Fraunhofer IAO and FORMIT. 2008. "eBSN eBusiness Guide for SMEs: eBusiness Software and Services in the European Market." Study done for the European Commission. Final report, March. Brussels.

Gilchrist, S., V. Gurbaxani, and R. Town. 2001. "Productivity and the PC Revolution," April. Center for Research on Information Technology and Organizations. Working Paper. Available at http://www.crito.uci.edu/itr/publications/pdf/prod_pc_revolution.pdf

Hempell, T., G. van Leeuwen, and H. Henry van der Wiel. 2004. "ICT, Innovation and Business Performance in Services: Evidence for Germany and the Netherlands." ZEW Discussion Paper No. 04-06, Manheim, published as a chapter in OECD publication: *The Economic Impact of ICT, Measurement, Evidence and Implications*. Paris: OECD. 131–52. Available at ftp://ftp.zew.de/pub/zew-docs/dp/dp0406.pdf.

Mason, G., M, O'Mahoney, and B. van Ark, 2004. "The Policy Framework: Does the EU Need a Productivity Agenda?" *E.U. Productivity and Competitiveness: An Industry Perspective*, eds. M. O'Mahony and B. van Ark, Brussels: European Commission, 2004

OECD (Organisation for Economic Co-operation and Development). 2004. *The Economic Impact of ICT: Measurement, Evidence, and Implications*. Paris: OECD.

Violino, B. 2004. "Productivity Gains: Quantity Plus Quality." *Optimize Magazine* 28 (February). Available at http://www.informationweek.com/management/showArticle.jhtml?articleID=18200222.

Part 3

Country/Economy Profiles

How to Read the Country/Economy Profiles

PEARL SAMANDARI, World Economic Forum

The following pages present the profiles of the 127 economies covered by the *Global Information Technology Report 2007–2008*. They provide a quick picture of the level of ICT development of an economy by grouping information under the following sections:

❶ Key macroeconomic and ICT indicators, which present data for population, gross domestic product (GDP) per capita, Internet users per 100 inhabitants, and Internet bandwidth per 10,000 inhabitants.[1]

❷ Overall Networked Readiness Index (NRI) ranking for 2007–2008, which gives immediate insight into overall ICT readiness. One can compare this ranking with those of the NRI 2005–2006 and NRI 2006–2007 if the economy was covered by the Index in those years. Also shown is the economy's ranking in the World Economic Forum's Global Competitiveness Index 2007–2008.[2]

❸ Three component subindexes, each consisting of a list of variables. Detailed rankings for the economy presented can be found for each of the variables listed and taken into consideration for the current NRI study.

This information, which identifies key areas of relative over- and underperformance, provides a rapid understanding of an economy's ICT readiness. For example, the rankings of the variables of venture capital availability and the state of cluster development in the environment component subindex enable the reader to identify key parameters contributing to the economy's performance.

The inferences that can be derived from the ranking of a given economy can be augmented by a closer inspection of the relative performance of other economies. The numbers next to the title of the variables refer to the numbering of the Data Tables presented at the end of this *Report*.

Notes

1 Sources for population include the UNFPA's *State of World Population 2006*, the UN Department of Economic and Social Affairs' *Population Division Database* (June 2007), and national sources. GDP figures were obtained from the IMF *World Economic Outlook Database* (April and September 2007 editions). Data on Internet users and bandwidth are from the International Telecommunication Union's *World Telecommunication Indicators 2007* and from national sources.

2 See World Economic Forum, *The Global Competitiveness Report 2007–2008*. Hampshire: Palgrave Macmillan.

List of Countries/Economies

Country/Economy	Page
Albania	162
Algeria	163
Argentina	164
Armenia	165
Australia	166
Austria	167
Azerbaijan	168
Bahrain	169
Bangladesh	170
Barbados	171
Belgium	172
Benin	173
Bolivia	174
Bosnia and Herzegovina	175
Botswana	176
Brazil	177
Bulgaria	178
Burkina Faso	179
Burundi	180
Cambodia	181
Cameroon	182
Canada	183
Chad	184
Chile	185
China	186
Colombia	187
Costa Rica	188
Croatia	189
Cyprus	190
Czech Republic	191
Denmark	192
Dominican Republic	193
Ecuador	194
Egypt	195
El Salvador	196
Estonia	197
Ethiopia	198
Finland	199
France	200
Gambia	201
Georgia	202
Germany	203
Greece	204

Country/Economy	Page
Guatemala	205
Guyana	206
Honduras	207
Hong Kong SAR	208
Hungary	209
Iceland	210
India	211
Indonesia	212
Ireland	213
Israel	214
Italy	215
Jamaica	216
Japan	217
Jordan	218
Kazakhstan	219
Kenya	220
Korea, Rep.	221
Kuwait	222
Kyrgyz Republic	223
Latvia	224
Lesotho	225
Libya	226
Lithuania	227
Luxembourg	228
Macedonia, FYR	229
Madagascar	230
Malaysia	231
Mali	232
Malta	233
Mauritania	234
Mauritius	235
Mexico	236
Moldova	237
Mongolia	238
Morocco	239
Mozambique	240
Namibia	241
Nepal	242
Netherlands	243
New Zealand	244
Nicaragua	245
Nigeria	246
Norway	247

Country/Economy	Page
Oman	248
Pakistan	249
Panama	250
Paraguay	251
Peru	252
Philippines	253
Poland	254
Portugal	255
Puerto Rico	256
Qatar	257
Romania	258
Russian Federation	259
Saudi Arabia	260
Senegal	261
Singapore	262
Slovak Republic	263
Slovenia	264
South Africa	265
Spain	266
Sri Lanka	267
Suriname	268
Sweden	269
Switzerland	270
Syria	271
Taiwan, China	272
Tajikistan	273
Tanzania	274
Thailand	275
Trinidad and Tobago	276
Tunisia	277
Turkey	278
Uganda	279
Ukraine	280
United Arab Emirates	281
United Kingdom	282
United States	283
Uruguay	284
Venezuela	285
Vietnam	286
Zambia	287
Zimbabwe	288

Albania

Key indicators

Population (millions), 2006...3.1
GDP (PPP) per capita (US$), 2006.......................5,727.4
Internet users per 100 inhabitants, 2006 ....15.0
Internet bandwidth (mB/s) per 10,000 inhabitants, 2005.........0.0

Networked Readiness Index

Year (number of economies)	Rank
2007–2008 (127)	**108**
2006–2007 (122)	107
2005–2006 (115)	106

Global Competitiveness Index 2007–2008 (131)   109

Environment component	115
Market environment	**106**
1.01 Venture capital availability, 2007	91
1.02 Financial market sophistication, 2007	119
1.03 Availability of latest technologies, 2007	99
1.04 State of cluster development, 2007	67
1.05 Utility patents,* 2006	86
1.06 High-tech exports,* 2005	86
1.07 Burden of government regulation, 2007	73
1.08 Extent and effect of taxation, 2007	80
1.09 Total tax rate,* 2007	70
1.10 Time required to start a business,* 2007	84
1.11 No. of procedures required to start a business,* 2007	74
1.12 Intensity of local competition, 2007	121
1.13 Freedom of the press, 2007	80
1.14 Accessibility of digital content, 2007	121
Political and regulatory environment	**111**
2.01 Effectiveness of law-making bodies, 2007	61
2.02 Laws relating to ICT, 2007	112
2.03 Judicial independence, 2007	115
2.04 Intellectual property protection, 2007	120
2.05 Efficiency of legal framework, 2007	114
2.06 Property rights, 2007	120
2.07 Quality of competition in the ISP sector, 2007	111
2.08 No. of procedures to enforce a contract,* 2007	75
2.09 Time to enforce a contract,* 2007	29
Infrastructure environment	**107**
3.01 Telephone lines,* 2005	81
3.02 Secure Internet servers,* 2006	85
3.03 Electricity production,* 2004	73
3.04 Availability of scientists and engineers, 2007	108
3.05 Quality of scientific research institutions, 2007	126
3.06 Tertiary enrollment,* 2004	79
3.07 Education expenditure,* 2005	94

Readiness component	99
Individual readiness	**86**
4.01 Quality of math and science education, 2007	71
4.02 Quality of the educational system, 2007	86
4.03 Internet access in schools, 2007	117
4.04 Buyer sophistication, 2007	98
4.05 Residential telephone connection charge,* 2004	96
4.06 Residential monthly telephone subscription,* 2005	7
4.07 High-speed monthly broadband subscription,* 2006	88
4.08 Lowest cost of broadband,* 2006	82
4.09 Cost of mobile telephone call,* 2005	84
Business readiness	**119**
5.01 Extent of staff training, 2007	98
5.02 Local availability of research and training, 2007	123
5.03 Quality of management schools, 2007	112
5.04 Company spending on R&D, 2007	126
5.05 University-industry research collaboration, 2007	127
5.06 Business telephone connection charge*	n/a
5.07 Business monthly telephone subscription,* 2005	54
5.08 Local supplier quality, 2007	120
5.09 Local supplier quantity, 2007	106
5.10 Computer, comm., and other services imports,* 2005	82
Government readiness	**103**
6.01 Government prioritization of ICT, 2007	80
6.02 Gov't procurement of advanced tech products, 2007	127
6.03 Importance of ICT to gov't vision of the future, 2007	95
6.04 E-Government Readiness Index,* 2007	77

Usage component	116
Individual usage	**82**
7.01 Mobile telephone subscribers,* 2005	81
7.02 Personal computers,* 2005	100
7.03 Broadband Internet subscribers,* 2005	108
7.04 Internet users,* 2006	67
7.05 Internet bandwidth,* 2005	116
Business usage	**118**
8.01 Prevalence of foreign technology licensing, 2007	88
8.02 Firm-level technology absorption, 2007	110
8.03 Capacity for innovation, 2007	127
8.04 Availability of new telephone lines, 2007	120
8.05 Extent of business Internet use, 2007	115
Government usage	**119**
9.01 Government success in ICT promotion, 2007	121
9.02 Availability of government online services, 2007	122
9.03 ICT use and government efficiency, 2007	126
9.04 Presence of ICT in government offices, 2007	55
9.05 E-Participation Index,* 2007	110

* Hard data

Note: For further details and explanation, please refer to the section "How to Read the Country/Economy Profiles" at the beginning of this chapter.

Algeria

Key indicators

Population (millions), 2006	33.4
GDP (PPP) per capita (US$), 2006	7,746.9
Internet users per 100 inhabitants, 2006	7.4
Internet bandwidth (mB/s) per 10,000 inhabitants, 2005	0.0

Networked Readiness Index

Year (number of economies)	Rank
2007–2008 (127)	**88**
2006–2007 (122)	80
2005–2006 (115)	87

Global Competitiveness Index 2007–2008 (131)	81

Environment component — 97
Market environment — 117

1.01	Venture capital availability, 2007	106
1.02	Financial market sophistication, 2007	123
1.03	Availability of latest technologies, 2007	106
1.04	State of cluster development, 2007	108
1.05	Utility patents,* 2006	83
1.06	High-tech exports,* 2004	106
1.07	Burden of government regulation, 2007	85
1.08	Extent and effect of taxation, 2007	41
1.09	Total tax rate,* 2007	111
1.10	Time required to start a business,* 2007	50
1.11	No. of procedures required to start a business,* 2007	112
1.12	Intensity of local competition, 2007	94
1.13	Freedom of the press, 2007	87
1.14	Accessibility of digital content, 2007	107

Political and regulatory environment — 96

2.01	Effectiveness of law-making bodies, 2007	83
2.02	Laws relating to ICT, 2007	105
2.03	Judicial independence, 2007	70
2.04	Intellectual property protection, 2007	94
2.05	Efficiency of legal framework, 2007	54
2.06	Property rights, 2007	73
2.07	Quality of competition in the ISP sector, 2007	92
2.08	No. of procedures to enforce a contract,* 2007	114
2.09	Time to enforce a contract,* 2007	86

Infrastructure environment — 80

3.01	Telephone lines,* 2006	90
3.02	Secure Internet servers,* 2006	101
3.03	Electricity production,* 2004	83
3.04	Availability of scientists and engineers, 2007	25
3.05	Quality of scientific research institutions, 2007	91
3.06	Tertiary enrollment,* 2005	76
3.07	Education expenditure,* 2005	47

Readiness component — 83
Individual readiness — 81

4.01	Quality of math and science education, 2007	82
4.02	Quality of the educational system, 2007	100
4.03	Internet access in schools, 2007	93
4.04	Buyer sophistication, 2007	77
4.05	Residential telephone connection charge,* 2006	68
4.06	Residential monthly telephone subscription,* 2006	36
4.07	High-speed monthly broadband subscription,* 2006	93
4.08	Lowest cost of broadband,* 2006	96
4.09	Cost of mobile telephone call,* 2006	49

Business readiness — 86

5.01	Extent of staff training, 2007	110
5.02	Local availability of research and training, 2007	102
5.03	Quality of management schools, 2007	99
5.04	Company spending on R&D, 2007	89
5.05	University-industry research collaboration, 2007	110
5.06	Business telephone connection charge,* 2006	60
5.07	Business monthly telephone subscription,* 2006	28
5.08	Local supplier quality, 2007	117
5.09	Local supplier quantity, 2007	98
5.10	Computer, comm., and other services imports*	n/a

Government readiness — 74

6.01	Government prioritization of ICT, 2007	49
6.02	Gov't procurement of advanced tech products, 2007	68
6.03	Importance of ICT to gov't vision of the future, 2007	61
6.04	E-Government Readiness Index,* 2007	97

Usage component — 97
Individual usage — 79

7.01	Mobile telephone subscribers,* 2006	68
7.02	Personal computers,* 2005	112
7.03	Broadband Internet subscribers,* 2005	74
7.04	Internet users,* 2006	92
7.05	Internet bandwidth,* 2005	111

Business usage — 108

8.01	Prevalence of foreign technology licensing, 2007	103
8.02	Firm-level technology absorption, 2007	96
8.03	Capacity for innovation, 2007	123
8.04	Availability of new telephone lines, 2007	75
8.05	Extent of business Internet use, 2007	126

Government usage — 96

9.01	Government success in ICT promotion, 2007	47
9.02	Availability of government online services, 2007	111
9.03	ICT use and government efficiency, 2007	92
9.04	Presence of ICT in government offices, 2007	66
9.05	E-Participation Index,* 2007	110

* Hard data

Note: For further details and explanation, please refer to the section "How to Read the Country/Economy Profiles" at the beginning of this chapter.

Argentina

Key indicators

Population (millions), 2006	39.1
GDP (PPP) per capita (US$), 2006	16,080.5
Internet users per 100 inhabitants, 2006	20.9
Internet bandwidth (mB/s) per 10,000 inhabitants, 2006	6.9

Networked Readiness Index

Year (number of economies)	Rank
2007–2008 (127)	**77**
2006–2007 (122)	63
2005–2006 (115)	71

Global Competitiveness Index 2007–2008 (131)	85

Environment component — 92

Market environment — 118

1.01	Venture capital availability, 2007	81
1.02	Financial market sophistication, 2007	74
1.03	Availability of latest technologies, 2007	85
1.04	State of cluster development, 2007	62
1.05	Utility patents,* 2006	46
1.06	High-tech exports,* 2005	60
1.07	Burden of government regulation, 2007	113
1.08	Extent and effect of taxation, 2007	125
1.09	Total tax rate,* 2007	119
1.10	Time required to start a business,* 2007	68
1.11	No. of procedures required to start a business,* 2007	112
1.12	Intensity of local competition, 2007	107
1.13	Freedom of the press, 2007	114
1.14	Accessibility of digital content, 2007	60

Political and regulatory environment — 115

2.01	Effectiveness of law-making bodies, 2007	124
2.02	Laws relating to ICT, 2007	96
2.03	Judicial independence, 2007	119
2.04	Intellectual property protection, 2007	99
2.05	Efficiency of legal framework, 2007	121
2.06	Property rights, 2007	124
2.07	Quality of competition in the ISP sector, 2007	71
2.08	No. of procedures to enforce a contract,* 2007	53
2.09	Time to enforce a contract,* 2007	75

Infrastructure environment — 49

3.01	Telephone lines,* 2006	54
3.02	Secure Internet servers,* 2006	58
3.03	Electricity production,* 2004	62
3.04	Availability of scientists and engineers, 2007	75
3.05	Quality of scientific research institutions, 2007	85
3.06	Tertiary enrollment,* 2004	21
3.07	Education expenditure,* 2005	64

Readiness component — 74

Individual readiness — 66

4.01	Quality of math and science education, 2007	92
4.02	Quality of the educational system, 2007	102
4.03	Internet access in schools, 2007	83
4.04	Buyer sophistication, 2007	61
4.05	Residential telephone connection charge,* 2005	65
4.06	Residential monthly telephone subscription,* 2005	52
4.07	High-speed monthly broadband subscription,* 2006	37
4.08	Lowest cost of broadband,* 2006	44
4.09	Cost of mobile telephone call,* 2006	50

Business readiness — 51

5.01	Extent of staff training, 2007	74
5.02	Local availability of research and training, 2007	45
5.03	Quality of management schools, 2007	30
5.04	Company spending on R&D, 2007	85
5.05	University-industry research collaboration, 2007	78
5.06	Business telephone connection charge,* 2005	57
5.07	Business monthly telephone subscription,* 2005	58
5.08	Local supplier quality, 2007	68
5.09	Local supplier quantity, 2007	63
5.10	Computer, comm., and other services imports,* 2005	55

Government readiness — 106

6.01	Government prioritization of ICT, 2007	119
6.02	Gov't procurement of advanced tech products, 2007	111
6.03	Importance of ICT to gov't vision of the future, 2007	120
6.04	E-Government Readiness Index,* 2007	39

Usage component — 67

Individual usage — 51

7.01	Mobile telephone subscribers,* 2006	47
7.02	Personal computers,* 2005	62
7.03	Broadband Internet subscribers,* 2006	47
7.04	Internet users,* 2006	55
7.05	Internet bandwidth,* 2006	43

Business usage — 82

8.01	Prevalence of foreign technology licensing, 2007	81
8.02	Firm-level technology absorption, 2007	97
8.03	Capacity for innovation, 2007	80
8.04	Availability of new telephone lines, 2007	72
8.05	Extent of business Internet use, 2007	73

Government usage — 76

9.01	Government success in ICT promotion, 2007	119
9.02	Availability of government online services, 2007	59
9.03	ICT use and government efficiency, 2007	84
9.04	Presence of ICT in government offices, 2007	110
9.05	E-Participation Index,* 2007	22

* Hard data

Note: For further details and explanation, please refer to the section "How to Read the Country/Economy Profiles" at the beginning of this chapter.

Armenia

Key indicators

Population (millions), 2006	3.0
GDP (PPP) per capita (US$), 2006	5,176.8
Internet users per 100 inhabitants, 2006	5.7
Internet bandwidth (mB/s) per 10,000 inhabitants, 2004	0.1

Networked Readiness Index

Year (number of economies)	Rank
2007–2008 (127)	**106**
2006–2007 (122)	96
2005–2006 (115)	86
Global Competitiveness Index 2007–2008 (131)	93

Environment component — 100
Market environment — 102
1.01	Venture capital availability, 2007	120
1.02	Financial market sophistication, 2007	109
1.03	Availability of latest technologies, 2007	110
1.04	State of cluster development, 2007	114
1.05	Utility patents,* 2006	52
1.06	High-tech exports,* 2005	81
1.07	Burden of government regulation, 2007	76
1.08	Extent and effect of taxation, 2007	70
1.09	Total tax rate,* 2007	37
1.10	Time required to start a business,* 2007	38
1.11	No. of procedures required to start a business,* 2007	58
1.12	Intensity of local competition, 2007	122
1.13	Freedom of the press, 2007	117
1.14	Accessibility of digital content, 2007	104

Political and regulatory environment — 107
2.01	Effectiveness of law-making bodies, 2007	92
2.02	Laws relating to ICT, 2007	93
2.03	Judicial independence, 2007	116
2.04	Intellectual property protection, 2007	106
2.05	Efficiency of legal framework, 2007	101
2.06	Property rights, 2007	68
2.07	Quality of competition in the ISP sector, 2007	121
2.08	No. of procedures to enforce a contract,* 2007	117
2.09	Time to enforce a contract,* 2007	14

Infrastructure environment — 81
3.01	Telephone lines,* 2005	61
3.02	Secure Internet servers,* 2006	78
3.03	Electricity production,* 2004	69
3.04	Availability of scientists and engineers, 2007	57
3.05	Quality of scientific research institutions, 2007	81
3.06	Tertiary enrollment,* 2005	70
3.07	Education expenditure,* 2005	87

Readiness component — 103
Individual readiness — 101
4.01	Quality of math and science education, 2007	62
4.02	Quality of the educational system, 2007	91
4.03	Internet access in schools, 2007	104
4.04	Buyer sophistication, 2007	92
4.05	Residential telephone connection charge,* 2005	76
4.06	Residential monthly telephone subscription,* 2005	63
4.07	High-speed monthly broadband subscription,* 2006	102
4.08	Lowest cost of broadband,* 2006	106
4.09	Cost of mobile telephone call,* 2005	72

Business readiness — 101
5.01	Extent of staff training, 2007	111
5.02	Local availability of research and training, 2007	108
5.03	Quality of management schools, 2007	118
5.04	Company spending on R&D, 2007	107
5.05	University-industry research collaboration, 2007	101
5.06	Business telephone connection charge,* 2005	71
5.07	Business monthly telephone subscription,* 2005	84
5.08	Local supplier quality, 2007	111
5.09	Local supplier quantity, 2007	107
5.10	Computer, comm., and other services imports,* 2005	104

Government readiness — 107
6.01	Government prioritization of ICT, 2007	106
6.02	Gov't procurement of advanced tech products, 2007	109
6.03	Importance of ICT to gov't vision of the future, 2007	107
6.04	E-Government Readiness Index,* 2007	88

Usage component — 112
Individual usage — 106
7.01	Mobile telephone subscribers,* 2005	116
7.02	Personal computers,* 2005	59
7.03	Broadband Internet subscribers,* 2005	98
7.04	Internet users,* 2006	97
7.05	Internet bandwidth,* 2004	102

Business usage — 103
8.01	Prevalence of foreign technology licensing, 2007	112
8.02	Firm-level technology absorption, 2007	80
8.03	Capacity for innovation, 2007	71
8.04	Availability of new telephone lines, 2007	111
8.05	Extent of business Internet use, 2007	109

Government usage — 111
9.01	Government success in ICT promotion, 2007	109
9.02	Availability of government online services, 2007	120
9.03	ICT use and government efficiency, 2007	114
9.04	Presence of ICT in government offices, 2007	83
9.05	E-Participation Index,* 2007	100

* Hard data

Note: For further details and explanation, please refer to the section "How to Read the Country/Economy Profiles" at the beginning of this chapter.

Australia

Key indicators

Population (millions), 2006..20.4
GDP (PPP) per capita (US$), 2006.....................................33,036.6
Internet users per 100 inhabitants, 2006 ....75.1
Internet bandwidth (mB/s) per 10,000 inhabitants, 2006.....117.6

Networked Readiness Index

Year (number of economies)	Rank
2007–2008 (127) **14**	
2006–2007 (122) 15	
2005–2006 (115) 15	

Global Competitiveness Index 2007–2008 (131)   19

Environment component — 12

Market environment — 21

1.01 Venture capital availability, 2007..........................13
1.02 Financial market sophistication, 2007 8
1.03 Availability of latest technologies, 2007 19
1.04 State of cluster development, 2007....................48
1.05 Utility patents,* 2006 17
1.06 High-tech exports,* 2005..50
1.07 Burden of government regulation, 2007 67
1.08 Extent and effect of taxation, 2007......................73
1.09 Total tax rate,* 2007 81
1.10 Time required to start a business,* 2007.............1
1.11 No. of procedures required to start a business,* 2007 1
1.12 Intensity of local competition, 2007 15
1.13 Freedom of the press, 2007...................................18
1.14 Accessibility of digital content, 2007..................23

Political and regulatory environment — 7

2.01 Effectiveness of law-making bodies, 2007 3
2.02 Laws relating to ICT, 2007......................................19
2.03 Judicial independence, 2007..................................6
2.04 Intellectual property protection, 2007 10
2.05 Efficiency of legal framework, 2007....................11
2.06 Property rights, 2007...8
2.07 Quality of competition in the ISP sector, 2007 27
2.08 No. of procedures to enforce a contract,* 2007 11
2.09 Time to enforce a contract,* 2007 9

Infrastructure environment — 10

3.01 Telephone lines,* 2006..18
3.02 Secure Internet servers,* 2006................................6
3.03 Electricity production,* 2004 10
3.04 Availability of scientists and engineers, 2007 34
3.05 Quality of scientific research institutions, 2007 15
3.06 Tertiary enrollment,* 2005......................................13
3.07 Education expenditure,* 2005................................44

Readiness component — 24

Individual readiness — 13

4.01 Quality of math and science education, 2007...................23
4.02 Quality of the educational system, 2007..............8
4.03 Internet access in schools, 2007..........................15
4.04 Buyer sophistication, 2007 20
4.05 Residential telephone connection charge,* 2005 40
4.06 Residential monthly telephone subscription,* 2005 18
4.07 High-speed monthly broadband subscription,* 2006........19
4.08 Lowest cost of broadband,* 2006 29
4.09 Cost of mobile telephone call,* 2005...................47

Business readiness — 24

5.01 Extent of staff training, 2007..................................20
5.02 Local availability of research and training, 2007.............16
5.03 Quality of management schools, 2007 16
5.04 Company spending on R&D, 2007.......................25
5.05 University-industry research collaboration, 2007...........22
5.06 Business telephone connection charge,* 2005 31
5.07 Business monthly telephone subscription,* 2005 34
5.08 Local supplier quality, 2007 16
5.09 Local supplier quantity, 2007................................33
5.10 Computer, comm., and other services imports,* 2005 76

Government readiness — 26

6.01 Government prioritization of ICT, 2007..............48
6.02 Gov't procurement of advanced tech products, 2007 27
6.03 Importance of ICT to gov't vision of the future, 2007.......40
6.04 E-Government Readiness Index,* 2007................8

Usage component — 11

Individual usage — 7

7.01 Mobile telephone subscribers,* 2006..................33
7.02 Personal computers,* 2005 6
7.03 Broadband Internet subscribers,* 2006 18
7.04 Internet users,* 2006..4
7.05 Internet bandwidth,* 2006..7

Business usage — 21

8.01 Prevalence of foreign technology licensing, 2007...............8
8.02 Firm-level technology absorption, 2007 18
8.03 Capacity for innovation, 2007................................30
8.04 Availability of new telephone lines, 2007..........39
8.05 Extent of business Internet use, 2007................18

Government usage — 9

9.01 Government success in ICT promotion, 2007...................46
9.02 Availability of government online services, 2007.............15
9.03 ICT use and government efficiency, 2007..........29
9.04 Presence of ICT in government offices, 2007 15
9.05 E-Participation Index,* 2007....................................5

* Hard data

Note: For further details and explanation, please refer to the section "How to Read the Country/Economy Profiles" at the beginning of this chapter.

Austria

Key indicators

Population (millions), 2006	8.2
GDP (PPP) per capita (US$), 2006	36,367.7
Internet users per 100 inhabitants, 2006	51.2
Internet bandwidth (mB/s) per 10,000 inhabitants, 2005	66.6

Networked Readiness Index

Year (number of economies)	Rank
2007–2008 (127)	**15**
2006–2007 (122)	17
2005–2006 (115)	18

Global Competitiveness Index 2007–2008 (131)	15

Environment component — 20
Market environment — 22
1.01	Venture capital availability, 2007	28
1.02	Financial market sophistication, 2007	21
1.03	Availability of latest technologies, 2007	17
1.04	State of cluster development, 2007	15
1.05	Utility patents,* 2006	15
1.06	High-tech exports,* 2005	33
1.07	Burden of government regulation, 2007	28
1.08	Extent and effect of taxation, 2007	36
1.09	Total tax rate,* 2007	97
1.10	Time required to start a business,* 2007	62
1.11	No. of procedures required to start a business,* 2007	44
1.12	Intensity of local competition, 2007	2
1.13	Freedom of the press, 2007	8
1.14	Accessibility of digital content, 2007	6

Political and regulatory environment — 6
2.01	Effectiveness of law-making bodies, 2007	26
2.02	Laws relating to ICT, 2007	6
2.03	Judicial independence, 2007	10
2.04	Intellectual property protection, 2007	11
2.05	Efficiency of legal framework, 2007	6
2.06	Property rights, 2007	4
2.07	Quality of competition in the ISP sector, 2007	5
2.08	No. of procedures to enforce a contract,* 2007	5
2.09	Time to enforce a contract,* 2007	32

Infrastructure environment — 20
3.01	Telephone lines,* 2006	24
3.02	Secure Internet servers,* 2006	19
3.03	Electricity production,* 2004	24
3.04	Availability of scientists and engineers, 2007	26
3.05	Quality of scientific research institutions, 2007	20
3.06	Tertiary enrollment,* 2005	35
3.07	Education expenditure,* 2005	27

Readiness component — 8
Individual readiness — 10
4.01	Quality of math and science education, 2007	25
4.02	Quality of the educational system, 2007	14
4.03	Internet access in schools, 2007	8
4.04	Buyer sophistication, 2007	6
4.05	Residential telephone connection charge,* 2005	32
4.06	Residential monthly telephone subscription,* 2005	29
4.07	High-speed monthly broadband subscription,* 2006	23
4.08	Lowest cost of broadband,* 2006	26
4.09	Cost of mobile telephone call,* 2005	31

Business readiness — 5
5.01	Extent of staff training, 2007	6
5.02	Local availability of research and training, 2007	15
5.03	Quality of management schools, 2007	24
5.04	Company spending on R&D, 2007	14
5.05	University-industry research collaboration, 2007	19
5.06	Business telephone connection charge,* 2005	37
5.07	Business monthly telephone subscription,* 2005	23
5.08	Local supplier quality, 2007	2
5.09	Local supplier quantity, 2007	3
5.10	Computer, comm., and other services imports,* 2005	6

Government readiness — 23
6.01	Government prioritization of ICT, 2007	27
6.02	Gov't procurement of advanced tech products, 2007	21
6.03	Importance of ICT to gov't vision of the future, 2007	22
6.04	E-Government Readiness Index,* 2007	16

Usage component — 17
Individual usage — 16
7.01	Mobile telephone subscribers,* 2006	13
7.02	Personal computers,* 2005	13
7.03	Broadband Internet subscribers,* 2006	21
7.04	Internet users,* 2006	21
7.05	Internet bandwidth,* 2005	15

Business usage — 13
8.01	Prevalence of foreign technology licensing, 2007	34
8.02	Firm-level technology absorption, 2007	12
8.03	Capacity for innovation, 2007	11
8.04	Availability of new telephone lines, 2007	11
8.05	Extent of business Internet use, 2007	16

Government usage — 13
9.01	Government success in ICT promotion, 2007	26
9.02	Availability of government online services, 2007	8
9.03	ICT use and government efficiency, 2007	17
9.04	Presence of ICT in government offices, 2007	7
9.05	E-Participation Index,* 2007	19

* Hard data

Note: For further details and explanation, please refer to the section "How to Read the Country/Economy Profiles" at the beginning of this chapter.

Azerbaijan

Key indicators

Population (millions), 2006..8.5
GDP (PPP) per capita (US$), 2006...............................6,475.6
Internet users per 100 inhabitants, 2006 ....9.8
Internet bandwidth (mB/s) per 10,000 inhabitants, 2005........0.4

Networked Readiness Index

Year (number of economies)	Rank
2007–2008 (127)	**67**
2006–2007 (122)	71
2005–2006 (115)	73

Global Competitiveness Index 2007–2008 (131)   66

Environment component — 76

Market environment — 81

1.01 Venture capital availability, 2007..64
1.02 Financial market sophistication, 2007 79
1.03 Availability of latest technologies, 2007 70
1.04 State of cluster development, 2007.......................................66
1.05 Utility patents,* 2006 73
1.06 High-tech exports,* 2005 101
1.07 Burden of government regulation, 2007 39
1.08 Extent and effect of taxation, 2007 54
1.09 Total tax rate,* 2007 54
1.10 Time required to start a business,* 2007 67
1.11 No. of procedures required to start a business,* 2007 ..103
1.12 Intensity of local competition, 2007 116
1.13 Freedom of the press, 2007...93
1.14 Accessibility of digital content, 2007 71

Political and regulatory environment — 74

2.01 Effectiveness of law-making bodies, 2007 72
2.02 Laws relating to ICT, 2007..60
2.03 Judicial independence, 2007..104
2.04 Intellectual property protection, 2007 92
2.05 Efficiency of legal framework, 2007......................................84
2.06 Property rights, 2007...101
2.07 Quality of competition in the ISP sector, 2007 64
2.08 No. of procedures to enforce a contract,* 2007 75
2.09 Time to enforce a contract,* 2007 10

Infrastructure environment — 83

3.01 Telephone lines,* 2006..75
3.02 Secure Internet servers,* 2006...101
3.03 Electricity production,* 2004..64
3.04 Availability of scientists and engineers, 2007 51
3.05 Quality of scientific research institutions, 2007 56
3.06 Tertiary enrollment,* 2005..91
3.07 Education expenditure,* 2005..79

Readiness component — 62

Individual readiness — 78

4.01 Quality of math and science education, 2007 81
4.02 Quality of the educational system, 2007.............................95
4.03 Internet access in schools, 2007..79
4.04 Buyer sophistication, 2007 79
4.05 Residential telephone connection charge,* 2005 101
4.06 Residential monthly telephone subscription,* 2005 23
4.07 High-speed monthly broadband subscription,* 2006........80
4.08 Lowest cost of broadband,* 2006 94
4.09 Cost of mobile telephone call,* 2005...................................73

Business readiness — 56

5.01 Extent of staff training, 2007..84
5.02 Local availability of research and training, 2007................75
5.03 Quality of management schools, 2007 115
5.04 Company spending on R&D, 2007......................................50
5.05 University-industry research collaboration, 2007...............58
5.06 Business telephone connection charge,* 2005 101
5.07 Business monthly telephone subscription,* 2005 83
5.08 Local supplier quality, 2007...88
5.09 Local supplier quantity, 2007...85
5.10 Computer, comm., and other services imports,* 2005 1

Government readiness — 47

6.01 Government prioritization of ICT, 2007...............................36
6.02 Gov't procurement of advanced tech products, 2007 37
6.03 Importance of ICT to gov't vision of the future, 2007........55
6.04 E-Government Readiness Index,* 2007..............................79

Usage component — 66

Individual usage — 90

7.01 Mobile telephone subscribers,* 2006.................................84
7.02 Personal computers,* 2005 95
7.03 Broadband Internet subscribers,* 2005 103
7.04 Internet users,* 2006..82
7.05 Internet bandwidth,* 2005 85

Business usage — 65

8.01 Prevalence of foreign technology licensing, 2007.............83
8.02 Firm-level technology absorption, 2007 58
8.03 Capacity for innovation, 2007 45
8.04 Availability of new telephone lines, 2007...........................82
8.05 Extent of business Internet use, 2007 62

Government usage — 48

9.01 Government success in ICT promotion, 2007....................33
9.02 Availability of government online services, 2007 67
9.03 ICT use and government efficiency, 2007...........................50
9.04 Presence of ICT in government offices, 2007 41
9.05 E-Participation Index,* 2007...47

* Hard data

Note: For further details and explanation, please refer to the section "How to Read the Country/Economy Profiles" at the beginning of this chapter.

Bahrain

Key indicators

Population (millions), 2006..0.7
GDP (PPP) per capita (US$), 2006..................................24,066.7
Internet users per 100 inhabitants, 2005..............................21.3
Internet bandwidth (mB/s) per 10,000 inhabitants, 2005.........5.6

Networked Readiness Index

Year (number of economies)	Rank
2007–2008 (127)	**45**
2006–2007 (122)	50
2005–2006 (115)	49

Global Competitiveness Index 2007–2008 (131)	43

Environment component — 50
Market environment — 42

1.01 Venture capital availability, 2007..38
1.02 Financial market sophistication, 2007 22
1.03 Availability of latest technologies, 2007 26
1.04 State of cluster development, 2007......................................74
1.05 Utility patents,* 2006 86
1.06 High-tech exports,* 2004 88
1.07 Burden of government regulation, 2007 18
1.08 Extent and effect of taxation, 2007..1
1.09 Total tax rate* ....n/a
1.10 Time required to start a business* ....n/a
1.11 No. of procedures required to start a business*...............n/a
1.12 Intensity of local competition, 2007 56
1.13 Freedom of the press, 2007..101
1.14 Accessibility of digital content, 2007 21

Political and regulatory environment — 57

2.01 Effectiveness of law-making bodies, 2007 80
2.02 Laws relating to ICT, 2007..38
2.03 Judicial independence, 2007 57
2.04 Intellectual property protection, 2007 33
2.05 Efficiency of legal framework, 2007 55
2.06 Property rights, 2007 35
2.07 Quality of competition in the ISP sector, 2007 96
2.08 No. of procedures to enforce a contract* ....n/a
2.09 Time to enforce a contract* ....n/a

Infrastructure environment — 54

3.01 Telephone lines,* 2006...49
3.02 Secure Internet servers,* 2006 34
3.03 Electricity production,* 2003 11
3.04 Availability of scientists and engineers, 2007 98
3.05 Quality of scientific research institutions, 2007 113
3.06 Tertiary enrollment,* 2005..55
3.07 Education expenditure,* 2005...54

Readiness component — 47
Individual readiness — 41

4.01 Quality of math and science education, 2007 77
4.02 Quality of the educational system, 2007.............................64
4.03 Internet access in schools, 2007..40
4.04 Buyer sophistication, 2007 36
4.05 Residential telephone connection charge,* 2006 24
4.06 Residential monthly telephone subscription,* 2006 4
4.07 High-speed monthly broadband subscription,* 2006..........43
4.08 Lowest cost of broadband,* 2006 56
4.09 Cost of mobile telephone call,* 2005..................................18

Business readiness — 79

5.01 Extent of staff training, 2007..59
5.02 Local availability of research and training, 2007 89
5.03 Quality of management schools, 2007 84
5.04 Company spending on R&D, 2007.....................................106
5.05 University-industry research collaboration, 2007..............117
5.06 Business telephone connection charge,* 2006 20
5.07 Business monthly telephone subscription,* 2005 6
5.08 Local supplier quality, 2007 41
5.09 Local supplier quantity, 2007 36
5.10 Computer, comm., and other services imports,* 2005 ..110

Government readiness — 31

6.01 Government prioritization of ICT, 2007................................33
6.02 Gov't procurement of advanced tech products, 2007 32
6.03 Importance of ICT to gov't vision of the future, 2007........27
6.04 E-Government Readiness Index,* 2007...............................42

Usage component — 39
Individual usage — 43

7.01 Mobile telephone subscribers,* 2006....................................8
7.02 Personal computers,* 2005 42
7.03 Broadband Internet subscribers,* 2006 42
7.04 Internet users,* 2005 53
7.05 Internet bandwidth,* 2005 47

Business usage — 56

8.01 Prevalence of foreign technology licensing, 2007...............25
8.02 Firm-level technology absorption, 2007 40
8.03 Capacity for innovation, 2007...124
8.04 Availability of new telephone lines, 2007...........................40
8.05 Extent of business Internet use, 2007 83

Government usage — 39

9.01 Government success in ICT promotion, 2007.....................25
9.02 Availability of government online services, 2007 51
9.03 ICT use and government efficiency, 2007...........................49
9.04 Presence of ICT in government offices, 2007 42
9.05 E-Participation Index,* 2007...34

* Hard data

Note: For further details and explanation, please refer to the section "How to Read the Country/Economy Profiles" at the beginning of this chapter.

Bangladesh

Key indicators

Population (millions), 2006	144.4
GDP (PPP) per capita (US$), 2006	2,129.8
Internet users per 100 inhabitants, 2006	0.3
Internet bandwidth (mB/s) per 10,000 inhabitants, 2006	0.1

Networked Readiness Index

Year (number of economies)	Rank
2007–2008 (127)	**124**
2006–2007 (122)	118
2005–2006 (115)	110

Global Competitiveness Index 2007–2008 (131)	107

Environment component — 123

Market environment — 100

1.01	Venture capital availability, 2007	111
1.02	Financial market sophistication, 2007	108
1.03	Availability of latest technologies, 2007	109
1.04	State of cluster development, 2007	73
1.05	Utility patents,* 2006	86
1.06	High-tech exports,* 2005	105
1.07	Burden of government regulation, 2007	102
1.08	Extent and effect of taxation, 2007	37
1.09	Total tax rate,* 2007	49
1.10	Time required to start a business,* 2007	111
1.11	No. of procedures required to start a business,* 2007	44
1.12	Intensity of local competition, 2007	69
1.13	Freedom of the press, 2007	60
1.14	Accessibility of digital content, 2007	118

Political and regulatory environment — 124

2.01	Effectiveness of law-making bodies, 2007	101
2.02	Laws relating to ICT, 2007	121
2.03	Judicial independence, 2007	105
2.04	Intellectual property protection, 2007	127
2.05	Efficiency of legal framework, 2007	111
2.06	Property rights, 2007	104
2.07	Quality of competition in the ISP sector, 2007	75
2.08	No. of procedures to enforce a contract,* 2007	94
2.09	Time to enforce a contract,* 2007	119

Infrastructure environment — 123

3.01	Telephone lines,* 2006	117
3.02	Secure Internet servers,* 2006	101
3.03	Electricity production,* 2004	108
3.04	Availability of scientists and engineers, 2007	72
3.05	Quality of scientific research institutions, 2007	97
3.06	Tertiary enrollment,* 2005	101
3.07	Education expenditure,* 2005	113

Readiness component — 124

Individual readiness — 121

4.01	Quality of math and science education, 2007	113
4.02	Quality of the educational system, 2007	104
4.03	Internet access in schools, 2007	121
4.04	Buyer sophistication, 2007	94
4.05	Residential telephone connection charge,* 2006	119
4.06	Residential monthly telephone subscription,* 2006	100
4.07	High-speed monthly broadband subscription,* 2006	106
4.08	Lowest cost of broadband,* 2006	111
4.09	Cost of mobile telephone call,* 2005	103

Business readiness — 125

5.01	Extent of staff training, 2007	123
5.02	Local availability of research and training, 2007	125
5.03	Quality of management schools, 2007	107
5.04	Company spending on R&D, 2007	116
5.05	University-industry research collaboration, 2007	120
5.06	Business telephone connection charge,* 2006	117
5.07	Business monthly telephone subscription,* 2006	89
5.08	Local supplier quality, 2007	100
5.09	Local supplier quantity, 2007	93
5.10	Computer, comm., and other services imports,* 2005	107

Government readiness — 115

6.01	Government prioritization of ICT, 2007	95
6.02	Gov't procurement of advanced tech products, 2007	116
6.03	Importance of ICT to gov't vision of the future, 2007	106
6.04	E-Government Readiness Index,* 2007	110

Usage component — 123

Individual usage — 116

7.01	Mobile telephone subscribers,* 2006	112
7.02	Personal computers,* 2006	92
7.03	Broadband Internet subscribers,* 2005	118
7.04	Internet users,* 2006	125
7.05	Internet bandwidth,* 2006	103

Business usage — 120

8.01	Prevalence of foreign technology licensing, 2007	100
8.02	Firm-level technology absorption, 2007	104
8.03	Capacity for innovation, 2007	119
8.04	Availability of new telephone lines, 2007	125
8.05	Extent of business Internet use, 2007	110

Government usage — 124

9.01	Government success in ICT promotion, 2007	116
9.02	Availability of government online services, 2007	126
9.03	ICT use and government efficiency, 2007	109
9.04	Presence of ICT in government offices, 2007	124
9.05	E-Participation Index,* 2007	69

* Hard data

Note: For further details and explanation, please refer to the section "How to Read the Country/Economy Profiles" at the beginning of this chapter.

Barbados

Key indicators

Population (millions), 2006	0.3
GDP (PPP) per capita (US$), 2006	19,273.9
Internet users per 100 inhabitants, 2005	59.5
Internet bandwidth (mB/s) per 10,000 inhabitants, 2005	22.2

Networked Readiness Index

Year (number of economies)	Rank
2007–2008 (127)	**38**
2006–2007 (122)	40
2005–2006 (115)	n/a

Global Competitiveness Index 2007–2008 (131)	50

Environment component — 27
Market environment — 59

1.01	Venture capital availability, 2007	71
1.02	Financial market sophistication, 2007	52
1.03	Availability of latest technologies, 2007	36
1.04	State of cluster development, 2007	96
1.05	Utility patents,* 2006	86
1.06	High-tech exports*	n/a
1.07	Burden of government regulation, 2007	30
1.08	Extent and effect of taxation, 2007	39
1.09	Total tax rate*	n/a
1.10	Time required to start a business*	n/a
1.11	No. of procedures required to start a business*	n/a
1.12	Intensity of local competition, 2007	90
1.13	Freedom of the press, 2007	48
1.14	Accessibility of digital content, 2007	43

Political and regulatory environment — 27

2.01	Effectiveness of law-making bodies, 2007	13
2.02	Laws relating to ICT, 2007	46
2.03	Judicial independence, 2007	17
2.04	Intellectual property protection, 2007	38
2.05	Efficiency of legal framework, 2007	22
2.06	Property rights, 2007	33
2.07	Quality of competition in the ISP sector, 2007	65
2.08	No. of procedures to enforce a contract*	n/a
2.09	Time to enforce a contract*	n/a

Infrastructure environment — 19

3.01	Telephone lines,* 2005	16
3.02	Secure Internet servers,* 2006	21
3.03	Electricity production*	n/a
3.04	Availability of scientists and engineers, 2007	62
3.05	Quality of scientific research institutions, 2007	51
3.06	Tertiary enrollment,* 2001	54
3.07	Education expenditure,* 2005	9

Readiness component — 40
Individual readiness — 34

4.01	Quality of math and science education, 2007	16
4.02	Quality of the educational system, 2007	20
4.03	Internet access in schools, 2007	44
4.04	Buyer sophistication, 2007	40
4.05	Residential telephone connection charge,* 2005	35
4.06	Residential monthly telephone subscription,* 2005	69
4.07	High-speed monthly broadband subscription,* 2006	54
4.08	Lowest cost of broadband,* 2006	49
4.09	Cost of mobile telephone call,* 2005	37

Business readiness — 65

5.01	Extent of staff training, 2007	42
5.02	Local availability of research and training, 2007	78
5.03	Quality of management schools, 2007	42
5.04	Company spending on R&D, 2007	55
5.05	University-industry research collaboration, 2007	66
5.06	Business telephone connection charge,* 2005	29
5.07	Business monthly telephone subscription,* 2005	85
5.08	Local supplier quality, 2007	63
5.09	Local supplier quantity, 2007	96
5.10	Computer, comm., and other services imports,* 2005	84

Government readiness — 39

6.01	Government prioritization of ICT, 2007	29
6.02	Gov't procurement of advanced tech products, 2007	64
6.03	Importance of ICT to gov't vision of the future, 2007	58
6.04	E-Government Readiness Index,* 2007	46

Usage component — 50
Individual usage — 32

7.01	Mobile telephone subscribers,* 2005	52
7.02	Personal computers,* 2005	47
7.03	Broadband Internet subscribers,* 2005	30
7.04	Internet users,* 2005	14
7.05	Internet bandwidth,* 2005	28

Business usage — 66

8.01	Prevalence of foreign technology licensing, 2007	70
8.02	Firm-level technology absorption, 2007	57
8.03	Capacity for innovation, 2007	75
8.04	Availability of new telephone lines, 2007	69
8.05	Extent of business Internet use, 2007	66

Government usage — 87

9.01	Government success in ICT promotion, 2007	41
9.02	Availability of government online services, 2007	102
9.03	ICT use and government efficiency, 2007	99
9.04	Presence of ICT in government offices, 2007	71
9.05	E-Participation Index,* 2007	69

* Hard data

Note: For further details and explanation, please refer to the section "How to Read the Country/Economy Profiles" at the beginning of this chapter.

Belgium

Key indicators

Population (millions), 2006...10.4
GDP (PPP) per capita (US$), 2006..........................34,749.3
Internet users per 100 inhabitants, 2005 ....45.7
Internet bandwidth (mB/s) per 10,000 inhabitants, 2004.....112.5

Networked Readiness Index

Year (number of economies)	Rank
2007–2008 (127)	**25**
2006–2007 (122)	24
2005–2006 (115)	25

Global Competitiveness Index 2007–2008 (131)   20

Environment component — 25

Market environment — 26

1.01 Venture capital availability, 2007..25
1.02 Financial market sophistication, 2007 18
1.03 Availability of latest technologies, 2007 18
1.04 State of cluster development, 2007.....................................26
1.05 Utility patents,* 2006 18
1.06 High-tech exports,* 2005 31
1.07 Burden of government regulation, 2007 93
1.08 Extent and effect of taxation, 2007...................................126
1.09 Total tax rate,* 2007 107
1.10 Time required to start a business,* 2007............................3
1.11 No. of procedures required to start a business,* 2007 4
1.12 Intensity of local competition, 2007 7
1.13 Freedom of the press, 2007...10
1.14 Accessibility of digital content, 2007...................................18

Political and regulatory environment — 23

2.01 Effectiveness of law-making bodies, 2007 54
2.02 Laws relating to ICT, 2007..28
2.03 Judicial independence, 2007 24
2.04 Intellectual property protection, 2007 14
2.05 Efficiency of legal framework, 2007....................................36
2.06 Property rights, 2007...19
2.07 Quality of competition in the ISP sector, 2007 30
2.08 No. of procedures to enforce a contract,* 2007.................8
2.09 Time to enforce a contract,* 2007 54

Infrastructure environment — 22

3.01 Telephone lines,* 2006...21
3.02 Secure Internet servers,* 2006..26
3.03 Electricity production,* 2004..20
3.04 Availability of scientists and engineers, 2007 18
3.05 Quality of scientific research institutions, 2007 7
3.06 Tertiary enrollment,* 2005..23
3.07 Education expenditure,* 2005..88

Readiness component — 22

Individual readiness — 5

4.01 Quality of math and science education, 2007 2
4.02 Quality of the educational system, 2007.............................5
4.03 Internet access in schools, 2007..25
4.04 Buyer sophistication, 2007 7
4.05 Residential telephone connection charge,* 2005 19
4.06 Residential monthly telephone subscription,* 2005 31
4.07 High-speed monthly broadband subscription,* 2006........16
4.08 Lowest cost of broadband,* 2006 16
4.09 Cost of mobile telephone call,* 2005.................................36

Business readiness — 7

5.01 Extent of staff training, 2007...12
5.02 Local availability of research and training, 2007 8
5.03 Quality of management schools, 2007 2
5.04 Company spending on R&D, 2007.....................................15
5.05 University-industry research collaboration, 2007...............10
5.06 Business telephone connection charge,* 2005 17
5.07 Business monthly telephone subscription,* 2005 17
5.08 Local supplier quality, 2007 6
5.09 Local supplier quantity, 2007 8
5.10 Computer, comm., and other services imports,* 2005 29

Government readiness — 35

6.01 Government prioritization of ICT, 2007..............................54
6.02 Gov't procurement of advanced tech products, 2007 49
6.03 Importance of ICT to gov' vision of the future, 2007.......57
6.04 E-Government Readiness Index,* 2007.............................24

Usage component — 24

Individual usage — 20

7.01 Mobile telephone subscribers,* 2006.................................37
7.02 Personal computers,* 2005 26
7.03 Broadband Internet subscribers,* 2005 19
7.04 Internet users,* 2005 27
7.05 Internet bandwidth,* 2004 9

Business usage — 20

8.01 Prevalence of foreign technology licensing, 2007.............26
8.02 Firm-level technology absorption, 2007 31
8.03 Capacity for innovation, 2007...13
8.04 Availability of new telephone lines, 2007..........................16
8.05 Extent of business Internet use, 2007 26

Government usage — 41

9.01 Government success in ICT promotion, 2007...................61
9.02 Availability of government online services, 2007 33
9.03 ICT use and government efficiency, 2007.........................53
9.04 Presence of ICT in government offices, 2007 64
9.05 E-Participation Index,* 2007...27

* Hard data

Note: For further details and explanation, please refer to the section "How to Read the Country/Economy Profiles" at the beginning of this chapter.

Benin

Key indicators

Population (millions), 2006..8.7
GDP (PPP) per capita (US$), 2006.....................................1,404.4
Internet users per 100 inhabitants, 2006 ....8.0
Internet bandwidth (mB/s) per 10,000 inhabitants, 2006.........0.1

Networked Readiness Index

Year (number of economies)	Rank
2007–2008 (127)	**113**
2006–2007 (122)	109
2005–2006 (115)	108

Global Competitiveness Index 2007–2008 (131)   108

Environment component   108
Market environment   109
1.01 Venture capital availability, 2007..101
1.02 Financial market sophistication, 2007 100
1.03 Availability of latest technologies, 2007 103
1.04 State of cluster development, 2007..................................121
1.05 Utility patents,* 2006 86
1.06 High-tech exports,* 2005 109
1.07 Burden of government regulation, 2007 96
1.08 Extent and effect of taxation, 2007...................................117
1.09 Total tax rate,* 2007..112
1.10 Time required to start a business,* 2007............................68
1.11 No. of procedures required to start a business,* 2007 34
1.12 Intensity of local competition, 2007 99
1.13 Freedom of the press, 2007 52
1.14 Accessibility of digital content, 2007...................................96

Political and regulatory environment   84
2.01 Effectiveness of law-making bodies, 2007 46
2.02 Laws relating to ICT, 2007...92
2.03 Judicial independence, 2007 64
2.04 Intellectual property protection, 2007 71
2.05 Efficiency of legal framework, 2007....................................75
2.06 Property rights, 2007..102
2.07 Quality of competition in the ISP sector, 2007 87
2.08 No. of procedures to enforce a contract,* 2007 100
2.09 Time to enforce a contract,* 2007 92

Infrastructure environment   117
3.01 Telephone lines,* 2006...114
3.02 Secure Internet servers,* 2006..101
3.03 Electricity production,* 2004 113
3.04 Availability of scientists and engineers, 2007 58
3.05 Quality of scientific research institutions, 2007 102
3.06 Tertiary enrollment,* 2001 113
3.07 Education expenditure,* 2005..108

Readiness component   118
Individual readiness   119
4.01 Quality of math and science education, 2007 56
4.02 Quality of the educational system, 2007............................93
4.03 Internet access in schools, 2007.......................................106
4.04 Buyer sophistication, 2007 103
4.05 Residential telephone connection charge,* 2005 120
4.06 Residential monthly telephone subscription,* 2005 111
4.07 High-speed monthly broadband subscription,* 2006 103
4.08 Lowest cost of broadband,* 2006 108
4.09 Cost of mobile telephone call,* 2006...............................114

Business readiness   108
5.01 Extent of staff training, 2007...114
5.02 Local availability of research and training, 2007................90
5.03 Quality of management schools, 2007 55
5.04 Company spending on R&D, 2007....................................102
5.05 University-industry research collaboration, 2007..............105
5.06 Business telephone connection charge,* 2005 113
5.07 Business monthly telephone subscription,* 2005 104
5.08 Local supplier quality, 2007...80
5.09 Local supplier quantity, 2007...105
5.10 Computer, comm., and other services imports,* 2004 ..100

Government readiness   98
6.01 Government prioritization of ICT, 2007...............................51
6.02 Gov't procurement of advanced tech products, 2007 46
6.03 Importance of ICT to gov't vision of the future, 2007.......59
6.04 E-Government Readiness Index,* 2007...........................119

Usage component   102
Individual usage   110
7.01 Mobile telephone subscribers,* 2006..............................113
7.02 Personal computers,* 2005 120
7.03 Broadband Internet subscribers,* 2006 113
7.04 Internet users,* 2006..87
7.05 Internet bandwidth,* 2006..110

Business usage   113
8.01 Prevalence of foreign technology licensing, 2007...........107
8.02 Firm-level technology absorption, 2007 81
8.03 Capacity for innovation, 2007..68
8.04 Availability of new telephone lines, 2007.........................126
8.05 Extent of business Internet use, 2007.............................104

Government usage   74
9.01 Government success in ICT promotion, 2007....................44
9.02 Availability of government online services, 2007 93
9.03 ICT use and government efficiency, 2007..........................80
9.04 Presence of ICT in government offices, 2007 49
9.05 E-Participation Index,* 2007...76

* Hard data

Note: For further details and explanation, please refer to the section "How to Read the Country/Economy Profiles" at the beginning of this chapter.

Bolivia

Key indicators

Population (millions), 2006	9.4
GDP (PPP) per capita (US$), 2006	2,931.4
Internet users per 100 inhabitants, 2006	6.2
Internet bandwidth (mB/s) per 10,000 inhabitants, 2005	0.4

Networked Readiness Index

Year (number of economies)	Rank
2007–2008 (127)	**111**
2006–2007 (122)	104
2005–2006 (115)	109

Global Competitiveness Index 2007–2008 (131)	105

Environment component — 113

Market environment — 120

1.01	Venture capital availability, 2007	104
1.02	Financial market sophistication, 2007	103
1.03	Availability of latest technologies, 2007	121
1.04	State of cluster development, 2007	103
1.05	Utility patents,* 2006	86
1.06	High-tech exports,* 2005	66
1.07	Burden of government regulation, 2007	110
1.08	Extent and effect of taxation, 2007	61
1.09	Total tax rate,* 2007	115
1.10	Time required to start a business,* 2007	100
1.11	No. of procedures required to start a business,* 2007	115
1.12	Intensity of local competition, 2007	110
1.13	Freedom of the press, 2007	69
1.14	Accessibility of digital content, 2007	100

Political and regulatory environment — 120

2.01	Effectiveness of law-making bodies, 2007	115
2.02	Laws relating to ICT, 2007	119
2.03	Judicial independence, 2007	112
2.04	Intellectual property protection, 2007	124
2.05	Efficiency of legal framework, 2007	120
2.06	Property rights, 2007	121
2.07	Quality of competition in the ISP sector, 2007	94
2.08	No. of procedures to enforce a contract,* 2007	60
2.09	Time to enforce a contract,* 2007	76

Infrastructure environment — 82

3.01	Telephone lines,* 2006	95
3.02	Secure Internet servers,* 2006	78
3.03	Electricity production,* 2004	102
3.04	Availability of scientists and engineers, 2007	121
3.05	Quality of scientific research institutions, 2007	123
3.06	Tertiary enrollment,* 2004	51
3.07	Education expenditure,* 2005	14

Readiness component — 105

Individual readiness — 100

4.01	Quality of math and science education, 2007	122
4.02	Quality of the educational system, 2007	122
4.03	Internet access in schools, 2007	114
4.04	Buyer sophistication, 2007	122
4.05	Residential telephone connection charge,* 2005	92
4.06	Residential monthly telephone subscription,* 2005	97
4.07	High-speed monthly broadband subscription,* 2006	89
4.08	Lowest cost of broadband,* 2006	97
4.09	Cost of mobile telephone call,* 2005	101

Business readiness — 110

5.01	Extent of staff training, 2007	120
5.02	Local availability of research and training, 2007	107
5.03	Quality of management schools, 2007	110
5.04	Company spending on R&D, 2007	119
5.05	University industry research collaboration, 2007	119
5.06	Business telephone connection charge,* 2005	79
5.07	Business monthly telephone subscription,* 2005	96
5.08	Local supplier quality, 2007	121
5.09	Local supplier quantity, 2007	123
5.10	Computer, comm., and other services imports,* 2005	88

Government readiness — 116

6.01	Government prioritization of ICT, 2007	118
6.02	Gov't procurement of advanced tech products, 2007	126
6.03	Importance of ICT to gov't vision of the future, 2007	117
6.04	E-Government Readiness Index,* 2007	67

Usage component — 108

Individual usage — 96

7.01	Mobile telephone subscribers,* 2006	94
7.02	Personal computers,* 2005	93
7.03	Broadband Internet subscribers,* 2005	94
7.04	Internet users,* 2006	96
7.05	Internet bandwidth,* 2005	81

Business usage — 121

8.01	Prevalence of foreign technology licensing, 2007	126
8.02	Firm-level technology absorption, 2007	127
8.03	Capacity for innovation, 2007	114
8.04	Availability of new telephone lines, 2007	95
8.05	Extent of business Internet use, 2007	114

Government usage — 90

9.01	Government success in ICT promotion, 2007	124
9.02	Availability of government online services, 2007	65
9.03	ICT use and government efficiency, 2007	87
9.04	Presence of ICT in government offices, 2007	116
9.05	E-Participation Index,* 2007	27

* Hard data

Note: For further details and explanation, please refer to the section "How to Read the Country/Economy Profiles" at the beginning of this chapter.

Bosnia and Herzegovina

Key indicators

Population (millions), 2006..3.9
GDP (PPP) per capita (US$), 2006.....................................9,253.4
Internet users per 100 inhabitants, 2006 ....24.3
Internet bandwidth (mB/s) per 10,000 inhabitants, 2005..........0.4

Networked Readiness Index

Year (number of economies)	Rank
2007–2008 (127)	**95**
2006–2007 (122)	89
2005–2006 (115)	97

Global Competitiveness Index 2007–2008 (131)   106

Environment component	111
Market environment	**104**

1.01 Venture capital availability, 2007...90
1.02 Financial market sophistication, 2007 102
1.03 Availability of latest technologies, 2007 118
1.04 State of cluster development, 2007..................................124
1.05 Utility patents,* 2006 86
1.06 High-tech exports* ....n/a
1.07 Burden of government regulation, 2007 122
1.08 Extent and effect of taxation, 2007...................................124
1.09 Total tax rate,* 2007..60
1.10 Time required to start a business,* 2007.........................102
1.11 No. of procedures required to start a business,* 2007 98
1.12 Intensity of local competition, 2007 100
1.13 Freedom of the press, 2007..76
1.14 Accessibility of digital content, 2007..................................87

Political and regulatory environment	**116**

2.01 Effectiveness of law-making bodies, 2007 117
2.02 Laws relating to ICT, 2007...113
2.03 Judicial independence, 2007...89
2.04 Intellectual property protection, 2007 117
2.05 Efficiency of legal framework, 2007..................................118
2.06 Property rights, 2007..117
2.07 Quality of competition in the ISP sector, 2007 105
2.08 No. of procedures to enforce a contract,* 2007 65
2.09 Time to enforce a contract,* 2007 78

Infrastructure environment	**94**

3.01 Telephone lines,* 2006..51
3.02 Secure Internet servers,* 2006..73
3.03 Electricity production,* 2004..57
3.04 Availability of scientists and engineers, 2007 105
3.05 Quality of scientific research institutions, 2007 114
3.06 Tertiary enrollment* ....n/a
3.07 Education expenditure* ....n/a

Readiness component	91
Individual readiness	**68**

4.01 Quality of math and science education, 2007 52
4.02 Quality of the educational system, 2007............................82
4.03 Internet access in schools, 2007..86
4.04 Buyer sophistication, 2007 101
4.05 Residential telephone connection charge,* 2005 93
4.06 Residential monthly telephone subscription,* 2005 64
4.07 High-speed monthly broadband subscription,* 2006........52
4.08 Lowest cost of broadband,* 2006 39
4.09 Cost of mobile telephone call,* 2005..................................79

Business readiness	**97**

5.01 Extent of staff training, 2007...106
5.02 Local availability of research and training, 2007...............95
5.03 Quality of management schools, 2007 101
5.04 Company spending on R&D, 2007......................................94
5.05 University-industry research collaboration, 2007............104
5.06 Business telephone connection charge,* 2005 80
5.07 Business monthly telephone subscription,* 2005 78
5.08 Local supplier quality, 2007..95
5.09 Local supplier quantity, 2007...111
5.10 Computer, comm., and other services imports,* 2005 98

Government readiness	**114**

6.01 Government prioritization of ICT, 2007............................108
6.02 Gov't procurement of advanced tech products, 2007 119
6.03 Importance of ICT to gov't vision of the future, 2007.....125
6.04 E-Government Readiness Index,* 2007..............................83

Usage component	101
Individual usage	**68**

7.01 Mobile telephone subscribers,* 2006..................................82
7.02 Personal computers,* 2005 74
7.03 Broadband Internet subscribers,* 2006 65
7.04 Internet users,* 2006...50
7.05 Internet bandwidth,* 2005..82

Business usage	**100**

8.01 Prevalence of foreign technology licensing, 2007...........106
8.02 Firm-level technology absorption, 2007 124
8.03 Capacity for innovation, 2007..108
8.04 Availability of new telephone lines, 2007 76
8.05 Extent of business Internet use, 2007 82

Government usage	**116**

9.01 Government success in ICT promotion, 2007..................117
9.02 Availability of government online services, 2007 109
9.03 ICT use and government efficiency, 2007........................120
9.04 Presence of ICT in government offices, 2007 111
9.05 E-Participation Index,* 2007...82

* Hard data

Note: For further details and explanation, please refer to the section "How to Read the Country/Economy Profiles" at the beginning of this chapter.

Botswana

Key indicators

Population (millions), 2006...1.8
GDP (PPP) per capita (US$), 2006..............................15,692.1
Internet users per 100 inhabitants, 2005 ....3.4
Internet bandwidth (mB/s) per 10,000 inhabitants, 2006.........0.2

Networked Readiness Index

Year (number of economies)	Rank
2007–2008 (127)	**78**
2006–2007 (122)	67
2005–2006 (115)	56

Global Competitiveness Index 2007–2008 (131)	76

Environment component — 65
Market environment — 63

1.01 Venture capital availability, 2007...52
1.02 Financial market sophistication, 2007 71
1.03 Availability of latest technologies, 2007 68
1.04 State of cluster development, 2007.....................................81
1.05 Utility patents,* 2006 86
1.06 High-tech exports* ....n/a
1.07 Burden of government regulation, 2007 65
1.08 Extent and effect of taxation, 2007......................................17
1.09 Total tax rate,* 2007 5
1.10 Time required to start a business,* 2007..........................118
1.11 No. of procedures required to start a business,* 2007 88
1.12 Intensity of local competition, 2007 75
1.13 Freedom of the press, 2007...62
1.14 Accessibility of digital content, 2007.................................109

Political and regulatory environment — 49

2.01 Effectiveness of law-making bodies, 2007 27
2.02 Laws relating to ICT, 2007..94
2.03 Judicial independence, 2007 29
2.04 Intellectual property protection, 2007 87
2.05 Efficiency of legal framework, 2007.....................................33
2.06 Property rights, 2007...57
2.07 Quality of competition in the ISP sector, 2007 93
2.08 No. of procedures to enforce a contract,* 2007 13
2.09 Time to enforce a contract,* 2007 110

Infrastructure environment — 93

3.01 Telephone lines,* 2006...94
3.02 Secure Internet servers,* 2006..90
3.03 Electricity production,* 2004..90
3.04 Availability of scientists and engineers, 2007 113
3.05 Quality of scientific research institutions, 2007 64
3.06 Tertiary enrollment,* 2005..106
3.07 Education expenditure,* 2005..25

Readiness component — 77
Individual readiness — 62

4.01 Quality of math and science education, 2007 79
4.02 Quality of the educational system, 2007............................54
4.03 Internet access in schools, 2007..90
4.04 Buyer sophistication, 2007 81
4.05 Residential telephone connection charge,* 2006 48
4.06 Residential monthly telephone subscription,* 2006 49
4.07 High-speed monthly broadband subscription,* 2006........51
4.08 Lowest cost of broadband,* 2006 59
4.09 Cost of mobile telephone call,* 2005..................................69

Business readiness — 90

5.01 Extent of staff training, 2007..64
5.02 Local availability of research and training, 2007..............103
5.03 Quality of management schools, 2007 102
5.04 Company spending on R&D, 2007......................................91
5.05 University-industry research collaboration, 2007...............85
5.06 Business telephone connection charge,* 2006 49
5.07 Business monthly telephone subscription,* 2006 48
5.08 Local supplier quality, 2007 107
5.09 Local supplier quantity, 2007...124
5.10 Computer, comm., and other services imports,* 2005 72

Government readiness — 88

6.01 Government prioritization of ICT, 2007...............................68
6.02 Gov't procurement of advanced tech products, 2007 76
6.03 Importance of ICT to gov't vision of the future, 2007.......78
6.04 E-Government Readiness Index,* 2007..............................94

Usage component — 88
Individual usage — 87

7.01 Mobile telephone subscribers,* 2006..................................70
7.02 Personal computers,* 2005 78
7.03 Broadband Internet subscribers,* 2005 95
7.04 Internet users,* 2005...109
7.05 Internet bandwidth,* 2006..97

Business usage — 96

8.01 Prevalence of foreign technology licensing, 2007.............79
8.02 Firm-level technology absorption, 2007 84
8.03 Capacity for innovation, 2007...107
8.04 Availability of new telephone lines, 2007..........................100
8.05 Extent of business Internet use, 2007...............................102

Government usage — 80

9.01 Government success in ICT promotion, 2007....................71
9.02 Availability of government online services, 2007 94
9.03 ICT use and government efficiency, 2007.........................103
9.04 Presence of ICT in government offices, 2007 75
9.05 E-Participation Index,* 2007...39

* Hard data

Note: For further details and explanation, please refer to the section "How to Read the Country/Economy Profiles" at the beginning of this chapter.

Brazil

Key indicators

Population (millions), 2006	188.9
GDP (PPP) per capita (US$), 2006	10,072.7
Internet users per 100 inhabitants, 2005	17.2
Internet bandwidth (mB/s) per 10,000 inhabitants, 2005	1.5

Networked Readiness Index

Year (number of economies)	Rank
2007–2008 (127)	**59**
2006–2007 (122)	53
2005–2006 (115)	52

Global Competitiveness Index 2007–2008 (131)	72

Environment component — 86
Market environment — 116

1.01	Venture capital availability, 2007	99
1.02	Financial market sophistication, 2007	31
1.03	Availability of latest technologies, 2007	59
1.04	State of cluster development, 2007	40
1.05	Utility patents,* 2006	53
1.06	High-tech exports,* 2005	35
1.07	Burden of government regulation, 2007	125
1.08	Extent and effect of taxation, 2007	127
1.09	Total tax rate,* 2007	109
1.10	Time required to start a business,* 2007	120
1.11	No. of procedures required to start a business,* 2007	119
1.12	Intensity of local competition, 2007	45
1.13	Freedom of the press, 2007	36
1.14	Accessibility of digital content, 2007	72

Political and regulatory environment — 86

2.01	Effectiveness of law-making bodies, 2007	116
2.02	Laws relating to ICT, 2007	51
2.03	Judicial independence, 2007	88
2.04	Intellectual property protection, 2007	72
2.05	Efficiency of legal framework, 2007	102
2.06	Property rights, 2007	69
2.07	Quality of competition in the ISP sector, 2007	33
2.08	No. of procedures to enforce a contract,* 2007	110
2.09	Time to enforce a contract,* 2007	84

Infrastructure environment — 63

3.01	Telephone lines,* 2005	58
3.02	Secure Internet servers,* 2006	56
3.03	Electricity production,* 2004	67
3.04	Availability of scientists and engineers, 2007	59
3.05	Quality of scientific research institutions, 2007	41
3.06	Tertiary enrollment,* 2004	74
3.07	Education expenditure,* 2005	63

Readiness component — 55
Individual readiness — 77

4.01	Quality of math and science education, 2007	114
4.02	Quality of the educational system, 2007	117
4.03	Internet access in schools, 2007	69
4.04	Buyer sophistication, 2007	65
4.05	Residential telephone connection charge,* 2005	43
4.06	Residential monthly telephone subscription,* 2005	91
4.07	High-speed monthly broadband subscription,* 2006	56
4.08	Lowest cost of broadband,* 2006	37
4.09	Cost of mobile telephone call,* 2005	83

Business readiness — 36

5.01	Extent of staff training, 2007	45
5.02	Local availability of research and training, 2007	32
5.03	Quality of management schools, 2007	65
5.04	Company spending on R&D, 2007	35
5.05	University-industry research collaboration, 2007	45
5.06	Business telephone connection charge,* 2005	35
5.07	Business monthly telephone subscription,* 2005	88
5.08	Local supplier quality, 2007	40
5.09	Local supplier quantity, 2007	21
5.10	Computer, comm., and other services imports,* 2005	13

Government readiness — 61

6.01	Government prioritization of ICT, 2007	100
6.02	Gov't procurement of advanced tech products, 2007	66
6.03	Importance of ICT to gov't vision of the future, 2007	75
6.04	E-Government Readiness Index,* 2007	45

Usage component — 41
Individual usage — 64

7.01	Mobile telephone subscribers,* 2005	83
7.02	Personal computers,* 2005	45
7.03	Broadband Internet subscribers,* 2005	54
7.04	Internet users,* 2005	62
7.05	Internet bandwidth,* 2005	63

Business usage — 36

8.01	Prevalence of foreign technology licensing, 2007	49
8.02	Firm-level technology absorption, 2007	54
8.03	Capacity for innovation, 2007	29
8.04	Availability of new telephone lines, 2007	50
8.05	Extent of business Internet use, 2007	28

Government usage — 33

9.01	Government success in ICT promotion, 2007	68
9.02	Availability of government online services, 2007	28
9.03	ICT use and government efficiency, 2007	27
9.04	Presence of ICT in government offices, 2007	53
9.05	E-Participation Index,* 2007	22

* Hard data

Note: For further details and explanation, please refer to the section "How to Read the Country/Economy Profiles" at the beginning of this chapter.

Bulgaria

Key indicators

Population (millions), 2006...7.7
GDP (PPP) per capita (US$), 2006...................................10,021.9
Internet users per 100 inhabitants, 2006 ....24.4
Internet bandwidth (mB/s) per 10,000 inhabitants, 2006.......17.5

Networked Readiness Index

Year (number of economies)	Rank
2007–2008 (127)	**68**
2006–2007 (122)	72
2005–2006 (115)	64

Global Competitiveness Index 2007–2008 (131)   79

Environment component — 71

Market environment — 82

1.01 Venture capital availability, 2007..58
1.02 Financial market sophistication, 2007 97
1.03 Availability of latest technologies, 2007 90
1.04 State of cluster development, 2007..................................106
1.05 Utility patents,* 2006 63
1.06 High-tech exports,* 2005 56
1.07 Burden of government regulation, 2007 82
1.08 Extent and effect of taxation, 2007....................................87
1.09 Total tax rate,* 2007 38
1.10 Time required to start a business,* 2007 73
1.11 No. of procedures required to start a business,* 2007 58
1.12 Intensity of local competition, 2007 86
1.13 Freedom of the press, 2007 96
1.14 Accessibility of digital content, 2007.................................48

Political and regulatory environment — 89

2.01 Effectiveness of law-making bodies, 2007 94
2.02 Laws relating to ICT, 2007..41
2.03 Judicial independence, 2007 101
2.04 Intellectual property protection, 2007 103
2.05 Efficiency of legal framework, 2007.................................109
2.06 Property rights, 2007..96
2.07 Quality of competition in the ISP sector, 2007 67
2.08 No. of procedures to enforce a contract,* 2007 89
2.09 Time to enforce a contract,* 2007 66

Infrastructure environment — 53

3.01 Telephone lines,* 2006...37
3.02 Secure Internet servers,* 2006..59
3.03 Electricity production,* 2004 40
3.04 Availability of scientists and engineers, 2007 64
3.05 Quality of scientific research institutions, 2007 72
3.06 Tertiary enrollment,* 2005...43
3.07 Education expenditure,* 2005..81

Readiness component — 69

Individual readiness — 61

4.01 Quality of math and science education, 2007....................48
4.02 Quality of the educational system, 2007............................73
4.03 Internet access in schools, 2007..53
4.04 Buyer sophistication, 2007...88
4.05 Residential telephone connection charge,* 2005 69
4.06 Residential monthly telephone subscription,* 2005 76
4.07 High-speed monthly broadband subscription,* 2006........55
4.08 Lowest cost of broadband,* 2006 52
4.09 Cost of mobile telephone call,* 2005................................77

Business readiness — 84

5.01 Extent of staff training, 2007..116
5.02 Local availability of research and training, 2007 74
5.03 Quality of management schools, 2007 81
5.04 Company spending on R&D, 2007....................................100
5.05 University-industry research collaboration, 2007...............92
5.06 Business telephone connection charge,* 2005 62
5.07 Business monthly telephone subscription,* 2005 68
5.08 Local supplier quality, 2007..76
5.09 Local supplier quantity, 2007..70
5.10 Computer, comm., and other services imports,* 2005 64

Government readiness — 71

6.01 Government prioritization of ICT, 2007..............................99
6.02 Gov't procurement of advanced tech products, 2007 83
6.03 Importance of ICT to gov't vision of the future, 2007.......90
6.04 E-Government Readiness Index,* 2007............................43

Usage component — 68

Individual usage — 46

7.01 Mobile telephone subscribers,* 2006................................20
7.02 Personal computers,* 2005 70
7.03 Broadband Internet subscribers,* 2006.............................44
7.04 Internet users,* 2006 49
7.05 Internet bandwidth,* 2006 33

Business usage — 97

8.01 Prevalence of foreign technology licensing, 2007.............98
8.02 Firm-level technology absorption, 2007 117
8.03 Capacity for innovation, 2007...78
8.04 Availability of new telephone lines, 2007..........................80
8.05 Extent of business Internet use, 2007 87

Government usage — 82

9.01 Government success in ICT promotion, 2007...................96
9.02 Availability of government online services, 2007 57
9.03 ICT use and government efficiency, 2007.........................97
9.04 Presence of ICT in government offices, 2007 44
9.05 E-Participation Index,* 2007..100

* Hard data

Note: For further details and explanation, please refer to the section "How to Read the Country/Economy Profiles" at the beginning of this chapter.

Burkina Faso

Key indicators

Population (millions), 2006...13.6
GDP (PPP) per capita (US$), 2006.....................................1,406.4
Internet users per 100 inhabitants, 2006 ....0.6
Internet bandwidth (mB/s) per 10,000 inhabitants, 2006.........0.2

Networked Readiness Index

Year (number of economies)	Rank
2007–2008 (127)	**103**
2006–2007 (122)	99
2005–2006 (115)	n/a

Global Competitiveness Index 2007–2008 (131) — 112

Environment component — 95
Market environment — 92
1.01 Venture capital availability, 2007...118
1.02 Financial market sophistication, 2007 99
1.03 Availability of latest technologies, 2007 107
1.04 State of cluster development, 2007.....................................117
1.05 Utility patents,* 2006 86
1.06 High-tech exports,* 2004 70
1.07 Burden of government regulation, 2007 42
1.08 Extent and effect of taxation, 2007.......................................76
1.09 Total tax rate,* 2007..77
1.10 Time required to start a business,* 2007 38
1.11 No. of procedures required to start a business,* 2007 19
1.12 Intensity of local competition, 2007 79
1.13 Freedom of the press, 2007..90
1.14 Accessibility of digital content, 2007...................................111

Political and regulatory environment — 69
2.01 Effectiveness of law-making bodies, 2007 51
2.02 Laws relating to ICT, 2007...100
2.03 Judicial independence, 2007 97
2.04 Intellectual property protection, 2007 54
2.05 Efficiency of legal framework, 2007......................................82
2.06 Property rights, 2007...70
2.07 Quality of competition in the ISP sector, 2007 85
2.08 No. of procedures to enforce a contract,* 2007 60
2.09 Time to enforce a contract,* 2007 43

Infrastructure environment — 109
3.01 Telephone lines,* 2006..118
3.02 Secure Internet servers,* 2006...101
3.03 Electricity production* ....n/a
3.04 Availability of scientists and engineers, 2007 107
3.05 Quality of scientific research institutions, 2007 73
3.06 Tertiary enrollment,* 2005..118
3.07 Education expenditure,* 2005...107

Readiness component — 114
Individual readiness — 120
4.01 Quality of math and science education, 2007 86
4.02 Quality of the educational system, 2007............................110
4.03 Internet access in schools, 2007..122
4.04 Buyer sophistication, 2007 121
4.05 Residential telephone connection charge,* 2005 113
4.06 Residential monthly telephone subscription,* 2005 114
4.07 High-speed monthly broadband subscription,* 2006........104
4.08 Lowest cost of broadband,* 2006 109
4.09 Cost of mobile telephone call,* 2005.................................118

Business readiness — 96
5.01 Extent of staff training, 2007..117
5.02 Local availability of research and training, 2007 86
5.03 Quality of management schools, 2007 74
5.04 Company spending on R&D, 2007..96
5.05 University-industry research collaboration, 2007.................99
5.06 Business telephone connection charge,* 2005 107
5.07 Business monthly telephone subscription,* 2005 107
5.08 Local supplier quality, 2007..86
5.09 Local supplier quantity, 2007..72
5.10 Computer, comm., and other services imports* ....n/a

Government readiness — 99
6.01 Government prioritization of ICT, 2007................................67
6.02 Gov't procurement of advanced tech products, 2007 44
6.03 Importance of ICT to gov't vision of the future, 2007........33
6.04 E-Government Readiness Index,* 2007............................123

Usage component — 96
Individual usage — 121
7.01 Mobile telephone subscribers,* 2006................................119
7.02 Personal computers,* 2005 124
7.03 Broadband Internet subscribers,* 2006 107
7.04 Internet users,* 2006 121
7.05 Internet bandwidth,* 2006 98

Business usage — 98
8.01 Prevalence of foreign technology licensing, 2007............108
8.02 Firm-level technology absorption, 2007 82
8.03 Capacity for innovation, 2007...82
8.04 Availability of new telephone lines, 2007..........................102
8.05 Extent of business Internet use, 2007................................98

Government usage — 66
9.01 Government success in ICT promotion, 2007.....................28
9.02 Availability of government online services, 2007 98
9.03 ICT use and government efficiency, 2007...........................60
9.04 Presence of ICT in government offices, 2007 67
9.05 E-Participation Index,* 2007...58

* Hard data

Note: For further details and explanation, please refer to the section "How to Read the Country/Economy Profiles" at the beginning of this chapter.

Burundi

Key indicators

Population (millions), 2006..7.8
GDP (PPP) per capita (US$), 2006......................................676.9
Internet users per 100 inhabitants, 2006 ....0.8
Internet bandwidth (mB/s) per 10,000 inhabitants, 2005.........0.0

Networked Readiness Index

Year (number of economies)	Rank
2007–2008 (127)	**126**
2006–2007 (122)	121
2005–2006 (115)	n/a

Global Competitiveness Index 2007–2008 (131)	130

Environment component — 126
Market environment — 126
1.01 Venture capital availability, 2007...126
1.02 Financial market sophistication, 2007 124
1.03 Availability of latest technologies, 2007 127
1.04 State of cluster development, 2007.....................................127
1.05 Utility patents,* 2006 86
1.06 High-tech exports,* 2005...109
1.07 Burden of government regulation, 2007 68
1.08 Extent and effect of taxation, 2007.....................................102
1.09 Total tax rate,* 2007..120
1.10 Time required to start a business,* 2007..............................91
1.11 No. of procedures required to start a business,* 2007 88
1.12 Intensity of local competition, 2007 118
1.13 Freedom of the press, 2007...105
1.14 Accessibility of digital content, 2007...................................126

Political and regulatory environment — 123
2.01 Effectiveness of law-making bodies, 2007 102
2.02 Laws relating to ICT, 2007...122
2.03 Judicial independence, 2007..122
2.04 Intellectual property protection, 2007 123
2.05 Efficiency of legal framework, 2007....................................115
2.06 Property rights, 2007..116
2.07 Quality of competition in the ISP sector, 2007 122
2.08 No. of procedures to enforce a contract,* 2007 104
2.09 Time to enforce a contract,* 2007 64

Infrastructure environment — 111
3.01 Telephone lines,* 2005..122
3.02 Secure Internet servers,* 2006 101
3.03 Electricity production* ....n/a
3.04 Availability of scientists and engineers, 2007 117
3.05 Quality of scientific research institutions, 2007 121
3.06 Tertiary enrollment,* 2005...119
3.07 Education expenditure,* 2005...71

Readiness component — 127
Individual readiness — 122
4.01 Quality of math and science education, 2007 88
4.02 Quality of the educational system, 2007............................107
4.03 Internet access in schools, 2007...126
4.04 Buyer sophistication, 2007..126
4.05 Residential telephone connection charge,* 2005 107
4.06 Residential monthly telephone subscription,* 2005 93
4.07 High-speed monthly broadband subscription* ....n/a
4.08 Lowest cost of broadband,* 2006 117
4.09 Cost of mobile telephone call,* 2006..................................122

Business readiness — 127
5.01 Extent of staff training, 2007...126
5.02 Local availability of research and training, 2007...............127
5.03 Quality of management schools, 2007 119
5.04 Company spending on R&D, 2007.......................................122
5.05 University-industry research collaboration, 2007..............122
5.06 Business telephone connection charge,* 2005 118
5.07 Business monthly telephone subscription,* 2005 75
5.08 Local supplier quality, 2007 122
5.09 Local supplier quantity, 2007..112
5.10 Computer, comm., and other services imports,* 2005 94

Government readiness — 125
6.01 Government prioritization of ICT, 2007...............................121
6.02 Gov't procurement of advanced tech products, 2007 115
6.03 Importance of ICT to gov't vision of the future, 2007.....122
6.04 E-Government Readiness Index,* 2007..............................121

Usage component — 125
Individual usage — 126
7.01 Mobile telephone subscribers,* 2005.................................126
7.02 Personal computers,* 2005 116
7.03 Broadband Internet subscribers,* 2005 118
7.04 Internet users,* 2006 119
7.05 Internet bandwidth,* 2005 124

Business usage — 125
8.01 Prevalence of foreign technology licensing, 2007............125
8.02 Firm-level technology absorption, 2007 112
8.03 Capacity for innovation, 2007..120
8.04 Availability of new telephone lines, 2007..........................116
8.05 Extent of business Internet use, 2007...............................125

Government usage — 118
9.01 Government success in ICT promotion, 2007......................91
9.02 Availability of government online services, 2007 114
9.03 ICT use and government efficiency, 2007..........................118
9.04 Presence of ICT in government offices, 2007 121
9.05 E-Participation Index,* 2007..100

* Hard data

Note: For further details and explanation, please refer to the section "How to Read the Country/Economy Profiles" at the beginning of this chapter.

Cambodia

Key indicators

Population (millions), 2006..14.4
GDP (PPP) per capita (US$), 2006.....................................3,374.1
Internet users per 100 inhabitants, 2005 ....0.3
Internet bandwidth (mB/s) per 10,000 inhabitants, 2005.........0.0

Networked Readiness Index

Year (number of economies)	Rank
2007–2008 (127)	**115**
2006–2007 (122)	106
2005–2006 (115)	104

Global Competitiveness Index 2007–2008 (131)   110

Environment component — 119
Market environment — 99
1.01 Venture capital availability, 2007..97
1.02 Financial market sophistication, 2007 106
1.03 Availability of latest technologies, 2007 101
1.04 State of cluster development, 2007.......................................59
1.05 Utility patents,* 2006 86
1.06 High-tech exports,* 2005 96
1.07 Burden of government regulation, 2007 63
1.08 Extent and effect of taxation, 2007..34
1.09 Total tax rate,* 2007 9
1.10 Time required to start a business,* 2007..........................114
1.11 No. of procedures required to start a business,* 2007 74
1.12 Intensity of local competition, 2007 106
1.13 Freedom of the press, 2007..110
1.14 Accessibility of digital content, 2007....................................88

Political and regulatory environment — 105
2.01 Effectiveness of law-making bodies, 2007 63
2.02 Laws relating to ICT, 2007..115
2.03 Judicial independence, 2007 114
2.04 Intellectual property protection, 2007 111
2.05 Efficiency of legal framework, 2007......................................92
2.06 Property rights, 2007..109
2.07 Quality of competition in the ISP sector, 2007 99
2.08 No. of procedures to enforce a contract,* 2007...............104
2.09 Time to enforce a contract,* 2007 34

Infrastructure environment — 127
3.01 Telephone lines,* 2006...126
3.02 Secure Internet servers,* 2006..101
3.03 Electricity production,* 2004 111
3.04 Availability of scientists and engineers, 2007 125
3.05 Quality of scientific research institutions, 2007 115
3.06 Tertiary enrollment,* 2005..111
3.07 Education expenditure,* 2005..111

Readiness component — 109
Individual readiness — 110
4.01 Quality of math and science education, 2007 115
4.02 Quality of the educational system, 2007..............................92
4.03 Internet access in schools, 2007...101
4.04 Buyer sophistication, 2007 70
4.05 Residential telephone connection charge,* 2005 103
4.06 Residential monthly telephone subscription,* 2005 106
4.07 High-speed monthly broadband subscription,* 2006......100
4.08 Lowest cost of broadband,* 2006 107
4.09 Cost of mobile telephone call,* 2005....................................92

Business readiness — 114
5.01 Extent of staff training, 2007..97
5.02 Local availability of research and training, 2007..............104
5.03 Quality of management schools, 2007 113
5.04 Company spending on R&D, 2007...65
5.05 University-industry research collaboration, 2007...............90
5.06 Business telephone connection charge,* 2005 108
5.07 Business monthly telephone subscription,* 2005 114
5.08 Local supplier quality, 2007 110
5.09 Local supplier quantity, 2007...118
5.10 Computer, comm., and other services imports,* 2005 74

Government readiness — 94
6.01 Government prioritization of ICT, 2007................................82
6.02 Gov't procurement of advanced tech products, 2007 47
6.03 Importance of ICT to gov't vision of the future, 2007.......77
6.04 E-Government Readiness Index,* 2007.............................107

Usage component — 109
Individual usage — 122
7.01 Mobile telephone subscribers,* 2006.................................118
7.02 Personal computers,* 2005 123
7.03 Broadband Internet subscribers,* 2005 109
7.04 Internet users,* 2005...124
7.05 Internet bandwidth,* 2005..119

Business usage — 109
8.01 Prevalence of foreign technology licensing, 2007............115
8.02 Firm-level technology absorption, 2007 100
8.03 Capacity for innovation, 2007..110
8.04 Availability of new telephone lines, 2007...........................110
8.05 Extent of business Internet use, 2007..................................99

Government usage — 98
9.01 Government success in ICT promotion, 2007.....................88
9.02 Availability of government online services, 2007 118
9.03 ICT use and government efficiency, 2007............................58
9.04 Presence of ICT in government offices, 2007 113
9.05 E-Participation Index,* 2007..53

* Hard data

Note: For further details and explanation, please refer to the section "How to Read the Country/Economy Profiles" at the beginning of this chapter.

Cameroon

Key indicators

Population (millions), 2006	16.6
GDP (PPP) per capita (US$), 2006	2,188.0
Internet users per 100 inhabitants, 2006	2.2
Internet bandwidth (mB/s) per 10,000 inhabitants, 2005	0.1

Networked Readiness Index

Year (number of economies)	Rank
2007–2008 (127)	**118**
2006–2007 (122)	113
2005–2006 (115)	99

Global Competitiveness Index 2007–2008 (131)	116

Environment component — 124

Market environment — 122

1.01	Venture capital availability, 2007	122
1.02	Financial market sophistication, 2007	125
1.03	Availability of latest technologies, 2007	105
1.04	State of cluster development, 2007	119
1.05	Utility patents,* 2006	86
1.06	High-tech exports,* 2005	99
1.07	Burden of government regulation, 2007	123
1.08	Extent and effect of taxation, 2007	120
1.09	Total tax rate,* 2007	90
1.10	Time required to start a business,* 2007	85
1.11	No. of procedures required to start a business,* 2007	103
1.12	Intensity of local competition, 2007	97
1.13	Freedom of the press, 2007	84
1.14	Accessibility of digital content, 2007	116

Political and regulatory environment — 118

2.01	Effectiveness of law-making bodies, 2007	111
2.02	Laws relating to ICT, 2007	120
2.03	Judicial independence, 2007	117
2.04	Intellectual property protection, 2007	65
2.05	Efficiency of legal framework, 2007	104
2.06	Property rights, 2007	100
2.07	Quality of competition in the ISP sector, 2007	102
2.08	No. of procedures to enforce a contract,* 2007	103
2.09	Time to enforce a contract,* 2007	99

Infrastructure environment — 112

3.01	Telephone lines,* 2005	120
3.02	Secure Internet servers,* 2006	101
3.03	Electricity production,* 2004	104
3.04	Availability of scientists and engineers, 2007	80
3.05	Quality of scientific research institutions, 2007	112
3.06	Tertiary enrollment,* 2005	103
3.07	Education expenditure,* 2005	84

Readiness component — 110

Individual readiness — 109

4.01	Quality of math and science education, 2007	84
4.02	Quality of the educational system, 2007	81
4.03	Internet access in schools, 2007	119
4.04	Buyer sophistication, 2007	119
4.05	Residential telephone connection charge,* 2005	105
4.06	Residential monthly telephone subscription,* 2005	102
4.07	High-speed monthly broadband subscription,* 2006	98
4.08	Lowest cost of broadband,* 2006	100
4.09	Cost of mobile telephone call,* 2006	110

Business readiness — 93

5.01	Extent of staff training, 2007	112
5.02	Local availability of research and training, 2007	100
5.03	Quality of management schools, 2007	95
5.04	Company spending on R&D, 2007	108
5.05	University-industry research collaboration, 2007	116
5.06	Business telephone connection charge,* 2005	99
5.07	Business monthly telephone subscription,* 2005	72
5.08	Local supplier quality, 2007	101
5.09	Local supplier quantity, 2007	86
5.10	Computer, comm., and other services imports*	n/a

Government readiness — 120

6.01	Government prioritization of ICT, 2007	114
6.02	Gov't procurement of advanced tech products, 2007	101
6.03	Importance of ICT to gov't vision of the future, 2007	112
6.04	E-Government Readiness Index,* 2007	112

Usage component — 118

Individual usage — 114

7.01	Mobile telephone subscribers,* 2005	111
7.02	Personal computers,* 2005	110
7.03	Broadband Internet subscribers,* 2005	114
7.04	Internet users,* 2006	114
7.05	Internet bandwidth,* 2005	101

Business usage — 114

8.01	Prevalence of foreign technology licensing, 2007	109
8.02	Firm-level technology absorption, 2007	93
8.03	Capacity for innovation, 2007	117
8.04	Availability of new telephone lines, 2007	114
8.05	Extent of business Internet use, 2007	124

Government usage — 108

9.01	Government success in ICT promotion, 2007	74
9.02	Availability of government online services, 2007	116
9.03	ICT use and government efficiency, 2007	111
9.04	Presence of ICT in government offices, 2007	112
9.05	E-Participation Index,* 2007	67

* Hard data

Note: For further details and explanation, please refer to the section "How to Read the Country/Economy Profiles" at the beginning of this chapter.

Canada

Key indicators

Population (millions), 2006..32.6
GDP (PPP) per capita (US$), 2006.................................35,513.8
Internet users per 100 inhabitants, 2005 ....67.9
Internet bandwidth (mB/s) per 10,000 inhabitants, 2005.......67.3

Networked Readiness Index

Year (number of economies)	Rank
2007–2008 (127) **13**
2006–2007 (122) 11
2005–2006 (115) 6

Global Competitiveness Index 2007–2008 (131)   13

Environment component — 8
Market environment — 16
1.01 Venture capital availability, 2007..20
1.02 Financial market sophistication, 2007 6
1.03 Availability of latest technologies, 2007 13
1.04 State of cluster development, 2007 23
1.05 Utility patents,* 2006 10
1.06 High-tech exports,* 2005 32
1.07 Burden of government regulation, 2007 45
1.08 Extent and effect of taxation, 2007......................................77
1.09 Total tax rate,* 2007 65
1.10 Time required to start a business,* 2007..............................2
1.11 No. of procedures required to start a business,* 2007 1
1.12 Intensity of local competition, 2007 18
1.13 Freedom of the press, 2007..11
1.14 Accessibility of digital content, 2007 16

Political and regulatory environment — 19
2.01 Effectiveness of law-making bodies, 2007 11
2.02 Laws relating to ICT, 2007...16
2.03 Judicial independence, 2007 14
2.04 Intellectual property protection, 2007 15
2.05 Efficiency of legal framework, 2007.....................................16
2.06 Property rights, 2007..15
2.07 Quality of competition in the ISP sector, 2007 15
2.08 No. of procedures to enforce a contract,* 2007 53
2.09 Time to enforce a contract,* 2007 71

Infrastructure environment — 5
3.01 Telephone lines,* 2005..4
3.02 Secure Internet servers,* 2006...3
3.03 Electricity production,* 2004..3
3.04 Availability of scientists and engineers, 2007 8
3.05 Quality of scientific research institutions, 2007 8
3.06 Tertiary enrollment,* 2004...24
3.07 Education expenditure,* 2005..33

Readiness component — 20
Individual readiness — 11
4.01 Quality of math and science education, 2007 15
4.02 Quality of the educational system, 2007.............................11
4.03 Internet access in schools, 2007..13
4.04 Buyer sophistication, 2007 17
4.05 Residential telephone connection charge,* 2005 12
4.06 Residential monthly telephone subscription,* 2005 24
4.07 High-speed monthly broadband subscription,* 2006........10
4.08 Lowest cost of broadband,* 2006 16
4.09 Cost of mobile telephone call,* 2005...................................19

Business readiness — 19
5.01 Extent of staff training, 2007...25
5.02 Local availability of research and training, 2007 10
5.03 Quality of management schools, 2007 4
5.04 Company spending on R&D, 2007 21
5.05 University-industry research collaboration, 2007................15
5.06 Business telephone connection charge*..........................n/a
5.07 Business monthly telephone subscription,* 2005 35
5.08 Local supplier quality, 2007 12
5.09 Local supplier quantity, 2007..13
5.10 Computer, comm., and other services imports,* 2005 30

Government readiness — 25
6.01 Government prioritization of ICT, 2007................................34
6.02 Gov't procurement of advanced tech products, 2007 28
6.03 Importance of ICT to gov't vision of the future, 2007........47
6.04 E-Government Readiness Index,* 2007................................7

Usage component — 15
Individual usage — 12
7.01 Mobile telephone subscribers,* 2005..................................75
7.02 Personal computers,* 2005 2
7.03 Broadband Internet subscribers,* 2006 10
7.04 Internet users,* 2005..9
7.05 Internet bandwidth,* 2005 14

Business usage — 16
8.01 Prevalence of foreign technology licensing, 2007...............3
8.02 Firm-level technology absorption, 2007 21
8.03 Capacity for innovation, 2007...17
8.04 Availability of new telephone lines, 2007 15
8.05 Extent of business Internet use, 2007 11

Government usage — 15
9.01 Government success in ICT promotion, 2007....................42
9.02 Availability of government online services, 2007 16
9.03 ICT use and government efficiency, 2007...........................24
9.04 Presence of ICT in government offices, 2007 21
9.05 E-Participation Index,* 2007..11

* Hard data

Note: For further details and explanation, please refer to the section "How to Read the Country/Economy Profiles" at the beginning of this chapter.

Chad

Key indicators

Population (millions), 2006..10.0
GDP (PPP) per capita (US$), 2006..1,748.8
Internet users per 100 inhabitants, 2006...................................0.6
Internet bandwidth (mB/s) per 10,000 inhabitants, 2006.........0.0

Networked Readiness Index

Year (number of economies)	Rank
2007–2008 (127)	**127**
2006–2007 (122)	122
2005–2006 (115)	114

Global Competitiveness Index 2007–2008 (131)   131

Environment component   127
Market environment   127
1.01 Venture capital availability, 2007..113
1.02 Financial market sophistication, 2007...................................126
1.03 Availability of latest technologies, 2007................................126
1.04 State of cluster development, 2007.......................................125
1.05 Utility patents,* 2006...86
1.06 High-tech exports*..n/a
1.07 Burden of government regulation, 2007................................116
1.08 Extent and effect of taxation, 2007..109
1.09 Total tax rate,* 2007..105
1.10 Time required to start a business,* 2007..............................112
1.11 No. of procedures required to start a business,* 2007 ..121
1.12 Intensity of local competition, 2007......................................127
1.13 Freedom of the press, 2007..123
1.14 Accessibility of digital content, 2007.....................................120

Political and regulatory environment   126
2.01 Effectiveness of law-making bodies, 2007...........................119
2.02 Laws relating to ICT, 2007..123
2.03 Judicial independence, 2007...123
2.04 Intellectual property protection, 2007....................................121
2.05 Efficiency of legal framework, 2007.......................................122
2.06 Property rights, 2007...125
2.07 Quality of competition in the ISP sector, 2007.....................125
2.08 No. of procedures to enforce a contract,* 2007...................94
2.09 Time to enforce a contract,* 2007..95

Infrastructure environment   125
3.01 Telephone lines,* 2006..127
3.02 Secure Internet servers*..n/a
3.03 Electricity production*...n/a
3.04 Availability of scientists and engineers, 2007......................123
3.05 Quality of scientific research institutions, 2007...................124
3.06 Tertiary enrollment,* 2005...123
3.07 Education expenditure,* 2005...116

Readiness component   125
Individual readiness   123
4.01 Quality of math and science education, 2007......................121
4.02 Quality of the educational system, 2007..............................125
4.03 Internet access in schools, 2007..127
4.04 Buyer sophistication, 2007..127
4.05 Residential telephone connection charge,* 2005...............116
4.06 Residential monthly telephone subscription,* 2005...........113
4.07 High-speed monthly broadband subscription*....................n/a
4.08 Lowest cost of broadband*...n/a
4.09 Cost of mobile telephone call,* 2006...................................113

Business readiness   122
5.01 Extent of staff training, 2007...127
5.02 Local availability of research and training, 2007.................110
5.03 Quality of management schools, 2007.................................126
5.04 Company spending on R&D, 2007..120
5.05 University-industry research collaboration, 2007................126
5.06 Business telephone connection charge,* 2005...................109
5.07 Business monthly telephone subscription,* 2005...............105
5.08 Local supplier quality, 2007...123
5.09 Local supplier quantity, 2007..91
5.10 Computer, comm., and other services imports*.................n/a

Government readiness   127
6.01 Government prioritization of ICT, 2007.................................123
6.02 Gov't procurement of advanced tech products, 2007.......107
6.03 Importance of ICT to gov't vision of the future, 2007.........118
6.04 E-Government Readiness Index,* 2007...............................124

Usage component   126
Individual usage   123
7.01 Mobile telephone subscribers,* 2006...................................123
7.02 Personal computers,* 2005..125
7.03 Broadband Internet subscribers,* 2005...............................118
7.04 Internet users,* 2006...120
7.05 Internet bandwidth,* 2006...123

Business usage   127
8.01 Prevalence of foreign technology licensing, 2007...............127
8.02 Firm-level technology absorption, 2007...............................122
8.03 Capacity for innovation, 2007..111
8.04 Availability of new telephone lines, 2007.............................119
8.05 Extent of business Internet use, 2007..................................127

Government usage   123
9.01 Government success in ICT promotion, 2007......................120
9.02 Availability of government online services, 2007................100
9.03 ICT use and government efficiency, 2007............................112
9.04 Presence of ICT in government offices, 2007.....................119
9.05 E-Participation Index,* 2007...117

* Hard data

Note: For further details and explanation, please refer to the section "How to Read the Country/Economy Profiles" at the beginning of this chapter.

Chile

Key indicators

Population (millions), 2006...16.5
GDP (PPP) per capita (US$), 2006....................................12,810.8
Internet users per 100 inhabitants, 2006 ....25.2
Internet bandwidth (mB/s) per 10,000 inhabitants, 2005.........7.8

Networked Readiness Index

Year (number of economies)	Rank
2007–2008 (127)	**34**
2006–2007 (122)	31
2005–2006 (115)	29

Global Competitiveness Index 2007–2008 (131)	26

Environment component — 35
Market environment — 30

1.01 Venture capital availability, 2007..34
1.02 Financial market sophistication, 2007 27
1.03 Availability of latest technologies, 2007 34
1.04 State of cluster development, 2007..................................52
1.05 Utility patents,* 2006 48
1.06 High-tech exports,* 2005 80
1.07 Burden of government regulation, 2007 24
1.08 Extent and effect of taxation, 2007..................................35
1.09 Total tax rate,* 2007..12
1.10 Time required to start a business,* 2007.........................59
1.11 No. of procedures required to start a business,* 2007 58
1.12 Intensity of local competition, 2007 14
1.13 Freedom of the press, 2007..30
1.14 Accessibility of digital content, 2007................................27

Political and regulatory environment — 31

2.01 Effectiveness of law-making bodies, 2007 49
2.02 Laws relating to ICT, 2007..25
2.03 Judicial independence, 2007 53
2.04 Intellectual property protection, 2007 49
2.05 Efficiency of legal framework, 2007 35
2.06 Property rights, 2007..40
2.07 Quality of competition in the ISP sector, 2007 17
2.08 No. of procedures to enforce a contract,* 2007 53
2.09 Time to enforce a contract,* 2007 51

Infrastructure environment — 50

3.01 Telephone lines,* 2006...59
3.02 Secure Internet servers,* 2006...51
3.03 Electricity production,* 2004 56
3.04 Availability of scientists and engineers, 2007 31
3.05 Quality of scientific research institutions, 2007 50
3.06 Tertiary enrollment,* 2005..37
3.07 Education expenditure,* 2005...72

Readiness component — 36
Individual readiness — 53

4.01 Quality of math and science education, 2007.................104
4.02 Quality of the educational system, 2007..........................75
4.03 Internet access in schools, 2007......................................39
4.04 Buyer sophistication, 2007 29
4.05 Residential telephone connection charge,* 2005 41
4.06 Residential monthly telephone subscription,* 2005 59
4.07 High-speed monthly broadband subscription,* 2006........48
4.08 Lowest cost of broadband,* 2006 46
4.09 Cost of mobile telephone call,* 2005................................76

Business readiness — 35

5.01 Extent of staff training, 2007..40
5.02 Local availability of research and training, 2007...............34
5.03 Quality of management schools, 2007 19
5.04 Company spending on R&D, 2007....................................59
5.05 University-industry research collaboration, 2007..............42
5.06 Business telephone connection charge,* 2005 32
5.07 Business monthly telephone subscription,* 2005 42
5.08 Local supplier quality, 2007 27
5.09 Local supplier quantity, 2007..24
5.10 Computer, comm., and other services imports,* 2005 71

Government readiness — 33

6.01 Government prioritization of ICT, 2007.............................40
6.02 Gov't procurement of advanced tech products, 2007 39
6.03 Importance of ICT to gov't vision of the future, 2007.......20
6.04 E-Government Readiness Index,* 2007............................40

Usage component — 35
Individual usage — 48

7.01 Mobile telephone subscribers,* 2006...............................53
7.02 Personal computers,* 2005 48
7.03 Broadband Internet subscribers,* 2006 37
7.04 Internet users,* 2006 46
7.05 Internet bandwidth,* 2005 42

Business usage — 31

8.01 Prevalence of foreign technology licensing, 2007.............40
8.02 Firm-level technology absorption, 2007 38
8.03 Capacity for innovation, 2007...49
8.04 Availability of new telephone lines, 2007.........................20
8.05 Extent of business Internet use, 2007 27

Government usage — 28

9.01 Government success in ICT promotion, 2007...................53
9.02 Availability of government online services, 2007 12
9.03 ICT use and government efficiency, 2007..........................9
9.04 Presence of ICT in government offices, 2007 25
9.05 E-Participation Index,* 2007..65

* Hard data

Note: For further details and explanation, please refer to the section "How to Read the Country/Economy Profiles" at the beginning of this chapter.

China

Key indicators

Population (millions), 2006	1323.6
GDP (PPP) per capita (US$), 2006	7,721.9
Internet users per 100 inhabitants, 2006	10.4
Internet bandwidth (mB/s) per 10,000 inhabitants, 2006	1.9

Networked Readiness Index

Year (number of economies)	Rank
2007–2008 (127)	**57**
2006–2007 (122)	59
2005–2006 (115)	50

Global Competitiveness Index 2007–2008 (131)	34

Environment component — 66

Market environment — 69

1.01	Venture capital availability, 2007	70
1.02	Financial market sophistication, 2007	89
1.03	Availability of latest technologies, 2007	78
1.04	State of cluster development, 2007	29
1.05	Utility patents,* 2006	57
1.06	High-tech exports,* 2004	8
1.07	Burden of government regulation, 2007	35
1.08	Extent and effect of taxation, 2007	45
1.09	Total tax rate,* 2007	113
1.10	Time required to start a business,* 2007	81
1.11	No. of procedures required to start a business,* 2007	103
1.12	Intensity of local competition, 2007	39
1.13	Freedom of the press, 2007	119
1.14	Accessibility of digital content, 2007	52

Political and regulatory environment — 58

2.01	Effectiveness of law-making bodies, 2007	37
2.02	Laws relating to ICT, 2007	56
2.03	Judicial independence, 2007	81
2.04	Intellectual property protection, 2007	70
2.05	Efficiency of legal framework, 2007	70
2.06	Property rights, 2007	75
2.07	Quality of competition in the ISP sector, 2007	59
2.08	No. of procedures to enforce a contract,* 2007	46
2.09	Time to enforce a contract,* 2007	36

Infrastructure environment — 86

3.01	Telephone lines,* 2006	45
3.02	Secure Internet servers,* 2006	101
3.03	Electricity production,* 2004	76
3.04	Availability of scientists and engineers, 2007	77
3.05	Quality of scientific research institutions, 2007	55
3.06	Tertiary enrollment,* 2005	77
3.07	Education expenditure,* 2005	110

Readiness component — 54

Individual readiness — 59

4.01	Quality of math and science education, 2007	55
4.02	Quality of the educational system, 2007	70
4.03	Internet access in schools, 2007	46
4.04	Buyer sophistication, 2007	39
4.05	Residential telephone connection charge*	n/a
4.06	Residential monthly telephone subscription,* 2005	74
4.07	High-speed monthly broadband subscription,* 2006	46
4.08	Lowest cost of broadband,* 2006	50
4.09	Cost of mobile telephone call,* 2005	64

Business readiness — 58

5.01	Extent of staff training, 2007	61
5.02	Local availability of research and training, 2007	39
5.03	Quality of management schools, 2007	87
5.04	Company spending on R&D, 2007	32
5.05	University-industry research collaboration, 2007	25
5.06	Business telephone connection charge*	n/a
5.07	Business monthly telephone subscription,* 2005	63
5.08	Local supplier quality, 2007	72
5.09	Local supplier quantity, 2007	35
5.10	Computer, comm., and other services imports,* 2005	40

Government readiness — 42

6.01	Government prioritization of ICT, 2007	74
6.02	Gov't procurement of advanced tech products, 2007	22
6.03	Importance of ICT to gov't vision of the future, 2007	29
6.04	E-Government Readiness Index,* 2007	62

Usage component — 54

Individual usage — 80

7.01	Mobile telephone subscribers,* 2006	87
7.02	Personal computers,* 2005	84
7.03	Broadband Internet subscribers,* 2006	48
7.04	Internet users,* 2006	79
7.05	Internet bandwidth,* 2006	59

Business usage — 59

8.01	Prevalence of foreign technology licensing, 2007	87
8.02	Firm-level technology absorption, 2007	50
8.03	Capacity for innovation, 2007	34
8.04	Availability of new telephone lines, 2007	71
8.05	Extent of business Internet use, 2007	60

Government usage — 34

9.01	Government success in ICT promotion, 2007	48
9.02	Availability of government online services, 2007	39
9.03	ICT use and government efficiency, 2007	38
9.04	Presence of ICT in government offices, 2007	40
9.05	E-Participation Index,* 2007	19

* Hard data

Note: For further details and explanation, please refer to the section "How to Read the Country/Economy Profiles" at the beginning of this chapter.

Colombia

Key indicators

Population (millions), 2006	46.3
GDP (PPP) per capita (US$), 2006	8,260.3
Internet users per 100 inhabitants, 2006	14.5
Internet bandwidth (mB/s) per 10,000 inhabitants, 2006	5.5

Networked Readiness Index

Year (number of economies)	Rank
2007–2008 (127)	**69**
2006–2007 (122)	64
2005–2006 (115)	62

Global Competitiveness Index 2007–2008 (131)	69

Environment component — 80

Market environment — 96

1.01	Venture capital availability, 2007	75
1.02	Financial market sophistication, 2007	61
1.03	Availability of latest technologies, 2007	86
1.04	State of cluster development, 2007	78
1.05	Utility patents,* 2006	75
1.06	High-tech exports,* 2005	62
1.07	Burden of government regulation, 2007	108
1.08	Extent and effect of taxation, 2007	106
1.09	Total tax rate,* 2007	117
1.10	Time required to start a business,* 2007	90
1.11	No. of procedures required to start a business,* 2007	88
1.12	Intensity of local competition, 2007	64
1.13	Freedom of the press, 2007	46
1.14	Accessibility of digital content, 2007	77

Political and regulatory environment — 79

2.01	Effectiveness of law-making bodies, 2007	87
2.02	Laws relating to ICT, 2007	54
2.03	Judicial independence, 2007	63
2.04	Intellectual property protection, 2007	62
2.05	Efficiency of legal framework, 2007	63
2.06	Property rights, 2007	67
2.07	Quality of competition in the ISP sector, 2007	58
2.08	No. of procedures to enforce a contract,* 2007	40
2.09	Time to enforce a contract,* 2007	116

Infrastructure environment — 74

3.01	Telephone lines,* 2006	67
3.02	Secure Internet servers,* 2006	63
3.03	Electricity production,* 2004	82
3.04	Availability of scientists and engineers, 2007	82
3.05	Quality of scientific research institutions, 2007	86
3.06	Tertiary enrollment,* 2005	67
3.07	Education expenditure,* 2005	40

Readiness component — 64

Individual readiness — 74

4.01	Quality of math and science education, 2007	78
4.02	Quality of the educational system, 2007	57
4.03	Internet access in schools, 2007	75
4.04	Buyer sophistication, 2007	72
4.05	Residential telephone connection charge,* 2005	78
4.06	Residential monthly telephone subscription,* 2005	105
4.07	High-speed monthly broadband subscription,* 2006	62
4.08	Lowest cost of broadband,* 2006	77
4.09	Cost of mobile telephone call,* 2005	66

Business readiness — 55

5.01	Extent of staff training, 2007	69
5.02	Local availability of research and training, 2007	69
5.03	Quality of management schools, 2007	46
5.04	Company spending on R&D, 2007	75
5.05	University-industry research collaboration, 2007	51
5.06	Business telephone connection charge,* 2005	70
5.07	Business monthly telephone subscription,* 2005	56
5.08	Local supplier quality, 2007	48
5.09	Local supplier quantity, 2007	54
5.10	Computer, comm., and other services imports,* 2005	73

Government readiness — 57

6.01	Government prioritization of ICT, 2007	69
6.02	Gov't procurement of advanced tech products, 2007	67
6.03	Importance of ICT to gov't vision of the future, 2007	72
6.04	E-Government Readiness Index,* 2007	51

Usage component — 64

Individual usage — 65

7.01	Mobile telephone subscribers,* 2006	65
7.02	Personal computers,* 2005	86
7.03	Broadband Internet subscribers,* 2006	63
7.04	Internet users,* 2006	69
7.05	Internet bandwidth,* 2006	49

Business usage — 74

8.01	Prevalence of foreign technology licensing, 2007	84
8.02	Firm-level technology absorption, 2007	94
8.03	Capacity for innovation, 2007	64
8.04	Availability of new telephone lines, 2007	49
8.05	Extent of business Internet use, 2007	74

Government usage — 53

9.01	Government success in ICT promotion, 2007	76
9.02	Availability of government online services, 2007	63
9.03	ICT use and government efficiency, 2007	63
9.04	Presence of ICT in government offices, 2007	88
9.05	E-Participation Index,* 2007	24

* Hard data

Note: For further details and explanation, please refer to the section "How to Read the Country/Economy Profiles" at the beginning of this chapter.

Costa Rica

Key indicators

Population (millions), 2006	4.4
GDP (PPP) per capita (US$), 2006	11,862.1
Internet users per 100 inhabitants, 2006	27.6
Internet bandwidth (mB/s) per 10,000 inhabitants, 2006	1.8

Networked Readiness Index

Year (number of economies)	Rank
2007–2008 (127)	**60**
2006–2007 (122)	56
2005–2006 (115)	69

Global Competitiveness Index 2007–2008 (131)	63

Environment component — 61

Market environment — 70

1.01	Venture capital availability, 2007	85
1.02	Financial market sophistication, 2007	66
1.03	Availability of latest technologies, 2007	71
1.04	State of cluster development, 2007	68
1.05	Utility patents,* 2006	45
1.06	High-tech exports,* 2005	12
1.07	Burden of government regulation, 2007	91
1.08	Extent and effect of taxation, 2007	47
1.09	Total tax rate,* 2007	99
1.10	Time required to start a business,* 2007	113
1.11	No. of procedures required to start a business,* 2007	98
1.12	Intensity of local competition, 2007	50
1.13	Freedom of the press, 2007	24
1.14	Accessibility of digital content, 2007	83

Political and regulatory environment — 71

2.01	Effectiveness of law-making bodies, 2007	113
2.02	Laws relating to ICT, 2007	59
2.03	Judicial independence, 2007	36
2.04	Intellectual property protection, 2007	58
2.05	Efficiency of legal framework, 2007	40
2.06	Property rights, 2007	64
2.07	Quality of competition in the ISP sector, 2007	124
2.08	No. of procedures to enforce a contract,* 2007	89
2.09	Time to enforce a contract,* 2007	107

Infrastructure environment — 52

3.01	Telephone lines,* 2006	38
3.02	Secure Internet servers,* 2006	30
3.03	Electricity production,* 2004	71
3.04	Availability of scientists and engineers, 2007	39
3.05	Quality of scientific research institutions, 2007	34
3.06	Tertiary enrollment,* 2005	71
3.07	Education expenditure,* 2005	66

Readiness component — 48

Individual readiness — 52

4.01	Quality of math and science education, 2007	65
4.02	Quality of the educational system, 2007	35
4.03	Internet access in schools, 2007	73
4.04	Buyer sophistication, 2007	35
4.05	Residential telephone connection charge,* 2005	58
4.06	Residential monthly telephone subscription,* 2005	48
4.07	High-speed monthly broadband subscription,* 2006	82
4.08	Lowest cost of broadband,* 2006	60
4.09	Cost of mobile telephone call,* 2005	39

Business readiness — 34

5.01	Extent of staff training, 2007	27
5.02	Local availability of research and training, 2007	36
5.03	Quality of management schools, 2007	27
5.04	Company spending on R&D, 2007	30
5.05	University-industry research collaboration, 2007	35
5.06	Business telephone connection charge,* 2005	48
5.07	Business monthly telephone subscription,* 2005	38
5.08	Local supplier quality, 2007	35
5.09	Local supplier quantity, 2007	40
5.10	Computer, comm., and other services imports,* 2005	79

Government readiness — 66

6.01	Government prioritization of ICT, 2007	77
6.02	Gov't procurement of advanced tech products, 2007	60
6.03	Importance of ICT to gov't vision of the future, 2007	89
6.04	E-Government Readiness Index,* 2007	56

Usage component — 69

Individual usage — 61

7.01	Mobile telephone subscribers,* 2006	89
7.02	Personal computers,* 2005	35
7.03	Broadband Internet subscribers,* 2006	64
7.04	Internet users,* 2006	45
7.05	Internet bandwidth,* 2006	60

Business usage — 76

8.01	Prevalence of foreign technology licensing, 2007	57
8.02	Firm-level technology absorption, 2007	55
8.03	Capacity for innovation, 2007	37
8.04	Availability of new telephone lines, 2007	117
8.05	Extent of business Internet use, 2007	71

Government usage — 64

9.01	Government success in ICT promotion, 2007	82
9.02	Availability of government online services, 2007	70
9.03	ICT use and government efficiency, 2007	93
9.04	Presence of ICT in government offices, 2007	80
9.05	E-Participation Index,* 2007	32

* Hard data

Note: For further details and explanation, please refer to the section "How to Read the Country/Economy Profiles" at the beginning of this chapter.

Croatia

Key indicators

Population (millions), 2006	4.6
GDP (PPP) per capita (US$), 2006	14,522.6
Internet users per 100 inhabitants, 2006	34.6
Internet bandwidth (mB/s) per 10,000 inhabitants, 2006	10.4

Networked Readiness Index

Year (number of economies)	Rank
2007–2008 (127)	**49**
2006–2007 (122)	46
2005–2006 (115)	57

Global Competitiveness Index 2007–2008 (131)	57

Environment component — 52

Market environment — 61

1.01	Venture capital availability, 2007	72
1.02	Financial market sophistication, 2007	67
1.03	Availability of latest technologies, 2007	75
1.04	State of cluster development, 2007	64
1.05	Utility patents,* 2006	33
1.06	High-tech exports,* 2005	39
1.07	Burden of government regulation, 2007	89
1.08	Extent and effect of taxation, 2007	83
1.09	Total tax rate,* 2007	22
1.10	Time required to start a business,* 2007	89
1.11	No. of procedures required to start a business,* 2007	44
1.12	Intensity of local competition, 2007	63
1.13	Freedom of the press, 2007	71
1.14	Accessibility of digital content, 2007	44

Political and regulatory environment — 63

2.01	Effectiveness of law-making bodies, 2007	59
2.02	Laws relating to ICT, 2007	45
2.03	Judicial independence, 2007	85
2.04	Intellectual property protection, 2007	57
2.05	Efficiency of legal framework, 2007	79
2.06	Property rights, 2007	77
2.07	Quality of competition in the ISP sector, 2007	57
2.08	No. of procedures to enforce a contract,* 2007	65
2.09	Time to enforce a contract,* 2007	65

Infrastructure environment — 44

3.01	Telephone lines,* 2006	32
3.02	Secure Internet servers,* 2006	37
3.03	Electricity production,* 2004	58
3.04	Availability of scientists and engineers, 2007	46
3.05	Quality of scientific research institutions, 2007	53
3.06	Tertiary enrollment,* 2004	46
3.07	Education expenditure,* 2005	61

Readiness component — 42

Individual readiness — 44

4.01	Quality of math and science education, 2007	27
4.02	Quality of the educational system, 2007	59
4.03	Internet access in schools, 2007	42
4.04	Buyer sophistication, 2007	69
4.05	Residential telephone connection charge,* 2005	63
4.06	Residential monthly telephone subscription,* 2005	60
4.07	High-speed monthly broadband subscription,* 2006	45
4.08	Lowest cost of broadband,* 2006	40
4.09	Cost of mobile telephone call,* 2005	48

Business readiness — 45

5.01	Extent of staff training, 2007	60
5.02	Local availability of research and training, 2007	38
5.03	Quality of management schools, 2007	70
5.04	Company spending on R&D, 2007	46
5.05	University-industry research collaboration, 2007	37
5.06	Business telephone connection charge,* 2005	56
5.07	Business monthly telephone subscription,* 2005	44
5.08	Local supplier quality, 2007	71
5.09	Local supplier quantity, 2007	81
5.10	Computer, comm., and other services imports,* 2005	7

Government readiness — 54

6.01	Government prioritization of ICT, 2007	61
6.02	Gov't procurement of advanced tech products, 2007	79
6.03	Importance of ICT to gov't vision of the future, 2007	76
6.04	E-Government Readiness Index,* 2007	47

Usage component — 48

Individual usage — 41

7.01	Mobile telephone subscribers,* 2006	31
7.02	Personal computers,* 2005	39
7.03	Broadband Internet subscribers,* 2006	41
7.04	Internet users,* 2006	36
7.05	Internet bandwidth,* 2005	37

Business usage — 52

8.01	Prevalence of foreign technology licensing, 2007	45
8.02	Firm-level technology absorption, 2007	92
8.03	Capacity for innovation, 2007	47
8.04	Availability of new telephone lines, 2007	41
8.05	Extent of business Internet use, 2007	65

Government usage — 62

9.01	Government success in ICT promotion, 2007	65
9.02	Availability of government online services, 2007	69
9.03	ICT use and government efficiency, 2007	82
9.04	Presence of ICT in government offices, 2007	34
9.05	E-Participation Index,* 2007	69

* Hard data

Note: For further details and explanation, please refer to the section "How to Read the Country/Economy Profiles" at the beginning of this chapter.

Cyprus

Key indicators

Population (millions), 2006	0.8
GDP (PPP) per capita (US$), 2006	29,870.1
Internet users per 100 inhabitants, 2006	42.2
Internet bandwidth (mB/s) per 10,000 inhabitants, 2004	3.7

Networked Readiness Index

Year (number of economies)	Rank
2007–2008 (127)	41
2006–2007 (122)	43
2005–2006 (115)	33

Global Competitiveness Index 2007–2008 (131)	55

Environment component — 30

Market environment — 40

1.01	Venture capital availability, 2007	44
1.02	Financial market sophistication, 2007	45
1.03	Availability of latest technologies, 2007	49
1.04	State of cluster development, 2007	47
1.05	Utility patents,* 2006	29
1.06	High-tech exports,* 2004	16
1.07	Burden of government regulation, 2007	27
1.08	Extent and effect of taxation, 2007	19
1.09	Total tax rate*	n/a
1.10	Time required to start a business*	n/a
1.11	No. of procedures required to start a business*	n/a
1.12	Intensity of local competition, 2007	36
1.13	Freedom of the press, 2007	38
1.14	Accessibility of digital content, 2007	68

Political and regulatory environment — 33

2.01	Effectiveness of law-making bodies, 2007	34
2.02	Laws relating to ICT, 2007	58
2.03	Judicial independence, 2007	33
2.04	Intellectual property protection, 2007	39
2.05	Efficiency of legal framework, 2007	32
2.06	Property rights, 2007	36
2.07	Quality of competition in the ISP sector, 2007	38
2.08	No. of procedures to enforce a contract*	n/a
2.09	Time to enforce a contract*	n/a

Infrastructure environment — 30

3.01	Telephone lines,* 2006	19
3.02	Secure Internet servers,* 2006	20
3.03	Electricity production,* 2003	44
3.04	Availability of scientists and engineers, 2007	33
3.05	Quality of scientific research institutions, 2007	75
3.06	Tertiary enrollment,* 2005	59
3.07	Education expenditure,* 2005	22

Readiness component — 45

Individual readiness — 32

4.01	Quality of math and science education, 2007	18
4.02	Quality of the educational system, 2007	23
4.03	Internet access in schools, 2007	43
4.04	Buyer sophistication, 2007	38
4.05	Residential telephone connection charge,* 2006	33
4.06	Residential monthly telephone subscription,* 2006	41
4.07	High-speed monthly broadband subscription,* 2006	35
4.08	Lowest cost of broadband,* 2006	36
4.09	Cost of mobile telephone call,* 2005	14

Business readiness — 60

5.01	Extent of staff training, 2007	71
5.02	Local availability of research and training, 2007	68
5.03	Quality of management schools, 2007	53
5.04	Company spending on R&D, 2007	80
5.05	University-industry research collaboration, 2007	73
5.06	Business telephone connection charge,* 2006	26
5.07	Business monthly telephone subscription,* 2006	30
5.08	Local supplier quality, 2007	46
5.09	Local supplier quantity, 2007	76
5.10	Computer, comm., and other services imports,* 2005	92

Government readiness — 52

6.01	Government prioritization of ICT, 2007	85
6.02	Gov't procurement of advanced tech products, 2007	77
6.03	Importance of ICT to gov't vision of the future, 2007	74
6.04	E-Government Readiness Index,* 2007	35

Usage component — 46

Individual usage — 37

7.01	Mobile telephone subscribers,* 2006	38
7.02	Personal computers,* 2005	29
7.03	Broadband Internet subscribers,* 2006	38
7.04	Internet users,* 2006	30
7.05	Internet bandwidth,* 2004	53

Business usage — 54

8.01	Prevalence of foreign technology licensing, 2007	66
8.02	Firm-level technology absorption, 2007	64
8.03	Capacity for innovation, 2007	69
8.04	Availability of new telephone lines, 2007	34
8.05	Extent of business Internet use, 2007	48

Government usage — 63

9.01	Government success in ICT promotion, 2007	75
9.02	Availability of government online services, 2007	46
9.03	ICT use and government efficiency, 2007	47
9.04	Presence of ICT in government offices, 2007	77
9.05	E-Participation Index,* 2007	82

* Hard data

Note: For further details and explanation, please refer to the section "How to Read the Country/Economy Profiles" at the beginning of this chapter.

Czech Republic

Key indicators

Population (millions), 2006...10.2
GDP (PPP) per capita (US$), 2006....................................23,399.1
Internet users per 100 inhabitants, 2006 ....34.7
Internet bandwidth (mB/s) per 10,000 inhabitants, 2005.......21.8

Networked Readiness Index

Year (number of economies)	Rank
2007–2008 (127)	**36**
2006–2007 (122)	34
2005–2006 (115)	32

Global Competitiveness Index 2007–2008 (131)   33

Environment component — 42
Market environment — 46
1.01 Venture capital availability, 2007..66
1.02 Financial market sophistication, 2007 53
1.03 Availability of latest technologies, 2007 44
1.04 State of cluster development, 2007 31
1.05 Utility patents,* 2006 32
1.06 High-tech exports,* 2005 26
1.07 Burden of government regulation, 2007 119
1.08 Extent and effect of taxation, 2007 85
1.09 Total tax rate,* 2007 75
1.10 Time required to start a business,* 2007 36
1.11 No. of procedures required to start a business,* 2007 74
1.12 Intensity of local competition, 2007 17
1.13 Freedom of the press, 2007...37
1.14 Accessibility of digital content, 2007 26

Political and regulatory environment — 54
2.01 Effectiveness of law-making bodies, 2007 82
2.02 Laws relating to ICT, 2007..44
2.03 Judicial independence, 2007 56
2.04 Intellectual property protection, 2007 51
2.05 Efficiency of legal framework, 2007.....................................77
2.06 Property rights, 2007 65
2.07 Quality of competition in the ISP sector, 2007 53
2.08 No. of procedures to enforce a contract,* 2007 8
2.09 Time to enforce a contract,* 2007 101

Infrastructure environment — 34
3.01 Telephone lines,* 2005..36
3.02 Secure Internet servers,* 2006 31
3.03 Electricity production,* 2004 19
3.04 Availability of scientists and engineers, 2007 5
3.05 Quality of scientific research institutions, 2007 30
3.06 Tertiary enrollment,* 2005..36
3.07 Education expenditure,* 2005 59

Readiness component — 33
Individual readiness — 31
4.01 Quality of math and science education, 2007......................9
4.02 Quality of the educational system, 2007.............................32
4.03 Internet access in schools, 2007...23
4.04 Buyer sophistication, 2007 46
4.05 Residential telephone connection charge,* 2005 71
4.06 Residential monthly telephone subscription,* 2005 58
4.07 High-speed monthly broadband subscription,* 2006........40
4.08 Lowest cost of broadband,* 2006 30
4.09 Cost of mobile telephone call,* 2005...................................35

Business readiness — 25
5.01 Extent of staff training, 2007..35
5.02 Local availability of research and training, 2007................25
5.03 Quality of management schools, 2007 38
5.04 Company spending on R&D, 2007.......................................29
5.05 University-industry research collaboration, 2007...............27
5.06 Business telephone connection charge,* 2005 64
5.07 Business monthly telephone subscription,* 2005 57
5.08 Local supplier quality, 2007...26
5.09 Local supplier quantity, 2007...17
5.10 Computer, comm., and other services imports,* 2005 16

Government readiness — 49
6.01 Government prioritization of ICT, 2007...............................76
6.02 Gov't procurement of advanced tech products, 2007 45
6.03 Importance of ICT to gov't vision of the future, 2007.....103
6.04 E-Government Readiness Index,* 2007..............................25

Usage component — 37
Individual usage — 31
7.01 Mobile telephone subscribers,* 2006....................................9
7.02 Personal computers,* 2005 31
7.03 Broadband Internet subscribers,* 2006 32
7.04 Internet users,* 2006 35
7.05 Internet bandwidth,* 2005 29

Business usage — 25
8.01 Prevalence of foreign technology licensing, 2007.............39
8.02 Firm-level technology absorption, 2007 35
8.03 Capacity for innovation, 2007..25
8.04 Availability of new telephone lines, 2007............................27
8.05 Extent of business Internet use, 2007.................................20

Government usage — 92
9.01 Government success in ICT promotion, 2007..................103
9.02 Availability of government online services, 2007 84
9.03 ICT use and government efficiency, 2007.........................101
9.04 Presence of ICT in government offices, 2007 76
9.05 E-Participation Index,* 2007..58

* Hard data

Note: For further details and explanation, please refer to the section "How to Read the Country/Economy Profiles" at the beginning of this chapter.

Denmark

Key indicators

Population (millions), 2006	5.4
GDP (PPP) per capita (US$), 2006	36,920.4
Internet users per 100 inhabitants, 2006	58.2
Internet bandwidth (mB/s) per 10,000 inhabitants, 2005	349.0

Networked Readiness Index

Year (number of economies)	Rank
2007–2008 (127)	**1**
2006–2007 (122)	1
2005–2006 (115)	3

Global Competitiveness Index 2007–2008 (131) — 3

Environment component — 2

Market environment — 11

1.01	Venture capital availability, 2007	8
1.02	Financial market sophistication, 2007	13
1.03	Availability of latest technologies, 2007	5
1.04	State of cluster development, 2007	19
1.05	Utility patents,* 2006	13
1.06	High-tech exports,* 2005	25
1.07	Burden of government regulation, 2007	23
1.08	Extent and effect of taxation, 2007	107
1.09	Total tax rate,* 2007	26
1.10	Time required to start a business,* 2007	6
1.11	No. of procedures required to start a business,* 2007	7
1.12	Intensity of local competition, 2007	26
1.13	Freedom of the press, 2007	2
1.14	Accessibility of digital content, 2007	4

Political and regulatory environment — 2

2.01	Effectiveness of law-making bodies, 2007	2
2.02	Laws relating to ICT, 2007	1
2.03	Judicial independence, 2007	3
2.04	Intellectual property protection, 2007	4
2.05	Efficiency of legal framework, 2007	1
2.06	Property rights, 2007	2
2.07	Quality of competition in the ISP sector, 2007	16
2.08	No. of procedures to enforce a contract,* 2007	40
2.09	Time to enforce a contract,* 2007	27

Infrastructure environment — 4

3.01	Telephone lines,* 2006	8
3.02	Secure Internet servers,* 2006	4
3.03	Electricity production,* 2004	25
3.04	Availability of scientists and engineers, 2007	11
3.05	Quality of scientific research institutions, 2007	14
3.06	Tertiary enrollment,* 2005	9
3.07	Education expenditure,* 2005	1

Readiness component — 2

Individual readiness — 6

4.01	Quality of math and science education, 2007	19
4.02	Quality of the educational system, 2007	4
4.03	Internet access in schools, 2007	5
4.04	Buyer sophistication, 2007	13
4.05	Residential telephone connection charge,* 2005	31
4.06	Residential monthly telephone subscription,* 2005	19
4.07	High-speed monthly broadband subscription,* 2006	14
4.08	Lowest cost of broadband,* 2006	22
4.09	Cost of mobile telephone call,* 2005	9

Business readiness — 6

5.01	Extent of staff training, 2007	1
5.02	Local availability of research and training, 2007	11
5.03	Quality of management schools, 2007	9
5.04	Company spending on R&D, 2007	8
5.05	University-industry research collaboration, 2007	11
5.06	Business telephone connection charge,* 2005	25
5.07	Business monthly telephone subscription,* 2005	10
5.08	Local supplier quality, 2007	8
5.09	Local supplier quantity, 2007	19
5.10	Computer, comm., and other services imports,* 2004	39

Government readiness — 2

6.01	Government prioritization of ICT, 2007	3
6.02	Gov't procurement of advanced tech products, 2007	13
6.03	Importance of ICT to gov't vision of the future, 2007	6
6.04	E-Government Readiness Index,* 2007	2

Usage component — 1

Individual usage — 2

7.01	Mobile telephone subscribers,* 2006	21
7.02	Personal computers,* 2005	9
7.03	Broadband Internet subscribers,* 2006	1
7.04	Internet users,* 2006	16
7.05	Internet bandwidth,* 2005	1

Business usage — 5

8.01	Prevalence of foreign technology licensing, 2007	9
8.02	Firm-level technology absorption, 2007	10
8.03	Capacity for innovation, 2007	6
8.04	Availability of new telephone lines, 2007	4
8.05	Extent of business Internet use, 2007	7

Government usage — 1

9.01	Government success in ICT promotion, 2007	10
9.02	Availability of government online services, 2007	3
9.03	ICT use and government efficiency, 2007	3
9.04	Presence of ICT in government offices, 2007	5
9.05	E-Participation Index,* 2007	3

* Hard data

Note: For further details and explanation, please refer to the section "How to Read the Country/Economy Profiles" at the beginning of this chapter.

Dominican Republic

Key indicators

Population (millions), 2006..9.0
GDP (PPP) per capita (US$), 2006.........................9,376.7
Internet users per 100 inhabitants, 2006 ....22.2
Internet bandwidth (mB/s) per 10,000 inhabitants, 2006.........0.1

Networked Readiness Index

Year (number of economies)	Rank
2007–2008 (127)	**75**
2006–2007 (122)	66
2005–2006 (115)	89

Global Competitiveness Index 2007–2008 (131)   96

Environment component — 83
Market environment — 62
1.01 Venture capital availability, 2007..100
1.02 Financial market sophistication, 2007 83
1.03 Availability of latest technologies, 2007 62
1.04 State of cluster development, 2007.....................................95
1.05 Utility patents,* 2006 74
1.06 High-tech exports* ....n/a
1.07 Burden of government regulation, 2007 75
1.08 Extent and effect of taxation, 2007..................................116
1.09 Total tax rate,* 2007 50
1.10 Time required to start a business,* 2007 47
1.11 No. of procedures required to start a business,* 2007 58
1.12 Intensity of local competition, 2007 96
1.13 Freedom of the press, 2007..65
1.14 Accessibility of digital content, 2007.................................46

Political and regulatory environment — 68
2.01 Effectiveness of law-making bodies, 2007 107
2.02 Laws relating to ICT, 2007...62
2.03 Judicial independence, 2007 87
2.04 Intellectual property protection, 2007 76
2.05 Efficiency of legal framework, 2007...................................98
2.06 Property rights, 2007..80
2.07 Quality of competition in the ISP sector, 2007 49
2.08 No. of procedures to enforce a contract,* 2007 40
2.09 Time to enforce a contract,* 2007 45

Infrastructure environment — 108
3.01 Telephone lines,* 2006..87
3.02 Secure Internet servers,* 2006...63
3.03 Electricity production,* 2004 78
3.04 Availability of scientists and engineers, 2007 115
3.05 Quality of scientific research institutions, 2007 119
3.06 Tertiary enrollment,* 2004...60
3.07 Education expenditure,* 2005...118

Readiness component — 79
Individual readiness — 82
4.01 Quality of math and science education, 2007.................124
4.02 Quality of the educational system, 2007.........................124
4.03 Internet access in schools, 2007..85
4.04 Buyer sophistication, 2007 67
4.05 Residential telephone connection charge,* 2006 57
4.06 Residential monthly telephone subscription,* 2006 95
4.07 High-speed monthly broadband subscription,* 2006........59
4.08 Lowest cost of broadband,* 2006 64
4.09 Cost of mobile telephone call,* 2005.................................70

Business readiness — 92
5.01 Extent of staff training, 2007...90
5.02 Local availability of research and training, 2007................94
5.03 Quality of management schools, 2007 89
5.04 Company spending on R&D, 2007......................................97
5.05 University-industry research collaboration, 2007...............95
5.06 Business telephone connection charge,* 2006 61
5.07 Business monthly telephone subscription,* 2005 71
5.08 Local supplier quality, 2007 87
5.09 Local supplier quantity, 2007...88
5.10 Computer, comm., and other services imports,* 2005 ..108

Government readiness — 51
6.01 Government prioritization of ICT, 2007...............................39
6.02 Gov't procurement of advanced tech products, 2007 91
6.03 Importance of ICT to gov't vision of the future, 2007.......43
6.04 E-Government Readiness Index,* 2007.............................65

Usage component — 56
Individual usage — 72
7.01 Mobile telephone subscribers,* 2006.................................79
7.02 Personal computers,* 2005 94
7.03 Broadband Internet subscribers,* 2006 70
7.04 Internet users,* 2006 51
7.05 Internet bandwidth,* 2006 107

Business usage — 62
8.01 Prevalence of foreign technology licensing, 2007.............62
8.02 Firm-level technology absorption, 2007 62
8.03 Capacity for innovation, 2007..97
8.04 Availability of new telephone lines, 2007 36
8.05 Extent of business Internet use, 2007...............................72

Government usage — 44
9.01 Government success in ICT promotion, 2007....................66
9.02 Availability of government online services, 2007 37
9.03 ICT use and government efficiency, 2007..........................31
9.04 Presence of ICT in government offices, 2007 81
9.05 E-Participation Index,* 2007..36

* Hard data

Note: For further details and explanation, please refer to the section "How to Read the Country/Economy Profiles" at the beginning of this chapter.

Ecuador

Key indicators

Population (millions), 2006	13.4
GDP (PPP) per capita (US$), 2006	4,834.9
Internet users per 100 inhabitants, 2006	11.5
Internet bandwidth (mB/s) per 10,000 inhabitants, 2006	2.2

Networked Readiness Index

Year (number of economies)	Rank
2007–2008 (127)	107
2006–2007 (122)	97
2005–2006 (115)	107

Global Competitiveness Index 2007–2008 (131)	103

Environment component — 121

Market environment — 110

1.01	Venture capital availability, 2007	112
1.02	Financial market sophistication, 2007	85
1.03	Availability of latest technologies, 2007	112
1.04	State of cluster development, 2007	87
1.05	Utility patents,* 2006	64
1.06	High-tech exports,* 2005	75
1.07	Burden of government regulation, 2007	99
1.08	Extent and effect of taxation, 2007	74
1.09	Total tax rate,* 2007	31
1.10	Time required to start a business,* 2007	107
1.11	No. of procedures required to start a business,* 2007	112
1.12	Intensity of local competition, 2007	101
1.13	Freedom of the press, 2007	63
1.14	Accessibility of digital content, 2007	110

Political and regulatory environment — 119

2.01	Effectiveness of law-making bodies, 2007	126
2.02	Laws relating to ICT, 2007	99
2.03	Judicial independence, 2007	121
2.04	Intellectual property protection, 2007	109
2.05	Efficiency of legal framework, 2007	125
2.06	Property rights, 2007	113
2.07	Quality of competition in the ISP sector, 2007	104
2.08	No. of procedures to enforce a contract,* 2007	75
2.09	Time to enforce a contract,* 2007	53

Infrastructure environment — 119

3.01	Telephone lines,* 2006	77
3.02	Secure Internet servers,* 2006	69
3.03	Electricity production,* 2004	84
3.04	Availability of scientists and engineers, 2007	110
3.05	Quality of scientific research institutions, 2007	116
3.06	Tertiary enrollment*	n/a
3.07	Education expenditure,* 2005	117

Readiness component — 97

Individual readiness — 90

4.01	Quality of math and science education, 2007	116
4.02	Quality of the educational system, 2007	119
4.03	Internet access in schools, 2007	102
4.04	Buyer sophistication, 2007	100
4.05	Residential telephone connection charge,* 2005	80
4.06	Residential monthly telephone subscription,* 2005	78
4.07	High-speed monthly broadband subscription,* 2006	67
4.08	Lowest cost of broadband,* 2006	84
4.09	Cost of mobile telephone call,* 2005	98

Business readiness — 94

5.01	Extent of staff training, 2007	113
5.02	Local availability of research and training, 2007	98
5.03	Quality of management schools, 2007	96
5.04	Company spending on R&D, 2007	109
5.05	University-industry research collaboration, 2007	97
5.06	Business telephone connection charge,* 2005	72
5.07	Business monthly telephone subscription,* 2005	80
5.08	Local supplier quality, 2007	94
5.09	Local supplier quantity, 2007	102
5.10	Computer, comm., and other services imports,* 2005	70

Government readiness — 122

6.01	Government prioritization of ICT, 2007	127
6.02	Gov't procurement of advanced tech products, 2007	117
6.03	Importance of ICT to gov't vision of the future, 2007	121
6.04	E-Government Readiness Index,* 2007	69

Usage component — 107

Individual usage — 73

7.01	Mobile telephone subscribers,* 2006	66
7.02	Personal computers,* 2005	69
7.03	Broadband Internet subscribers,* 2005	89
7.04	Internet users,* 2006	77
7.05	Internet bandwidth,* 2006	58

Business usage — 112

8.01	Prevalence of foreign technology licensing, 2007	113
8.02	Firm-level technology absorption, 2007	109
8.03	Capacity for innovation, 2007	99
8.04	Availability of new telephone lines, 2007	115
8.05	Extent of business Internet use, 2007	107

Government usage — 109

9.01	Government success in ICT promotion, 2007	125
9.02	Availability of government online services, 2007	80
9.03	ICT use and government efficiency, 2007	100
9.04	Presence of ICT in government offices, 2007	120
9.05	E-Participation Index,* 2007	76

* Hard data

Note: For further details and explanation, please refer to the section "How to Read the Country/Economy Profiles" at the beginning of this chapter.

Egypt

Key indicators

Population (millions), 2006 .... 75.4
GDP (PPP) per capita (US$), 2006 .... 4,895.4
Internet users per 100 inhabitants, 2006 .... 8.0
Internet bandwidth (mB/s) per 10,000 inhabitants, 2006 .... 1.2

Networked Readiness Index

Year (number of economies)	Rank
2007–2008 (127)	**63**
2006–2007 (122)	77
2005–2006 (115)	63

Global Competitiveness Index 2007–2008 (131)   77

Environment component — 60
Market environment — 66
1.01 Venture capital availability, 2007 77
1.02 Financial market sophistication, 2007 84
1.03 Availability of latest technologies, 2007 64
1.04 State of cluster development, 2007 60
1.05 Utility patents,* 2006 82
1.06 High-tech exports,* 2005 103
1.07 Burden of government regulation, 2007 56
1.08 Extent and effect of taxation, 2007 33
1.09 Total tax rate,* 2007 73
1.10 Time required to start a business,* 2007 16
1.11 No. of procedures required to start a business,* 2007 34
1.12 Intensity of local competition, 2007 73
1.13 Freedom of the press, 2007 92
1.14 Accessibility of digital content, 2007 67

Political and regulatory environment — 61
2.01 Effectiveness of law-making bodies, 2007 65
2.02 Laws relating to ICT, 2007 78
2.03 Judicial independence, 2007 41
2.04 Intellectual property protection, 2007 63
2.05 Efficiency of legal framework, 2007 47
2.06 Property rights, 2007 51
2.07 Quality of competition in the ISP sector, 2007 32
2.08 No. of procedures to enforce a contract,* 2007 100
2.09 Time to enforce a contract,* 2007 111

Infrastructure environment — 64
3.01 Telephone lines,* 2006 74
3.02 Secure Internet servers,* 2006 90
3.03 Electricity production,* 2004 80
3.04 Availability of scientists and engineers, 2007 29
3.05 Quality of scientific research institutions, 2007 90
3.06 Tertiary enrollment,* 2005 57
3.07 Education expenditure,* 2005 50

Readiness component — 70
Individual readiness — 83
4.01 Quality of math and science education, 2007 103
4.02 Quality of the educational system, 2007 116
4.03 Internet access in schools, 2007 81
4.04 Buyer sophistication, 2007 118
4.05 Residential telephone connection charge,* 2006 91
4.06 Residential monthly telephone subscription,* 2006 65
4.07 High-speed monthly broadband subscription,* 2006 86
4.08 Lowest cost of broadband,* 2006 79
4.09 Cost of mobile telephone call,* 2005 1

Business readiness — 73
5.01 Extent of staff training, 2007 80
5.02 Local availability of research and training, 2007 81
5.03 Quality of management schools, 2007 97
5.04 Company spending on R&D, 2007 69
5.05 University-industry research collaboration, 2007 83
5.06 Business telephone connection charge,* 2006 97
5.07 Business monthly telephone subscription,* 2006 59
5.08 Local supplier quality, 2007 69
5.09 Local supplier quantity, 2007 37
5.10 Computer, comm., and other services imports,* 2005 43

Government readiness — 48
6.01 Government prioritization of ICT, 2007 57
6.02 Gov't procurement of advanced tech products, 2007 57
6.03 Importance of ICT to gov't vision of the future, 2007 36
6.04 E-Government Readiness Index,* 2007 71

Usage component — 72
Individual usage — 94
7.01 Mobile telephone subscribers,* 2006 100
7.02 Personal computers,* 2006 83
7.03 Broadband Internet subscribers,* 2006 82
7.04 Internet users,* 2006 86
7.05 Internet bandwidth,* 2006 68

Business usage — 57
8.01 Prevalence of foreign technology licensing, 2007 54
8.02 Firm-level technology absorption, 2007 67
8.03 Capacity for innovation, 2007 77
8.04 Availability of new telephone lines, 2007 37
8.05 Extent of business Internet use, 2007 57

Government usage — 55
9.01 Government success in ICT promotion, 2007 38
9.02 Availability of government online services, 2007 61
9.03 ICT use and government efficiency, 2007 59
9.04 Presence of ICT in government offices, 2007 87
9.05 E-Participation Index,* 2007 47

* Hard data

Note: For further details and explanation, please refer to the section "How to Read the Country/Economy Profiles" at the beginning of this chapter.

El Salvador

Key indicators

Population (millions), 2006	7.0
GDP (PPP) per capita (US$), 2006	5,599.6
Internet users per 100 inhabitants, 2005	9.3
Internet bandwidth (mB/s) per 10,000 inhabitants, 2006	0.2

Networked Readiness Index

Year (number of economies)	Rank
2007–2008 (127)	66
2006–2007 (122)	61
2005–2006 (115)	59

Global Competitiveness Index 2007–2008 (131)	67

Environment component — 78

Market environment — 53

1.01	Venture capital availability, 2007	76
1.02	Financial market sophistication, 2007	42
1.03	Availability of latest technologies, 2007	74
1.04	State of cluster development, 2007	92
1.05	Utility patents,* 2006	71
1.06	High-tech exports,* 2005	68
1.07	Burden of government regulation, 2007	47
1.08	Extent and effect of taxation, 2007	25
1.09	Total tax rate,* 2007	27
1.10	Time required to start a business,* 2007	54
1.11	No. of procedures required to start a business,* 2007	58
1.12	Intensity of local competition, 2007	67
1.13	Freedom of the press, 2007	40
1.14	Accessibility of digital content, 2007	57

Political and regulatory environment — 76

2.01	Effectiveness of law-making bodies, 2007	109
2.02	Laws relating to ICT, 2007	71
2.03	Judicial independence, 2007	90
2.04	Intellectual property protection, 2007	77
2.05	Efficiency of legal framework, 2007	95
2.06	Property rights, 2007	71
2.07	Quality of competition in the ISP sector, 2007	42
2.08	No. of procedures to enforce a contract,* 2007	15
2.09	Time to enforce a contract,* 2007	98

Infrastructure environment — 106

3.01	Telephone lines,* 2006	72
3.02	Secure Internet servers,* 2006	63
3.03	Electricity production,* 2004	93
3.04	Availability of scientists and engineers, 2007	116
3.05	Quality of scientific research institutions, 2007	118
3.06	Tertiary enrollment,* 2005	80
3.07	Education expenditure,* 2005	97

Readiness component — 68

Individual readiness — 70

4.01	Quality of math and science education, 2007	99
4.02	Quality of the educational system, 2007	84
4.03	Internet access in schools, 2007	78
4.04	Buyer sophistication, 2007	62
4.05	Residential telephone connection charge,* 2005	23
4.06	Residential monthly telephone subscription,* 2005	14
4.07	High-speed monthly broadband subscription*	n/a
4.08	Lowest cost of broadband,* 2006	73
4.09	Cost of mobile telephone call,* 2005	13

Business readiness — 78

5.01	Extent of staff training, 2007	68
5.02	Local availability of research and training, 2007	82
5.03	Quality of management schools, 2007	63
5.04	Company spending on R&D, 2007	105
5.05	University-industry research collaboration, 2007	112
5.06	Business telephone connection charge,* 2005	19
5.07	Business monthly telephone subscription,* 2005	27
5.08	Local supplier quality, 2007	74
5.09	Local supplier quantity, 2007	90
5.10	Computer, comm., and other services imports,* 2005	90

Government readiness — 56

6.01	Government prioritization of ICT, 2007	59
6.02	Gov't procurement of advanced tech products, 2007	89
6.03	Importance of ICT to gov't vision of the future, 2007	44
6.04	E-Government Readiness Index,* 2007	64

Usage component — 58

Individual usage — 77

7.01	Mobile telephone subscribers,* 2006	72
7.02	Personal computers,* 2005	76
7.03	Broadband Internet subscribers,* 2005	71
7.04	Internet users,* 2005	84
7.05	Internet bandwidth,* 2006	90

Business usage — 64

8.01	Prevalence of foreign technology licensing, 2007	75
8.02	Firm-level technology absorption, 2007	85
8.03	Capacity for innovation, 2007	86
8.04	Availability of new telephone lines, 2007	25
8.05	Extent of business Internet use, 2007	68

Government usage — 43

9.01	Government success in ICT promotion, 2007	64
9.02	Availability of government online services, 2007	43
9.03	ICT use and government efficiency, 2007	45
9.04	Presence of ICT in government offices, 2007	52
9.05	E-Participation Index,* 2007	30

* Hard data

Note: For further details and explanation, please refer to the section "How to Read the Country/Economy Profiles" at the beginning of this chapter.

Estonia

Key indicators

Population (millions), 2006..1.3
GDP (PPP) per capita (US$), 2006..................................19,692.2
Internet users per 100 inhabitants, 2006 ....57.4
Internet bandwidth (mB/s) per 10,000 inhabitants, 2006.....115.4

Networked Readiness Index

Year (number of economies)	Rank
2007–2008 (127)	**20**
2006–2007 (122)	20
2005–2006 (115)	23

Global Competitiveness Index 2007–2008 (131)   27

Environment component — 24

Market environment — 23

1.01 Venture capital availability, 2007..24
1.02 Financial market sophistication, 2007 29
1.03 Availability of latest technologies, 2007 25
1.04 State of cluster development, 2007.....................................71
1.05 Utility patents,* 2006 42
1.06 High-tech exports,* 2005 28
1.07 Burden of government regulation, 2007 10
1.08 Extent and effect of taxation, 2007......................................12
1.09 Total tax rate,* 2007..78
1.10 Time required to start a business,* 2007.............................9
1.11 No. of procedures required to start a business,* 2007 9
1.12 Intensity of local competition, 2007 24
1.13 Freedom of the press, 2007...17
1.14 Accessibility of digital content, 2007.....................................5

Political and regulatory environment — 24

2.01 Effectiveness of law-making bodies, 2007 30
2.02 Laws relating to ICT, 2007..2
2.03 Judicial independence, 2007 27
2.04 Intellectual property protection, 2007 34
2.05 Efficiency of legal framework, 2007.....................................29
2.06 Property rights, 2007..26
2.07 Quality of competition in the ISP sector, 2007 7
2.08 No. of procedures to enforce a contract,* 2007................53
2.09 Time to enforce a contract,* 2007 41

Infrastructure environment — 24

3.01 Telephone lines,* 2006...31
3.02 Secure Internet servers,* 2006..25
3.03 Electricity production,* 2004 22
3.04 Availability of scientists and engineers, 2007 67
3.05 Quality of scientific research institutions, 2007 26
3.06 Tertiary enrollment,* 2005...18
3.07 Education expenditure,* 2005..35

Readiness component — 23

Individual readiness — 26

4.01 Quality of math and science education, 2007....................21
4.02 Quality of the educational system, 2007............................34
4.03 Internet access in schools, 2007...6
4.04 Buyer sophistication, 2007 47
4.05 Residential telephone connection charge,* 2005 53
4.06 Residential monthly telephone subscription,* 2005 45
4.07 High-speed monthly broadband subscription,* 2006........32
4.08 Lowest cost of broadband,* 2006 41
4.09 Cost of mobile telephone call,* 2005....................................33

Business readiness — 31

5.01 Extent of staff training, 2007..30
5.02 Local availability of research and training, 2007...............27
5.03 Quality of management schools, 2007 31
5.04 Company spending on R&D, 2007.......................................37
5.05 University-industry research collaboration, 2007...............32
5.06 Business telephone connection charge,* 2005 43
5.07 Business monthly telephone subscription,* 2005 37
5.08 Local supplier quality, 2007..34
5.09 Local supplier quantity, 2007...53
5.10 Computer, comm., and other services imports,* 2005 44

Government readiness — 8

6.01 Government prioritization of ICT, 2007..................................4
6.02 Gov't procurement of advanced tech products, 2007 23
6.03 Importance of ICT to gov't vision of the future, 2007.........9
6.04 E-Government Readiness Index,* 2007.............................13

Usage component — 8

Individual usage — 11

7.01 Mobile telephone subscribers,* 2006...................................5
7.02 Personal computers,* 2005 23
7.03 Broadband Internet subscribers,* 2006 22
7.04 Internet users,* 2006...17
7.05 Internet bandwidth,* 2006..8

Business usage — 23

8.01 Prevalence of foreign technology licensing, 2007.............50
8.02 Firm-level technology absorption, 2007 26
8.03 Capacity for innovation, 2007..39
8.04 Availability of new telephone lines, 2007............................24
8.05 Extent of business Internet use, 2007..................................2

Government usage — 2

9.01 Government success in ICT promotion, 2007.....................4
9.02 Availability of government online services, 2007 1
9.03 ICT use and government efficiency, 2007...........................2
9.04 Presence of ICT in government offices, 2007 2
9.05 E-Participation Index,* 2007...8

* Hard data

Note: For further details and explanation, please refer to the section "How to Read the Country/Economy Profiles" at the beginning of this chapter.

Ethiopia

Key indicators

Population (millions), 2006	79.3
GDP (PPP) per capita (US$), 2006	1,122.9
Internet users per 100 inhabitants, 2005	0.2
Internet bandwidth (mB/s) per 10,000 inhabitants, 2005	0.0

Networked Readiness Index

Year (number of economies)	Rank
2007–2008 (127)	**123**
2006–2007 (122)	119
2005–2006 (115)	115
Global Competitiveness Index 2007–2008 (131)	123

Environment component — 118

Market environment — 105

1.01	Venture capital availability, 2007	117
1.02	Financial market sophistication, 2007	120
1.03	Availability of latest technologies, 2007	123
1.04	State of cluster development, 2007	99
1.05	Utility patents,* 2006	86
1.06	High-tech exports,* 2005	109
1.07	Burden of government regulation, 2007	36
1.08	Extent and effect of taxation, 2007	48
1.09	Total tax rate,* 2007	19
1.10	Time required to start a business,* 2007	33
1.11	No. of procedures required to start a business,* 2007	34
1.12	Intensity of local competition, 2007	115
1.13	Freedom of the press, 2007	126
1.14	Accessibility of digital content, 2007	125

Political and regulatory environment — 113

2.01	Effectiveness of law-making bodies, 2007	99
2.02	Laws relating to ICT, 2007	110
2.03	Judicial independence, 2007	103
2.04	Intellectual property protection, 2007	96
2.05	Efficiency of legal framework, 2007	89
2.06	Property rights, 2007	82
2.07	Quality of competition in the ISP sector, 2007	126
2.08	No. of procedures to enforce a contract,* 2007	75
2.09	Time to enforce a contract,* 2007	90

Infrastructure environment — 124

3.01	Telephone lines,* 2006	113
3.02	Secure Internet servers,* 2006	101
3.03	Electricity production,* 2004	112
3.04	Availability of scientists and engineers, 2007	118
3.05	Quality of scientific research institutions, 2007	78
3.06	Tertiary enrollment,* 2005	115
3.07	Education expenditure,* 2005	89

Readiness component — 123

Individual readiness — 124

4.01	Quality of math and science education, 2007	96
4.02	Quality of the educational system, 2007	94
4.03	Internet access in schools, 2007	112
4.04	Buyer sophistication, 2007	120
4.05	Residential telephone connection charge,* 2006	121
4.06	Residential monthly telephone subscription,* 2006	99
4.07	High-speed monthly broadband subscription,* 2006	109
4.08	Lowest cost of broadband,* 2006	115
4.09	Cost of mobile telephone call,* 2005	116

Business readiness — 123

5.01	Extent of staff training, 2007	119
5.02	Local availability of research and training, 2007	109
5.03	Quality of management schools, 2007	104
5.04	Company spending on R&D, 2007	123
5.05	University-industry research collaboration, 2007	107
5.06	Business telephone connection charge,* 2006	114
5.07	Business monthly telephone subscription,* 2006	110
5.08	Local supplier quality, 2007	119
5.09	Local supplier quantity, 2007	114
5.10	Computer, comm., and other services imports,* 2005	67

Government readiness — 109

6.01	Government prioritization of ICT, 2007	87
6.02	Gov't procurement of advanced tech products, 2007	96
6.03	Importance of ICT to gov't vision of the future, 2007	66
6.04	E-Government Readiness Index,* 2007	120

Usage component — 117

Individual usage — 127

7.01	Mobile telephone subscribers,* 2006	127
7.02	Personal computers,* 2005	122
7.03	Broadband Internet subscribers,* 2005	117
7.04	Internet users,* 2005	127
7.05	Internet bandwidth,* 2005	127

Business usage — 110

8.01	Prevalence of foreign technology licensing, 2007	110
8.02	Firm-level technology absorption, 2007	119
8.03	Capacity for innovation, 2007	103
8.04	Availability of new telephone lines, 2007	103
8.05	Extent of business Internet use, 2007	106

Government usage — 104

9.01	Government success in ICT promotion, 2007	85
9.02	Availability of government online services, 2007	99
9.03	ICT use and government efficiency, 2007	89
9.04	Presence of ICT in government offices, 2007	99
9.05	E-Participation Index,* 2007	117

* Hard data

Note: For further details and explanation, please refer to the section "How to Read the Country/Economy Profiles" at the beginning of this chapter.

Finland

Key indicators

Population (millions), 2006..5.3
GDP (PPP) per capita (US$), 2006..................................35,558.9
Internet users per 100 inhabitants, 2005 ....53.3
Internet bandwidth (mB/s) per 10,000 inhabitants, 2005.......43.5

Networked Readiness Index

Year (number of economies)	Rank
2007–2008 (127)	**6**
2006–2007 (122)	4
2005–2006 (115)	5

Global Competitiveness Index 2007–2008 (131)   6

Environment component   3
Market environment   5
1.01 Venture capital availability, 2007..2
1.02 Financial market sophistication, 2007 14
1.03 Availability of latest technologies, 2007 2
1.04 State of cluster development, 2007.....................................11
1.05 Utility patents,* 2006 4
1.06 High-tech exports,* 2005 17
1.07 Burden of government regulation, 2007 4
1.08 Extent and effect of taxation, 2007..................................112
1.09 Total tax rate,* 2007..............................72
1.10 Time required to start a business,* 2007..........................27
1.11 No. of procedures required to start a business,* 2007 4
1.12 Intensity of local competition, 2007 16
1.13 Freedom of the press, 2007..............................6
1.14 Accessibility of digital content, 2007.....................................9

Political and regulatory environment   4
2.01 Effectiveness of law-making bodies, 2007 6
2.02 Laws relating to ICT, 2007..............................9
2.03 Judicial independence, 2007 4
2.04 Intellectual property protection, 2007 2
2.05 Efficiency of legal framework, 2007.....................................4
2.06 Property rights, 2007..............................7
2.07 Quality of competition in the ISP sector, 2007 14
2.08 No. of procedures to enforce a contract,* 2007 35
2.09 Time to enforce a contract,* 2007 8

Infrastructure environment   7
3.01 Telephone lines,* 2006.....................................34
3.02 Secure Internet servers,* 2006..............................15
3.03 Electricity production,* 2004..............................6
3.04 Availability of scientists and engineers, 2007 1
3.05 Quality of scientific research institutions, 2007 6
3.06 Tertiary enrollment,* 2005..............................1
3.07 Education expenditure,* 2005..............................15

Readiness component   5
Individual readiness   1
4.01 Quality of math and science education, 2007 3
4.02 Quality of the educational system, 2007.............................2
4.03 Internet access in schools, 2007..............................2
4.04 Buyer sophistication, 2007 8
4.05 Residential telephone connection charge,* 2006 28
4.06 Residential monthly telephone subscription,* 2006 15
4.07 High-speed monthly broadband subscription,* 2006........26
4.08 Lowest cost of broadband,* 2006 3
4.09 Cost of mobile telephone call,* 2005................................10

Business readiness   3
5.01 Extent of staff training, 2007..............................13
5.02 Local availability of research and training, 2007 9
5.03 Quality of management schools, 2007 12
5.04 Company spending on R&D, 2007..............................9
5.05 University-industry research collaboration, 2007................4
5.06 Business telephone connection charge,* 2006 23
5.07 Business monthly telephone subscription,* 2006 11
5.08 Local supplier quality, 2007..............................9
5.09 Local supplier quantity, 2007..............................25
5.10 Computer, comm., and other services imports,* 2005 11

Government readiness   9
6.01 Government prioritization of ICT, 2007..............................12
6.02 Gov't procurement of advanced tech products, 2007 11
6.03 Importance of ICT to gov't vision of the future, 2007.......13
6.04 E-Government Readiness Index,* 2007............................15

Usage component   16
Individual usage   14
7.01 Mobile telephone subscribers,* 2006..............................19
7.02 Personal computers,* 2005 22
7.03 Broadband Internet subscribers,* 2006 7
7.04 Internet users,* 2005..............................19
7.05 Internet bandwidth,* 2005 17

Business usage   6
8.01 Prevalence of foreign technology licensing, 2007.............28
8.02 Firm-level technology absorption, 2007..............................7
8.03 Capacity for innovation, 2007..............................5
8.04 Availability of new telephone lines, 2007 2
8.05 Extent of business Internet use, 2007..............................13

Government usage   20
9.01 Government success in ICT promotion, 2007....................15
9.02 Availability of government online services, 2007 17
9.03 ICT use and government efficiency, 2007.........................16
9.04 Presence of ICT in government offices, 2007 9
9.05 E-Participation Index,* 2007..............................43

* Hard data

Note: For further details and explanation, please refer to the section "How to Read the Country/Economy Profiles" at the beginning of this chapter.

France

Key indicators

Population (millions), 2006...60.7
GDP (PPP) per capita (US$), 2006..................................31,825.5
Internet users per 100 inhabitants, 2006 ....49.6
Internet bandwidth (mB/s) per 10,000 inhabitants, 2005.......33.1

Networked Readiness Index

Year (number of economies)	Rank
2007–2008 (127)	**21**
2006–2007 (122)	23
2005–2006 (115)	22

Global Competitiveness Index 2007–2008 (131)   18

Environment component   22

Market environment   25

1.01 Venture capital availability, 2007..30
1.02 Financial market sophistication, 2007 16
1.03 Availability of latest technologies, 2007 15
1.04 State of cluster development, 2007..................................27
1.05 Utility patents,* 2006 20
1.06 High-tech exports,* 2005 22
1.07 Burden of government regulation, 2007 111
1.08 Extent and effect of taxation, 2007..................................92
1.09 Total tax rate,* 2007..108
1.10 Time required to start a business,* 2007...........................9
1.11 No. of procedures required to start a business,* 2007 9
1.12 Intensity of local competition, 2007 12
1.13 Freedom of the press, 2007...15
1.14 Accessibility of digital content, 2007.................................19

Political and regulatory environment   16

2.01 Effectiveness of law-making bodies, 2007 28
2.02 Laws relating to ICT, 2007..20
2.03 Judicial independence, 2007 28
2.04 Intellectual property protection, 2007 9
2.05 Efficiency of legal framework, 2007..................................20
2.06 Property rights, 2007..17
2.07 Quality of competition in the ISP sector, 2007 20
2.08 No. of procedures to enforce a contract,* 2007 15
2.09 Time to enforce a contract,* 2007 23

Infrastructure environment   18

3.01 Telephone lines,* 2006...11
3.02 Secure Internet servers,* 2006..28
3.03 Electricity production,* 2004 13
3.04 Availability of scientists and engineers, 2007 7
3.05 Quality of scientific research institutions, 2007 19
3.06 Tertiary enrollment,* 2005..30
3.07 Education expenditure,* 2005...34

Readiness component   16

Individual readiness   15

4.01 Quality of math and science education, 2007.....................6
4.02 Quality of the educational system, 2007..........................27
4.03 Internet access in schools, 2007......................................28
4.04 Buyer sophistication, 2007 21
4.05 Residential telephone connection charge,* 2005 15
4.06 Residential monthly telephone subscription,* 2005 26
4.07 High-speed monthly broadband subscription,* 2006.........9
4.08 Lowest cost of broadband,* 2006 3
4.09 Cost of mobile telephone call,* 2005...............................42

Business readiness   15

5.01 Extent of staff training, 2007..24
5.02 Local availability of research and training, 2007..............12
5.03 Quality of management schools, 2007 1
5.04 Company spending on R&D, 2007...................................17
5.05 University-industry research collaboration, 2007.............30
5.06 Business telephone connection charge,* 2005 13
5.07 Business monthly telephone subscription,* 2005 13
5.08 Local supplier quality, 2007..10
5.09 Local supplier quantity, 2007..5
5.10 Computer, comm., and other services imports,* 2005 30

Government readiness   18

6.01 Government prioritization of ICT, 2007............................43
6.02 Gov't procurement of advanced tech products, 2007 14
6.03 Importance of ICT to gov't vision of the future, 2007.......31
6.04 E-Government Readiness Index,* 2007.............................9

Usage component   19

Individual usage   23

7.01 Mobile telephone subscribers,* 2006...............................43
7.02 Personal computers,* 2005 17
7.03 Broadband Internet subscribers,* 2006 12
7.04 Internet users,* 2006...23
7.05 Internet bandwidth,* 2005..20

Business usage   18

8.01 Prevalence of foreign technology licensing, 2007............44
8.02 Firm-level technology absorption, 2007 28
8.03 Capacity for innovation, 2007...8
8.04 Availability of new telephone lines, 2007.........................10
8.05 Extent of business Internet use, 2007..............................23

Government usage   10

9.01 Government success in ICT promotion, 2007...................27
9.02 Availability of government online services, 2007 20
9.03 ICT use and government efficiency, 2007........................23
9.04 Presence of ICT in government offices, 2007 39
9.05 E-Participation Index,* 2007...3

* Hard data

Note: For further details and explanation, please refer to the section "How to Read the Country/Economy Profiles" at the beginning of this chapter.

Gambia, The

Key indicators

Population (millions), 2006...1.6
GDP (PPP) per capita (US$), 2006.....................................2,244.6
Internet users per 100 inhabitants, 2005 ....3.8
Internet bandwidth (mB/s) per 10,000 inhabitants, 2005.........0.1

Networked Readiness Index

Year (number of economies)	Rank
2007–2008 (127)	**101**
2006–2007 (122)	n/a
2005–2006 (115)	n/a

Global Competitiveness Index 2007–2008 (131)   102

Environment component — 94
Market environment — 103
1.01 Venture capital availability, 2007..92
1.02 Financial market sophistication, 2007 90
1.03 Availability of latest technologies, 2007 80
1.04 State of cluster development, 2007......................................76
1.05 Utility patents,* 2006 86
1.06 High-tech exports,* 2005 109
1.07 Burden of government regulation, 2007 13
1.08 Extent and effect of taxation, 2007......................................38
1.09 Total tax rate,* 2007 121
1.10 Time required to start a business,* 2007............................73
1.11 No. of procedures required to start a business,* 2007 58
1.12 Intensity of local competition, 2007 87
1.13 Freedom of the press, 2007...121
1.14 Accessibility of digital content, 2007...................................93

Political and regulatory environment — 56
2.01 Effectiveness of law-making bodies, 2007 52
2.02 Laws relating to ICT, 2007...81
2.03 Judicial independence, 2007 55
2.04 Intellectual property protection, 2007 81
2.05 Efficiency of legal framework, 2007....................................53
2.06 Property rights, 2007...72
2.07 Quality of competition in the ISP sector, 2007 63
2.08 No. of procedures to enforce a contract,* 2007................29
2.09 Time to enforce a contract,* 2007 42

Infrastructure environment — 122
3.01 Telephone lines,* 2006..105
3.02 Secure Internet servers,* 2006...90
3.03 Electricity production* ....n/a
3.04 Availability of scientists and engineers, 2007 120
3.05 Quality of scientific research institutions, 2007 88
3.06 Tertiary enrollment,* 2004...124
3.07 Education expenditure,* 2005...109

Readiness component — 117
Individual readiness — 115
4.01 Quality of math and science education, 2007....................94
4.02 Quality of the educational system, 2007............................49
4.03 Internet access in schools, 2007...95
4.04 Buyer sophistication, 2007 97
4.05 Residential telephone connection charge*......................n/a
4.06 Residential monthly telephone subscription*..................n/a
4.07 High-speed monthly broadband subscription,* 2006........96
4.08 Lowest cost of broadband,* 2006 103
4.09 Cost of mobile telephone call* ....n/a

Business readiness — 124
5.01 Extent of staff training, 2007...77
5.02 Local availability of research and training, 2007..............106
5.03 Quality of management schools, 2007 79
5.04 Company spending on R&D, 2007....................................111
5.05 University-industry research collaboration, 2007.............106
5.06 Business telephone connection charge*.........................n/a
5.07 Business monthly telephone subscription*.....................n/a
5.08 Local supplier quality, 2007...91
5.09 Local supplier quantity, 2007...97
5.10 Computer, comm., and other services imports,* 2005 ..114

Government readiness — 76
6.01 Government prioritization of ICT, 2007...............................25
6.02 Gov't procurement of advanced tech products, 2007 58
6.03 Importance of ICT to gov't vision of the future, 2007.......32
6.04 E-Government Readiness Index,* 2007..........................117

Usage component — 85
Individual usage — 103
7.01 Mobile telephone subscribers,* 2006.................................96
7.02 Personal computers,* 2005 103
7.03 Broadband Internet subscribers,* 2005 110
7.04 Internet users,* 2005 107
7.05 Internet bandwidth,* 2005 108

Business usage — 85
8.01 Prevalence of foreign technology licensing, 2007.............72
8.02 Firm-level technology absorption, 2007 76
8.03 Capacity for innovation, 2007..91
8.04 Availability of new telephone lines, 2007 87
8.05 Extent of business Internet use, 2007 86

Government usage — 65
9.01 Government success in ICT promotion, 2007....................19
9.02 Availability of government online services, 2007 82
9.03 ICT use and government efficiency, 2007..........................56
9.04 Presence of ICT in government offices, 2007 46
9.05 E-Participation Index,* 2007...110

* Hard data

Note: For further details and explanation, please refer to the section "How to Read the Country/Economy Profiles" at the beginning of this chapter.

Georgia

Key indicators

Population (millions), 2006	4.4
GDP (PPP) per capita (US$), 2006	3,642.1
Internet users per 100 inhabitants, 2006	7.5
Internet bandwidth (mB/s) per 10,000 inhabitants, 2005	0.1

Networked Readiness Index

Year (number of economies)	Rank
2007–2008 (127)	**91**
2006–2007 (122)	93
2005–2006 (115)	96

Global Competitiveness Index 2007–2008 (131)	90

Environment component — 79

Market environment — 68

1.01	Venture capital availability, 2007	88
1.02	Financial market sophistication, 2007	92
1.03	Availability of latest technologies, 2007	97
1.04	State of cluster development, 2007	116
1.05	Utility patents,* 2006	51
1.06	High-tech exports,* 2005	42
1.07	Burden of government regulation, 2007	14
1.08	Extent and effect of taxation, 2007	31
1.09	Total tax rate,* 2007	46
1.10	Time required to start a business,* 2007	19
1.11	No. of procedures required to start a business,* 2007	9
1.12	Intensity of local competition, 2007	113
1.13	Freedom of the press, 2007	86
1.14	Accessibility of digital content, 2007	76

Political and regulatory environment — 91

2.01	Effectiveness of law-making bodies, 2007	73
2.02	Laws relating to ICT, 2007	104
2.03	Judicial independence, 2007	108
2.04	Intellectual property protection, 2007	104
2.05	Efficiency of legal framework, 2007	113
2.06	Property rights, 2007	114
2.07	Quality of competition in the ISP sector, 2007	56
2.08	No. of procedures to enforce a contract,* 2007	53
2.09	Time to enforce a contract,* 2007	14

Infrastructure environment — 85

3.01	Telephone lines,* 2006	78
3.02	Secure Internet servers,* 2006	69
3.03	Electricity production,* 2004	79
3.04	Availability of scientists and engineers, 2007	90
3.05	Quality of scientific research institutions, 2007	105
3.06	Tertiary enrollment,* 2005	40
3.07	Education expenditure,* 2005	92

Readiness component — 92

Individual readiness — 76

4.01	Quality of math and science education, 2007	74
4.02	Quality of the educational system, 2007	90
4.03	Internet access in schools, 2007	72
4.04	Buyer sophistication, 2007	87
4.05	Residential telephone connection charge,* 2005	99
4.06	Residential monthly telephone subscription,* 2005	67
4.07	High-speed monthly broadband subscription,* 2006	61
4.08	Lowest cost of broadband,* 2006	70
4.09	Cost of mobile telephone call,* 2005	86

Business readiness — 109

5.01	Extent of staff training, 2007	87
5.02	Local availability of research and training, 2007	113
5.03	Quality of management schools, 2007	111
5.04	Company spending on R&D, 2007	110
5.05	University-industry research collaboration, 2007	115
5.06	Business telephone connection charge,* 2005	86
5.07	Business monthly telephone subscription,* 2005	76
5.08	Local supplier quality, 2007	126
5.09	Local supplier quantity, 2007	126
5.10	Computer, comm., and other services imports,* 2005	105

Government readiness — 104

6.01	Government prioritization of ICT, 2007	105
6.02	Gov't procurement of advanced tech products, 2007	106
6.03	Importance of ICT to gov't vision of the future, 2007	109
6.04	E-Government Readiness Index,* 2007	80

Usage component — 100

Individual usage — 89

7.01	Mobile telephone subscribers,* 2006	85
7.02	Personal computers,* 2005	79
7.03	Broadband Internet subscribers,* 2006	72
7.04	Internet users,* 2006	91
7.05	Internet bandwidth,* 2005	105

Business usage — 99

8.01	Prevalence of foreign technology licensing, 2007	102
8.02	Firm-level technology absorption, 2007	107
8.03	Capacity for innovation, 2007	98
8.04	Availability of new telephone lines, 2007	85
8.05	Extent of business Internet use, 2007	95

Government usage — 105

9.01	Government success in ICT promotion, 2007	102
9.02	Availability of government online services, 2007	112
9.03	ICT use and government efficiency, 2007	96
9.04	Presence of ICT in government offices, 2007	86
9.05	E-Participation Index,* 2007	100

* Hard data

Note: For further details and explanation, please refer to the section "How to Read the Country/Economy Profiles" at the beginning of this chapter.

Germany

Key indicators

Population (millions), 2006	82.7
GDP (PPP) per capita (US$), 2006	31,389.7
Internet users per 100 inhabitants, 2006	46.7
Internet bandwidth (mB/s) per 10,000 inhabitants, 2005	68.4

Networked Readiness Index

Year (number of economies)	Rank
2007–2008 (127)	**16**
2006–2007 (122)	16
2005–2006 (115)	17

Global Competitiveness Index 2007–2008 (131)	5

Environment component — 11
Market environment — 17
1.01	Venture capital availability, 2007	19
1.02	Financial market sophistication, 2007	11
1.03	Availability of latest technologies, 2007	8
1.04	State of cluster development, 2007	10
1.05	Utility patents,* 2006	9
1.06	High-tech exports,* 2005	23
1.07	Burden of government regulation, 2007	66
1.08	Extent and effect of taxation, 2007	82
1.09	Total tax rate,* 2007	82
1.10	Time required to start a business,* 2007	38
1.11	No. of procedures required to start a business,* 2007	58
1.12	Intensity of local competition, 2007	1
1.13	Freedom of the press, 2007	1
1.14	Accessibility of digital content, 2007	13

Political and regulatory environment — 3
2.01	Effectiveness of law-making bodies, 2007	14
2.02	Laws relating to ICT, 2007	4
2.03	Judicial independence, 2007	1
2.04	Intellectual property protection, 2007	1
2.05	Efficiency of legal framework, 2007	2
2.06	Property rights, 2007	1
2.07	Quality of competition in the ISP sector, 2007	2
2.08	No. of procedures to enforce a contract,* 2007	35
2.09	Time to enforce a contract,* 2007	31

Infrastructure environment — 14
3.01	Telephone lines,* 2006	2
3.02	Secure Internet servers,* 2006	16
3.03	Electricity production,* 2004	26
3.04	Availability of scientists and engineers, 2007	16
3.05	Quality of scientific research institutions, 2007	5
3.06	Tertiary enrollment,* 2003	34
3.07	Education expenditure,* 2005	56

Readiness component — 13
Individual readiness — 21
4.01	Quality of math and science education, 2007	35
4.02	Quality of the educational system, 2007	22
4.03	Internet access in schools, 2007	24
4.04	Buyer sophistication, 2007	15
4.05	Residential telephone connection charge,* 2005	17
4.06	Residential monthly telephone subscription,* 2005	33
4.07	High-speed monthly broadband subscription,* 2006	6
4.08	Lowest cost of broadband,* 2006	10
4.09	Cost of mobile telephone call,* 2005	40

Business readiness — 2
5.01	Extent of staff training, 2007	9
5.02	Local availability of research and training, 2007	3
5.03	Quality of management schools, 2007	25
5.04	Company spending on R&D, 2007	4
5.05	University-industry research collaboration, 2007	6
5.06	Business telephone connection charge,* 2005	15
5.07	Business monthly telephone subscription,* 2005	19
5.08	Local supplier quality, 2007	1
5.09	Local supplier quantity, 2007	1
5.10	Computer, comm., and other services imports,* 2005	33

Government readiness — 27
6.01	Government prioritization of ICT, 2007	31
6.02	Gov't procurement of advanced tech products, 2007	10
6.03	Importance of ICT to gov't vision of the future, 2007	63
6.04	E-Government Readiness Index,* 2007	22

Usage component — 22
Individual usage — 21
7.01	Mobile telephone subscribers,* 2006	28
7.02	Personal computers,* 2005	14
7.03	Broadband Internet subscribers,* 2006	23
7.04	Internet users,* 2006	24
7.05	Internet bandwidth,* 2005	13

Business usage — 2
8.01	Prevalence of foreign technology licensing, 2007	20
8.02	Firm-level technology absorption, 2007	14
8.03	Capacity for innovation, 2007	1
8.04	Availability of new telephone lines, 2007	3
8.05	Extent of business Internet use, 2007	5

Government usage — 38
9.01	Government success in ICT promotion, 2007	39
9.02	Availability of government online services, 2007	31
9.03	ICT use and government efficiency, 2007	35
9.04	Presence of ICT in government offices, 2007	20
9.05	E-Participation Index,* 2007	67

* Hard data

Note: For further details and explanation, please refer to the section "How to Read the Country/Economy Profiles" at the beginning of this chapter.

Greece

Key indicators

Population (millions), 2006	11.1
GDP (PPP) per capita (US$), 2006	33,004.0
Internet users per 100 inhabitants, 2005	18.0
Internet bandwidth (mB/s) per 10,000 inhabitants, 2005	5.9

Networked Readiness Index

Year (number of economies)	Rank
2007–2008 (127)	**56**
2006–2007 (122)	48
2005–2006 (115)	43
Global Competitiveness Index 2007–2008 (131)	65

Environment component — 46

Market environment — 77

1.01	Venture capital availability, 2007	61
1.02	Financial market sophistication, 2007	43
1.03	Availability of latest technologies, 2007	66
1.04	State of cluster development, 2007	88
1.05	Utility patents,* 2006	40
1.06	High-tech exports,* 2005	59
1.07	Burden of government regulation, 2007	106
1.08	Extent and effect of taxation, 2007	72
1.09	Total tax rate,* 2007	75
1.10	Time required to start a business,* 2007	86
1.11	No. of procedures required to start a business,* 2007	115
1.12	Intensity of local competition, 2007	65
1.13	Freedom of the press, 2007	22
1.14	Accessibility of digital content, 2007	91

Political and regulatory environment — 55

2.01	Effectiveness of law-making bodies, 2007	45
2.02	Laws relating to ICT, 2007	68
2.03	Judicial independence, 2007	48
2.04	Intellectual property protection, 2007	45
2.05	Efficiency of legal framework, 2007	50
2.06	Property rights, 2007	46
2.07	Quality of competition in the ISP sector, 2007	62
2.08	No. of procedures to enforce a contract,* 2007	75
2.09	Time to enforce a contract,* 2007	100

Infrastructure environment — 25

3.01	Telephone lines,* 2006	12
3.02	Secure Internet servers,* 2006	39
3.03	Electricity production,* 2004	41
3.04	Availability of scientists and engineers, 2007	17
3.05	Quality of scientific research institutions, 2007	74
3.06	Tertiary enrollment,* 2005	3
3.07	Education expenditure,* 2005	86

Readiness component — 57

Individual readiness — 50

4.01	Quality of math and science education, 2007	50
4.02	Quality of the educational system, 2007	80
4.03	Internet access in schools, 2007	61
4.04	Buyer sophistication, 2007	51
4.05	Residential telephone connection charge,* 2005	13
4.06	Residential monthly telephone subscription,* 2005	30
4.07	High-speed monthly broadband subscription,* 2006	34
4.08	Lowest cost of broadband,* 2006	43
4.09	Cost of mobile telephone call,* 2005	44

Business readiness — 63

5.01	Extent of staff training, 2007	55
5.02	Local availability of research and training, 2007	73
5.03	Quality of management schools, 2007	75
5.04	Company spending on R&D, 2007	83
5.05	University-industry research collaboration, 2007	80
5.06	Business telephone connection charge,* 2005	9
5.07	Business monthly telephone subscription,* 2005	16
5.08	Local supplier quality, 2007	54
5.09	Local supplier quantity, 2007	71
5.10	Computer, comm., and other services imports,* 2005	85

Government readiness — 70

6.01	Government prioritization of ICT, 2007	94
6.02	Gov't procurement of advanced tech products, 2007	97
6.03	Importance of ICT to gov't vision of the future, 2007	86
6.04	E-Government Readiness Index,* 2007	44

Usage component — 62

Individual usage — 50

7.01	Mobile telephone subscribers,* 2006	29
7.02	Personal computers,* 2005	61
7.03	Broadband Internet subscribers,* 2006	46
7.04	Internet users,* 2005	60
7.05	Internet bandwidth,* 2005	46

Business usage — 69

8.01	Prevalence of foreign technology licensing, 2007	43
8.02	Firm-level technology absorption, 2007	89
8.03	Capacity for innovation, 2007	73
8.04	Availability of new telephone lines, 2007	56
8.05	Extent of business Internet use, 2007	97

Government usage — 91

9.01	Government success in ICT promotion, 2007	99
9.02	Availability of government online services, 2007	68
9.03	ICT use and government efficiency, 2007	69
9.04	Presence of ICT in government offices, 2007	85
9.05	E-Participation Index,* 2007	82

* Hard data

Note: For further details and explanation, please refer to the section "How to Read the Country/Economy Profiles" at the beginning of this chapter.

Guatemala

Key indicators

Population (millions), 2006..12.9
GDP (PPP) per capita (US$), 2006.....................................4,335.0
Internet users per 100 inhabitants, 2006 ....10.2
Internet bandwidth (mB/s) per 10,000 inhabitants, 2005.........0.6

Networked Readiness Index

Year (number of economies)	Rank
2007–2008 (127)	**80**
2006–2007 (122)	79
2005–2006 (115)	98

Global Competitiveness Index 2007–2008 (131) 87

Environment component	90
Market environment	**55**

1.01 Venture capital availability, 2007...74
1.02 Financial market sophistication, 2007 73
1.03 Availability of latest technologies, 2007 61
1.04 State of cluster development, 2007.......................................70
1.05 Utility patents,* 2006 79
1.06 High-tech exports,* 2005 57
1.07 Burden of government regulation, 2007 41
1.08 Extent and effect of taxation, 2007..42
1.09 Total tax rate,* 2007...42
1.10 Time required to start a business,* 2007..............................54
1.11 No. of procedures required to start a business,* 2007 88
1.12 Intensity of local competition, 2007 58
1.13 Freedom of the press, 2007..31
1.14 Accessibility of digital content, 2007.....................................33

Political and regulatory environment	**95**

2.01 Effectiveness of law-making bodies, 2007 120
2.02 Laws relating to ICT, 2007..88
2.03 Judicial independence, 2007 86
2.04 Intellectual property protection, 2007 90
2.05 Efficiency of legal framework, 2007......................................96
2.06 Property rights, 2007...84
2.07 Quality of competition in the ISP sector, 2007 21
2.08 No. of procedures to enforce a contract,* 2007 11
2.09 Time to enforce a contract,* 2007 120

Infrastructure environment	**115**

3.01 Telephone lines,* 2006..85
3.02 Secure Internet servers,* 2006..63
3.03 Electricity production,* 2004..97
3.04 Availability of scientists and engineers, 2007 96
3.05 Quality of scientific research institutions, 2007 100
3.06 Tertiary enrollment,* 2003..100
3.07 Education expenditure,* 2005..115

Readiness component	81
Individual readiness	**84**

4.01 Quality of math and science education, 2007..................118
4.02 Quality of the educational system, 2007...........................111
4.03 Internet access in schools, 2007...92
4.04 Buyer sophistication, 2007 73
4.05 Residential telephone connection charge,* 2006 90
4.06 Residential monthly telephone subscription,* 2006 85
4.07 High-speed monthly broadband subscription,* 2006........81
4.08 Lowest cost of broadband,* 2006 87
4.09 Cost of mobile telephone call,* 2006...................................71

Business readiness	**70**

5.01 Extent of staff training, 2007..62
5.02 Local availability of research and training, 2007................53
5.03 Quality of management schools, 2007 60
5.04 Company spending on R&D, 2007...63
5.05 University-industry research collaboration, 2007................55
5.06 Business telephone connection charge,* 2005 84
5.07 Business monthly telephone subscription,* 2006 65
5.08 Local supplier quality, 2007..51
5.09 Local supplier quantity, 2007...56
5.10 Computer, comm., and other services imports,* 2005 ..112

Government readiness	**83**

6.01 Government prioritization of ICT, 2007.................................90
6.02 Gov't procurement of advanced tech products, 2007 84
6.03 Importance of ICT to gov't vision of the future, 2007.......70
6.04 E-Government Readiness Index,* 2007...............................85

Usage component	65
Individual usage	**81**

7.01 Mobile telephone subscribers,* 2006...................................71
7.02 Personal computers,* 2005 98
7.03 Broadband Internet subscribers,* 2005 86
7.04 Internet users,* 2006 80
7.05 Internet bandwidth,* 2005 77

Business usage	**47**

8.01 Prevalence of foreign technology licensing, 2007.............77
8.02 Firm-level technology absorption, 2007 59
8.03 Capacity for innovation, 2007...58
8.04 Availability of new telephone lines, 2007............................28
8.05 Extent of business Internet use, 2007..................................37

Government usage	**69**

9.01 Government success in ICT promotion, 2007.....................90
9.02 Availability of government online services, 2007 41
9.03 ICT use and government efficiency, 2007...........................39
9.04 Presence of ICT in government offices, 2007 79
9.05 E-Participation Index,* 2007...100

* Hard data

Note: For further details and explanation, please refer to the section "How to Read the Country/Economy Profiles" at the beginning of this chapter.

Guyana

Key indicators

Population (millions), 2006	0.7
GDP (PPP) per capita (US$), 2006	5,004.4
Internet users per 100 inhabitants, 2005	21.3
Internet bandwidth (mB/s) per 10,000 inhabitants, 2005	0.5

Networked Readiness Index

Year (number of economies)	Rank
2007–2008 (127)	**102**
2006–2007 (122)	98
2005–2006 (115)	111

Global Competitiveness Index 2007–2008 (131)	126

Environment component — 107

Market environment — 112

1.01	Venture capital availability, 2007	115
1.02	Financial market sophistication, 2007	118
1.03	Availability of latest technologies, 2007	116
1.04	State of cluster development, 2007	105
1.05	Utility patents,* 2006	86
1.06	High-tech exports,* 2004	102
1.07	Burden of government regulation, 2007	83
1.08	Extent and effect of taxation, 2007	118
1.09	Total tax rate,* 2007	47
1.10	Time required to start a business,* 2007	94
1.11	No. of procedures required to start a business,* 2007	44
1.12	Intensity of local competition, 2007	102
1.13	Freedom of the press, 2007	94
1.14	Accessibility of digital content, 2007	99

Political and regulatory environment — 112

2.01	Effectiveness of law-making bodies, 2007	91
2.02	Laws relating to ICT, 2007	118
2.03	Judicial independence, 2007	99
2.04	Intellectual property protection, 2007	125
2.05	Efficiency of legal framework, 2007	117
2.06	Property rights, 2007	111
2.07	Quality of competition in the ISP sector, 2007	89
2.08	No. of procedures to enforce a contract,* 2007	53
2.09	Time to enforce a contract,* 2007	74

Infrastructure environment — 89

3.01	Telephone lines,* 2006	73
3.02	Secure Internet servers,* 2006	78
3.03	Electricity production*	n/a
3.04	Availability of scientists and engineers, 2007	124
3.05	Quality of scientific research institutions, 2007	107
3.06	Tertiary enrollment,* 2005	99
3.07	Education expenditure,* 2005	41

Readiness component — 93

Individual readiness — 91

4.01	Quality of math and science education, 2007	90
4.02	Quality of the educational system, 2007	79
4.03	Internet access in schools, 2007	107
4.04	Buyer sophistication, 2007	105
4.05	Residential telephone connection charge,* 2005	21
4.06	Residential monthly telephone subscription,* 2005	82
4.07	High-speed monthly broadband subscription*	n/a
4.08	Lowest cost of broadband,* 2006	86
4.09	Cost of mobile telephone call,* 2005	95

Business readiness — 95

5.01	Extent of staff training, 2007	94
5.02	Local availability of research and training, 2007	121
5.03	Quality of management schools, 2007	105
5.04	Company spending on R&D, 2007	93
5.05	University-industry research collaboration, 2007	114
5.06	Business telephone connection charge,* 2005	66
5.07	Business monthly telephone subscription,* 2005	99
5.08	Local supplier quality, 2007	99
5.09	Local supplier quantity, 2007	99
5.10	Computer, comm., and other services imports,* 2005	50

Government readiness — 105

6.01	Government prioritization of ICT, 2007	83
6.02	Gov't procurement of advanced tech products, 2007	108
6.03	Importance of ICT to gov't vision of the future, 2007	115
6.04	E-Government Readiness Index,* 2007	84

Usage component — 114

Individual usage — 78

7.01	Mobile telephone subscribers,* 2005	86
7.02	Personal computers,* 2005	87
7.03	Broadband Internet subscribers,* 2005	83
7.04	Internet users,* 2005	54
7.05	Internet bandwidth,* 2005	80

Business usage — 119

8.01	Prevalence of foreign technology licensing, 2007	121
8.02	Firm-level technology absorption, 2007	114
8.03	Capacity for innovation, 2007	101
8.04	Availability of new telephone lines, 2007	123
8.05	Extent of business Internet use, 2007	94

Government usage — 114

9.01	Government success in ICT promotion, 2007	94
9.02	Availability of government online services, 2007	121
9.03	ICT use and government efficiency, 2007	122
9.04	Presence of ICT in government offices, 2007	98
9.05	E-Participation Index,* 2007	91

* Hard data

Note: For further details and explanation, please refer to the section "How to Read the Country/Economy Profiles" at the beginning of this chapter.

Honduras

Key indicators

Population (millions), 2006..7.4
GDP (PPP) per capita (US$), 2006.....................................3,199.0
Internet users per 100 inhabitants, 2006 ....4.6
Internet bandwidth (mB/s) per 10,000 inhabitants, 2005.........0.1

Networked Readiness Index

Year (number of economies)	Rank
2007–2008 (127)	**90**
2006–2007 (122)	94
2005–2006 (115)	100

Global Competitiveness Index 2007–2008 (131)	83

Environment component — 88
Market environment — 76

1.01 Venture capital availability, 2007..62
1.02 Financial market sophistication, 2007 78
1.03 Availability of latest technologies, 2007 94
1.04 State of cluster development, 2007......................................58
1.05 Utility patents,* 2006 72
1.06 High-tech exports,* 2005 92
1.07 Burden of government regulation, 2007 37
1.08 Extent and effect of taxation, 2007.......................................53
1.09 Total tax rate,* 2007 87
1.10 Time required to start a business,* 2007.............................44
1.11 No. of procedures required to start a business,* 2007 ..103
1.12 Intensity of local competition, 2007....................................104
1.13 Freedom of the press, 2007..34
1.14 Accessibility of digital content, 2007....................................74

Political and regulatory environment — 85

2.01 Effectiveness of law-making bodies, 2007 74
2.02 Laws relating to ICT, 2007..83
2.03 Judicial independence, 2007...93
2.04 Intellectual property protection, 2007 73
2.05 Efficiency of legal framework, 2007.....................................86
2.06 Property rights, 2007...85
2.07 Quality of competition in the ISP sector, 2007 48
2.08 No. of procedures to enforce a contract,* 2007..............110
2.09 Time to enforce a contract,* 2007 51

Infrastructure environment — 104

3.01 Telephone lines,* 2006..88
3.02 Secure Internet servers,* 2006..73
3.03 Electricity production,* 2004..91
3.04 Availability of scientists and engineers, 2007 104
3.05 Quality of scientific research institutions, 2007 117
3.06 Tertiary enrollment,* 2004..88
3.07 Education expenditure,* 2005...77

Readiness component — 90
Individual readiness — 95

4.01 Quality of math and science education, 2007...................112
4.02 Quality of the educational system, 2007...........................114
4.03 Internet access in schools, 2007..96
4.04 Buyer sophistication, 2007 93
4.05 Residential telephone connection charge,* 2005 82
4.06 Residential monthly telephone subscription,* 2005 75
4.07 High-speed monthly broadband subscription* ....n/a
4.08 Lowest cost of broadband,* 2006 89
4.09 Cost of mobile telephone call,* 2005................................102

Business readiness — 89

5.01 Extent of staff training, 2007..70
5.02 Local availability of research and training, 2007................70
5.03 Quality of management schools, 2007 93
5.04 Company spending on R&D, 2007......................................98
5.05 University-industry research collaboration, 2007...............91
5.06 Business telephone connection charge,* 2005 88
5.07 Business monthly telephone subscription,* 2005 82
5.08 Local supplier quality, 2007..85
5.09 Local supplier quantity, 2007..94
5.10 Computer, comm., and other services imports,* 2005 78

Government readiness — 102

6.01 Government prioritization of ICT, 2007................................91
6.02 Gov't procurement of advanced tech products, 2007 87
6.03 Importance of ICT to gov't vision of the future, 2007.....100
6.04 E-Government Readiness Index,* 2007..............................90

Usage component — 94
Individual usage — 100

7.01 Mobile telephone subscribers,* 2006..................................92
7.02 Personal computers,* 2005 102
7.03 Broadband Internet subscribers,* 2005 118
7.04 Internet users,* 2006..102
7.05 Internet bandwidth,* 2005 109

Business usage — 94

8.01 Prevalence of foreign technology licensing, 2007..............93
8.02 Firm-level technology absorption, 2007 98
8.03 Capacity for innovation, 2007...84
8.04 Availability of new telephone lines, 2007.........................106
8.05 Extent of business Internet use, 2007................................63

Government usage — 89

9.01 Government success in ICT promotion, 2007..................101
9.02 Availability of government online services, 2007 77
9.03 ICT use and government efficiency, 2007...........................88
9.04 Presence of ICT in government offices, 2007 96
9.05 E-Participation Index,* 2007...43

* Hard data

Note: For further details and explanation, please refer to the section "How to Read the Country/Economy Profiles" at the beginning of this chapter.

Hong Kong SAR

Key indicators

Population (millions), 2006...7.1
GDP (PPP) per capita (US$), 2006...................................38,713.6
Internet users per 100 inhabitants, 2006 ....53.0
Internet bandwidth (mB/s) per 10,000 inhabitants, 2006.....129.8

Networked Readiness Index

Year (number of economies)	Rank
2007–2008 (127)	**11**
2006–2007 (122)	12
2005–2006 (115)	11

Global Competitiveness Index 2007–2008 (131) — 12

Environment component — 16
Market environment — 2
1.01 Venture capital availability, 2007..11
1.02 Financial market sophistication, 2007 3
1.03 Availability of latest technologies, 2007 23
1.04 State of cluster development, 2007....................................14
1.05 Utility patents,* 2006 22
1.06 High-tech exports,* 2005 6
1.07 Burden of government regulation, 2007 3
1.08 Extent and effect of taxation, 2007.......................................4
1.09 Total tax rate,* 2007..11
1.10 Time required to start a business,* 2007...........................19
1.11 No. of procedures required to start a business,* 2007 9
1.12 Intensity of local competition, 2007......................................4
1.13 Freedom of the press, 2007...32
1.14 Accessibility of digital content, 2007...................................12

Political and regulatory environment — 10
2.01 Effectiveness of law-making bodies, 2007 35
2.02 Laws relating to ICT, 2007..18
2.03 Judicial independence, 2007 16
2.04 Intellectual property protection, 2007 21
2.05 Efficiency of legal framework, 2007.....................................9
2.06 Property rights, 2007 13
2.07 Quality of competition in the ISP sector, 2007 8
2.08 No. of procedures to enforce a contract,* 2007 3
2.09 Time to enforce a contract,* 2007 4

Infrastructure environment — 33
3.01 Telephone lines,* 2006...13
3.02 Secure Internet servers,* 2006...22
3.03 Electricity production,* 2004...39
3.04 Availability of scientists and engineers, 2007 35
3.05 Quality of scientific research institutions, 2007 25
3.06 Tertiary enrollment,* 2005..63
3.07 Education expenditure,* 2005..73

Readiness component — 15
Individual readiness — 4
4.01 Quality of math and science education, 2007 4
4.02 Quality of the educational system, 2007.............................9
4.03 Internet access in schools, 2007..7
4.04 Buyer sophistication, 2007 4
4.05 Residential telephone connection charge,* 2005 1
4.06 Residential monthly telephone subscription,* 2005 22
4.07 High-speed monthly broadband subscription,* 2006........25
4.08 Lowest cost of broadband,* 2006 16
4.09 Cost of mobile telephone call,* 2005...................................3

Business readiness — 21
5.01 Extent of staff training, 2007...28
5.02 Local availability of research and training, 2007...............19
5.03 Quality of management schools, 2007 17
5.04 Company spending on R&D, 2007......................................23
5.05 University-industry research collaboration, 2007..............21
5.06 Business telephone connection charge,* 2005 1
5.07 Business monthly telephone subscription,* 2005 15
5.08 Local supplier quality, 2007 15
5.09 Local supplier quantity, 2007 11
5.10 Computer, comm., and other services imports,* 2004 68

Government readiness — 19
6.01 Government prioritization of ICT, 2007..............................17
6.02 Gov't procurement of advanced tech products, 2007 15
6.03 Importance of ICT to gov't vision of the future, 2007.......12
6.04 E-Government Readiness Index* ....n/a

Usage component — 5
Individual usage — 5
7.01 Mobile telephone subscribers,* 2006...................................3
7.02 Personal computers,* 2005 16
7.03 Broadband Internet subscribers,* 2006 9
7.04 Internet users,* 2006 20
7.05 Internet bandwidth,* 2006 6

Business usage — 19
8.01 Prevalence of foreign technology licensing, 2007.............16
8.02 Firm-level technology absorption, 2007 16
8.03 Capacity for innovation, 2007..26
8.04 Availability of new telephone lines, 2007 9
8.05 Extent of business Internet use, 2007...............................22

Government usage — 7
9.01 Government success in ICT promotion, 2007....................17
9.02 Availability of government online services, 2007 13
9.03 ICT use and government efficiency, 2007...........................8
9.04 Presence of ICT in government offices, 2007 10
9.05 E-Participation Index* ....n/a

* Hard data

Note: For further details and explanation, please refer to the section "How to Read the Country/Economy Profiles" at the beginning of this chapter.

Hungary

Key indicators

Population (millions), 2006..10.1
GDP (PPP) per capita (US$), 2006.....................................20,047.4
Internet users per 100 inhabitants, 2006................................34.8
Internet bandwidth (mB/s) per 10,000 inhabitants, 2006.........9.9

Networked Readiness Index

Year (number of economies)	Rank
2007–2008 (127)	**37**
2006–2007 (122)	33
2005–2006 (115)	38

Global Competitiveness Index 2007–2008 (131)   47

Environment component — 32
Market environment — 38

1.01 Venture capital availability, 2007..50
1.02 Financial market sophistication, 2007 47
1.03 Availability of latest technologies, 2007 55
1.04 State of cluster development, 2007..6
1.05 Utility patents,* 2006..30
1.06 High-tech exports,* 2005 14
1.07 Burden of government regulation, 2007 107
1.08 Extent and effect of taxation, 2007.......................................114
1.09 Total tax rate,* 2007 98
1.10 Time required to start a business,* 2007...............................33
1.11 No. of procedures required to start a business,* 2007 19
1.12 Intensity of local competition, 2007 32
1.13 Freedom of the press, 2007..47
1.14 Accessibility of digital content, 2007......................................41

Political and regulatory environment — 40

2.01 Effectiveness of law-making bodies, 2007 78
2.02 Laws relating to ICT, 2007..47
2.03 Judicial independence, 2007...49
2.04 Intellectual property protection, 2007 37
2.05 Efficiency of legal framework, 2007.......................................56
2.06 Property rights, 2007..37
2.07 Quality of competition in the ISP sector, 2007 78
2.08 No. of procedures to enforce a contract,* 2007...................35
2.09 Time to enforce a contract,* 2007 24

Infrastructure environment — 28

3.01 Telephone lines,* 2006...35
3.02 Secure Internet servers,* 2006...41
3.03 Electricity production,* 2004..53
3.04 Availability of scientists and engineers, 2007 40
3.05 Quality of scientific research institutions, 2007 24
3.06 Tertiary enrollment,* 2005..20
3.07 Education expenditure,* 2005...18

Readiness component — 39
Individual readiness — 42

4.01 Quality of math and science education, 2007 22
4.02 Quality of the educational system, 2007...............................63
4.03 Internet access in schools, 2007..27
4.04 Buyer sophistication, 2007 89
4.05 Residential telephone connection charge,* 2005 75
4.06 Residential monthly telephone subscription,* 2005 70
4.07 High-speed monthly broadband subscription,* 2006...........39
4.08 Lowest cost of broadband,* 2006 35
4.09 Cost of mobile telephone call,* 2005.....................................43

Business readiness — 47

5.01 Extent of staff training, 2007..73
5.02 Local availability of research and training, 2007..................60
5.03 Quality of management schools, 2007 57
5.04 Company spending on R&D, 2007...67
5.05 University-industry research collaboration, 2007..................34
5.06 Business telephone connection charge,* 2005 76
5.07 Business monthly telephone subscription,* 2005 55
5.08 Local supplier quality, 2007..59
5.09 Local supplier quantity, 2007..69
5.10 Computer, comm., and other services imports,* 2005 9

Government readiness — 44

6.01 Government prioritization of ICT, 2007..................................72
6.02 Gov't procurement of advanced tech products, 2007 85
6.03 Importance of ICT to gov't vision of the future, 2007.........64
6.04 E-Government Readiness Index,* 2007.................................30

Usage component — 38
Individual usage — 38

7.01 Mobile telephone subscribers,* 2006.....................................30
7.02 Personal computers,* 2005 46
7.03 Broadband Internet subscribers,* 2006.................................34
7.04 Internet users,* 2006..34
7.05 Internet bandwidth,* 2006..40

Business usage — 41

8.01 Prevalence of foreign technology licensing, 2007................52
8.02 Firm-level technology absorption, 2007 48
8.03 Capacity for innovation, 2007 38
8.04 Availability of new telephone lines, 2007..............................23
8.05 Extent of business Internet use, 2007..................................50

Government usage — 54

9.01 Government success in ICT promotion, 2007.......................83
9.02 Availability of government online services, 2007 48
9.03 ICT use and government efficiency, 2007.............................61
9.04 Presence of ICT in government offices, 2007 50
9.05 E-Participation Index,* 2007...58

* Hard data

Note: For further details and explanation, please refer to the section "How to Read the Country/Economy Profiles" at the beginning of this chapter.

Iceland

Key indicators

Population (millions), 2006...0.3
GDP (PPP) per capita (US$), 2006...........................40,112.3
Internet users per 100 inhabitants, 2006........................65.3
Internet bandwidth (mB/s) per 10,000 inhabitants, 2004.......42.3

Networked Readiness Index

Year (number of economies)	Rank
2007–2008 (127)	**8**
2006–2007 (122)	8
2005–2006 (115)	4

Global Competitiveness Index 2007–2008 (131)   23

Environment component — 1

Market environment — 10
1.01 Venture capital availability, 2007..........................12
1.02 Financial market sophistication, 2007..................20
1.03 Availability of latest technologies, 2007................3
1.04 State of cluster development, 2007......................41
1.05 Utility patents*, 2006...16
1.06 High-tech exports*, 2004..72
1.07 Burden of government regulation, 2007.................2
1.08 Extent and effect of taxation, 2007.........................9
1.09 Total tax rate*, 2007..14
1.10 Time required to start a business*, 2007...............4
1.11 No. of procedures required to start a business*, 2007 ...9
1.12 Intensity of local competition, 2007......................40
1.13 Freedom of the press, 2007...................................13
1.14 Accessibility of digital content, 2007......................7

Political and regulatory environment — 9
2.01 Effectiveness of law-making bodies, 2007.............8
2.02 Laws relating to ICT, 2007......................................13
2.03 Judicial independence, 2007..................................11
2.04 Intellectual property protection, 2007...................12
2.05 Efficiency of legal framework, 2007......................13
2.06 Property rights, 2007..10
2.07 Quality of competition in the ISP sector, 2007....12
2.08 No. of procedures to enforce a contract*, 2007....5
2.09 Time to enforce a contract*, 2007.........................30

Infrastructure environment — 1
3.01 Telephone lines*, 2006...3
3.02 Secure Internet servers*, 2006................................1
3.03 Electricity production*, 2003....................................1
3.04 Availability of scientists and engineers, 2007.....20
3.05 Quality of scientific research institutions, 2007..29
3.06 Tertiary enrollment*, 2005.....................................14
3.07 Education expenditure*, 2005.................................3

Readiness component — 18

Individual readiness — 8
4.01 Quality of math and science education, 2007....33
4.02 Quality of the educational system, 2007................6
4.03 Internet access in schools, 2007.............................1
4.04 Buyer sophistication, 2007.....................................25
4.05 Residential telephone connection charge*, 2005....4
4.06 Residential monthly telephone subscription*, 2005....16
4.07 High-speed monthly broadband subscription*, 2006....21
4.08 Lowest cost of broadband*, 2006..........................13
4.09 Cost of mobile telephone call*, 2005...................12

Business readiness — 22
5.01 Extent of staff training, 2007.................................14
5.02 Local availability of research and training, 2007....22
5.03 Quality of management schools, 2007.................20
5.04 Company spending on R&D, 2007........................20
5.05 University-industry research collaboration, 2007....20
5.06 Business telephone connection charge*, 2005.....4
5.07 Business monthly telephone subscription*, 2005....14
5.08 Local supplier quality, 2007...................................22
5.09 Local supplier quantity, 2007................................28
5.10 Computer, comm., and other services imports*, 2005 ...66

Government readiness — 15
6.01 Government prioritization of ICT, 2007................14
6.02 Gov't procurement of advanced tech products, 2007....33
6.03 Importance of ICT to gov't vision of the future, 2007....10
6.04 E-Government Readiness Index*, 2007...............21

Usage component — 14

Individual usage — 10
7.01 Mobile telephone subscribers*, 2006...................15
7.02 Personal computers*, 2005....................................24
7.03 Broadband Internet subscribers*, 2006..................3
7.04 Internet users*, 2006..10
7.05 Internet bandwidth*, 2004......................................18

Business usage — 10
8.01 Prevalence of foreign technology licensing, 2007....17
8.02 Firm-level technology absorption, 2007..................1
8.03 Capacity for innovation, 2007................................21
8.04 Availability of new telephone lines, 2007...............5
8.05 Extent of business Internet use, 2007..................10

Government usage — 21
9.01 Government success in ICT promotion, 2007.....13
9.02 Availability of government online services, 2007....7
9.03 ICT use and government efficiency, 2007..............4
9.04 Presence of ICT in government offices, 2007.......8
9.05 E-Participation Index*, 2007..................................91

* Hard data

Note: For further details and explanation, please refer to the section "How to Read the Country/Economy Profiles" at the beginning of this chapter.

India

Key indicators

Population (millions), 2006..1119.5
GDP (PPP) per capita (US$), 2006...3,802.0
Internet users per 100 inhabitants, 2005 ....5.4
Internet bandwidth (mB/s) per 10,000 inhabitants, 2006.............0.2

Networked Readiness Index

Year (number of economies)	Rank
2007–2008 (127)	**50**
2006–2007 (122)	44
2005–2006 (115)	40

Global Competitiveness Index 2007–2008 (131) 48

Environment component — 54
Market environment — 49
1.01 Venture capital availability, 2007..29
1.02 Financial market sophistication, 2007 33
1.03 Availability of latest technologies, 2007 31
1.04 State of cluster development, 2007......................................24
1.05 Utility patents,* 2006 60
1.06 High-tech exports,* 2005 44
1.07 Burden of government regulation, 2007 78
1.08 Extent and effect of taxation, 2007.......................................29
1.09 Total tax rate,* 2007..110
1.10 Time required to start a business,* 2007.............................75
1.11 No. of procedures required to start a business,* 2007 ..103
1.12 Intensity of local competition, 2007 10
1.13 Freedom of the press, 2007..20
1.14 Accessibility of digital content, 2007....................................65

Political and regulatory environment — 47
2.01 Effectiveness of law-making bodies, 2007 24
2.02 Laws relating to ICT, 2007...36
2.03 Judicial independence, 2007...26
2.04 Intellectual property protection, 2007 48
2.05 Efficiency of legal framework, 2007.....................................34
2.06 Property rights, 2007...44
2.07 Quality of competition in the ISP sector, 2007 23
2.08 No. of procedures to enforce a contract,* 2007 112
2.09 Time to enforce a contract,* 2007 118

Infrastructure environment — 71
3.01 Telephone lines,* 2005..100
3.02 Secure Internet servers,* 2006...90
3.03 Electricity production,* 2004..95
3.04 Availability of scientists and engineers, 2007 4
3.05 Quality of scientific research institutions, 2007 22
3.06 Tertiary enrollment,* 2005..95
3.07 Education expenditure,* 2005...68

Readiness component — 37
Individual readiness — 46
4.01 Quality of math and science education, 2007....................11
4.02 Quality of the educational system, 2007.............................31
4.03 Internet access in schools, 2007..56
4.04 Buyer sophistication, 2007 31
4.05 Residential telephone connection charge,* 2005 87
4.06 Residential monthly telephone subscription,* 2005 94
4.07 High-speed monthly broadband subscription,* 2006........65
4.08 Lowest cost of broadband,* 2006 81
4.09 Cost of mobile telephone call,* 2005..................................56

Business readiness — 28
5.01 Extent of staff training, 2007..33
5.02 Local availability of research and training, 2007................31
5.03 Quality of management schools, 2007 8
5.04 Company spending on R&D, 2007 28
5.05 University-industry research collaboration, 2007...............43
5.06 Business telephone connection charge,* 2005 75
5.07 Business monthly telephone subscription,* 2005 98
5.08 Local supplier quality, 2007..33
5.09 Local supplier quantity, 2007..6
5.10 Computer, comm., and other services imports,* 2005 18

Government readiness — 45
6.01 Government prioritization of ICT, 2007................................16
6.02 Gov't procurement of advanced tech products, 2007 70
6.03 Importance of ICT to gov't vision of the future, 2007.......21
6.04 E-Government Readiness Index,* 2007..............................91

Usage component — 51
Individual usage — 109
7.01 Mobile telephone subscribers,* 2006.............................107
7.02 Personal computers,* 2005 104
7.03 Broadband Internet subscribers,* 2006 88
7.04 Internet users,* 2005 101
7.05 Internet bandwidth,* 2006 87

Business usage — 26
8.01 Prevalence of foreign technology licensing, 2007............22
8.02 Firm-level technology absorption, 2007 22
8.03 Capacity for innovation, 2007..31
8.04 Availability of new telephone lines, 2007.........................33
8.05 Extent of business Internet use, 2007..............................35

Government usage — 40
9.01 Government success in ICT promotion, 2007..................18
9.02 Availability of government online services, 2007 44
9.03 ICT use and government efficiency, 2007........................30
9.04 Presence of ICT in government offices, 2007 56
9.05 E-Participation Index,* 2007..47

* Hard data

Note: For further details and explanation, please refer to the section "How to Read the Country/Economy Profiles" at the beginning of this chapter.

Indonesia

Key indicators

Population (millions), 2006	225.5
GDP (PPP) per capita (US$), 2006	4,356.3
Internet users per 100 inhabitants, 2005	7.2
Internet bandwidth (mB/s) per 10,000 inhabitants, 2005	0.1

Networked Readiness Index

Year (number of economies)	Rank
2007–2008 (127)	**76**
2006–2007 (122)	62
2005–2006 (115)	68

Global Competitiveness Index 2007–2008 (131)	54

Environment component — 74
Market environment — 52

1.01	Venture capital availability, 2007	35
1.02	Financial market sophistication, 2007	81
1.03	Availability of latest technologies, 2007	51
1.04	State of cluster development, 2007	8
1.05	Utility patents,* 2006	84
1.06	High-tech exports,* 2005	34
1.07	Burden of government regulation, 2007	22
1.08	Extent and effect of taxation, 2007	8
1.09	Total tax rate,* 2007	41
1.10	Time required to start a business,* 2007	117
1.11	No. of procedures required to start a business,* 2007	98
1.12	Intensity of local competition, 2007	28
1.13	Freedom of the press, 2007	53
1.14	Accessibility of digital content, 2007	64

Political and regulatory environment — 81

2.01	Effectiveness of law-making bodies, 2007	77
2.02	Laws relating to ICT, 2007	79
2.03	Judicial independence, 2007	96
2.04	Intellectual property protection, 2007	86
2.05	Efficiency of legal framework, 2007	74
2.06	Property rights, 2007	112
2.07	Quality of competition in the ISP sector, 2007	36
2.08	No. of procedures to enforce a contract,* 2007	75
2.09	Time to enforce a contract,* 2007	71

Infrastructure environment — 99

3.01	Telephone lines,* 2006	97
3.02	Secure Internet servers,* 2006	90
3.03	Electricity production,* 2004	100
3.04	Availability of scientists and engineers, 2007	27
3.05	Quality of scientific research institutions, 2007	28
3.06	Tertiary enrollment,* 2005	86
3.07	Education expenditure,* 2005	119

Readiness component — 58
Individual readiness — 38

4.01	Quality of math and science education, 2007	31
4.02	Quality of the educational system, 2007	29
4.03	Internet access in schools, 2007	64
4.04	Buyer sophistication, 2007	9
4.05	Residential telephone connection charge,* 2005	83
4.06	Residential monthly telephone subscription,* 2005	86
4.07	High-speed monthly broadband subscription,* 2006	69
4.08	Lowest cost of broadband,* 2006	75
4.09	Cost of mobile telephone call,* 2004	54

Business readiness — 33

5.01	Extent of staff training, 2007	34
5.02	Local availability of research and training, 2007	29
5.03	Quality of management schools, 2007	32
5.04	Company spending on R&D, 2007	27
5.05	University-industry research collaboration, 2007	62
5.06	Business telephone connection charge,* 2005	78
5.07	Business monthly telephone subscription,* 2005	81
5.08	Local supplier quality, 2007	52
5.09	Local supplier quantity, 2007	31
5.10	Computer, comm., and other services imports,* 2005	12

Government readiness — 111

6.01	Government prioritization of ICT, 2007	124
6.02	Gov't procurement of advanced tech products, 2007	65
6.03	Importance of ICT to gov't vision of the future, 2007	114
6.04	E-Government Readiness Index,* 2007	89

Usage component — 93
Individual usage — 97

7.01	Mobile telephone subscribers,* 2006	95
7.02	Personal computers,* 2005	105
7.03	Broadband Internet subscribers,* 2005	99
7.04	Internet users,* 2005	93
7.05	Internet bandwidth,* 2005	106

Business usage — 48

8.01	Prevalence of foreign technology licensing, 2007	4
8.02	Firm-level technology absorption, 2007	66
8.03	Capacity for innovation, 2007	50
8.04	Availability of new telephone lines, 2007	91
8.05	Extent of business Internet use, 2007	56

Government usage — 112

9.01	Government success in ICT promotion, 2007	114
9.02	Availability of government online services, 2007	87
9.03	ICT use and government efficiency, 2007	115
9.04	Presence of ICT in government offices, 2007	115
9.05	E-Participation Index,* 2007	100

* Hard data

Note: For further details and explanation, please refer to the section "How to Read the Country/Economy Profiles" at the beginning of this chapter.

Ireland

Key indicators

Population (millions), 2006...4.2
GDP (PPP) per capita (US$), 2006..................................44,676.0
Internet users per 100 inhabitants, 2006 ....34.1
Internet bandwidth (mB/s) per 10,000 inhabitants, 2005.......60.0

Networked Readiness Index

Year (number of economies)	Rank
2007–2008 (127)	**23**
2006–2007 (122)	21
2005–2006 (115)	20

Global Competitiveness Index 2007–2008 (131)   22

Environment component — 15
Market environment — 15

1.01 Venture capital availability, 2007..9
1.02 Financial market sophistication, 2007 9
1.03 Availability of latest technologies, 2007 33
1.04 State of cluster development, 2007......................................33
1.05 Utility patents,* 2006 23
1.06 High-tech exports,* 2004 9
1.07 Burden of government regulation, 2007 34
1.08 Extent and effect of taxation, 2007 11
1.09 Total tax rate,* 2007..16
1.10 Time required to start a business,* 2007 24
1.11 No. of procedures required to start a business,* 2007 7
1.12 Intensity of local competition, 2007 30
1.13 Freedom of the press, 2007..23
1.14 Accessibility of digital content, 2007....................................38

Political and regulatory environment — 17

2.01 Effectiveness of law-making bodies, 2007 21
2.02 Laws relating to ICT, 2007..27
2.03 Judicial independence, 2007...15
2.04 Intellectual property protection, 2007 19
2.05 Efficiency of legal framework, 2007.....................................21
2.06 Property rights, 2007 11
2.07 Quality of competition in the ISP sector, 2007 68
2.08 No. of procedures to enforce a contract,* 2007...................1
2.09 Time to enforce a contract,* 2007 59

Infrastructure environment — 15

3.01 Telephone lines,* 2006..17
3.02 Secure Internet servers,* 2006...11
3.03 Electricity production,* 2004 33
3.04 Availability of scientists and engineers, 2007 15
3.05 Quality of scientific research institutions, 2007 16
3.06 Tertiary enrollment,* 2005...27
3.07 Education expenditure,* 2005...43

Readiness component — 19
Individual readiness — 16

4.01 Quality of math and science education, 2007 20
4.02 Quality of the educational system, 2007...............................7
4.03 Internet access in schools, 2007...38
4.04 Buyer sophistication, 2007 10
4.05 Residential telephone connection charge,* 2005 29
4.06 Residential monthly telephone subscription,* 2005 38
4.07 High-speed monthly broadband subscription,* 2006..........15
4.08 Lowest cost of broadband,* 2006 23
4.09 Cost of mobile telephone call,* 2005...................................25

Business readiness — 8

5.01 Extent of staff training, 2007...15
5.02 Local availability of research and training, 2007 23
5.03 Quality of management schools, 2007 14
5.04 Company spending on R&D, 2007..16
5.05 University-industry research collaboration, 2007................18
5.06 Business telephone connection charge,* 2005 24
5.07 Business monthly telephone subscription,* 2005 24
5.08 Local supplier quality, 2007 18
5.09 Local supplier quantity, 2007 34
5.10 Computer, comm., and other services imports,* 2005 2

Government readiness — 28

6.01 Government prioritization of ICT, 2007................................52
6.02 Gov't procurement of advanced tech products, 2007 25
6.03 Importance of ICT to gov't vision of the future, 2007........34
6.04 E-Government Readiness Index,* 2007...............................19

Usage component — 25
Individual usage — 26

7.01 Mobile telephone subscribers,* 2006...................................14
7.02 Personal computers,* 2005 20
7.03 Broadband Internet subscribers,* 2006 29
7.04 Internet users,* 2006 38
7.05 Internet bandwidth,* 2005 16

Business usage — 28

8.01 Prevalence of foreign technology licensing, 2007..............33
8.02 Firm-level technology absorption, 2007 23
8.03 Capacity for innovation, 2007 24
8.04 Availability of new telephone lines, 2007 73
8.05 Extent of business Internet use, 2007 24

Government usage — 24

9.01 Government success in ICT promotion, 2007.....................50
9.02 Availability of government online services, 2007 5
9.03 ICT use and government efficiency, 2007...........................18
9.04 Presence of ICT in government offices, 2007 24
9.05 E-Participation Index,* 2007..47

* Hard data

Note: For further details and explanation, please refer to the section "How to Read the Country/Economy Profiles" at the beginning of this chapter.

Israel

Key indicators

Population (millions), 2006...6.8
GDP (PPP) per capita (US$), 2006.............................31,560.9
Internet users per 100 inhabitants, 2005 ....24.4
Internet bandwidth (mB/s) per 10,000 inhabitants, 2005.......25.4

Networked Readiness Index

Year (number of economies)	Rank
2007–2008 (127)	**18**
2006–2007 (122)	18
2005–2006 (115)	19

Global Competitiveness Index 2007–2008 (131)   17

Environment component   19
Market environment   8

1.01 Venture capital availability, 2007..5
1.02 Financial market sophistication, 2007 17
1.03 Availability of latest technologies, 2007................................4
1.04 State of cluster development, 2007.....................................28
1.05 Utility patents,* 2006...5
1.06 High-tech exports,* 2005...27
1.07 Burden of government regulation, 2007 31
1.08 Extent and effect of taxation, 2007.....................................66
1.09 Total tax rate,* 2007..35
1.10 Time required to start a business,* 2007............................78
1.11 No. of procedures required to start a business,* 2007 9
1.12 Intensity of local competition, 2007....................................21
1.13 Freedom of the press, 2007..12
1.14 Accessibility of digital content, 2007..................................17

Political and regulatory environment   25

2.01 Effectiveness of law-making bodies, 2007 40
2.02 Laws relating to ICT, 2007...21
2.03 Judicial independence, 2007..13
2.04 Intellectual property protection, 2007 26
2.05 Efficiency of legal framework, 2007....................................26
2.06 Property rights, 2007..25
2.07 Quality of competition in the ISP sector, 2007 3
2.08 No. of procedures to enforce a contract,* 2007................46
2.09 Time to enforce a contract,* 2007 109

Infrastructure environment   13

3.01 Telephone lines,* 2006..23
3.02 Secure Internet servers,* 2006...23
3.03 Electricity production,* 2004...27
3.04 Availability of scientists and engineers, 2007 3
3.05 Quality of scientific research institutions, 2007 3
3.06 Tertiary enrollment,* 2005...28
3.07 Education expenditure,* 2005...4

Readiness component   14
Individual readiness   18

4.01 Quality of math and science education, 2007....................30
4.02 Quality of the educational system, 2007............................25
4.03 Internet access in schools, 2007...17
4.04 Buyer sophistication, 2007..26
4.05 Residential telephone connection charge,* 2005 26
4.06 Residential monthly telephone subscription,* 2005 25
4.07 High-speed monthly broadband subscription,* 2006.........30
4.08 Lowest cost of broadband,* 2006.......................................31
4.09 Cost of mobile telephone call,* 2005..................................28

Business readiness   13

5.01 Extent of staff training, 2007...23
5.02 Local availability of research and training, 2007................13
5.03 Quality of management schools, 2007 15
5.04 Company spending on R&D, 2007..7
5.05 University-industry research collaboration, 2007.................8
5.06 Business telephone connection charge,* 2005 22
5.07 Business monthly telephone subscription,* 2005 12
5.08 Local supplier quality, 2007...20
5.09 Local supplier quantity, 2007...42
5.10 Computer, comm., and other services imports,* 2005 25

Government readiness   17

6.01 Government prioritization of ICT, 2007...............................26
6.02 Gov't procurement of advanced tech products, 2007 7
6.03 Importance of ICT to gov't vision of the future, 2007.......26
6.04 E-Government Readiness Index,* 2007.............................17

Usage component   18
Individual usage   13

7.01 Mobile telephone subscribers,* 2006...................................7
7.02 Personal computers,* 2005..1
7.03 Broadband Internet subscribers,* 2006..............................13
7.04 Internet users,* 2005...48
7.05 Internet bandwidth,* 2005...27

Business usage   9

8.01 Prevalence of foreign technology licensing, 2007..............14
8.02 Firm-level technology absorption, 2007 5
8.03 Capacity for innovation, 2007..10
8.04 Availability of new telephone lines, 2007...........................14
8.05 Extent of business Internet use, 2007................................14

Government usage   26

9.01 Government success in ICT promotion, 2007....................20
9.02 Availability of government online services, 2007 27
9.03 ICT use and government efficiency, 2007..........................21
9.04 Presence of ICT in government offices, 2007 31
9.05 E-Participation Index,* 2007..36

* Hard data

Note: For further details and explanation, please refer to the section "How to Read the Country/Economy Profiles" at the beginning of this chapter.

Italy

Key indicators

Population (millions), 2006	58.1
GDP (PPP) per capita (US$), 2006	31,051.1
Internet users per 100 inhabitants, 2006	49.6
Internet bandwidth (mB/s) per 10,000 inhabitants, 2005	20.6

Networked Readiness Index

Year (number of economies)	Rank
2007–2008 (127)	**42**
2006–2007 (122)	38
2005–2006 (115)	42

Global Competitiveness Index 2007–2008 (131)	46

Environment component — 55

Market environment — 71

1.01	Venture capital availability, 2007	79
1.02	Financial market sophistication, 2007	57
1.03	Availability of latest technologies, 2007	54
1.04	State of cluster development, 2007	21
1.05	Utility patents,* 2006	25
1.06	High-tech exports,* 2005	36
1.07	Burden of government regulation, 2007	124
1.08	Extent and effect of taxation, 2007	123
1.09	Total tax rate,* 2007	114
1.10	Time required to start a business,* 2007	24
1.11	No. of procedures required to start a business,* 2007	58
1.12	Intensity of local competition, 2007	78
1.13	Freedom of the press, 2007	66
1.14	Accessibility of digital content, 2007	69

Political and regulatory environment — 75

2.01	Effectiveness of law-making bodies, 2007	93
2.02	Laws relating to ICT, 2007	42
2.03	Judicial independence, 2007	65
2.04	Intellectual property protection, 2007	42
2.05	Efficiency of legal framework, 2007	97
2.06	Property rights, 2007	53
2.07	Quality of competition in the ISP sector, 2007	45
2.08	No. of procedures to enforce a contract,* 2007	94
2.09	Time to enforce a contract,* 2007	113

Infrastructure environment — 36

3.01	Telephone lines,* 2005	25
3.02	Secure Internet servers,* 2006	36
3.03	Electricity production,* 2004	43
3.04	Availability of scientists and engineers, 2007	48
3.05	Quality of scientific research institutions, 2007	94
3.06	Tertiary enrollment,* 2005	19
3.07	Education expenditure,* 2005	46

Readiness component — 46

Individual readiness — 47

4.01	Quality of math and science education, 2007	57
4.02	Quality of the educational system, 2007	74
4.03	Internet access in schools, 2007	54
4.04	Buyer sophistication, 2007	32
4.05	Residential telephone connection charge,* 2005	51
4.06	Residential monthly telephone subscription,* 2005	40
4.07	High-speed monthly broadband subscription,* 2006	12
4.08	Lowest cost of broadband,* 2006	3
4.09	Cost of mobile telephone call,* 2005	2

Business readiness — 39

5.01	Extent of staff training, 2007	79
5.02	Local availability of research and training, 2007	28
5.03	Quality of management schools, 2007	52
5.04	Company spending on R&D, 2007	71
5.05	University-industry research collaboration, 2007	70
5.06	Business telephone connection charge,* 2005	41
5.07	Business monthly telephone subscription,* 2005	40
5.08	Local supplier quality, 2007	28
5.09	Local supplier quantity, 2007	20
5.10	Computer, comm., and other services imports,* 2005	15

Government readiness — 64

6.01	Government prioritization of ICT, 2007	110
6.02	Gov't procurement of advanced tech products, 2007	95
6.03	Importance of ICT to gov't vision of the future, 2007	92
6.04	E-Government Readiness Index,* 2007	27

Usage component — 33

Individual usage — 25

7.01	Mobile telephone subscribers,* 2005	6
7.02	Personal computers,* 2005	27
7.03	Broadband Internet subscribers,* 2006	25
7.04	Internet users,* 2006	22
7.05	Internet bandwidth,* 2005	31

Business usage — 45

8.01	Prevalence of foreign technology licensing, 2007	56
8.02	Firm-level technology absorption, 2007	78
8.03	Capacity for innovation, 2007	20
8.04	Availability of new telephone lines, 2007	70
8.05	Extent of business Internet use, 2007	54

Government usage — 47

9.01	Government success in ICT promotion, 2007	97
9.02	Availability of government online services, 2007	58
9.03	ICT use and government efficiency, 2007	5
9.04	Presence of ICT in government offices, 2007	54
9.05	E-Participation Index,* 2007	53

* Hard data

Note: For further details and explanation, please refer to the section "How to Read the Country/Economy Profiles" at the beginning of this chapter.

Jamaica

Key indicators

Population (millions), 2006...2.7
GDP (PPP) per capita (US$), 2006.....................................4,493.7
Internet users per 100 inhabitants, 2005 ....46.5
Internet bandwidth (mB/s) per 10,000 inhabitants, 2005.....155.6

Networked Readiness Index

Year (number of economies)	Rank
2007–2008 (127)	**46**
2006–2007 (122)	45
2005–2006 (115)	54

Global Competitiveness Index 2007–2008 (131) — 78

Environment component — 53

Market environment — 39

1.01	Venture capital availability, 2007	94
1.02	Financial market sophistication, 2007	37
1.03	Availability of latest technologies, 2007	42
1.04	State of cluster development, 2007	94
1.05	Utility patents,* 2006	86
1.06	High-tech exports*	n/a
1.07	Burden of government regulation, 2007	100
1.08	Extent and effect of taxation, 2007	99
1.09	Total tax rate,* 2007	86
1.10	Time required to start a business,* 2007	15
1.11	No. of procedures required to start a business,* 2007	19
1.12	Intensity of local competition, 2007	46
1.13	Freedom of the press, 2007	50
1.14	Accessibility of digital content, 2007	42

Political and regulatory environment — 52

2.01	Effectiveness of law-making bodies, 2007	60
2.02	Laws relating to ICT, 2007	70
2.03	Judicial independence, 2007	54
2.04	Intellectual property protection, 2007	67
2.05	Efficiency of legal framework, 2007	73
2.06	Property rights, 2007	55
2.07	Quality of competition in the ISP sector, 2007	43
2.08	No. of procedures to enforce a contract,* 2007	40
2.09	Time to enforce a contract,* 2007	67

Infrastructure environment — 73

3.01	Telephone lines,* 2005	80
3.02	Secure Internet servers,* 2006	53
3.03	Electricity production,* 2004	60
3.04	Availability of scientists and engineers, 2007	88
3.05	Quality of scientific research institutions, 2007	39
3.06	Tertiary enrollment,* 2003	81
3.07	Education expenditure,* 2005	36

Readiness component — 59

Individual readiness — 65

4.01	Quality of math and science education, 2007	102
4.02	Quality of the educational system, 2007	88
4.03	Internet access in schools, 2007	63
4.04	Buyer sophistication, 2007	56
4.05	Residential telephone connection charge,* 2005	27
4.06	Residential monthly telephone subscription,* 2005	81
4.07	High-speed monthly broadband subscription,* 2006	57
4.08	Lowest cost of broadband,* 2006	65
4.09	Cost of mobile telephone call,* 2005	65

Business readiness — 54

5.01	Extent of staff training, 2007	67
5.02	Local availability of research and training, 2007	59
5.03	Quality of management schools, 2007	59
5.04	Company spending on R&D, 2007	43
5.05	University-industry research collaboration, 2007	47
5.06	Business telephone connection charge,* 2005	28
5.07	Business monthly telephone subscription,* 2005	91
5.08	Local supplier quality, 2007	61
5.09	Local supplier quantity, 2007	83
5.10	Computer, comm., and other services imports,* 2005	46

Government readiness — 55

6.01	Government prioritization of ICT, 2007	44
6.02	Gov't procurement of advanced tech products, 2007	69
6.03	Importance of ICT to gov't vision of the future, 2007	56
6.04	E-Government Readiness Index,* 2007	76

Usage component — 36

Individual usage — 28

7.01	Mobile telephone subscribers,* 2005	25
7.02	Personal computers,* 2005	67
7.03	Broadband Internet subscribers,* 2005	60
7.04	Internet users,* 2005	26
7.05	Internet bandwidth,* 2005	4

Business usage — 58

8.01	Prevalence of foreign technology licensing, 2007	51
8.02	Firm-level technology absorption, 2007	53
8.03	Capacity for innovation, 2007	67
8.04	Availability of new telephone lines, 2007	67
8.05	Extent of business Internet use, 2007	43

Government usage — 52

9.01	Government success in ICT promotion, 2007	58
9.02	Availability of government online services, 2007	45
9.03	ICT use and government efficiency, 2007	42
9.04	Presence of ICT in government offices, 2007	51
9.05	E-Participation Index,* 2007	76

* Hard data

Note: For further details and explanation, please refer to the section "How to Read the Country/Economy Profiles" at the beginning of this chapter.

Japan

Key indicators

Population (millions), 2006	128.2
GDP (PPP) per capita (US$), 2006	32,529.7
Internet users per 100 inhabitants, 2006	68.3
Internet bandwidth (mB/s) per 10,000 inhabitants, 2005	10.4

Networked Readiness Index

Year (number of economies)	Rank
2007–2008 (127)	**19**
2006–2007 (122)	14
2005–2006 (115)	16

Global Competitiveness Index 2007–2008 (131)	8

Environment component — 18
Market environment — 14

1.01	Venture capital availability, 2007	37
1.02	Financial market sophistication, 2007	34
1.03	Availability of latest technologies, 2007	10
1.04	State of cluster development, 2007	12
1.05	Utility patents,* 2006	2
1.06	High-tech exports,* 2005	13
1.07	Burden of government regulation, 2007	16
1.08	Extent and effect of taxation, 2007	64
1.09	Total tax rate,* 2007	91
1.10	Time required to start a business,* 2007	48
1.11	No. of procedures required to start a business,* 2007	44
1.12	Intensity of local competition, 2007	3
1.13	Freedom of the press, 2007	33
1.14	Accessibility of digital content, 2007	20

Political and regulatory environment — 14

2.01	Effectiveness of law-making bodies, 2007	18
2.02	Laws relating to ICT, 2007	29
2.03	Judicial independence, 2007	21
2.04	Intellectual property protection, 2007	17
2.05	Efficiency of legal framework, 2007	15
2.06	Property rights, 2007	14
2.07	Quality of competition in the ISP sector, 2007	6
2.08	No. of procedures to enforce a contract,* 2007	15
2.09	Time to enforce a contract,* 2007	21

Infrastructure environment — 21

3.01	Telephone lines,* 2006	26
3.02	Secure Internet servers,* 2006	17
3.03	Electricity production,* 2004	18
3.04	Availability of scientists and engineers, 2007	2
3.05	Quality of scientific research institutions, 2007	12
3.06	Tertiary enrollment,* 2005	32
3.07	Education expenditure,* 2005	85

Readiness component — 12
Individual readiness — 27

4.01	Quality of math and science education, 2007	28
4.02	Quality of the educational system, 2007	28
4.03	Internet access in schools, 2007	26
4.04	Buyer sophistication, 2007	3
4.05	Residential telephone connection charge,* 2005	62
4.06	Residential monthly telephone subscription,* 2005	21
4.07	High-speed monthly broadband subscription,* 2006	5
4.08	Lowest cost of broadband,* 2006	1
4.09	Cost of mobile telephone call*	n/a

Business readiness — 9

5.01	Extent of staff training, 2007	4
5.02	Local availability of research and training, 2007	6
5.03	Quality of management schools, 2007	67
5.04	Company spending on R&D, 2007	3
5.05	University-industry research collaboration, 2007	14
5.06	Business telephone connection charge,* 2005	54
5.07	Business monthly telephone subscription,* 2005	29
5.08	Local supplier quality, 2007	4
5.09	Local supplier quantity, 2007	2
5.10	Computer, comm., and other services imports,* 2005	32

Government readiness — 14

6.01	Government prioritization of ICT, 2007	15
6.02	Gov't procurement of advanced tech products, 2007	16
6.03	Importance of ICT to gov't vision of the future, 2007	25
6.04	E-Government Readiness Index,* 2007	11

Usage component — 21
Individual usage — 22

7.01	Mobile telephone subscribers,* 2006	49
7.02	Personal computers,* 2005	11
7.03	Broadband Internet subscribers,* 2006	14
7.04	Internet users,* 2006	8
7.05	Internet bandwidth,* 2005	39

Business usage — 3

8.01	Prevalence of foreign technology licensing, 2007	12
8.02	Firm-level technology absorption, 2007	3
8.03	Capacity for innovation, 2007	3
8.04	Availability of new telephone lines, 2007	8
8.05	Extent of business Internet use, 2007	9

Government usage — 31

9.01	Government success in ICT promotion, 2007	34
9.02	Availability of government online services, 2007	49
9.03	ICT use and government efficiency, 2007	65
9.04	Presence of ICT in government offices, 2007	37
9.05	E-Participation Index,* 2007	11

* Hard data

Note: For further details and explanation, please refer to the section "How to Read the Country/Economy Profiles" at the beginning of this chapter.

Jordan

Key indicators

Population (millions), 2006...5.8
GDP (PPP) per capita (US$), 2006............................5,610.7
Internet users per 100 inhabitants, 2006 ....13.7
Internet bandwidth (mB/s) per 10,000 inhabitants, 2005.........0.5

Networked Readiness Index

Year (number of economies)	Rank
2007–2008 (127)	**47**
2006–2007 (122)	57
2005–2006 (115)	47

Global Competitiveness Index 2007–2008 (131)　　49

Environment component — 49
Market environment — 54
1.01　Venture capital availability, 2007..55
1.02　Financial market sophistication, 2007 64
1.03　Availability of latest technologies, 2007................................37
1.04　State of cluster development, 2007......................................56
1.05　Utility patents,* 2006 67
1.06　High-tech exports,* 2005 49
1.07　Burden of government regulation, 2007 25
1.08　Extent and effect of taxation, 2007 71
1.09　Total tax rate,* 2007 19
1.10　Time required to start a business,* 2007 27
1.11　No. of procedures required to start a business,* 2007 74
1.12　Intensity of local competition, 2007 33
1.13　Freedom of the press, 2007 116
1.14　Accessibility of digital content, 2007 47

Political and regulatory environment — 38
2.01　Effectiveness of law-making bodies, 2007 71
2.02　Laws relating to ICT, 2007..65
2.03　Judicial independence, 2007 40
2.04　Intellectual property protection, 2007 40
2.05　Efficiency of legal framework, 2007......................................38
2.06　Property rights, 2007 29
2.07　Quality of competition in the ISP sector, 2007 22
2.08　No. of procedures to enforce a contract,* 2007 75
2.09　Time to enforce a contract,* 2007 89

Infrastructure environment — 57
3.01　Telephone lines,* 2006...84
3.02　Secure Internet servers,* 2006 73
3.03　Electricity production,* 2004 77
3.04　Availability of scientists and engineers, 2007 38
3.05　Quality of scientific research institutions, 2007 59
3.06　Tertiary enrollment,* 2005..53
3.07　Education expenditure,* 2005..24

Readiness component — 52
Individual readiness — 55
4.01　Quality of math and science education, 2007.....................45
4.02　Quality of the educational system, 2007.............................36
4.03　Internet access in schools, 2007...47
4.04　Buyer sophistication, 2007 90
4.05　Residential telephone connection charge,* 2005 81
4.06　Residential monthly telephone subscription,* 2005 88
4.07　High-speed monthly broadband subscription,* 2006........44
4.08　Lowest cost of broadband,* 2006 47
4.09　Cost of mobile telephone call,* 2005....................................55

Business readiness — 77
5.01　Extent of staff training, 2007..57
5.02　Local availability of research and training, 2007.................58
5.03　Quality of management schools, 2007 64
5.04　Company spending on R&D, 2007...74
5.05　University-industry research collaboration, 2007................67
5.06　Business telephone connection charge,* 2005 82
5.07　Business monthly telephone subscription,* 2005 94
5.08　Local supplier quality, 2007 66
5.09　Local supplier quantity, 2007 51
5.10　Computer, comm., and other services imports,* 2005 ..101

Government readiness — 34
6.01　Government prioritization of ICT, 2007................................23
6.02　Gov't procurement of advanced tech products, 2007 38
6.03　Importance of ICT to gov't vision of the future, 2007.......23
6.04　E-Government Readiness Index,* 2007................................49

Usage component — 47
Individual usage — 63
7.01　Mobile telephone subscribers,* 2006...................................55
7.02　Personal computers,* 2006 71
7.03　Broadband Internet subscribers,* 2006 68
7.04　Internet users,* 2006 70
7.05　Internet bandwidth,* 2005 78

Business usage — 39
8.01　Prevalence of foreign technology licensing, 2007..............31
8.02　Firm-level technology absorption, 2007 42
8.03　Capacity for innovation, 2007..61
8.04　Availability of new telephone lines, 2007............................18
8.05　Extent of business Internet use, 2007..................................41

Government usage — 36
9.01　Government success in ICT promotion, 2007.....................22
9.02　Availability of government online services, 2007 83
9.03　ICT use and government efficiency, 2007...........................48
9.04　Presence of ICT in government offices, 2007 45
9.05　E-Participation Index,* 2007..15

* Hard data

Note: For further details and explanation, please refer to the section "How to Read the Country/Economy Profiles" at the beginning of this chapter.

Kazakhstan

Key indicators

Population (millions), 2006...14.8
GDP (PPP) per capita (US$), 2006.......................................9,568.1
Internet users per 100 inhabitants, 2006 ....8.4
Internet bandwidth (mB/s) per 10,000 inhabitants, 2006.........0.6

Networked Readiness Index

Year (number of economies)	Rank
2007–2008 (127)	71
2006–2007 (122)	73
2005–2006 (115)	60

Global Competitiveness Index 2007–2008 (131)   61

Environment component   59
Market environment   72

1.01 Venture capital availability, 2007...49
1.02 Financial market sophistication, 2007 72
1.03 Availability of latest technologies, 2007 88
1.04 State of cluster development, 2007......................................91
1.05 Utility patents,* 2006 81
1.06 High-tech exports,* 2005 87
1.07 Burden of government regulation, 2007 58
1.08 Extent and effect of taxation, 2007.......................................79
1.09 Total tax rate,* 2007...38
1.10 Time required to start a business,* 2007............................44
1.11 No. of procedures required to start a business,* 2007 44
1.12 Intensity of local competition, 2007 74
1.13 Freedom of the press, 2007..112
1.14 Accessibility of digital content, 2007 50

Political and regulatory environment   67

2.01 Effectiveness of law-making bodies, 2007 44
2.02 Laws relating to ICT, 2007...63
2.03 Judicial independence, 2007...98
2.04 Intellectual property protection, 2007 79
2.05 Efficiency of legal framework, 2007.....................................71
2.06 Property rights, 2007..90
2.07 Quality of competition in the ISP sector, 2007 98
2.08 No. of procedures to enforce a contract,* 2007 65
2.09 Time to enforce a contract,* 2007 6

Infrastructure environment   55

3.01 Telephone lines,* 2006...60
3.02 Secure Internet servers,* 2006...90
3.03 Electricity production,* 2004 47
3.04 Availability of scientists and engineers, 2007 95
3.05 Quality of scientific research institutions, 2007 61
3.06 Tertiary enrollment,* 2005...33
3.07 Education expenditure,* 2005...49

Readiness component   78
Individual readiness   96

4.01 Quality of math and science education, 2007....................67
4.02 Quality of the educational system, 2007............................62
4.03 Internet access in schools, 2007..50
4.04 Buyer sophistication, 2007 50
4.05 Residential telephone connection charge,* 2005 79
4.06 Residential monthly telephone subscription*...................n/a
4.07 High-speed monthly broadband subscription,* 2006........97
4.08 Lowest cost of broadband,* 2006 93
4.09 Cost of mobile telephone call,* 2005...................................75

Business readiness   72

5.01 Extent of staff training, 2007..92
5.02 Local availability of research and training, 2007 80
5.03 Quality of management schools, 2007 92
5.04 Company spending on R&D, 2007 64
5.05 University-industry research collaboration, 2007...............69
5.06 Business telephone connection charge,* 2005 94
5.07 Business monthly telephone subscription*......................n/a
5.08 Local supplier quality, 2007..81
5.09 Local supplier quantity, 2007..79
5.10 Computer, comm., and other services imports,* 2005 3

Government readiness   50

6.01 Government prioritization of ICT, 2007...............................56
6.02 Gov't procurement of advanced tech products, 2007 61
6.03 Importance of ICT to gov't vision of the future, 2007.......41
6.04 E-Government Readiness Index,* 2007..............................72

Usage component   79
Individual usage   76

7.01 Mobile telephone subscribers,* 2006..................................73
7.02 Personal computers*..n/a
7.03 Broadband Internet subscribers,* 2006 87
7.04 Internet users,* 2006..85
7.05 Internet bandwidth,* 2006...76

Business usage   86

8.01 Prevalence of foreign technology licensing, 2007.............91
8.02 Firm-level technology absorption, 2007 74
8.03 Capacity for innovation, 2007 63
8.04 Availability of new telephone lines, 2007...........................92
8.05 Extent of business Internet use, 2007................................77

Government usage   58

9.01 Government success in ICT promotion, 2007....................52
9.02 Availability of government online services, 2007 54
9.03 ICT use and government efficiency, 2007...........................57
9.04 Presence of ICT in government offices, 2007 65
9.05 E-Participation Index,* 2007...82

* Hard data

Note: For further details and explanation, please refer to the section "How to Read the Country/Economy Profiles" at the beginning of this chapter.

Kenya

Key indicators

Population (millions), 2006...35.1
GDP (PPP) per capita (US$), 2006...13,57.1
Internet users per 100 inhabitants, 2006 ....7.9
Internet bandwidth (mB/s) per 10,000 inhabitants, 2006..........0.2

Networked Readiness Index

Year (number of economies)   Rank

2007–2008 (127) 92
2006–2007 (122) 95
2005–2006 (115) 91

Global Competitiveness Index 2007–2008 (131)   99

Environment component   84
Market environment   98

1.01 Venture capital availability, 2007..67
1.02 Financial market sophistication, 2007 65
1.03 Availability of latest technologies, 2007................................87
1.04 State of cluster development, 2007......................................61
1.05 Utility patents,* 2006..78
1.06 High-tech exports,* 2005 83
1.07 Burden of government regulation, 2007 71
1.08 Extent and effect of taxation, 2007....................................110
1.09 Total tax rate,* 2007...84
1.10 Time required to start a business,* 2007..........................94
1.11 No. of procedures required to start a business,* 2007 98
1.12 Intensity of local competition, 2007 55
1.13 Freedom of the press, 2007...107
1.14 Accessibility of digital content, 2007.................................108

Political and regulatory environment   88

2.01 Effectiveness of law-making bodies, 2007 85
2.02 Laws relating to ICT, 2007..77
2.03 Judicial independence, 2007 95
2.04 Intellectual property protection, 2007 93
2.05 Efficiency of legal framework, 2007....................................90
2.06 Property rights, 2007..86
2.07 Quality of competition in the ISP sector, 2007 61
2.08 No. of procedures to enforce a contract,* 2007.............104
2.09 Time to enforce a contract,* 2007 47

Infrastructure environment   77

3.01 Telephone lines,* 2006..115
3.02 Secure Internet servers,* 2006...101
3.03 Electricity production,* 2004 106
3.04 Availability of scientists and engineers, 2007 50
3.05 Quality of scientific research institutions, 2007 31
3.06 Tertiary enrollment,* 2004...114
3.07 Education expenditure,* 2005..13

Readiness component   95
Individual readiness   107

4.01 Quality of math and science education, 2007...................69
4.02 Quality of the educational system, 2007...........................33
4.03 Internet access in schools, 2007......................................110
4.04 Buyer sophistication, 2007 85
4.05 Residential telephone connection charge,* 2005 100
4.06 Residential monthly telephone subscription,* 2005 116
4.07 High-speed monthly broadband subscription,* 2006........95
4.08 Lowest cost of broadband,* 2006 105
4.09 Cost of mobile telephone call,* 2005...............................108

Business readiness   66

5.01 Extent of staff training, 2007...54
5.02 Local availability of research and training, 2007...............42
5.03 Quality of management schools, 2007 69
5.04 Company spending on R&D, 2007.....................................31
5.05 University-industry research collaboration, 2007..............46
5.06 Business telephone connection charge,* 2005 87
5.07 Business monthly telephone subscription,* 2005 109
5.08 Local supplier quality, 2007 67
5.09 Local supplier quantity, 2007 47
5.10 Computer, comm., and other services imports,* 2005 53

Government readiness   93

6.01 Government prioritization of ICT, 2007............................103
6.02 Gov't procurement of advanced tech products, 2007 54
6.03 Importance of ICT to gov't vision of the future, 2007.......67
6.04 E-Government Readiness Index,* 2007 98

Usage component   91
Individual usage   105

7.01 Mobile telephone subscribers,* 2006.............................105
7.02 Personal computers,* 2005 106
7.03 Broadband Internet subscribers,* 2005 118
7.04 Internet users,* 2006 88
7.05 Internet bandwidth,* 2006 91

Business usage   78

8.01 Prevalence of foreign technology licensing, 2007.............48
8.02 Firm-level technology absorption, 2007 56
8.03 Capacity for innovation, 2007 56
8.04 Availability of new telephone lines, 2007........................113
8.05 Extent of business Internet use, 2007 75

Government usage   95

9.01 Government success in ICT promotion, 2007...................67
9.02 Availability of government online services, 2007 78
9.03 ICT use and government efficiency, 2007.........................72
9.04 Presence of ICT in government offices, 2007 97
9.05 E-Participation Index,* 2007...100

* Hard data

Note: For further details and explanation, please refer to the section "How to Read the Country/Economy Profiles" at the beginning of this chapter.

Korea, Rep.

Key indicators

Population (millions), 2006..48.0
GDP (PPP) per capita (US$), 2006.................................24,084.0
Internet users per 100 inhabitants, 2006 ....71.1
Internet bandwidth (mB/s) per 10,000 inhabitants, 2006.......10.4

Networked Readiness Index

Year (number of economies)	Rank
2007–2008 (127)	**9**
2006–2007 (122)	19
2005–2006 (115)	14

Global Competitiveness Index 2007–2008 (131)	11

Environment component — 17
Market environment — 7
1.01 Venture capital availability, 2007..17
1.02 Financial market sophistication, 2007 32
1.03 Availability of latest technologies, 2007 20
1.04 State of cluster development, 2007......................................3
1.05 Utility patents,* 2006 8
1.06 High-tech exports,* 2005 7
1.07 Burden of government regulation, 2007 8
1.08 Extent and effect of taxation, 2007.....................................30
1.09 Total tax rate,* 2007 29
1.10 Time required to start a business,* 2007..........................36
1.11 No. of procedures required to start a business,* 2007 74
1.12 Intensity of local competition, 2007 23
1.13 Freedom of the press, 2007..51
1.14 Accessibility of digital content, 2007....................................3

Political and regulatory environment — 20
2.01 Effectiveness of law-making bodies, 2007 32
2.02 Laws relating to ICT, 2007...7
2.03 Judicial independence, 2007 35
2.04 Intellectual property protection, 2007 23
2.05 Efficiency of legal framework, 2007...................................28
2.06 Property rights, 2007..24
2.07 Quality of competition in the ISP sector, 2007 1
2.08 No. of procedures to enforce a contract,* 2007 46
2.09 Time to enforce a contract,* 2007 6

Infrastructure environment — 17
3.01 Telephone lines,* 2006..10
3.02 Secure Internet servers,* 2006...51
3.03 Electricity production,* 2004 23
3.04 Availability of scientists and engineers, 2007 13
3.05 Quality of scientific research institutions, 2007 11
3.06 Tertiary enrollment,* 2006..2
3.07 Education expenditure,* 2005..75

Readiness component — 3
Individual readiness — 7
4.01 Quality of math and science education, 2007...................10
4.02 Quality of the educational system, 2007...........................19
4.03 Internet access in schools, 2007...4
4.04 Buyer sophistication, 2007 2
4.05 Residential telephone connection charge,* 2005 34
4.06 Residential monthly telephone subscription,* 2005 10
4.07 High-speed monthly broadband subscription,* 2006........27
4.08 Lowest cost of broadband,* 2006 3
4.09 Cost of mobile telephone call,* 2005.................................21

Business readiness — 11
5.01 Extent of staff training, 2007..5
5.02 Local availability of research and training, 2007.................14
5.03 Quality of management schools, 2007 26
5.04 Company spending on R&D, 2007..6
5.05 University-industry research collaboration, 2007................5
5.06 Business telephone connection charge,* 2005 27
5.07 Business monthly telephone subscription,* 2005 5
5.08 Local supplier quality, 2007..17
5.09 Local supplier quantity, 2007..7
5.10 Computer, comm., and other services imports,* 2005 34

Government readiness — 3
6.01 Government prioritization of ICT, 2007................................6
6.02 Gov't procurement of advanced tech products, 2007 2
6.03 Importance of ICT to gov't vision of the future, 2007.........7
6.04 E-Government Readiness Index,* 2007..............................6

Usage component — 4
Individual usage — 15
7.01 Mobile telephone subscribers,* 2006................................45
7.02 Personal computers,* 2005 19
7.03 Broadband Internet subscribers,* 2006 5
7.04 Internet users,* 2006 6
7.05 Internet bandwidth,* 2006 38

Business usage — 7
8.01 Prevalence of foreign technology licensing, 2007.............27
8.02 Firm-level technology absorption, 2007 13
8.03 Capacity for innovation, 2007...7
8.04 Availability of new telephone lines, 2007 26
8.05 Extent of business Internet use, 2007.................................1

Government usage — 3
9.01 Government success in ICT promotion, 2007.....................7
9.02 Availability of government online services, 2007................9
9.03 ICT use and government efficiency, 2007.........................12
9.04 Presence of ICT in government offices, 2007 3
9.05 E-Participation Index,* 2007..2

* Hard data

Note: For further details and explanation, please refer to the section "How to Read the Country/Economy Profiles" at the beginning of this chapter.

Kuwait

Key indicators

Population (millions), 2006...2.8
GDP (PPP) per capita (US$), 2006........................20,886.4
Internet users per 100 inhabitants, 2006 ....29.5
Internet bandwidth (mB/s) per 10,000 inhabitants, 2005.........3.3

Networked Readiness Index

Year (number of economies)	Rank
2007–2008 (127)	**52**
2006–2007 (122)	54
2005–2006 (115)	46

Global Competitiveness Index 2007–2008 (131)   30

Environment component   36
Market environment   29
1.01 Venture capital availability, 2007..........................32
1.02 Financial market sophistication, 2007 48
1.03 Availability of latest technologies, 2007................43
1.04 State of cluster development, 2007......................22
1.05 Utility patents,* 2006...35
1.06 High-tech exports* ....n/a
1.07 Burden of government regulation, 2007...............86
1.08 Extent and effect of taxation, 2007.........................5
1.09 Total tax rate,* 2007..1
1.10 Time required to start a business,* 2007.............81
1.11 No. of procedures required to start a business,* 2007 ..103
1.12 Intensity of local competition, 2007......................60
1.13 Freedom of the press, 2007..................................79
1.14 Accessibility of digital content, 2007....................53

Political and regulatory environment   51
2.01 Effectiveness of law-making bodies, 2007 42
2.02 Laws relating to ICT, 2007....................................87
2.03 Judicial independence, 2007................................31
2.04 Intellectual property protection, 2007 60
2.05 Efficiency of legal framework, 2007......................25
2.06 Property rights, 2007...42
2.07 Quality of competition in the ISP sector, 2007 52
2.08 No. of procedures to enforce a contract,* 2007..117
2.09 Time to enforce a contract,* 2007 70

Infrastructure environment   37
3.01 Telephone lines,* 2005..63
3.02 Secure Internet servers,* 2006..............................42
3.03 Electricity production,* 2004...................................5
3.04 Availability of scientists and engineers, 2007......49
3.05 Quality of scientific research institutions, 2007....46
3.06 Tertiary enrollment,* 2005......................................78
3.07 Education expenditure,* 2005................................10

Readiness component   60
Individual readiness   48
4.01 Quality of math and science education, 2007......73
4.02 Quality of the educational system, 2007..............77
4.03 Internet access in schools, 2007..........................45
4.04 Buyer sophistication, 2007....................................48
4.05 Residential telephone connection charge,* 2005....37
4.06 Residential monthly telephone subscription,* 2005....11
4.07 High-speed monthly broadband subscription,* 2006....47
4.08 Lowest cost of broadband,* 2006.........................48
4.09 Cost of mobile telephone call,* 2005....................60

Business readiness   53
5.01 Extent of staff training, 2007.................................48
5.02 Local availability of research and training, 2007....51
5.03 Quality of management schools, 2007 68
5.04 Company spending on R&D, 2007.......................70
5.05 University-industry research collaboration, 2007....71
5.06 Business telephone connection charge,* 2005....55
5.07 Business monthly telephone subscription,* 2005....33
5.08 Local supplier quality, 2007..................................36
5.09 Local supplier quantity, 2007................................12
5.10 Computer, comm., and other services imports,* 2005..115

Government readiness   80
6.01 Government prioritization of ICT, 2007................97
6.02 Gov't procurement of advanced tech products, 2007....80
6.03 Importance of ICT to gov't vision of the future, 2007....99
6.04 E-Government Readiness Index,* 2007...............55

Usage component   60
Individual usage   47
7.01 Mobile telephone subscribers,* 2005....................40
7.02 Personal computers,* 2005...................................36
7.03 Broadband Internet subscribers,* 2005................66
7.04 Internet users,* 2006...43
7.05 Internet bandwidth,* 2005.....................................56

Business usage   51
8.01 Prevalence of foreign technology licensing, 2007....38
8.02 Firm-level technology absorption, 2007 32
8.03 Capacity for innovation, 2007.............................106
8.04 Availability of new telephone lines, 2007.............51
8.05 Extent of business Internet use, 2007..................61

Government usage   97
9.01 Government success in ICT promotion, 2007......86
9.02 Availability of government online services, 2007....97
9.03 ICT use and government efficiency, 2007............98
9.04 Presence of ICT in government offices, 2007......78
9.05 E-Participation Index,* 2007..................................91

* Hard data

Note: For further details and explanation, please refer to the section "How to Read the Country/Economy Profiles" at the beginning of this chapter.

Kyrgyz Republic

Key indicators

Population (millions), 2006	5.3
GDP (PPP) per capita (US$), 2006	2,121.1
Internet users per 100 inhabitants, 2006	5.6
Internet bandwidth (mB/s) per 10,000 inhabitants, 2005	0.4

Networked Readiness Index

Year (number of economies)	Rank
2007–2008 (127)	**114**
2006–2007 (122)	105
2005–2006 (115)	103

Global Competitiveness Index 2007–2008 (131)	119

Environment component — 104

Market environment — 115

1.01	Venture capital availability, 2007	95
1.02	Financial market sophistication, 2007	114
1.03	Availability of latest technologies, 2007	124
1.04	State of cluster development, 2007	111
1.05	Utility patents,* 2006	86
1.06	High-tech exports,* 2005	79
1.07	Burden of government regulation, 2007	117
1.08	Extent and effect of taxation, 2007	113
1.09	Total tax rate,* 2007	102
1.10	Time required to start a business,* 2007	44
1.11	No. of procedures required to start a business,* 2007	44
1.12	Intensity of local competition, 2007	124
1.13	Freedom of the press, 2007	95
1.14	Accessibility of digital content, 2007	90

Political and regulatory environment — 103

2.01	Effectiveness of law-making bodies, 2007	86
2.02	Laws relating to ICT, 2007	117
2.03	Judicial independence, 2007	120
2.04	Intellectual property protection, 2007	102
2.05	Efficiency of legal framework, 2007	112
2.06	Property rights, 2007	118
2.07	Quality of competition in the ISP sector, 2007	101
2.08	No. of procedures to enforce a contract,* 2007	75
2.09	Time to enforce a contract,* 2007	2

Infrastructure environment — 84

3.01	Telephone lines,* 2005	91
3.02	Secure Internet servers,* 2006	90
3.03	Electricity production,* 2004	59
3.04	Availability of scientists and engineers, 2007	114
3.05	Quality of scientific research institutions, 2007	110
3.06	Tertiary enrollment,* 2005	47
3.07	Education expenditure,* 2005	53

Readiness component — 106

Individual readiness — 97

4.01	Quality of math and science education, 2007	72
4.02	Quality of the educational system, 2007	69
4.03	Internet access in schools, 2007	80
4.04	Buyer sophistication, 2007	104
4.05	Residential telephone connection charge,* 2005	115
4.06	Residential monthly telephone subscription,* 2005	90
4.07	High-speed monthly broadband subscription,* 2006	91
4.08	Lowest cost of broadband,* 2006	102
4.09	Cost of mobile telephone call,* 2005	94

Business readiness — 115

5.01	Extent of staff training, 2007	121
5.02	Local availability of research and training, 2007	115
5.03	Quality of management schools, 2007	114
5.04	Company spending on R&D, 2007	114
5.05	University-industry research collaboration, 2007	109
5.06	Business telephone connection charge,* 2005	112
5.07	Business monthly telephone subscription,* 2005	97
5.08	Local supplier quality, 2007	118
5.09	Local supplier quantity, 2007	120
5.10	Computer, comm., and other services imports,* 2005	47

Government readiness — 119

6.01	Government prioritization of ICT, 2007	111
6.02	Gov't procurement of advanced tech products, 2007	124
6.03	Importance of ICT to gov't vision of the future, 2007	123
6.04	E-Government Readiness Index,* 2007	87

Usage component — 120

Individual usage — 112

7.01	Mobile telephone subscribers,* 2005	117
7.02	Personal computers,* 2005	99
7.03	Broadband Internet subscribers,* 2005	100
7.04	Internet users,* 2006	98
7.05	Internet bandwidth,* 2005	84

Business usage — 115

8.01	Prevalence of foreign technology licensing, 2007	122
8.02	Firm-level technology absorption, 2007	120
8.03	Capacity for innovation, 2007	81
8.04	Availability of new telephone lines, 2007	107
8.05	Extent of business Internet use, 2007	116

Government usage — 122

9.01	Government success in ICT promotion, 2007	122
9.02	Availability of government online services, 2007	113
9.03	ICT use and government efficiency, 2007	119
9.04	Presence of ICT in government offices, 2007	122
9.05	E-Participation Index,* 2007	69

* Hard data

Note: For further details and explanation, please refer to the section "How to Read the Country/Economy Profiles" at the beginning of this chapter.

Latvia

Key indicators

Population (millions), 2006	2.3
GDP (PPP) per capita (US$), 2006	15,806.2
Internet users per 100 inhabitants, 2006	46.6
Internet bandwidth (mB/s) per 10,000 inhabitants, 2006	32.1

Networked Readiness Index

Year (number of economies)	Rank
2007–2008 (127)	**44**
2006–2007 (122)	42
2005–2006 (115)	51

Global Competitiveness Index 2007–2008 (131)	45

Environment component — 44
Market environment — 45

1.01	Venture capital availability, 2007	46
1.02	Financial market sophistication, 2007	62
1.03	Availability of latest technologies, 2007	58
1.04	State of cluster development, 2007	83
1.05	Utility patents,* 2006	47
1.06	High-tech exports,* 2005	55
1.07	Burden of government regulation, 2007	55
1.08	Extent and effect of taxation, 2007	51
1.09	Total tax rate,* 2007	24
1.10	Time required to start a business,* 2007	33
1.11	No. of procedures required to start a business,* 2007	9
1.12	Intensity of local competition, 2007	62
1.13	Freedom of the press, 2007	56
1.14	Accessibility of digital content, 2007	59

Political and regulatory environment — 43

2.01	Effectiveness of law-making bodies, 2007	67
2.02	Laws relating to ICT, 2007	61
2.03	Judicial independence, 2007	61
2.04	Intellectual property protection, 2007	69
2.05	Efficiency of legal framework, 2007	72
2.06	Property rights, 2007	54
2.07	Quality of competition in the ISP sector, 2007	51
2.08	No. of procedures to enforce a contract,* 2007	8
2.09	Time to enforce a contract,* 2007	12

Infrastructure environment — 40

3.01	Telephone lines,* 2006	40
3.02	Secure Internet servers,* 2006	38
3.03	Electricity production,* 2004	68
3.04	Availability of scientists and engineers, 2007	102
3.05	Quality of scientific research institutions, 2007	68
3.06	Tertiary enrollment,* 2005	12
3.07	Education expenditure,* 2005	26

Readiness component — 53
Individual readiness — 37

4.01	Quality of math and science education, 2007	41
4.02	Quality of the educational system, 2007	41
4.03	Internet access in schools, 2007	34
4.04	Buyer sophistication, 2007	66
4.05	Residential telephone connection charge,* 2005	61
4.06	Residential monthly telephone subscription,* 2005	50
4.07	High-speed monthly broadband subscription,* 2006	70
4.08	Lowest cost of broadband,* 2006	67
4.09	Cost of mobile telephone call,* 2005	8

Business readiness — 50

5.01	Extent of staff training, 2007	49
5.02	Local availability of research and training, 2007	64
5.03	Quality of management schools, 2007	45
5.04	Company spending on R&D, 2007	57
5.05	University industry research collaboration, 2007	61
5.06	Business telephone connection charge,* 2005	52
5.07	Business monthly telephone subscription,* 2005	52
5.08	Local supplier quality, 2007	55
5.09	Local supplier quantity, 2007	89
5.10	Computer, comm., and other services imports,* 2005	59

Government readiness — 67

6.01	Government prioritization of ICT, 2007	89
6.02	Gov't procurement of advanced tech products, 2007	94
6.03	Importance of ICT to gov't vision of the future, 2007	93
6.04	E-Government Readiness Index,* 2007	36

Usage component — 44
Individual usage — 35

7.01	Mobile telephone subscribers,* 2006	35
7.02	Personal computers,* 2005	32
7.03	Broadband Internet subscribers,* 2006	45
7.04	Internet users,* 2006	25
7.05	Internet bandwidth,* 2006	22

Business usage — 55

8.01	Prevalence of foreign technology licensing, 2007	76
8.02	Firm-level technology absorption, 2007	65
8.03	Capacity for innovation, 2007	54
8.04	Availability of new telephone lines, 2007	53
8.05	Extent of business Internet use, 2007	39

Government usage — 61

9.01	Government success in ICT promotion, 2007	98
9.02	Availability of government online services, 2007	74
9.03	ICT use and government efficiency, 2007	76
9.04	Presence of ICT in government offices, 2007	33
9.05	E-Participation Index,* 2007	53

* Hard data

Note: For further details and explanation, please refer to the section "How to Read the Country/Economy Profiles" at the beginning of this chapter.

Lesotho

Key indicators

Population (millions), 2006..1.8
GDP (PPP) per capita (US$), 2006......................................2,251.0
Internet users per 100 inhabitants, 2005 ....2.9
Internet bandwidth (mB/s) per 10,000 inhabitants, 2005.........0.0

Networked Readiness Index

Year (number of economies)	Rank
2007–2008 (127)	**122**
2006–2007 (122)	116
2005–2006 (115)	n/a

Global Competitiveness Index 2007–2008 (131) 124

Environment component — 102

Market environment — 113

1.01 Venture capital availability, 2007 121
1.02 Financial market sophistication, 2007 121
1.03 Availability of latest technologies, 2007 117
1.04 State of cluster development, 2007 97
1.05 Utility patents,* 2006 86
1.06 High-tech exports* ....n/a
1.07 Burden of government regulation, 2007 118
1.08 Extent and effect of taxation, 2007 95
1.09 Total tax rate,* 2007 6
1.10 Time required to start a business,* 2007 110
1.11 No. of procedures required to start a business,* 2007 44
1.12 Intensity of local competition, 2007 117
1.13 Freedom of the press, 2007 108
1.14 Accessibility of digital content, 2007 127

Political and regulatory environment — 114

2.01 Effectiveness of law-making bodies, 2007 96
2.02 Laws relating to ICT, 2007 109
2.03 Judicial independence, 2007 75
2.04 Intellectual property protection, 2007 115
2.05 Efficiency of legal framework, 2007 85
2.06 Property rights, 2007 123
2.07 Quality of competition in the ISP sector, 2007 117
2.08 No. of procedures to enforce a contract,* 2007 94
2.09 Time to enforce a contract,* 2007 91

Infrastructure environment — 75

3.01 Telephone lines,* 2005 107
3.02 Secure Internet servers* ....n/a
3.03 Electricity production* ....n/a
3.04 Availability of scientists and engineers, 2007 122
3.05 Quality of scientific research institutions, 2007 120
3.06 Tertiary enrollment,* 2005 110
3.07 Education expenditure,* 2005 12

Readiness component — 122

Individual readiness — 116

4.01 Quality of math and science education, 2007 117
4.02 Quality of the educational system, 2007 97
4.03 Internet access in schools, 2007 125
4.04 Buyer sophistication, 2007 115
4.05 Residential telephone connection charge,* 2005 109
4.06 Residential monthly telephone subscription,* 2005 117
4.07 High-speed monthly broadband subscription* ....n/a
4.08 Lowest cost of broadband* ....n/a
4.09 Cost of mobile telephone call,* 2005 105

Business readiness — 126

5.01 Extent of staff training, 2007 103
5.02 Local availability of research and training, 2007 122
5.03 Quality of management schools, 2007 122
5.04 Company spending on R&D, 2007 121
5.05 University-industry research collaboration, 2007 123
5.06 Business telephone connection charge,* 2005 103
5.07 Business monthly telephone subscription,* 2005 111
5.08 Local supplier quality, 2007 127
5.09 Local supplier quantity, 2007 127
5.10 Computer, comm., and other services imports,* 2005 ..116

Government readiness — 117

6.01 Government prioritization of ICT, 2007 116
6.02 Gov't procurement of advanced tech products, 2007 113
6.03 Importance of ICT to gov't vision of the future, 2007 119
6.04 E-Government Readiness Index,* 2007 92

Usage component — 122

Individual usage — 113

7.01 Mobile telephone subscribers,* 2005 110
7.02 Personal computers,* 2005 126
7.03 Broadband Internet subscribers,* 2005 112
7.04 Internet users,* 2005 111
7.05 Internet bandwidth,* 2005 117

Business usage — 122

8.01 Prevalence of foreign technology licensing, 2007 114
8.02 Firm-level technology absorption, 2007 115
8.03 Capacity for innovation, 2007 122
8.04 Availability of new telephone lines, 2007 121
8.05 Extent of business Internet use, 2007 122

Government usage — 121

9.01 Government success in ICT promotion, 2007 112
9.02 Availability of government online services, 2007 107
9.03 ICT use and government efficiency, 2007 121
9.04 Presence of ICT in government offices, 2007 123
9.05 E-Participation Index,* 2007 82

* Hard data

Note: For further details and explanation, please refer to the section "How to Read the Country/Economy Profiles" at the beginning of this chapter.

Libya

Key indicators

Population (millions), 2006..6.0
GDP (PPP) per capita (US$), 2006.................................12,847.6
Internet users per 100 inhabitants, 2005..............................4.0
Internet bandwidth (mB/s) per 10,000 inhabitants, 2006.........0.2

Networked Readiness Index

Year (number of economies)	Rank
2007–2008 (127)	**105**
2006–2007 (122)	n/a
2005–2006 (115)	n/a

Global Competitiveness Index 2007–2008 (131)	88

Environment component — 109
Market environment — 123

1.01 Venture capital availability, 2007...114
1.02 Financial market sophistication, 2007..................................127
1.03 Availability of latest technologies, 2007................................83
1.04 State of cluster development, 2007.....................................115
1.05 Utility patents,* 2006...86
1.06 High-tech exports*..n/a
1.07 Burden of government regulation, 2007................................97
1.08 Extent and effect of taxation, 2007..44
1.09 Total tax rate*..n/a
1.10 Time required to start a business*.......................................n/a
1.11 No. of procedures required to start a business*................n/a
1.12 Intensity of local competition, 2007....................................114
1.13 Freedom of the press, 2007...124
1.14 Accessibility of digital content, 2007...................................117

Political and regulatory environment — 102

2.01 Effectiveness of law-making bodies, 2007............................57
2.02 Laws relating to ICT, 2007..126
2.03 Judicial independence, 2007...60
2.04 Intellectual property protection, 2007....................................91
2.05 Efficiency of legal framework, 2007.......................................64
2.06 Property rights, 2007...97
2.07 Quality of competition in the ISP sector, 2007...................110
2.08 No. of procedures to enforce a contract*...........................n/a
2.09 Time to enforce a contract*...n/a

Infrastructure environment — 72

3.01 Telephone lines,* 2006..93
3.02 Secure Internet servers,* 2006...101
3.03 Electricity production,* 2004...52
3.04 Availability of scientists and engineers, 2007.......................53
3.05 Quality of scientific research institutions, 2007....................99
3.06 Tertiary enrollment,* 2003..31
3.07 Education expenditure*...n/a

Readiness component — 98
Individual readiness — 93

4.01 Quality of math and science education, 2007.......................95
4.02 Quality of the educational system, 2007.............................121
4.03 Internet access in schools, 2007..123
4.04 Buyer sophistication, 2007..108
4.05 Residential telephone connection charge,* 2006.................38
4.06 Residential monthly telephone subscription,* 2006..............3
4.07 High-speed monthly broadband subscription*...................n/a
4.08 Lowest cost of broadband,* 2006..88
4.09 Cost of mobile telephone call,* 2006....................................38

Business readiness — 98

5.01 Extent of staff training, 2007..104
5.02 Local availability of research and training, 2007................111
5.03 Quality of management schools, 2007................................123
5.04 Company spending on R&D, 2007.......................................117
5.05 University-industry research collaboration, 2007...............121
5.06 Business telephone connection charge,* 2006....................69
5.07 Business monthly telephone subscription,* 2006................51
5.08 Local supplier quality, 2007...89
5.09 Local supplier quantity, 2007...74
5.10 Computer, comm., and other services imports,* 2005.....103

Government readiness — 113

6.01 Government prioritization of ICT, 2007................................109
6.02 Gov't procurement of advanced tech products, 2007........114
6.03 Importance of ICT to gov't vision of the future, 2007........111
6.04 E-Government Readiness Index,* 2007.................................96

Usage component — 115
Individual usage — 84

7.01 Mobile telephone subscribers,* 2006....................................64
7.02 Personal computers,* 2005...96
7.03 Broadband Internet subscribers,* 2005...............................118
7.04 Internet users,* 2005...106
7.05 Internet bandwidth,* 2006..92

Business usage — 117

8.01 Prevalence of foreign technology licensing, 2007................95
8.02 Firm-level technology absorption, 2007..............................106
8.03 Capacity for innovation, 2007...126
8.04 Availability of new telephone lines, 2007............................122
8.05 Extent of business Internet use, 2007.................................117

Government usage — 117

9.01 Government success in ICT promotion, 2007.....................105
9.02 Availability of government online services, 2007...............125
9.03 ICT use and government efficiency, 2007...........................124
9.04 Presence of ICT in government offices, 2007.....................114
9.05 E-Participation Index,* 2007...58

* Hard data

Note: For further details and explanation, please refer to the section "How to Read the Country/Economy Profiles" at the beginning of this chapter.

Lithuania

Key indicators

Population (millions), 2006..3.4
GDP (PPP) per capita (US$), 2006.....................................16,373.5
Internet users per 100 inhabitants, 2006 ....31.7
Internet bandwidth (mB/s) per 10,000 inhabitants, 2006.......27.1

Networked Readiness Index

Year (number of economies)	Rank
2007–2008 (127)	**33**
2006–2007 (122)	39
2005–2006 (115)	44

Global Competitiveness Index 2007–2008 (131) — 38

Environment component — 34
Market environment — 47
1.01 Venture capital availability, 2007..47
1.02 Financial market sophistication, 2007 54
1.03 Availability of latest technologies, 2007 56
1.04 State of cluster development, 2007.......................................57
1.05 Utility patents,* 2006 34
1.06 High-tech exports,* 2005 46
1.07 Burden of government regulation, 2007 43
1.08 Extent and effect of taxation, 2007..68
1.09 Total tax rate,* 2007 74
1.10 Time required to start a business,* 2007..............................54
1.11 No. of procedures required to start a business,* 2007 34
1.12 Intensity of local competition, 2007 37
1.13 Freedom of the press, 2007..35
1.14 Accessibility of digital content, 2007.....................................34

Political and regulatory environment — 37
2.01 Effectiveness of law-making bodies, 2007 70
2.02 Laws relating to ICT, 2007..39
2.03 Judicial independence, 2007 73
2.04 Intellectual property protection, 2007 59
2.05 Efficiency of legal framework, 2007......................................69
2.06 Property rights, 2007 48
2.07 Quality of competition in the ISP sector, 2007 31
2.08 No. of procedures to enforce a contract,* 2007 15
2.09 Time to enforce a contract,* 2007 3

Infrastructure environment — 32
3.01 Telephone lines,* 2006...56
3.02 Secure Internet servers,* 2006...48
3.03 Electricity production,* 2004...38
3.04 Availability of scientists and engineers, 2007 43
3.05 Quality of scientific research institutions, 2007 42
3.06 Tertiary enrollment,* 2005...11
3.07 Education expenditure,* 2005...20

Readiness component — 38
Individual readiness — 35
4.01 Quality of math and science education, 2007.....................17
4.02 Quality of the educational system, 2007..............................43
4.03 Internet access in schools, 2007..32
4.04 Buyer sophistication, 2007..57
4.05 Residential telephone connection charge,* 2005 67
4.06 Residential monthly telephone subscription,* 2005 56
4.07 High-speed monthly broadband subscription,* 2006........33
4.08 Lowest cost of broadband,* 2006 27
4.09 Cost of mobile telephone call,* 2005....................................41

Business readiness — 48
5.01 Extent of staff training, 2007..41
5.02 Local availability of research and training, 2007 48
5.03 Quality of management schools, 2007 48
5.04 Company spending on R&D, 2007...48
5.05 University-industry research collaboration, 2007................50
5.06 Business telephone connection charge,* 2005 59
5.07 Business monthly telephone subscription,* 2005 45
5.08 Local supplier quality, 2007..43
5.09 Local supplier quantity, 2007..49
5.10 Computer, comm., and other services imports,* 2005 96

Government readiness — 38
6.01 Government prioritization of ICT, 2007.................................41
6.02 Gov't procurement of advanced tech products, 2007 62
6.03 Importance of ICT to gov't vision of the future, 2007.......73
6.04 E-Government Readiness Index,* 2007...............................28

Usage component — 31
Individual usage — 30
7.01 Mobile telephone subscribers,* 2006.....................................2
7.02 Personal computers,* 2005 41
7.03 Broadband Internet subscribers,* 2006 31
7.04 Internet users,* 2006..41
7.05 Internet bandwidth,* 2006...26

Business usage — 42
8.01 Prevalence of foreign technology licensing, 2007.............60
8.02 Firm-level technology absorption, 2007 45
8.03 Capacity for innovation, 2007...44
8.04 Availability of new telephone lines, 2007.............................48
8.05 Extent of business Internet use, 2007 33

Government usage — 32
9.01 Government success in ICT promotion, 2007.....................45
9.02 Availability of government online services, 2007 34
9.03 ICT use and government efficiency, 2007............................44
9.04 Presence of ICT in government offices, 2007 29
9.05 E-Participation Index,* 2007...19

* Hard data

Note: For further details and explanation, please refer to the section "How to Read the Country/Economy Profiles" at the beginning of this chapter.

Luxembourg

Key indicators

Population (millions), 2006..0.5
GDP (PPP) per capita (US$), 2006.................................81,510.6
Internet users per 100 inhabitants, 2006...........................72.0
Internet bandwidth (mB/s) per 10,000 inhabitants, 2004.......32.4

Networked Readiness Index

Year (number of economies)   Rank
2007–2008 (127) **24**
2006–2007 (122) 25
2005–2006 (115) 26

Global Competitiveness Index 2007–2008 (131)   25

Environment component — 23
Market environment — 20
1.01 Venture capital availability, 2007..........................10
1.02 Financial market sophistication, 2007 4
1.03 Availability of latest technologies, 2007................39
1.04 State of cluster development, 2007........................34
1.05 Utility patents,* 2006 12
1.06 High-tech exports,* 2004 53
1.07 Burden of government regulation, 2007................21
1.08 Extent and effect of taxation, 2007........................13
1.09 Total tax rate,* 2007...31
1.10 Time required to start a business,* 2007..............54
1.11 No. of procedures required to start a business,* 2007....19
1.12 Intensity of local competition, 2007......................48
1.13 Freedom of the press, 2007..................................28
1.14 Accessibility of digital content, 2007.....................28

Political and regulatory environment — 18
2.01 Effectiveness of law-making bodies, 2007............17
2.02 Laws relating to ICT, 2007.....................................26
2.03 Judicial independence, 2007.................................20
2.04 Intellectual property protection, 2007...................18
2.05 Efficiency of legal framework, 2007......................19
2.06 Property rights, 2007..20
2.07 Quality of competition in the ISP sector, 2007.....46
2.08 No. of procedures to enforce a contract,* 2007......5
2.09 Time to enforce a contract,* 2007.........................22

Infrastructure environment — 35
3.01 Telephone lines,* 2006...14
3.02 Secure Internet servers,* 2006................................7
3.03 Electricity production,* 2003..................................35
3.04 Availability of scientists and engineers, 2007.......81
3.05 Quality of scientific research institutions, 2007....54
3.06 Tertiary enrollment,* 2004......................................93
3.07 Education expenditure,* 2005................................76

Readiness component — 26
Individual readiness — 24
4.01 Quality of math and science education, 2007......38
4.02 Quality of the educational system, 2007..............37
4.03 Internet access in schools, 2007............................19
4.04 Buyer sophistication, 2007....................................14
4.05 Residential telephone connection charge,* 2005....5
4.06 Residential monthly telephone subscription,* 2005....8
4.07 High-speed monthly broadband subscription,* 2006....7
4.08 Lowest cost of broadband,* 2006..........................20
4.09 Cost of mobile telephone call,* 2006......................5

Business readiness — 38
5.01 Extent of staff training, 2007.................................18
5.02 Local availability of research and training, 2007..44
5.03 Quality of management schools, 2007..................88
5.04 Company spending on R&D, 2007.........................22
5.05 University-industry research collaboration, 2007....40
5.06 Business telephone connection charge,* 2005.......5
5.07 Business monthly telephone subscription,* 2005....3
5.08 Local supplier quality, 2007...................................31
5.09 Local supplier quantity, 2007.................................68
5.10 Computer, comm., and other services imports,* 2005....62

Government readiness — 21
6.01 Government prioritization of ICT, 2007.................37
6.02 Gov't procurement of advanced tech products, 2007....9
6.03 Importance of ICT to gov's vision of the future, 2007....30
6.04 E-Government Readiness Index,* 2007................14

Usage component — 20
Individual usage — 9
7.01 Mobile telephone subscribers,* 2006......................1
7.02 Personal computers,* 2005....................................12
7.03 Broadband Internet subscribers,* 2006.................15
7.04 Internet users,* 2006..5
7.05 Internet bandwidth,* 2004......................................21

Business usage — 27
8.01 Prevalence of foreign technology licensing, 2007....42
8.02 Firm-level technology absorption, 2007................36
8.03 Capacity for innovation, 2007................................18
8.04 Availability of new telephone lines, 2007.............38
8.05 Extent of business Internet use, 2007...................30

Government usage — 25
9.01 Government success in ICT promotion, 2007.......29
9.02 Availability of government online services, 2007....38
9.03 ICT use and government efficiency, 2007.............41
9.04 Presence of ICT in government offices, 2007.......30
9.05 E-Participation Index,* 2007..................................11

* Hard data

Note: For further details and explanation, please refer to the section "How to Read the Country/Economy Profiles" at the beginning of this chapter.

Macedonia, FYR

Key indicators

Population (millions), 2006...2.0
GDP (PPP) per capita (US$), 2006.......................7,680.5
Internet users per 100 inhabitants, 2006 ....13.2
Internet bandwidth (mB/s) per 10,000 inhabitants, 2006.........0.2

Networked Readiness Index

Year (number of economies)	Rank
2007–2008 (127)	**83**
2006–2007 (122)	81
2005–2006 (115)	82

Global Competitiveness Index 2007–2008 (131) — 94

Environment component — 82
Market environment — 93
1.01 Venture capital availability, 2007..........................59
1.02 Financial market sophistication, 2007 91
1.03 Availability of latest technologies, 2007 111
1.04 State of cluster development, 2007 113
1.05 Utility patents,* 2006 86
1.06 High-tech exports,* 2005 74
1.07 Burden of government regulation, 2007 74
1.08 Extent and effect of taxation, 2007........................67
1.09 Total tax rate,* 2007...79
1.10 Time required to start a business,* 2007.............30
1.11 No. of procedures required to start a business,* 2007 58
1.12 Intensity of local competition, 2007 98
1.13 Freedom of the press, 2007.....................................81
1.14 Accessibility of digital content, 2007...................112

Political and regulatory environment — 101
2.01 Effectiveness of law-making bodies, 2007 90
2.02 Laws relating to ICT, 2007..85
2.03 Judicial independence, 2007 106
2.04 Intellectual property protection, 2007 114
2.05 Efficiency of legal framework, 2007....................107
2.06 Property rights, 2007...103
2.07 Quality of competition in the ISP sector, 2007 ..116
2.08 No. of procedures to enforce a contract,* 2007 ...75
2.09 Time to enforce a contract,* 2007 28

Infrastructure environment — 59
3.01 Telephone lines,* 2006..55
3.02 Secure Internet servers,* 2006 85
3.03 Electricity production,* 2004 55
3.04 Availability of scientists and engineers, 2007 63
3.05 Quality of scientific research institutions, 2007 ..87
3.06 Tertiary enrollment,* 2005..66
3.07 Education expenditure,* 2005..................................39

Readiness component — 75
Individual readiness — 69
4.01 Quality of math and science education, 2007.....49
4.02 Quality of the educational system, 2007..............55
4.03 Internet access in schools, 2007.............................98
4.04 Buyer sophistication, 2007 102
4.05 Residential telephone connection charge,* 2006 ..59
4.06 Residential monthly telephone subscription,* 2006 89
4.07 High-speed monthly broadband subscription,* 2006.....84
4.08 Lowest cost of broadband,* 2006 62
4.09 Cost of mobile telephone call,* 2006.....................93

Business readiness — 81
5.01 Extent of staff training, 2007...................................78
5.02 Local availability of research and training, 2007....93
5.03 Quality of management schools, 2007 91
5.04 Company spending on R&D, 2007.......................104
5.05 University-industry research collaboration, 2007....79
5.06 Business telephone connection charge,* 2006 ..50
5.07 Business monthly telephone subscription,* 2006 ..87
5.08 Local supplier quality, 2007 97
5.09 Local supplier quantity, 2007 100
5.10 Computer, comm., and other services imports,* 2005 22

Government readiness — 84
6.01 Government prioritization of ICT, 2007.................92
6.02 Gov't procurement of advanced tech products, 2007 105
6.03 Importance of ICT to gov't vision of the future, 2007.......79
6.04 E-Government Readiness Index,* 2007................68

Usage component — 92
Individual usage — 58
7.01 Mobile telephone subscribers,* 2006....................61
7.02 Personal computers,* 2005 37
7.03 Broadband Internet subscribers,* 2006 57
7.04 Internet users,* 2006..71
7.05 Internet bandwidth,* 2006 96

Business usage — 102
8.01 Prevalence of foreign technology licensing, 2007 101
8.02 Firm-level technology absorption, 2007 125
8.03 Capacity for innovation, 2007 83
8.04 Availability of new telephone lines, 2007............63
8.05 Extent of business Internet use, 2007 123

Government usage — 100
9.01 Government success in ICT promotion, 2007.....92
9.02 Availability of government online services, 2007 89
9.03 ICT use and government efficiency, 2007..........102
9.04 Presence of ICT in government offices, 2007 92
9.05 E-Participation Index,* 2007..................................110

* Hard data

Note: For further details and explanation, please refer to the section "How to Read the Country/Economy Profiles" at the beginning of this chapter.

Madagascar

Key indicators

Population (millions), 2006...19.1
GDP (PPP) per capita (US$), 2006.....................................954.2
Internet users per 100 inhabitants, 2005 ....0.5
Internet bandwidth (mB/s) per 10,000 inhabitants, 2006.........0.0

Networked Readiness Index

Year (number of economies) Rank
2007–2008 (127) 104
2006–2007 (122) 102
2005–2006 (115) 102

Global Competitiveness Index 2007–2008 (131) 118

Environment component — 106
Market environment — 91
1.01 Venture capital availability, 2007 93
1.02 Financial market sophistication, 2007 115
1.03 Availability of latest technologies, 2007 89
1.04 State of cluster development, 2007 100
1.05 Utility patents,* 2006 86
1.06 High-tech exports,* 2005 89
1.07 Burden of government regulation, 2007 92
1.08 Extent and effect of taxation, 2007 75
1.09 Total tax rate,* 2007 68
1.10 Time required to start a business,* 2007 9
1.11 No. of procedures required to start a business,* 2007 9
1.12 Intensity of local competition, 2007 108
1.13 Freedom of the press, 2007 103
1.14 Accessibility of digital content, 2007 119

Political and regulatory environment — 99
2.01 Effectiveness of law-making bodies, 2007 84
2.02 Laws relating to ICT, 2007 102
2.03 Judicial independence, 2007 94
2.04 Intellectual property protection, 2007 80
2.05 Efficiency of legal framework, 2007 83
2.06 Property rights, 2007 108
2.07 Quality of competition in the ISP sector, 2007 ..95
2.08 No. of procedures to enforce a contract,* 2007 65
2.09 Time to enforce a contract,* 2007 105

Infrastructure environment — 105
3.01 Telephone lines,* 2006 119
3.02 Secure Internet servers,* 2006 101
3.03 Electricity production* ....n/a
3.04 Availability of scientists and engineers, 2007 61
3.05 Quality of scientific research institutions, 2007 ..103
3.06 Tertiary enrollment,* 2005 116
3.07 Education expenditure,* 2005 105

Readiness component — 104
Individual readiness — 112
4.01 Quality of math and science education, 2007 80
4.02 Quality of the educational system, 2007 98
4.03 Internet access in schools, 2007 113
4.04 Buyer sophistication, 2007 124
4.05 Residential telephone connection charge,* 2006 106
4.06 Residential monthly telephone subscription,* 2006 118
4.07 High-speed monthly broadband subscription* ......n/a
4.08 Lowest cost of broadband,* 2006 95
4.09 Cost of mobile telephone call,* 2006 115

Business readiness — 102
5.01 Extent of staff training, 2007 105
5.02 Local availability of research and training, 2007 105
5.03 Quality of management schools, 2007 72
5.04 Company spending on R&D, 2007 84
5.05 University-industry research collaboration, 2007 93
5.06 Business telephone connection charge,* 2006 100
5.07 Business monthly telephone subscription,* 2006 115
5.08 Local supplier quality, 2007 106
5.09 Local supplier quantity, 2007 92
5.10 Computer, comm., and other services imports,* 2005 40

Government readiness — 77
6.01 Government prioritization of ICT, 2007 53
6.02 Gov't procurement of advanced tech products, 2007 52
6.03 Importance of ICT to gov't vision of the future, 2007 60
6.04 E-Government Readiness Index,* 2007 105

Usage component — 104
Individual usage — 120
7.01 Mobile telephone subscribers,* 2006 122
7.02 Personal computers,* 2005 117
7.03 Broadband Internet subscribers,* 2004 79
7.04 Internet users,* 2005 122
7.05 Internet bandwidth,* 2006 118

Business usage — 107
8.01 Prevalence of foreign technology licensing, 2007 117
8.02 Firm-level technology absorption, 2007 69
8.03 Capacity for innovation, 2007 90
8.04 Availability of new telephone lines, 2007 112
8.05 Extent of business Internet use, 2007 118

Government usage — 81
9.01 Government success in ICT promotion, 2007 31
9.02 Availability of government online services, 2007 104
9.03 ICT use and government efficiency, 2007 54
9.04 Presence of ICT in government offices, 2007 90
9.05 E-Participation Index,* 2007 69

* Hard data

Note: For further details and explanation, please refer to the section "How to Read the Country/Economy Profiles" at the beginning of this chapter.

Malaysia

Key indicators

Population (millions), 2006	25.8
GDP (PPP) per capita (US$), 2006	11,957.4
Internet users per 100 inhabitants, 2006	43.8
Internet bandwidth (mB/s) per 10,000 inhabitants, 2005	1.3

Networked Readiness Index

Year (number of economies)	Rank
2007–2008 (127)	**26**
2006–2007 (122)	26
2005–2006 (115)	24

Global Competitiveness Index 2007–2008 (131)	21

Environment component — 26

Market environment — 18

1.01	Venture capital availability, 2007	18
1.02	Financial market sophistication, 2007	30
1.03	Availability of latest technologies, 2007	22
1.04	State of cluster development, 2007	5
1.05	Utility patents,* 2006	31
1.06	High-tech exports,* 2005	1
1.07	Burden of government regulation, 2007	5
1.08	Extent and effect of taxation, 2007	15
1.09	Total tax rate,* 2007	35
1.10	Time required to start a business,* 2007	50
1.11	No. of procedures required to start a business,* 2007	58
1.12	Intensity of local competition, 2007	19
1.13	Freedom of the press, 2007	100
1.14	Accessibility of digital content, 2007	32

Political and regulatory environment — 21

2.01	Effectiveness of law-making bodies, 2007	4
2.02	Laws relating to ICT, 2007	14
2.03	Judicial independence, 2007	30
2.04	Intellectual property protection, 2007	25
2.05	Efficiency of legal framework, 2007	18
2.06	Property rights, 2007	23
2.07	Quality of competition in the ISP sector, 2007	26
2.08	No. of procedures to enforce a contract,* 2007	15
2.09	Time to enforce a contract,* 2007	80

Infrastructure environment — 41

3.01	Telephone lines,* 2006	68
3.02	Secure Internet servers,* 2006	55
3.03	Electricity production,* 2004	54
3.04	Availability of scientists and engineers, 2007	21
3.05	Quality of scientific research institutions, 2007	17
3.06	Tertiary enrollment,* 2004	61
3.07	Education expenditure,* 2005	19

Readiness component — 11

Individual readiness — 22

4.01	Quality of math and science education, 2007	13
4.02	Quality of the educational system, 2007	15
4.03	Internet access in schools, 2007	31
4.04	Buyer sophistication, 2007	24
4.05	Residential telephone connection charge,* 2005	25
4.06	Residential monthly telephone subscription,* 2005	61
4.07	High-speed monthly broadband subscription,* 2006	38
4.08	Lowest cost of broadband,* 2006	42
4.09	Cost of mobile telephone call,* 2005	52

Business readiness — 18

5.01	Extent of staff training, 2007	16
5.02	Local availability of research and training, 2007	21
5.03	Quality of management schools, 2007	23
5.04	Company spending on R&D, 2007	11
5.05	University-industry research collaboration, 2007	16
5.06	Business telephone connection charge,* 2005	21
5.07	Business monthly telephone subscription,* 2005	60
5.08	Local supplier quality, 2007	25
5.09	Local supplier quantity, 2007	16
5.10	Computer, comm., and other services imports,* 2005	23

Government readiness — 7

6.01	Government prioritization of ICT, 2007	2
6.02	Gov't procurement of advanced tech products, 2007	3
6.03	Importance of ICT to gov't vision of the future, 2007	5
6.04	E-Government Readiness Index,* 2007	34

Usage component — 28

Individual usage — 45

7.01	Mobile telephone subscribers,* 2006	54
7.02	Personal computers,* 2005	38
7.03	Broadband Internet subscribers,* 2006	50
7.04	Internet users,* 2006	28
7.05	Internet bandwidth,* 2005	66

Business usage — 22

8.01	Prevalence of foreign technology licensing, 2007	10
8.02	Firm-level technology absorption, 2007	15
8.03	Capacity for innovation, 2007	22
8.04	Availability of new telephone lines, 2007	43
8.05	Extent of business Internet use, 2007	29

Government usage — 16

9.01	Government success in ICT promotion, 2007	5
9.02	Availability of government online services, 2007	19
9.03	ICT use and government efficiency, 2007	13
9.04	Presence of ICT in government offices, 2007	14
9.05	E-Participation Index,* 2007	39

* Hard data

Note: For further details and explanation, please refer to the section "How to Read the Country/Economy Profiles" at the beginning of this chapter.

Mali

Key indicators

Population (millions), 2006	13.9
GDP (PPP) per capita (US$), 2006	1,307.8
Internet users per 100 inhabitants, 2006	0.5
Internet bandwidth (mB/s) per 10,000 inhabitants, 2006	0.2

Networked Readiness Index

Year (number of economies)	Rank
2007–2008 (127)	**99**
2006–2007 (122)	101
2005–2006 (115)	95

Global Competitiveness Index 2007–2008 (131)	115

Environment component — 85

Market environment — 78

1.01	Venture capital availability, 2007	107
1.02	Financial market sophistication, 2007	113
1.03	Availability of latest technologies, 2007	92
1.04	State of cluster development, 2007	120
1.05	Utility patents,* 2006	86
1.06	High-tech exports*	n/a
1.07	Burden of government regulation, 2007	33
1.08	Extent and effect of taxation, 2007	56
1.09	Total tax rate,* 2007	87
1.10	Time required to start a business,* 2007	54
1.11	No. of procedures required to start a business,* 2007	88
1.12	Intensity of local competition, 2007	93
1.13	Freedom of the press, 2007	45
1.14	Accessibility of digital content, 2007	89

Political and regulatory environment — 73

2.01	Effectiveness of law-making bodies, 2007	36
2.02	Laws relating to ICT, 2007	107
2.03	Judicial independence, 2007	68
2.04	Intellectual property protection, 2007	75
2.05	Efficiency of legal framework, 2007	58
2.06	Property rights, 2007	81
2.07	Quality of competition in the ISP sector, 2007	44
2.08	No. of procedures to enforce a contract,* 2007	75
2.09	Time to enforce a contract,* 2007	104

Infrastructure environment — 103

3.01	Telephone lines,* 2006	121
3.02	Secure Internet servers,* 2006	101
3.03	Electricity production*	n/a
3.04	Availability of scientists and engineers, 2007	74
3.05	Quality of scientific research institutions, 2007	84
3.06	Tertiary enrollment,* 2005	117
3.07	Education expenditure,* 2005	98

Readiness component — 116

Individual readiness — 118

4.01	Quality of math and science education, 2007	100
4.02	Quality of the educational system, 2007	105
4.03	Internet access in schools, 2007	94
4.04	Buyer sophistication, 2007	116
4.05	Residential telephone connection charge,* 2005	108
4.06	Residential monthly telephone subscription,* 2006	120
4.07	High-speed monthly broadband subscription*	n/a
4.08	Lowest cost of broadband*	n/a
4.09	Cost of mobile telephone call,* 2006	117

Business readiness — 118

5.01	Extent of staff training, 2007	122
5.02	Local availability of research and training, 2007	85
5.03	Quality of management schools, 2007	94
5.04	Company spending on R&D, 2007	99
5.05	University-industry research collaboration, 2007	108
5.06	Business telephone connection charge,* 2005	102
5.07	Business monthly telephone subscription,* 2006	118
5.08	Local supplier quality, 2007	98
5.09	Local supplier quantity, 2007	80
5.10	Computer, comm., and other services imports,* 2005	95

Government readiness — 75

6.01	Government prioritization of ICT, 2007	42
6.02	Gov't procurement of advanced tech products, 2007	29
6.03	Importance of ICT to gov't vision of the future, 2007	18
6.04	E-Government Readiness Index,* 2007	122

Usage component — 89

Individual usage — 118

7.01	Mobile telephone subscribers,* 2006	115
7.02	Personal computers,* 2005	121
7.03	Broadband Internet subscribers,* 2006	105
7.04	Internet users,* 2006	123
7.05	Internet bandwidth,* 2006	89

Business usage — 91

8.01	Prevalence of foreign technology licensing, 2007	97
8.02	Firm-level technology absorption, 2007	77
8.03	Capacity for innovation, 2007	89
8.04	Availability of new telephone lines, 2007	79
8.05	Extent of business Internet use, 2007	89

Government usage — 59

9.01	Government success in ICT promotion, 2007	14
9.02	Availability of government online services, 2007	90
9.03	ICT use and government efficiency, 2007	51
9.04	Presence of ICT in government offices, 2007	57
9.05	E-Participation Index,* 2007	82

* Hard data

Note: For further details and explanation, please refer to the section "How to Read the Country/Economy Profiles" at the beginning of this chapter.

Malta

Key indicators

Population (millions), 2006...0.4
GDP (PPP) per capita (US$), 2006.....................................22,238.6
Internet users per 100 inhabitants, 2005 ....31.7
Internet bandwidth (mB/s) per 10,000 inhabitants, 2004.......19.4

Networked Readiness Index

Year (number of economies)	Rank
2007–2008 (127)	**27**
2006–2007 (122)	27
2005–2006 (115)	30

Global Competitiveness Index 2007–2008 (131) — 56

Environment component — 29
Market environment — 34

1.01 Venture capital availability, 2007..57
1.02 Financial market sophistication, 2007 35
1.03 Availability of latest technologies, 2007 27
1.04 State of cluster development, 2007................................101
1.05 Utility patents,* 2006 35
1.06 High-tech exports,* 2004 5
1.07 Burden of government regulation, 2007 95
1.08 Extent and effect of taxation, 2007....................................63
1.09 Total tax rate* ....n/a
1.10 Time required to start a business* ....n/a
1.11 No. of procedures required to start a business*..............n/a
1.12 Intensity of local competition, 2007 20
1.13 Freedom of the press, 2007...39
1.14 Accessibility of digital content, 2007.................................24

Political and regulatory environment — 28

2.01 Effectiveness of law-making bodies, 2007 25
2.02 Laws relating to ICT, 2007..22
2.03 Judicial independence, 2007 25
2.04 Intellectual property protection, 2007 41
2.05 Efficiency of legal framework, 2007...................................39
2.06 Property rights, 2007...43
2.07 Quality of competition in the ISP sector, 2007 29
2.08 No. of procedures to enforce a contract* ....n/a
2.09 Time to enforce a contract* ....n/a

Infrastructure environment — 29

3.01 Telephone lines,* 2006...15
3.02 Secure Internet servers,* 2006...10
3.03 Electricity production,* 2003..37
3.04 Availability of scientists and engineers, 2007 70
3.05 Quality of scientific research institutions, 2007 77
3.06 Tertiary enrollment,* 2005...62
3.07 Education expenditure,* 2005..52

Readiness component — 30
Individual readiness — 30

4.01 Quality of math and science education, 2007 34
4.02 Quality of the educational system, 2007...........................26
4.03 Internet access in schools, 2007..18
4.04 Buyer sophistication, 2007 53
4.05 Residential telephone connection charge,* 2005 39
4.06 Residential monthly telephone subscription,* 2005 27
4.07 High-speed monthly broadband subscription,* 2006 1
4.08 Lowest cost of broadband,* 2006 13
4.09 Cost of mobile telephone call,* 2005.................................62

Business readiness — 49

5.01 Extent of staff training, 2007..43
5.02 Local availability of research and training, 2007..............91
5.03 Quality of management schools, 2007 41
5.04 Company spending on R&D, 2007.......................................58
5.05 University-industry research collaboration, 2007..............77
5.06 Business telephone connection charge,* 2005 53
5.07 Business monthly telephone subscription,* 2005 43
5.08 Local supplier quality, 2007 53
5.09 Local supplier quantity, 2007..55
5.10 Computer, comm., and other services imports,* 2005 57

Government readiness — 13

6.01 Government prioritization of ICT, 2007................................5
6.02 Gov't procurement of advanced tech products, 2007 40
6.03 Importance of ICT to gov't vision of the future, 2007.........3
6.04 E-Government Readiness Index,* 2007............................29

Usage component — 26
Individual usage — 39

7.01 Mobile telephone subscribers,* 2006................................42
7.02 Personal computers,* 2005 44
7.03 Broadband Internet subscribers,* 2006 33
7.04 Internet users,* 2005...40
7.05 Internet bandwidth,* 2004 32

Business usage — 37

8.01 Prevalence of foreign technology licensing, 2007.............35
8.02 Firm-level technology absorption, 2007 41
8.03 Capacity for innovation, 2007...60
8.04 Availability of new telephone lines, 2007.........................29
8.05 Extent of business Internet use, 2007..............................32

Government usage — 11

9.01 Government success in ICT promotion, 2007.....................3
9.02 Availability of government online services, 2007 6
9.03 ICT use and government efficiency, 2007...........................6
9.04 Presence of ICT in government offices, 2007 12
9.05 E-Participation Index,* 2007..30

* Hard data

Note: For further details and explanation, please refer to the section "How to Read the Country/Economy Profiles" at the beginning of this chapter.

Mauritania

Key indicators

Population (millions), 2006...3.2
GDP (PPP) per capita (US$), 2006..........................2,504.1
Internet users per 100 inhabitants, 2006.....................3.2
Internet bandwidth (mB/s) per 10,000 inhabitants, 2006.........0.3

Networked Readiness Index

Year (number of economies)	Rank
2007–2008 (127)	**97**
2006–2007 (122)	87
2005–2006 (115)	n/a

Global Competitiveness Index 2007–2008 (131) 125

Environment component — 112
Market environment — 108

1.01 Venture capital availability, 2007.........................105
1.02 Financial market sophistication, 2007..................110
1.03 Availability of latest technologies, 2007................93
1.04 State of cluster development, 2007........................84
1.05 Utility patents,* 2006..86
1.06 High-tech exports*..n/a
1.07 Burden of government regulation, 2007................15
1.08 Extent and effect of taxation, 2007........................22
1.09 Total tax rate,* 2007..118
1.10 Time required to start a business,* 2007.............107
1.11 No. of procedures required to start a business,* 2007....88
1.12 Intensity of local competition, 2007......................120
1.13 Freedom of the press, 2007.....................................72
1.14 Accessibility of digital content, 2007....................115

Political and regulatory environment — 98

2.01 Effectiveness of law-making bodies, 2007.............95
2.02 Laws relating to ICT, 2007.....................................114
2.03 Judicial independence, 2007....................................80
2.04 Intellectual property protection, 2007....................88
2.05 Efficiency of legal framework, 2007........................61
2.06 Property rights, 2007..87
2.07 Quality of competition in the ISP sector, 2007...120
2.08 No. of procedures to enforce a contract,* 2007...112
2.09 Time to enforce a contract,* 2007..........................33

Infrastructure environment — 116

3.01 Telephone lines,* 2006...112
3.02 Secure Internet servers,* 2006................................90
3.03 Electricity production*..n/a
3.04 Availability of scientists and engineers, 2007......97
3.05 Quality of scientific research institutions, 2007..125
3.06 Tertiary enrollment,* 2005....................................112
3.07 Education expenditure,* 2005.................................83

Readiness component — 108
Individual readiness — 117

4.01 Quality of math and science education, 2007.....105
4.02 Quality of the educational system, 2007.............123
4.03 Internet access in schools, 2007...........................116
4.04 Buyer sophistication, 2007....................................114
4.05 Residential telephone connection charge,* 2005...84
4.06 Residential monthly telephone subscription,* 2005...108
4.07 High-speed monthly broadband subscription,* 2006...107
4.08 Lowest cost of broadband,* 2006.........................113
4.09 Cost of mobile telephone call,* 2005...................106

Business readiness — 105

5.01 Extent of staff training, 2007................................102
5.02 Local availability of research and training, 2007...124
5.03 Quality of management schools, 2007.................127
5.04 Company spending on R&D, 2007.........................127
5.05 University-industry research collaboration, 2007...124
5.06 Business telephone connection charge,* 2005......73
5.07 Business monthly telephone subscription,* 2005..100
5.08 Local supplier quality, 2007..................................105
5.09 Local supplier quantity, 2007...............................103
5.10 Computer, comm., and other services imports*...n/a

Government readiness — 63

6.01 Government prioritization of ICT, 2007.................20
6.02 Gov't procurement of advanced tech products, 2007...34
6.03 Importance of ICT to gov't vision of the future, 2007...19
6.04 E-Government Readiness Index,* 2007................118

Usage component — 74
Individual usage — 98

7.01 Mobile telephone subscribers,* 2006......................88
7.02 Personal computers,* 2005......................................90
7.03 Broadband Internet subscribers,* 2006.................104
7.04 Internet users,* 2006..110
7.05 Internet bandwidth,* 2006.......................................86

Business usage — 72

8.01 Prevalence of foreign technology licensing, 2007...80
8.02 Firm-level technology absorption, 2007.................39
8.03 Capacity for innovation, 2007.................................93
8.04 Availability of new telephone lines, 2007..............60
8.05 Extent of business Internet use, 2007....................93

Government usage — 50

9.01 Government success in ICT promotion, 2007........12
9.02 Availability of government online services, 2007..76
9.03 ICT use and government efficiency, 2007..............34
9.04 Presence of ICT in government offices, 2007.......43
9.05 E-Participation Index,* 2007...................................76

* Hard data

Note: For further details and explanation, please refer to the section "How to Read the Country/Economy Profiles" at the beginning of this chapter.

Mauritius

Key indicators

Population (millions), 2006..1.3
GDP (PPP) per capita (US$), 2006.....................................13,281.1
Internet users per 100 inhabitants, 2006 ....14.5
Internet bandwidth (mB/s) per 10,000 inhabitants, 2006.........1.5

Networked Readiness Index

Year (number of economies)	Rank
2007–2008 (127)	**54**
2006–2007 (122)	51
2005–2006 (115)	45

Global Competitiveness Index 2007–2008 (131) 60

Environment component — 48
Market environment — 33

1.01 Venture capital availability, 2007..54
1.02 Financial market sophistication, 2007 51
1.03 Availability of latest technologies, 2007 53
1.04 State of cluster development, 2007....................................69
1.05 Utility patents,* 2006 86
1.06 High-tech exports,* 2005...29
1.07 Burden of government regulation, 2007 64
1.08 Extent and effect of taxation, 2007......................................18
1.09 Total tax rate,* 2007 8
1.10 Time required to start a business,* 2007............................9
1.11 No. of procedures required to start a business,* 2007 19
1.12 Intensity of local competition, 2007 76
1.13 Freedom of the press, 2007...42
1.14 Accessibility of digital content, 2007..................................66

Political and regulatory environment — 41

2.01 Effectiveness of law-making bodies, 2007 22
2.02 Laws relating to ICT, 2007..43
2.03 Judicial independence, 2007 45
2.04 Intellectual property protection, 2007 43
2.05 Efficiency of legal framework, 2007.....................................37
2.06 Property rights, 2007..27
2.07 Quality of competition in the ISP sector, 2007 97
2.08 No. of procedures to enforce a contract,* 2007...............60
2.09 Time to enforce a contract,* 2007 96

Infrastructure environment — 62

3.01 Telephone lines,* 2006..41
3.02 Secure Internet servers,* 2006...53
3.03 Electricity production* ....n/a
3.04 Availability of scientists and engineers, 2007 103
3.05 Quality of scientific research institutions, 2007 67
3.06 Tertiary enrollment,* 2005..87
3.07 Education expenditure,* 2005..70

Readiness component — 50
Individual readiness — 54

4.01 Quality of math and science education, 2007...................60
4.02 Quality of the educational system, 2007...........................51
4.03 Internet access in schools, 2007..65
4.04 Buyer sophistication, 2007 63
4.05 Residential telephone connection charge,* 2005 54
4.06 Residential monthly telephone subscription,* 2005 37
4.07 High-speed monthly broadband subscription,* 2006........73
4.08 Lowest cost of broadband,* 2006 63
4.09 Cost of mobile telephone call,* 2006...................................23

Business readiness — 57

5.01 Extent of staff training, 2007..29
5.02 Local availability of research and training, 2007................87
5.03 Quality of management schools, 2007 86
5.04 Company spending on R&D, 2007 81
5.05 University-industry research collaboration, 2007...............75
5.06 Business telephone connection charge,* 2005 65
5.07 Business monthly telephone subscription,* 2005 49
5.08 Local supplier quality, 2007 57
5.09 Local supplier quantity, 2007...62
5.10 Computer, comm., and other services imports,* 2005 54

Government readiness — 41

6.01 Government prioritization of ICT, 2007................................19
6.02 Gov't procurement of advanced tech products, 2007 63
6.03 Importance of ICT to gov't vision of the future, 2007.......48
6.04 E-Government Readiness Index,* 2007..............................60

Usage component — 70
Individual usage — 59

7.01 Mobile telephone subscribers,* 2006..................................69
7.02 Personal computers,* 2005 43
7.03 Broadband Internet subscribers,* 2006 58
7.04 Internet users,* 2006 68
7.05 Internet bandwidth,* 2006 64

Business usage — 71

8.01 Prevalence of foreign technology licensing, 2007.............55
8.02 Firm-level technology absorption, 2007 72
8.03 Capacity for innovation, 2007..94
8.04 Availability of new telephone lines, 2007...........................57
8.05 Extent of business Internet use, 2007 88

Government usage — 72

9.01 Government success in ICT promotion, 2007....................40
9.02 Availability of government online services, 2007 66
9.03 ICT use and government efficiency, 2007...........................86
9.04 Presence of ICT in government offices, 2007 68
9.05 E-Participation Index,* 2007..76

* Hard data

Note: For further details and explanation, please refer to the section "How to Read the Country/Economy Profiles" at the beginning of this chapter.

Mexico

Key indicators

Population (millions), 2006..108.3
GDP (PPP) per capita (US$), 2006..................................11,369.0
Internet users per 100 inhabitants, 2005 ....16.9
Internet bandwidth (mB/s) per 10,000 inhabitants, 2005.........1.1

Networked Readiness Index

Year (number of economies)	Rank
2007–2008 (127)	**58**
2006–2007 (122)	49
2005–2006 (115)	55

Global Competitiveness Index 2007–2008 (131)   52

Environment component — 62

Market environment — 57

1.01 Venture capital availability, 2007..84
1.02 Financial market sophistication, 2007 49
1.03 Availability of latest technologies, 2007 72
1.04 State of cluster development, 2007......................................53
1.05 Utility patents,* 2006...54
1.06 High-tech exports,* 2005 20
1.07 Burden of government regulation, 2007 109
1.08 Extent and effect of taxation, 2007 78
1.09 Total tax rate,* 2007..85
1.10 Time required to start a business,* 2007............................59
1.11 No. of procedures required to start a business,* 2007 44
1.12 Intensity of local competition, 2007 66
1.13 Freedom of the press, 2007..44
1.14 Accessibility of digital content, 2007...................................79

Political and regulatory environment — 70

2.01 Effectiveness of law-making bodies, 2007 108
2.02 Laws relating to ICT, 2007...52
2.03 Judicial independence, 2007 74
2.04 Intellectual property protection, 2007 64
2.05 Efficiency of legal framework, 2007.....................................93
2.06 Property rights, 2007..76
2.07 Quality of competition in the ISP sector, 2007 72
2.08 No. of procedures to enforce a contract,* 2007 65
2.09 Time to enforce a contract,* 2007 38

Infrastructure environment — 67

3.01 Telephone lines,* 2006..65
3.02 Secure Internet servers,* 2006...60
3.03 Electricity production,* 2004 65
3.04 Availability of scientists and engineers, 2007 93
3.05 Quality of scientific research institutions, 2007 63
3.06 Tertiary enrollment,* 2005...73
3.07 Education expenditure,* 2005...32

Readiness component — 63

Individual readiness — 67

4.01 Quality of math and science education, 2007..................110
4.02 Quality of the educational system, 2007............................89
4.03 Internet access in schools, 2007..62
4.04 Buyer sophistication, 2007 54
4.05 Residential telephone connection charge,* 2005 72
4.06 Residential monthly telephone subscription,* 2005 77
4.07 High-speed monthly broadband subscription,* 2006........79
4.08 Lowest cost of broadband,* 2006 51
4.09 Cost of mobile telephone call,* 2005..................................45

Business readiness — 64

5.01 Extent of staff training, 2007..65
5.02 Local availability of research and training, 2007................52
5.03 Quality of management schools, 2007 49
5.04 Company spending on R&D, 2007..68
5.05 University-industry research collaboration, 2007...............57
5.06 Business telephone connection charge,* 2005 67
5.07 Business monthly telephone subscription,* 2005 62
5.08 Local supplier quality, 2007..49
5.09 Local supplier quantity, 2007..66
5.10 Computer, comm., and other services imports,* 2005 ..109

Government readiness — 53

6.01 Government prioritization of ICT, 2007...............................73
6.02 Gov't procurement of advanced tech products, 2007 92
6.03 Importance of ICT to gov't vision of the future, 2007.......62
6.04 E-Government Readiness Index,* 2007..............................37

Usage component — 49

Individual usage — 62

7.01 Mobile telephone subscribers,* 2006..................................74
7.02 Personal computers,* 2005...51
7.03 Broadband Internet subscribers,* 2006 51
7.04 Internet users,* 2005...64
7.05 Internet bandwidth,* 2005 70

Business usage — 63

8.01 Prevalence of foreign technology licensing, 2007.............61
8.02 Firm-level technology absorption, 2007 87
8.03 Capacity for innovation, 2007...57
8.04 Availability of new telephone lines, 2007...........................61
8.05 Extent of business Internet use, 2007................................64

Government usage — 29

9.01 Government success in ICT promotion, 2007....................79
9.02 Availability of government online services, 2007 40
9.03 ICT use and government efficiency, 2007...........................37
9.04 Presence of ICT in government offices, 2007 70
9.05 E-Participation Index,* 2007...7

* Hard data

Note: For further details and explanation, please refer to the section "How to Read the Country/Economy Profiles" at the beginning of this chapter.

Moldova

Key indicators

Population (millions), 2006...4.2
GDP (PPP) per capita (US$), 2006......................................2,869.1
Internet users per 100 inhabitants, 2006 ....17.3
Internet bandwidth (mB/s) per 10,000 inhabitants, 2006.........1.3

Networked Readiness Index

Year (number of economies)	Rank
2007–2008 (127)	**96**
2006–2007 (122)	92
2005–2006 (115)	94

Global Competitiveness Index 2007–2008 (131) — 97

Environment component — 89
Market environment — 114

1.01 Venture capital availability, 2007..108
1.02 Financial market sophistication, 2007 105
1.03 Availability of latest technologies, 2007 125
1.04 State of cluster development, 2007.....................................126
1.05 Utility patents,* 2006 86
1.06 High-tech exports,* 2005 71
1.07 Burden of government regulation, 2007 103
1.08 Extent and effect of taxation, 2007.....................................103
1.09 Total tax rate,* 2007 59
1.10 Time required to start a business,* 2007..............................48
1.11 No. of procedures required to start a business,* 2007 58
1.12 Intensity of local competition, 2007 84
1.13 Freedom of the press, 2007..118
1.14 Accessibility of digital content, 2007..................................106

Political and regulatory environment — 82

2.01 Effectiveness of law-making bodies, 2007 75
2.02 Laws relating to ICT, 2007...90
2.03 Judicial independence, 2007 113
2.04 Intellectual property protection, 2007 85
2.05 Efficiency of legal framework, 2007....................................110
2.06 Property rights, 2007...105
2.07 Quality of competition in the ISP sector, 2007 91
2.08 No. of procedures to enforce a contract,* 2007..................26
2.09 Time to enforce a contract,* 2007 26

Infrastructure environment — 79

3.01 Telephone lines,* 2006..53
3.02 Secure Internet servers,* 2006...73
3.03 Electricity production,* 2004...86
3.04 Availability of scientists and engineers, 2007 100
3.05 Quality of scientific research institutions, 2007 108
3.06 Tertiary enrollment,* 2005...56
3.07 Education expenditure,* 2005...60

Readiness component — 102
Individual readiness — 102

4.01 Quality of math and science education, 2007 59
4.02 Quality of the educational system, 2007..............................72
4.03 Internet access in schools, 2007..87
4.04 Buyer sophistication, 2007 112
4.05 Residential telephone connection charge,* 2005 117
4.06 Residential monthly telephone subscription,* 2005 79
4.07 High-speed monthly broadband subscription,* 2006.........94
4.08 Lowest cost of broadband,* 2006 98
4.09 Cost of mobile telephone call,* 2005.................................119

Business readiness — 107

5.01 Extent of staff training, 2007..101
5.02 Local availability of research and training, 2007...............101
5.03 Quality of management schools, 2007 106
5.04 Company spending on R&D, 2007.....................................112
5.05 University-industry research collaboration, 2007..............113
5.06 Business telephone connection charge,* 2005 110
5.07 Business monthly telephone subscription,* 2005 77
5.08 Local supplier quality, 2007 116
5.09 Local supplier quantity, 2007...116
5.10 Computer, comm., and other services imports,* 2005 69

Government readiness — 100

6.01 Government prioritization of ICT, 2007................................78
6.02 Gov't procurement of advanced tech products, 2007 121
6.03 Importance of ICT to gov't vision of the future, 2007........88
6.04 E-Government Readiness Index,* 2007..............................82

Usage component — 99
Individual usage — 83

7.01 Mobile telephone subscribers,* 2006..................................91
7.02 Personal computers,* 2005 64
7.03 Broadband Internet subscribers,* 2006 78
7.04 Internet users,* 2006 61
7.05 Internet bandwidth,* 2006 65

Business usage — 104

8.01 Prevalence of foreign technology licensing, 2007............120
8.02 Firm-level technology absorption, 2007 108
8.03 Capacity for innovation, 2007 72
8.04 Availability of new telephone lines, 2007 81
8.05 Extent of business Internet use, 2007..............................119

Government usage — 99

9.01 Government success in ICT promotion, 2007.....................93
9.02 Availability of government online services, 2007 110
9.03 ICT use and government efficiency, 2007.........................108
9.04 Presence of ICT in government offices, 2007 47
9.05 E-Participation Index,* 2007...91

* Hard data

Note: For further details and explanation, please refer to the section "How to Read the Country/Economy Profiles" at the beginning of this chapter.

Mongolia

Key indicators

Population (millions), 2006...2.7
GDP (PPP) per capita (US$), 2006......................................2,891.2
Internet users per 100 inhabitants, 2005 ....10.1
Internet bandwidth (mB/s) per 10,000 inhabitants, 2005.........0.1

Networked Readiness Index

Year (number of economies)	Rank
2007–2008 (127)	**87**
2006–2007 (122)	90
2005–2006 (115)	92

Global Competitiveness Index 2007–2008 (131)   101

Environment component   72
Market environment   95
1.01 Venture capital availability, 2007..124
1.02 Financial market sophistication, 2007 104
1.03 Availability of latest technologies, 2007.............................102
1.04 State of cluster development, 2007...................................109
1.05 Utility patents,* 2006 86
1.06 High-tech exports,* 2005 109
1.07 Burden of government regulation, 2007 90
1.08 Extent and effect of taxation, 2007.....................................96
1.09 Total tax rate,* 2007 44
1.10 Time required to start a business,* 2007............................42
1.11 No. of procedures required to start a business,* 2007 44
1.12 Intensity of local competition, 2007 82
1.13 Freedom of the press, 2007..89
1.14 Accessibility of digital content, 2007...................................85

Political and regulatory environment   97
2.01 Effectiveness of law-making bodies, 2007 105
2.02 Laws relating to ICT, 2007...108
2.03 Judicial independence, 2007 110
2.04 Intellectual property protection, 2007 116
2.05 Efficiency of legal framework, 2007...................................116
2.06 Property rights, 2007...88
2.07 Quality of competition in the ISP sector, 2007 76
2.08 No. of procedures to enforce a contract,* 2007 29
2.09 Time to enforce a contract,* 2007 20

Infrastructure environment   51
3.01 Telephone lines,* 2005..98
3.02 Secure Internet servers,* 2006...73
3.03 Electricity production* ....n/a
3.04 Availability of scientists and engineers, 2007 52
3.05 Quality of scientific research institutions, 2007 95
3.06 Tertiary enrollment,* 2005...44
3.07 Education expenditure,* 2005...28

Readiness component   88
Individual readiness   92
4.01 Quality of math and science education, 2007....................61
4.02 Quality of the educational system, 2007..........................108
4.03 Internet access in schools, 2007..97
4.04 Buyer sophistication, 2007 95
4.05 Residential telephone connection charge,* 2005 98
4.06 Residential monthly telephone subscription,* 2005 42
4.07 High-speed monthly broadband subscription,* 2006........92
4.08 Lowest cost of broadband,* 2006 99
4.09 Cost of mobile telephone call,* 2005.................................96

Business readiness   103
5.01 Extent of staff training, 2007..93
5.02 Local availability of research and training, 2007................88
5.03 Quality of management schools, 2007 120
5.04 Company spending on R&D, 2007.....................................95
5.05 University-industry research collaboration, 2007...............86
5.06 Business telephone connection charge,* 2005 91
5.07 Business monthly telephone subscription,* 2005 90
5.08 Local supplier quality, 2007 124
5.09 Local supplier quantity, 2007..125
5.10 Computer, comm., and other services imports,* 2004 ..102

Government readiness   60
6.01 Government prioritization of ICT, 2007..............................30
6.02 Gov't procurement of advanced tech products, 2007 104
6.03 Importance of ICT to gov't vision of the future, 2007.......53
6.04 E-Government Readiness Index,* 2007..............................73

Usage component   95
Individual usage   91
7.01 Mobile telephone subscribers,* 2005...............................104
7.02 Personal computers,* 2005 53
7.03 Broadband Internet subscribers,* 2005 97
7.04 Internet users,* 2005...81
7.05 Internet bandwidth,* 2005 99

Business usage   105
8.01 Prevalence of foreign technology licensing, 2007............104
8.02 Firm-level technology absorption, 2007 105
8.03 Capacity for innovation, 2007...95
8.04 Availability of new telephone lines, 2007 105
8.05 Extent of business Internet use, 2007 100

Government usage   79
9.01 Government success in ICT promotion, 2007....................57
9.02 Availability of government online services, 2007 108
9.03 ICT use and government efficiency, 2007........................104
9.04 Presence of ICT in government offices, 2007 48
9.05 E-Participation Index,* 2007..43

* Hard data

Note: For further details and explanation, please refer to the section "How to Read the Country/Economy Profiles" at the beginning of this chapter.

Morocco

Key indicators

Population (millions), 2006...31.9
GDP (PPP) per capita (US$), 2006.......................................5,764.9
Internet users per 100 inhabitants, 2006 ....19.8
Internet bandwidth (mB/s) per 10,000 inhabitants, 2006.........3.6

Networked Readiness Index

Year (number of economies)	Rank
2007–2008 (127)	**74**
2006–2007 (122)	76
2005–2006 (115)	77

Global Competitiveness Index 2007–2008 (131)	64

Environment component — 67
Market environment — 65
1.01 Venture capital availability, 2007..73
1.02 Financial market sophistication, 2007 77
1.03 Availability of latest technologies, 2007 63
1.04 State of cluster development, 2007 55
1.05 Utility patents,* 2006 77
1.06 High-tech exports,* 2005 38
1.07 Burden of government regulation, 2007 46
1.08 Extent and effect of taxation, 2007 59
1.09 Total tax rate,* 2007 94
1.10 Time required to start a business,* 2007 22
1.11 No. of procedures required to start a business,* 2007 19
1.12 Intensity of local competition, 2007 83
1.13 Freedom of the press, 2007 106
1.14 Accessibility of digital content, 2007 70

Political and regulatory environment — 65
2.01 Effectiveness of law-making bodies, 2007 56
2.02 Laws relating to ICT, 2007 84
2.03 Judicial independence, 2007 62
2.04 Intellectual property protection, 2007 53
2.05 Efficiency of legal framework, 2007 51
2.06 Property rights, 2007 62
2.07 Quality of competition in the ISP sector, 2007 88
2.08 No. of procedures to enforce a contract,* 2007 89
2.09 Time to enforce a contract,* 2007 83

Infrastructure environment — 78
3.01 Telephone lines,* 2006..104
3.02 Secure Internet servers,* 2006...90
3.03 Electricity production,* 2004 94
3.04 Availability of scientists and engineers, 2007 36
3.05 Quality of scientific research institutions, 2007 79
3.06 Tertiary enrollment,* 2005..96
3.07 Education expenditure,* 2005..16

Readiness component — 76
Individual readiness — 79
4.01 Quality of math and science education, 2007 40
4.02 Quality of the educational system, 2007 87
4.03 Internet access in schools, 2007...60
4.04 Buyer sophistication, 2007 82
4.05 Residential telephone connection charge,* 2005 88
4.06 Residential monthly telephone subscription,* 2005 104
4.07 High-speed monthly broadband subscription,* 2006........74
4.08 Lowest cost of broadband,* 2006 55
4.09 Cost of mobile telephone call,* 2006..................................97

Business readiness — 76
5.01 Extent of staff training, 2007..72
5.02 Local availability of research and training, 2007 57
5.03 Quality of management schools, 2007 36
5.04 Company spending on R&D, 2007 62
5.05 University-industry research collaboration, 2007...............68
5.06 Business telephone connection charge,* 2005 95
5.07 Business monthly telephone subscription,* 2005 103
5.08 Local supplier quality, 2007 77
5.09 Local supplier quantity, 2007 57
5.10 Computer, comm., and other services imports,* 2005 58

Government readiness — 79
6.01 Government prioritization of ICT, 2007...............................63
6.02 Gov't procurement of advanced tech products, 2007 42
6.03 Importance of ICT to gov't vision of the future, 2007.......45
6.04 E-Government Readiness Index,* 2007..........................109

Usage component — 77
Individual usage — 71
7.01 Mobile telephone subscribers,* 2006.................................77
7.02 Personal computers,* 2005 91
7.03 Broadband Internet subscribers,* 2005 69
7.04 Internet users,* 2006 57
7.05 Internet bandwidth,* 2006 54

Business usage — 68
8.01 Prevalence of foreign technology licensing, 2007.............71
8.02 Firm-level technology absorption, 2007 51
8.03 Capacity for innovation, 2007 85
8.04 Availability of new telephone lines, 2007 42
8.05 Extent of business Internet use, 2007 105

Government usage — 77
9.01 Government success in ICT promotion, 2007....................36
9.02 Availability of government online services, 2007 75
9.03 ICT use and government efficiency, 2007..........................62
9.04 Presence of ICT in government offices, 2007 69
9.05 E-Participation Index,* 2007..117

* Hard data

Note: For further details and explanation, please refer to the section "How to Read the Country/Economy Profiles" at the beginning of this chapter.

Mozambique

Key indicators

Population (millions), 2006...20.2
GDP (PPP) per capita (US$), 2006....................................1,494.3
Internet users per 100 inhabitants, 2005 ....0.9
Internet bandwidth (mB/s) per 10,000 inhabitants, 2005..........0.0

Networked Readiness Index

Year (number of economies)	Rank
2007–2008 (127)	**121**
2006–2007 (122)	115
2005–2006 (115)	101

Global Competitiveness Index 2007–2008 (131) — 128

Environment component — 120
Market environment — 111

1.01 Venture capital availability, 2007.......................................125
1.02 Financial market sophistication, 2007 116
1.03 Availability of latest technologies, 2007 104
1.04 State of cluster development, 2007...................................123
1.05 Utility patents,* 2006 86
1.06 High-tech exports,* 2005 78
1.07 Burden of government regulation, 2007 84
1.08 Extent and effect of taxation, 2007.....................................88
1.09 Total tax rate,* 2007 28
1.10 Time required to start a business,* 2007...........................64
1.11 No. of procedures required to start a business,* 2007 74
1.12 Intensity of local competition, 2007 123
1.13 Freedom of the press, 2007..82
1.14 Accessibility of digital content, 2007.................................101

Political and regulatory environment — 104

2.01 Effectiveness of law-making bodies, 2007 76
2.02 Laws relating to ICT, 2007...111
2.03 Judicial independence, 2007...100
2.04 Intellectual property protection, 2007 112
2.05 Efficiency of legal framework, 2007..................................105
2.06 Property rights, 2007...95
2.07 Quality of competition in the ISP sector, 2007 100
2.08 No. of procedures to enforce a contract,* 2007 26
2.09 Time to enforce a contract,* 2007 111

Infrastructure environment — 126

3.01 Telephone lines,* 2006..125
3.02 Secure Internet servers,* 2006...101
3.03 Electricity production,* 2004...96
3.04 Availability of scientists and engineers, 2007 119
3.05 Quality of scientific research institutions, 2007 106
3.06 Tertiary enrollment,* 2005...121
3.07 Education expenditure,* 2005...112

Readiness component — 121
Individual readiness — 125

4.01 Quality of math and science education, 2007..................111
4.02 Quality of the educational system, 2007..........................112
4.03 Internet access in schools, 2007.......................................111
4.04 Buyer sophistication, 2007 123
4.05 Residential telephone connection charge,* 2006 97
4.06 Residential monthly telephone subscription,* 2006 121
4.07 High-speed monthly broadband subscription,* 2006......105
4.08 Lowest cost of broadband,* 2006 112
4.09 Cost of mobile telephone call,* 2005................................107

Business readiness — 120

5.01 Extent of staff training, 2007...89
5.02 Local availability of research and training, 2007.............112
5.03 Quality of management schools, 2007 121
5.04 Company spending on R&D, 2007....................................115
5.05 University-industry research collaboration, 2007..............94
5.06 Business telephone connection charge,* 2006 85
5.07 Business monthly telephone subscription,* 2005 119
5.08 Local supplier quality, 2007 125
5.09 Local supplier quantity, 2007..119
5.10 Computer, comm., and other services imports,* 2005 45

Government readiness — 108

6.01 Government prioritization of ICT, 2007..............................81
6.02 Gov't procurement of advanced tech products, 2007 100
6.03 Importance of ICT to gov't vision of the future, 2007.......83
6.04 E-Government Readiness Index,* 2007..........................114

Usage component — 105
Individual usage — 117

7.01 Mobile telephone subscribers,* 2006..............................114
7.02 Personal computers,* 2005...107
7.03 Broadband Internet subscribers,* 2005 118
7.04 Internet users,* 2005 118
7.05 Internet bandwidth,* 2005...122

Business usage — 106

8.01 Prevalence of foreign technology licensing, 2007.............96
8.02 Firm-level technology absorption, 2007 116
8.03 Capacity for innovation, 2007...113
8.04 Availability of new telephone lines, 2007..........................89
8.05 Extent of business Internet use, 2007 113

Government usage — 93

9.01 Government success in ICT promotion, 2007...................78
9.02 Availability of government online services, 2007 117
9.03 ICT use and government efficiency, 2007.......................106
9.04 Presence of ICT in government offices, 2007 107
9.05 E-Participation Index,* 2007...24

* Hard data

Note: For further details and explanation, please refer to the section "How to Read the Country/Economy Profiles" at the beginning of this chapter.

Namibia

Key indicators

Population (millions), 2006..2.1
GDP (PPP) per capita (US$), 2006..................................8,576.8
Internet users per 100 inhabitants, 2005 ....4.0
Internet bandwidth (mB/s) per 10,000 inhabitants, 2005.........0.2

Networked Readiness Index

Year (number of economies)	Rank
2007–2008 (127)	**93**
2006–2007 (122)	85
2005–2006 (115)	78

Global Competitiveness Index 2007–2008 (131)   89

Environment component — 68
Market environment — 85

1.01 Venture capital availability, 2007..65
1.02 Financial market sophistication, 2007 56
1.03 Availability of latest technologies, 2007 73
1.04 State of cluster development, 2007......................................107
1.05 Utility patents,* 2006 86
1.06 High-tech exports,* 2005 73
1.07 Burden of government regulation, 2007 72
1.08 Extent and effect of taxation, 2007...57
1.09 Total tax rate,* 2007 13
1.10 Time required to start a business,* 2007..............................116
1.11 No. of procedures required to start a business,* 2007 74
1.12 Intensity of local competition, 2007 77
1.13 Freedom of the press, 2007..58
1.14 Accessibility of digital content, 2007.................................114

Political and regulatory environment — 39

2.01 Effectiveness of law-making bodies, 2007 53
2.02 Laws relating to ICT, 2007...91
2.03 Judicial independence, 2007 34
2.04 Intellectual property protection, 2007 46
2.05 Efficiency of legal framework, 2007..42
2.06 Property rights, 2007...41
2.07 Quality of competition in the ISP sector, 2007 113
2.08 No. of procedures to enforce a contract,* 2007 35
2.09 Time to enforce a contract,* 2007 11

Infrastructure environment — 92

3.01 Telephone lines,* 2005..96
3.02 Secure Internet servers,* 2006..61
3.03 Electricity production,* 2004 87
3.04 Availability of scientists and engineers, 2007 127
3.05 Quality of scientific research institutions, 2007 109
3.06 Tertiary enrollment,* 2004...102
3.07 Education expenditure,* 2005...5

Readiness component — 100
Individual readiness — 98

4.01 Quality of math and science education, 2007 123
4.02 Quality of the educational system, 2007..........................115
4.03 Internet access in schools, 2007...91
4.04 Buyer sophistication, 2007 68
4.05 Residential telephone connection charge,* 2006 70
4.06 Residential monthly telephone subscription,* 2006 80
4.07 High-speed monthly broadband subscription* ....n/a
4.08 Lowest cost of broadband*...n/a
4.09 Cost of mobile telephone call,* 2005................................91

Business readiness — 91

5.01 Extent of staff training, 2007...58
5.02 Local availability of research and training, 2007..............126
5.03 Quality of management schools, 2007 125
5.04 Company spending on R&D, 2007..88
5.05 University-industry research collaboration, 2007...............88
5.06 Business telephone connection charge,* 2006 63
5.07 Business monthly telephone subscription,* 2006 67
5.08 Local supplier quality, 2007 83
5.09 Local supplier quantity, 2007..122
5.10 Computer, comm., and other services imports,* 2004 37

Government readiness — 112

6.01 Government prioritization of ICT, 2007.............................115
6.02 Gov't procurement of advanced tech products, 2007 102
6.03 Importance of ICT to gov't vision of the future, 2007.....113
6.04 E-Government Readiness Index,* 2007...........................101

Usage component — 103
Individual usage — 93

7.01 Mobile telephone subscribers,* 2005.....................................99
7.02 Personal computers,* 2005 55
7.03 Broadband Internet subscribers,* 2005 118
7.04 Internet users,* 2005...105
7.05 Internet bandwidth,* 2005 94

Business usage — 88

8.01 Prevalence of foreign technology licensing, 2007.............63
8.02 Firm-level technology absorption, 2007 86
8.03 Capacity for innovation, 2007..115
8.04 Availability of new telephone lines, 2007 77
8.05 Extent of business Internet use, 2007....................................92

Government usage — 113

9.01 Government success in ICT promotion, 2007..................111
9.02 Availability of government online services, 2007............106
9.03 ICT use and government efficiency, 2007........................117
9.04 Presence of ICT in government offices, 2007 101
9.05 E-Participation Index,* 2007...100

* Hard data

Note: For further details and explanation, please refer to the section "How to Read the Country/Economy Profiles" at the beginning of this chapter.

Nepal

Key indicators

Population (millions), 2006	27.7
GDP (PPP) per capita (US$), 2006	1,947.3
Internet users per 100 inhabitants, 2006	0.9
Internet bandwidth (mB/s) per 10,000 inhabitants, 2006	0.0

Networked Readiness Index

Year (number of economies)	Rank
2007-2008 (127)	**119**
2006-2007 (122)	108
2005-2006 (115)	n/a

Global Competitiveness Index 2007-2008 (131)	114

Environment component — 110

Market environment — 86

1.01	Venture capital availability, 2007	110
1.02	Financial market sophistication, 2007	111
1.03	Availability of latest technologies, 2007	114
1.04	State of cluster development, 2007	90
1.05	Utility patents,* 2006	86
1.06	High-tech exports,* 2005	98
1.07	Burden of government regulation, 2007	88
1.08	Extent and effect of taxation, 2007	50
1.09	Total tax rate,* 2007	22
1.10	Time required to start a business,* 2007	68
1.11	No. of procedures required to start a business,* 2007	34
1.12	Intensity of local competition, 2007	80
1.13	Freedom of the press, 2007	67
1.14	Accessibility of digital content, 2007	113

Political and regulatory environment — 100

2.01	Effectiveness of law-making bodies, 2007	98
2.02	Laws relating to ICT, 2007	116
2.03	Judicial independence, 2007	69
2.04	Intellectual property protection, 2007	118
2.05	Efficiency of legal framework, 2007	100
2.06	Property rights, 2007	92
2.07	Quality of competition in the ISP sector, 2007	66
2.08	No. of procedures to enforce a contract,* 2007	75
2.09	Time to enforce a contract,* 2007	94

Infrastructure environment — 121

3.01	Telephone lines,* 2006	110
3.02	Secure Internet servers,* 2006	90
3.03	Electricity production,* 2004	109
3.04	Availability of scientists and engineers, 2007	99
3.05	Quality of scientific research institutions, 2007	101
3.06	Tertiary enrollment,* 2004	104
3.07	Education expenditure,* 2005	102

Readiness component — 119

Individual readiness — 113

4.01	Quality of math and science education, 2007	93
4.02	Quality of the educational system, 2007	96
4.03	Internet access in schools, 2007	99
4.04	Buyer sophistication, 2007	110
4.05	Residential telephone connection charge,* 2005	104
4.06	Residential monthly telephone subscription,* 2005	109
4.07	High-speed monthly broadband subscription*	n/a
4.08	Lowest cost of broadband,* 2006	114
4.09	Cost of mobile telephone call,* 2006	87

Business readiness — 112

5.01	Extent of staff training, 2007	124
5.02	Local availability of research and training, 2007	120
5.03	Quality of management schools, 2007	108
5.04	Company spending on R&D, 2007	113
5.05	University-industry research collaboration, 2007	118
5.06	Business telephone connection charge,* 2005	96
5.07	Business monthly telephone subscription,* 2005	101
5.08	Local supplier quality, 2007	112
5.09	Local supplier quantity, 2007	110
5.10	Computer, comm., and other services imports,* 2005	91

Government readiness — 118

6.01	Government prioritization of ICT, 2007	86
6.02	Gov't procurement of advanced tech products, 2007	118
6.03	Importance of ICT to gov't vision of the future, 2007	110
6.04	E-Government Readiness Index,* 2007	113

Usage component — 119

Individual usage — 124

7.01	Mobile telephone subscribers,* 2006	125
7.02	Personal computers,* 2005	119
7.03	Broadband Internet subscribers,* 2005	118
7.04	Internet users,* 2006	117
7.05	Internet bandwidth,* 2006	112

Business usage — 111

8.01	Prevalence of foreign technology licensing, 2007	99
8.02	Firm-level technology absorption, 2007	111
8.03	Capacity for innovation, 2007	121
8.04	Availability of new telephone lines, 2007	108
8.05	Extent of business Internet use, 2007	103

Government usage — 115

9.01	Government success in ICT promotion, 2007	100
9.02	Availability of government online services, 2007	115
9.03	ICT use and government efficiency, 2007	105
9.04	Presence of ICT in government offices, 2007	118
9.05	E-Participation Index,* 2007	110

* Hard data

Note: For further details and explanation, please refer to the section "How to Read the Country/Economy Profiles" at the beginning of this chapter.

Netherlands

Key indicators

Population (millions), 2006	16.4
GDP (PPP) per capita (US$), 2006	36,936.6
Internet users per 100 inhabitants, 2006	88.9
Internet bandwidth (mB/s) per 10,000 inhabitants, 2005	205.3

Networked Readiness Index

Year (number of economies)	Rank
2007–2008 (127)	**7**
2006–2007 (122)	6
2005–2006 (115)	12

Global Competitiveness Index 2007–2008 (131)	10

Environment component — 13

Market environment — 12

1.01	Venture capital availability, 2007	3
1.02	Financial market sophistication, 2007	10
1.03	Availability of latest technologies, 2007	14
1.04	State of cluster development, 2007	20
1.05	Utility patents,* 2006	14
1.06	High-tech exports,* 2005	18
1.07	Burden of government regulation, 2007	54
1.08	Extent and effect of taxation, 2007	49
1.09	Total tax rate,* 2007	58
1.10	Time required to start a business,* 2007	17
1.11	No. of procedures required to start a business,* 2007	19
1.12	Intensity of local competition, 2007	9
1.13	Freedom of the press, 2007	3
1.14	Accessibility of digital content, 2007	11

Political and regulatory environment — 5

2.01	Effectiveness of law-making bodies, 2007	16
2.02	Laws relating to ICT, 2007	15
2.03	Judicial independence, 2007	5
2.04	Intellectual property protection, 2007	6
2.05	Efficiency of legal framework, 2007	7
2.06	Property rights, 2007	6
2.07	Quality of competition in the ISP sector, 2007	4
2.08	No. of procedures to enforce a contract,* 2007	4
2.09	Time to enforce a contract,* 2007	58

Infrastructure environment — 16

3.01	Telephone lines,* 2005	20
3.02	Secure Internet servers,* 2006	12
3.03	Electricity production,* 2004	34
3.04	Availability of scientists and engineers, 2007	30
3.05	Quality of scientific research institutions, 2007	10
3.06	Tertiary enrollment,* 2005	25
3.07	Education expenditure,* 2005	38

Readiness component — 17

Individual readiness — 19

4.01	Quality of math and science education, 2007	14
4.02	Quality of the educational system, 2007	13
4.03	Internet access in schools, 2007	11
4.04	Buyer sophistication, 2007	11
4.05	Residential telephone connection charge*	n/a
4.06	Residential monthly telephone subscription*	n/a
4.07	High-speed monthly broadband subscription,* 2006	3
4.08	Lowest cost of broadband,* 2006	1
4.09	Cost of mobile telephone call,* 2005	32

Business readiness — 16

5.01	Extent of staff training, 2007	8
5.02	Local availability of research and training, 2007	7
5.03	Quality of management schools, 2007	11
5.04	Company spending on R&D, 2007	13
5.05	University-industry research collaboration, 2007	13
5.06	Business telephone connection charge*	n/a
5.07	Business monthly telephone subscription*	n/a
5.08	Local supplier quality, 2007	7
5.09	Local supplier quantity, 2007	14
5.10	Computer, comm., and other services imports,* 2005	8

Government readiness — 16

6.01	Government prioritization of ICT, 2007	32
6.02	Gov't procurement of advanced tech products, 2007	19
6.03	Importance of ICT to gov't vision of the future, 2007	46
6.04	E-Government Readiness Index,* 2007	5

Usage component — 3

Individual usage — 1

7.01	Mobile telephone subscribers,* 2005	32
7.02	Personal computers,* 2005	4
7.03	Broadband Internet subscribers,* 2006	2
7.04	Internet users,* 2006	1
7.05	Internet bandwidth,* 2005	2

Business usage — 12

8.01	Prevalence of foreign technology licensing, 2007	6
8.02	Firm-level technology absorption, 2007	27
8.03	Capacity for innovation, 2007	12
8.04	Availability of new telephone lines, 2007	13
8.05	Extent of business Internet use, 2007	12

Government usage — 19

9.01	Government success in ICT promotion, 2007	43
9.02	Availability of government online services, 2007	24
9.03	ICT use and government efficiency, 2007	28
9.04	Presence of ICT in government offices, 2007	16
9.05	E-Participation Index,* 2007	16

* Hard data

Note: For further details and explanation, please refer to the section "How to Read the Country/Economy Profiles" at the beginning of this chapter.

New Zealand

Key indicators

Population (millions), 2006...4.1
GDP (PPP) per capita (US$), 2006..................................25,874.2
Internet users per 100 inhabitants, 2006................................78.8
Internet bandwidth (mB/s) per 10,000 inhabitants, 2005.......11.4

Networked Readiness Index

Year (number of economies)	Rank
2007–2008 (127)	**22**
2006–2007 (122)	22
2005–2006 (115)	21

Global Competitiveness Index 2007–2008 (131)	24

Environment component — 14

Market environment — 27

1.01 Venture capital availability, 2007..14
1.02 Financial market sophistication, 2007 25
1.03 Availability of latest technologies, 2007................................29
1.04 State of cluster development, 2007......................................54
1.05 Utility patents,* 2006 24
1.06 High-tech exports,* 2005 45
1.07 Burden of government regulation, 2007 50
1.08 Extent and effect of taxation, 2007.......................................65
1.09 Total tax rate,* 2007 30
1.10 Time required to start a business,* 2007.............................22
1.11 No. of procedures required to start a business,* 2007 1
1.12 Intensity of local competition, 2007 34
1.13 Freedom of the press, 2007...9
1.14 Accessibility of digital content, 2007....................................56

Political and regulatory environment — 15

2.01 Effectiveness of law-making bodies, 2007 12
2.02 Laws relating to ICT, 2007..17
2.03 Judicial independence, 2007 2
2.04 Intellectual property protection, 2007 13
2.05 Efficiency of legal framework, 2007 12
2.06 Property rights, 2007...16
2.07 Quality of competition in the ISP sector, 2007 106
2.08 No. of procedures to enforce a contract,* 2007..................15
2.09 Time to enforce a contract,* 2007 5

Infrastructure environment — 8

3.01 Telephone lines,* 2005..27
3.02 Secure Internet servers,* 2006...5
3.03 Electricity production,* 2004...12
3.04 Availability of scientists and engineers, 2007 60
3.05 Quality of scientific research institutions, 2007 18
3.06 Tertiary enrollment,* 2005..6
3.07 Education expenditure,* 2005...6

Readiness component — 27

Individual readiness — 20

4.01 Quality of math and science education, 2007.....................29
4.02 Quality of the educational system, 2007.............................21
4.03 Internet access in schools, 2007..22
4.04 Buyer sophistication, 2007 23
4.05 Residential telephone connection charge,* 2005 11
4.06 Residential monthly telephone subscription,* 2005 53
4.07 High-speed monthly broadband subscription,* 2006.........20
4.08 Lowest cost of broadband,* 2006 23
4.09 Cost of mobile telephone call,* 2004...................................59

Business readiness — 26

5.01 Extent of staff training, 2007..22
5.02 Local availability of research and training, 2007.................24
5.03 Quality of management schools, 2007 28
5.04 Company spending on R&D, 2007..38
5.05 University-industry research collaboration, 2007................23
5.06 Business telephone connection charge,* 2005 10
5.07 Business monthly telephone subscription,* 2005 50
5.08 Local supplier quality, 2007 21
5.09 Local supplier quantity, 2007..41
5.10 Computer, comm., and other services imports,* 2005 52

Government readiness — 30

6.01 Government prioritization of ICT, 2007................................58
6.02 Gov't procurement of advanced tech products, 2007 50
6.03 Importance of ICT to gov't vision of the future, 2007........51
6.04 E-Government Readiness Index,* 2007...............................18

Usage component — 23

Individual usage — 24

7.01 Mobile telephone subscribers,* 2005..................................41
7.02 Personal computers,* 2005 21
7.03 Broadband Internet subscribers,* 2006 26
7.04 Internet users,* 2006 2
7.05 Internet bandwidth,* 2005 36

Business usage — 24

8.01 Prevalence of foreign technology licensing, 2007..............13
8.02 Firm-level technology absorption, 2007 25
8.03 Capacity for innovation, 2007...27
8.04 Availability of new telephone lines, 2007............................47
8.05 Extent of business Internet use, 2007.................................25

Government usage — 14

9.01 Government success in ICT promotion, 2007.....................80
9.02 Availability of government online services, 2007 18
9.03 ICT use and government efficiency, 2007............................36
9.04 Presence of ICT in government offices, 2007 19
9.05 E-Participation Index,* 2007...6

* Hard data

Note: For further details and explanation, please refer to the section "How to Read the Country/Economy Profiles" at the beginning of this chapter.

Nicaragua

Key indicators

Population (millions), 2006..5.6
GDP (PPP) per capita (US$), 2006......................................3,886.1
Internet users per 100 inhabitants, 2006 ....2.8
Internet bandwidth (mB/s) per 10,000 inhabitants, 2005.........0.0

Networked Readiness Index

Year (number of economies)	Rank
2007–2008 (127)	**116**
2006–2007 (122)	103
2005–2006 (115)	112

Global Competitiveness Index 2007–2008 (131)   111

Environment component — 116
Market environment — 97
1.01 Venture capital availability, 2007..109
1.02 Financial market sophistication, 2007 93
1.03 Availability of latest technologies, 2007 115
1.04 State of cluster development, 2007......................................93
1.05 Utility patents,* 2006 86
1.06 High-tech exports,* 2005 90
1.07 Burden of government regulation, 2007 60
1.08 Extent and effect of taxation, 2007......................................97
1.09 Total tax rate,* 2007 104
1.10 Time required to start a business,* 2007 87
1.11 No. of procedures required to start a business,* 2007 19
1.12 Intensity of local competition, 2007 112
1.13 Freedom of the press, 2007..29
1.14 Accessibility of digital content, 2007..................................92

Political and regulatory environment — 117
2.01 Effectiveness of law-making bodies, 2007 123
2.02 Laws relating to ICT, 2007..103
2.03 Judicial independence, 2007 125
2.04 Intellectual property protection, 2007 101
2.05 Efficiency of legal framework, 2007...................................124
2.06 Property rights, 2007..106
2.07 Quality of competition in the ISP sector, 2007 103
2.08 No. of procedures to enforce a contract,* 2007 46
2.09 Time to enforce a contract,* 2007 63

Infrastructure environment — 114
3.01 Telephone lines,* 2006...101
3.02 Secure Internet servers,* 2006...78
3.03 Electricity production,* 2004 101
3.04 Availability of scientists and engineers, 2007 112
3.05 Quality of scientific research institutions, 2007 122
3.06 Tertiary enrollment,* 2003...84
3.07 Education expenditure,* 2005...91

Readiness component — 112
Individual readiness — 105
4.01 Quality of math and science education, 2007..................120
4.02 Quality of the educational system, 2007..........................120
4.03 Internet access in schools, 2007...105
4.04 Buyer sophistication, 2007 99
4.05 Residential telephone connection charge,* 2005 114
4.06 Residential monthly telephone subscription,* 2005 101
4.07 High-speed monthly broadband subscription,* 2006........85
4.08 Lowest cost of broadband,* 2006 92
4.09 Cost of mobile telephone call,* 2005................................112

Business readiness — 121
5.01 Extent of staff training, 2007..107
5.02 Local availability of research and training, 2007 97
5.03 Quality of management schools, 2007 71
5.04 Company spending on R&D, 2007......................................118
5.05 University-industry research collaboration, 2007.............111
5.06 Business telephone connection charge,* 2005 116
5.07 Business monthly telephone subscription,* 2005 112
5.08 Local supplier quality, 2007 108
5.09 Local supplier quantity, 2007..113
5.10 Computer, comm., and other services imports,* 2005 96

Government readiness — 110
6.01 Government prioritization of ICT, 2007.............................117
6.02 Gov't procurement of advanced tech products, 2007 110
6.03 Importance of ICT to gov't vision of the future, 2007.......98
6.04 E-Government Readiness Index,* 2007..............................93

Usage component — 113
Individual usage — 95
7.01 Mobile telephone subscribers,* 2006..................................90
7.02 Personal computers,* 2005 88
7.03 Broadband Internet subscribers,* 2006 81
7.04 Internet users,* 2006...112
7.05 Internet bandwidth,* 2005 121

Business usage — 116
8.01 Prevalence of foreign technology licensing, 2007...........119
8.02 Firm-level technology absorption, 2007 123
8.03 Capacity for innovation, 2007 105
8.04 Availability of new telephone lines, 2007........................109
8.05 Extent of business Internet use, 2007 108

Government usage — 107
9.01 Government success in ICT promotion, 2007...................115
9.02 Availability of government online services, 2007 85
9.03 ICT use and government efficiency, 2007..........................94
9.04 Presence of ICT in government offices, 2007 95
9.05 E-Participation Index,* 2007...117

* Hard data

Note: For further details and explanation, please refer to the section "How to Read the Country/Economy Profiles" at the beginning of this chapter.

Nigeria

Key indicators

Population (millions), 2006..134.4
GDP (PPP) per capita (US$), 2006....................................1,226.8
Internet users per 100 inhabitants, 2005 ....3.8
Internet bandwidth (mB/s) per 10,000 inhabitants, 2005.........0.0

Networked Readiness Index

Year (number of economies)	Rank
2007–2008 (127)	**94**
2006–2007 (122)	88
2005–2006 (115)	90

Global Competitiveness Index 2007–2008 (131)   95

Environment component   91
Market environment   73

1.01 Venture capital availability, 2007..82
1.02 Financial market sophistication, 2007 80
1.03 Availability of latest technologies, 2007 98
1.04 State of cluster development, 2007.......................................43
1.05 Utility patents,* 2006 86
1.06 High-tech exports,* 2005 107
1.07 Burden of government regulation, 2007 48
1.08 Extent and effect of taxation, 2007.......................................27
1.09 Total tax rate,* 2007..18
1.10 Time required to start a business,* 2007..............................78
1.11 No. of procedures required to start a business,* 2007 58
1.12 Intensity of local competition, 2007......................................88
1.13 Freedom of the press, 2007..88
1.14 Accessibility of digital content, 2007....................................97

Political and regulatory environment   78

2.01 Effectiveness of law-making bodies, 2007 62
2.02 Laws relating to ICT, 2007...74
2.03 Judicial independence, 2007 77
2.04 Intellectual property protection, 2007 95
2.05 Efficiency of legal framework, 2007......................................80
2.06 Property rights, 2007..98
2.07 Quality of competition in the ISP sector, 2007 70
2.08 No. of procedures to enforce a contract,* 2007 75
2.09 Time to enforce a contract,* 2007 44

Infrastructure environment   120

3.01 Telephone lines,* 2006..111
3.02 Secure Internet servers,* 2006...101
3.03 Electricity production,* 2004 107
3.04 Availability of scientists and engineers, 2007 76
3.05 Quality of scientific research institutions, 2007 57
3.06 Tertiary enrollment,* 2004...98
3.07 Education expenditure,* 2005...120

Readiness component   94
Individual readiness   108

4.01 Quality of math and science education, 2007 97
4.02 Quality of the educational system, 2007.............................68
4.03 Internet access in schools, 2007..100
4.04 Buyer sophistication, 2007 84
4.05 Residential telephone connection charge,* 2005 111
4.06 Residential monthly telephone subscription,* 2005 110
4.07 High-speed monthly broadband subscription* ....n/a
4.08 Lowest cost of broadband*..n/a
4.09 Cost of mobile telephone call,* 2005.................................111

Business readiness   62

5.01 Extent of staff training, 2007 75
5.02 Local availability of research and training, 2007 56
5.03 Quality of management schools, 2007 85
5.04 Company spending on R&D, 2007 44
5.05 University-industry research collaboration, 2007................64
5.06 Business telephone connection charge,* 2005 105
5.07 Business monthly telephone subscription,* 2005 102
5.08 Local supplier quality, 2007 90
5.09 Local supplier quantity, 2007..59
5.10 Computer, comm., and other services imports,* 2005 5

Government readiness   92

6.01 Government prioritization of ICT, 2007................................84
6.02 Gov't procurement of advanced tech products, 2007 41
6.03 Importance of ICT to gov't vision of the future, 2007........68
6.04 E-Government Readiness Index,* 2007............................106

Usage component   90
Individual usage   107

7.01 Mobile telephone subscribers,* 2006................................101
7.02 Personal computers,* 2005 114
7.03 Broadband Internet subscribers,* 2005 116
7.04 Internet users,* 2005...108
7.05 Internet bandwidth,* 2005 120

Business usage   81

8.01 Prevalence of foreign technology licensing, 2007..............74
8.02 Firm-level technology absorption, 2007 79
8.03 Capacity for innovation, 2007 65
8.04 Availability of new telephone lines, 2007 88
8.05 Extent of business Internet use, 2007 81

Government usage   86

9.01 Government success in ICT promotion, 2007.....................63
9.02 Availability of government online services, 2007 64
9.03 ICT use and government efficiency, 2007...........................73
9.04 Presence of ICT in government offices, 2007 93
9.05 E-Participation Index,* 2007...91

* Hard data

Note: For further details and explanation, please refer to the section "How to Read the Country/Economy Profiles" at the beginning of this chapter.

Norway

Key indicators

Population (millions), 2006..4.6
GDP (PPP) per capita (US$), 2006...........................44,648.1
Internet users per 100 inhabitants, 2005 ....58.5
Internet bandwidth (mB/s) per 10,000 inhabitants, 2005.......93.5

Networked Readiness Index

Year (number of economies)	Rank
2007–2008 (127)	**10**
2006–2007 (122)	10
2005–2006 (115)	13

Global Competitiveness Index 2007–2008 (131)　　16

Environment component　　7
Market environment　　19
1.01　Venture capital availability, 2007..4
1.02　Financial market sophistication, 2007 19
1.03　Availability of latest technologies, 2007 9
1.04　State of cluster development, 2007......................................25
1.05　Utility patents,* 2006 21
1.06　High-tech exports,* 2005 54
1.07　Burden of government regulation, 2007 29
1.08　Extent and effect of taxation, 2007......................................62
1.09　Total tax rate,* 2007 57
1.10　Time required to start a business,* 2007............................17
1.11　No. of procedures required to start a business,* 2007 19
1.12　Intensity of local competition, 2007 22
1.13　Freedom of the press, 2007...5
1.14　Accessibility of digital content, 2007...................................10

Political and regulatory environment　　13
2.01　Effectiveness of law-making bodies, 2007 7
2.02　Laws relating to ICT, 2007..8
2.03　Judicial independence, 2007..9
2.04　Intellectual property protection, 2007 16
2.05　Efficiency of legal framework, 2007......................................8
2.06　Property rights, 2007...12
2.07　Quality of competition in the ISP sector, 2007 10
2.08　No. of procedures to enforce a contract,* 2007................35
2.09　Time to enforce a contract,* 2007 19

Infrastructure environment　　6
3.01　Telephone lines,* 2006...22
3.02　Secure Internet servers,* 2006..14
3.03　Electricity production,* 2004 2
3.04　Availability of scientists and engineers, 2007 23
3.05　Quality of scientific research institutions, 2007 21
3.06　Tertiary enrollment,* 2005..10
3.07　Education expenditure,* 2005..8

Readiness component　　10
Individual readiness　　17
4.01　Quality of math and science education, 2007....................51
4.02　Quality of the educational system, 2007............................10
4.03　Internet access in schools, 2007...21
4.04　Buyer sophistication, 2007 22
4.05　Residential telephone connection charge,* 2005 22
4.06　Residential monthly telephone subscription,* 2005 13
4.07　High-speed monthly broadband subscription,* 2006..........8
4.08　Lowest cost of broadband,* 2006 16
4.09　Cost of mobile telephone call,* 2005....................................7

Business readiness　　20
5.01　Extent of staff training, 2007...10
5.02　Local availability of research and training, 2007................18
5.03　Quality of management schools, 2007 21
5.04　Company spending on R&D, 2007.......................................19
5.05　University-industry research collaboration, 2007...............17
5.06　Business telephone connection charge,* 2005 18
5.07　Business monthly telephone subscription,* 2005 8
5.08　Local supplier quality, 2007...14
5.09　Local supplier quantity, 2007...23
5.10　Computer, comm., and other services imports,* 2005 56

Government readiness　　6
6.01　Government prioritization of ICT, 2007...............................22
6.02　Gov't procurement of advanced tech products, 2007 20
6.03　Importance of ICT to gov't vision of the future, 2007.......15
6.04　E-Government Readiness Index,* 2007...............................3

Usage component　　10
Individual usage　　8
7.01　Mobile telephone subscribers,* 2006.................................18
7.02　Personal computers,* 2005 15
7.03　Broadband Internet subscribers,* 2006................................6
7.04　Internet users,* 2005 15
7.05　Internet bandwidth,* 2005 11

Business usage　　14
8.01　Prevalence of foreign technology licensing, 2007.............24
8.02　Firm-level technology absorption, 2007 11
8.03　Capacity for innovation, 2007..15
8.04　Availability of new telephone lines, 2007 12
8.05　Extent of business Internet use, 2007...............................15

Government usage　　12
9.01　Government success in ICT promotion, 2007....................23
9.02　Availability of government online services, 2007..............11
9.03　ICT use and government efficiency, 2007..........................19
9.04　Presence of ICT in government offices, 2007 11
9.05　E-Participation Index,* 2007..16

* Hard data

Note: For further details and explanation, please refer to the section "How to Read the Country/Economy Profiles" at the beginning of this chapter.

Oman

Key indicators

Population (millions), 2006..2.6
GDP (PPP) per capita (US$), 2006..............................18,497.8
Internet users per 100 inhabitants, 2006...........................12.2
Internet bandwidth (mB/s) per 10,000 inhabitants, 2006.........1.7

Networked Readiness Index

Year (number of economies)	Rank
2007–2008 (127)	**53**
2006–2007 (122)	n/a
2005–2006 (115)	n/a

Global Competitiveness Index 2007–2008 (131)　　42

Environment component　　56

Market environment　　44

1.01 Venture capital availability, 2007...21
1.02 Financial market sophistication, 2007..................................44
1.03 Availability of latest technologies, 2007..............................46
1.04 State of cluster development, 2007.....................................36
1.05 Utility patents,* 2006...86
1.06 High-tech exports,* 2005..93
1.07 Burden of government regulation, 2007................................9
1.08 Extent and effect of taxation, 2007......................................16
1.09 Total tax rate,* 2007...7
1.10 Time required to start a business,* 2007............................78
1.11 No. of procedures required to start a business,* 2007 58
1.12 Intensity of local competition, 2007....................................95
1.13 Freedom of the press, 2007...122
1.14 Accessibility of digital content, 2007..................................82

Political and regulatory environment　　46

2.01 Effectiveness of law-making bodies, 2007.........................20
2.02 Laws relating to ICT, 2007..40
2.03 Judicial independence, 2007..46
2.04 Intellectual property protection, 2007.................................32
2.05 Efficiency of legal framework, 2007....................................31
2.06 Property rights, 2007..59
2.07 Quality of competition in the ISP sector, 2007..................79
2.08 No. of procedures to enforce a contract,* 2007...............120
2.09 Time to enforce a contract,* 2007.......................................79

Infrastructure environment　　76

3.01 Telephone lines,* 2006...83
3.02 Secure Internet servers,* 2006..78
3.03 Electricity production,* 2004..46
3.04 Availability of scientists and engineers, 2007....................84
3.05 Quality of scientific research institutions, 2007.................38
3.06 Tertiary enrollment,* 2005..83
3.07 Education expenditure,* 2005..57

Readiness component　　41

Individual readiness　　49

4.01 Quality of math and science education, 2007....................63
4.02 Quality of the educational system, 2007............................48
4.03 Internet access in schools, 2007...51
4.04 Buyer sophistication, 2007...49
4.05 Residential telephone connection charge,* 2005..............16
4.06 Residential monthly telephone subscription,* 2005.........43
4.07 High-speed monthly broadband subscription,* 2006........76
4.08 Lowest cost of broadband,* 2006.......................................69
4.09 Cost of mobile telephone call,* 2005..................................27

Business readiness　　46

5.01 Extent of staff training, 2007..38
5.02 Local availability of research and training, 2007................54
5.03 Quality of management schools, 2007...............................61
5.04 Company spending on R&D, 2007......................................33
5.05 University industry research collaboration, 2007...............29
5.06 Business telephone connection charge,* 2005..................14
5.07 Business monthly telephone subscription,* 2005.............26
5.08 Local supplier quality, 2007..75
5.09 Local supplier quantity, 2007...84
5.10 Computer, comm., and other services imports,* 2005 40

Government readiness　　46

6.01 Government prioritization of ICT, 2007...............................66
6.02 Gov't procurement of advanced tech products, 2007.......36
6.03 Importance of ICT to gov't vision of the future, 2007.......24
6.04 E-Government Readiness Index,* 2007..............................75

Usage component　　59

Individual usage　　69

7.01 Mobile telephone subscribers,* 2006..................................60
7.02 Personal computers,* 2005..77
7.03 Broadband Internet subscribers,* 2006..............................76
7.04 Internet users,* 2006..75
7.05 Internet bandwidth,* 2006...61

Business usage　　67

8.01 Prevalence of foreign technology licensing, 2007.............69
8.02 Firm-level technology absorption, 2007.............................95
8.03 Capacity for innovation, 2007..32
8.04 Availability of new telephone lines, 2007...........................98
8.05 Extent of business Internet use, 2007................................44

Government usage　　46

9.01 Government success in ICT promotion, 2007....................56
9.02 Availability of government online services, 2007..............30
9.03 ICT use and government efficiency, 2007..........................52
9.04 Presence of ICT in government offices, 2007....................63
9.05 E-Participation Index,* 2007..58

* Hard data

Note: For further details and explanation, please refer to the section "How to Read the Country/Economy Profiles" at the beginning of this chapter.

Pakistan

Key indicators

Population (millions), 2006	161.2
GDP (PPP) per capita (US$), 2006	2,744.5
Internet users per 100 inhabitants, 2006	7.6
Internet bandwidth (mB/s) per 10,000 inhabitants, 2005	0.0

Networked Readiness Index

Year (number of economies)	Rank
2007–2008 (127)	**89**
2006–2007 (122)	84
2005–2006 (115)	67

Global Competitiveness Index 2007–2008 (131)	92

Environment component — 101
Market environment — 75

1.01	Venture capital availability, 2007	87
1.02	Financial market sophistication, 2007	70
1.03	Availability of latest technologies, 2007	77
1.04	State of cluster development, 2007	65
1.05	Utility patents,* 2006	85
1.06	High-tech exports,* 2005	65
1.07	Burden of government regulation, 2007	69
1.08	Extent and effect of taxation, 2007	32
1.09	Total tax rate,* 2007	52
1.10	Time required to start a business,* 2007	50
1.11	No. of procedures required to start a business,* 2007	88
1.12	Intensity of local competition, 2007	103
1.13	Freedom of the press, 2007	74
1.14	Accessibility of digital content, 2007	94

Political and regulatory environment — 93

2.01	Effectiveness of law-making bodies, 2007	66
2.02	Laws relating to ICT, 2007	69
2.03	Judicial independence, 2007	78
2.04	Intellectual property protection, 2007	61
2.05	Efficiency of legal framework, 2007	88
2.06	Property rights, 2007	91
2.07	Quality of competition in the ISP sector, 2007	60
2.08	No. of procedures to enforce a contract,* 2007	114
2.09	Time to enforce a contract,* 2007	108

Infrastructure environment — 118

3.01	Telephone lines,* 2006	106
3.02	Secure Internet servers,* 2006	101
3.03	Electricity production,* 2004	98
3.04	Availability of scientists and engineers, 2007	85
3.05	Quality of scientific research institutions, 2007	71
3.06	Tertiary enrollment,* 2005	107
3.07	Education expenditure,* 2005	114

Readiness component — 89
Individual readiness — 103

4.01	Quality of math and science education, 2007	98
4.02	Quality of the educational system, 2007	85
4.03	Internet access in schools, 2007	68
4.04	Buyer sophistication, 2007	91
4.05	Residential telephone connection charge,* 2006	74
4.06	Residential monthly telephone subscription,* 2006	92
4.07	High-speed monthly broadband subscription,* 2006	99
4.08	Lowest cost of broadband,* 2006	104
4.09	Cost of mobile telephone call,* 2005	89

Business readiness — 68

5.01	Extent of staff training, 2007	115
5.02	Local availability of research and training, 2007	92
5.03	Quality of management schools, 2007	77
5.04	Company spending on R&D, 2007	72
5.05	University-industry research collaboration, 2007	60
5.06	Business telephone connection charge,* 2006	68
5.07	Business monthly telephone subscription,* 2006	79
5.08	Local supplier quality, 2007	79
5.09	Local supplier quantity, 2007	48
5.10	Computer, comm., and other services imports,* 2005	19

Government readiness — 73

6.01	Government prioritization of ICT, 2007	38
6.02	Gov't procurement of advanced tech products, 2007	48
6.03	Importance of ICT to gov't vision of the future, 2007	65
6.04	E-Government Readiness Index,* 2007	102

Usage component — 86
Individual usage — 102

7.01	Mobile telephone subscribers,* 2006	103
7.02	Personal computers,* 2005	118
7.03	Broadband Internet subscribers,* 2005	101
7.04	Internet users,* 2006	90
7.05	Internet bandwidth,* 2005	113

Business usage — 75

8.01	Prevalence of foreign technology licensing, 2007	64
8.02	Firm-level technology absorption, 2007	68
8.03	Capacity for innovation, 2007	70
8.04	Availability of new telephone lines, 2007	78
8.05	Extent of business Internet use, 2007	85

Government usage — 85

9.01	Government success in ICT promotion, 2007	55
9.02	Availability of government online services, 2007	88
9.03	ICT use and government efficiency, 2007	64
9.04	Presence of ICT in government offices, 2007	89
9.05	E-Participation Index,* 2007	82

* Hard data

Note: For further details and explanation, please refer to the section "How to Read the Country/Economy Profiles" at the beginning of this chapter.

Panama

Key indicators

Population (millions), 2006..3.3
GDP (PPP) per capita (US$), 2006.....................................8,593.3
Internet users per 100 inhabitants, 2006 ....6.7
Internet bandwidth (mB/s) per 10,000 inhabitants, 2005.........2.9

Networked Readiness Index

Year (number of economies)	Rank
2007–2008 (127)	**64**
2006–2007 (122)	65
2005–2006 (115)	66

Global Competitiveness Index 2007–2008 (131) 59

Environment component	57
Market environment	**50**

1.01 Venture capital availability, 2007..36
1.02 Financial market sophistication, 2007 28
1.03 Availability of latest technologies, 2007 48
1.04 State of cluster development, 2007......................................49
1.05 Utility patents,* 2006 86
1.06 High-tech exports,* 2005 108
1.07 Burden of government regulation, 2007 51
1.08 Extent and effect of taxation, 2007......................................84
1.09 Total tax rate,* 2007..82
1.10 Time required to start a business,* 2007.............................41
1.11 No. of procedures required to start a business,* 2007 34
1.12 Intensity of local competition, 2007.....................................68
1.13 Freedom of the press, 2007..57
1.14 Accessibility of digital content, 2007...................................58

Political and regulatory environment	**66**

2.01 Effectiveness of law-making bodies, 2007 110
2.02 Laws relating to ICT, 2007..53
2.03 Judicial independence, 2007 111
2.04 Intellectual property protection, 2007 47
2.05 Efficiency of legal framework, 2007....................................99
2.06 Property rights, 2007...49
2.07 Quality of competition in the ISP sector, 2007 39
2.08 No. of procedures to enforce a contract,* 2007...............26
2.09 Time to enforce a contract,* 2007 88

Infrastructure environment	**69**

3.01 Telephone lines,* 2006..76
3.02 Secure Internet servers,* 2006 33
3.03 Electricity production,* 2004 72
3.04 Availability of scientists and engineers, 2007 94
3.05 Quality of scientific research institutions, 2007 93
3.06 Tertiary enrollment,* 2005...42
3.07 Education expenditure,* 2005...48

Readiness component	71
Individual readiness	**64**

4.01 Quality of math and science education, 2007..................108
4.02 Quality of the educational system, 2007..........................103
4.03 Internet access in schools, 2007...66
4.04 Buyer sophistication, 2007 42
4.05 Residential telephone connection charge,* 2006 56
4.06 Residential monthly telephone subscription,* 2006 46
4.07 High-speed monthly broadband subscription,* 2006........64
4.08 Lowest cost of broadband,* 2006 76
4.09 Cost of mobile telephone call,* 2006..................................58

Business readiness	**71**

5.01 Extent of staff training, 2007..56
5.02 Local availability of research and training, 2007 67
5.03 Quality of management schools, 2007 80
5.04 Company spending on R&D, 2007 77
5.05 University industry research collaboration, 2007...............81
5.06 Business telephone connection charge,* 2005 47
5.07 Business monthly telephone subscription,* 2005.............69
5.08 Local supplier quality, 2007 56
5.09 Local supplier quantity, 2007...61
5.10 Computer, comm., and other services imports,* 2005 99

Government readiness	**82**

6.01 Government prioritization of ICT, 2007.............................107
6.02 Gov't procurement of advanced tech products, 2007 78
6.03 Importance of ICT to gov't vision of the future, 2007.......80
6.04 E-Government Readiness Index,* 2007..............................74

Usage component	76
Individual usage	**85**

7.01 Mobile telephone subscribers,* 2005.................................76
7.02 Personal computers,* 2005 81
7.03 Broadband Internet subscribers,* 2005 77
7.04 Internet users,* 2006...95
7.05 Internet bandwidth,* 2005 57

Business usage	**53**

8.01 Prevalence of foreign technology licensing, 2007.............46
8.02 Firm-level technology absorption, 2007 49
8.03 Capacity for innovation, 2007..102
8.04 Availability of new telephone lines, 2007...........................54
8.05 Extent of business Internet use, 2007 40

Government usage	**84**

9.01 Government success in ICT promotion, 2007..................104
9.02 Availability of government online services, 2007 55
9.03 ICT use and government efficiency, 2007..........................66
9.04 Presence of ICT in government offices, 2007 91
9.05 E-Participation Index,* 2007...76

* Hard data

Note: For further details and explanation, please refer to the section "How to Read the Country/Economy Profiles" at the beginning of this chapter.

Paraguay

Key indicators

Population (millions), 2006..6.3
GDP (PPP) per capita (US$), 2006.......................................5,339.2
Internet users per 100 inhabitants, 2006 ....4.1
Internet bandwidth (mB/s) per 10,000 inhabitants, 2006.........0.8

Networked Readiness Index

Year (number of economies)	Rank
2007–2008 (127)	**120**
2006–2007 (122)	114
2005–2006 (115)	113

Global Competitiveness Index 2007–2008 (131)   121

Environment component — 114
Market environment — 89
1.01 Venture capital availability, 2007..116
1.02 Financial market sophistication, 2007 112
1.03 Availability of latest technologies, 2007 122
1.04 State of cluster development, 2007...................................110
1.05 Utility patents,* 2006 68
1.06 High-tech exports,* 2005 82
1.07 Burden of government regulation, 2007 70
1.08 Extent and effect of taxation, 2007......................................28
1.09 Total tax rate,* 2007 31
1.10 Time required to start a business,* 2007..........................81
1.11 No. of procedures required to start a business,* 2007 34
1.12 Intensity of local competition, 2007 109
1.13 Freedom of the press, 2007..55
1.14 Accessibility of digital content, 2007..................................95

Political and regulatory environment — 125
2.01 Effectiveness of law-making bodies, 2007 125
2.02 Laws relating to ICT, 2007..125
2.03 Judicial independence, 2007 126
2.04 Intellectual property protection, 2007 119
2.05 Efficiency of legal framework, 2007...................................126
2.06 Property rights, 2007...122
2.07 Quality of competition in the ISP sector, 2007 115
2.08 No. of procedures to enforce a contract,* 2007 65
2.09 Time to enforce a contract,* 2007 76

Infrastructure environment — 100
3.01 Telephone lines,* 2006..99
3.02 Secure Internet servers,* 2006...90
3.03 Electricity production,* 2004 15
3.04 Availability of scientists and engineers, 2007 126
3.05 Quality of scientific research institutions, 2007 127
3.06 Tertiary enrollment,* 2004..72
3.07 Education expenditure,* 2005...58

Readiness component — 115
Individual readiness — 104
4.01 Quality of math and science education, 2007.................126
4.02 Quality of the educational system, 2007..........................127
4.03 Internet access in schools, 2007..124
4.04 Buyer sophistication, 2007 111
4.05 Residential telephone connection charge,* 2005 110
4.06 Residential monthly telephone subscription,* 2005 84
4.07 High-speed monthly broadband subscription* ....n/a
4.08 Lowest cost of broadband,* 2006 78
4.09 Cost of mobile telephone call,* 2005..................................82

Business readiness — 116
5.01 Extent of staff training, 2007..118
5.02 Local availability of research and training, 2007..............114
5.03 Quality of management schools, 2007 116
5.04 Company spending on R&D, 2007.......................................125
5.05 University-industry research collaboration, 2007.............125
5.06 Business telephone connection charge,* 2005 104
5.07 Business monthly telephone subscription,* 2005 73
5.08 Local supplier quality, 2007 109
5.09 Local supplier quantity, 2007..108
5.10 Computer, comm., and other services imports,* 2005 ..113

Government readiness — 123
6.01 Government prioritization of ICT, 2007.............................126
6.02 Gov't procurement of advanced tech products, 2007 125
6.03 Importance of ICT to gov't vision of the future, 2007.....124
6.04 E-Government Readiness Index,* 2007..............................78

Usage component — 121
Individual usage — 86
7.01 Mobile telephone subscribers,* 2006..................................78
7.02 Personal computers,* 2005 65
7.03 Broadband Internet subscribers,* 2006 84
7.04 Internet users,* 2006 104
7.05 Internet bandwidth,* 2006 75

Business usage — 124
8.01 Prevalence of foreign technology licensing, 2007...........124
8.02 Firm-level technology absorption, 2007 126
8.03 Capacity for innovation, 2007 116
8.04 Availability of new telephone lines, 2007........................118
8.05 Extent of business Internet use, 2007 121

Government usage — 125
9.01 Government success in ICT promotion, 2007..................127
9.02 Availability of government online services, 2007 105
9.03 ICT use and government efficiency, 2007........................113
9.04 Presence of ICT in government offices, 2007 125
9.05 E-Participation Index,* 2007...91

* Hard data

Note: For further details and explanation, please refer to the section "How to Read the Country/Economy Profiles" at the beginning of this chapter.

Peru

Key indicators

Population (millions), 2006	28.4
GDP (PPP) per capita (US$), 2006	6,855.5
Internet users per 100 inhabitants, 2006	21.5
Internet bandwidth (mB/s) per 10,000 inhabitants, 2005	3.6

Networked Readiness Index

Year (number of economies)	Rank
2007–2008 (127)	**84**
2006–2007 (122)	78
2005–2006 (115)	85

Global Competitiveness Index 2007–2008 (131)	86

Environment component — 98

Market environment — 79

1.01	Venture capital availability, 2007	68
1.02	Financial market sophistication, 2007	60
1.03	Availability of latest technologies, 2007	81
1.04	State of cluster development, 2007	77
1.05	Utility patents,* 2006	76
1.06	High-tech exports,* 2005	84
1.07	Burden of government regulation, 2007	121
1.08	Extent and effect of taxation, 2007	89
1.09	Total tax rate,* 2007	56
1.10	Time required to start a business,* 2007	109
1.11	No. of procedures required to start a business,* 2007	74
1.12	Intensity of local competition, 2007	53
1.13	Freedom of the press, 2007	19
1.14	Accessibility of digital content, 2007	86

Political and regulatory environment — 109

2.01	Effectiveness of law-making bodies, 2007	121
2.02	Laws relating to ICT, 2007	72
2.03	Judicial independence, 2007	118
2.04	Intellectual property protection, 2007	110
2.05	Efficiency of legal framework, 2007	119
2.06	Property rights, 2007	107
2.07	Quality of competition in the ISP sector, 2007	74
2.08	No. of procedures to enforce a contract,* 2007	94
2.09	Time to enforce a contract,* 2007	48

Infrastructure environment — 98

3.01	Telephone lines,* 2006	92
3.02	Secure Internet servers,* 2006	63
3.03	Electricity production,* 2004	85
3.04	Availability of scientists and engineers, 2007	89
3.05	Quality of scientific research institutions, 2007	111
3.06	Tertiary enrollment,* 2005	58
3.07	Education expenditure,* 2005	93

Readiness component — 85

Individual readiness — 89

4.01	Quality of math and science education, 2007	127
4.02	Quality of the educational system, 2007	126
4.03	Internet access in schools, 2007	74
4.04	Buyer sophistication, 2007	64
4.05	Residential telephone connection charge,* 2006	46
4.06	Residential monthly telephone subscription,* 2006	98
4.07	High-speed monthly broadband subscription,* 2006	60
4.08	Lowest cost of broadband,* 2006	74
4.09	Cost of mobile telephone call,* 2006	88

Business readiness — 67

5.01	Extent of staff training, 2007	85
5.02	Local availability of research and training, 2007	76
5.03	Quality of management schools, 2007	47
5.04	Company spending on R&D, 2007	73
5.05	University industry research collaboration, 2007	98
5.06	Business telephone connection charge,* 2006	38
5.07	Business monthly telephone subscription,* 2006	92
5.08	Local supplier quality, 2007	47
5.09	Local supplier quantity, 2007	46
5.10	Computer, comm., and other services imports,* 2005	65

Government readiness — 101

6.01	Government prioritization of ICT, 2007	113
6.02	Gov't procurement of advanced tech products, 2007	112
6.03	Importance of ICT to gov't vision of the future, 2007	102
6.04	E-Government Readiness Index,* 2007	54

Usage component — 82

Individual usage — 75

7.01	Mobile telephone subscribers,* 2006	93
7.02	Personal computers,* 2005	57
7.03	Broadband Internet subscribers,* 2006	59
7.04	Internet users,* 2006	52
7.05	Internet bandwidth,* 2005	55

Business usage — 77

8.01	Prevalence of foreign technology licensing, 2007	94
8.02	Firm-level technology absorption, 2007	91
8.03	Capacity for innovation, 2007	66
8.04	Availability of new telephone lines, 2007	55
8.05	Extent of business Internet use, 2007	70

Government usage — 88

9.01	Government success in ICT promotion, 2007	113
9.02	Availability of government online services, 2007	52
9.03	ICT use and government efficiency, 2007	55
9.04	Presence of ICT in government offices, 2007	103
9.05	E-Participation Index,* 2007	69

* Hard data

Note: For further details and explanation, please refer to the section "How to Read the Country/Economy Profiles" at the beginning of this chapter.

Philippines

Key indicators

Population (millions), 2006	84.5
GDP (PPP) per capita (US$), 2006	5,365.3
Internet users per 100 inhabitants, 2005	5.5
Internet bandwidth (mB/s) per 10,000 inhabitants, 2005	0.4

Networked Readiness Index

Year (number of economies)	Rank
2007–2008 (127)	**81**
2006–2007 (122)	69
2005–2006 (115)	70

Global Competitiveness Index 2007–2008 (131)	71

Environment component — 77

Market environment — 56

1.01	Venture capital availability, 2007	78
1.02	Financial market sophistication, 2007	63
1.03	Availability of latest technologies, 2007	57
1.04	State of cluster development, 2007	51
1.05	Utility patents,* 2006	62
1.06	High-tech exports,* 2005	1
1.07	Burden of government regulation, 2007	114
1.08	Extent and effect of taxation, 2007	55
1.09	Total tax rate,* 2007	92
1.10	Time required to start a business,* 2007	103
1.11	No. of procedures required to start a business,* 2007	115
1.12	Intensity of local competition, 2007	57
1.13	Freedom of the press, 2007	61
1.14	Accessibility of digital content, 2007	61

Political and regulatory environment — 80

2.01	Effectiveness of law-making bodies, 2007	103
2.02	Laws relating to ICT, 2007	55
2.03	Judicial independence, 2007	84
2.04	Intellectual property protection, 2007	89
2.05	Efficiency of legal framework, 2007	91
2.06	Property rights, 2007	74
2.07	Quality of competition in the ISP sector, 2007	34
2.08	No. of procedures to enforce a contract,* 2007	60
2.09	Time to enforce a contract,* 2007	103

Infrastructure environment — 101

3.01	Telephone lines,* 2006	103
3.02	Secure Internet servers,* 2006	78
3.03	Electricity production,* 2004	92
3.04	Availability of scientists and engineers, 2007	92
3.05	Quality of scientific research institutions, 2007	83
3.06	Tertiary enrollment,* 2005	69
3.07	Education expenditure,* 2005	95

Readiness component — 87

Individual readiness — 87

4.01	Quality of math and science education, 2007	106
4.02	Quality of the educational system, 2007	52
4.03	Internet access in schools, 2007	58
4.04	Buyer sophistication, 2007	52
4.05	Residential telephone connection charge,* 2005	86
4.06	Residential monthly telephone subscription,* 2005	112
4.07	High-speed monthly broadband subscription,* 2006	83
4.08	Lowest cost of broadband,* 2006	57
4.09	Cost of mobile telephone call,* 2005	90

Business readiness — 88

5.01	Extent of staff training, 2007	31
5.02	Local availability of research and training, 2007	62
5.03	Quality of management schools, 2007	35
5.04	Company spending on R&D, 2007	52
5.05	University-industry research collaboration, 2007	65
5.06	Business telephone connection charge,* 2005	90
5.07	Business monthly telephone subscription,* 2005	117
5.08	Local supplier quality, 2007	60
5.09	Local supplier quantity, 2007	60
5.10	Computer, comm., and other services imports,* 2005	87

Government readiness — 90

6.01	Government prioritization of ICT, 2007	104
6.02	Gov't procurement of advanced tech products, 2007	99
6.03	Importance of ICT to gov't vision of the future, 2007	91
6.04	E-Government Readiness Index,* 2007	63

Usage component — 78

Individual usage — 88

7.01	Mobile telephone subscribers,* 2006	80
7.02	Personal computers,* 2005	75
7.03	Broadband Internet subscribers,* 2005	92
7.04	Internet users,* 2005	99
7.05	Internet bandwidth,* 2005	83

Business usage — 60

8.01	Prevalence of foreign technology licensing, 2007	47
8.02	Firm-level technology absorption, 2007	52
8.03	Capacity for innovation, 2007	59
8.04	Availability of new telephone lines, 2007	74
8.05	Extent of business Internet use, 2007	67

Government usage — 75

9.01	Government success in ICT promotion, 2007	81
9.02	Availability of government online services, 2007	72
9.03	ICT use and government efficiency, 2007	68
9.04	Presence of ICT in government offices, 2007	94
9.05	E-Participation Index,* 2007	43

* Hard data

Note: For further details and explanation, please refer to the section "How to Read the Country/Economy Profiles" at the beginning of this chapter.

Poland

Key indicators

Population (millions), 2006	38.5
GDP (PPP) per capita (US$), 2006	15,149.0
Internet users per 100 inhabitants, 2006	28.6
Internet bandwidth (mB/s) per 10,000 inhabitants, 2005	5.6

Networked Readiness Index

Year (number of economies)	Rank
2007–2008 (127)	**62**
2006–2007 (122)	58
2005–2006 (115)	53

Global Competitiveness Index 2007–2008 (131)	51

Environment component — 58

Market environment — 74

1.01	Venture capital availability, 2007	43
1.02	Financial market sophistication, 2007	68
1.03	Availability of latest technologies, 2007	79
1.04	State of cluster development, 2007	85
1.05	Utility patents,* 2006	50
1.06	High-tech exports,* 2005	51
1.07	Burden of government regulation, 2007	94
1.08	Extent and effect of taxation, 2007	98
1.09	Total tax rate,* 2007	44
1.10	Time required to start a business,* 2007	68
1.11	No. of procedures required to start a business,* 2007	74
1.12	Intensity of local competition, 2007	70
1.13	Freedom of the press, 2007	75
1.14	Accessibility of digital content, 2007	78

Political and regulatory environment — 90

2.01	Effectiveness of law-making bodies, 2007	104
2.02	Laws relating to ICT, 2007	67
2.03	Judicial independence, 2007	76
2.04	Intellectual property protection, 2007	66
2.05	Efficiency of legal framework, 2007	87
2.06	Property rights, 2007	89
2.07	Quality of competition in the ISP sector, 2007	90
2.08	No. of procedures to enforce a contract,* 2007	65
2.09	Time to enforce a contract,* 2007	102

Infrastructure environment — 38

3.01	Telephone lines,* 2006	39
3.02	Secure Internet servers,* 2006	40
3.03	Electricity production,* 2004	49
3.04	Availability of scientists and engineers, 2007	73
3.05	Quality of scientific research institutions, 2007	62
3.06	Tertiary enrollment,* 2005	22
3.07	Education expenditure,* 2005	23

Readiness component — 65

Individual readiness — 51

4.01	Quality of math and science education, 2007	46
4.02	Quality of the educational system, 2007	47
4.03	Internet access in schools, 2007	48
4.04	Buyer sophistication, 2007	74
4.05	Residential telephone connection charge,* 2005	66
4.06	Residential monthly telephone subscription,* 2005	71
4.07	High-speed monthly broadband subscription,* 2006	50
4.08	Lowest cost of broadband,* 2006	33
4.09	Cost of mobile telephone call,* 2005	53

Business readiness — 59

5.01	Extent of staff training, 2007	66
5.02	Local availability of research and training, 2007	41
5.03	Quality of management schools, 2007	50
5.04	Company spending on R&D, 2007	41
5.05	University-industry research collaboration, 2007	56
5.06	Business telephone connection charge,* 2005	58
5.07	Business monthly telephone subscription*	n/a
5.08	Local supplier quality, 2007	65
5.09	Local supplier quantity, 2007	77
5.10	Computer, comm., and other services imports,* 2005	26

Government readiness — 96

6.01	Government prioritization of ICT, 2007	120
6.02	Gov't procurement of advanced tech products, 2007	88
6.03	Importance of ICT to gov't vision of the future, 2007	108
6.04	E-Government Readiness Index,* 2007	33

Usage component — 63

Individual usage — 42

7.01	Mobile telephone subscribers,* 2006	34
7.02	Personal computers,* 2005	33
7.03	Broadband Internet subscribers,* 2006	36
7.04	Internet users,* 2006	44
7.05	Internet bandwidth,* 2005	48

Business usage — 70

8.01	Prevalence of foreign technology licensing, 2007	82
8.02	Firm-level technology absorption, 2007	75
8.03	Capacity for innovation, 2007	43
8.04	Availability of new telephone lines, 2007	99
8.05	Extent of business Internet use, 2007	38

Government usage — 103

9.01	Government success in ICT promotion, 2007	118
9.02	Availability of government online services, 2007	91
9.03	ICT use and government efficiency, 2007	107
9.04	Presence of ICT in government offices, 2007	108
9.05	E-Participation Index,* 2007	53

* Hard data

Note: For further details and explanation, please refer to the section "How to Read the Country/Economy Profiles" at the beginning of this chapter.

Portugal

Key indicators

Population (millions), 2006...10.5
GDP (PPP) per capita (US$), 2006..................................22,936.8
Internet users per 100 inhabitants, 2006 ....30.5
Internet bandwidth (mB/s) per 10,000 inhabitants, 2005.........8.3

Networked Readiness Index

Year (number of economies)	Rank
2007–2008 (127)	**28**
2006–2007 (122)	28
2005–2006 (115)	27

Global Competitiveness Index 2007–2008 (131)	40

Environment component — 28
Market environment — 32
1.01 Venture capital availability, 2007..40
1.02 Financial market sophistication, 2007 26
1.03 Availability of latest technologies, 2007 35
1.04 State of cluster development, 2007.....................................72
1.05 Utility patents,* 2006 43
1.06 High-tech exports,* 2005 37
1.07 Burden of government regulation, 2007 61
1.08 Extent and effect of taxation, 2007......................................81
1.09 Total tax rate,* 2007 63
1.10 Time required to start a business,* 2007 9
1.11 No. of procedures required to start a business,* 2007 34
1.12 Intensity of local competition, 2007 44
1.13 Freedom of the press, 2007...14
1.14 Accessibility of digital content, 2007...................................30

Political and regulatory environment — 30
2.01 Effectiveness of law-making bodies, 2007 41
2.02 Laws relating to ICT, 2007..23
2.03 Judicial independence, 2007 18
2.04 Intellectual property protection, 2007 29
2.05 Efficiency of legal framework, 2007....................................52
2.06 Property rights, 2007...28
2.07 Quality of competition in the ISP sector, 2007 35
2.08 No. of procedures to enforce a contract,* 2007................46
2.09 Time to enforce a contract,* 2007 73

Infrastructure environment — 27
3.01 Telephone lines,* 2006..33
3.02 Secure Internet servers,* 2006..31
3.03 Electricity production,* 2004..48
3.04 Availability of scientists and engineers, 2007 32
3.05 Quality of scientific research institutions, 2007 32
3.06 Tertiary enrollment,* 2005..29
3.07 Education expenditure,* 2005..21

Readiness component — 31
Individual readiness — 45
4.01 Quality of math and science education, 2007 89
4.02 Quality of the educational system, 2007............................65
4.03 Internet access in schools, 2007..29
4.04 Buyer sophistication, 2007 45
4.05 Residential telephone connection charge,* 2005 52
4.06 Residential monthly telephone subscription,* 2005 55
4.07 High-speed monthly broadband subscription,* 2006........36
4.08 Lowest cost of broadband,* 2006 21
4.09 Cost of mobile telephone call,* 2005..................................26

Business readiness — 44
5.01 Extent of staff training, 2007..53
5.02 Local availability of research and training, 2007 37
5.03 Quality of management schools, 2007 34
5.04 Company spending on R&D, 2007......................................54
5.05 University-industry research collaboration, 2007...............39
5.06 Business telephone connection charge,* 2005 42
5.07 Business monthly telephone subscription,* 2005 41
5.08 Local supplier quality, 2007..44
5.09 Local supplier quantity, 2007..43
5.10 Computer, comm., and other services imports,* 2005 42

Government readiness — 12
6.01 Government prioritization of ICT, 2007.................................8
6.02 Gov't procurement of advanced tech products, 2007 30
6.03 Importance of ICT to gov't vision of the future, 2007.........2
6.04 E-Government Readiness Index,* 2007.............................31

Usage component — 29
Individual usage — 33
7.01 Mobile telephone subscribers,* 2006.................................12
7.02 Personal computers,* 2005 50
7.03 Broadband Internet subscribers,* 2006 27
7.04 Internet users,* 2006...42
7.05 Internet bandwidth,* 2005 41

Business usage — 29
8.01 Prevalence of foreign technology licensing, 2007...............7
8.02 Firm-level technology absorption, 2007 43
8.03 Capacity for innovation, 2007 33
8.04 Availability of new telephone lines, 2007 31
8.05 Extent of business Internet use, 2007 36

Government usage — 23
9.01 Government success in ICT promotion, 2007....................16
9.02 Availability of government online services, 2007 26
9.03 ICT use and government efficiency, 2007..........................10
9.04 Presence of ICT in government offices, 2007 28
9.05 E-Participation Index,* 2007...47

* Hard data

Note: For further details and explanation, please refer to the section "How to Read the Country/Economy Profiles" at the beginning of this chapter.

Puerto Rico

Key indicators

Population (millions), 2006..4.0
GDP (PPP) per capita (US$), 2006..n/a
Internet users per 100 inhabitants, 2006 ....25.0
Internet bandwidth (mB/s) per 10,000 inhabitants, 2005.........5.0

Networked Readiness Index

Year (number of economies)	Rank
2007–2008 (127)	**39**
2006–2007 (122)	n/a
2005–2006 (115)	n/a

Global Competitiveness Index 2007–2008 (131)   36

Environment component | 31
Market environment | **28**
1.01 Venture capital availability, 2007..31
1.02 Financial market sophistication, 2007 23
1.03 Availability of latest technologies, 2007 24
1.04 State of cluster development, 2007..................................32
1.05 Utility patents,* 2006 28
1.06 High-tech exports,* 2006 10
1.07 Burden of government regulation, 2007 126
1.08 Extent and effect of taxation, 2007......................................91
1.09 Total tax rate,* 2007 61
1.10 Time required to start a business,* 2007............................9
1.11 No. of procedures required to start a business,* 2007 34
1.12 Intensity of local competition, 2007 11
1.13 Freedom of the press, 2007...16
1.14 Accessibility of digital content, 2007..................................25

Political and regulatory environment | **34**
2.01 Effectiveness of law-making bodies, 2007 112
2.02 Laws relating to ICT, 2007..34
2.03 Judicial independence, 2007 38
2.04 Intellectual property protection, 2007 20
2.05 Efficiency of legal framework, 2007....................................41
2.06 Property rights, 2007..21
2.07 Quality of competition in the ISP sector, 2007 24
2.08 No. of procedures to enforce a contract,* 2007...............94
2.09 Time to enforce a contract,* 2007 85

Infrastructure environment | **43**
3.01 Telephone lines,* 2005...48
3.02 Secure Internet servers,* 2006...43
3.03 Electricity production,* 2006...32
3.04 Availability of scientists and engineers, 2007 19
3.05 Quality of scientific research institutions, 2007 35
3.06 Tertiary enrollment,* 2002..48
3.07 Education expenditure* ....n/a

Readiness component | 43
Individual readiness | **60**
4.01 Quality of math and science education, 2007...................87
4.02 Quality of the educational system, 2007............................58
4.03 Internet access in schools, 2007..57
4.04 Buyer sophistication, 2007 34
4.05 Residential telephone connection charge,* 2005 20
4.06 Residential monthly telephone subscription,* 2006 9
4.07 High-speed monthly broadband subscription,* 2006........11
4.08 Lowest cost of broadband*..n/a
4.09 Cost of mobile telephone call,* 2005..................................22

Business readiness | **23**
5.01 Extent of staff training, 2007...26
5.02 Local availability of research and training, 2007................30
5.03 Quality of management schools, 2007 39
5.04 Company spending on R&D, 2007 34
5.05 University-industry research collaboration, 2007...............26
5.06 Business telephone connection charge,* 2006 46
5.07 Business monthly telephone subscription,* 2006 1
5.08 Local supplier quality, 2007...23
5.09 Local supplier quantity, 2007..45
5.10 Computer, comm., and other services imports*..............n/a

Government readiness | **72**
6.01 Government prioritization of ICT, 2007...............................62
6.02 Gov't procurement of advanced tech products, 2007 59
6.03 Importance of ICT to gov't vision of the future, 2007.......97
6.04 E-Government Readiness Index* ....n/a

Usage component | 42
Individual usage | **52**
7.01 Mobile telephone subscribers,* 2006..................................44
7.02 Personal computers,* 2005 115
7.03 Broadband Internet subscribers,* 2005 53
7.04 Internet users,* 2006..47
7.05 Internet bandwidth,* 2005...50

Business usage | **30**
8.01 Prevalence of foreign technology licensing, 2007.............32
8.02 Firm-level technology absorption, 2007 20
8.03 Capacity for innovation, 2007...51
8.04 Availability of new telephone lines, 2007...........................64
8.05 Extent of business Internet use, 2007 21

Government usage | **45**
9.01 Government success in ICT promotion, 2007....................70
9.02 Availability of government online services, 2007..............47
9.03 ICT use and government efficiency, 2007...........................83
9.04 Presence of ICT in government offices, 2007 72
9.05 E-Participation Index* ....n/a

* Hard data

Note: For further details and explanation, please refer to the section "How to Read the Country/Economy Profiles" at the beginning of this chapter.

Qatar

Key indicators

Population (millions), 2006..0.9
GDP (PPP) per capita (US$), 2006.................................36,631.8
Internet users per 100 inhabitants, 2006 ....34.5
Internet bandwidth (mB/s) per 10,000 inhabitants, 2004........6.2

Networked Readiness Index

Year (number of economies)	Rank
2007–2008 (127)	**32**
2006–2007 (122)	36
2005–2006 (115)	39

Global Competitiveness Index 2007–2008 (131) 31

Environment component — 43
Market environment — 48
1.01 Venture capital availability, 2007..33
1.02 Financial market sophistication, 2007 46
1.03 Availability of latest technologies, 2007 28
1.04 State of cluster development, 2007......................................42
1.05 Utility patents,* 2006 39
1.06 High-tech exports,* 2004 97
1.07 Burden of government regulation, 2007 12
1.08 Extent and effect of taxation, 2007..3
1.09 Total tax rate* ....n/a
1.10 Time required to start a business* ....n/a
1.11 No. of procedures required to start a business* ....n/a
1.12 Intensity of local competition, 2007 59
1.13 Freedom of the press, 2007..83
1.14 Accessibility of digital content, 2007 29

Political and regulatory environment — 32
2.01 Effectiveness of law-making bodies, 2007 38
2.02 Laws relating to ICT, 2007..37
2.03 Judicial independence, 2007 22
2.04 Intellectual property protection, 2007 27
2.05 Efficiency of legal framework, 2007....................................24
2.06 Property rights, 2007 38
2.07 Quality of competition in the ISP sector, 2007 118
2.08 No. of procedures to enforce a contract* ....n/a
2.09 Time to enforce a contract* ....n/a

Infrastructure environment — 46
3.01 Telephone lines,* 2006..46
3.02 Secure Internet servers,* 2006..45
3.03 Electricity production,* 2003 7
3.04 Availability of scientists and engineers, 2007 66
3.05 Quality of scientific research institutions, 2007 45
3.06 Tertiary enrollment,* 2005..82
3.07 Education expenditure* ....n/a

Readiness component — 28
Individual readiness — 28
4.01 Quality of math and science education, 2007 24
4.02 Quality of the educational system, 2007............................24
4.03 Internet access in schools, 2007..35
4.04 Buyer sophistication, 2007 44
4.05 Residential telephone connection charge,* 2005 8
4.06 Residential monthly telephone subscription,* 2005 5
4.07 High-speed monthly broadband subscription,* 2006........22
4.08 Lowest cost of broadband,* 2006 27
4.09 Cost of mobile telephone call,* 2005..................................11

Business readiness — 41
5.01 Extent of staff training, 2007..46
5.02 Local availability of research and training, 2007................55
5.03 Quality of management schools, 2007 37
5.04 Company spending on R&D, 2007......................................40
5.05 University-industry research collaboration, 2007...............41
5.06 Business telephone connection charge,* 2005 6
5.07 Business monthly telephone subscription,* 2005 21
5.08 Local supplier quality, 2007 73
5.09 Local supplier quantity, 2007...67
5.10 Computer, comm., and other services imports* ....n/a

Government readiness — 24
6.01 Government prioritization of ICT, 2007..............................10
6.02 Gov't procurement of advanced tech products, 2007 18
6.03 Importance of ICT to gov't vision of the future, 2007........8
6.04 E-Government Readiness Index,* 2007............................52

Usage component — 34
Individual usage — 40
7.01 Mobile telephone subscribers,* 2006.................................16
7.02 Personal computers,* 2005 40
7.03 Broadband Internet subscribers,* 2006 40
7.04 Internet users,* 2006 37
7.05 Internet bandwidth,* 2004 44

Business usage — 46
8.01 Prevalence of foreign technology licensing, 2007.............21
8.02 Firm-level technology absorption, 2007 33
8.03 Capacity for innovation, 2007..88
8.04 Availability of new telephone lines, 2007...........................62
8.05 Extent of business Internet use, 2007 59

Government usage — 27
9.01 Government success in ICT promotion, 2007...................11
9.02 Availability of government online services, 2007 23
9.03 ICT use and government efficiency, 2007..........................15
9.04 Presence of ICT in government offices, 2007 26
9.05 E-Participation Index,* 2007..65

* Hard data

Note: For further details and explanation, please refer to the section "How to Read the Country/Economy Profiles" at the beginning of this chapter.

Romania

Key indicators

Population (millions), 2006..21.6
GDP (PPP) per capita (US$), 2006..................................10,125.0
Internet users per 100 inhabitants, 2006..............................32.4
Internet bandwidth (mB/s) per 10,000 inhabitants, 2006.......15.0

Networked Readiness Index

Year (number of economies)	Rank
2007–2008 (127)	**61**
2006–2007 (122)	55
2005–2006 (115)	58

Global Competitiveness Index 2007–2008 (131)   74

Environment component   63
Market environment   60

1.01 Venture capital availability, 2007..69
1.02 Financial market sophistication, 2007 87
1.03 Availability of latest technologies, 2007 91
1.04 State of cluster development, 2007 7
1.05 Utility patents,* 2006 61
1.06 High-tech exports,* 2005 52
1.07 Burden of government regulation, 2007 44
1.08 Extent and effect of taxation, 2007................................105
1.09 Total tax rate,* 2007 71
1.10 Time required to start a business,* 2007..........................27
1.11 No. of procedures required to start a business,* 2007 19
1.12 Intensity of local competition, 2007 81
1.13 Freedom of the press, 2007 64
1.14 Accessibility of digital content, 2007.................................54

Political and regulatory environment   77

2.01 Effectiveness of law-making bodies, 2007 100
2.02 Laws relating to ICT, 2007..66
2.03 Judicial independence, 2007 92
2.04 Intellectual property protection, 2007 74
2.05 Efficiency of legal framework, 2007 94
2.06 Property rights, 2007...83
2.07 Quality of competition in the ISP sector, 2007 81
2.08 No. of procedures to enforce a contract,* 2007 29
2.09 Time to enforce a contract,* 2007 62

Infrastructure environment   61

3.01 Telephone lines,* 2006..62
3.02 Secure Internet servers,* 2006..62
3.03 Electricity production,* 2004..63
3.04 Availability of scientists and engineers, 2007 47
3.05 Quality of scientific research institutions, 2007................70
3.06 Tertiary enrollment,* 2005..41
3.07 Education expenditure,* 2005...82

Readiness component   56
Individual readiness   43

4.01 Quality of math and science education, 2007....................12
4.02 Quality of the educational system, 2007.............................56
4.03 Internet access in schools, 2007...49
4.04 Buyer sophistication, 2007 71
4.05 Residential telephone connection charge,* 2005 18
4.06 Residential monthly telephone subscription,* 2005 57
4.07 High-speed monthly broadband subscription,* 2006........42
4.08 Lowest cost of broadband,* 2006 45
4.09 Cost of mobile telephone call,* 2005....................................63

Business readiness   61

5.01 Extent of staff training, 2007...83
5.02 Local availability of research and training, 2007................49
5.03 Quality of management schools, 2007 78
5.04 Company spending on R&D, 2007 87
5.05 University-industry research collaboration, 2007...............87
5.06 Business telephone connection charge,* 2005 16
5.07 Business monthly telephone subscription,* 2005 53
5.08 Local supplier quality, 2007...92
5.09 Local supplier quantity, 2007..87
5.10 Computer, comm., and other services imports,* 2005 24

Government readiness   69

6.01 Government prioritization of ICT, 2007............................101
6.02 Gov't procurement of advanced tech products, 2007 81
6.03 Importance of ICT to gov't vision of the future, 2007.......81
6.04 E-Government Readiness Index,* 2007..............................50

Usage component   55
Individual usage   44

7.01 Mobile telephone subscribers,* 2006...................................48
7.02 Personal computers,* 2005 52
7.03 Broadband Internet subscribers,* 2006 35
7.04 Internet users,* 2006...39
7.05 Internet bandwidth,* 2006...34

Business usage   80

8.01 Prevalence of foreign technology licensing, 2007.............78
8.02 Firm-level technology absorption, 2007 83
8.03 Capacity for innovation, 2007 62
8.04 Availability of new telephone lines, 2007 86
8.05 Extent of business Internet use, 2007 78

Government usage   73

9.01 Government success in ICT promotion, 2007....................73
9.02 Availability of government online services, 2007 73
9.03 ICT use and government efficiency, 2007...........................71
9.04 Presence of ICT in government offices, 2007 35
9.05 E-Participation Index,* 2007...100

* Hard data

Note: For further details and explanation, please refer to the section "How to Read the Country/Economy Profiles" at the beginning of this chapter.

Russian Federation

Key indicators

Population (millions), 2006..142.5
GDP (PPP) per capita (US$), 2006.............................12,177.7
Internet users per 100 inhabitants, 2006 ....18.0
Internet bandwidth (mB/s) per 10,000 inhabitants, 2005.........1.0

Networked Readiness Index

Year (number of economies)	Rank
2007–2008 (127)	**72**
2006–2007 (122)	70
2005–2006 (115)	72

Global Competitiveness Index 2007–2008 (131)   58

Environment component — 64
Market environment — 88
1.01 Venture capital availability, 2007..60
1.02 Financial market sophistication, 2007 86
1.03 Availability of latest technologies, 2007 96
1.04 State of cluster development, 2007...................................82
1.05 Utility patents,* 2006 44
1.06 High-tech exports,* 2005 63
1.07 Burden of government regulation, 2007 115
1.08 Extent and effect of taxation, 2007...................................94
1.09 Total tax rate,* 2007...87
1.10 Time required to start a business,* 2007.........................64
1.11 No. of procedures required to start a business,* 2007 44
1.12 Intensity of local competition, 2007 91
1.13 Freedom of the press, 2007 102
1.14 Accessibility of digital content, 2007................................63

Political and regulatory environment — 92
2.01 Effectiveness of law-making bodies, 2007 81
2.02 Laws relating to ICT, 2007...82
2.03 Judicial independence, 2007 102
2.04 Intellectual property protection, 2007 113
2.05 Efficiency of legal framework, 2007................................103
2.06 Property rights, 2007..119
2.07 Quality of competition in the ISP sector, 2007 73
2.08 No. of procedures to enforce a contract,* 2007..............60
2.09 Time to enforce a contract,* 2007 13

Infrastructure environment — 39
3.01 Telephone lines,* 2005..44
3.02 Secure Internet servers,* 2006...78
3.03 Electricity production,* 2004 31
3.04 Availability of scientists and engineers, 2007 37
3.05 Quality of scientific research institutions, 2007 43
3.06 Tertiary enrollment,* 2005...15
3.07 Education expenditure,* 2005...78

Readiness component — 67
Individual readiness — 56
4.01 Quality of math and science education, 2007..................37
4.02 Quality of the educational system, 2007..........................44
4.03 Internet access in schools, 2007..55
4.04 Buyer sophistication, 2007 58
4.05 Residential telephone connection charge,* 2005 95
4.06 Residential monthly telephone subscription,* 2005 62
4.07 High-speed monthly broadband subscription,* 2006........75
4.08 Lowest cost of broadband,* 2006 85
4.09 Cost of mobile telephone call,* 2005................................51

Business readiness — 69
5.01 Extent of staff training, 2007..95
5.02 Local availability of research and training, 2007.................77
5.03 Quality of management schools, 2007 76
5.04 Company spending on R&D, 2007....................................49
5.05 University-industry research collaboration, 2007..............59
5.06 Business telephone connection charge,* 2005 98
5.07 Business monthly telephone subscription,* 2005 46
5.08 Local supplier quality, 2007 84
5.09 Local supplier quantity, 2007 73
5.10 Computer, comm., and other services imports,* 2005 38

Government readiness — 89
6.01 Government prioritization of ICT, 2007.............................98
6.02 Gov't procurement of advanced tech products, 2007 82
6.03 Importance of ICT to gov't vision of the future, 2007.....105
6.04 E-Government Readiness Index,* 2007...........................57

Usage component — 84
Individual usage — 53
7.01 Mobile telephone subscribers,* 2005...............................46
7.02 Personal computers,* 2005 56
7.03 Broadband Internet subscribers,* 2006 55
7.04 Internet users,* 2006..59
7.05 Internet bandwidth,* 2005...73

Business usage — 87
8.01 Prevalence of foreign technology licensing, 2007...........105
8.02 Firm-level technology absorption, 2007 101
8.03 Capacity for innovation, 2007 53
8.04 Availability of new telephone lines, 2007........................94
8.05 Extent of business Internet use, 2007..............................53

Government usage — 101
9.01 Government success in ICT promotion, 2007................106
9.02 Availability of government online services, 2007..............92
9.03 ICT use and government efficiency, 2007........................95
9.04 Presence of ICT in government offices, 2007 102
9.05 E-Participation Index,* 2007...82

* Hard data

Note: For further details and explanation, please refer to the section "How to Read the Country/Economy Profiles" at the beginning of this chapter.

Saudi Arabia

Key indicators

Population (millions), 2006..25.2
GDP (PPP) per capita (US$), 2006.....................................16,505.3
Internet users per 100 inhabitants, 2006 ....18.7
Internet bandwidth (mB/s) per 10,000 inhabitants, 2006.........1.2

Networked Readiness Index

Year (number of economies)	Rank
2007–2008 (127)	**48**
2006–2007 (122)	n/a
2005–2006 (115)	n/a

Global Competitiveness Index 2007–2008 (131)　　35

Environment component　　45

Market environment　　37
1.01　Venture capital availability, 2007..42
1.02　Financial market sophistication, 2007 69
1.03　Availability of latest technologies, 2007 45
1.04　State of cluster development, 2007......................................46
1.05　Utility patents,* 2006 49
1.06　High-tech exports,* 2005 94
1.07　Burden of government regulation, 2007 20
1.08　Extent and effect of taxation, 2007...7
1.09　Total tax rate,* 2007 3
1.10　Time required to start a business,* 2007............................30
1.11　No. of procedures required to start a business,* 2007 34
1.12　Intensity of local competition, 2007 51
1.13　Freedom of the press, 2007..109
1.14　Accessibility of digital content, 2007....................................80

Political and regulatory environment　　53
2.01　Effectiveness of law-making bodies, 2007 50
2.02　Laws relating to ICT, 2007..57
2.03　Judicial independence, 2007 51
2.04　Intellectual property protection, 2007 52
2.05　Efficiency of legal framework, 2007......................................44
2.06　Property rights, 2007 47
2.07　Quality of competition in the ISP sector, 2007 47
2.08　No. of procedures to enforce a contract,* 2007................104
2.09　Time to enforce a contract,* 2007 87

Infrastructure environment　　45
3.01　Telephone lines,* 2006..70
3.02　Secure Internet servers,* 2006...69
3.03　Electricity production,* 2004 28
3.04　Availability of scientists and engineers, 2007 56
3.05　Quality of scientific research institutions, 2007 52
3.06　Tertiary enrollment,* 2005...68
3.07　Education expenditure,* 2005...7

Readiness component　　49

Individual readiness　　71
4.01　Quality of math and science education, 2007 64
4.02　Quality of the educational system, 2007.............................76
4.03　Internet access in schools, 2007..59
4.04　Buyer sophistication, 2007 83
4.05　Residential telephone connection charge,* 2005 49
4.06　Residential monthly telephone subscription,* 2005 32
4.07　High-speed monthly broadband subscription* ....n/a
4.08　Lowest cost of broadband,* 2006 101
4.09　Cost of mobile telephone call,* 2005.................................24

Business readiness　　40
5.01　Extent of staff training, 2007..76
5.02　Local availability of research and training, 2007................66
5.03　Quality of management schools, 2007 73
5.04　Company spending on R&D, 2007......................................45
5.05　University-industry research collaboration, 2007...............49
5.06　Business telephone connection charge,* 2005 39
5.07　Business monthly telephone subscription,* 2005 18
5.08　Local supplier quality, 2007..50
5.09　Local supplier quantity, 2007..39
5.10　Computer, comm., and other services imports,* 2005 4

Government readiness　　40
6.01　Government prioritization of ICT, 2007...............................50
6.02　Gov't procurement of advanced tech products, 2007 31
6.03　Importance of ICT to gov't vision of the future, 2007.......35
6.04　E-Government Readiness Index,* 2007.............................66

Usage component　　53

Individual usage　　56
7.01　Mobile telephone subscribers,* 2006..................................50
7.02　Personal computers,* 2005..54
7.03　Broadband Internet subscribers,* 2006 67
7.04　Internet users,* 2006 58
7.05　Internet bandwidth,* 2006..69

Business usage　　49
8.01　Prevalence of foreign technology licensing, 2007.............68
8.02　Firm-level technology absorption, 2007 47
8.03　Capacity for innovation, 2007...48
8.04　Availability of new telephone lines, 2007 59
8.05　Extent of business Internet use, 2007................................51

Government usage　　51
9.01　Government success in ICT promotion, 2007....................35
9.02　Availability of government online services, 2007 60
9.03　ICT use and government efficiency, 2007...........................70
9.04　Presence of ICT in government offices, 2007 60
9.05　E-Participation Index,* 2007...36

* Hard data

Note: For further details and explanation, please refer to the section "How to Read the Country/Economy Profiles" at the beginning of this chapter.

Senegal

Key indicators

Population (millions), 2006...11.9
GDP (PPP) per capita (US$), 2006.......................................1,981.0
Internet users per 100 inhabitants, 2006 ....5.4
Internet bandwidth (mB/s) per 10,000 inhabitants, 2006.........1.0

Networked Readiness Index

Year (number of economies)	Rank
2007–2008 (127)	**85**
2006–2007 (122)	n/a
2005–2006 (115)	n/a

Global Competitiveness Index 2007–2008 (131)   100

Environment component — 103
Market environment — 84
1.01 Venture capital availability, 2007.......................................119
1.02 Financial market sophistication, 2007 94
1.03 Availability of latest technologies, 2007 30
1.04 State of cluster development, 2007...................................98
1.05 Utility patents,* 2006 86
1.06 High-tech exports,* 2005 43
1.07 Burden of government regulation, 2007 104
1.08 Extent and effect of taxation, 2007...................................90
1.09 Total tax rate,* 2007 66
1.10 Time required to start a business,* 2007........................103
1.11 No. of procedures required to start a business,* 2007 74
1.12 Intensity of local competition, 2007 47
1.13 Freedom of the press, 2007..68
1.14 Accessibility of digital content, 2007.................................49

Political and regulatory environment — 110
2.01 Effectiveness of law-making bodies, 2007 114
2.02 Laws relating to ICT, 2007...86
2.03 Judicial independence, 2007 109
2.04 Intellectual property protection, 2007 83
2.05 Efficiency of legal framework, 2007................................106
2.06 Property rights, 2007..94
2.07 Quality of competition in the ISP sector, 2007 69
2.08 No. of procedures to enforce a contract,* 2007 104
2.09 Time to enforce a contract,* 2007 97

Infrastructure environment — 102
3.01 Telephone lines,* 2006..109
3.02 Secure Internet servers,* 2006..101
3.03 Electricity production,* 2004...105
3.04 Availability of scientists and engineers, 2007 68
3.05 Quality of scientific research institutions, 2007 60
3.06 Tertiary enrollment,* 2005...105
3.07 Education expenditure,* 2005...74

Readiness component — 86
Individual readiness — 94
4.01 Quality of math and science education, 2007...................75
4.02 Quality of the educational system, 2007...........................78
4.03 Internet access in schools, 2007.......................................88
4.04 Buyer sophistication, 2007 117
4.05 Residential telephone connection charge,* 2005 102
4.06 Residential monthly telephone subscription,* 2005 103
4.07 High-speed monthly broadband subscription,* 2006........87
4.08 Lowest cost of broadband,* 2006 91
4.09 Cost of mobile telephone call,* 2006..............................104

Business readiness — 75
5.01 Extent of staff training, 2007...108
5.02 Local availability of research and training, 2007...............46
5.03 Quality of management schools, 2007 40
5.04 Company spending on R&D, 2007....................................78
5.05 University-industry research collaboration, 2007..............84
5.06 Business telephone connection charge,* 2005 93
5.07 Business monthly telephone subscription,* 2005 95
5.08 Local supplier quality, 2007...70
5.09 Local supplier quantity, 2007...44
5.10 Computer, comm., and other services imports,* 2004 60

Government readiness — 81
6.01 Government prioritization of ICT, 2007.............................46
6.02 Gov't procurement of advanced tech products, 2007 43
6.03 Importance of ICT to gov't vision of the future, 2007.......50
6.04 E-Government Readiness Index,* 2007..........................115

Usage component — 80
Individual usage — 101
7.01 Mobile telephone subscribers,* 2006...............................98
7.02 Personal computers,* 2005 97
7.03 Broadband Internet subscribers,* 2006 85
7.04 Internet users,* 2006...100
7.05 Internet bandwidth,* 2006...71

Business usage — 61
8.01 Prevalence of foreign technology licensing, 2007.............90
8.02 Firm-level technology absorption, 2007 24
8.03 Capacity for innovation, 2007..92
8.04 Availability of new telephone lines, 2007..........................66
8.05 Extent of business Internet use, 2007..............................51

Government usage — 57
9.01 Government success in ICT promotion, 2007...................24
9.02 Availability of government online services, 2007 86
9.03 ICT use and government efficiency, 2007.........................78
9.04 Presence of ICT in government offices, 2007 58
9.05 E-Participation Index,* 2007..58

* Hard data

Note: For further details and explanation, please refer to the section "How to Read the Country/Economy Profiles" at the beginning of this chapter.

Singapore

Key indicators

Population (millions), 2006...4.4
GDP (PPP) per capita (US$), 2006.................................33,471.4
Internet users per 100 inhabitants, 2006...........................39.2
Internet bandwidth (mB/s) per 10,000 inhabitants, 2005.......71.2

Networked Readiness Index

Year (number of economies)	Rank
2007–2008 (127)	**5**
2006–2007 (122)	3
2005–2006 (115)	2

Global Competitiveness Index 2007–2008 (131) — 7

Environment component — 9
Market environment — 1
1.01 Venture capital availability, 2007...15
1.02 Financial market sophistication, 2007..................................12
1.03 Availability of latest technologies, 2007..............................12
1.04 State of cluster development, 2007......................................4
1.05 Utility patents,* 2006..11
1.06 High-tech exports,* 2005...1
1.07 Burden of government regulation, 2007...............................1
1.08 Extent and effect of taxation, 2007.......................................6
1.09 Total tax rate,* 2007...10
1.10 Time required to start a business,* 2007.............................4
1.11 No. of procedures required to start a business,* 2007.......9
1.12 Intensity of local competition, 2007....................................29
1.13 Freedom of the press, 2007...115
1.14 Accessibility of digital content, 2007..................................15

Political and regulatory environment — 1
2.01 Effectiveness of law-making bodies, 2007...........................1
2.02 Laws relating to ICT, 2007..3
2.03 Judicial independence, 2007..19
2.04 Intellectual property protection, 2007...................................5
2.05 Efficiency of legal framework, 2007....................................10
2.06 Property rights, 2007..5
2.07 Quality of competition in the ISP sector, 2007..................19
2.08 No. of procedures to enforce a contract,* 2007..................2
2.09 Time to enforce a contract,* 2007..1

Infrastructure environment — 26
3.01 Telephone lines,* 2006...30
3.02 Secure Internet servers,* 2006..18
3.03 Electricity production,* 2004..16
3.04 Availability of scientists and engineers, 2007....................22
3.05 Quality of scientific research institutions, 2007.................13
3.06 Tertiary enrollment,* 2004..39
3.07 Education expenditure,* 2005..99

Readiness component — 1
Individual readiness — 2
4.01 Quality of math and science education, 2007......................1
4.02 Quality of the educational system, 2007..............................1
4.03 Internet access in schools, 2007...9
4.04 Buyer sophistication, 2007...19
4.05 Residential telephone connection charge,* 2006................6
4.06 Residential monthly telephone subscription,* 2006............6
4.07 High-speed monthly broadband subscription,* 2006........29
4.08 Lowest cost of broadband,* 2006...3
4.09 Cost of mobile telephone call,* 2006..................................16

Business readiness — 12
5.01 Extent of staff training, 2007...7
5.02 Local availability of research and training, 2007...............17
5.03 Quality of management schools, 2007.................................7
5.04 Company spending on R&D, 2007......................................10
5.05 University-industry research collaboration, 2007................7
5.06 Business telephone connection charge,* 2006...................8
5.07 Business monthly telephone subscription,* 2006...............4
5.08 Local supplier quality, 2007...24
5.09 Local supplier quantity, 2007..50
5.10 Computer, comm., and other services imports,* 2005....27

Government readiness — 1
6.01 Government prioritization of ICT, 2007................................1
6.02 Gov't procurement of advanced tech products, 2007........1
6.03 Importance of ICT to gov't vision of the future, 2007.........1
6.04 E-Government Readiness Index,* 2007..............................23

Usage component — 7
Individual usage — 18
7.01 Mobile telephone subscribers,* 2006.................................17
7.02 Personal computers,* 2005..10
7.03 Broadband Internet subscribers,* 2006.............................20
7.04 Internet users,* 2006..32
7.05 Internet bandwidth,* 2005...12

Business usage — 15
8.01 Prevalence of foreign technology licensing, 2007..............1
8.02 Firm-level technology absorption, 2007...............................9
8.03 Capacity for innovation, 2007...23
8.04 Availability of new telephone lines, 2007............................6
8.05 Extent of business Internet use, 2007...............................19

Government usage — 4
9.01 Government success in ICT promotion, 2007......................1
9.02 Availability of government online services, 2007................2
9.03 ICT use and government efficiency, 2007............................1
9.04 Presence of ICT in government offices, 2007.....................1
9.05 E-Participation Index,* 2007..10

* Hard data

Note: For further details and explanation, please refer to the section "How to Read the Country/Economy Profiles" at the beginning of this chapter.

Slovak Republic

Key indicators

Population (millions), 2006..5.4
GDP (PPP) per capita (US$), 2006.................................17,913.5
Internet users per 100 inhabitants, 2006 ....41.8
Internet bandwidth (mB/s) per 10,000 inhabitants, 2006.......29.1

Networked Readiness Index

Year (number of economies)	Rank
2007–2008 (127) **43**
2006–2007 (122) 41
2005–2006 (115) 41

Global Competitiveness Index 2007–2008 (131)   41

Environment component — 47
Market environment — 36
1.01 Venture capital availability, 2007...39
1.02 Financial market sophistication, 2007 41
1.03 Availability of latest technologies, 2007 52
1.04 State of cluster development, 2007....................................63
1.05 Utility patents,* 2006 86
1.06 High-tech exports,* 2005 30
1.07 Burden of government regulation, 2007 81
1.08 Extent and effect of taxation, 2007.....................................10
1.09 Total tax rate,* 2007 80
1.10 Time required to start a business,* 2007..........................53
1.11 No. of procedures required to start a business,* 2007 58
1.12 Intensity of local competition, 2007 38
1.13 Freedom of the press, 2007...25
1.14 Accessibility of digital content, 2007..................................37

Political and regulatory environment — 50
2.01 Effectiveness of law-making bodies, 2007 68
2.02 Laws relating to ICT, 2007..50
2.03 Judicial independence, 2007 71
2.04 Intellectual property protection, 2007 55
2.05 Efficiency of legal framework, 2007....................................78
2.06 Property rights, 2007 52
2.07 Quality of competition in the ISP sector, 2007 54
2.08 No. of procedures to enforce a contract,* 2007 15
2.09 Time to enforce a contract,* 2007 67

Infrastructure environment — 48
3.01 Telephone lines,* 2006..57
3.02 Secure Internet servers,* 2006..45
3.03 Electricity production,* 2004 36
3.04 Availability of scientists and engineers, 2007 24
3.05 Quality of scientific research institutions, 2007 69
3.06 Tertiary enrollment,* 2005..50
3.07 Education expenditure,* 2005..65

Readiness component — 44
Individual readiness — 39
4.01 Quality of math and science education, 2007...................26
4.02 Quality of the educational system, 2007...........................61
4.03 Internet access in schools, 2007...36
4.04 Buyer sophistication, 2007 76
4.05 Residential telephone connection charge,* 2005 36
4.06 Residential monthly telephone subscription,* 2005 54
4.07 High-speed monthly broadband subscription,* 2006........58
4.08 Lowest cost of broadband,* 2006 38
4.09 Cost of mobile telephone call,* 2005..................................57

Business readiness — 42
5.01 Extent of staff training, 2007..44
5.02 Local availability of research and training, 2007..............47
5.03 Quality of management schools, 2007 66
5.04 Company spending on R&D, 2007......................................51
5.05 University-industry research collaboration, 2007..............36
5.06 Business telephone connection charge,* 2005 30
5.07 Business monthly telephone subscription,* 2005 47
5.08 Local supplier quality, 2007 45
5.09 Local supplier quantity, 2007...38
5.10 Computer, comm., and other services imports,* 2005 20

Government readiness — 62
6.01 Government prioritization of ICT, 2007..............................88
6.02 Gov't procurement of advanced tech products, 2007 86
6.03 Importance of ICT to gov't vision of the future, 2007.......87
6.04 E-Government Readiness Index,* 2007.............................38

Usage component — 40
Individual usage — 34
7.01 Mobile telephone subscribers,* 2006.................................39
7.02 Personal computers,* 2005 28
7.03 Broadband Internet subscribers,* 2006 39
7.04 Internet users,* 2006..31
7.05 Internet bandwidth,* 2006 24

Business usage — 38
8.01 Prevalence of foreign technology licensing, 2007.............37
8.02 Firm-level technology absorption, 2007 34
8.03 Capacity for innovation, 2007..52
8.04 Availability of new telephone lines, 2007 21
8.05 Extent of business Internet use, 2007 49

Government usage — 78
9.01 Government success in ICT promotion, 2007...................95
9.02 Availability of government online services, 2007 79
9.03 ICT use and government efficiency, 2007..........................79
9.04 Presence of ICT in government offices, 2007 32
9.05 E-Participation Index,* 2007...91

* Hard data

Note: For further details and explanation, please refer to the section "How to Read the Country/Economy Profiles" at the beginning of this chapter.

Slovenia

Key indicators

Population (millions), 2006	2.0
GDP (PPP) per capita (US$), 2006	24,570.6
Internet users per 100 inhabitants, 2006	63.6
Internet bandwidth (mB/s) per 10,000 inhabitants, 2005	12.6

Networked Readiness Index

Year (number of economies)	Rank
2007–2008 (127)	**30**
2006–2007 (122)	30
2005–2006 (115)	35

Global Competitiveness Index 2007–2008 (131)	39

Environment component — 37

Market environment — 58

1.01	Venture capital availability, 2007	48
1.02	Financial market sophistication, 2007	55
1.03	Availability of latest technologies, 2007	50
1.04	State of cluster development, 2007	30
1.05	Utility patents,* 2006	26
1.06	High-tech exports,* 2005	41
1.07	Burden of government regulation, 2007	52
1.08	Extent and effect of taxation, 2007	101
1.09	Total tax rate,* 2007	48
1.10	Time required to start a business,* 2007	105
1.11	No. of procedures required to start a business,* 2007	58
1.12	Intensity of local competition, 2007	43
1.13	Freedom of the press, 2007	85
1.14	Accessibility of digital content, 2007	36

Political and regulatory environment — 48

2.01	Effectiveness of law-making bodies, 2007	55
2.02	Laws relating to ICT, 2007	30
2.03	Judicial independence, 2007	47
2.04	Intellectual property protection, 2007	36
2.05	Efficiency of legal framework, 2007	48
2.06	Property rights, 2007	56
2.07	Quality of competition in the ISP sector, 2007	37
2.08	No. of procedures to enforce a contract,* 2007	29
2.09	Time to enforce a contract,* 2007	117

Infrastructure environment — 23

3.01	Telephone lines,* 2006	28
3.02	Secure Internet servers,* 2006	28
3.03	Electricity production,* 2004	21
3.04	Availability of scientists and engineers, 2007	91
3.05	Quality of scientific research institutions, 2007	33
3.06	Tertiary enrollment,* 2005	8
3.07	Education expenditure,* 2005	29

Readiness component — 32

Individual readiness — 29

4.01	Quality of math and science education, 2007	36
4.02	Quality of the educational system, 2007	42
4.03	Internet access in schools, 2007	20
4.04	Buyer sophistication, 2007	27
4.05	Residential telephone connection charge,* 2005	45
4.06	Residential monthly telephone subscription,* 2005	39
4.07	High-speed monthly broadband subscription,* 2006	31
4.08	Lowest cost of broadband,* 2006	25
4.09	Cost of mobile telephone call,* 2005	15

Business readiness — 29

5.01	Extent of staff training, 2007	37
5.02	Local availability of research and training, 2007	35
5.03	Quality of management schools, 2007	44
5.04	Company spending on R&D, 2007	24
5.05	University-industry research collaboration, 2007	33
5.06	Business telephone connection charge,* 2005	36
5.07	Business monthly telephone subscription,* 2005	25
5.08	Local supplier quality, 2007	32
5.09	Local supplier quantity, 2007	58
5.10	Computer, comm., and other services imports,* 2005	20

Government readiness — 37

6.01	Government prioritization of ICT, 2007	65
6.02	Gov't procurement of advanced tech products, 2007	75
6.03	Importance of ICT to gov't vision of the future, 2007	38
6.04	E-Government Readiness Index,* 2007	26

Usage component — 30

Individual usage — 27

7.01	Mobile telephone subscribers,* 2006	36
7.02	Personal computers,* 2005	25
7.03	Broadband Internet subscribers,* 2006	28
7.04	Internet users,* 2006	12
7.05	Internet bandwidth,* 2005	35

Business usage — 34

8.01	Prevalence of foreign technology licensing, 2007	58
8.02	Firm-level technology absorption, 2007	61
8.03	Capacity for innovation, 2007	19
8.04	Availability of new telephone lines, 2007	52
8.05	Extent of business Internet use, 2007	34

Government usage — 42

9.01	Government success in ICT promotion, 2007	62
9.02	Availability of government online services, 2007	35
9.03	ICT use and government efficiency, 2007	46
9.04	Presence of ICT in government offices, 2007	27
9.05	E-Participation Index,* 2007	53

* Hard data

Note: For further details and explanation, please refer to the section "How to Read the Country/Economy Profiles" at the beginning of this chapter.

South Africa

Key indicators

Population (millions), 2006..47.6
GDP (PPP) per capita (US$), 2006..................................13,018.1
Internet users per 100 inhabitants, 2005 ....10.8
Internet bandwidth (mB/s) per 10,000 inhabitants, 2005.........0.2

Networked Readiness Index

Year (number of economies)	Rank
2007–2008 (127)	**51**
2006–2007 (122)	47
2005–2006 (115)	37

Global Competitiveness Index 2007–2008 (131)   44

Environment component   40
Market environment   35

1.01 Venture capital availability, 2007..41
1.02 Financial market sophistication, 2007 15
1.03 Availability of latest technologies, 2007 40
1.04 State of cluster development, 2007...................................44
1.05 Utility patents,* 2006 38
1.06 High-tech exports,* 2005 47
1.07 Burden of government regulation, 2007 98
1.08 Extent and effect of taxation, 2007....................................26
1.09 Total tax rate,* 2007..40
1.10 Time required to start a business,* 2007...........................68
1.11 No. of procedures required to start a business,* 2007 44
1.12 Intensity of local competition, 2007 52
1.13 Freedom of the press, 2007...26
1.14 Accessibility of digital content, 2007..................................55

Political and regulatory environment   26

2.01 Effectiveness of law-making bodies, 2007 19
2.02 Laws relating to ICT, 2007..32
2.03 Judicial independence, 2007 23
2.04 Intellectual property protection, 2007 24
2.05 Efficiency of legal framework, 2007....................................17
2.06 Property rights, 2007...22
2.07 Quality of competition in the ISP sector, 2007 108
2.08 No. of procedures to enforce a contract,* 2007 15
2.09 Time to enforce a contract,* 2007 80

Infrastructure environment   66

3.01 Telephone lines,* 2005..86
3.02 Secure Internet servers,* 2006 50
3.03 Electricity production,* 2004 42
3.04 Availability of scientists and engineers, 2007 101
3.05 Quality of scientific research institutions, 2007 27
3.06 Tertiary enrollment,* 2005...90
3.07 Education expenditure,* 2005..31

Readiness component   51
Individual readiness   72

4.01 Quality of math and science education, 2007..................125
4.02 Quality of the educational system, 2007..........................101
4.03 Internet access in schools, 2007...84
4.04 Buyer sophistication, 2007 33
4.05 Residential telephone connection charge,* 2005 55
4.06 Residential monthly telephone subscription,* 2005 87
4.07 High-speed monthly broadband subscription,* 2006........63
4.08 Lowest cost of broadband,* 2006 68
4.09 Cost of mobile telephone call,* 2005.................................78

Business readiness   30

5.01 Extent of staff training, 2007...21
5.02 Local availability of research and training, 2007................33
5.03 Quality of management schools, 2007 22
5.04 Company spending on R&D, 2007......................................26
5.05 University-industry research collaboration, 2007..............24
5.06 Business telephone connection charge,* 2005 45
5.07 Business monthly telephone subscription,* 2005 74
5.08 Local supplier quality, 2007...29
5.09 Local supplier quantity, 2007...26
5.10 Computer, comm., and other services imports,* 2005 77

Government readiness   59

6.01 Government prioritization of ICT, 2007..............................60
6.02 Gov't procurement of advanced tech products, 2007 51
6.03 Importance of ICT to gov't vision of the future, 2007.......85
6.04 E-Government Readiness Index,* 2007.............................58

Usage component   57
Individual usage   67

7.01 Mobile telephone subscribers,* 2005.................................57
7.02 Personal computers,* 2005 63
7.03 Broadband Internet subscribers,* 2005 80
7.04 Internet users,* 2005...78
7.05 Internet bandwidth,* 2005..93

Business usage   44

8.01 Prevalence of foreign technology licensing, 2007.............11
8.02 Firm-level technology absorption, 2007 30
8.03 Capacity for innovation, 2007..42
8.04 Availability of new telephone lines, 2007 97
8.05 Extent of business Internet use, 2007...............................45

Government usage   60

9.01 Government success in ICT promotion, 2007...................77
9.02 Availability of government online services, 2007 62
9.03 ICT use and government efficiency, 2007.........................85
9.04 Presence of ICT in government offices, 2007 61
9.05 E-Participation Index,* 2007..47

* Hard data

Note: For further details and explanation, please refer to the section "How to Read the Country/Economy Profiles" at the beginning of this chapter.

Spain

Key indicators

Population (millions), 2006...43.4
GDP (PPP) per capita (US$), 2006..................................27,914.1
Internet users per 100 inhabitants, 2006 ....42.8
Internet bandwidth (mB/s) per 10,000 inhabitants, 2005.......27.9

Networked Readiness Index

Year (number of economies)	Rank
2007–2008 (127)	**31**
2006–2007 (122)	32
2005–2006 (115)	31

Global Competitiveness Index 2007–2008 (131)   29

Environment component — 33
Market environment — 43

1.01 Venture capital availability, 2007..26
1.02 Financial market sophistication, 2007 24
1.03 Availability of latest technologies, 2007 38
1.04 State of cluster development, 2007.......................................39
1.05 Utility patents,* 2006 27
1.06 High-tech exports,* 2005 40
1.07 Burden of government regulation, 2007 59
1.08 Extent and effect of taxation, 2007..69
1.09 Total tax rate,* 2007..103
1.10 Time required to start a business,* 2007..............................97
1.11 No. of procedures required to start a business,* 2007 74
1.12 Intensity of local competition, 2007 25
1.13 Freedom of the press, 2007...41
1.14 Accessibility of digital content, 2007....................................31

Political and regulatory environment — 36

2.01 Effectiveness of law-making bodies, 2007 39
2.02 Laws relating to ICT, 2007..31
2.03 Judicial independence, 2007 67
2.04 Intellectual property protection, 2007 28
2.05 Efficiency of legal framework, 2007......................................46
2.06 Property rights, 2007...32
2.07 Quality of competition in the ISP sector, 2007 55
2.08 No. of procedures to enforce a contract,* 2007................75
2.09 Time to enforce a contract,* 2007 59

Infrastructure environment — 31

3.01 Telephone lines,* 2006..29
3.02 Secure Internet servers,* 2006..27
3.03 Electricity production,* 2004 30
3.04 Availability of scientists and engineers, 2007 45
3.05 Quality of scientific research institutions, 2007 48
3.06 Tertiary enrollment,* 2005..17
3.07 Education expenditure,* 2005..62

Readiness component — 34
Individual readiness — 36

4.01 Quality of math and science education, 2007....................66
4.02 Quality of the educational system, 2007.............................50
4.03 Internet access in schools, 2007..41
4.04 Buyer sophistication, 2007 30
4.05 Residential telephone connection charge,* 2006 1
4.06 Residential monthly telephone subscription,* 2006 35
4.07 High-speed monthly broadband subscription,* 2006........24
4.08 Lowest cost of broadband,* 2006 34
4.09 Cost of mobile telephone call,* 2005..................................29

Business readiness — 27

5.01 Extent of staff training, 2007...50
5.02 Local availability of research and training, 2007................40
5.03 Quality of management schools, 2007 5
5.04 Company spending on R&D, 2007...47
5.05 University-industry research collaboration, 2007...............44
5.06 Business telephone connection charge,* 2006 1
5.07 Business monthly telephone subscription,* 2005 22
5.08 Local supplier quality, 2007 30
5.09 Local supplier quantity, 2007...15
5.10 Computer, comm., and other services imports,* 2005 17

Government readiness — 36

6.01 Government prioritization of ICT, 2007................................71
6.02 Gov't procurement of advanced tech products, 2007 55
6.03 Importance of ICT to gov't vision of the future, 2007.......69
6.04 E-Government Readiness Index,* 2007...............................20

Usage component — 32
Individual usage — 29

7.01 Mobile telephone subscribers,* 2006..................................23
7.02 Personal computers,* 2005 30
7.03 Broadband Internet subscribers,* 2006 24
7.04 Internet users,* 2006..29
7.05 Internet bandwidth,* 2005 25

Business usage — 40

8.01 Prevalence of foreign technology licensing, 2007.............30
8.02 Firm-level technology absorption, 2007 60
8.03 Capacity for innovation, 2007..35
8.04 Availability of new telephone lines, 2007 45
8.05 Extent of business Internet use, 2007.................................46

Government usage — 37

9.01 Government success in ICT promotion, 2007....................89
9.02 Availability of government online services, 2007 32
9.03 ICT use and government efficiency, 2007...........................32
9.04 Presence of ICT in government offices, 2007 38
9.05 E-Participation Index,* 2007..32

* Hard data

Note: For further details and explanation, please refer to the section "How to Read the Country/Economy Profiles" at the beginning of this chapter.

Sri Lanka

Key indicators

Population (millions), 2006...20.9
GDP (PPP) per capita (US$), 2006................................5,386.5
Internet users per 100 inhabitants, 2006 ....2.0
Internet bandwidth (mB/s) per 10,000 inhabitants, 2006.........0.2

Networked Readiness Index

Year (number of economies)	Rank
2007–2008 (127)	**79**
2006–2007 (122)	86
2005–2006 (115)	83

Global Competitiveness Index 2007–2008 (131)   70

Environment component   75
Market environment   64
1.01 Venture capital availability, 2007..45
1.02 Financial market sophistication, 2007 59
1.03 Availability of latest technologies, 2007 67
1.04 State of cluster development, 2007......................................37
1.05 Utility patents,* 2006 70
1.06 High-tech exports,* 2005 69
1.07 Burden of government regulation, 2007 49
1.08 Extent and effect of taxation, 2007.......................................52
1.09 Total tax rate,* 2007..105
1.10 Time required to start a business,* 2007..............................87
1.11 No. of procedures required to start a business,* 2007 9
1.12 Intensity of local competition, 2007 54
1.13 Freedom of the press, 2007..91
1.14 Accessibility of digital content, 2007....................................75

Political and regulatory environment   72
2.01 Effectiveness of law-making bodies, 2007 58
2.02 Laws relating to ICT, 2007...64
2.03 Judicial independence, 2007..59
2.04 Intellectual property protection, 2007 56
2.05 Efficiency of legal framework, 2007......................................59
2.06 Property rights, 2007..60
2.07 Quality of competition in the ISP sector, 2007 40
2.08 No. of procedures to enforce a contract,* 2007 89
2.09 Time to enforce a contract,* 2007 114

Infrastructure environment   95
3.01 Telephone lines,* 2006..89
3.02 Secure Internet servers,* 2006 85
3.03 Electricity production,* 2004 103
3.04 Availability of scientists and engineers, 2007 44
3.05 Quality of scientific research institutions, 2007 40
3.06 Tertiary enrollment,* 2002...97
3.07 Education expenditure,* 2005...104

Readiness component   80
Individual readiness   88
4.01 Quality of math and science education, 2007.....................53
4.02 Quality of the educational system, 2007..............................53
4.03 Internet access in schools, 2007..76
4.04 Buyer sophistication, 2007 43
4.05 Residential telephone connection charge,* 2005 118
4.06 Residential monthly telephone subscription,* 2005 96
4.07 High-speed monthly broadband subscription,* 2006.........77
4.08 Lowest cost of broadband,* 2006 71
4.09 Cost of mobile telephone call,* 2005...................................81

Business readiness   87
5.01 Extent of staff training, 2007...51
5.02 Local availability of research and training, 2007.................65
5.03 Quality of management schools, 2007 56
5.04 Company spending on R&D, 2007 39
5.05 University-industry research collaboration, 2007................38
5.06 Business telephone connection charge,* 2005 111
5.07 Business monthly telephone subscription,* 2005 106
5.08 Local supplier quality, 2007 58
5.09 Local supplier quantity, 2007 65
5.10 Computer, comm., and other services imports,* 2005 93

Government readiness   58
6.01 Government prioritization of ICT, 2007................................47
6.02 Gov't procurement of advanced tech products, 2007 53
6.03 Importance of ICT to gov't vision of the future, 2007.......54
6.04 E-Government Readiness Index,* 2007...............................86

Usage component   81
Individual usage   104
7.01 Mobile telephone subscribers,* 2006..................................97
7.02 Personal computers,* 2005 89
7.03 Broadband Internet subscribers,* 2006 93
7.04 Internet users,* 2006..115
7.05 Internet bandwidth,* 2006 88

Business usage   50
8.01 Prevalence of foreign technology licensing, 2007..............59
8.02 Firm-level technology absorption, 2007 63
8.03 Capacity for innovation, 2007..36
8.04 Availability of new telephone lines, 2007............................58
8.05 Extent of business Internet use, 2007 58

Government usage   83
9.01 Government success in ICT promotion, 2007....................59
9.02 Availability of government online services, 2007 71
9.03 ICT use and government efficiency, 2007...........................74
9.04 Presence of ICT in government offices, 2007 82
9.05 E-Participation Index,* 2007..91

* Hard data

Note: For further details and explanation, please refer to the section "How to Read the Country/Economy Profiles" at the beginning of this chapter.

Suriname

Key indicators

Population (millions), 2006...0.5
GDP (PPP) per capita (US$), 2006..............................6,571.4
Internet users per 100 inhabitants, 2005 ....7.1
Internet bandwidth (mB/s) per 10,000 inhabitants, 2004.........1.0

Networked Readiness Index

Year (number of economies)	Rank
2007–2008 (127)	**117**
2006–2007 (122)	110
2005–2006 (115)	n/a

Global Competitiveness Index 2007–2008 (131)	113

Environment component — 125

Market environment — 119

1.01 Venture capital availability, 2007........................127
1.02 Financial market sophistication, 2007 101
1.03 Availability of latest technologies, 2007 120
1.04 State of cluster development, 2007.....................112
1.05 Utility patents,* 2006 86
1.06 High-tech exports* ....n/a
1.07 Burden of government regulation, 2007 87
1.08 Extent and effect of taxation, 2007......................111
1.09 Total tax rate,* 2007 15
1.10 Time required to start a business,* 2007...........121
1.11 No. of procedures required to start a business,* 2007..103
1.12 Intensity of local competition, 2007.....................85
1.13 Freedom of the press, 2007..................................54
1.14 Accessibility of digital content, 2007.................123

Political and regulatory environment — 127

2.01 Effectiveness of law-making bodies, 2007 122
2.02 Laws relating to ICT, 2007..................................127
2.03 Judicial independence, 2007 44
2.04 Intellectual property protection, 2007 126
2.05 Efficiency of legal framework, 2007....................65
2.06 Property rights, 2007..99
2.07 Quality of competition in the ISP sector, 2007..127
2.08 No. of procedures to enforce a contract,* 2007..104
2.09 Time to enforce a contract,* 2007 121

Infrastructure environment — 96

3.01 Telephone lines,* 2006..66
3.02 Secure Internet servers,* 2006..............................56
3.03 Electricity production*..n/a
3.04 Availability of scientists and engineers, 2007..109
3.05 Quality of scientific research institutions, 2007..98
3.06 Tertiary enrollment,* 2002.....................................92
3.07 Education expenditure*......................................n/a

Readiness component — 101

Individual readiness — 85

4.01 Quality of math and science education, 2007....85
4.02 Quality of the educational system, 2007..........118
4.03 Internet access in schools, 2007.......................115
4.04 Buyer sophistication, 2007 107
4.05 Residential telephone connection charge,* 2005..94
4.06 Residential monthly telephone subscription,* 2005..12
4.07 High-speed monthly broadband subscription,* 2006..72
4.08 Lowest cost of broadband,* 2006 90
4.09 Cost of mobile telephone call,* 2005.................74

Business readiness — 85

5.01 Extent of staff training, 2007............................109
5.02 Local availability of research and training, 2007..119
5.03 Quality of management schools, 2007 103
5.04 Company spending on R&D, 2007......................90
5.05 University-industry research collaboration, 2007..96
5.06 Business telephone connection charge,* 2005..81
5.07 Business monthly telephone subscription,* 2005..7
5.08 Local supplier quality, 2007...............................104
5.09 Local supplier quantity, 2007............................115
5.10 Computer, comm., and other services imports,* 2005..10

Government readiness — 124

6.01 Government prioritization of ICT, 2007............125
6.02 Gov't procurement of advanced tech products, 2007..122
6.03 Importance of ICT to gov't vision of the future, 2007..126
6.04 E-Government Readiness Index,* 2007.............99

Usage component — 124

Individual usage — 74

7.01 Mobile telephone subscribers,* 2006................59
7.02 Personal computers,* 2005.................................82
7.03 Broadband Internet subscribers,* 2006............75
7.04 Internet users,* 2005..94
7.05 Internet bandwidth,* 2004....................................72

Business usage — 123

8.01 Prevalence of foreign technology licensing, 2007..123
8.02 Firm-level technology absorption, 2007..........121
8.03 Capacity for innovation, 2007.............................96
8.04 Availability of new telephone lines, 2007........124
8.05 Extent of business Internet use, 2007.............112

Government usage — 127

9.01 Government success in ICT promotion, 2007..126
9.02 Availability of government online services, 2007..127
9.03 ICT use and government efficiency, 2007.......125
9.04 Presence of ICT in government offices, 2007..127
9.05 E-Participation Index,* 2007.............................117

* Hard data

Note: For further details and explanation, please refer to the section "How to Read the Country/Economy Profiles" at the beginning of this chapter.

Sweden

Key indicators

Population (millions), 2006..9.1
GDP (PPP) per capita (US$), 2006.....................................34,734.9
Internet users per 100 inhabitants, 2006 ....77.0
Internet bandwidth (mB/s) per 10,000 inhabitants, 2005.....175.2

Networked Readiness Index

Year (number of economies)	Rank
2007–2008 (127)	**2**
2006–2007 (122)	2
2005–2006 (115)	8

Global Competitiveness Index 2007–2008 (131) 4

Environment component — 4
Market environment — 9

1.01 Venture capital availability, 2007..7
1.02 Financial market sophistication, 2007 7
1.03 Availability of latest technologies, 2007 1
1.04 State of cluster development, 2007.......................................18
1.05 Utility patents,* 2006 7
1.06 High-tech exports,* 2005 24
1.07 Burden of government regulation, 2007 53
1.08 Extent and effect of taxation, 2007.....................................122
1.09 Total tax rate,* 2007...96
1.10 Time required to start a business,* 2007.............................30
1.11 No. of procedures required to start a business,* 2007 4
1.12 Intensity of local competition, 2007 5
1.13 Freedom of the press, 2007..4
1.14 Accessibility of digital content, 2007......................................1

Political and regulatory environment — 11

2.01 Effectiveness of law-making bodies, 2007 9
2.02 Laws relating to ICT, 2007...5
2.03 Judicial independence, 2007...8
2.04 Intellectual property protection, 2007 7
2.05 Efficiency of legal framework, 2007.......................................5
2.06 Property rights, 2007..9
2.07 Quality of competition in the ISP sector, 2007 11
2.08 No. of procedures to enforce a contract,* 2007 15
2.09 Time to enforce a contract,* 2007 55

Infrastructure environment — 3

3.01 Telephone lines,* 2006..6
3.02 Secure Internet servers,* 2006...13
3.03 Electricity production,* 2004...4
3.04 Availability of scientists and engineers, 2007 6
3.05 Quality of scientific research institutions, 2007 9
3.06 Tertiary enrollment,* 2005...7
3.07 Education expenditure,* 2005...2

Readiness component — 4
Individual readiness — 9

4.01 Quality of math and science education, 2007....................32
4.02 Quality of the educational system, 2007............................16
4.03 Internet access in schools, 2007..3
4.04 Buyer sophistication, 2007..5
4.05 Residential telephone connection charge,* 2005 30
4.06 Residential monthly telephone subscription,* 2005 20
4.07 High-speed monthly broadband subscription,* 2006........17
4.08 Lowest cost of broadband,* 2006 3
4.09 Cost of mobile telephone call,* 2005....................................6

Business readiness — 10

5.01 Extent of staff training, 2007..3
5.02 Local availability of research and training, 2007..................4
5.03 Quality of management schools, 2007 13
5.04 Company spending on R&D, 2007...5
5.05 University-industry research collaboration, 2007.................3
5.06 Business telephone connection charge*..........................n/a
5.07 Business monthly telephone subscription*......................n/a
5.08 Local supplier quality, 2007 5
5.09 Local supplier quantity, 2007 10
5.10 Computer, comm., and other services imports,* 2005 14

Government readiness — 4

6.01 Government prioritization of ICT, 2007...............................11
6.02 Gov't procurement of advanced tech products, 2007 6
6.03 Importance of ICT to gov't vision of the future, 2007.......16
6.04 E-Government Readiness Index,* 2007...............................1

Usage component — 2
Individual usage — 3

7.01 Mobile telephone subscribers,* 2006..............................24
7.02 Personal computers,* 2005 5
7.03 Broadband Internet subscribers,* 2006 8
7.04 Internet users,* 2006 3
7.05 Internet bandwidth,* 2005 3

Business usage — 1

8.01 Prevalence of foreign technology licensing, 2007...............2
8.02 Firm-level technology absorption, 2007 2
8.03 Capacity for innovation, 2007...2
8.04 Availability of new telephone lines, 2007.............................7
8.05 Extent of business Internet use, 2007..................................3

Government usage — 6

9.01 Government success in ICT promotion, 2007......................8
9.02 Availability of government online services, 2007................4
9.03 ICT use and government efficiency, 2007............................7
9.04 Presence of ICT in government offices, 2007 6
9.05 E-Participation Index,* 2007...9

* Hard data

Note: For further details and explanation, please refer to the section "How to Read the Country/Economy Profiles" at the beginning of this chapter.

Switzerland

Key indicators

Population (millions), 2006...7.3
GDP (PPP) per capita (US$), 2006....................38,705.8
Internet users per 100 inhabitants, 2006................60.0
Internet bandwidth (mB/s) per 10,000 inhabitants, 2005.......97.9

Networked Readiness Index

Year (number of economies)	Rank
2007–2008 (127)	**3**
2006–2007 (122)	5
2005–2006 (115)	9

Global Competitiveness Index 2007–2008 (131)	2

Environment component — 6

Market environment — 4

1.01 Venture capital availability, 2007........................22
1.02 Financial market sophistication, 2007 1
1.03 Availability of latest technologies, 2007..................7
1.04 State of cluster development, 2007......................13
1.05 Utility patents,* 2006 6
1.06 High-tech exports,* 2005..21
1.07 Burden of government regulation, 2007 11
1.08 Extent and effect of taxation, 2007.......................14
1.09 Total tax rate,* 2007...17
1.10 Time required to start a business,* 2007............42
1.11 No. of procedures required to start a business,* 2007 19
1.12 Intensity of local competition, 2007 27
1.13 Freedom of the press, 2007....................................7
1.14 Accessibility of digital content, 2007......................2

Political and regulatory environment — 8

2.01 Effectiveness of law-making bodies, 2007 10
2.02 Laws relating to ICT, 2007.....................................10
2.03 Judicial independence, 2007...................................7
2.04 Intellectual property protection, 2007 3
2.05 Efficiency of legal framework, 2007.......................3
2.06 Property rights, 2007..3
2.07 Quality of competition in the ISP sector, 2007 ...18
2.08 No. of procedures to enforce a contract,* 2007.....29
2.09 Time to enforce a contract,* 2007 39

Infrastructure environment — 9

3.01 Telephone lines,* 2006..1
3.02 Secure Internet servers,* 2006...............................8
3.03 Electricity production,* 2004................................17
3.04 Availability of scientists and engineers, 2007 10
3.05 Quality of scientific research institutions, 2007....1
3.06 Tertiary enrollment,* 2005....................................38
3.07 Education expenditure,* 2005...............................37

Readiness component — 6

Individual readiness — 3

4.01 Quality of math and science education, 2007......5
4.02 Quality of the educational system, 2007...............3
4.03 Internet access in schools, 2007..........................10
4.04 Buyer sophistication, 2007......................................1
4.05 Residential telephone connection charge,* 2005...........3
4.06 Residential monthly telephone subscription,* 2005 17
4.07 High-speed monthly broadband subscription,* 2006........4
4.08 Lowest cost of broadband,* 2006 13
4.09 Cost of mobile telephone call,* 2006..................20

Business readiness — 1

5.01 Extent of staff training, 2007..................................2
5.02 Local availability of research and training, 2007...1
5.03 Quality of management schools, 2007 3
5.04 Company spending on R&D, 2007........................1
5.05 University-industry research collaboration, 2007...2
5.06 Business telephone connection charge,* 2005 ...3
5.07 Business monthly telephone subscription,* 2005 9
5.08 Local supplier quality, 2007....................................3
5.09 Local supplier quantity, 2007..................................4
5.10 Computer, comm., and other services imports,* 2005 35

Government readiness — 20

6.01 Government prioritization of ICT, 2007..............24
6.02 Gov't procurement of advanced tech products, 2007 12
6.03 Importance of ICT to gov't vision of the future, 2007.......39
6.04 E-Government Readiness Index,* 2007.............12

Usage component — 6

Individual usage — 4

7.01 Mobile telephone subscribers,* 2006..................26
7.02 Personal computers,* 2005 3
7.03 Broadband Internet subscribers,* 2006.................4
7.04 Internet users,* 2006...13
7.05 Internet bandwidth,* 2005....................................10

Business usage — 4

8.01 Prevalence of foreign technology licensing, 2007.............18
8.02 Firm-level technology absorption, 2007................6
8.03 Capacity for innovation, 2007.................................4
8.04 Availability of new telephone lines, 2007.............1
8.05 Extent of business Internet use, 2007..................8

Government usage — 18

9.01 Government success in ICT promotion, 2007....32
9.02 Availability of government online services, 2007..............21
9.03 ICT use and government efficiency, 2007...........25
9.04 Presence of ICT in government offices, 2007 4
9.05 E-Participation Index,* 2007.................................27

* Hard data

Note: For further details and explanation, please refer to the section "How to Read the Country/Economy Profiles" at the beginning of this chapter.

Syria

Key indicators

Population (millions), 2006...19.5
GDP (PPP) per capita (US$), 2006.................................4,324.5
Internet users per 100 inhabitants, 2006 ....7.7
Internet bandwidth (mB/s) per 10,000 inhabitants, 2006.........0.1

Networked Readiness Index

Year (number of economies)	Rank
2007–2008 (127)	**110**
2006–2007 (122)	n/a
2005–2006 (115)	n/a

Global Competitiveness Index 2007–2008 (131)   80

Environment component — 105
Market environment — 107
1.01 Venture capital availability, 2007..103
1.02 Financial market sophistication, 2007 122
1.03 Availability of latest technologies, 2007 60
1.04 State of cluster development, 2007 89
1.05 Utility patents,* 2006 69
1.06 High-tech exports,* 2005 100
1.07 Burden of government regulation, 2007 77
1.08 Extent and effect of taxation, 2007 40
1.09 Total tax rate,* 2007 69
1.10 Time required to start a business,* 2007 91
1.11 No. of procedures required to start a business,* 2007 ..103
1.12 Intensity of local competition, 2007 49
1.13 Freedom of the press, 2007..113
1.14 Accessibility of digital content, 2007..................................122

Political and regulatory environment — 106
2.01 Effectiveness of law-making bodies, 2007 64
2.02 Laws relating to ICT, 2007...124
2.03 Judicial independence, 2007 79
2.04 Intellectual property protection, 2007 78
2.05 Efficiency of legal framework, 2007 76
2.06 Property rights, 2007...31
2.07 Quality of competition in the ISP sector, 2007 107
2.08 No. of procedures to enforce a contract,* 2007.............121
2.09 Time to enforce a contract,* 2007 106

Infrastructure environment — 87
3.01 Telephone lines,* 2006...69
3.02 Secure Internet servers,* 2006..101
3.03 Electricity production,* 2004 74
3.04 Availability of scientists and engineers, 2007 55
3.05 Quality of scientific research institutions, 2007 89
3.06 Tertiary enrollment* ....n/a
3.07 Education expenditure,* 2005...103

Readiness component — 111
Individual readiness — 111
4.01 Quality of math and science education, 2007 68
4.02 Quality of the educational system, 2007............................99
4.03 Internet access in schools, 2007..118
4.04 Buyer sophistication, 2007 113
4.05 Residential telephone connection charge*......................n/a
4.06 Residential monthly telephone subscription*..................n/a
4.07 High-speed monthly broadband subscription* ....n/a
4.08 Lowest cost of broadband*..n/a
4.09 Cost of mobile telephone call,* 2005..................................68

Business readiness — 117
5.01 Extent of staff training, 2007...99
5.02 Local availability of research and training, 2007 96
5.03 Quality of management schools, 2007 98
5.04 Company spending on R&D, 2007....................................101
5.05 University-industry research collaboration, 2007............102
5.06 Business telephone connection charge*..........................n/a
5.07 Business monthly telephone subscription*......................n/a
5.08 Local supplier quality, 2007 64
5.09 Local supplier quantity, 2007..32
5.10 Computer, comm., and other services imports,* 2005 ..111

Government readiness — 95
6.01 Government prioritization of ICT, 2007...............................70
6.02 Gov't procurement of advanced tech products, 2007 93
6.03 Importance of ICT to gov't vision of the future, 2007.......84
6.04 E-Government Readiness Index,* 2007..............................95

Usage component — 106
Individual usage — 99
7.01 Mobile telephone subscribers,* 2006...............................102
7.02 Personal computers,* 2005 85
7.03 Broadband Internet subscribers,* 2006 102
7.04 Internet users,* 2006 89
7.05 Internet bandwidth,* 2006 104

Business usage — 95
8.01 Prevalence of foreign technology licensing, 2007.............85
8.02 Firm-level technology absorption, 2007 102
8.03 Capacity for innovation, 2007 104
8.04 Availability of new telephone lines, 2007 68
8.05 Extent of business Internet use, 2007 111

Government usage — 110
9.01 Government success in ICT promotion, 2007....................69
9.02 Availability of government online services, 2007 123
9.03 ICT use and government efficiency, 2007........................110
9.04 Presence of ICT in government offices, 2007 106
9.05 E-Participation Index,* 2007..100

* Hard data

Note: For further details and explanation, please refer to the section "How to Read the Country/Economy Profiles" at the beginning of this chapter.

Taiwan, China

Key indicators

Population (millions), 2006..22.7
GDP (PPP) per capita (US$), 2006.....................................30,687.1
Internet users per 100 inhabitants, 2006 ....63.7
Internet bandwidth (mB/s) per 10,000 inhabitants, 2004.......31.4

Networked Readiness Index

Year (number of economies)	Rank
2007–2008 (127)	**17**
2006–2007 (122)	13
2005–2006 (115)	7

Global Competitiveness Index 2007–2008 (131) — 14

Environment component — 21
Market environment — 6
1.01 Venture capital availability, 2007..23
1.02 Financial market sophistication, 2007 40
1.03 Availability of latest technologies, 2007 21
1.04 State of cluster development, 2007..1
1.05 Utility patents,* 2006 3
1.06 High-tech exports,* 2004 1
1.07 Burden of government regulation, 2007 17
1.08 Extent and effect of taxation, 2007......................................24
1.09 Total tax rate,* 2007 51
1.10 Time required to start a business,* 2007............................98
1.11 No. of procedures required to start a business,* 2007 44
1.12 Intensity of local competition, 2007 13
1.13 Freedom of the press, 2007..43
1.14 Accessibility of digital content, 2007...................................22

Political and regulatory environment — 42
2.01 Effectiveness of law-making bodies, 2007 88
2.02 Laws relating to ICT, 2007..24
2.03 Judicial independence, 2007 52
2.04 Intellectual property protection, 2007 30
2.05 Efficiency of legal framework, 2007....................................45
2.06 Property rights, 2007...39
2.07 Quality of competition in the ISP sector, 2007 25
2.08 No. of procedures to enforce a contract,* 2007 114
2.09 Time to enforce a contract,* 2007 56

Infrastructure environment — 12
3.01 Telephone lines,* 2006...5
3.02 Secure Internet servers,* 2006...24
3.03 Electricity production,* 2003 14
3.04 Availability of scientists and engineers, 2007 14
3.05 Quality of scientific research institutions, 2007 23
3.06 Tertiary enrollment,* 2005...5
3.07 Education expenditure*...n/a

Readiness component — 9
Individual readiness — 12
4.01 Quality of math and science education, 2007......................8
4.02 Quality of the educational system, 2007............................18
4.03 Internet access in schools, 2007...16
4.04 Buyer sophistication, 2007 16
4.05 Residential telephone connection charge,* 2005 50
4.06 Residential monthly telephone subscription,* 2005 2
4.07 High-speed monthly broadband subscription,* 2006........18
4.08 Lowest cost of broadband,* 2006 10
4.09 Cost of mobile telephone call,* 2005.................................34

Business readiness — 17
5.01 Extent of staff training, 2007..19
5.02 Local availability of research and training, 2007................20
5.03 Quality of management schools, 2007 29
5.04 Company spending on R&D, 2007..18
5.05 University-industry research collaboration, 2007.................9
5.06 Business telephone connection charge,* 2005 40
5.07 Business monthly telephone subscription,* 2005 20
5.08 Local supplier quality, 2007 13
5.09 Local supplier quantity, 2007..18
5.10 Computer, comm., and other services imports,* 2004 28

Government readiness — 11
6.01 Government prioritization of ICT, 2007.................................9
6.02 Gov't procurement of advanced tech products, 2007 8
6.03 Importance of ICT to gov't vision of the future, 2007.......14
6.04 E-Government Readiness Index* ....n/a

Usage component — 13
Individual usage — 19
7.01 Mobile telephone subscribers,* 2006.................................27
7.02 Personal computers,* 2005 18
7.03 Broadband Internet subscribers,* 2006 16
7.04 Internet users,* 2006 11
7.05 Internet bandwidth,* 2004 23

Business usage — 17
8.01 Prevalence of foreign technology licensing, 2007...............5
8.02 Firm-level technology absorption, 2007 8
8.03 Capacity for innovation, 2007..16
8.04 Availability of new telephone lines, 2007 30
8.05 Extent of business Internet use, 2007................................17

Government usage — 8
9.01 Government success in ICT promotion, 2007......................9
9.02 Availability of government online services, 2007 22
9.03 ICT use and government efficiency, 2007..........................14
9.04 Presence of ICT in government offices, 2007 13
9.05 E-Participation Index* ....n/a

* Hard data

Note: For further details and explanation, please refer to the section "How to Read the Country/Economy Profiles" at the beginning of this chapter.

Tajikistan

Key indicators

Population (millions), 2006..6.6
GDP (PPP) per capita (US$), 2006.........................1,494.1
Internet users per 100 inhabitants, 2005 ....0.3
Internet bandwidth (mB/s) per 10,000 inhabitants, 2005.........0.0

Networked Readiness Index

Year (number of economies)	Rank
2007–2008 (127)	**98**
2006–2007 (122)	n/a
2005–2006 (115)	93

Global Competitiveness Index 2007–2008 (131) — 117

Environment component — 96
Market environment — 121

1.01 Venture capital availability, 2007..........................98
1.02 Financial market sophistication, 2007 117
1.03 Availability of latest technologies, 2007 119
1.04 State of cluster development, 2007....................122
1.05 Utility patents,* 2006 86
1.06 High-tech exports* ....n/a
1.07 Burden of government regulation, 2007 112
1.08 Extent and effect of taxation, 2007......................93
1.09 Total tax rate,* 2007 116
1.10 Time required to start a business,* 2007............99
1.11 No. of procedures required to start a business,* 2007 ..103
1.12 Intensity of local competition, 2007 111
1.13 Freedom of the press, 2007.................................120
1.14 Accessibility of digital content, 2007...................84

Political and regulatory environment — 64

2.01 Effectiveness of law-making bodies, 2007 48
2.02 Laws relating to ICT, 2007.....................................97
2.03 Judicial independence, 2007.................................83
2.04 Intellectual property protection, 2007 97
2.05 Efficiency of legal framework, 2007....................66
2.06 Property rights, 2007..79
2.07 Quality of competition in the ISP sector, 2007 ...82
2.08 No. of procedures to enforce a contract,* 2007 ..40
2.09 Time to enforce a contract,* 2007 16

Infrastructure environment — 97

3.01 Telephone lines,* 2005..102
3.02 Secure Internet servers* ....n/a
3.03 Electricity production,* 2004................................61
3.04 Availability of scientists and engineers, 2007 ..111
3.05 Quality of scientific research institutions, 2007 ..76
3.06 Tertiary enrollment,* 2005....................................85
3.07 Education expenditure,* 2005............................101

Readiness component — 96
Individual readiness — 99

4.01 Quality of math and science education, 2007 ..119
4.02 Quality of the educational system, 2007..........106
4.03 Internet access in schools, 2007..........................89
4.04 Buyer sophistication, 2007 106
4.05 Residential telephone connection charge,* 2005 ..64
4.06 Residential monthly telephone subscription,* 2005 47
4.07 High-speed monthly broadband subscription* ..n/a
4.08 Lowest cost of broadband* ....n/a
4.09 Cost of mobile telephone call,* 2005..................99

Business readiness — 104

5.01 Extent of staff training, 2007..............................100
5.02 Local availability of research and training, 2007 ..118
5.03 Quality of management schools, 2007 124
5.04 Company spending on R&D, 2007......................103
5.05 University-industry research collaboration, 2007 ..100
5.06 Business telephone connection charge,* 2005 ..83
5.07 Business monthly telephone subscription,* 2005 ..86
5.08 Local supplier quality, 2007................................115
5.09 Local supplier quantity, 2007.............................117
5.10 Computer, comm., and other services imports,* 2005 81

Government readiness — 87

6.01 Government prioritization of ICT, 2007...............45
6.02 Gov't procurement of advanced tech products, 2007 71
6.03 Importance of ICT to gov't vision of the future, 2007.......82
6.04 E-Government Readiness Index,* 2007..........103

Usage component — 110
Individual usage — 125

7.01 Mobile telephone subscribers,* 2005...............124
7.02 Personal computers,* 2005 109
7.03 Broadband Internet subscribers,* 2005 115
7.04 Internet users,* 2005...126
7.05 Internet bandwidth,* 2005..................................126

Business usage — 101

8.01 Prevalence of foreign technology licensing, 2007...........116
8.02 Firm-level technology absorption, 2007 113
8.03 Capacity for innovation, 2007..............................79
8.04 Availability of new telephone lines, 2007..........90
8.05 Extent of business Internet use, 2007................96

Government usage — 102

9.01 Government success in ICT promotion, 2007....60
9.02 Availability of government online services, 2007 ..103
9.03 ICT use and government efficiency, 2007..........90
9.04 Presence of ICT in government offices, 2007 ..105
9.05 E-Participation Index,* 2007...............................117

* Hard data

Note: For further details and explanation, please refer to the section "How to Read the Country/Economy Profiles" at the beginning of this chapter.

Tanzania

Key indicators

Population (millions), 2006..39.0
GDP (PPP) per capita (US$), 2006..806.5
Internet users per 100 inhabitants, 2005 ....1.0
Internet bandwidth (mB/s) per 10,000 inhabitants, 2005.........0.0

Networked Readiness Index

Year (number of economies)	Rank
2007–2008 (127)	**100**
2006–2007 (122)	91
2005–2006 (115)	84

Global Competitiveness Index 2007–2008 (131)   104

Environment component — 87
Market environment — 90
1.01 Venture capital availability, 2007..83
1.02 Financial market sophistication, 2007 98
1.03 Availability of latest technologies, 2007 84
1.04 State of cluster development, 2007......................................80
1.05 Utility patents,* 2006 86
1.06 High-tech exports,* 2005 104
1.07 Burden of government regulation, 2007 32
1.08 Extent and effect of taxation, 2007......................................60
1.09 Total tax rate,* 2007 61
1.10 Time required to start a business,* 2007 64
1.11 No. of procedures required to start a business,* 2007 98
1.12 Intensity of local competition, 2007 89
1.13 Freedom of the press, 2007..78
1.14 Accessibility of digital content, 2007....................................98

Political and regulatory environment — 62
2.01 Effectiveness of law-making bodies, 2007 23
2.02 Laws relating to ICT, 2007..89
2.03 Judicial independence, 2007 58
2.04 Intellectual property protection, 2007 82
2.05 Efficiency of legal framework, 2007....................................67
2.06 Property rights, 2007..93
2.07 Quality of competition in the ISP sector, 2007 80
2.08 No. of procedures to enforce a contract,* 2007 65
2.09 Time to enforce a contract,* 2007 46

Infrastructure environment — 110
3.01 Telephone lines,* 2006..123
3.02 Secure Internet servers,* 2006..101
3.03 Electricity production,* 2004 110
3.04 Availability of scientists and engineers, 2007 86
3.05 Quality of scientific research institutions, 2007 47
3.06 Tertiary enrollment,* 2005...122
3.07 Education expenditure,* 2005...106

Readiness component — 107
Individual readiness — 114
4.01 Quality of math and science education, 2007..................107
4.02 Quality of the educational system, 2007............................83
4.03 Internet access in schools, 2007..103
4.04 Buyer sophistication, 2007 86
4.05 Residential telephone connection charge,* 2005 112
4.06 Residential monthly telephone subscription,* 2005 115
4.07 High-speed monthly broadband subscription* ....n/a
4.08 Lowest cost of broadband*..n/a
4.09 Cost of mobile telephone call,* 2005................................120

Business readiness — 100
5.01 Extent of staff training, 2007..91
5.02 Local availability of research and training, 2007................79
5.03 Quality of management schools, 2007 109
5.04 Company spending on R&D, 2007.......................................60
5.05 University-industry research collaboration, 2007...............54
5.06 Business telephone connection charge,* 2005 106
5.07 Business monthly telephone subscription,* 2005 108
5.08 Local supplier quality, 2007 103
5.09 Local supplier quantity, 2007..95
5.10 Computer, comm., and other services imports,* 2005 83

Government readiness — 78
6.01 Government prioritization of ICT, 2007...............................55
6.02 Gov't procurement of advanced tech products, 2007 56
6.03 Importance of ICT to gov't vision of the future, 2007.......52
6.04 E-Government Readiness Index,* 2007............................111

Usage component — 98
Individual usage — 115
7.01 Mobile telephone subscribers,* 2006..............................108
7.02 Personal computers,* 2005 113
7.03 Broadband Internet subscribers,* 2005 118
7.04 Internet users,* 2005...116
7.05 Internet bandwidth,* 2005 125

Business usage — 93
8.01 Prevalence of foreign technology licensing, 2007.............92
8.02 Firm-level technology absorption, 2007 88
8.03 Capacity for innovation, 2007 100
8.04 Availability of new telephone lines, 2007 93
8.05 Extent of business Internet use, 2007 90

Government usage — 94
9.01 Government success in ICT promotion, 2007....................51
9.02 Availability of government online services, 2007 96
9.03 ICT use and government efficiency, 2007..........................81
9.04 Presence of ICT in government offices, 2007 84
9.05 E-Participation Index,* 2007..110

* Hard data

Note: For further details and explanation, please refer to the section "How to Read the Country/Economy Profiles" at the beginning of this chapter.

Thailand

Key indicators

Population (millions), 2006..64.8
GDP (PPP) per capita (US$), 2006.......................................9,193.5
Internet users per 100 inhabitants, 2006 ....13.1
Internet bandwidth (mB/s) per 10,000 inhabitants, 2006........1.5

Networked Readiness Index

Year (number of economies)	Rank
2007–2008 (127)	**40**
2006–2007 (122)	37
2005–2006 (115)	34

Global Competitiveness Index 2007–2008 (131)   28

Environment component   41
Market environment   31
1.01   Venture capital availability, 2007..51
1.02   Financial market sophistication, 2007 38
1.03   Availability of latest technologies, 2007 41
1.04   State of cluster development, 2007 38
1.05   Utility patents,* 2006 58
1.06   High-tech exports,* 2005 15
1.07   Burden of government regulation, 2007 26
1.08   Extent and effect of taxation, 2007.....................................21
1.09   Total tax rate,* 2007 43
1.10   Time required to start a business,* 2007...........................75
1.11   No. of procedures required to start a business,* 2007 44
1.12   Intensity of local competition, 2007 42
1.13   Freedom of the press, 2007...73
1.14   Accessibility of digital content, 2007..................................45

Political and regulatory environment   35
2.01   Effectiveness of law-making bodies, 2007 43
2.02   Laws relating to ICT, 2007..48
2.03   Judicial independence, 2007 43
2.04   Intellectual property protection, 2007 44
2.05   Efficiency of legal framework, 2007....................................43
2.06   Property rights, 2007 50
2.07   Quality of competition in the ISP sector, 2007 28
2.08   No. of procedures to enforce a contract,* 2007................46
2.09   Time to enforce a contract,* 2007 50

Infrastructure environment   58
3.01   Telephone lines,* 2006..82
3.02   Secure Internet servers,* 2006...63
3.03   Electricity production,* 2004 70
3.04   Availability of scientists and engineers, 2007 42
3.05   Quality of scientific research institutions, 2007 44
3.06   Tertiary enrollment,* 2006...45
3.07   Education expenditure,* 2005..45

Readiness component   35
Individual readiness   40
4.01   Quality of math and science education, 2007 39
4.02   Quality of the educational system, 2007............................40
4.03   Internet access in schools, 2007...37
4.04   Buyer sophistication, 2007 41
4.05   Residential telephone connection charge,* 2005 85
4.06   Residential monthly telephone subscription,* 2005 51
4.07   High-speed monthly broadband subscription,* 2006........49
4.08   Lowest cost of broadband,* 2006 53
4.09   Cost of mobile telephone call,* 2005..................................67

Business readiness   43
5.01   Extent of staff training, 2007...36
5.02   Local availability of research and training, 2007 61
5.03   Quality of management schools, 2007 33
5.04   Company spending on R&D, 2007 42
5.05   University-industry research collaboration, 2007...............28
5.06   Business telephone connection charge,* 2005 74
5.07   Business monthly telephone subscription,* 2005 36
5.08   Local supplier quality, 2007 38
5.09   Local supplier quantity, 2007...29
5.10   Computer, comm., and other services imports,* 2005 63

Government readiness   32
6.01   Government prioritization of ICT, 2007...............................28
6.02   Gov't procurement of advanced tech products, 2007 24
6.03   Importance of ICT to gov't vision of the future, 2007.......17
6.04   E-Government Readiness Index,* 2007..............................61

Usage component   43
Individual usage   70
7.01   Mobile telephone subscribers,* 2006.................................67
7.02   Personal computers,* 2005 66
7.03   Broadband Internet subscribers,* 2005 91
7.04   Internet users,* 2006 72
7.05   Internet bandwidth,* 2006 62

Business usage   35
8.01   Prevalence of foreign technology licensing, 2007.............29
8.02   Firm-level technology absorption, 2007 44
8.03   Capacity for innovation, 2007..55
8.04   Availability of new telephone lines, 2007..........................44
8.05   Extent of business Internet use, 2007................................31

Government usage   30
9.01   Government success in ICT promotion, 2007....................30
9.02   Availability of government online services, 2007 29
9.03   ICT use and government efficiency, 2007..........................22
9.04   Presence of ICT in government offices, 2007 36
9.05   E-Participation Index,* 2007..39

* Hard data

Note: For further details and explanation, please refer to the section "How to Read the Country/Economy Profiles" at the beginning of this chapter.

Trinidad and Tobago

Key indicators

Population (millions), 2006	1.3
GDP (PPP) per capita (US$), 2006	17,493.8
Internet users per 100 inhabitants, 2005	12.5
Internet bandwidth (mB/s) per 10,000 inhabitants, 2005	3.8

Networked Readiness Index

Year (number of economies)	Rank
2007–2008 (127)	**82**
2006–2007 (122)	68
2005–2006 (115)	74

Global Competitiveness Index 2007–2008 (131)	84

Environment component — 81

Market environment — 67

1.01	Venture capital availability, 2007	53
1.02	Financial market sophistication, 2007	58
1.03	Availability of latest technologies, 2007	69
1.04	State of cluster development, 2007	79
1.05	Utility patents,* 2006	37
1.06	High-tech exports,* 2005	76
1.07	Burden of government regulation, 2007	80
1.08	Extent and effect of taxation, 2007	23
1.09	Total tax rate,* 2007	25
1.10	Time required to start a business,* 2007	91
1.11	No. of procedures required to start a business,* 2007	58
1.12	Intensity of local competition, 2007	72
1.13	Freedom of the press, 2007	59
1.14	Accessibility of digital content, 2007	102

Political and regulatory environment — 108

2.01	Effectiveness of law-making bodies, 2007	89
2.02	Laws relating to ICT, 2007	101
2.03	Judicial independence, 2007	66
2.04	Intellectual property protection, 2007	84
2.05	Efficiency of legal framework, 2007	68
2.06	Property rights, 2007	63
2.07	Quality of competition in the ISP sector, 2007	123
2.08	No. of procedures to enforce a contract,* 2007	100
2.09	Time to enforce a contract,* 2007	115

Infrastructure environment — 70

3.01	Telephone lines,* 2006	52
3.02	Secure Internet servers,* 2006	45
3.03	Electricity production,* 2004	45
3.04	Availability of scientists and engineers, 2007	65
3.05	Quality of scientific research institutions, 2007	65
3.06	Tertiary enrollment,* 2005	94
3.07	Education expenditure,* 2005	67

Readiness component — 82

Individual readiness — 57

4.01	Quality of math and science education, 2007	54
4.02	Quality of the educational system, 2007	46
4.03	Internet access in schools, 2007	71
4.04	Buyer sophistication, 2007	59
4.05	Residential telephone connection charge,* 2004	9
4.06	Residential monthly telephone subscription*	n/a
4.07	High-speed monthly broadband subscription,* 2006	41
4.08	Lowest cost of broadband,* 2006	72
4.09	Cost of mobile telephone call,* 2005	46

Business readiness — 99

5.01	Extent of staff training, 2007	52
5.02	Local availability of research and training, 2007	84
5.03	Quality of management schools, 2007	43
5.04	Company spending on R&D, 2007	76
5.05	University-industry research collaboration, 2007	72
5.06	Business telephone connection charge*	n/a
5.07	Business monthly telephone subscription*	n/a
5.08	Local supplier quality, 2007	62
5.09	Local supplier quantity, 2007	78
5.10	Computer, comm., and other services imports,* 2004	89

Government readiness — 86

6.01	Government prioritization of ICT, 2007	96
6.02	Gov't procurement of advanced tech products, 2007	98
6.03	Importance of ICT to gov't vision of the future, 2007	101
6.04	E-Government Readiness Index,* 2007	53

Usage component — 83

Individual usage — 49

7.01	Mobile telephone subscribers,* 2006	4
7.02	Personal computers,* 2005	58
7.03	Broadband Internet subscribers,* 2006	61
7.04	Internet users,* 2005	74
7.05	Internet bandwidth,* 2005	52

Business usage — 89

8.01	Prevalence of foreign technology licensing, 2007	53
8.02	Firm-level technology absorption, 2007	70
8.03	Capacity for innovation, 2007	109
8.04	Availability of new telephone lines, 2007	104
8.05	Extent of business Internet use, 2007	79

Government usage — 106

9.01	Government success in ICT promotion, 2007	87
9.02	Availability of government online services, 2007	119
9.03	ICT use and government efficiency, 2007	116
9.04	Presence of ICT in government offices, 2007	100
9.05	E-Participation Index,* 2007	58

* Hard data

Note: For further details and explanation, please refer to the section "How to Read the Country/Economy Profiles" at the beginning of this chapter.

Tunisia

Key indicators

Population (millions), 2006..10.2
GDP (PPP) per capita (US$), 2006......................................8,974.7
Internet users per 100 inhabitants, 2006 ....12.7
Internet bandwidth (mB/s) per 10,000 inhabitants, 2006.........1.3

Networked Readiness Index

Year (number of economies)	Rank
2007–2008 (127)	**35**
2006–2007 (122)	35
2005–2006 (115)	36

Global Competitiveness Index 2007–2008 (131) — 32

Environment component — 38
Market environment — 41
1.01 Venture capital availability, 2007..27
1.02 Financial market sophistication, 2007 50
1.03 Availability of latest technologies, 2007 32
1.04 State of cluster development, 2007......................................35
1.05 Utility patents,* 2006 66
1.06 High-tech exports,* 2005 48
1.07 Burden of government regulation, 2007 7
1.08 Extent and effect of taxation, 2007.......................................20
1.09 Total tax rate,* 2007 101
1.10 Time required to start a business,* 2007.............................19
1.11 No. of procedures required to start a business,* 2007 74
1.12 Intensity of local competition, 2007 41
1.13 Freedom of the press, 2007..98
1.14 Accessibility of digital content, 2007....................................51

Political and regulatory environment — 29
2.01 Effectiveness of law-making bodies, 2007 15
2.02 Laws relating to ICT, 2007...35
2.03 Judicial independence, 2007 32
2.04 Intellectual property protection, 2007 35
2.05 Efficiency of legal framework, 2007.....................................23
2.06 Property rights, 2007..34
2.07 Quality of competition in the ISP sector, 2007 41
2.08 No. of procedures to enforce a contract,* 2007 75
2.09 Time to enforce a contract,* 2007 67

Infrastructure environment — 47
3.01 Telephone lines,* 2006..79
3.02 Secure Internet servers,* 2006...85
3.03 Electricity production,* 2004..81
3.04 Availability of scientists and engineers, 2007 9
3.05 Quality of scientific research institutions, 2007 36
3.06 Tertiary enrollment,* 2005..65
3.07 Education expenditure,* 2005...17

Readiness component — 29
Individual readiness — 25
4.01 Quality of math and science education, 2007......................7
4.02 Quality of the educational system, 2007............................12
4.03 Internet access in schools, 2007..33
4.04 Buyer sophistication, 2007 28
4.05 Residential telephone connection charge,* 2006 42
4.06 Residential monthly telephone subscription,* 2005 44
4.07 High-speed monthly broadband subscription,* 2006........78
4.08 Lowest cost of broadband,* 2006 80
4.09 Cost of mobile telephone call,* 2005..................................61

Business readiness — 32
5.01 Extent of staff training, 2007..32
5.02 Local availability of research and training, 2007................26
5.03 Quality of management schools, 2007 18
5.04 Company spending on R&D, 2007 36
5.05 University-industry research collaboration, 2007...............31
5.06 Business telephone connection charge,* 2006 34
5.07 Business monthly telephone subscription,* 2006 32
5.08 Local supplier quality, 2007 37
5.09 Local supplier quantity, 2007..30
5.10 Computer, comm., and other services imports,* 2005 80

Government readiness — 29
6.01 Government prioritization of ICT, 2007...............................13
6.02 Gov't procurement of advanced tech products, 2007 4
6.03 Importance of ICT to gov't vision of the future, 2007.......11
6.04 E-Government Readiness Index,* 2007..........................100

Usage component — 45
Individual usage — 66
7.01 Mobile telephone subscribers,* 2006..................................56
7.02 Personal computers,* 2006 72
7.03 Broadband Internet subscribers,* 2005 90
7.04 Internet users,* 2006...73
7.05 Internet bandwidth,* 2006 67

Business usage — 33
8.01 Prevalence of foreign technology licensing, 2007.............36
8.02 Firm-level technology absorption, 2007 37
8.03 Capacity for innovation, 2007...28
8.04 Availability of new telephone lines, 2007...........................35
8.05 Extent of business Internet use, 2007................................47

Government usage — 35
9.01 Government success in ICT promotion, 2007......................2
9.02 Availability of government online services, 2007 36
9.03 ICT use and government efficiency, 2007..........................26
9.04 Presence of ICT in government offices, 2007 23
9.05 E-Participation Index,* 2007...110

* Hard data

Note: For further details and explanation, please refer to the section "How to Read the Country/Economy Profiles" at the beginning of this chapter.

Turkey

Key indicators

Population (millions), 2006	74.2
GDP (PPP) per capita (US$), 2006	9,240.0
Internet users per 100 inhabitants, 2006	16.6
Internet bandwidth (mB/s) per 10,000 inhabitants, 2006	6.2

Networked Readiness Index

Year (number of economies)	Rank
2007–2008 (127)	**55**
2006–2007 (122)	52
2005–2006 (115)	48

Global Competitiveness Index 2007–2008 (131)	53

Environment component — 51
Market environment — 51

1.01	Venture capital availability, 2007	80
1.02	Financial market sophistication, 2007	36
1.03	Availability of latest technologies, 2007	47
1.04	State of cluster development, 2007	45
1.05	Utility patents,* 2006	65
1.06	High-tech exports,* 2005	67
1.07	Burden of government regulation, 2007	79
1.08	Extent and effect of taxation, 2007	100
1.09	Total tax rate,* 2007	64
1.10	Time required to start a business,* 2007	6
1.11	No. of procedures required to start a business,* 2007	19
1.12	Intensity of local competition, 2007	31
1.13	Freedom of the press, 2007	70
1.14	Accessibility of digital content, 2007	39

Political and regulatory environment — 44

2.01	Effectiveness of law-making bodies, 2007	33
2.02	Laws relating to ICT, 2007	49
2.03	Judicial independence, 2007	50
2.04	Intellectual property protection, 2007	68
2.05	Efficiency of legal framework, 2007	62
2.06	Property rights, 2007	58
2.07	Quality of competition in the ISP sector, 2007	50
2.08	No. of procedures to enforce a contract,* 2007	53
2.09	Time to enforce a contract,* 2007	40

Infrastructure environment — 60

3.01	Telephone lines,* 2006	50
3.02	Secure Internet servers,* 2006	49
3.03	Electricity production,* 2004	66
3.04	Availability of scientists and engineers, 2007	41
3.05	Quality of scientific research institutions, 2007	49
3.06	Tertiary enrollment,* 2005	64
3.07	Education expenditure,* 2005	80

Readiness component — 61
Individual readiness — 63

4.01	Quality of math and science education, 2007	58
4.02	Quality of the educational system, 2007	67
4.03	Internet access in schools, 2007	52
4.04	Buyer sophistication, 2007	60
4.05	Residential telephone connection charge,* 2005	10
4.06	Residential monthly telephone subscription,* 2005	72
4.07	High-speed monthly broadband subscription,* 2006	71
4.08	Lowest cost of broadband,* 2006	66
4.09	Cost of mobile telephone call*	n/a

Business readiness — 52

5.01	Extent of staff training, 2007	47
5.02	Local availability of research and training, 2007	43
5.03	Quality of management schools, 2007	54
5.04	Company spending on R&D, 2007	61
5.05	University-industry research collaboration, 2007	48
5.06	Business telephone connection charge,* 2005	7
5.07	Business monthly telephone subscription,* 2005	93
5.08	Local supplier quality, 2007	39
5.09	Local supplier quantity, 2007	22
5.10	Computer, comm., and other services imports,* 2005	105

Government readiness — 65

6.01	Government prioritization of ICT, 2007	75
6.02	Gov't procurement of advanced tech products, 2007	72
6.03	Importance of ICT to gov't vision of the future, 2007	71
6.04	E-Government Readiness Index,* 2007	70

Usage component — 52
Individual usage — 57

7.01	Mobile telephone subscribers,* 2006	58
7.02	Personal computers,* 2005	73
7.03	Broadband Internet subscribers,* 2006	49
7.04	Internet users,* 2006	65
7.05	Internet bandwidth,* 2006	45

Business usage — 43

8.01	Prevalence of foreign technology licensing, 2007	41
8.02	Firm-level technology absorption, 2007	29
8.03	Capacity for innovation, 2007	46
8.04	Availability of new telephone lines, 2007	46
8.05	Extent of business Internet use, 2007	55

Government usage — 56

9.01	Government success in ICT promotion, 2007	72
9.02	Availability of government online services, 2007	53
9.03	ICT use and government efficiency, 2007	40
9.04	Presence of ICT in government offices, 2007	59
9.05	E-Participation Index,* 2007	69

* Hard data

Note: For further details and explanation, please refer to the section "How to Read the Country/Economy Profiles" at the beginning of this chapter.

Uganda

Key indicators

Population (millions), 2006..29.9
GDP (PPP) per capita (US$), 2006.......................................1,642.9
Internet users per 100 inhabitants, 2006 ....2.5
Internet bandwidth (mB/s) per 10,000 inhabitants, 2006..........0.0

Networked Readiness Index

Year (number of economies)	Rank
2007–2008 (127)	**109**
2006–2007 (122)	100
2005–2006 (115)	79

Global Competitiveness Index 2007–2008 (131)   120

Environment component — 93
Market environment — 101
1.01 Venture capital availability, 2007..86
1.02 Financial market sophistication, 2007 107
1.03 Availability of latest technologies, 2007 100
1.04 State of cluster development, 2007 75
1.05 Utility patents,* 2006 86
1.06 High-tech exports,* 2005 64
1.07 Burden of government regulation, 2007 38
1.08 Extent and effect of taxation, 2007.................................108
1.09 Total tax rate,* 2007 21
1.10 Time required to start a business,* 2007 62
1.11 No. of procedures required to start a business,* 2007 ..119
1.12 Intensity of local competition, 2007 71
1.13 Freedom of the press, 2007...97
1.14 Accessibility of digital content, 2007...............................103

Political and regulatory environment — 87
2.01 Effectiveness of law-making bodies, 2007 69
2.02 Laws relating to ICT, 2007..95
2.03 Judicial independence, 2007 82
2.04 Intellectual property protection, 2007 108
2.05 Efficiency of legal framework, 2007...................................81
2.06 Property rights, 2007..110
2.07 Quality of competition in the ISP sector, 2007 86
2.08 No. of procedures to enforce a contract,* 2007 65
2.09 Time to enforce a contract,* 2007 61

Infrastructure environment — 88
3.01 Telephone lines,* 2006...124
3.02 Secure Internet servers,* 2006...101
3.03 Electricity production* ....n/a
3.04 Availability of scientists and engineers, 2007 83
3.05 Quality of scientific research institutions, 2007 37
3.06 Tertiary enrollment,* 2004...109
3.07 Education expenditure,* 2005...69

Readiness component — 120
Individual readiness — 126
4.01 Quality of math and science education, 2007.................101
4.02 Quality of the educational system, 2007...........................71
4.03 Internet access in schools, 2007......................................109
4.04 Buyer sophistication, 2007 109
4.05 Residential telephone connection charge,* 2006 122
4.06 Residential monthly telephone subscription,* 2006 119
4.07 High-speed monthly broadband subscription,* 2006......108
4.08 Lowest cost of broadband,* 2006 116
4.09 Cost of mobile telephone call,* 2005...............................121

Business readiness — 106
5.01 Extent of staff training, 2007..81
5.02 Local availability of research and training, 2007..............63
5.03 Quality of management schools, 2007 100
5.04 Company spending on R&D, 2007......................................86
5.05 University-industry research collaboration, 2007..............52
5.06 Business telephone connection charge,* 2006 115
5.07 Business monthly telephone subscription,* 2006 116
5.08 Local supplier quality, 2007..114
5.09 Local supplier quantity, 2007..75
5.10 Computer, comm., and other services imports,* 2005 36

Government readiness — 85
6.01 Government prioritization of ICT, 2007..............................64
6.02 Gov't procurement of advanced tech products, 2007 73
6.03 Importance of ICT to gov't vision of the future, 2007.......49
6.04 E-Government Readiness Index,* 2007..........................104

Usage component — 87
Individual usage — 119
7.01 Mobile telephone subscribers,* 2006..............................120
7.02 Personal computers,* 2006 101
7.03 Broadband Internet subscribers,* 2006 111
7.04 Internet users,* 2006...113
7.05 Internet bandwidth,* 2006 114

Business usage — 84
8.01 Prevalence of foreign technology licensing, 2007.............65
8.02 Firm-level technology absorption, 2007 103
8.03 Capacity for innovation, 2007...87
8.04 Availability of new telephone lines, 2007 83
8.05 Extent of business Internet use, 2007...............................84

Government usage — 68
9.01 Government success in ICT promotion, 2007....................49
9.02 Availability of government online services, 2007 56
9.03 ICT use and government efficiency, 2007..........................67
9.04 Presence of ICT in government offices, 2007 74
9.05 E-Participation Index,* 2007..82

* Hard data

Note: For further details and explanation, please refer to the section "How to Read the Country/Economy Profiles" at the beginning of this chapter.

Ukraine

Key indicators

Population (millions), 2006	46.0
GDP (PPP) per capita (US$), 2006	7,831.9
Internet users per 100 inhabitants, 2006	12.1
Internet bandwidth (mB/s) per 10,000 inhabitants, 2005	0.2

Networked Readiness Index

Year (number of economies)	Rank
2007–2008 (127)	**70**
2006–2007 (122)	75
2005–2006 (115)	76

Global Competitiveness Index 2007–2008 (131)	73

Environment component — 70
Market environment — 94

1.01	Venture capital availability, 2007	56
1.02	Financial market sophistication, 2007	88
1.03	Availability of latest technologies, 2007	95
1.04	State of cluster development, 2007	86
1.05	Utility patents,* 2006	56
1.06	High-tech exports,* 2005	58
1.07	Burden of government regulation, 2007	101
1.08	Extent and effect of taxation, 2007	119
1.09	Total tax rate,* 2007	100
1.10	Time required to start a business,* 2007	59
1.11	No. of procedures required to start a business,* 2007	74
1.12	Intensity of local competition, 2007	92
1.13	Freedom of the press, 2007	77
1.14	Accessibility of digital content, 2007	73

Political and regulatory environment — 94

2.01	Effectiveness of law-making bodies, 2007	106
2.02	Laws relating to ICT, 2007	80
2.03	Judicial independence, 2007	107
2.04	Intellectual property protection, 2007	107
2.05	Efficiency of legal framework, 2007	108
2.06	Property rights, 2007	115
2.07	Quality of competition in the ISP sector, 2007	109
2.08	No. of procedures to enforce a contract,* 2007	15
2.09	Time to enforce a contract,* 2007	25

Infrastructure environment — 42

3.01	Telephone lines,* 2006	47
3.02	Secure Internet servers,* 2006	85
3.03	Electricity production,* 2004	50
3.04	Availability of scientists and engineers, 2007	69
3.05	Quality of scientific research institutions, 2007	58
3.06	Tertiary enrollment,* 2005	16
3.07	Education expenditure,* 2005	51

Readiness component — 72
Individual readiness — 58

4.01	Quality of math and science education, 2007	42
4.02	Quality of the educational system, 2007	45
4.03	Internet access in schools, 2007	77
4.04	Buyer sophistication, 2007	80
4.05	Residential telephone connection charge,* 2006	73
4.06	Residential monthly telephone subscription,* 2006	66
4.07	High-speed monthly broadband subscription,* 2006	53
4.08	Lowest cost of broadband,* 2006	54
4.09	Cost of mobile telephone call,* 2005	85

Business readiness — 80

5.01	Extent of staff training, 2007	96
5.02	Local availability of research and training, 2007	83
5.03	Quality of management schools, 2007	82
5.04	Company spending on R&D, 2007	66
5.05	University-industry research collaboration, 2007	63
5.06	Business telephone connection charge,* 2006	92
5.07	Business monthly telephone subscription,* 2006	66
5.08	Local supplier quality, 2007	78
5.09	Local supplier quantity, 2007	64
5.10	Computer, comm., and other services imports,* 2005	61

Government readiness — 91

6.01	Government prioritization of ICT, 2007	112
6.02	Gov't procurement of advanced tech products, 2007	74
6.03	Importance of ICT to gov't vision of the future, 2007	116
6.04	E-Government Readiness Index,* 2007	41

Usage component — 71
Individual usage — 54

7.01	Mobile telephone subscribers,* 2006	22
7.02	Personal computers,* 2006	80
7.03	Broadband Internet subscribers,* 2006	62
7.04	Internet users,* 2006	76
7.05	Internet bandwidth,* 2005	95

Business usage — 90

8.01	Prevalence of foreign technology licensing, 2007	111
8.02	Firm-level technology absorption, 2007	90
8.03	Capacity for innovation, 2007	40
8.04	Availability of new telephone lines, 2007	101
8.05	Extent of business Internet use, 2007	76

Government usage — 67

9.01	Government success in ICT promotion, 2007	107
9.02	Availability of government online services, 2007	81
9.03	ICT use and government efficiency, 2007	91
9.04	Presence of ICT in government offices, 2007	104
9.05	E-Participation Index,* 2007	14

* Hard data

Note: For further details and explanation, please refer to the section "How to Read the Country/Economy Profiles" at the beginning of this chapter.

United Arab Emirates

Key indicators

Population (millions), 2006..4.7
GDP (PPP) per capita (US$), 2006..............................34,109.5
Internet users per 100 inhabitants, 2006 ....36.7
Internet bandwidth (mB/s) per 10,000 inhabitants, 2006.......21.4

Networked Readiness Index

Year (number of economies)	Rank
2007–2008 (127)	**29**
2006–2007 (122)	29
2005–2006 (115)	28

Global Competitiveness Index 2007–2008 (131) 37

Environment component — 39
Market environment — 24

1.01 Venture capital availability, 2007..16
1.02 Financial market sophistication, 2007 39
1.03 Availability of latest technologies, 2007............................16
1.04 State of cluster development, 2007.....................................17
1.05 Utility patents,* 2006 41
1.06 High-tech exports* ....n/a
1.07 Burden of government regulation, 2007 6
1.08 Extent and effect of taxation, 2007..2
1.09 Total tax rate,* 2007 1
1.10 Time required to start a business,* 2007........................106
1.11 No. of procedures required to start a business,* 2007 88
1.12 Intensity of local competition, 2007 35
1.13 Freedom of the press, 2007..104
1.14 Accessibility of digital content, 2007..................................40

Political and regulatory environment — 45

2.01 Effectiveness of law-making bodies, 2007 31
2.02 Laws relating to ICT, 2007..33
2.03 Judicial independence, 2007 39
2.04 Intellectual property protection, 2007 31
2.05 Efficiency of legal framework, 2007....................................27
2.06 Property rights, 2007..45
2.07 Quality of competition in the ISP sector, 2007 112
2.08 No. of procedures to enforce a contract,* 2007 117
2.09 Time to enforce a contract,* 2007 82

Infrastructure environment — 56

3.01 Telephone lines,* 2006..43
3.02 Secure Internet servers,* 2006..35
3.03 Electricity production,* 2004 9
3.04 Availability of scientists and engineers, 2007 79
3.05 Quality of scientific research institutions, 2007 66
3.06 Tertiary enrollment,* 2003..75
3.07 Education expenditure* ....n/a

Readiness component — 25
Individual readiness — 33

4.01 Quality of math and science education, 2007 47
4.02 Quality of the educational system, 2007...........................38
4.03 Internet access in schools, 2007..30
4.04 Buyer sophistication, 2007 37
4.05 Residential telephone connection charge,* 2005 14
4.06 Residential monthly telephone subscription,* 2005 1
4.07 High-speed monthly broadband subscription,* 2006.......28
4.08 Lowest cost of broadband,* 2006 32
4.09 Cost of mobile telephone call,* 2005....................................4

Business readiness — 37

5.01 Extent of staff training, 2007...39
5.02 Local availability of research and training, 2007.............50
5.03 Quality of management schools, 2007 58
5.04 Company spending on R&D, 2007......................................53
5.05 University-industry research collaboration, 2007............53
5.06 Business telephone connection charge,* 2005 11
5.07 Business monthly telephone subscription,* 2005 2
5.08 Local supplier quality, 2007...42
5.09 Local supplier quantity, 2007..52
5.10 Computer, comm., and other services imports*............n/a

Government readiness — 10

6.01 Government prioritization of ICT, 2007.................................7
6.02 Gov't procurement of advanced tech products, 2007 17
6.03 Importance of ICT to gov't vision of the future, 2007.........4
6.04 E-Government Readiness Index,* 2007............................32

Usage component — 27
Individual usage — 36

7.01 Mobile telephone subscribers,* 2006.................................10
7.02 Personal computers,* 2005 34
7.03 Broadband Internet subscribers,* 2006 43
7.04 Internet users,* 2006 33
7.05 Internet bandwidth,* 2006 30

Business usage — 32

8.01 Prevalence of foreign technology licensing, 2007.............19
8.02 Firm-level technology absorption, 2007 17
8.03 Capacity for innovation, 2007...76
8.04 Availability of new telephone lines, 2007..........................17
8.05 Extent of business Internet use, 2007................................42

Government usage — 17

9.01 Government success in ICT promotion, 2007.....................6
9.02 Availability of government online services, 2007 25
9.03 ICT use and government efficiency, 2007..........................11
9.04 Presence of ICT in government offices, 2007 17
9.05 E-Participation Index,* 2007..39

* Hard data

Note: For further details and explanation, please refer to the section "How to Read the Country/Economy Profiles" at the beginning of this chapter.

United Kingdom

Key indicators

Population (millions), 2006..59.8
GDP (PPP) per capita (US$), 2006..................................35,485.9
Internet users per 100 inhabitants, 2006 ....56.0
Internet bandwidth (mB/s) per 10,000 inhabitants, 2004.....130.7

Networked Readiness Index

Year (number of economies)	Rank
2007–2008 (127)	**12**
2006–2007 (122)	9
2005–2006 (115)	10

Global Competitiveness Index 2007–2008 (131) 9

Environment component — 10

Market environment — 13

1.01 Venture capital availability, 2007..6
1.02 Financial market sophistication, 2007 2
1.03 Availability of latest technologies, 2007 11
1.04 State of cluster development, 2007..9
1.05 Utility patents,* 2006 19
1.06 High-tech exports,* 2005 19
1.07 Burden of government regulation, 2007 57
1.08 Extent and effect of taxation, 2007......................................43
1.09 Total tax rate,* 2007 34
1.10 Time required to start a business,* 2007............................24
1.11 No. of procedures required to start a business,* 2007 19
1.12 Intensity of local competition, 2007 6
1.13 Freedom of the press, 2007..21
1.14 Accessibility of digital content, 2007..................................14

Political and regulatory environment — 12

2.01 Effectiveness of law-making bodies, 2007 5
2.02 Laws relating to ICT, 2007...11
2.03 Judicial independence, 2007..12
2.04 Intellectual property protection, 2007 8
2.05 Efficiency of legal framework, 2007....................................14
2.06 Property rights, 2007..18
2.07 Quality of competition in the ISP sector, 2007 9
2.08 No. of procedures to enforce a contract,* 2007................15
2.09 Time to enforce a contract,* 2007 35

Infrastructure environment — 11

3.01 Telephone lines,* 2006..9
3.02 Secure Internet servers,* 2006..9
3.03 Electricity production,* 2004...29
3.04 Availability of scientists and engineers, 2007 28
3.05 Quality of scientific research institutions, 2007 4
3.06 Tertiary enrollment,* 2005..26
3.07 Education expenditure,* 2005...30

Readiness component — 21

Individual readiness — 23

4.01 Quality of math and science education, 2007....................44
4.02 Quality of the educational system, 2007...........................30
4.03 Internet access in schools, 2007..14
4.04 Buyer sophistication, 2007 18
4.05 Residential telephone connection charge,* 2006 47
4.06 Residential monthly telephone subscription,* 2006 28
4.07 High-speed monthly broadband subscription,* 2006........13
4.08 Lowest cost of broadband,* 2006 10
4.09 Cost of mobile telephone call,* 2005.................................17

Business readiness — 14

5.01 Extent of staff training, 2007...17
5.02 Local availability of research and training, 2007.................5
5.03 Quality of management schools, 2007 10
5.04 Company spending on R&D, 2007......................................12
5.05 University-industry research collaboration, 2007...............12
5.06 Business telephone connection charge,* 2006 33
5.07 Business monthly telephone subscription,* 2006 31
5.08 Local supplier quality, 2007 19
5.09 Local supplier quantity, 2007...27
5.10 Computer, comm., and other services imports,* 2005 47

Government readiness — 22

6.01 Government prioritization of ICT, 2007..............................21
6.02 Gov't procurement of advanced tech products, 2007 26
6.03 Importance of ICT to gov't vision of the future, 2007.......42
6.04 E-Government Readiness Index,* 2007............................10

Usage component — 12

Individual usage — 6

7.01 Mobile telephone subscribers,* 2006.................................11
7.02 Personal computers,* 2005 7
7.03 Broadband Internet subscribers,* 2006 11
7.04 Internet users,* 2006 18
7.05 Internet bandwidth,* 2004 5

Business usage — 11

8.01 Prevalence of foreign technology licensing, 2007.............15
8.02 Firm-level technology absorption, 2007 19
8.03 Capacity for innovation, 2007 14
8.04 Availability of new telephone lines, 2007...........................19
8.05 Extent of business Internet use, 2007 4

Government usage — 22

9.01 Government success in ICT promotion, 2007...................54
9.02 Availability of government online services, 2007 14
9.03 ICT use and government efficiency, 2007..........................33
9.04 Presence of ICT in government offices, 2007 22
9.05 E-Participation Index,* 2007...24

* Hard data

Note: For further details and explanation, please refer to the section "How to Read the Country/Economy Profiles" at the beginning of this chapter.

United States

Key indicators

Population (millions), 2006..301.0
GDP (PPP) per capita (US$), 2006....................................43,223.5
Internet users per 100 inhabitants, 2006 ....69.1
Internet bandwidth (mB/s) per 10,000 inhabitants, 2004.......33.1

Networked Readiness Index

Year (number of economies)	Rank
2007–2008 (127)	**4**
2006–2007 (122)	7
2005–2006 (115)	1

Global Competitiveness Index 2007–2008 (131)   1

Environment component   5
Market environment   3
1.01 Venture capital availability, 2007..1
1.02 Financial market sophistication, 2007 5
1.03 Availability of latest technologies, 2007 6
1.04 State of cluster development, 2007 2
1.05 Utility patents,* 2006 1
1.06 High-tech exports,* 2005 11
1.07 Burden of government regulation, 2007 40
1.08 Extent and effect of taxation, 2007 46
1.09 Total tax rate,* 2007 67
1.10 Time required to start a business,* 2007 6
1.11 No. of procedures required to start a business,* 2007 19
1.12 Intensity of local competition, 2007 8
1.13 Freedom of the press, 2007..27
1.14 Accessibility of digital content, 2007.................................8

Political and regulatory environment   22
2.01 Effectiveness of law-making bodies, 2007 29
2.02 Laws relating to ICT, 2007..12
2.03 Judicial independence, 2007 37
2.04 Intellectual property protection, 2007 22
2.05 Efficiency of legal framework, 2007..................................30
2.06 Property rights, 2007..30
2.07 Quality of competition in the ISP sector, 2007 13
2.08 No. of procedures to enforce a contract,* 2007 29
2.09 Time to enforce a contract,* 2007 18

Infrastructure environment   2
3.01 Telephone lines,* 2006..7
3.02 Secure Internet servers,* 2006..2
3.03 Electricity production,* 2004...8
3.04 Availability of scientists and engineers, 2007 12
3.05 Quality of scientific research institutions, 2007 2
3.06 Tertiary enrollment,* 2005..4
3.07 Education expenditure,* 2005..42

Readiness component   7
Individual readiness   14
4.01 Quality of math and science education, 2007...................43
4.02 Quality of the educational system, 2007..........................17
4.03 Internet access in schools, 2007.......................................12
4.04 Buyer sophistication, 2007 12
4.05 Residential telephone connection charge,* 2005 7
4.06 Residential monthly telephone subscription,* 2005 34
4.07 High-speed monthly broadband subscription,* 2006..........2
4.08 Lowest cost of broadband,* 2006 3
4.09 Cost of mobile telephone call,* 2005...............................30

Business readiness   4
5.01 Extent of staff training, 2007...11
5.02 Local availability of research and training, 2007 2
5.03 Quality of management schools, 2007 6
5.04 Company spending on R&D, 2007....................................2
5.05 University-industry research collaboration, 2007................1
5.06 Business telephone connection charge,* 2005 12
5.07 Business monthly telephone subscription,* 2005 39
5.08 Local supplier quality, 2007 11
5.09 Local supplier quantity, 2007 9
5.10 Computer, comm., and other services imports,* 2005 51

Government readiness   5
6.01 Government prioritization of ICT, 2007............................18
6.02 Gov't procurement of advanced tech products, 2007 5
6.03 Importance of ICT to gov't vision of the future, 2007......28
6.04 E-Government Readiness Index,* 2007.............................4

Usage component   9
Individual usage   17
7.01 Mobile telephone subscribers,* 2006...............................51
7.02 Personal computers,* 2004 8
7.03 Broadband Internet subscribers,* 2006 17
7.04 Internet users,* 2006...7
7.05 Internet bandwidth,* 2004 19

Business usage   8
8.01 Prevalence of foreign technology licensing, 2007.............23
8.02 Firm-level technology absorption, 2007 4
8.03 Capacity for innovation, 2007 9
8.04 Availability of new telephone lines, 2007 22
8.05 Extent of business Internet use, 2007 6

Government usage   5
9.01 Government success in ICT promotion, 2007...................21
9.02 Availability of government online services, 2007 10
9.03 ICT use and government efficiency, 2007........................20
9.04 Presence of ICT in government offices, 2007 18
9.05 E-Participation Index,* 2007..1

* Hard data

Note: For further details and explanation, please refer to the section "How to Read the Country/Economy Profiles" at the beginning of this chapter.

Uruguay

Key indicators

Population (millions), 2006	3.5
GDP (PPP) per capita (US$), 2006	11,969.4
Internet users per 100 inhabitants, 2005	20.6
Internet bandwidth (mB/s) per 10,000 inhabitants, 2005	4.6

Networked Readiness Index

Year (number of economies)	Rank
2007–2008 (127)	**65**
2006–2007 (122)	60
2005–2006 (115)	65

Global Competitiveness Index 2007–2008 (131)	75

Environment component — 69
Market environment — 83

1.01	Venture capital availability, 2007	102
1.02	Financial market sophistication, 2007	82
1.03	Availability of latest technologies, 2007	65
1.04	State of cluster development, 2007	104
1.05	Utility patents,* 2006	55
1.06	High-tech exports,* 2005	77
1.07	Burden of government regulation, 2007	62
1.08	Extent and effect of taxation, 2007	104
1.09	Total tax rate,* 2007	52
1.10	Time required to start a business,* 2007	94
1.11	No. of procedures required to start a business,* 2007	88
1.12	Intensity of local competition, 2007	105
1.13	Freedom of the press, 2007	49
1.14	Accessibility of digital content, 2007	35

Political and regulatory environment — 60

2.01	Effectiveness of law-making bodies, 2007	79
2.02	Laws relating to ICT, 2007	75
2.03	Judicial independence, 2007	42
2.04	Intellectual property protection, 2007	50
2.05	Efficiency of legal framework, 2007	49
2.06	Property rights, 2007	61
2.07	Quality of competition in the ISP sector, 2007	77
2.08	No. of procedures to enforce a contract,* 2007	89
2.09	Time to enforce a contract,* 2007	92

Infrastructure environment — 68

3.01	Telephone lines,* 2006	42
3.02	Secure Internet servers,* 2006	44
3.03	Electricity production,* 2004	75
3.04	Availability of scientists and engineers, 2007	71
3.05	Quality of scientific research institutions, 2007	82
3.06	Tertiary enrollment,* 2004	52
3.07	Education expenditure,* 2005	100

Readiness component — 73
Individual readiness — 73

4.01	Quality of math and science education, 2007	83
4.02	Quality of the educational system, 2007	66
4.03	Internet access in schools, 2007	70
4.04	Buyer sophistication, 2007	75
4.05	Residential telephone connection charge,* 2005	60
4.06	Residential monthly telephone subscription,* 2005	73
4.07	High-speed monthly broadband subscription,* 2006	68
4.08	Lowest cost of broadband,* 2006	61
4.09	Cost of mobile telephone call*	n/a

Business readiness — 82

5.01	Extent of staff training, 2007	88
5.02	Local availability of research and training, 2007	71
5.03	Quality of management schools, 2007	51
5.04	Company spending on R&D, 2007	92
5.05	University-industry research collaboration, 2007	89
5.06	Business telephone connection charge,* 2005	51
5.07	Business monthly telephone subscription,* 2005	70
5.08	Local supplier quality, 2007	82
5.09	Local supplier quantity, 2007	101
5.10	Computer, comm., and other services imports.* 2005	85

Government readiness — 68

6.01	Government prioritization of ICT, 2007	79
6.02	Gov't procurement of advanced tech products, 2007	90
6.03	Importance of ICT to gov't vision of the future, 2007	94
6.04	E-Government Readiness Index,* 2007	48

Usage component — 61
Individual usage — 55

7.01	Mobile telephone subscribers,* 2006	63
7.02	Personal computers,* 2005	49
7.03	Broadband Internet subscribers,* 2006	52
7.04	Internet users,* 2005	56
7.05	Internet bandwidth,* 2005	51

Business usage — 73

8.01	Prevalence of foreign technology licensing, 2007	86
8.02	Firm-level technology absorption, 2007	99
8.03	Capacity for innovation, 2007	74
8.04	Availability of new telephone lines, 2007	32
8.05	Extent of business Internet use, 2007	69

Government usage — 70

9.01	Government success in ICT promotion, 2007	84
9.02	Availability of government online services, 2007	50
9.03	ICT use and government efficiency, 2007	43
9.04	Presence of ICT in government offices, 2007	73
9.05	E-Participation Index,* 2007	91

* Hard data

Note: For further details and explanation, please refer to the section "How to Read the Country/Economy Profiles" at the beginning of this chapter.

Venezuela

Key indicators

Population (millions), 2006..27.2
GDP (PPP) per capita (US$), 2006....................................7,480.5
Internet users per 100 inhabitants, 2006 ....15.2
Internet bandwidth (mB/s) per 10,000 inhabitants, 2005.........0.5

Networked Readiness Index

Year (number of economies)	Rank
2007–2008 (127)	**86**
2006–2007 (122)	83
2005–2006 (115)	81

Global Competitiveness Index 2007–2008 (131)	98

Environment component — 117
Market environment — 124

1.01 Venture capital availability, 2007...89
1.02 Financial market sophistication, 2007 75
1.03 Availability of latest technologies, 2007 76
1.04 State of cluster development, 2007.....................................102
1.05 Utility patents,* 2006 59
1.06 High-tech exports,* 2005 91
1.07 Burden of government regulation, 2007 127
1.08 Extent and effect of taxation, 2007.......................................86
1.09 Total tax rate,* 2007...95
1.10 Time required to start a business,* 2007..........................119
1.11 No. of procedures required to start a business,* 2007 ..118
1.12 Intensity of local competition, 2007 119
1.13 Freedom of the press, 2007..125
1.14 Accessibility of digital content, 2007.....................................62

Political and regulatory environment — 121

2.01 Effectiveness of law-making bodies, 2007 127
2.02 Laws relating to ICT, 2007..76
2.03 Judicial independence, 2007..127
2.04 Intellectual property protection, 2007 122
2.05 Efficiency of legal framework, 2007....................................127
2.06 Property rights, 2007..126
2.07 Quality of competition in the ISP sector, 2007 83
2.08 No. of procedures to enforce a contract,* 2007................13
2.09 Time to enforce a contract,* 2007 56

Infrastructure environment — 65

3.01 Telephone lines,* 2006...71
3.02 Secure Internet servers,* 2006...69
3.03 Electricity production,* 2004 51
3.04 Availability of scientists and engineers, 2007 78
3.05 Quality of scientific research institutions, 2007 104
3.06 Tertiary enrollment,* 2004...49
3.07 Education expenditure,* 2005...55

Readiness component — 84
Individual readiness — 75

4.01 Quality of math and science education, 2007 109
4.02 Quality of the educational system, 2007...........................113
4.03 Internet access in schools, 2007..82
4.04 Buyer sophistication, 2007 78
4.05 Residential telephone connection charge,* 2005 44
4.06 Residential monthly telephone subscription,* 2005 68
4.07 High-speed monthly broadband subscription,* 2006........66
4.08 Lowest cost of broadband,* 2006 58
4.09 Cost of mobile telephone call,* 2005...................................80

Business readiness — 83

5.01 Extent of staff training, 2007...86
5.02 Local availability of research and training, 2007................99
5.03 Quality of management schools, 2007 62
5.04 Company spending on R&D, 2007.......................................82
5.05 University-industry research collaboration, 2007...............74
5.06 Business telephone connection charge,* 2005 44
5.07 Business monthly telephone subscription,* 2005 61
5.08 Local supplier quality, 2007 93
5.09 Local supplier quantity, 2007..109
5.10 Computer, comm., and other services imports,* 2005 75

Government readiness — 97

6.01 Government prioritization of ICT, 2007.............................102
6.02 Gov't procurement of advanced tech products, 2007 103
6.03 Importance of ICT to gov't vision of the future, 2007.....104
6.04 E-Government Readiness Index,* 2007..............................59

Usage component — 73
Individual usage — 60

7.01 Mobile telephone subscribers,* 2006..................................62
7.02 Personal computers,* 2005 60
7.03 Broadband Internet subscribers,* 2006 56
7.04 Internet users,* 2006 66
7.05 Internet bandwidth,* 2005 79

Business usage — 83

8.01 Prevalence of foreign technology licensing, 2007.............67
8.02 Firm-level technology absorption, 2007 71
8.03 Capacity for innovation, 2007...112
8.04 Availability of new telephone lines, 2007...........................84
8.05 Extent of business Internet use, 2007................................80

Government usage — 71

9.01 Government success in ICT promotion, 2007.................110
9.02 Availability of government online services, 2007 42
9.03 ICT use and government efficiency, 2007..........................77
9.04 Presence of ICT in government offices, 2007 109
9.05 E-Participation Index,* 2007..34

* Hard data

Note: For further details and explanation, please refer to the section "How to Read the Country/Economy Profiles" at the beginning of this chapter.

Vietnam

Key indicators

Population (millions), 2006...85.3
GDP (PPP) per capita (US$), 2006..3,393.2
Internet users per 100 inhabitants, 2006 ....17.2
Internet bandwidth (mB/s) per 10,000 inhabitants, 2006.........0.8

Networked Readiness Index

Year (number of economies)	Rank
2007–2008 (127)	**73**
2006–2007 (122)	82
2005–2006 (115)	75

Global Competitiveness Index 2007–2008 (131)	68

Environment component — 73
Market environment — 80

1.01 Venture capital availability, 2007...63
1.02 Financial market sophistication, 2007 95
1.03 Availability of latest technologies, 2007 82
1.04 State of cluster development, 2007.......................................16
1.05 Utility patents,* 2006 86
1.06 High-tech exports,* 2005 61
1.07 Burden of government regulation, 2007 105
1.08 Extent and effect of taxation, 2007..58
1.09 Total tax rate,* 2007 55
1.10 Time required to start a business,* 2007............................100
1.11 No. of procedures required to start a business,* 2007 88
1.12 Intensity of local competition, 2007 61
1.13 Freedom of the press, 2007..99
1.14 Accessibility of digital content, 2007.....................................81

Political and regulatory environment — 59

2.01 Effectiveness of law-making bodies, 2007 47
2.02 Laws relating to ICT, 2007...73
2.03 Judicial independence, 2007...72
2.04 Intellectual property protection, 2007 100
2.05 Efficiency of legal framework, 2007......................................57
2.06 Property rights, 2007...78
2.07 Quality of competition in the ISP sector, 2007 84
2.08 No. of procedures to enforce a contract,* 2007 40
2.09 Time to enforce a contract,* 2007 16

Infrastructure environment — 91

3.01 Telephone lines,* 2005..64
3.02 Secure Internet servers,* 2006...101
3.03 Electricity production,* 2004 99
3.04 Availability of scientists and engineers, 2007 54
3.05 Quality of scientific research institutions, 2007 92
3.06 Tertiary enrollment,* 2005...89
3.07 Education expenditure,* 2005...96

Readiness component — 66
Individual readiness — 80

4.01 Quality of math and science education, 2007......................76
4.02 Quality of the educational system, 2007............................109
4.03 Internet access in schools, 2007..67
4.04 Buyer sophistication, 2007 55
4.05 Residential telephone connection charge,* 2006 89
4.06 Residential monthly telephone subscription,* 2006 83
4.07 High-speed monthly broadband subscription,* 2006..........90
4.08 Lowest cost of broadband,* 2006 83
4.09 Cost of mobile telephone call,* 2006..................................100

Business readiness — 74

5.01 Extent of staff training, 2007...82
5.02 Local availability of research and training, 2007..................72
5.03 Quality of management schools, 2007 117
5.04 Company spending on R&D, 2007..56
5.05 University-industry research collaboration, 2007.................76
5.06 Business telephone connection charge,* 2006 77
5.07 Business monthly telephone subscription,* 2006 64
5.08 Local supplier quality, 2007 96
5.09 Local supplier quantity, 2007 82
5.10 Computer, comm., and other services imports* ....n/a

Government readiness — 43

6.01 Government prioritization of ICT, 2007.................................35
6.02 Gov't procurement of advanced tech products, 2007 35
6.03 Importance of ICT to gov't vision of the future, 2007.........37
6.04 E-Government Readiness Index,* 2007...............................81

Usage component — 75
Individual usage — 92

7.01 Mobile telephone subscribers,* 2006.................................106
7.02 Personal computers,* 2005 108
7.03 Broadband Internet subscribers,* 2006 73
7.04 Internet users,* 2006 63
7.05 Internet bandwidth,* 2006...74

Business usage — 79

8.01 Prevalence of foreign technology licensing, 2007.............118
8.02 Firm-level technology absorption, 2007 46
8.03 Capacity for innovation, 2007..41
8.04 Availability of new telephone lines, 2007.............................65
8.05 Extent of business Internet use, 2007................................101

Government usage — 49

9.01 Government success in ICT promotion, 2007......................37
9.02 Availability of government online services, 2007 95
9.03 ICT use and government efficiency, 2007............................75
9.04 Presence of ICT in government offices, 2007 62
9.05 E-Participation Index,* 2007..16

* Hard data

Note: For further details and explanation, please refer to the section "How to Read the Country/Economy Profiles" at the beginning of this chapter.

Zambia

Key indicators

Population (millions), 2006..11.9
GDP (PPP) per capita (US$), 2006.................................1,087.6
Internet users per 100 inhabitants, 2006 ....4.2
Internet bandwidth (mB/s) per 10,000 inhabitants, 2006.........0.1

Networked Readiness Index

Year (number of economies)	Rank
2007–2008 (127)	**112**
2006–2007 (122)	112
2005–2006 (115)	n/a

Global Competitiveness Index 2007–2008 (131)   122

Environment component — 99
Market environment — 87
1.01 Venture capital availability, 2007..123
1.02 Financial market sophistication, 2007 96
1.03 Availability of latest technologies, 2007 108
1.04 State of cluster development, 2007 50
1.05 Utility patents,* 2006 86
1.06 High-tech exports,* 2004 95
1.07 Burden of government regulation, 2007 19
1.08 Extent and effect of taxation, 2007 115
1.09 Total tax rate,* 2007 4
1.10 Time required to start a business,* 2007 75
1.11 No. of procedures required to start a business,* 2007 19
1.12 Intensity of local competition, 2007 125
1.13 Freedom of the press, 2007 111
1.14 Accessibility of digital content, 2007 105

Political and regulatory environment — 83
2.01 Effectiveness of law-making bodies, 2007 97
2.02 Laws relating to ICT, 2007...98
2.03 Judicial independence, 2007 91
2.04 Intellectual property protection, 2007 105
2.05 Efficiency of legal framework, 2007 60
2.06 Property rights, 2007 66
2.07 Quality of competition in the ISP sector, 2007 114
2.08 No. of procedures to enforce a contract,* 2007 46
2.09 Time to enforce a contract,* 2007 49

Infrastructure environment — 113
3.01 Telephone lines,* 2006..116
3.02 Secure Internet servers,* 2006 101
3.03 Electricity production,* 2004 89
3.04 Availability of scientists and engineers, 2007 87
3.05 Quality of scientific research institutions, 2007 96
3.06 Tertiary enrollment,* 2000...120
3.07 Education expenditure,* 2005 90

Readiness component — 113
Individual readiness — 106
4.01 Quality of math and science education, 2007 91
4.02 Quality of the educational system, 2007 60
4.03 Internet access in schools, 2007 120
4.04 Buyer sophistication, 2007 125
4.05 Residential telephone connection charge,* 2005 77
4.06 Residential monthly telephone subscription,* 2005 107
4.07 High-speed monthly broadband subscription* ....n/a
4.08 Lowest cost of broadband* ....n/a
4.09 Cost of mobile telephone call,* 2004 109

Business readiness — 113
5.01 Extent of staff training, 2007 125
5.02 Local availability of research and training, 2007 116
5.03 Quality of management schools, 2007 90
5.04 Company spending on R&D, 2007 124
5.05 University-industry research collaboration, 2007 103
5.06 Business telephone connection charge,* 2005 89
5.07 Business monthly telephone subscription,* 2005 113
5.08 Local supplier quality, 2007 113
5.09 Local supplier quantity, 2007 121
5.10 Computer, comm., and other services imports* ....n/a

Government readiness — 121
6.01 Government prioritization of ICT, 2007 93
6.02 Gov't procurement of advanced tech products, 2007 120
6.03 Importance of ICT to gov't vision of the future, 2007.......96
6.04 E-Government Readiness Index,* 2007 116

Usage component — 111
Individual usage — 111
7.01 Mobile telephone subscribers,* 2006 109
7.02 Personal computers,* 2005 111
7.03 Broadband Internet subscribers,* 2006 106
7.04 Internet users,* 2006 103
7.05 Internet bandwidth,* 2006 100

Business usage — 92
8.01 Prevalence of foreign technology licensing, 2007.................73
8.02 Firm-level technology absorption, 2007 73
8.03 Capacity for innovation, 2007 118
8.04 Availability of new telephone lines, 2007 96
8.05 Extent of business Internet use, 2007 91

Government usage — 120
9.01 Government success in ICT promotion, 2007.....................108
9.02 Availability of government online services, 2007 101
9.03 ICT use and government efficiency, 2007............................123
9.04 Presence of ICT in government offices, 2007 117
9.05 E-Participation Index,* 2007 117

* Hard data

Note: For further details and explanation, please refer to the section "How to Read the Country/Economy Profiles" at the beginning of this chapter.

Zimbabwe

Key indicators

Population (millions), 2006..13.1
GDP (PPP) per capita (US$), 2006......................................2,488.0
Internet users per 100 inhabitants, 2006 ....9.3
Internet bandwidth (mB/s) per 10,000 inhabitants, 2006.........0.0

Networked Readiness Index

Year (number of economies)	Rank
2007–2008 (127)	**125**
2006–2007 (122)	117
2005–2006 (115)	105

Global Competitiveness Index 2007–2008 (131)   129

Environment component — 122

Market environment — 125

1.01 Venture capital availability, 2007..96
1.02 Financial market sophistication, 2007 76
1.03 Availability of latest technologies, 2007 113
1.04 State of cluster development, 2007.................................118
1.05 Utility patents,* 2006 80
1.06 High-tech exports,* 2004 85
1.07 Burden of government regulation, 2007 120
1.08 Extent and effect of taxation, 2007..................................121
1.09 Total tax rate,* 2007 93
1.10 Time required to start a business,* 2007........................115
1.11 No. of procedures required to start a business,* 2007 74
1.12 Intensity of local competition, 2007 126
1.13 Freedom of the press, 2007...127
1.14 Accessibility of digital content, 2007................................124

Political and regulatory environment — 122

2.01 Effectiveness of law-making bodies, 2007 118
2.02 Laws relating to ICT, 2007..106
2.03 Judicial independence, 2007 124
2.04 Intellectual property protection, 2007 98
2.05 Efficiency of legal framework, 2007.................................123
2.06 Property rights, 2007 127
2.07 Quality of competition in the ISP sector, 2007 119
2.08 No. of procedures to enforce a contract,* 2007.............65
2.09 Time to enforce a contract,* 2007 37

Infrastructure environment — 90

3.01 Telephone lines,* 2006...108
3.02 Secure Internet servers,* 2006...101
3.03 Electricity production,* 2004 88
3.04 Availability of scientists and engineers, 2007 106
3.05 Quality of scientific research institutions, 2007 80
3.06 Tertiary enrollment,* 2003...108
3.07 Education expenditure,* 2005...11

Readiness component — 126

Individual readiness — 127

4.01 Quality of math and science education, 2007 70
4.02 Quality of the educational system, 2007...........................39
4.03 Internet access in schools, 2007..108
4.04 Buyer sophistication, 2007 96
4.05 Residential telephone connection charge*......................n/a
4.06 Residential monthly telephone subscription,* 2005 122
4.07 High-speed monthly broadband subscription,* 2006......101
4.08 Lowest cost of broadband,* 2006 110
4.09 Cost of mobile telephone call,* 2006...............................123

Business readiness — 111

5.01 Extent of staff training, 2007..63
5.02 Local availability of research and training, 2007.............117
5.03 Quality of management schools, 2007 83
5.04 Company spending on R&D, 2007......................................79
5.05 University-industry research collaboration, 2007.............82
5.06 Business telephone connection charge*...........................n/a
5.07 Business monthly telephone subscription*.....................n/a
5.08 Local supplier quality, 2007 102
5.09 Local supplier quantity, 2007 104
5.10 Computer, comm., and other services imports*..............n/a

Government readiness — 126

6.01 Government prioritization of ICT, 2007............................122
6.02 Gov't procurement of advanced tech products, 2007 123
6.03 Importance of ICT to gov't vision of the future, 2007.....127
6.04 E-Government Readiness Index,* 2007...........................108

Usage component — 127

Individual usage — 108

7.01 Mobile telephone subscribers,* 2006...............................121
7.02 Personal computers,* 2006 68
7.03 Broadband Internet subscribers,* 2006 96
7.04 Internet users,* 2006 83
7.05 Internet bandwidth,* 2006 115

Business usage — 126

8.01 Prevalence of foreign technology licensing, 2007.............89
8.02 Firm-level technology absorption, 2007 118
8.03 Capacity for innovation, 2007...125
8.04 Availability of new telephone lines, 2007 127
8.05 Extent of business Internet use, 2007 120

Government usage — 126

9.01 Government success in ICT promotion, 2007.................123
9.02 Availability of government online services, 2007 124
9.03 ICT use and government efficiency, 2007........................127
9.04 Presence of ICT in government offices, 2007 126
9.05 E-Participation Index,* 2007...117

* Hard data

Note: For further details and explanation, please refer to the section "How to Read the Country/Economy Profiles" at the beginning of this chapter.

Part 4
Data Tables

How to Read the Data Tables

PEARL SAMANDARI, World Economic Forum

The following pages present the data for all 127 economies included in the *Global Information Technology Report 2007–2008*.

The tables are organized in nine sections, which correspond to the nine pillars of the NRI.

Environment
1. Market environment
2. Political and regulatory environment
3. Infrastructure environment

Readiness
4. Individual readiness
5. Business readiness
6. Government readiness

Usage
7. Individual usage
8. Business usage
9. Government usage

Two types of data are used in the NRI: Survey data and hard data.

- **Survey data**: average responses in each economy to questions included in the World Economic Forum's Executive Opinion Survey, conducted in the first quarter of 2006 and 2007.

- **Hard data:** indicators obtained from a variety of sources.

Survey data

❶ Data yielded from the World Economic Forum's Executive Opinion Survey are presented in blue-colored bar graphs. Questions asked for responses on a scale of 1 to 7, where an answer of 1 corresponds to the lowest possible score and an answer of 7 corresponds to the highest possible score. For each Survey variable, the original question and the two extreme answers are shown.

We report the average score for each economy, that is, the arithmetic mean of responses from each economy. Variable 1.02, for example, asks about the sophistication of the financial markets in the respondent's economy. On this particular variable, Switzerland, with a score of 6.75, ranks first and therefore appears at the top. We report responses rounded to two decimal points, but use the exact figures to determine rankings. For example, in the case of variable 8.01 on the prevalence of foreign technology licensing, New Zealand's average score is 5.56990099009901 and Israel's average score is 5.56916996047431. These economies are therefore ranked 13th and 14th respectively, although they are both listed with the same rounded score of 5.57

❷ A dotted line on the graph indicates the mean score across the sample of 127 economies.

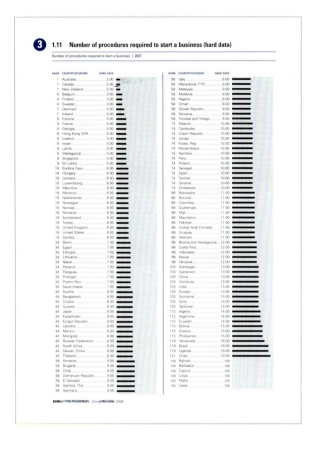

Hard data

③ While Survey data provide qualitative information, hard data are an objective measure of a quantity (e.g., gross domestic product, cost of a mobile telephone call, number of personal computers, number of procedures required to start a business, and so on). We use the latest data available from international organizations (the International Telecommunication Union, the World Bank, United Nations' agencies, and so on), completed, if necessary, by national sources. In the following pages, hard data variables are presented in gray-shaded bar graphs. Detailed description and full source for each variable can be found in the Technical Notes and Sources section at the end of this *Report*.

When data are not available or are too old, "n/a" is used in lieu of the rank and the value.

In the case of hard data, true ties between two or more countries are possible. In such cases, shared rankings are indicated accordingly. For example, the number of days required to start a business is the same—six—in Denmark, Turkey, and the United States. Therefore, the three countries share the sixth place for variable 1.10.

Index of Data Tables

Subindex A Environment component

1st pillar: Market environment 295
- 1.01 Venture capital availability 296
- 1.02 Financial market sophistication 297
- 1.03 Availability of latest technologies 298
- 1.04 State of cluster development 299
- 1.05 Utility patents (hard data) 300
- 1.06 High-tech exports (hard data) 301
- 1.07 Burden of government regulation 302
- 1.08 Extent and effect of taxation 303
- 1.09 Total tax rate (hard data) 304
- 1.10 Time required to start a business (hard data) 305
- 1.11 Number of procedures required to start a business (hard data) 306
- 1.12 Intensity of local competition 307
- 1.13 Freedom of the press 308
- 1.14 Accessibility of digital content 309

2nd pillar: Political and regulatory environment 311
- 2.01 Effectiveness of law-making bodies 312
- 2.02 Laws relating to ICT 313
- 2.03 Judicial independence 314
- 2.04 Intellectual property protection 315
- 2.05 Efficiency of legal framework for disputes 316
- 2.06 Property rights 317
- 2.07 Quality of competition in the ISP sector 318
- 2.08 Number of procedures to enforce a contract (hard data) 319
- 2.09 Time to enforce a contract (hard data) 320

3rd pillar: Infrastructure environment 321
- 3.01 Telephone lines (hard data) 322
- 3.02 Secure Internet servers (hard data) 323
- 3.03 Electricity production (hard data) 324
- 3.04 Availability of scientists and engineers 325
- 3.05 Quality of scientific research institutions 326
- 3.06 Tertiary enrollment (hard data) 327
- 3.07 Education expenditure (hard data) 328

Subindex B Readiness component

4th pillar: Individual readiness 329
- 4.01 Quality of math and science education 330
- 4.02 Quality of the educational system 331
- 4.03 Internet access in schools 332
- 4.04 Buyer sophistication 333
- 4.05 Residential telephone connection charge (hard data) 334
- 4.06 Residential monthly telephone subscription (hard data) ...335
- 4.07 High-speed monthly broadband subscription (hard data)...336
- 4.08 Lowest cost of broadband (hard data) 337
- 4.09 Cost of mobile telephone call (hard data) 338

5th pillar: Business readiness 339
- 5.01 Extent of staff training 340
- 5.02 Local availability of specialized research and training services 341
- 5.03 Quality of management schools 342
- 5.04 Company spending on R&D..343
- 5.05 University-industry research collaboration 344
- 5.06 Business telephone connection charge (hard data) 345
- 5.07 Business monthly telephone subscription (hard data) ...346
- 5.08 Local supplier quality..347
- 5.09 Local supplier quantity 348
- 5.10 Computer, communications, and other services imports (hard data) 349

6th pillar: Government readiness 351
- 6.01 Government prioritization of ICT 352
- 6.02 Government procurement of advanced technology products 353
- 6.03 Importance of ICT to government vision of the future......354
- 6.04 E-Government Readiness Index (hard data) 355

Subindex C Usage component

7th pillar: Individual usage 357
- 7.01 Mobile telephone subscribers (hard data) 358
- 7.02 Personal computers (hard data) 359
- 7.03 Broadband Internet subscribers (hard data) 360
- 7.04 Internet users (hard data) 361
- 7.05 Internet bandwidth (hard data) 362

8th pillar: Business usage 363
- 8.01 Prevalence of foreign technology licensing 364
- 8.02 Firm-level technology absorption 365
- 8.03 Capacity for innovation 366
- 8.04 Availability of new telephone lines 367
- 8.05 Extent of business Internet use 368

9th pillar: Government usage 369
- 9.01 Government success in ICT promotion 370
- 9.02 Availability of government online services 371
- 9.03 ICT use and government efficiency 372
- 9.04 Presence of ICT in government offices 373
- 9.05 E-Participation Index (hard data) 374

Subindex A Environment component

1st pillar
Market environment

1.01 Venture capital availability

Entrepreneurs with innovative but risky projects can generally find venture capital in your country (1 = not true, 7 = true)

RANK	COUNTRY/ECONOMY	SCORE
1	United States	5.28
2	Finland	5.21
3	Netherlands	5.19
4	Norway	5.18
5	Israel	5.16
6	United Kingdom	5.07
7	Sweden	4.92
8	Denmark	4.90
9	Ireland	4.89
10	Luxembourg	4.87
11	Hong Kong SAR	4.87
12	Iceland	4.72
13	Australia	4.66
14	New Zealand	4.64
15	Singapore	4.64
16	United Arab Emirates	4.54
17	Korea, Rep.	4.50
18	Malaysia	4.49
19	Germany	4.42
20	Canada	4.37
21	Oman	4.32
22	Switzerland	4.31
23	Taiwan, China	4.31
24	Estonia	4.24
25	Belgium	4.21
26	Spain	4.21
27	Tunisia	4.20
28	Austria	4.18
29	India	4.12
30	France	4.08
31	Puerto Rico	4.05
32	Kuwait	4.02
33	Qatar	3.95
34	Chile	3.89
35	Indonesia	3.87
36	Panama	3.87
37	Japan	3.86
38	Bahrain	3.78
39	Slovak Republic	3.75
40	Portugal	3.74
41	South Africa	3.72
42	Saudi Arabia	3.66
43	Poland	3.58
44	Cyprus	3.56
45	Sri Lanka	3.53
46	Latvia	3.50
47	Lithuania	3.48
48	Slovenia	3.46
49	Kazakhstan	3.44
50	Hungary	3.37
51	Thailand	3.37
52	Botswana	3.33
53	Trinidad and Tobago	3.25
54	Mauritius	3.22
55	Jordan	3.20
56	Ukraine	3.19
57	Malta	3.17
58	Bulgaria	3.16
59	Macedonia, FYR	3.15
60	Russian Federation	3.15
61	Greece	3.12
62	Honduras	3.12
63	Vietnam	3.12
64	Azerbaijan	3.11
65	Namibia	3.09
66	Czech Republic	3.04
67	Kenya	3.03
68	Peru	3.02
69	Romania	2.99
70	China	2.98
71	Barbados	2.97
72	Croatia	2.96
73	Morocco	2.95
74	Guatemala	2.94
75	Colombia	2.94
76	El Salvador	2.93
77	Egypt	2.91
78	Philippines	2.89
79	Italy	2.89
80	Turkey	2.85
81	Argentina	2.84
82	Nigeria	2.84
83	Tanzania	2.83
84	Mexico	2.83
85	Costa Rica	2.82
86	Uganda	2.81
87	Pakistan	2.81
88	Georgia	2.70
89	Venezuela	2.67
90	Bosnia and Herzegovina	2.67
91	Albania	2.67
92	Gambia, The	2.65
93	Madagascar	2.64
94	Jamaica	2.63
95	Kyrgyz Republic	2.60
96	Zimbabwe	2.60
97	Cambodia	2.59
98	Tajikistan	2.57
99	Brazil	2.52
100	Dominican Republic	2.50
101	Benin	2.43
102	Uruguay	2.42
103	Syria	2.42
104	Bolivia	2.34
105	Mauritania	2.34
106	Algeria	2.33
107	Mali	2.32
108	Moldova	2.30
109	Nicaragua	2.29
110	Nepal	2.26
111	Bangladesh	2.26
112	Ecuador	2.20
113	Chad	2.19
114	Libya	2.17
115	Guyana	2.15
116	Paraguay	2.15
117	Ethiopia	2.13
118	Burkina Faso	2.13
119	Senegal	2.13
120	Armenia	2.12
121	Lesotho	2.08
122	Cameroon	2.00
123	Zambia	1.98
124	Mongolia	1.93
125	Mozambique	1.89
126	Burundi	1.87
127	Suriname	1.81

MEAN: 3.29

SOURCE: World Economic Forum, Executive Opinion Survey 2006, 2007

1.02 Financial market sophistication

The level of sophistication of financial markets in your country is (1 = lower than international norms, 7 = higher than international norms)

RANK	COUNTRY/ECONOMY	SCORE
1	Switzerland	6.75
2	United Kingdom	6.66
3	Hong Kong SAR	6.53
4	Luxembourg	6.34
5	United States	6.33
6	Canada	6.29
7	Sweden	6.28
8	Australia	6.26
9	Ireland	6.24
10	Netherlands	6.23
11	Germany	6.19
12	Singapore	6.16
13	Denmark	6.09
14	Finland	6.01
15	South Africa	6.00
16	France	5.98
17	Israel	5.91
18	Belgium	5.90
19	Norway	5.87
20	Iceland	5.81
21	Austria	5.77
22	Bahrain	5.77
23	Puerto Rico	5.76
24	Spain	5.69
25	New Zealand	5.64
26	Portugal	5.55
27	Chile	5.52
28	Panama	5.49
29	Estonia	5.46
30	Malaysia	5.42
31	Brazil	5.41
32	Korea, Rep.	5.20
33	India	5.18
34	Japan	5.18
35	Malta	4.91
36	Turkey	4.85
37	Jamaica	4.83
38	Thailand	4.80
39	United Arab Emirates	4.78
40	Taiwan, China	4.78
41	Slovak Republic	4.77
42	El Salvador	4.72
43	Greece	4.68
44	Oman	4.67
45	Cyprus	4.65
46	Qatar	4.60
47	Hungary	4.59
48	Kuwait	4.59
49	Mexico	4.57
50	Tunisia	4.48
51	Mauritius	4.43
52	Barbados	4.42
53	Czech Republic	4.39
54	Lithuania	4.35
55	Slovenia	4.33
56	Namibia	4.32
57	Italy	4.30
58	Trinidad and Tobago	4.26
59	Sri Lanka	4.24
60	Peru	4.23
61	Colombia	4.22
62	Latvia	4.20
63	Philippines	4.19
64	Jordan	4.15
65	Kenya	4.13
66	Costa Rica	4.13
67	Croatia	4.12
68	Poland	4.11
69	Saudi Arabia	4.11
70	Pakistan	4.04
71	Botswana	4.01
72	Kazakhstan	3.93
73	Guatemala	3.91
74	Argentina	3.86
75	Venezuela	3.75
76	Zimbabwe	3.74
77	Morocco	3.74
78	Honduras	3.72
79	Azerbaijan	3.70
80	Nigeria	3.67
81	Indonesia	3.59
82	Uruguay	3.54
83	Dominican Republic	3.53
84	Egypt	3.44
85	Ecuador	3.36
86	Russian Federation	3.33
87	Romania	3.29
88	Ukraine	3.25
89	China	3.25
90	Gambia, The	3.19
91	Macedonia, FYR	3.14
92	Georgia	3.08
93	Nicaragua	3.07
94	Senegal	3.04
95	Vietnam	3.01
96	Zambia	3.01
97	Bulgaria	2.98
98	Tanzania	2.95
99	Burkina Faso	2.92
100	Benin	2.88
101	Suriname	2.87
102	Bosnia and Herzegovina	2.83
103	Bolivia	2.80
104	Mongolia	2.75
105	Moldova	2.70
106	Cambodia	2.70
107	Uganda	2.70
108	Bangladesh	2.70
109	Armenia	2.67
110	Mauritania	2.62
111	Nepal	2.56
112	Paraguay	2.56
113	Mali	2.54
114	Kyrgyz Republic	2.50
115	Madagascar	2.46
116	Mozambique	2.46
117	Tajikistan	2.38
118	Guyana	2.31
119	Albania	2.26
120	Ethiopia	2.22
121	Lesotho	2.17
122	Syria	2.17
123	Algeria	2.11
124	Burundi	2.07
125	Cameroon	1.84
126	Chad	1.83
127	Libya	1.80

MEAN: 4.16

SOURCE: World Economic Forum, Executive Opinion Survey 2006, 2007

1.03 Availability of latest technologies

In your country, the latest technologies are: (1 = not widely available and used, 7 = widely available and used)

RANK	COUNTRY/ECONOMY	SCORE
1	Sweden	6.55
2	Finland	6.54
3	Iceland	6.43
4	Israel	6.35
5	Denmark	6.35
6	United States	6.32
7	Switzerland	6.26
8	Germany	6.26
9	Norway	6.23
10	Japan	6.23
11	United Kingdom	6.08
12	Singapore	6.06
13	Canada	6.02
14	Netherlands	5.87
15	France	5.83
16	United Arab Emirates	5.82
17	Austria	5.78
18	Belgium	5.70
19	Australia	5.70
20	Korea, Rep.	5.67
21	Taiwan, China	5.61
22	Malaysia	5.61
23	Hong Kong SAR	5.59
24	Puerto Rico	5.44
25	Estonia	5.42
26	Bahrain	5.26
27	Malta	5.26
28	Qatar	5.23
29	New Zealand	5.21
30	Senegal	5.16
31	India	5.16
32	Tunisia	5.15
33	Ireland	5.13
34	Chile	5.11
35	Portugal	5.10
36	Barbados	5.09
37	Jordan	5.05
38	Spain	5.03
39	Luxembourg	4.97
40	South Africa	4.94
41	Thailand	4.93
42	Jamaica	4.92
43	Kuwait	4.88
44	Czech Republic	4.86
45	Saudi Arabia	4.83
46	Oman	4.76
47	Turkey	4.73
48	Panama	4.72
49	Cyprus	4.70
50	Slovenia	4.67
51	Indonesia	4.66
52	Slovak Republic	4.63
53	Mauritius	4.54
54	Italy	4.51
55	Hungary	4.47
56	Lithuania	4.33
57	Philippines	4.32
58	Latvia	4.31
59	Brazil	4.31
60	Syria	4.30
61	Guatemala	4.30
62	Dominican Republic	4.28
63	Morocco	4.27
64	Egypt	4.26
65	Uruguay	4.24
66	Greece	4.22
67	Sri Lanka	4.21
68	Botswana	4.16
69	Trinidad and Tobago	4.16
70	Azerbaijan	4.11
71	Costa Rica	4.09
72	Mexico	4.05
73	Namibia	4.04
74	El Salvador	4.03
75	Croatia	4.03
76	Venezuela	4.00
77	Pakistan	3.93
78	China	3.93
79	Poland	3.92
80	Gambia, The	3.84
81	Peru	3.82
82	Vietnam	3.81
83	Libya	3.76
84	Tanzania	3.75
85	Argentina	3.75
86	Colombia	3.72
87	Kenya	3.70
88	Kazakhstan	3.64
89	Madagascar	3.62
90	Bulgaria	3.62
91	Romania	3.60
92	Mali	3.55
93	Mauritania	3.50
94	Honduras	3.47
95	Ukraine	3.45
96	Russian Federation	3.39
97	Georgia	3.38
98	Nigeria	3.33
99	Albania	3.30
100	Uganda	3.29
101	Cambodia	3.22
102	Mongolia	3.22
103	Benin	3.21
104	Mozambique	3.21
105	Cameroon	3.20
106	Algeria	3.18
107	Burkina Faso	3.17
108	Zambia	3.16
109	Bangladesh	3.15
110	Armenia	3.10
111	Macedonia, FYR	3.10
112	Ecuador	3.08
113	Zimbabwe	3.06
114	Nepal	3.06
115	Nicaragua	3.05
116	Guyana	3.00
117	Lesotho	2.91
118	Bosnia and Herzegovina	2.88
119	Tajikistan	2.84
120	Suriname	2.82
121	Bolivia	2.80
122	Paraguay	2.72
123	Ethiopia	2.67
124	Kyrgyz Republic	2.62
125	Moldova	2.59
126	Chad	2.28
127	Burundi	2.27

MEAN: 4.35

SOURCE: World Economic Forum, Executive Opinion Survey 2006, 2007

1.04 State of cluster development

Strong and deep clusters are widespread throughout the economy (1 = strongly disagree, 7 = strongly agree)

RANK	COUNTRY/ECONOMY	SCORE
1	Taiwan, China	5.66
2	United States	5.28
3	Korea, Rep.	5.06
4	Singapore	5.06
5	Malaysia	4.98
6	Hungary	4.90
7	Romania	4.87
8	Indonesia	4.85
9	United Kingdom	4.84
10	Germany	4.84
11	Finland	4.83
12	Japan	4.74
13	Switzerland	4.68
14	Hong Kong SAR	4.68
15	Austria	4.61
16	Vietnam	4.59
17	United Arab Emirates	4.59
18	Sweden	4.55
19	Denmark	4.54
20	Netherlands	4.51
21	Italy	4.48
22	Kuwait	4.47
23	Canada	4.44
24	India	4.44
25	Norway	4.34
26	Belgium	4.34
27	France	4.33
28	Israel	4.29
29	China	4.27
30	Slovenia	4.25
31	Czech Republic	4.13
32	Puerto Rico	4.11
33	Ireland	4.10
34	Luxembourg	4.09
35	Tunisia	4.05
36	Oman	4.02
37	Sri Lanka	3.98
38	Thailand	3.97
39	Spain	3.94
40	Brazil	3.92
41	Iceland	3.92
42	Qatar	3.90
43	Nigeria	3.89
44	South Africa	3.85
45	Turkey	3.81
46	Saudi Arabia	3.80
47	Cyprus	3.78
48	Australia	3.77
49	Panama	3.74
50	Zambia	3.69
51	Philippines	3.68
52	Chile	3.67
53	Mexico	3.65
54	New Zealand	3.63
55	Morocco	3.63
56	Jordan	3.62
57	Lithuania	3.61
58	Honduras	3.59
59	Cambodia	3.58
60	Egypt	3.58
61	Kenya	3.58
62	Argentina	3.56
63	Slovak Republic	3.55
64	Croatia	3.54
65	Pakistan	3.53
66	Azerbaijan	3.51
67	Albania	3.50
68	Costa Rica	3.48
69	Mauritius	3.47
70	Guatemala	3.47
71	Estonia	3.46
72	Portugal	3.44
73	Bangladesh	3.44
74	Bahrain	3.44
75	Uganda	3.43
76	Gambia, The	3.42
77	Peru	3.42
78	Colombia	3.40
79	Trinidad and Tobago	3.36
80	Tanzania	3.32
81	Botswana	3.30
82	Russian Federation	3.28
83	Latvia	3.26
84	Mauritania	3.25
85	Poland	3.24
86	Ukraine	3.24
87	Ecuador	3.22
88	Greece	3.21
89	Syria	3.21
90	Nepal	3.20
91	Kazakhstan	3.17
92	El Salvador	3.17
93	Nicaragua	3.16
94	Jamaica	3.13
95	Dominican Republic	3.10
96	Barbados	3.10
97	Lesotho	3.10
98	Senegal	3.09
99	Ethiopia	3.08
100	Madagascar	3.08
101	Malta	3.07
102	Venezuela	3.04
103	Bolivia	3.00
104	Uruguay	2.98
105	Guyana	2.95
106	Bulgaria	2.88
107	Namibia	2.86
108	Algeria	2.82
109	Mongolia	2.82
110	Paraguay	2.78
111	Kyrgyz Republic	2.74
112	Suriname	2.68
113	Macedonia, FYR	2.67
114	Armenia	2.66
115	Libya	2.65
116	Georgia	2.60
117	Burkina Faso	2.52
118	Zimbabwe	2.51
119	Cameroon	2.48
120	Mali	2.44
121	Benin	2.44
122	Tajikistan	2.41
123	Mozambique	2.32
124	Bosnia and Herzegovina	2.32
125	Chad	2.29
126	Moldova	1.93
127	Burundi	1.85

MEAN: 3.61

SOURCE: World Economic Forum, Executive Opinion Survey 2006, 2007

1.05 Utility patents (hard data)

Number of utility patents (i.e., patents for invention) granted between January 1 and December 31, 2006, per million population | 2006

RANK	COUNTRY/ECONOMY	HARD DATA
1	United States	298.42
2	Japan	287.11
3	Taiwan, China	226.86
4	Finland	179.25
5	Israel	179.12
6	Switzerland	164.52
7	Sweden	136.59
8	Korea, Rep.	123.08
9	Germany	120.98
10	Canada	109.57
11	Singapore	93.64
12	Luxembourg	89.13
13	Denmark	81.30
14	Netherlands	80.67
15	Austria	70.37
16	Iceland	66.67
17	Australia	64.95
18	Belgium	60.10
19	United Kingdom	59.95
20	France	56.52
21	Norway	53.04
22	Hong Kong SAR	43.38
23	Ireland	41.43
24	New Zealand	33.17
25	Italy	25.47
26	Slovenia	10.50
27	Spain	6.80
28	Puerto Rico	6.25
29	Cyprus	5.00
30	Hungary	4.85
31	Malaysia	4.38
32	Czech Republic	3.33
33	Croatia	3.04
34	Lithuania	2.65
35	Kuwait	2.50
35	Malta	2.50
37	Trinidad and Tobago	2.31
38	South Africa	2.29
39	Qatar	2.22
40	Greece	1.80
41	United Arab Emirates	1.70
42	Estonia	1.54
43	Portugal	1.52
44	Russian Federation	1.21
45	Costa Rica	1.14
46	Argentina	0.97
47	Latvia	0.87
48	Chile	0.85
49	Saudi Arabia	0.75
50	Poland	0.75
51	Georgia	0.68
52	Armenia	0.67
53	Brazil	0.64
54	Mexico	0.61
55	Uruguay	0.57
56	Ukraine	0.52
57	China	0.50
58	Thailand	0.48
59	Venezuela	0.48
60	India	0.43
61	Romania	0.42
62	Philippines	0.41
63	Bulgaria	0.39
64	Ecuador	0.22
65	Turkey	0.22
66	Tunisia	0.20
67	Jordan	0.17
68	Paraguay	0.16
69	Syria	0.15
70	Sri Lanka	0.14
71	El Salvador	0.14
72	Honduras	0.14
73	Azerbaijan	0.12
74	Dominican Republic	0.11
75	Colombia	0.11
76	Peru	0.11
77	Morocco	0.09
78	Kenya	0.09
79	Guatemala	0.08
80	Zimbabwe	0.08
81	Kazakhstan	0.07
82	Egypt	0.05
83	Algeria	0.03
84	Indonesia	0.01
85	Pakistan	0.01
86	Albania	0.00
86	Bahrain	0.00
86	Bangladesh	0.00
86	Barbados	0.00
86	Benin	0.00
86	Bolivia	0.00
86	Bosnia and Herzegovina	0.00
86	Botswana	0.00
86	Burkina Faso	0.00
86	Burundi	0.00
86	Cambodia	0.00
86	Cameroon	0.00
86	Chad	0.00
86	Ethiopia	0.00
86	Gambia, The	0.00
86	Guyana	0.00
86	Jamaica	0.00
86	Kyrgyz Republic	0.00
86	Lesotho	0.00
86	Libya	0.00
86	Macedonia, FYR	0.00
86	Madagascar	0.00
86	Mali	0.00
86	Mauritania	0.00
86	Mauritius	0.00
86	Moldova	0.00
86	Mongolia	0.00
86	Mozambique	0.00
86	Namibia	0.00
86	Nepal	0.00
86	Nicaragua	0.00
86	Nigeria	0.00
86	Oman	0.00
86	Panama	0.00
86	Senegal	0.00
86	Slovak Republic	0.00
86	Suriname	0.00
86	Tajikistan	0.00
86	Tanzania	0.00
86	Uganda	0.00
86	Vietnam	0.00
86	Zambia	0.00

SOURCE: US Patent and Trademark Office (November 2007); UNFPA, *State of World Population 2006*

1.06 High-tech exports (hard data)

High-technology exports as a percentage of total exports | 2005 or most recent year available

RANK	COUNTRY/ECONOMY	HARD DATA
1	Philippines	58.35
1	Taiwan, China[1]	44.60
1	Singapore	37.06
1	Malaysia	35.55
5	Malta[1]	34.14
6	Hong Kong SAR	26.95
7	Korea, Rep.	24.98
8	China[1]	24.64
9	Ireland[1]	20.75
10	Puerto Rico[2]	19.00
11	United States	18.28
12	Costa Rica	18.27
13	Japan	18.10
14	Hungary	17.59
15	Thailand	17.31
16	Cyprus[1]	16.78
17	Finland	16.78
18	Netherlands	15.37
19	United Kingdom	14.10
20	Mexico	14.00
21	Switzerland	12.96
22	France	12.55
23	Germany	12.20
24	Sweden	9.59
25	Denmark	9.38
26	Czech Republic	8.61
27	Israel	8.53
28	Estonia	8.51
29	Mauritius	7.92
30	Slovak Republic	7.77
31	Belgium	7.16
32	Canada	6.96
33	Austria	6.79
34	Indonesia	6.63
35	Brazil	5.96
36	Italy	5.32
37	Portugal	4.95
38	Morocco	3.74
39	Croatia	3.65
40	Spain	3.61
41	Slovenia	3.55
42	Georgia	3.50
43	Senegal	3.44
44	India	3.43
45	New Zealand	3.10
46	Lithuania	2.76
47	South Africa	2.62
48	Tunisia	2.55
49	Jordan	2.43
50	Australia	2.42
51	Poland	2.39
52	Romania	2.31
53	Luxembourg[1]	2.27
54	Norway	2.26
55	Latvia	2.11
56	Bulgaria	2.03
57	Guatemala	1.98
58	Ukraine	1.96
59	Greece	1.92
60	Argentina	1.75
61	Vietnam	1.62
62	Colombia	1.48
63	Russian Federation	1.38
64	Uganda	1.34
65	Pakistan	1.11
66	Bolivia	0.89
67	Turkey	0.88
68	El Salvador	0.81
69	Sri Lanka	0.76
70	Burkina Faso[1]	0.73
71	Moldova	0.72
72	Iceland[1]	0.67
73	Namibia	0.65
74	Macedonia, FYR	0.64
75	Ecuador	0.56
76	Trinidad and Tobago	0.47
77	Uruguay	0.43
78	Mozambique	0.43
79	Kyrgyz Republic	0.42
80	Chile	0.41
81	Armenia	0.37
82	Paraguay	0.36
83	Kenya	0.35
84	Peru	0.33
85	Zimbabwe[1]	0.29
86	Albania	0.27
87	Kazakhstan	0.24
88	Bahrain[1]	0.23
89	Madagascar	0.22
90	Nicaragua	0.21
91	Venezuela	0.21
92	Honduras	0.18
93	Oman	0.13
94	Saudi Arabia	0.12
95	Zambia[1]	0.12
96	Cambodia	0.10
97	Qatar[1]	0.10
98	Nepal	0.08
99	Cameroon	0.07
100	Syria	0.06
101	Azerbaijan	0.06
102	Guyana[1]	0.06
103	Egypt	0.05
104	Tanzania	0.03
105	Bangladesh	0.03
106	Algeria[1]	0.02
107	Nigeria	0.02
108	Panama	0.01
109	Benin	0.00
109	Burundi	0.00
109	Ethiopia	0.00
109	Gambia, The	0.00
109	Mongolia	0.00
n/a	Barbados	n/a
n/a	Bosnia and Herzegovina	n/a
n/a	Botswana	n/a
n/a	Chad	n/a
n/a	Dominican Republic	n/a
n/a	Jamaica	n/a
n/a	Kuwait	n/a
n/a	Lesotho	n/a
n/a	Libya	n/a
n/a	Mali	n/a
n/a	Mauritania	n/a
n/a	Suriname	n/a
n/a	Tajikistan	n/a
n/a	United Arab Emirates	n/a

SOURCE: The World Bank, *World Development Indicators 2007*; national sources
[1] 2004   [2] 2006

1.07 Burden of government regulation

Complying with administrative requirements (permits, regulations, reporting) issued by the government in your country is (1 = burdensome, 7 = not burdensome)

RANK	COUNTRY/ECONOMY	SCORE
1	Singapore	5.30
2	Iceland	4.91
3	Hong Kong SAR	4.78
4	Finland	4.62
5	Malaysia	4.62
6	United Arab Emirates	4.60
7	Tunisia	4.44
8	Korea, Rep.	4.35
9	Oman	4.33
10	Estonia	4.31
11	Switzerland	4.28
12	Qatar	4.19
13	Gambia, The	4.14
14	Georgia	4.11
15	Mauritania	4.10
16	Japan	4.09
17	Taiwan, China	4.06
18	Bahrain	3.99
19	Zambia	3.98
20	Saudi Arabia	3.94
21	Luxembourg	3.90
22	Indonesia	3.88
23	Denmark	3.88
24	Chile	3.83
25	Jordan	3.81
26	Thailand	3.79
27	Cyprus	3.72
28	Austria	3.68
29	Norway	3.65
30	Barbados	3.64
31	Israel	3.61
32	Tanzania	3.59
33	Mali	3.59
34	Ireland	3.58
35	China	3.57
36	Ethiopia	3.56
37	Honduras	3.56
38	Uganda	3.55
39	Azerbaijan	3.53
40	United States	3.51
41	Guatemala	3.51
42	Burkina Faso	3.48
43	Lithuania	3.48
44	Romania	3.47
45	Canada	3.47
46	Morocco	3.46
47	El Salvador	3.37
48	Nigeria	3.33
49	Sri Lanka	3.32
50	New Zealand	3.26
51	Panama	3.25
52	Slovenia	3.24
53	Sweden	3.23
54	Netherlands	3.22
55	Latvia	3.20
56	Egypt	3.17
57	United Kingdom	3.16
58	Kazakhstan	3.16
59	Spain	3.14
60	Nicaragua	3.14
61	Portugal	3.13
62	Uruguay	3.12
63	Cambodia	3.09
64	Mauritius	3.08
65	Botswana	3.08
66	Germany	3.05
67	Australia	3.01
68	Burundi	3.00
69	Pakistan	2.99
70	Paraguay	2.99
71	Kenya	2.99
72	Namibia	2.98
73	Albania	2.98
74	Macedonia, FYR	2.98
75	Dominican Republic	2.97
76	Armenia	2.96
77	Syria	2.96
78	India	2.94
79	Turkey	2.94
80	Trinidad and Tobago	2.93
81	Slovak Republic	2.93
82	Bulgaria	2.93
83	Guyana	2.89
84	Mozambique	2.87
85	Algeria	2.87
86	Kuwait	2.87
87	Suriname	2.86
88	Nepal	2.86
89	Croatia	2.81
90	Mongolia	2.80
91	Costa Rica	2.80
92	Madagascar	2.78
93	Belgium	2.78
94	Poland	2.77
95	Malta	2.72
96	Benin	2.72
97	Libya	2.70
98	South Africa	2.68
99	Ecuador	2.68
100	Jamaica	2.68
101	Ukraine	2.67
102	Bangladesh	2.67
103	Moldova	2.65
104	Senegal	2.64
105	Vietnam	2.62
106	Greece	2.60
107	Hungary	2.59
108	Colombia	2.59
109	Mexico	2.59
110	Bolivia	2.57
111	France	2.57
112	Tajikistan	2.57
113	Argentina	2.54
114	Philippines	2.52
115	Russian Federation	2.47
116	Chad	2.45
117	Kyrgyz Republic	2.42
118	Lesotho	2.42
119	Czech Republic	2.36
120	Zimbabwe	2.27
121	Peru	2.25
122	Bosnia and Herzegovina	2.21
123	Cameroon	2.13
124	Italy	2.12
125	Brazil	1.85
126	Puerto Rico	1.83
127	Venezuela	1.56

MEAN: 3.21

SOURCE: World Economic Forum, Executive Opinion Survey 2006, 2007

1.08 Extent and effect of taxation

The level of taxes in your country (1 = significantly limits the incentives to work or invest, 7 = has little impact on the incentives to work or invest)

RANK	COUNTRY/ECONOMY	SCORE
1	Bahrain	6.31
2	United Arab Emirates	6.19
3	Qatar	5.89
4	Hong Kong SAR	5.85
5	Kuwait	5.82
6	Singapore	5.66
7	Saudi Arabia	5.46
8	Indonesia	5.42
9	Iceland	5.36
10	Slovak Republic	5.35
11	Ireland	5.11
12	Estonia	5.11
13	Luxembourg	5.06
14	Switzerland	5.04
15	Malaysia	5.01
16	Oman	4.94
17	Botswana	4.84
18	Mauritius	4.75
19	Cyprus	4.73
20	Tunisia	4.53
21	Thailand	4.52
22	Mauritania	4.48
23	Trinidad and Tobago	4.41
24	Taiwan, China	4.38
25	El Salvador	4.35
26	South Africa	4.32
27	Nigeria	4.29
28	Paraguay	4.25
29	India	4.25
30	Korea, Rep.	4.24
31	Georgia	4.21
32	Pakistan	4.16
33	Egypt	4.10
34	Cambodia	4.06
35	Chile	4.01
36	Austria	3.92
37	Bangladesh	3.91
38	Gambia, The	3.85
39	Barbados	3.82
40	Syria	3.80
41	Algeria	3.80
42	Guatemala	3.79
43	United Kingdom	3.78
44	Libya	3.77
45	China	3.73
46	United States	3.72
47	Costa Rica	3.72
48	Ethiopia	3.72
49	Netherlands	3.71
50	Nepal	3.68
51	Latvia	3.63
52	Sri Lanka	3.63
53	Honduras	3.62
54	Azerbaijan	3.61
55	Philippines	3.59
56	Mali	3.57
57	Namibia	3.55
58	Vietnam	3.55
59	Morocco	3.50
60	Tanzania	3.50
61	Bolivia	3.46
62	Norway	3.45
63	Malta	3.43
64	Japan	3.41
65	New Zealand	3.36
66	Israel	3.32
67	Macedonia, FYR	3.32
68	Lithuania	3.32
69	Spain	3.31
70	Armenia	3.29
71	Jordan	3.28
72	Greece	3.27
73	Australia	3.27
74	Ecuador	3.27
75	Madagascar	3.26
76	Burkina Faso	3.24
77	Canada	3.20
78	Mexico	3.19
79	Kazakhstan	3.13
80	Albania	3.12
81	Portugal	3.12
82	Germany	3.11
83	Croatia	3.05
84	Panama	3.03
85	Czech Republic	3.02
86	Venezuela	3.02
87	Bulgaria	2.99
88	Mozambique	2.99
89	Peru	2.99
90	Senegal	2.91
91	Puerto Rico	2.90
92	France	2.89
93	Tajikistan	2.89
94	Russian Federation	2.87
95	Lesotho	2.87
96	Mongolia	2.84
97	Nicaragua	2.83
98	Poland	2.83
99	Jamaica	2.83
100	Turkey	2.76
101	Slovenia	2.74
102	Burundi	2.70
103	Moldova	2.70
104	Uruguay	2.69
105	Romania	2.61
106	Colombia	2.60
107	Denmark	2.60
108	Uganda	2.56
109	Chad	2.55
110	Kenya	2.55
111	Suriname	2.55
112	Finland	2.55
113	Kyrgyz Republic	2.52
114	Hungary	2.51
115	Zambia	2.49
116	Dominican Republic	2.47
117	Benin	2.47
118	Guyana	2.44
119	Ukraine	2.43
120	Cameroon	2.39
121	Zimbabwe	2.39
122	Sweden	2.39
123	Italy	2.28
124	Bosnia and Herzegovina	2.26
125	Argentina	2.25
126	Belgium	2.08
127	Brazil	1.52

MEAN: 3.57

SOURCE: World Economic Forum, Executive Opinion Survey 2006, 2007

1.09 Total tax rate (hard data)

This variable is a combination of profit tax (% of profits), labor tax and contribution (% of profits), and other taxes (% of profits) | 2007

RANK	COUNTRY/ECONOMY	HARD DATA
1	Kuwait	14.40
1	United Arab Emirates	14.40
3	Saudi Arabia	14.50
4	Zambia	16.10
5	Botswana	17.20
6	Lesotho	20.80
7	Oman	21.60
8	Mauritius	21.70
9	Cambodia	22.60
10	Singapore	23.20
11	Hong Kong SAR	24.40
12	Chile	25.90
13	Namibia	26.50
14	Iceland	27.20
15	Suriname	27.90
16	Ireland	28.90
17	Switzerland	29.10
18	Nigeria	29.90
19	Ethiopia	31.10
19	Jordan	31.10
21	Uganda	32.30
22	Croatia	32.50
22	Nepal	32.50
24	Latvia	32.60
25	Trinidad and Tobago	33.10
26	Denmark	33.30
27	El Salvador	33.80
28	Mozambique	34.30
29	Korea, Rep.	34.90
30	New Zealand	35.10
31	Ecuador	35.30
31	Luxembourg	35.30
31	Paraguay	35.30
34	United Kingdom	35.70
35	Israel	36.00
35	Malaysia	36.00
37	Armenia	36.60
38	Bulgaria	36.70
38	Kazakhstan	36.70
40	South Africa	37.10
41	Indonesia	37.30
42	Guatemala	37.50
43	Thailand	37.70
44	Mongolia	38.40
44	Poland	38.40
46	Georgia	38.60
47	Guyana	39.00
48	Slovenia	39.20
49	Bangladesh	39.50
50	Dominican Republic	40.20
51	Taiwan, China	40.60
52	Pakistan	40.70
52	Uruguay	40.70
54	Azerbaijan	40.90
55	Vietnam	41.10
56	Peru	41.50
57	Norway	42.00
58	Netherlands	43.40
59	Moldova	44.00
60	Bosnia and Herzegovina	44.10
61	Puerto Rico	44.30
61	Tanzania	44.30
63	Portugal	44.80
64	Turkey	45.10
65	Canada	45.90
66	Senegal	46.00
67	United States	46.20
68	Madagascar	46.50
69	Syria	46.70
70	Albania	46.80
71	Romania	46.90
72	Finland	47.80
73	Egypt	47.90
74	Lithuania	48.30
75	Czech Republic	48.60
75	Greece	48.60
77	Burkina Faso	48.90
78	Estonia	49.20
79	Macedonia, FYR	49.80
80	Slovak Republic	50.50
81	Australia	50.60
82	Germany	50.80
82	Panama	50.80
84	Kenya	50.90
85	Mexico	51.20
86	Jamaica	51.30
87	Honduras	51.40
87	Mali	51.40
87	Russian Federation	51.40
90	Cameroon	51.90
91	Japan	52.00
92	Philippines	52.80
93	Zimbabwe	53.00
94	Morocco	53.10
95	Venezuela	53.30
96	Sweden	54.50
97	Austria	54.60
98	Hungary	55.10
99	Costa Rica	55.70
100	Ukraine	57.30
101	Tunisia	61.00
102	Kyrgyz Republic	61.40
103	Spain	62.00
104	Nicaragua	63.20
105	Chad	63.70
105	Sri Lanka	63.70
107	Belgium	64.30
108	France	66.30
109	Brazil	69.20
110	India	70.60
111	Algeria	72.60
112	Benin	73.30
113	China	73.90
114	Italy	76.20
115	Bolivia	78.10
116	Tajikistan	82.20
117	Colombia	82.40
118	Mauritania	107.50
119	Argentina	112.90
120	Burundi	278.70
121	Gambia, The	286.70
n/a	Bahrain	n/a
n/a	Barbados	n/a
n/a	Cyprus	n/a
n/a	Libya	n/a
n/a	Malta	n/a
n/a	Qatar	n/a

SOURCE: The World Bank, *Doing Business 2008*

1.10 Time required to start a business (hard data)

Number of days required to start a business | 2007

RANK	COUNTRY/ECONOMY	HARD DATA
1	Australia	2.00
2	Canada	3.00
3	Belgium	4.00
4	Iceland	5.00
4	Singapore	5.00
6	Denmark	6.00
6	Turkey	6.00
6	United States	6.00
9	Estonia	7.00
9	France	7.00
9	Madagascar	7.00
9	Mauritius	7.00
9	Portugal	7.00
9	Puerto Rico	7.00
15	Jamaica	8.00
16	Egypt	9.00
17	Netherlands	10.00
17	Norway	10.00
19	Georgia	11.00
19	Hong Kong SAR	11.00
19	Tunisia	11.00
22	Morocco	12.00
22	New Zealand	12.00
24	Ireland	13.00
24	Italy	13.00
24	United Kingdom	13.00
27	Finland	14.00
27	Jordan	14.00
27	Romania	14.00
30	Macedonia, FYR	15.00
30	Saudi Arabia	15.00
30	Sweden	15.00
33	Ethiopia	16.00
33	Hungary	16.00
33	Latvia	16.00
36	Czech Republic	17.00
36	Korea, Rep.	17.00
38	Armenia	18.00
38	Burkina Faso	18.00
38	Germany	18.00
41	Panama	19.00
42	Mongolia	20.00
42	Switzerland	20.00
44	Honduras	21.00
44	Kazakhstan	21.00
44	Kyrgyz Republic	21.00
47	Dominican Republic	22.00
48	Japan	23.00
48	Moldova	23.00
50	Algeria	24.00
50	Malaysia	24.00
50	Pakistan	24.00
53	Slovak Republic	25.00
54	El Salvador	26.00
54	Guatemala	26.00
54	Lithuania	26.00
54	Luxembourg	26.00
54	Mali	26.00
59	Chile	27.00
59	Mexico	27.00
59	Ukraine	27.00
62	Austria	28.00
62	Uganda	28.00
64	Mozambique	29.00
64	Russian Federation	29.00
64	Tanzania	29.00
67	Azerbaijan	30.00
68	Argentina	31.00
68	Benin	31.00
68	Nepal	31.00
68	Poland	31.00
68	South Africa	31.00
73	Bulgaria	32.00
73	Gambia, The	32.00
75	India	33.00
75	Thailand	33.00
75	Zambia	33.00
78	Israel	34.00
78	Nigeria	34.00
78	Oman	34.00
81	China	35.00
81	Kuwait	35.00
81	Paraguay	35.00
84	Albania	36.00
85	Cameroon	37.00
86	Greece	38.00
87	Nicaragua	39.00
87	Sri Lanka	39.00
89	Croatia	40.00
90	Colombia	42.00
91	Burundi	43.00
91	Syria	43.00
91	Trinidad and Tobago	43.00
94	Guyana	44.00
94	Kenya	44.00
94	Uruguay	44.00
97	Spain	47.00
98	Taiwan, China	48.00
99	Tajikistan	49.00
100	Bolivia	50.00
100	Vietnam	50.00
102	Bosnia and Herzegovina	54.00
103	Philippines	58.00
103	Senegal	58.00
105	Slovenia	60.00
106	United Arab Emirates	62.00
107	Ecuador	65.00
107	Mauritania	65.00
109	Peru	72.00
110	Lesotho	73.00
111	Bangladesh	74.00
112	Chad	75.00
113	Costa Rica	77.00
114	Cambodia	86.00
115	Zimbabwe	96.00
116	Namibia	99.00
117	Indonesia	105.00
118	Botswana	108.00
119	Venezuela	141.00
120	Brazil	152.00
121	Suriname	694.00
n/a	Bahrain	n/a
n/a	Barbados	n/a
n/a	Cyprus	n/a
n/a	Libya	n/a
n/a	Malta	n/a
n/a	Qatar	n/a

SOURCE: The World Bank, *Doing Business 2008*

1.11 Number of procedures required to start a business (hard data)

Number of procedures required to start a business | 2007

RANK	COUNTRY/ECONOMY	HARD DATA
1	Australia	2.00
1	Canada	2.00
1	New Zealand	2.00
4	Belgium	3.00
4	Finland	3.00
4	Sweden	3.00
7	Denmark	4.00
7	Ireland	4.00
9	Estonia	5.00
9	France	5.00
9	Georgia	5.00
9	Hong Kong SAR	5.00
9	Iceland	5.00
9	Israel	5.00
9	Latvia	5.00
9	Madagascar	5.00
9	Singapore	5.00
9	Sri Lanka	5.00
19	Burkina Faso	6.00
19	Hungary	6.00
19	Jamaica	6.00
19	Luxembourg	6.00
19	Mauritius	6.00
19	Morocco	6.00
19	Netherlands	6.00
19	Nicaragua	6.00
19	Norway	6.00
19	Romania	6.00
19	Switzerland	6.00
19	Turkey	6.00
19	United Kingdom	6.00
19	United States	6.00
19	Zambia	6.00
34	Benin	7.00
34	Egypt	7.00
34	Ethiopia	7.00
34	Lithuania	7.00
34	Nepal	7.00
34	Panama	7.00
34	Paraguay	7.00
34	Portugal	7.00
34	Puerto Rico	7.00
34	Saudi Arabia	7.00
44	Austria	8.00
44	Bangladesh	8.00
44	Croatia	8.00
44	Guyana	8.00
44	Japan	8.00
44	Kazakhstan	8.00
44	Kyrgyz Republic	8.00
44	Lesotho	8.00
44	Mexico	8.00
44	Mongolia	8.00
44	Russian Federation	8.00
44	South Africa	8.00
44	Taiwan, China	8.00
44	Thailand	8.00
58	Armenia	9.00
58	Bulgaria	9.00
58	Chile	9.00
58	Dominican Republic	9.00
58	El Salvador	9.00
58	Gambia, The	9.00
58	Germany	9.00
58	Italy	9.00
58	Macedonia, FYR	9.00
58	Malaysia	9.00
58	Moldova	9.00
58	Nigeria	9.00
58	Oman	9.00
58	Slovak Republic	9.00
58	Slovenia	9.00
58	Trinidad and Tobago	9.00
74	Albania	10.00
74	Cambodia	10.00
74	Czech Republic	10.00
74	Jordan	10.00
74	Korea, Rep.	10.00
74	Mozambique	10.00
74	Namibia	10.00
74	Peru	10.00
74	Poland	10.00
74	Senegal	10.00
74	Spain	10.00
74	Tunisia	10.00
74	Ukraine	10.00
74	Zimbabwe	10.00
88	Botswana	11.00
88	Burundi	11.00
88	Colombia	11.00
88	Guatemala	11.00
88	Mali	11.00
88	Mauritania	11.00
88	Pakistan	11.00
88	United Arab Emirates	11.00
88	Uruguay	11.00
88	Vietnam	11.00
98	Bosnia and Herzegovina	12.00
98	Costa Rica	12.00
98	Indonesia	12.00
98	Kenya	12.00
98	Tanzania	12.00
103	Azerbaijan	13.00
103	Cameroon	13.00
103	China	13.00
103	Honduras	13.00
103	India	13.00
103	Kuwait	13.00
103	Suriname	13.00
103	Syria	13.00
103	Tajikistan	13.00
112	Algeria	14.00
112	Argentina	14.00
112	Ecuador	14.00
115	Bolivia	15.00
115	Greece	15.00
115	Philippines	15.00
118	Venezuela	16.00
119	Brazil	18.00
119	Uganda	18.00
121	Chad	19.00
n/a	Bahrain	n/a
n/a	Barbados	n/a
n/a	Cyprus	n/a
n/a	Libya	n/a
n/a	Malta	n/a
n/a	Qatar	n/a

SOURCE: The World Bank, *Doing Business 2008*

1.12 Intensity of local competition

Competition in the local market is (1 = limited in most industries and price-cutting is rare, 7 = intense in most industries as market leadership changes over time)

RANK	COUNTRY/ECONOMY	SCORE
1	Germany	6.32
2	Austria	6.06
3	Japan	6.03
4	Hong Kong SAR	6.02
5	Sweden	6.02
6	United Kingdom	5.98
7	Belgium	5.97
8	United States	5.90
9	Netherlands	5.88
10	India	5.88
11	Puerto Rico	5.86
12	France	5.80
13	Taiwan, China	5.80
14	Chile	5.74
15	Australia	5.73
16	Finland	5.73
17	Czech Republic	5.73
18	Canada	5.67
19	Malaysia	5.66
20	Malta	5.66
21	Israel	5.64
22	Norway	5.60
23	Korea, Rep.	5.58
24	Estonia	5.57
25	Spain	5.57
26	Denmark	5.57
27	Switzerland	5.53
28	Indonesia	5.51
29	Singapore	5.48
30	Ireland	5.47
31	Turkey	5.45
32	Hungary	5.42
33	Jordan	5.41
34	New Zealand	5.40
35	United Arab Emirates	5.40
36	Cyprus	5.37
37	Lithuania	5.36
38	Slovak Republic	5.35
39	China	5.34
40	Iceland	5.32
41	Tunisia	5.32
42	Thailand	5.30
43	Slovenia	5.29
44	Portugal	5.28
45	Brazil	5.25
46	Jamaica	5.14
47	Senegal	5.13
48	Luxembourg	5.11
49	Syria	5.10
50	Costa Rica	5.10
51	Saudi Arabia	5.09
52	South Africa	5.09
53	Peru	5.09
54	Sri Lanka	5.09
55	Kenya	5.07
56	Bahrain	5.06
57	Philippines	5.02
58	Guatemala	5.01
59	Qatar	5.00
60	Kuwait	4.99
61	Vietnam	4.98
62	Latvia	4.98
63	Croatia	4.97
64	Colombia	4.94
65	Greece	4.93
66	Mexico	4.90
67	El Salvador	4.89
68	Panama	4.83
69	Bangladesh	4.74
70	Poland	4.72
71	Uganda	4.72
72	Trinidad and Tobago	4.72
73	Egypt	4.71
74	Kazakhstan	4.67
75	Botswana	4.66
76	Mauritius	4.66
77	Namibia	4.65
78	Italy	4.62
79	Burkina Faso	4.61
80	Nepal	4.59
81	Romania	4.58
82	Mongolia	4.58
83	Morocco	4.58
84	Moldova	4.57
85	Suriname	4.50
86	Bulgaria	4.50
87	Gambia, The	4.49
88	Nigeria	4.49
89	Tanzania	4.49
90	Barbados	4.47
91	Russian Federation	4.45
92	Ukraine	4.45
93	Mali	4.37
94	Algeria	4.36
95	Oman	4.36
96	Dominican Republic	4.36
97	Cameroon	4.35
98	Macedonia, FYR	4.34
99	Benin	4.33
100	Bosnia and Herzegovina	4.32
101	Ecuador	4.25
102	Guyana	4.24
103	Pakistan	4.22
104	Honduras	4.18
105	Uruguay	4.18
106	Cambodia	4.18
107	Argentina	4.16
108	Madagascar	4.14
109	Paraguay	4.12
110	Bolivia	4.09
111	Tajikistan	4.01
112	Nicaragua	4.01
113	Georgia	3.99
114	Libya	3.90
115	Ethiopia	3.90
116	Azerbaijan	3.84
117	Lesotho	3.82
118	Burundi	3.70
119	Venezuela	3.69
120	Mauritania	3.69
121	Albania	3.67
122	Armenia	3.63
123	Mozambique	3.61
124	Kyrgyz Republic	3.57
125	Zambia	3.43
126	Zimbabwe	3.42
127	Chad	3.22

MEAN: 4.87

SOURCE: World Economic Forum, Executive Opinion Survey 2006, 2007

1.13 Freedom of the press

How free is the press in your country? (1 = totally restricted, 7 = completely free)

RANK	COUNTRY/ECONOMY	SCORE
1	Germany	6.83
2	Denmark	6.81
3	Netherlands	6.81
4	Sweden	6.76
5	Norway	6.71
6	Finland	6.66
7	Switzerland	6.63
8	Austria	6.56
9	New Zealand	6.46
10	Belgium	6.44
11	Canada	6.44
12	Israel	6.44
13	Iceland	6.36
14	Portugal	6.35
15	France	6.33
16	Puerto Rico	6.29
17	Estonia	6.29
18	Australia	6.29
19	Peru	6.28
20	India	6.23
21	United Kingdom	6.22
22	Greece	6.18
23	Ireland	6.10
24	Costa Rica	6.04
25	Slovak Republic	6.04
26	South Africa	6.04
27	United States	6.01
28	Luxembourg	6.00
29	Nicaragua	5.99
30	Chile	5.98
31	Guatemala	5.98
32	Hong Kong SAR	5.97
33	Japan	5.89
34	Honduras	5.85
35	Lithuania	5.82
36	Brazil	5.81
37	Czech Republic	5.81
38	Cyprus	5.81
39	Malta	5.79
40	El Salvador	5.75
41	Spain	5.72
42	Mauritius	5.69
43	Taiwan, China	5.68
44	Mexico	5.66
45	Mali	5.60
46	Colombia	5.59
47	Hungary	5.58
48	Barbados	5.55
49	Uruguay	5.55
50	Jamaica	5.52
51	Korea, Rep.	5.51
52	Benin	5.49
53	Indonesia	5.46
54	Suriname	5.45
55	Paraguay	5.43
56	Latvia	5.42
57	Panama	5.38
58	Namibia	5.36
59	Trinidad and Tobago	5.36
60	Bangladesh	5.34
61	Philippines	5.28
62	Botswana	5.26
63	Ecuador	5.25
64	Romania	5.19
65	Dominican Republic	5.19
66	Italy	5.13
67	Nepal	5.05
68	Senegal	5.04
69	Bolivia	5.01
70	Turkey	5.00
71	Croatia	4.94
72	Mauritania	4.94
73	Thailand	4.89
74	Pakistan	4.84
75	Poland	4.84
76	Bosnia and Herzegovina	4.81
77	Ukraine	4.77
78	Tanzania	4.76
79	Kuwait	4.74
80	Albania	4.74
81	Macedonia, FYR	4.73
82	Mozambique	4.70
83	Qatar	4.67
84	Cameroon	4.65
85	Slovenia	4.65
86	Georgia	4.62
87	Algeria	4.56
88	Nigeria	4.55
89	Mongolia	4.55
90	Burkina Faso	4.53
91	Sri Lanka	4.50
92	Egypt	4.49
93	Azerbaijan	4.37
94	Guyana	4.33
95	Kyrgyz Republic	4.31
96	Bulgaria	4.30
97	Uganda	4.28
98	Tunisia	4.28
99	Vietnam	4.28
100	Malaysia	4.24
101	Bahrain	4.24
102	Russian Federation	4.23
103	Madagascar	4.21
104	United Arab Emirates	4.16
105	Burundi	4.07
106	Morocco	4.07
107	Kenya	4.06
108	Lesotho	4.04
109	Saudi Arabia	3.85
110	Cambodia	3.85
111	Zambia	3.77
112	Kazakhstan	3.74
113	Syria	3.71
114	Argentina	3.64
115	Singapore	3.62
116	Jordan	3.61
117	Armenia	3.56
118	Moldova	3.55
119	China	3.39
120	Tajikistan	3.38
121	Gambia, The	3.37
122	Oman	3.30
123	Chad	3.22
124	Libya	2.66
125	Venezuela	2.51
126	Ethiopia	2.41
127	Zimbabwe	1.77

MEAN: 5.08

SOURCE: World Economic Forum, Executive Opinion Survey 2006, 2007

1.14 Accessibility of digital content

In your country, is digital content (text and audiovisual content, software products) widely accessible via multiple platforms (fixed-line Internet, wireless Internet, mobile network, satellite, etc.)? (1 = no, there is no convergence across these sectors, 7 = yes, convergence is total and generating new products and services)

RANK	COUNTRY/ECONOMY	SCORE
1	Sweden	6.46
2	Switzerland	6.44
3	Korea, Rep.	6.39
4	Denmark	6.36
5	Estonia	6.29
6	Austria	6.21
7	Iceland	6.21
8	United States	6.18
9	Finland	6.17
10	Norway	6.15
11	Netherlands	6.12
12	Hong Kong SAR	6.12
13	Germany	6.11
14	United Kingdom	6.10
15	Singapore	6.07
16	Canada	6.00
17	Israel	5.95
18	Belgium	5.85
19	France	5.81
20	Japan	5.79
21	Bahrain	5.77
22	Taiwan, China	5.76
23	Australia	5.70
24	Malta	5.70
25	Puerto Rico	5.59
26	Czech Republic	5.58
27	Chile	5.55
28	Luxembourg	5.54
29	Qatar	5.52
30	Portugal	5.51
31	Spain	5.49
32	Malaysia	5.36
33	Guatemala	5.28
34	Lithuania	5.25
35	Uruguay	5.19
36	Slovenia	5.15
37	Slovak Republic	5.13
38	Ireland	5.10
39	Turkey	5.07
40	United Arab Emirates	5.07
41	Hungary	5.06
42	Jamaica	5.06
43	Barbados	5.04
44	Croatia	5.02
45	Thailand	5.02
46	Dominican Republic	4.95
47	Jordan	4.93
48	Bulgaria	4.89
49	Senegal	4.88
50	Kazakhstan	4.88
51	Tunisia	4.87
52	China	4.84
53	Kuwait	4.83
54	Romania	4.78
55	South Africa	4.78
56	New Zealand	4.76
57	El Salvador	4.75
58	Panama	4.71
59	Latvia	4.70
60	Argentina	4.68
61	Philippines	4.68
62	Venezuela	4.66
63	Russian Federation	4.66
64	Indonesia	4.65
65	India	4.65
66	Mauritius	4.64
67	Egypt	4.63
68	Cyprus	4.62
69	Italy	4.61
70	Morocco	4.60
71	Azerbaijan	4.58
72	Brazil	4.54
73	Ukraine	4.47
74	Honduras	4.45
75	Sri Lanka	4.45
76	Georgia	4.44
77	Colombia	4.43
78	Poland	4.42
79	Mexico	4.37
80	Saudi Arabia	4.35
81	Vietnam	4.33
82	Oman	4.30
83	Costa Rica	4.28
84	Tajikistan	4.25
85	Mongolia	4.24
86	Peru	4.24
87	Bosnia and Herzegovina	4.21
88	Cambodia	4.20
89	Mali	4.00
90	Kyrgyz Republic	3.98
91	Greece	3.94
92	Nicaragua	3.81
93	Gambia, The	3.78
94	Pakistan	3.77
95	Paraguay	3.76
96	Benin	3.73
97	Nigeria	3.71
98	Tanzania	3.70
99	Guyana	3.70
100	Bolivia	3.69
101	Mozambique	3.67
102	Trinidad and Tobago	3.64
103	Uganda	3.63
104	Armenia	3.63
105	Zambia	3.60
106	Moldova	3.52
107	Algeria	3.52
108	Kenya	3.52
109	Botswana	3.51
110	Ecuador	3.44
111	Burkina Faso	3.41
112	Macedonia, FYR	3.41
113	Nepal	3.37
114	Namibia	3.36
115	Mauritania	3.32
116	Cameroon	3.29
117	Libya	3.26
118	Bangladesh	3.22
119	Madagascar	3.15
120	Chad	3.02
121	Albania	2.90
122	Syria	2.84
123	Suriname	2.76
124	Zimbabwe	2.68
125	Ethiopia	2.64
126	Burundi	2.49
127	Lesotho	2.08

MEAN: 4.61

SOURCE: World Economic Forum, Executive Opinion Survey 2006, 2007

Subindex A **Environment component**

2nd pillar
Political and regulatory environment

2.01 Effectiveness of law-making bodies

How effective is your national parliament/congress as a law-making institution? (1 = very ineffective, 7 = very effective - among the best in the world)

RANK	COUNTRY/ECONOMY	SCORE
1	Singapore	6.09
2	Denmark	5.72
3	Australia	5.49
4	Malaysia	5.42
5	United Kingdom	5.29
6	Finland	5.27
7	Norway	5.15
8	Iceland	5.13
9	Sweden	5.06
10	Switzerland	5.02
11	Canada	5.00
12	New Zealand	5.00
13	Barbados	4.98
14	Germany	4.89
15	Tunisia	4.87
16	Netherlands	4.87
17	Luxembourg	4.86
18	Japan	4.76
19	South Africa	4.64
20	Oman	4.62
21	Ireland	4.55
22	Mauritius	4.53
23	Tanzania	4.51
24	India	4.51
25	Malta	4.51
26	Austria	4.50
27	Botswana	4.48
28	France	4.44
29	United States	4.44
30	Estonia	4.33
31	United Arab Emirates	4.28
32	Korea, Rep.	4.26
33	Turkey	4.26
34	Cyprus	4.19
35	Hong Kong SAR	4.16
36	Mali	4.14
37	China	4.13
38	Qatar	4.13
39	Spain	4.12
40	Israel	4.11
41	Portugal	4.10
42	Kuwait	3.98
43	Thailand	3.92
44	Kazakhstan	3.87
45	Greece	3.85
46	Benin	3.84
47	Vietnam	3.80
48	Tajikistan	3.79
49	Chile	3.77
50	Saudi Arabia	3.76
51	Burkina Faso	3.75
52	Gambia, The	3.70
53	Namibia	3.65
54	Belgium	3.63
55	Slovenia	3.61
56	Morocco	3.61
57	Libya	3.59
58	Sri Lanka	3.54
59	Croatia	3.50
60	Jamaica	3.50
61	Albania	3.44
62	Nigeria	3.43
63	Cambodia	3.43
64	Syria	3.43
65	Egypt	3.42
66	Pakistan	3.38
67	Latvia	3.38
68	Slovak Republic	3.37
69	Uganda	3.37
70	Lithuania	3.30
71	Jordan	3.30
72	Azerbaijan	3.28
73	Georgia	3.28
74	Honduras	3.25
75	Moldova	3.23
76	Mozambique	3.23
77	Indonesia	3.20
78	Hungary	3.15
79	Uruguay	3.13
80	Bahrain	3.09
81	Russian Federation	3.06
82	Czech Republic	3.04
83	Algeria	3.04
84	Madagascar	3.04
85	Kenya	3.03
86	Kyrgyz Republic	3.02
87	Colombia	3.01
88	Taiwan, China	2.98
89	Trinidad and Tobago	2.98
90	Macedonia, FYR	2.93
91	Guyana	2.92
92	Armenia	2.89
93	Italy	2.89
94	Bulgaria	2.83
95	Mauritania	2.79
96	Lesotho	2.75
97	Zambia	2.73
98	Nepal	2.72
99	Ethiopia	2.72
100	Romania	2.61
101	Bangladesh	2.57
102	Burundi	2.55
103	Philippines	2.53
104	Poland	2.51
105	Mongolia	2.50
106	Ukraine	2.48
107	Dominican Republic	2.44
108	Mexico	2.37
109	El Salvador	2.35
110	Panama	2.35
111	Cameroon	2.34
112	Puerto Rico	2.31
113	Costa Rica	2.24
114	Senegal	2.22
115	Bolivia	2.20
116	Brazil	2.18
117	Bosnia and Herzegovina	2.13
118	Zimbabwe	2.13
119	Chad	2.12
120	Guatemala	2.10
121	Peru	2.01
122	Suriname	1.99
123	Nicaragua	1.97
124	Argentina	1.91
125	Paraguay	1.81
126	Ecuador	1.60
127	Venezuela	1.56

SOURCE: World Economic Forum, Executive Opinion Survey 2006, 2007

2.02 Laws relating to ICT

Laws relating to the use of information and communication technologies (electronic commerce, digital signatures, consumer protection) are (1 = nonexistent, 7 = well developed and enforced)

RANK	COUNTRY/ECONOMY	SCORE
1	Denmark	6.01
2	Estonia	5.90
3	Singapore	5.88
4	Germany	5.76
5	Sweden	5.74
6	Austria	5.70
7	Korea, Rep.	5.69
8	Norway	5.63
9	Finland	5.58
10	Switzerland	5.57
11	United Kingdom	5.54
12	United States	5.42
13	Iceland	5.40
14	Malaysia	5.40
15	Netherlands	5.39
16	Canada	5.37
17	New Zealand	5.35
18	Hong Kong SAR	5.35
19	Australia	5.34
20	France	5.34
21	Israel	5.13
22	Malta	4.95
23	Portugal	4.94
24	Taiwan, China	4.93
25	Chile	4.92
26	Luxembourg	4.91
27	Ireland	4.91
28	Belgium	4.85
29	Japan	4.83
30	Slovenia	4.82
31	Spain	4.77
32	South Africa	4.75
33	United Arab Emirates	4.71
34	Puerto Rico	4.60
35	Tunisia	4.60
36	India	4.57
37	Qatar	4.42
38	Bahrain	4.42
39	Lithuania	4.31
40	Oman	4.30
41	Bulgaria	4.27
42	Italy	4.27
43	Mauritius	4.23
44	Czech Republic	4.21
45	Croatia	4.16
46	Barbados	4.13
47	Hungary	4.09
48	Thailand	4.08
49	Turkey	4.04
50	Slovak Republic	4.01
51	Brazil	4.00
52	Mexico	3.97
53	Panama	3.96
54	Colombia	3.95
55	Philippines	3.90
56	China	3.90
57	Saudi Arabia	3.88
58	Cyprus	3.88
59	Costa Rica	3.88
60	Azerbaijan	3.82
61	Latvia	3.82
62	Dominican Republic	3.81
63	Kazakhstan	3.80
64	Sri Lanka	3.80
65	Jordan	3.77
66	Romania	3.74
67	Poland	3.69
68	Greece	3.63
69	Pakistan	3.59
70	Jamaica	3.58
71	El Salvador	3.54
72	Peru	3.47
73	Vietnam	3.41
74	Nigeria	3.40
75	Uruguay	3.36
76	Venezuela	3.34
77	Kenya	3.34
78	Egypt	3.29
79	Indonesia	3.29
80	Ukraine	3.28
81	Gambia, The	3.24
82	Russian Federation	3.21
83	Honduras	3.21
84	Morocco	3.19
85	Macedonia, FYR	3.17
86	Senegal	3.17
87	Kuwait	3.15
88	Guatemala	3.13
89	Tanzania	3.12
90	Moldova	3.10
91	Namibia	3.09
92	Benin	3.07
93	Armenia	3.06
94	Botswana	2.99
95	Uganda	2.97
96	Argentina	2.92
97	Tajikistan	2.92
98	Zambia	2.86
99	Ecuador	2.84
100	Burkina Faso	2.81
101	Trinidad and Tobago	2.79
102	Madagascar	2.76
103	Nicaragua	2.71
104	Georgia	2.69
105	Algeria	2.67
106	Zimbabwe	2.66
107	Mali	2.62
108	Mongolia	2.62
109	Lesotho	2.60
110	Ethiopia	2.57
111	Mozambique	2.56
112	Albania	2.49
113	Bosnia and Herzegovina	2.44
114	Mauritania	2.40
115	Cambodia	2.39
116	Nepal	2.36
117	Kyrgyz Republic	2.35
118	Guyana	2.27
119	Bolivia	2.25
120	Cameroon	2.23
121	Bangladesh	2.21
122	Burundi	2.15
123	Chad	2.09
124	Syria	2.09
125	Paraguay	2.06
126	Libya	2.05
127	Suriname	1.53

MEAN: 3.81

SOURCE: World Economic Forum, Executive Opinion Survey 2006, 2007

2.03 Judicial independence

Is the judiciary in your country independent from political influences of members of government, citizens, or firms? (1 = no, heavily influenced, 7 = yes, entirely independent)

RANK	COUNTRY/ECONOMY	SCORE
1	Germany	6.53
2	New Zealand	6.49
3	Denmark	6.44
4	Finland	6.43
5	Netherlands	6.41
6	Australia	6.40
7	Switzerland	6.30
8	Sweden	6.16
9	Norway	6.09
10	Austria	6.06
11	Iceland	6.05
12	United Kingdom	6.04
13	Israel	6.03
14	Canada	6.01
15	Ireland	6.01
16	Hong Kong SAR	5.94
17	Barbados	5.83
18	Portugal	5.68
19	Singapore	5.60
20	Luxembourg	5.55
21	Japan	5.51
22	Qatar	5.50
23	South Africa	5.45
24	Belgium	5.37
25	Malta	5.31
26	India	5.30
27	Estonia	5.26
28	France	5.26
29	Botswana	5.25
30	Malaysia	5.24
31	Kuwait	5.23
32	Tunisia	5.17
33	Cyprus	5.17
34	Namibia	5.14
35	Korea, Rep.	5.13
36	Costa Rica	5.08
37	United States	5.06
38	Puerto Rico	5.00
39	United Arab Emirates	4.98
40	Jordan	4.88
41	Egypt	4.86
42	Uruguay	4.83
43	Thailand	4.72
44	Suriname	4.72
45	Mauritius	4.72
46	Oman	4.66
47	Slovenia	4.49
48	Greece	4.41
49	Hungary	4.41
50	Turkey	4.40
51	Saudi Arabia	4.39
52	Taiwan, China	4.30
53	Chile	4.25
54	Jamaica	4.22
55	Gambia, The	4.14
56	Czech Republic	4.10
57	Bahrain	4.09
58	Tanzania	4.04
59	Sri Lanka	3.96
60	Libya	3.93
61	Latvia	3.85
62	Morocco	3.84
63	Colombia	3.81
64	Benin	3.80
65	Italy	3.79
66	Trinidad and Tobago	3.79
67	Spain	3.76
68	Mali	3.73
69	Nepal	3.68
70	Algeria	3.65
71	Slovak Republic	3.61
72	Vietnam	3.61
73	Lithuania	3.60
74	Mexico	3.58
75	Lesotho	3.55
76	Poland	3.54
77	Nigeria	3.52
78	Pakistan	3.51
79	Syria	3.49
80	Mauritania	3.44
81	China	3.43
82	Uganda	3.37
83	Tajikistan	3.33
84	Philippines	3.31
85	Croatia	3.30
86	Guatemala	3.29
87	Dominican Republic	3.27
88	Brazil	3.14
89	Bosnia and Herzegovina	3.14
90	El Salvador	3.11
91	Zambia	3.09
92	Romania	3.09
93	Honduras	3.02
94	Madagascar	3.00
95	Kenya	2.98
96	Indonesia	2.97
97	Burkina Faso	2.95
98	Kazakhstan	2.85
99	Guyana	2.79
100	Mozambique	2.78
101	Bulgaria	2.75
102	Russian Federation	2.70
103	Ethiopia	2.69
104	Azerbaijan	2.68
105	Bangladesh	2.56
106	Macedonia, FYR	2.54
107	Ukraine	2.52
108	Georgia	2.52
109	Senegal	2.52
110	Mongolia	2.52
111	Panama	2.47
112	Bolivia	2.44
113	Moldova	2.43
114	Cambodia	2.41
115	Albania	2.38
116	Armenia	2.31
117	Cameroon	2.20
118	Peru	2.19
119	Argentina	2.17
120	Kyrgyz Republic	2.05
121	Ecuador	2.04
122	Burundi	2.02
123	Chad	1.90
124	Zimbabwe	1.82
125	Nicaragua	1.58
126	Paraguay	1.55
127	Venezuela	1.19

MEAN: 4.02

SOURCE: World Economic Forum, Executive Opinion Survey 2006, 2007

2.04 Intellectual property protection

Intellectual property protection in your country (1 = is weak and not enforced; 7 = is strong and enforced)

RANK	COUNTRY/ECONOMY	SCORE
1	Germany	6.48
2	Finland	6.33
3	Switzerland	6.31
4	Denmark	6.31
5	Singapore	6.17
6	Netherlands	6.03
7	Sweden	6.01
8	United Kingdom	5.96
9	France	5.91
10	Australia	5.90
11	Austria	5.87
12	Iceland	5.86
13	New Zealand	5.75
14	Belgium	5.70
15	Canada	5.66
16	Norway	5.64
17	Japan	5.63
18	Luxembourg	5.60
19	Ireland	5.51
20	Puerto Rico	5.50
21	Hong Kong SAR	5.45
22	United States	5.42
23	Korea, Rep.	5.37
24	South Africa	5.20
25	Malaysia	5.11
26	Israel	5.08
27	Qatar	5.02
28	Spain	4.92
29	Portugal	4.92
30	Taiwan, China	4.86
31	United Arab Emirates	4.84
32	Oman	4.79
33	Bahrain	4.74
34	Estonia	4.66
35	Tunisia	4.63
36	Slovenia	4.48
37	Hungary	4.44
38	Barbados	4.40
39	Cyprus	4.38
40	Jordan	4.37
41	Malta	4.32
42	Italy	4.31
43	Mauritius	4.13
44	Thailand	4.13
45	Greece	4.13
46	Namibia	4.10
47	Panama	4.09
48	India	3.99
49	Chile	3.96
50	Uruguay	3.93
51	Czech Republic	3.88
52	Saudi Arabia	3.86
53	Morocco	3.85
54	Burkina Faso	3.84
55	Slovak Republic	3.83
56	Sri Lanka	3.76
57	Croatia	3.75
58	Costa Rica	3.73
59	Lithuania	3.66
60	Kuwait	3.63
61	Pakistan	3.61
62	Colombia	3.53
63	Egypt	3.51
64	Mexico	3.51
65	Cameroon	3.49
66	Poland	3.48
67	Jamaica	3.48
68	Turkey	3.45
69	Latvia	3.45
70	China	3.42
71	Benin	3.33
72	Brazil	3.33
73	Honduras	3.30
74	Romania	3.29
75	Mali	3.28
76	Dominican Republic	3.28
77	El Salvador	3.27
78	Syria	3.26
79	Kazakhstan	3.26
80	Madagascar	3.25
81	Gambia, The	3.23
82	Tanzania	3.21
83	Senegal	3.19
84	Trinidad and Tobago	3.13
85	Moldova	3.13
86	Indonesia	3.11
87	Botswana	3.11
88	Mauritania	3.09
89	Philippines	3.08
90	Guatemala	3.07
91	Libya	3.06
92	Azerbaijan	3.03
93	Kenya	3.01
94	Algeria	3.00
95	Nigeria	2.94
96	Ethiopia	2.94
97	Tajikistan	2.94
98	Zimbabwe	2.93
99	Argentina	2.83
100	Vietnam	2.82
101	Nicaragua	2.79
102	Kyrgyz Republic	2.79
103	Bulgaria	2.78
104	Georgia	2.75
105	Zambia	2.72
106	Armenia	2.70
107	Ukraine	2.69
108	Uganda	2.69
109	Ecuador	2.68
110	Peru	2.67
111	Cambodia	2.66
112	Mozambique	2.60
113	Russian Federation	2.58
114	Macedonia, FYR	2.58
115	Lesotho	2.46
116	Mongolia	2.42
117	Bosnia and Herzegovina	2.37
118	Nepal	2.26
119	Paraguay	2.25
120	Albania	2.20
121	Chad	2.07
122	Venezuela	2.06
123	Burundi	2.05
124	Bolivia	2.04
125	Guyana	1.97
126	Suriname	1.96
127	Bangladesh	1.96

MEAN: 3.85

SOURCE: World Economic Forum, Executive Opinion Survey 2006, 2007

2.05 Efficiency of legal framework for disputes

The legal framework in your country for private businesses to settle disputes and challenge the legality of government actions and/or regulations (1 = is inefficient and subject to manipulation, 7 = is efficient and follows a clear, neutral process)

RANK	COUNTRY/ECONOMY	SCORE
1	Denmark	6.48
2	Germany	6.30
3	Switzerland	6.14
4	Finland	6.11
5	Sweden	6.10
6	Austria	6.07
7	Netherlands	6.05
8	Norway	6.05
9	Hong Kong SAR	5.99
10	Singapore	5.98
11	Australia	5.91
12	New Zealand	5.86
13	Iceland	5.83
14	United Kingdom	5.82
15	Japan	5.59
16	Canada	5.58
17	South Africa	5.43
18	Malaysia	5.37
19	Luxembourg	5.35
20	France	5.28
21	Ireland	5.26
22	Barbados	5.24
23	Tunisia	5.15
24	Qatar	5.13
25	Kuwait	5.06
26	Israel	4.98
27	United Arab Emirates	4.97
28	Korea, Rep.	4.96
29	Estonia	4.93
30	United States	4.88
31	Oman	4.87
32	Cyprus	4.85
33	Botswana	4.80
34	India	4.77
35	Chile	4.76
36	Belgium	4.70
37	Mauritius	4.67
38	Jordan	4.65
39	Malta	4.61
40	Costa Rica	4.60
41	Puerto Rico	4.57
42	Namibia	4.44
43	Thailand	4.39
44	Saudi Arabia	4.26
45	Taiwan, China	4.20
46	Spain	4.18
47	Egypt	4.17
48	Slovenia	4.08
49	Uruguay	4.07
50	Greece	4.05
51	Morocco	4.03
52	Portugal	3.93
53	Gambia, The	3.91
54	Algeria	3.89
55	Bahrain	3.82
56	Hungary	3.81
57	Vietnam	3.78
58	Mali	3.78
59	Sri Lanka	3.77
60	Zambia	3.75
61	Mauritania	3.75
62	Turkey	3.71
63	Colombia	3.70
64	Libya	3.70
65	Suriname	3.70
66	Tajikistan	3.67
67	Tanzania	3.66
68	Trinidad and Tobago	3.65
69	Lithuania	3.62
70	China	3.59
71	Kazakhstan	3.56
72	Latvia	3.54
73	Jamaica	3.53
74	Indonesia	3.52
75	Benin	3.49
76	Syria	3.46
77	Czech Republic	3.37
78	Slovak Republic	3.33
79	Croatia	3.29
80	Nigeria	3.29
81	Uganda	3.27
82	Burkina Faso	3.24
83	Madagascar	3.22
84	Azerbaijan	3.21
85	Lesotho	3.16
86	Honduras	3.15
87	Poland	3.13
88	Pakistan	3.12
89	Ethiopia	3.09
90	Kenya	3.08
91	Philippines	3.07
92	Cambodia	3.07
93	Mexico	3.05
94	Romania	3.03
95	El Salvador	3.03
96	Guatemala	3.01
97	Italy	2.99
98	Dominican Republic	2.95
99	Panama	2.92
100	Nepal	2.92
101	Armenia	2.87
102	Brazil	2.86
103	Russian Federation	2.84
104	Cameroon	2.81
105	Mozambique	2.80
106	Senegal	2.78
107	Macedonia, FYR	2.75
108	Ukraine	2.75
109	Bulgaria	2.75
110	Moldova	2.70
111	Bangladesh	2.68
112	Kyrgyz Republic	2.68
113	Georgia	2.62
114	Albania	2.61
115	Burundi	2.60
116	Mongolia	2.46
117	Guyana	2.43
118	Bosnia and Herzegovina	2.39
119	Peru	2.38
120	Bolivia	2.37
121	Argentina	2.36
122	Chad	2.35
123	Zimbabwe	2.28
124	Nicaragua	2.22
125	Ecuador	2.18
126	Paraguay	1.99
127	Venezuela	1.54

MEAN: 3.91

SOURCE: World Economic Forum, Executive Opinion Survey 2006, 2007

2.06 Property rights

Property rights, including over financial assets (1 = are poorly defined and not protected by law, 7 = are clearly defined and well protected by law)

RANK	COUNTRY/ECONOMY	SCORE
1	Germany	6.67
2	Denmark	6.59
3	Switzerland	6.58
4	Austria	6.54
5	Singapore	6.41
6	Netherlands	6.40
7	Finland	6.40
8	Australia	6.35
9	Sweden	6.34
10	Iceland	6.33
11	Ireland	6.32
12	Norway	6.31
13	Hong Kong SAR	6.27
14	Japan	6.19
15	Canada	6.08
16	New Zealand	6.07
17	France	6.06
18	United Kingdom	6.06
19	Belgium	6.04
20	Luxembourg	6.00
21	Puerto Rico	5.91
22	South Africa	5.78
23	Malaysia	5.71
24	Korea, Rep.	5.71
25	Israel	5.65
26	Estonia	5.65
27	Mauritius	5.65
28	Portugal	5.58
29	Jordan	5.57
30	United States	5.55
31	Syria	5.55
32	Spain	5.54
33	Barbados	5.51
34	Tunisia	5.49
35	Bahrain	5.48
36	Cyprus	5.45
37	Hungary	5.44
38	Qatar	5.43
39	Taiwan, China	5.42
40	Chile	5.41
41	Namibia	5.41
42	Kuwait	5.40
43	Malta	5.34
44	India	5.28
45	United Arab Emirates	5.18
46	Greece	5.18
47	Saudi Arabia	5.17
48	Lithuania	5.13
49	Panama	5.12
50	Thailand	5.10
51	Egypt	5.05
52	Slovak Republic	5.05
53	Italy	5.03
54	Latvia	5.01
55	Jamaica	4.96
56	Slovenia	4.91
57	Botswana	4.87
58	Turkey	4.80
59	Oman	4.77
60	Sri Lanka	4.72
61	Uruguay	4.71
62	Morocco	4.67
63	Trinidad and Tobago	4.67
64	Costa Rica	4.60
65	Czech Republic	4.58
66	Zambia	4.55
67	Colombia	4.53
68	Armenia	4.48
69	Brazil	4.46
70	Burkina Faso	4.46
71	El Salvador	4.42
72	Gambia, The	4.36
73	Algeria	4.35
74	Philippines	4.35
75	China	4.31
76	Mexico	4.30
77	Croatia	4.24
78	Vietnam	4.23
79	Tajikistan	4.21
80	Dominican Republic	4.20
81	Mali	4.14
82	Ethiopia	4.14
83	Romania	4.13
84	Guatemala	4.11
85	Honduras	4.10
86	Kenya	4.09
87	Mauritania	4.07
88	Mongolia	4.05
89	Poland	4.01
90	Kazakhstan	3.98
91	Pakistan	3.98
92	Nepal	3.95
93	Tanzania	3.95
94	Senegal	3.87
95	Mozambique	3.83
96	Bulgaria	3.82
97	Libya	3.81
98	Nigeria	3.81
99	Suriname	3.80
100	Cameroon	3.76
101	Azerbaijan	3.74
102	Benin	3.73
103	Macedonia, FYR	3.72
104	Bangladesh	3.69
105	Moldova	3.61
106	Nicaragua	3.60
107	Peru	3.59
108	Madagascar	3.59
109	Cambodia	3.59
110	Uganda	3.59
111	Guyana	3.46
112	Indonesia	3.38
113	Ecuador	3.35
114	Georgia	3.32
115	Ukraine	3.29
116	Burundi	3.25
117	Bosnia and Herzegovina	3.20
118	Kyrgyz Republic	3.17
119	Russian Federation	3.16
120	Albania	3.12
121	Bolivia	3.08
122	Paraguay	3.06
123	Lesotho	3.02
124	Argentina	2.97
125	Chad	2.62
126	Venezuela	2.29
127	Zimbabwe	2.14

MEAN: 4.69

SOURCE: World Economic Forum, Executive Opinion Survey 2006, 2007

2.07 Quality of competition in the ISP sector

Is there sufficient competition among Internet service providers in your country to ensure high quality, infrequent interruptions and low prices?
(1 = no, 7 = yes, equal to the best in the world)

RANK	COUNTRY/ECONOMY	SCORE
1	Korea, Rep.	6.19
2	Germany	6.04
3	Israel	5.99
4	Netherlands	5.97
5	Austria	5.92
6	Japan	5.87
7	Estonia	5.82
8	Hong Kong SAR	5.82
9	United Kingdom	5.69
10	Norway	5.63
11	Sweden	5.61
12	Iceland	5.60
13	United States	5.59
14	Finland	5.57
15	Canada	5.52
16	Denmark	5.48
17	Chile	5.46
18	Switzerland	5.43
19	Singapore	5.39
20	France	5.38
21	Guatemala	5.35
22	Jordan	5.29
23	India	5.28
24	Puerto Rico	5.27
25	Taiwan, China	5.17
26	Malaysia	5.13
27	Australia	5.09
28	Thailand	5.08
29	Malta	5.05
30	Belgium	5.03
31	Lithuania	4.96
32	Egypt	4.92
33	Brazil	4.91
34	Philippines	4.84
35	Portugal	4.69
36	Indonesia	4.64
37	Slovenia	4.62
38	Cyprus	4.62
39	Panama	4.60
40	Sri Lanka	4.59
41	Tunisia	4.59
42	El Salvador	4.59
43	Jamaica	4.58
44	Mali	4.52
45	Italy	4.51
46	Luxembourg	4.46
47	Saudi Arabia	4.45
48	Honduras	4.44
49	Dominican Republic	4.40
50	Turkey	4.39
51	Latvia	4.38
52	Kuwait	4.35
53	Czech Republic	4.34
54	Slovak Republic	4.28
55	Spain	4.27
56	Georgia	4.25
57	Croatia	4.20
58	Colombia	4.20
59	China	4.18
60	Pakistan	4.18
61	Kenya	4.18
62	Greece	4.15
63	Gambia, The	4.15
64	Azerbaijan	4.15
65	Barbados	4.14
66	Nepal	4.14
67	Bulgaria	4.12
68	Ireland	4.06
69	Senegal	4.05
70	Nigeria	4.01
71	Argentina	4.00
72	Mexico	3.92
73	Russian Federation	3.88
74	Peru	3.87
75	Bangladesh	3.87
76	Mongolia	3.83
77	Uruguay	3.83
78	Hungary	3.81
79	Oman	3.80
80	Tanzania	3.80
81	Romania	3.79
82	Tajikistan	3.79
83	Venezuela	3.77
84	Vietnam	3.71
85	Burkina Faso	3.71
86	Uganda	3.70
87	Benin	3.69
88	Morocco	3.68
89	Guyana	3.63
90	Poland	3.60
91	Moldova	3.58
92	Algeria	3.56
93	Botswana	3.55
94	Bolivia	3.53
95	Madagascar	3.53
96	Bahrain	3.46
97	Mauritius	3.45
98	Kazakhstan	3.44
99	Cambodia	3.41
100	Mozambique	3.41
101	Kyrgyz Republic	3.41
102	Cameroon	3.38
103	Nicaragua	3.38
104	Ecuador	3.36
105	Bosnia and Herzegovina	3.33
106	New Zealand	3.33
107	Syria	3.31
108	South Africa	3.28
109	Ukraine	3.25
110	Libya	3.20
111	Albania	3.19
112	United Arab Emirates	3.16
113	Namibia	3.13
114	Zambia	3.13
115	Paraguay	3.03
116	Macedonia, FYR	3.03
117	Lesotho	2.96
118	Qatar	2.90
119	Zimbabwe	2.88
120	Mauritania	2.87
121	Armenia	2.79
122	Burundi	2.78
123	Trinidad and Tobago	2.67
124	Costa Rica	2.38
125	Chad	2.33
126	Ethiopia	2.07
127	Suriname	1.86

MEAN: 4.20

SOURCE: World Economic Forum, Executive Opinion Survey 2006, 2007

2.08 Number of procedures to enforce a contract (hard data)

Number of procedures from the moment the plaintiff files a lawsuit in court until the moment of payment | 2007

RANK	COUNTRY/ECONOMY	HARD DATA
1	Ireland	20.00
2	Singapore	22.00
3	Hong Kong SAR	24.00
4	Netherlands	25.00
5	Austria	26.00
5	Iceland	26.00
5	Luxembourg	26.00
8	Belgium	27.00
8	Czech Republic	27.00
8	Latvia	27.00
11	Australia	28.00
11	Guatemala	28.00
13	Botswana	29.00
13	Venezuela	29.00
15	El Salvador	30.00
15	France	30.00
15	Japan	30.00
15	Lithuania	30.00
15	Malaysia	30.00
15	New Zealand	30.00
15	Slovak Republic	30.00
15	South Africa	30.00
15	Sweden	30.00
15	Ukraine	30.00
15	United Kingdom	30.00
26	Moldova	31.00
26	Mozambique	31.00
26	Panama	31.00
29	Gambia, The	32.00
29	Mongolia	32.00
29	Romania	32.00
29	Slovenia	32.00
29	Switzerland	32.00
29	United States	32.00
35	Finland	33.00
35	Germany	33.00
35	Hungary	33.00
35	Namibia	33.00
35	Norway	33.00
40	Colombia	34.00
40	Denmark	34.00
40	Dominican Republic	34.00
40	Jamaica	34.00
40	Tajikistan	34.00
40	Vietnam	34.00
46	China	35.00
46	Israel	35.00
46	Korea, Rep.	35.00
46	Nicaragua	35.00
46	Portugal	35.00
46	Thailand	35.00
46	Zambia	35.00
53	Argentina	36.00
53	Canada	36.00
53	Chile	36.00
53	Estonia	36.00
53	Georgia	36.00
53	Guyana	36.00
53	Turkey	36.00
60	Bolivia	37.00
60	Burkina Faso	37.00
60	Mauritius	37.00
60	Philippines	37.00
60	Russian Federation	37.00
65	Bosnia and Herzegovina	38.00
65	Croatia	38.00
65	Kazakhstan	38.00
65	Madagascar	38.00
65	Mexico	38.00
65	Paraguay	38.00
65	Poland	38.00
65	Tanzania	38.00
65	Uganda	38.00
65	Zimbabwe	38.00
75	Albania	39.00
75	Azerbaijan	39.00
75	Ecuador	39.00
75	Ethiopia	39.00
75	Greece	39.00
75	Indonesia	39.00
75	Jordan	39.00
75	Kyrgyz Republic	39.00
75	Macedonia, FYR	39.00
75	Mali	39.00
75	Nepal	39.00
75	Nigeria	39.00
75	Spain	39.00
75	Tunisia	39.00
89	Bulgaria	40.00
89	Costa Rica	40.00
89	Morocco	40.00
89	Sri Lanka	40.00
89	Uruguay	40.00
94	Bangladesh	41.00
94	Chad	41.00
94	Italy	41.00
94	Lesotho	41.00
94	Peru	41.00
94	Puerto Rico	41.00
100	Benin	42.00
100	Egypt	42.00
100	Trinidad and Tobago	42.00
103	Cameroon	43.00
104	Burundi	44.00
104	Cambodia	44.00
104	Kenya	44.00
104	Saudi Arabia	44.00
104	Senegal	44.00
104	Suriname	44.00
110	Brazil	45.00
110	Honduras	45.00
112	India	46.00
112	Mauritania	46.00
114	Algeria	47.00
114	Pakistan	47.00
114	Taiwan, China	47.00
117	Armenia	50.00
117	Kuwait	50.00
117	United Arab Emirates	50.00
120	Oman	51.00
121	Syria	55.00
n/a	Bahrain	n/a
n/a	Barbados	n/a
n/a	Cyprus	n/a
n/a	Libya	n/a
n/a	Malta	n/a
n/a	Qatar	n/a

SOURCE: The World Bank, *Doing Business 2008*

2.09 Time to enforce a contract (hard data)

Number of days required to resolve a dispute | 2007

RANK	COUNTRY/ECONOMY	HARD DATA
1	Singapore	120.00
2	Kyrgyz Republic	177.00
3	Lithuania	210.00
4	Hong Kong SAR	211.00
5	New Zealand	216.00
6	Kazakhstan	230.00
6	Korea, Rep.	230.00
8	Finland	235.00
9	Australia	262.00
10	Azerbaijan	267.00
11	Namibia	270.00
12	Latvia	279.00
13	Russian Federation	281.00
14	Armenia	285.00
14	Georgia	285.00
16	Tajikistan	295.00
16	Vietnam	295.00
18	United States	300.00
19	Norway	310.00
20	Mongolia	314.00
21	Japan	316.00
22	Luxembourg	321.00
23	France	331.00
24	Hungary	335.00
25	Ukraine	354.00
26	Moldova	365.00
27	Denmark	380.00
28	Macedonia, FYR	385.00
29	Albania	390.00
30	Iceland	393.00
31	Germany	394.00
32	Austria	397.00
33	Mauritania	400.00
34	Cambodia	401.00
35	United Kingdom	404.00
36	China	406.00
37	Zimbabwe	410.00
38	Mexico	415.00
39	Switzerland	417.00
40	Turkey	420.00
41	Estonia	425.00
42	Gambia, The	434.00
43	Burkina Faso	446.00
44	Nigeria	457.00
45	Dominican Republic	460.00
46	Tanzania	462.00
47	Kenya	465.00
48	Peru	468.00
49	Zambia	471.00
50	Thailand	479.00
51	Chile	480.00
51	Honduras	480.00
53	Ecuador	498.00
54	Belgium	505.00
55	Sweden	508.00
56	Taiwan, China	510.00
56	Venezuela	510.00
58	Netherlands	514.00
59	Ireland	515.00
59	Spain	515.00
61	Uganda	535.00
62	Romania	537.00
63	Nicaragua	540.00
64	Burundi	558.00
65	Croatia	561.00
66	Bulgaria	564.00
67	Jamaica	565.00
67	Slovak Republic	565.00
67	Tunisia	565.00
70	Kuwait	566.00
71	Canada	570.00
71	Indonesia	570.00
73	Portugal	577.00
74	Guyana	581.00
75	Argentina	590.00
76	Bolivia	591.00
76	Paraguay	591.00
78	Bosnia and Herzegovina	595.00
79	Oman	598.00
80	Malaysia	600.00
80	South Africa	600.00
82	United Arab Emirates	607.00
83	Morocco	615.00
84	Brazil	616.00
85	Puerto Rico	620.00
86	Algeria	630.00
87	Saudi Arabia	635.00
88	Panama	686.00
89	Jordan	689.00
90	Ethiopia	690.00
91	Lesotho	695.00
92	Benin	720.00
92	Uruguay	720.00
94	Nepal	735.00
95	Chad	743.00
96	Mauritius	750.00
97	Senegal	780.00
98	El Salvador	786.00
99	Cameroon	800.00
100	Greece	819.00
101	Czech Republic	820.00
102	Poland	830.00
103	Philippines	842.00
104	Mali	860.00
105	Madagascar	871.00
106	Syria	872.00
107	Costa Rica	877.00
108	Pakistan	880.00
109	Israel	890.00
110	Botswana	987.00
111	Egypt	1,010.00
111	Mozambique	1,010.00
113	Italy	1,210.00
114	Sri Lanka	1,318.00
115	Trinidad and Tobago	1,340.00
116	Colombia	1,346.00
117	Slovenia	1,350.00
118	India	1,420.00
119	Bangladesh	1,442.00
120	Guatemala	1,459.00
121	Suriname	1,715.00
n/a	Bahrain	n/a
n/a	Barbados	n/a
n/a	Cyprus	n/a
n/a	Libya	n/a
n/a	Malta	n/a
n/a	Qatar	n/a

SOURCE: The World Bank, *Doing Business 2008*

Subindex A Environment component

3rd pillar
Infrastructure environment

3.01 Telephone lines (hard data)

Main telephone lines per 100 inhabitants | 2006 or most recent year available

RANK	COUNTRY/ECONOMY	HARD DATA
1	Switzerland	69.38
2	Germany	65.53
3	Iceland	65.21
4	Canada[1]	64.12
5	Taiwan, China	63.58
6	Sweden	59.52
7	United States	57.15
8	Denmark	56.89
9	United Kingdom	56.15
10	Korea, Rep.	55.99
11	France	55.82
12	Greece	55.52
13	Hong Kong SAR	54.08
14	Luxembourg	52.40
15	Malta	50.16
16	Barbados[1]	50.14
17	Ireland	49.81
18	Australia	48.81
19	Cyprus	48.35
20	Netherlands[1]	46.63
21	Belgium	45.21
22	Norway	44.27
23	Israel	43.88
24	Austria	43.44
25	Italy[1]	43.12
26	Japan	43.02
27	New Zealand[1]	42.91
28	Slovenia	42.60
29	Spain	42.38
30	Singapore	42.32
31	Estonia	40.90
32	Croatia	40.22
33	Portugal	40.12
34	Finland	36.49
35	Hungary	33.27
36	Czech Republic[1]	31.48
37	Bulgaria	31.28
38	Costa Rica	30.72
39	Poland	29.81
40	Latvia	28.64
41	Mauritius	28.45
42	Uruguay	28.31
43	United Arab Emirates	28.12
44	Russian Federation[1]	27.94
45	China	27.79
46	Qatar	27.21
47	Ukraine	26.84
48	Puerto Rico[1]	26.24
49	Bahrain	26.18
50	Turkey	25.39
51	Bosnia and Herzegovina	25.28
52	Trinidad and Tobago	24.87
53	Moldova	24.27
54	Argentina	24.17
55	Macedonia, FYR	24.10
56	Lithuania	23.19
57	Slovak Republic	21.62
58	Brazil[1]	21.38
59	Chile	20.20
60	Kazakhstan	19.77
61	Armenia[1]	19.71
62	Romania	19.44
63	Kuwait[1]	18.99
64	Vietnam[1]	18.81
65	Mexico	18.33
66	Suriname	18.03
67	Colombia	17.00
68	Malaysia	16.83
69	Syria	16.62
70	Saudi Arabia	15.68
71	Venezuela	15.49
72	El Salvador	14.81
73	Guyana	14.66
74	Egypt	14.33
75	Azerbaijan	14.03
76	Panama	13.17
77	Ecuador	13.07
78	Georgia	12.48
79	Tunisia	12.42
80	Jamaica[1]	12.03
81	Albania[1]	11.30
82	Thailand	10.92
83	Oman	10.65
84	Jordan	10.52
85	Guatemala	10.49
86	South Africa[1]	9.97
87	Dominican Republic	9.94
88	Honduras	9.62
89	Sri Lanka	9.01
90	Algeria	8.52
91	Kyrgyz Republic[1]	8.37
92	Peru	8.22
93	Libya	8.09
94	Botswana	7.78
95	Bolivia	7.13
96	Namibia[1]	6.84
97	Indonesia	6.57
98	Mongolia[1]	5.90
99	Paraguay	5.25
100	India[1]	4.55
101	Nicaragua	4.43
102	Tajikistan[1]	4.31
103	Philippines	4.30
104	Morocco	4.12
105	Gambia, The	3.40
106	Pakistan	3.34
107	Lesotho[1]	2.67
108	Zimbabwe	2.54
109	Senegal	2.37
110	Nepal	2.15
111	Nigeria	1.26
112	Mauritania	1.10
113	Ethiopia	0.91
114	Benin	0.89
115	Kenya	0.84
116	Zambia	0.79
117	Bangladesh	0.79
118	Burkina Faso	0.70
119	Madagascar	0.68
120	Cameroon[1]	0.61
121	Mali	0.59
122	Burundi[1]	0.41
123	Tanzania	0.40
124	Uganda	0.36
125	Mozambique	0.33
126	Cambodia	0.23
127	Chad	0.13

SOURCE: International Telecommunication Union, *World Telecommunication Indicators 2007*

[1] 2005

3.02 Secure Internet servers (hard data)

Secure Internet servers per 1 million inhabitants | 2006

RANK	COUNTRY/ECONOMY	HARD DATA
1	Iceland	1,258.00
2	United States	869.00
3	Canada	646.00
4	Denmark	615.00
5	New Zealand	596.00
6	Australia	584.00
7	Luxembourg	582.00
8	Switzerland	580.00
9	United Kingdom	561.00
10	Malta	486.00
11	Ireland	420.00
12	Netherlands	412.00
13	Sweden	406.00
14	Norway	390.00
15	Finland	381.00
16	Germany	349.00
17	Japan	332.00
18	Singapore	298.00
19	Austria	285.00
20	Cyprus	268.00
21	Barbados	196.00
22	Hong Kong SAR	190.00
23	Israel	183.00
24	Taiwan, China	169.00
25	Estonia	163.00
26	Belgium	146.00
27	Spain	102.00
28	France	96.00
28	Slovenia	96.00
30	Costa Rica	67.00
31	Czech Republic	65.00
31	Portugal	65.00
33	Panama	57.00
34	Bahrain	55.00
35	United Arab Emirates	54.00
36	Italy	53.00
37	Croatia	48.00
38	Latvia	46.00
39	Greece	40.00
40	Poland	38.00
41	Hungary	36.00
42	Kuwait	35.00
43	Puerto Rico	33.00
44	Uruguay	29.00
45	Qatar	28.00
45	Slovak Republic	28.00
45	Trinidad and Tobago	28.00
48	Lithuania	26.00
49	Turkey	25.00
50	South Africa	24.00
51	Chile	22.00
51	Korea, Rep.	22.00
53	Jamaica	18.00
53	Mauritius	18.00
55	Malaysia	17.00
56	Brazil	16.00
56	Suriname	16.00
58	Argentina	12.00
59	Bulgaria	11.00
60	Mexico	10.00
61	Namibia	8.00
62	Romania	7.00
63	Colombia	6.00
63	Dominican Republic	6.00
63	El Salvador	6.00
63	Guatemala	6.00
63	Peru	6.00
63	Thailand	6.00
69	Ecuador	5.00
69	Georgia	5.00
69	Saudi Arabia	5.00
69	Venezuela	5.00
73	Bosnia and Herzegovina	4.00
73	Honduras	4.00
73	Jordan	4.00
73	Moldova	4.00
73	Mongolia	4.00
78	Armenia	3.00
78	Bolivia	3.00
78	Guyana	3.00
78	Nicaragua	3.00
78	Oman	3.00
78	Philippines	3.00
78	Russian Federation	3.00
85	Albania	2.00
85	Macedonia, FYR	2.00
85	Sri Lanka	2.00
85	Tunisia	2.00
85	Ukraine	2.00
90	Botswana	1.00
90	Egypt	1.00
90	Gambia, The	1.00
90	India	1.00
90	Indonesia	1.00
90	Kazakhstan	1.00
90	Kyrgyz Republic	1.00
90	Mauritania	1.00
90	Morocco	1.00
90	Nepal	1.00
90	Paraguay	1.00
101	Algeria	0.00
101	Azerbaijan	0.00
101	Bangladesh	0.00
101	Benin	0.00
101	Burkina Faso	0.00
101	Burundi	0.00
101	Cambodia	0.00
101	Cameroon	0.00
101	China	0.00
101	Ethiopia	0.00
101	Kenya	0.00
101	Libya	0.00
101	Madagascar	0.00
101	Mali	0.00
101	Mozambique	0.00
101	Nigeria	0.00
101	Pakistan	0.00
101	Senegal	0.00
101	Syria	0.00
101	Tanzania	0.00
101	Uganda	0.00
101	Vietnam	0.00
101	Zambia	0.00
101	Zimbabwe	0.00
n/a	Chad	n/a
n/a	Lesotho	n/a
n/a	Tajikistan	n/a

SOURCE: The World Bank, *World Development Indicators 2007*

3.03 Electricity production (hard data)

Per capita electricity production (kWh) | 2004 or most recent year available

RANK	COUNTRY/ECONOMY	HARD DATA
1	Iceland[1]	29,356.09
2	Norway	23,976.48
3	Canada	18,706.43
4	Sweden	16,870.55
5	Kuwait	16,792.03
6	Finland	16,411.32
7	Qatar[1]	16,382.15
8	United States	14,124.16
9	United Arab Emirates	12,129.63
10	Australia	11,910.21
11	Bahrain[1]	11,004.98
12	New Zealand	10,292.02
13	France	9,370.30
14	Taiwan, China[1]	9,248.74
15	Paraguay	8,966.67
16	Singapore	8,678.63
17	Switzerland	8,606.69
18	Japan	8,382.91
19	Czech Republic	8,210.05
20	Belgium	8,099.03
21	Slovenia	7,661.49
22	Estonia	7,635.29
23	Korea, Rep.	7,624.47
24	Austria	7,535.44
25	Denmark	7,498.33
26	Germany	7,392.51
27	Israel	7,216.87
28	Saudi Arabia	7,097.52
29	United Kingdom	6,571.51
30	Spain	6,490.68
31	Russian Federation	6,464.37
32	Puerto Rico[2]	6,380.21
33	Ireland	6,193.93
34	Netherlands	6,190.89
35	Luxembourg[1]	6,178.51
36	Slovak Republic	5,666.62
37	Malta[1]	5,604.01
38	Lithuania	5,472.12
39	Hong Kong SAR	5,390.40
40	Bulgaria	5,320.65
41	Greece	5,315.49
42	South Africa	5,224.33
43	Italy	5,036.53
44	Cyprus[1]	4,953.39
45	Trinidad and Tobago	4,918.16
46	Oman	4,538.64
47	Kazakhstan	4,456.14
48	Portugal	4,265.85
49	Poland	3,996.65
50	Ukraine	3,836.34
51	Venezuela	3,770.05
52	Libya	3,519.10
53	Hungary	3,334.32
54	Malaysia	3,330.12
55	Macedonia, FYR	3,299.68
56	Chile	3,225.01
57	Bosnia and Herzegovina	3,222.92
58	Croatia	2,971.03
59	Kyrgyz Republic	2,964.97
60	Jamaica	2,725.21
61	Tajikistan	2,690.39
62	Argentina	2,613.89
63	Romania	2,605.49
64	Azerbaijan	2,600.40
65	Mexico	2,195.98
66	Turkey	2,118.06
67	Brazil	2,107.01
68	Latvia	2,032.17
69	Armenia	1,982.75
70	Thailand	1,973.50
71	Costa Rica	1,928.05
72	Panama	1,826.54
73	Albania	1,799.66
74	Syria	1,727.48
75	Uruguay	1,715.37
76	China	1,696.96
77	Jordan	1,682.24
78	Dominican Republic	1,573.92
79	Georgia	1,527.22
80	Egypt	1,394.51
81	Tunisia	1,318.92
82	Colombia	1,117.67
83	Algeria	967.30
84	Ecuador	966.26
85	Peru	881.65
86	Moldova	853.51
87	Namibia	846.07
88	Zimbabwe	749.85
89	Zambia	740.48
90	Botswana	734.84
91	Honduras	695.20
92	Philippines	686.13
93	El Salvador	650.66
94	Morocco	647.13
95	India	618.51
96	Mozambique	602.35
97	Guatemala	569.34
98	Pakistan	563.59
99	Vietnam	559.87
100	Indonesia	552.42
101	Nicaragua	546.58
102	Bolivia	488.40
103	Sri Lanka	411.06
104	Cameroon	255.64
105	Senegal	210.79
106	Kenya	167.33
107	Nigeria	156.94
108	Bangladesh	154.44
109	Nepal	86.50
110	Tanzania	66.44
111	Cambodia	57.98
112	Ethiopia	35.73
113	Benin	12.23
n/a	Barbados	n/a
n/a	Burkina Faso	n/a
n/a	Burundi	n/a
n/a	Chad	n/a
n/a	Gambia, The	n/a
n/a	Guyana	n/a
n/a	Lesotho	n/a
n/a	Madagascar	n/a
n/a	Mali	n/a
n/a	Mauritania	n/a
n/a	Mauritius	n/a
n/a	Mongolia	n/a
n/a	Suriname	n/a
n/a	Uganda	n/a

SOURCE: The World Bank, *World Development Indicators 2007*

[1] 2003 [2] 2006

3.04 Availability of scientists and engineers

Scientists and engineers in your country are (1 = nonexistent or rare, 7 = widely available)

MEAN: 4.36

RANK	COUNTRY/ECONOMY	SCORE
1	Finland	6.04
2	Japan	5.95
3	Israel	5.92
4	India	5.92
5	Czech Republic	5.76
6	Sweden	5.76
7	France	5.68
8	Canada	5.66
9	Tunisia	5.65
10	Switzerland	5.64
11	Denmark	5.61
12	United States	5.60
13	Korea, Rep.	5.52
14	Taiwan, China	5.47
15	Ireland	5.44
16	Germany	5.44
17	Greece	5.41
18	Belgium	5.34
19	Puerto Rico	5.32
20	Iceland	5.29
21	Malaysia	5.28
22	Singapore	5.28
23	Norway	5.25
24	Slovak Republic	5.19
25	Algeria	5.16
26	Austria	5.13
27	Indonesia	5.05
28	United Kingdom	5.04
29	Egypt	5.00
30	Netherlands	4.99
31	Chile	4.94
32	Portugal	4.93
33	Cyprus	4.91
34	Australia	4.90
35	Hong Kong SAR	4.90
36	Morocco	4.89
37	Russian Federation	4.87
38	Jordan	4.82
39	Costa Rica	4.76
40	Hungary	4.74
41	Turkey	4.74
42	Thailand	4.73
43	Lithuania	4.72
44	Sri Lanka	4.72
45	Spain	4.71
46	Croatia	4.69
47	Romania	4.61
48	Italy	4.59
49	Kuwait	4.58
50	Kenya	4.57
51	Azerbaijan	4.56
52	Mongolia	4.55
53	Libya	4.54
54	Vietnam	4.53
55	Syria	4.50
56	Saudi Arabia	4.47
57	Armenia	4.45
58	Benin	4.43
59	Brazil	4.42
60	New Zealand	4.42
61	Madagascar	4.40
62	Barbados	4.40
63	Macedonia, FYR	4.38
64	Bulgaria	4.36
65	Trinidad and Tobago	4.36
66	Qatar	4.33
67	Estonia	4.33
68	Senegal	4.30
69	Ukraine	4.30
70	Malta	4.29
71	Uruguay	4.28
72	Bangladesh	4.26
73	Poland	4.25
74	Mali	4.20
75	Argentina	4.19
76	Nigeria	4.17
77	China	4.16
78	Venezuela	4.16
79	United Arab Emirates	4.07
80	Cameroon	4.07
81	Luxembourg	4.06
82	Colombia	4.06
83	Uganda	4.05
84	Oman	4.05
85	Pakistan	4.04
86	Tanzania	4.00
87	Zambia	3.98
88	Jamaica	3.97
89	Peru	3.89
90	Georgia	3.86
91	Slovenia	3.85
92	Philippines	3.85
93	Mexico	3.82
94	Panama	3.80
95	Kazakhstan	3.77
96	Guatemala	3.74
97	Mauritania	3.73
98	Bahrain	3.69
99	Nepal	3.69
100	Moldova	3.63
101	South Africa	3.62
102	Latvia	3.61
103	Mauritius	3.48
104	Honduras	3.47
105	Bosnia and Herzegovina	3.44
106	Zimbabwe	3.43
107	Burkina Faso	3.41
108	Albania	3.37
109	Suriname	3.37
110	Ecuador	3.36
111	Tajikistan	3.36
112	Nicaragua	3.35
113	Botswana	3.33
114	Kyrgyz Republic	3.33
115	Dominican Republic	3.32
116	El Salvador	3.29
117	Burundi	3.15
118	Ethiopia	3.09
119	Mozambique	3.08
120	Gambia, The	3.02
121	Bolivia	3.00
122	Lesotho	2.95
123	Chad	2.95
124	Guyana	2.88
125	Cambodia	2.82
126	Paraguay	2.74
127	Namibia	2.69

SOURCE: World Economic Forum, Executive Opinion Survey 2006, 2007

3.05 Quality of scientific research institutions

Scientific research institutions in your country (e.g., university laboratories, government laboratories) are (1 = nonexistent, 7 = the best in their fields internationally)

RANK	COUNTRY/ECONOMY	SCORE
1	Switzerland	6.22
2	United States	6.13
3	Israel	6.04
4	United Kingdom	5.92
5	Germany	5.82
6	Finland	5.71
7	Belgium	5.69
8	Canada	5.67
9	Sweden	5.64
10	Netherlands	5.57
11	Korea, Rep.	5.56
12	Japan	5.56
13	Singapore	5.54
14	Denmark	5.52
15	Australia	5.52
16	Ireland	5.39
17	Malaysia	5.31
18	New Zealand	5.21
19	France	5.18
20	Austria	5.18
21	Norway	5.08
22	India	5.06
23	Taiwan, China	4.97
24	Hungary	4.90
25	Hong Kong SAR	4.80
26	Estonia	4.80
27	South Africa	4.70
28	Indonesia	4.70
29	Iceland	4.65
30	Czech Republic	4.63
31	Kenya	4.57
32	Portugal	4.49
33	Slovenia	4.45
34	Costa Rica	4.43
35	Puerto Rico	4.41
36	Tunisia	4.41
37	Uganda	4.29
38	Oman	4.29
39	Jamaica	4.28
40	Sri Lanka	4.26
41	Brazil	4.26
42	Lithuania	4.24
43	Russian Federation	4.24
44	Thailand	4.22
45	Qatar	4.14
46	Kuwait	4.12
47	Tanzania	4.12
48	Spain	4.10
49	Turkey	4.04
50	Chile	4.03
51	Barbados	4.01
52	Saudi Arabia	4.01
53	Croatia	4.01
54	Luxembourg	4.01
55	China	3.98
56	Azerbaijan	3.97
57	Nigeria	3.95
58	Ukraine	3.94
59	Jordan	3.92
60	Senegal	3.90
61	Kazakhstan	3.87
62	Poland	3.82
63	Mexico	3.81
64	Botswana	3.77
65	Trinidad and Tobago	3.77
66	United Arab Emirates	3.75
67	Mauritius	3.74
68	Latvia	3.70
69	Slovak Republic	3.68
70	Romania	3.68
71	Pakistan	3.68
72	Bulgaria	3.68
73	Burkina Faso	3.63
74	Greece	3.61
75	Cyprus	3.60
76	Tajikistan	3.58
77	Malta	3.58
78	Ethiopia	3.58
79	Morocco	3.58
80	Zimbabwe	3.55
81	Armenia	3.54
82	Uruguay	3.51
83	Philippines	3.48
84	Mali	3.48
85	Argentina	3.48
86	Colombia	3.48
87	Macedonia, FYR	3.44
88	Gambia, The	3.44
89	Syria	3.40
90	Egypt	3.40
91	Algeria	3.39
92	Vietnam	3.37
93	Panama	3.36
94	Italy	3.36
95	Mongolia	3.33
96	Zambia	3.32
97	Bangladesh	3.27
98	Suriname	3.27
99	Libya	3.26
100	Guatemala	3.22
101	Nepal	3.20
102	Benin	3.19
103	Madagascar	3.18
104	Venezuela	3.17
105	Georgia	3.13
106	Mozambique	3.09
107	Guyana	3.07
108	Moldova	3.06
109	Namibia	3.01
110	Kyrgyz Republic	2.99
111	Peru	2.99
112	Cameroon	2.90
113	Bahrain	2.89
114	Bosnia and Herzegovina	2.89
115	Cambodia	2.85
116	Ecuador	2.83
117	Honduras	2.80
118	El Salvador	2.77
119	Dominican Republic	2.76
120	Lesotho	2.69
121	Burundi	2.58
122	Nicaragua	2.57
123	Bolivia	2.55
124	Chad	2.51
125	Mauritania	2.15
126	Albania	2.15
127	Paraguay	2.08

MEAN: 3.96

SOURCE: World Economic Forum, Executive Opinion Survey 2006, 2007

3.06 Tertiary enrollment (hard data)

Gross tertiary enrollment | 2005 or most recent year available

RANK	COUNTRY/ECONOMY	HARD DATA
1	Finland	91.69
2	Korea, Rep.[6]	91.04
3	Greece	89.10
4	United States	82.72
5	Taiwan, China	82.02
6	New Zealand	81.93
7	Sweden	81.66
8	Slovenia	81.19
9	Denmark	80.46
10	Norway	79.66
11	Lithuania	76.04
12	Latvia	74.36
13	Australia	71.83
14	Iceland	71.20
15	Russian Federation	71.04
16	Ukraine	68.96
17	Spain	66.87
18	Estonia	65.74
19	Italy	65.62
20	Hungary	65.22
21	Argentina[5]	65.03
22	Poland	63.41
23	Belgium	63.01
24	Canada[5]	62.34
25	Netherlands	60.71
26	United Kingdom	59.71
27	Ireland	59.31
28	Israel	57.87
29	Portugal	56.47
30	France	56.39
31	Libya[4]	56.24
32	Japan	55.31
33	Kazakhstan	53.00
34	Germany[4]	51.00
35	Austria	50.27
36	Czech Republic	47.99
37	Chile	47.83
38	Switzerland	47.42
39	Singapore[5]	47.00
40	Georgia	46.13
41	Romania	44.79
42	Panama	43.89
43	Bulgaria	43.64
44	Mongolia	43.20
45	Thailand[6]	42.74
46	Croatia[5]	41.80
47	Kyrgyz Republic	41.45
48	Puerto Rico[3]	41.42
49	Venezuela[5]	41.15
50	Slovak Republic	40.63
51	Bolivia[5]	40.62
52	Uruguay[5]	40.51
53	Jordan	39.19
54	Barbados[2]	37.75
55	Bahrain	35.51
56	Moldova	33.94
57	Egypt	33.91
58	Peru	33.45
59	Cyprus	33.22
60	Dominican Republic[5]	32.89
61	Malaysia[5]	32.01
62	Malta	31.82
63	Hong Kong SAR	31.39
64	Turkey	31.19
65	Tunisia	30.18
66	Macedonia, FYR	29.70
67	Colombia	29.27
68	Saudi Arabia	28.41
69	Philippines	28.08
70	Armenia	28.03
71	Costa Rica	25.34
72	Paraguay[5]	24.45
73	Mexico	23.99
74	Brazil[5]	23.78
75	United Arab Emirates[4]	22.49
76	Algeria	20.34
77	China	20.31
78	Kuwait	19.53
79	Albania[5]	19.28
80	El Salvador	19.01
81	Jamaica[4]	18.99
82	Qatar	18.56
83	Oman	18.36
84	Nicaragua[4]	17.87
85	Tajikistan	17.26
86	Indonesia	17.06
87	Mauritius	16.86
88	Honduras[5]	16.42
89	Vietnam	15.97
90	South Africa	15.30
91	Azerbaijan	14.92
92	Suriname[3]	12.44
93	Luxembourg[5]	12.39
94	Trinidad and Tobago	12.14
95	India	11.41
96	Morocco	11.27
97	Sri Lanka[3]	11.00
98	Nigeria[5]	10.18
99	Guyana	9.86
100	Guatemala[4]	9.58
101	Bangladesh	6.49
102	Namibia[5]	6.11
103	Cameroon	6.10
104	Nepal[5]	5.64
105	Senegal	5.40
106	Botswana	5.08
107	Pakistan	4.65
108	Zimbabwe[4]	3.67
109	Uganda[5]	3.44
110	Lesotho	3.43
111	Cambodia	3.35
112	Mauritania	3.18
113	Benin[2]	3.05
114	Kenya[5]	2.76
115	Ethiopia	2.68
116	Madagascar	2.61
117	Mali	2.56
118	Burkina Faso	2.38
119	Burundi	2.33
120	Zambia[1]	2.33
121	Mozambique	1.47
122	Tanzania	1.39
123	Chad	1.21
124	Gambia, The[5]	1.20
n/a	Bosnia and Herzegovina	n/a
n/a	Ecuador	n/a
n/a	Syria	n/a

SOURCE: UNESCO Institute for Statistics (June 2007); national sources

[1] 2000 [2] 2001 [3] 2002 [4] 2003 [5] 2004 [6] 2006

3.07 Education expenditure (hard data)

Education expenditure as a percentage of GNI | 2005

RANK	COUNTRY/ECONOMY	HARD DATA
1	Denmark	8.09
2	Sweden	8.04
3	Iceland	7.62
4	Israel	7.31
5	Namibia	7.28
6	New Zealand	7.23
7	Saudi Arabia	7.19
8	Norway	7.03
9	Barbados	6.99
10	Kuwait	6.87
11	Zimbabwe	6.87
12	Lesotho	6.69
13	Kenya	6.57
14	Bolivia	6.32
15	Finland	6.04
16	Morocco	6.03
17	Tunisia	5.91
18	Hungary	5.82
19	Malaysia	5.77
20	Lithuania	5.72
21	Portugal	5.66
22	Cyprus	5.63
23	Poland	5.62
24	Jordan	5.61
25	Botswana	5.61
26	Latvia	5.57
27	Austria	5.57
28	Mongolia	5.38
29	Slovenia	5.35
30	United Kingdom	5.33
31	South Africa	5.29
32	Mexico	5.25
33	Canada	5.23
34	France	5.16
35	Estonia	5.14
36	Jamaica	5.05
37	Switzerland	5.03
38	Netherlands	4.91
39	Macedonia, FYR	4.90
40	Colombia	4.90
41	Guyana	4.81
42	United States	4.79
43	Ireland	4.78
44	Australia	4.76
45	Thailand	4.75
46	Italy	4.61
47	Algeria	4.47
48	Panama	4.42
49	Kazakhstan	4.41
50	Egypt	4.41
51	Ukraine	4.41
52	Malta	4.40
53	Kyrgyz Republic	4.39
54	Bahrain	4.36
55	Venezuela	4.35
56	Germany	4.31
57	Oman	4.20
58	Paraguay	4.20
59	Czech Republic	4.16
60	Moldova	4.16
61	Croatia	4.15
62	Spain	4.12
63	Brazil	4.09
64	Argentina	4.09
65	Slovak Republic	4.08
66	Costa Rica	4.04
67	Trinidad and Tobago	4.01
68	India	3.99
69	Uganda	3.98
70	Mauritius	3.93
71	Burundi	3.92
72	Chile	3.92
73	Hong Kong SAR	3.75
74	Senegal	3.73
75	Korea, Rep.	3.73
76	Luxembourg	3.72
77	Honduras	3.55
78	Russian Federation	3.54
79	Azerbaijan	3.50
80	Turkey	3.49
81	Bulgaria	3.48
82	Romania	3.24
83	Mauritania	3.23
84	Cameroon	3.20
85	Japan	3.12
86	Greece	3.11
87	Armenia	3.05
88	Belgium	3.04
89	Ethiopia	2.96
90	Zambia	2.91
91	Nicaragua	2.91
92	Georgia	2.90
93	Peru	2.88
94	Albania	2.84
95	Philippines	2.82
96	Vietnam	2.81
97	El Salvador	2.78
98	Mali	2.72
99	Singapore	2.70
100	Uruguay	2.65
101	Tajikistan	2.65
102	Nepal	2.61
103	Syria	2.60
104	Sri Lanka	2.55
105	Madagascar	2.53
106	Tanzania	2.39
107	Burkina Faso	2.38
108	Benin	2.36
109	Gambia, The	2.04
110	China	1.97
111	Cambodia	1.83
112	Mozambique	1.80
113	Bangladesh	1.70
114	Pakistan	1.63
115	Guatemala	1.57
116	Chad	1.44
117	Ecuador	1.38
118	Dominican Republic	1.20
119	Indonesia	0.86
120	Nigeria	0.85
n/a	Bosnia and Herzegovina	n/a
n/a	Libya	n/a
n/a	Puerto Rico	n/a
n/a	Qatar	n/a
n/a	Suriname	n/a
n/a	Taiwan, China	n/a
n/a	United Arab Emirates	n/a

SOURCE: The World Bank, *World Development Indicators 2007*

Subindex B **Readiness component**

4th pillar
Individual readiness

4.01 Quality of math and science education

Math and science education in your country's schools (1 = lag far behind most other countries' schools, 7 = are among the best in the world)

RANK	COUNTRY/ECONOMY	SCORE
1	Singapore	6.34
2	Belgium	6.29
3	Finland	6.17
4	Hong Kong SAR	5.85
5	Switzerland	5.72
6	France	5.71
7	Tunisia	5.62
8	Taiwan, China	5.59
9	Czech Republic	5.53
10	Korea, Rep.	5.46
11	India	5.38
12	Romania	5.37
13	Malaysia	5.36
14	Netherlands	5.27
15	Canada	5.21
16	Barbados	5.19
17	Lithuania	5.19
18	Cyprus	5.18
19	Denmark	5.17
20	Ireland	5.16
21	Estonia	5.14
22	Hungary	5.12
23	Australia	5.11
24	Qatar	5.07
25	Austria	5.06
26	Slovak Republic	5.05
27	Croatia	5.05
28	Japan	5.03
29	New Zealand	4.97
30	Israel	4.94
31	Indonesia	4.94
32	Sweden	4.81
33	Iceland	4.80
34	Malta	4.79
35	Germany	4.79
36	Slovenia	4.78
37	Russian Federation	4.72
38	Luxembourg	4.68
39	Thailand	4.63
40	Morocco	4.62
41	Latvia	4.61
42	Ukraine	4.59
43	United States	4.54
44	United Kingdom	4.54
45	Jordan	4.53
46	Poland	4.52
47	United Arab Emirates	4.52
48	Bulgaria	4.51
49	Macedonia, FYR	4.49
50	Greece	4.47
51	Norway	4.44
52	Bosnia and Herzegovina	4.44
53	Sri Lanka	4.43
54	Trinidad and Tobago	4.41
55	China	4.38
56	Benin	4.28
57	Italy	4.27
58	Turkey	4.26
59	Moldova	4.25
60	Mauritius	4.20
61	Mongolia	4.17
62	Armenia	3.98
63	Oman	3.95
64	Saudi Arabia	3.94
65	Costa Rica	3.93
66	Spain	3.93
67	Kazakhstan	3.92
68	Syria	3.91
69	Kenya	3.90
70	Zimbabwe	3.90
71	Albania	3.90
72	Kyrgyz Republic	3.87
73	Kuwait	3.85
74	Georgia	3.85
75	Senegal	3.85
76	Vietnam	3.83
77	Bahrain	3.78
78	Colombia	3.78
79	Botswana	3.78
80	Madagascar	3.74
81	Azerbaijan	3.69
82	Algeria	3.67
83	Uruguay	3.63
84	Cameroon	3.61
85	Suriname	3.59
86	Burkina Faso	3.56
87	Puerto Rico	3.51
88	Burundi	3.44
89	Portugal	3.43
90	Guyana	3.39
91	Zambia	3.38
92	Argentina	3.32
93	Nepal	3.26
94	Gambia, The	3.25
95	Libya	3.23
96	Ethiopia	3.22
97	Nigeria	3.17
98	Pakistan	3.12
99	El Salvador	3.10
100	Mali	3.09
101	Uganda	3.08
102	Jamaica	3.08
103	Egypt	3.06
104	Chile	3.04
105	Mauritania	3.04
106	Philippines	2.95
107	Tanzania	2.93
108	Panama	2.92
109	Venezuela	2.92
110	Mexico	2.81
111	Mozambique	2.81
112	Honduras	2.78
113	Bangladesh	2.77
114	Brazil	2.76
115	Cambodia	2.73
116	Ecuador	2.72
117	Lesotho	2.71
118	Guatemala	2.70
119	Tajikistan	2.68
120	Nicaragua	2.61
121	Chad	2.56
122	Bolivia	2.55
123	Namibia	2.52
124	Dominican Republic	2.43
125	South Africa	2.35
126	Paraguay	2.31
127	Peru	2.06

MEAN: 4.07

SOURCE: World Economic Forum, Executive Opinion Survey 2006, 2007

4.02 Quality of the educational system

The educational system in your country (1 = does not meet the needs of a competitive economy, 7 = meets the needs of a competitive economy)

RANK	COUNTRY/ECONOMY	SCORE
1	Singapore	6.04
2	Finland	6.01
3	Switzerland	5.83
4	Denmark	5.79
5	Belgium	5.74
6	Iceland	5.71
7	Ireland	5.62
8	Australia	5.34
9	Hong Kong SAR	5.33
10	Norway	5.29
11	Canada	5.28
12	Tunisia	5.25
13	Netherlands	5.21
14	Austria	5.20
15	Malaysia	5.19
16	Sweden	5.17
17	United States	5.09
18	Taiwan, China	5.06
19	Korea, Rep.	4.98
20	Barbados	4.96
21	New Zealand	4.91
22	Germany	4.88
23	Cyprus	4.87
24	Qatar	4.87
25	Israel	4.84
26	Malta	4.80
27	France	4.78
28	Japan	4.69
29	Indonesia	4.61
30	United Kingdom	4.59
31	India	4.49
32	Czech Republic	4.44
33	Kenya	4.42
34	Estonia	4.31
35	Costa Rica	4.30
36	Jordan	4.28
37	Luxembourg	4.23
38	United Arab Emirates	4.22
39	Zimbabwe	4.22
40	Thailand	4.14
41	Latvia	4.14
42	Slovenia	4.14
43	Lithuania	4.07
44	Russian Federation	4.01
45	Ukraine	3.97
46	Trinidad and Tobago	3.97
47	Poland	3.97
48	Oman	3.92
49	Gambia, The	3.91
50	Spain	3.81
51	Mauritius	3.80
52	Philippines	3.79
53	Sri Lanka	3.79
54	Botswana	3.78
55	Macedonia, FYR	3.75
56	Romania	3.74
57	Colombia	3.72
58	Puerto Rico	3.68
59	Croatia	3.68
60	Zambia	3.68
61	Slovak Republic	3.67
62	Kazakhstan	3.66
63	Hungary	3.60
64	Bahrain	3.57
65	Portugal	3.54
66	Uruguay	3.52
67	Turkey	3.51
68	Nigeria	3.47
69	Kyrgyz Republic	3.45
70	China	3.43
71	Uganda	3.43
72	Moldova	3.40
73	Bulgaria	3.38
74	Italy	3.37
75	Chile	3.36
76	Saudi Arabia	3.36
77	Kuwait	3.33
78	Senegal	3.33
79	Guyana	3.30
80	Greece	3.28
81	Cameroon	3.24
82	Bosnia and Herzegovina	3.23
83	Tanzania	3.22
84	El Salvador	3.19
85	Pakistan	3.17
86	Albania	3.16
87	Morocco	3.08
88	Jamaica	3.05
89	Mexico	3.04
90	Georgia	3.02
91	Armenia	3.01
92	Cambodia	3.01
93	Benin	3.01
94	Ethiopia	2.96
95	Azerbaijan	2.94
96	Nepal	2.93
97	Lesotho	2.90
98	Madagascar	2.90
99	Syria	2.89
100	Algeria	2.87
101	South Africa	2.84
102	Argentina	2.83
103	Panama	2.80
104	Bangladesh	2.80
105	Mali	2.79
106	Tajikistan	2.70
107	Burundi	2.67
108	Mongolia	2.67
109	Vietnam	2.67
110	Burkina Faso	2.65
111	Guatemala	2.65
112	Mozambique	2.63
113	Venezuela	2.63
114	Honduras	2.61
115	Namibia	2.58
116	Egypt	2.51
117	Brazil	2.50
118	Suriname	2.49
119	Ecuador	2.41
120	Nicaragua	2.36
121	Libya	2.31
122	Bolivia	2.30
123	Mauritania	2.28
124	Dominican Republic	2.25
125	Chad	2.16
126	Peru	2.09
127	Paraguay	2.06

MEAN: 3.73

SOURCE: World Economic Forum, Executive Opinion Survey 2006, 2007

4.03 Internet access in schools

Internet access in schools is (1 = very limited; 7 = extensive – most children have frequent access)

RANK	COUNTRY/ECONOMY	SCORE
1	Iceland	6.50
2	Finland	6.35
3	Sweden	6.34
4	Korea, Rep.	6.31
5	Denmark	6.21
6	Estonia	6.19
7	Hong Kong SAR	6.12
8	Austria	6.09
9	Singapore	6.07
10	Switzerland	6.01
11	Netherlands	5.98
12	United States	5.84
13	Canada	5.83
14	United Kingdom	5.78
15	Australia	5.69
16	Taiwan, China	5.69
17	Israel	5.62
18	Malta	5.51
19	Luxembourg	5.51
20	Slovenia	5.47
21	Norway	5.47
22	New Zealand	5.43
23	Czech Republic	5.26
24	Germany	5.22
25	Belgium	5.20
26	Japan	5.15
27	Hungary	5.09
28	France	5.05
29	Portugal	5.02
30	United Arab Emirates	5.00
31	Malaysia	4.96
32	Lithuania	4.88
33	Tunisia	4.85
34	Latvia	4.82
35	Qatar	4.76
36	Slovak Republic	4.69
37	Thailand	4.60
38	Ireland	4.57
39	Chile	4.53
40	Bahrain	4.40
41	Spain	4.39
42	Croatia	4.25
43	Cyprus	4.25
44	Barbados	4.24
45	Kuwait	4.24
46	China	4.03
47	Jordan	3.91
48	Poland	3.87
49	Romania	3.82
50	Kazakhstan	3.81
51	Oman	3.80
52	Turkey	3.73
53	Bulgaria	3.71
54	Italy	3.69
55	Russian Federation	3.68
56	India	3.68
57	Puerto Rico	3.57
58	Philippines	3.51
59	Saudi Arabia	3.50
60	Morocco	3.49
61	Greece	3.47
62	Mexico	3.46
63	Jamaica	3.45
64	Indonesia	3.44
65	Mauritius	3.44
66	Panama	3.43
67	Vietnam	3.42
68	Pakistan	3.40
69	Brazil	3.31
70	Uruguay	3.30
71	Trinidad and Tobago	3.26
72	Georgia	3.24
73	Costa Rica	3.19
74	Peru	3.17
75	Colombia	3.16
76	Sri Lanka	3.16
77	Ukraine	3.16
78	El Salvador	3.12
79	Azerbaijan	3.12
80	Kyrgyz Republic	3.11
81	Egypt	3.07
82	Venezuela	3.07
83	Argentina	3.01
84	South Africa	3.01
85	Dominican Republic	3.00
86	Bosnia and Herzegovina	2.99
87	Moldova	2.94
88	Senegal	2.90
89	Tajikistan	2.81
90	Botswana	2.79
91	Namibia	2.74
92	Guatemala	2.69
93	Algeria	2.67
94	Mali	2.65
95	Gambia, The	2.64
96	Honduras	2.60
97	Mongolia	2.60
98	Macedonia, FYR	2.58
99	Nepal	2.54
100	Nigeria	2.50
101	Cambodia	2.41
102	Ecuador	2.38
103	Tanzania	2.33
104	Armenia	2.30
105	Nicaragua	2.28
106	Benin	2.24
107	Guyana	2.19
108	Zimbabwe	2.18
109	Uganda	2.12
110	Kenya	2.07
111	Mozambique	2.07
112	Ethiopia	2.05
113	Madagascar	2.02
114	Bolivia	2.00
115	Suriname	1.99
116	Mauritania	1.93
117	Albania	1.88
118	Syria	1.84
119	Cameroon	1.83
120	Zambia	1.81
121	Bangladesh	1.77
122	Burkina Faso	1.75
123	Libya	1.69
124	Paraguay	1.68
125	Lesotho	1.56
126	Burundi	1.34
127	Chad	1.29

MEAN: 3.70

SOURCE: World Economic Forum, Executive Opinion Survey 2006, 2007

4.04 Buyer sophistication

Buyers in your country make purchasing decisions (1 = based solely on the lowest price, 7 = based on a sophisticated analysis of performance attributes)

RANK	COUNTRY/ECONOMY	SCORE
1	Switzerland	5.72
2	Korea, Rep.	5.67
3	Japan	5.64
4	Hong Kong SAR	5.63
5	Sweden	5.53
6	Austria	5.44
7	Belgium	5.38
8	Finland	5.38
9	Indonesia	5.37
10	Ireland	5.36
11	Netherlands	5.34
12	United States	5.32
13	Denmark	5.32
14	Luxembourg	5.31
15	Germany	5.31
16	Taiwan, China	5.29
17	Canada	5.28
18	United Kingdom	5.28
19	Singapore	5.27
20	Australia	5.27
21	France	5.25
22	Norway	5.20
23	New Zealand	5.12
24	Malaysia	5.04
25	Iceland	4.93
26	Israel	4.93
27	Slovenia	4.81
28	Tunisia	4.73
29	Chile	4.73
30	Spain	4.71
31	India	4.67
32	Italy	4.56
33	South Africa	4.55
34	Puerto Rico	4.54
35	Costa Rica	4.50
36	Bahrain	4.48
37	United Arab Emirates	4.46
38	Cyprus	4.46
39	China	4.34
40	Barbados	4.32
41	Thailand	4.28
42	Panama	4.26
43	Sri Lanka	4.25
44	Qatar	4.25
45	Portugal	4.16
46	Czech Republic	4.16
47	Estonia	4.14
48	Kuwait	4.13
49	Oman	4.13
50	Kazakhstan	4.12
51	Greece	4.12
52	Philippines	4.11
53	Malta	4.09
54	Mexico	4.04
55	Vietnam	4.01
56	Jamaica	4.00
57	Lithuania	3.99
58	Russian Federation	3.95
59	Trinidad and Tobago	3.95
60	Turkey	3.92
61	Argentina	3.91
62	El Salvador	3.91
63	Mauritius	3.86
64	Peru	3.84
65	Brazil	3.83
66	Latvia	3.81
67	Dominican Republic	3.74
68	Namibia	3.70
69	Croatia	3.69
70	Cambodia	3.67
71	Romania	3.66
72	Colombia	3.64
73	Guatemala	3.64
74	Poland	3.63
75	Uruguay	3.61
76	Slovak Republic	3.56
77	Algeria	3.52
78	Venezuela	3.52
79	Azerbaijan	3.52
80	Ukraine	3.48
81	Botswana	3.48
82	Morocco	3.45
83	Saudi Arabia	3.44
84	Nigeria	3.43
85	Kenya	3.40
86	Tanzania	3.38
87	Georgia	3.31
88	Bulgaria	3.29
89	Hungary	3.25
90	Jordan	3.24
91	Pakistan	3.22
92	Armenia	3.18
93	Honduras	3.18
94	Bangladesh	3.18
95	Mongolia	3.14
96	Zimbabwe	3.08
97	Gambia, The	3.05
98	Albania	2.97
99	Nicaragua	2.92
100	Ecuador	2.92
101	Bosnia and Herzegovina	2.88
102	Macedonia, FYR	2.86
103	Benin	2.86
104	Kyrgyz Republic	2.84
105	Guyana	2.84
106	Tajikistan	2.83
107	Suriname	2.79
108	Libya	2.77
109	Uganda	2.76
110	Nepal	2.75
111	Paraguay	2.74
112	Moldova	2.73
113	Syria	2.65
114	Mauritania	2.65
115	Lesotho	2.65
116	Mali	2.61
117	Senegal	2.58
118	Egypt	2.56
119	Cameroon	2.55
120	Ethiopia	2.53
121	Burkina Faso	2.53
122	Bolivia	2.47
123	Mozambique	2.45
124	Madagascar	2.45
125	Zambia	2.37
126	Burundi	2.28
127	Chad	1.96

MEAN: 3.89

SOURCE: World Economic Forum, Executive Opinion Survey 2006, 2007

4.05 Residential telephone connection charge (hard data)

One-time residential telephone connection charge (US$) as a percentage of GDP per capita | 2005 or most recent year available

RANK	COUNTRY/ECONOMY	HARD DATA
1	Hong Kong SAR	0.00
1	Spain[2]	0.00
3	Switzerland	0.07
4	Iceland	0.09
5	Luxembourg	0.09
6	Singapore[2]	0.09
7	United States	0.10
8	Qatar	0.10
9	Trinidad and Tobago[1]	0.11
10	Turkey	0.11
11	New Zealand	0.12
12	Canada	0.13
13	Greece	0.14
14	United Arab Emirates	0.15
15	France	0.20
16	Oman	0.22
17	Germany	0.22
18	Romania	0.22
19	Belgium	0.23
20	Puerto Rico	0.23
21	Guyana	0.23
22	Norway	0.23
23	El Salvador	0.24
24	Bahrain[2]	0.26
25	Malaysia	0.26
26	Israel	0.28
27	Jamaica	0.30
28	Finland[2]	0.31
29	Ireland	0.31
30	Sweden	0.33
31	Denmark	0.33
32	Austria	0.33
33	Cyprus[2]	0.34
34	Korea, Rep.	0.36
35	Barbados	0.43
36	Slovak Republic	0.44
37	Kuwait	0.44
38	Libya[2]	0.45
39	Malta	0.46
40	Australia	0.46
41	Chile	0.49
42	Tunisia[2]	0.50
43	Brazil	0.50
44	Venezuela	0.52
45	Slovenia	0.53
46	Peru[2]	0.54
47	United Kingdom[2]	0.58
48	Botswana[2]	0.58
49	Saudi Arabia	0.59
50	Taiwan, China	0.60
51	Italy	0.61
52	Portugal	0.62
53	Estonia	0.63
54	Mauritius	0.69
55	South Africa	0.77
56	Panama[2]	0.77
57	Dominican Republic[2]	0.82
58	Costa Rica	0.84
59	Macedonia, FYR[2]	0.86
60	Uruguay	0.86
61	Latvia	0.89
62	Japan	0.94
63	Croatia	0.96
64	Tajikistan	1.06
65	Argentina	1.10
66	Poland	1.16
67	Lithuania	1.20
68	Algeria[2]	1.21
69	Bulgaria	1.26
70	Namibia[2]	1.28
71	Czech Republic	1.36
72	Mexico	1.39
73	Ukraine[2]	1.46
74	Pakistan[2]	1.52
75	Hungary	1.55
76	Armenia	1.78
77	Zambia	1.79
78	Colombia	1.94
79	Kazakhstan	1.99
80	Ecuador	2.13
81	Jordan	2.20
82	Honduras	2.27
83	Indonesia	2.32
84	Mauritania	2.86
85	Thailand	3.08
86	Philippines	3.13
87	India	3.19
88	Morocco	3.46
89	Vietnam[2]	3.46
90	Guatemala[2]	3.52
91	Egypt[2]	3.56
92	Bolivia	3.70
93	Bosnia and Herzegovina	3.96
94	Suriname	4.33
95	Russian Federation	4.78
96	Albania[1]	4.92
97	Mozambique[2]	5.00
98	Mongolia	5.07
99	Georgia	5.21
100	Kenya	5.32
101	Azerbaijan	5.41
102	Senegal	5.97
103	Cambodia	6.60
104	Nepal	7.10
105	Cameroon	8.02
106	Madagascar[2]	8.07
107	Burundi	8.65
108	Mali	8.76
109	Lesotho	8.78
110	Paraguay	9.42
111	Nigeria	10.17
112	Tanzania	10.54
113	Burkina Faso	11.05
114	Nicaragua	14.02
115	Kyrgyz Republic	15.20
116	Chad	15.45
117	Moldova	16.19
118	Sri Lanka	16.38
119	Bangladesh[2]	17.46
120	Benin	18.90
121	Ethiopia[2]	19.77
122	Uganda[2]	20.72
n/a	China	n/a
n/a	Gambia, The	n/a
n/a	Netherlands	n/a
n/a	Syria	n/a
n/a	Zimbabwe	n/a

SOURCE: International Telecommunication Union, *World Telecommunication Indicators 2007*; International Monetary Fund, *World Economic Outlook Database* (October 2007 edition); national sources

[1] 2004   [2] 2006

4.06 Residential monthly telephone subscription (hard data)

Residential monthly telephone subscription to the public switched telephone network (US$) as a percentage of monthly GDP per capita | 2005 or most recent year available

RANK	COUNTRY/ECONOMY	HARD DATA
1	United Arab Emirates	0.15
2	Taiwan, China	0.17
3	Libya[1]	0.18
4	Bahrain[1]	0.18
5	Qatar	0.21
6	Singapore[1]	0.22
7	Albania	0.22
8	Luxembourg	0.33
9	Puerto Rico[1]	0.36
10	Korea, Rep.	0.37
11	Kuwait	0.38
12	Suriname	0.43
13	Norway	0.45
14	El Salvador	0.46
15	Finland[1]	0.47
16	Iceland	0.47
17	Switzerland	0.47
18	Australia	0.49
19	Denmark	0.50
20	Sweden	0.51
21	Japan	0.52
22	Hong Kong SAR	0.53
23	Azerbaijan	0.54
24	Canada	0.56
25	Israel	0.58
26	France	0.60
27	Malta	0.60
28	United Kingdom[1]	0.61
29	Austria	0.62
30	Greece	0.70
31	Belgium	0.70
32	Saudi Arabia	0.70
33	Germany	0.71
34	United States	0.71
35	Spain[1]	0.72
36	Algeria[1]	0.73
37	Mauritius	0.74
38	Ireland	0.74
39	Slovenia	0.76
40	Italy	0.77
41	Cyprus[1]	0.77
42	Mongolia	0.77
43	Oman	0.78
44	Tunisia	0.85
45	Estonia	0.90
46	Panama[1]	0.93
47	Tajikistan	0.95
48	Costa Rica	1.01
49	Botswana[1]	1.06
50	Latvia	1.08
51	Thailand	1.10
52	Argentina	1.16
53	New Zealand	1.27
54	Slovak Republic	1.31
55	Portugal	1.31
56	Lithuania	1.33
57	Romania	1.34
58	Czech Republic	1.35
59	Chile	1.36
60	Croatia	1.38
61	Malaysia	1.57
62	Russian Federation	1.59
63	Armenia	1.60
64	Bosnia and Herzegovina	1.62
65	Egypt[1]	1.71
66	Ukraine[1]	1.71
67	Georgia	1.78
68	Venezuela	1.82
69	Barbados	1.83
70	Hungary	1.86
71	Poland	1.89
72	Turkey	2.03
73	Uruguay	2.08
74	China	2.13
75	Honduras	2.22
76	Bulgaria	2.27
77	Mexico	2.31
78	Ecuador	2.56
79	Moldova	2.59
80	Namibia[1]	2.70
81	Jamaica	2.73
82	Guyana	2.78
83	Vietnam[1]	2.80
84	Paraguay	3.01
85	Guatemala[1]	3.03
86	Indonesia	3.08
87	South Africa	3.18
88	Jordan	3.25
89	Macedonia, FYR[1]	3.31
90	Kyrgyz Republic	3.37
91	Brazil	4.01
92	Pakistan[1]	4.24
93	Burundi	4.36
94	India	4.60
95	Dominican Republic[1]	4.87
96	Sri Lanka	4.93
97	Bolivia	5.27
98	Peru[1]	6.10
99	Ethiopia[1]	6.22
100	Bangladesh[1]	6.29
101	Nicaragua	6.40
102	Cameroon	7.21
103	Senegal	7.39
104	Morocco	7.47
105	Colombia	7.55
106	Cambodia	7.92
107	Zambia	8.57
108	Mauritania	8.93
109	Nepal	9.46
110	Nigeria	9.49
111	Benin	11.23
112	Philippines	12.29
113	Chad	12.36
114	Burkina Faso	13.26
115	Tanzania	13.44
116	Kenya	13.88
117	Lesotho	16.71
118	Madagascar[1]	19.54
119	Uganda[1]	20.72
120	Mali[1]	21.21
121	Mozambique[1]	27.66
122	Zimbabwe	34.58
n/a	Gambia, The	n/a
n/a	Kazakhstan	n/a
n/a	Netherlands	n/a
n/a	Syria	n/a
n/a	Trinidad and Tobago	n/a

SOURCE: International Telecommunication Union, *World Telecommunication Indicators 2007*; International Monetary Fund, *World Economic Outlook Database* (October 2007 edition); national sources

[1] 2006

4.07 High-speed monthly broadband subscription

High-speed monthly broadband subscription charge (US$) as a percentage of monthly GDP per capita | 2006

RANK	COUNTRY/ECONOMY	HARD DATA
1	Malta	0.12
2	United States	0.55
3	Netherlands	0.83
4	Switzerland	0.88
5	Japan	1.04
6	Germany	1.06
7	Luxembourg	1.19
8	Norway	1.21
9	France	1.23
10	Canada	1.35
11	Puerto Rico	1.36
12	Italy	1.42
13	United Kingdom	1.56
14	Denmark	1.58
15	Ireland	1.58
16	Belgium	1.61
17	Sweden	1.62
18	Taiwan, China	1.69
19	Australia	1.73
20	New Zealand	1.85
21	Iceland	1.86
22	Qatar	2.09
23	Austria	2.11
24	Spain	2.15
25	Hong Kong SAR	2.24
26	Finland	2.59
27	Korea, Rep.	2.81
28	United Arab Emirates	2.95
29	Singapore	3.07
30	Israel	3.51
31	Slovenia	3.57
32	Estonia	3.85
33	Lithuania	3.93
34	Greece	4.73
35	Cyprus	4.96
36	Portugal	4.99
37	Argentina	5.55
38	Malaysia	5.72
39	Hungary	6.04
40	Czech Republic	6.15
41	Trinidad and Tobago	6.27
42	Romania	7.02
43	Bahrain	7.71
44	Jordan	7.95
45	Croatia	8.27
46	China	8.96
47	Kuwait	9.30
48	Chile	9.72
49	Thailand	10.07
50	Poland	10.49
51	Botswana	11.40
52	Bosnia and Herzegovina	15.47
53	Ukraine	15.47
54	Barbados	17.48
55	Bulgaria	18.51
56	Brazil	20.21
57	Jamaica	21.65
58	Slovak Republic	21.81
59	Dominican Republic	22.59
60	Peru	24.27
61	Georgia	24.28
62	Colombia	25.56
63	South Africa	26.30
64	Panama	27.64
65	India	27.82
66	Venezuela	29.09
67	Ecuador	31.36
68	Uruguay	38.53
69	Indonesia	39.83
70	Latvia	42.69
71	Turkey	43.75
72	Suriname	43.89
73	Mauritius	47.95
74	Morocco	50.08
75	Russian Federation	50.11
76	Oman	56.11
77	Sri Lanka	56.96
78	Tunisia	61.18
79	Mexico	62.68
80	Azerbaijan	67.44
81	Guatemala	74.05
82	Costa Rica	80.64
83	Philippines	86.34
84	Macedonia, FYR	94.93
85	Nicaragua	100.35
86	Egypt	100.46
87	Senegal	160.95
88	Albania	200.82
89	Bolivia	205.91
90	Vietnam	242.46
91	Kyrgyz Republic	265.69
92	Mongolia	294.74
93	Algeria	309.84
94	Moldova	449.06
95	Kenya	885.46
96	Gambia, The	920.35
97	Kazakhstan	965.63
98	Cameroon	1,446.75
99	Pakistan	1,608.59
100	Cambodia	1,633.66
101	Zimbabwe	2,955.74
102	Armenia	3,248.37
103	Benin	3,678.97
104	Burkina Faso	4,090.85
105	Mozambique	5,757.37
106	Bangladesh	5,959.18
107	Mauritania	8,904.40
108	Uganda	21,852.81
109	Ethiopia	31,103.21
n/a	Burundi	n/a
n/a	Chad	n/a
n/a	El Salvador	n/a
n/a	Guyana	n/a
n/a	Honduras	n/a
n/a	Lesotho	n/a
n/a	Libya	n/a
n/a	Madagascar	n/a
n/a	Mali	n/a
n/a	Namibia	n/a
n/a	Nepal	n/a
n/a	Nigeria	n/a
n/a	Paraguay	n/a
n/a	Saudi Arabia	n/a
n/a	Syria	n/a
n/a	Tajikistan	n/a
n/a	Tanzania	n/a
n/a	Zambia	n/a

SOURCE: International Telecommunication Union, *World Information Society Report 2007*; International Monetary Fund, *World Economic Outlook Database*, (October 2007 edition); national sources

4.08 Lowest cost of broadband (hard data)

Lowest sampled cost (US$) per 100 kb/s as a percentage of monthly income (GNI) | 2006

RANK	COUNTRY/ECONOMY	HARD DATA
1	Japan	0.00
1	Netherlands	0.00
3	Finland	0.01
3	France	0.01
3	Italy	0.01
3	Korea, Rep.	0.01
3	Singapore	0.01
3	Sweden	0.01
3	United States	0.01
10	Germany	0.02
10	Taiwan, China	0.02
10	United Kingdom	0.02
13	Iceland	0.03
13	Malta	0.03
13	Switzerland	0.03
16	Belgium	0.04
16	Canada	0.04
16	Hong Kong SAR	0.04
16	Norway	0.04
20	Luxembourg	0.05
21	Portugal	0.07
22	Denmark	0.08
23	Ireland	0.09
23	New Zealand	0.09
25	Slovenia	0.10
26	Austria	0.11
27	Lithuania	0.12
27	Qatar	0.12
29	Australia	0.13
30	Czech Republic	0.16
31	Israel	0.19
32	United Arab Emirates	0.20
33	Poland	0.21
34	Spain	0.23
35	Hungary	0.33
36	Cyprus	0.35
37	Brazil	0.42
38	Slovak Republic	0.43
39	Bosnia and Herzegovina	0.45
40	Croatia	0.48
41	Estonia	0.52
42	Malaysia	0.64
43	Greece	0.65
44	Argentina	0.66
45	Romania	0.67
46	Chile	0.72
47	Jordan	0.78
48	Kuwait	0.91
49	Barbados	1.00
50	China	1.01
51	Mexico	1.03
52	Bulgaria	1.07
53	Thailand	1.12
54	Ukraine	1.13
55	Morocco	1.52
56	Bahrain	1.69
57	Philippines	1.75
58	Venezuela	1.78
59	Botswana	1.94
60	Costa Rica	2.09
61	Uruguay	2.11
62	Macedonia, FYR	2.14
63	Mauritius	2.15
64	Dominican Republic	2.28
65	Jamaica	2.41
66	Turkey	2.51
67	Latvia	2.70
68	South Africa	2.78
69	Oman	2.83
70	Georgia	3.10
71	Sri Lanka	3.27
72	Trinidad and Tobago	3.29
73	El Salvador	3.35
74	Peru	3.48
75	Indonesia	4.98
76	Panama	5.06
77	Colombia	5.40
78	Paraguay	5.49
79	Egypt	5.84
80	Tunisia	5.92
81	India	5.93
82	Albania	6.78
83	Vietnam	6.90
84	Ecuador	7.12
85	Russian Federation	7.57
86	Guyana	8.12
87	Guatemala	9.38
88	Libya	12.46
89	Honduras	13.13
90	Suriname	13.77
91	Senegal	14.52
92	Nicaragua	19.31
93	Kazakhstan	21.57
94	Azerbaijan	24.81
95	Madagascar	34.60
96	Algeria	37.69
97	Bolivia	46.41
98	Moldova	49.40
99	Mongolia	50.78
100	Cameroon	55.91
101	Saudi Arabia	58.30
102	Kyrgyz Republic	63.92
103	Gambia, The	138.16
104	Pakistan	186.06
105	Kenya	194.96
106	Armenia	203.07
107	Cambodia	215.56
108	Benin	219.75
109	Burkina Faso	224.15
110	Zimbabwe	425.96
111	Bangladesh	1,028.74
112	Mozambique	1,400.63
113	Mauritania	1,456.59
114	Nepal	1,661.39
115	Ethiopia	1,683.59
116	Uganda	4,821.43
117	Burundi	7,593.75
n/a	Chad	n/a
n/a	Lesotho	n/a
n/a	Mali	n/a
n/a	Namibia	n/a
n/a	Nigeria	n/a
n/a	Puerto Rico	n/a
n/a	Syria	n/a
n/a	Tajikistan	n/a
n/a	Tanzania	n/a
n/a	Zambia	n/a

SOURCE: International Telecommunication Union, *World Information Society Report 2007*

4.09 Cost of mobile telephone call (hard data)

Cost of 3-minute local call during peak hours (US$) as a percentage of monthly GDP per capita | 2005 or most recent year available

RANK	COUNTRY/ECONOMY	HARD DATA
1	Egypt	0.00
2	Italy	0.00
3	Hong Kong SAR	0.00
4	United Arab Emirates	0.00
5	Luxembourg[2]	0.01
6	Sweden	0.01
7	Norway	0.01
8	Latvia	0.01
9	Denmark	0.01
10	Finland	0.01
11	Qatar	0.01
12	Iceland	0.01
13	El Salvador	0.01
14	Cyprus	0.01
15	Slovenia	0.02
16	Singapore[2]	0.02
17	United Kingdom	0.02
18	Bahrain	0.02
19	Canada	0.02
20	Switzerland[2]	0.02
21	Korea, Rep.	0.02
22	Puerto Rico	0.02
23	Mauritius[2]	0.03
24	Saudi Arabia	0.03
25	Ireland	0.03
26	Portugal	0.03
27	Oman	0.03
28	Israel	0.04
29	Spain	0.04
30	United States	0.04
31	Austria	0.04
32	Netherlands	0.04
33	Estonia	0.04
34	Taiwan, China	0.04
35	Czech Republic	0.04
36	Belgium	0.05
37	Barbados	0.05
38	Libya[2]	0.05
39	Costa Rica	0.05
40	Germany	0.05
41	Lithuania	0.06
42	France	0.06
43	Hungary	0.06
44	Greece	0.06
45	Mexico	0.07
46	Trinidad and Tobago	0.08
47	Australia	0.08
48	Croatia	0.08
49	Algeria[2]	0.09
50	Argentina[2]	0.09
51	Russian Federation	0.10
52	Malaysia	0.10
53	Poland	0.11
54	Indonesia[1]	0.11
55	Jordan	0.11
56	India	0.11
57	Slovak Republic	0.12
58	Panama[2]	0.12
59	New Zealand[1]	0.13
60	Kuwait	0.14
61	Tunisia	0.14
62	Malta	0.14
63	Romania	0.15
64	China	0.15
65	Jamaica	0.16
66	Colombia	0.17
67	Thailand	0.17
68	Syria	0.17
69	Botswana	0.19
70	Dominican Republic	0.20
71	Guatemala[2]	0.21
72	Armenia	0.21
73	Azerbaijan	0.23
74	Suriname	0.24
75	Kazakhstan	0.25
76	Chile	0.29
77	Bulgaria	0.29
78	South Africa	0.30
79	Bosnia and Herzegovina	0.30
80	Venezuela	0.30
81	Sri Lanka	0.33
82	Paraguay	0.33
83	Brazil	0.34
84	Albania	0.34
85	Ukraine	0.38
86	Georgia	0.39
87	Nepal[2]	0.40
88	Peru[2]	0.43
89	Pakistan	0.43
90	Philippines	0.45
91	Namibia	0.47
92	Cambodia	0.49
93	Macedonia, FYR[2]	0.57
94	Kyrgyz Republic	0.60
95	Guyana	0.62
96	Mongolia	0.63
97	Morocco[2]	0.63
98	Ecuador	0.64
99	Tajikistan	0.66
100	Vietnam[2]	0.71
101	Bolivia	0.74
102	Honduras	0.82
103	Bangladesh	0.84
104	Senegal[2]	0.89
105	Lesotho	0.91
106	Mauritania	0.93
107	Mozambique	1.32
108	Kenya	1.33
109	Zambia[1]	1.53
110	Cameroon[2]	1.58
111	Nigeria	1.59
112	Nicaragua	1.73
113	Chad[2]	1.84
114	Benin[2]	1.84
115	Madagascar[2]	1.86
116	Ethiopia	1.92
117	Mali[2]	2.10
118	Burkina Faso	2.16
119	Moldova	2.16
120	Tanzania	2.47
121	Uganda	2.65
122	Burundi[2]	5.87
123	Zimbabwe[2]	23.58
n/a	Gambia, The	n/a
n/a	Japan	n/a
n/a	Turkey	n/a
n/a	Uruguay	n/a

SOURCE: International Telecommunication Union, *World Telecommunication Indicators 2007*; International Monetary Fund, *World Economic Outlook Database* (October 2007 edition)

[1] 2004 [2] 2006

Subindex B **Readiness component**

5th pillar
Business readiness

5.01 Extent of staff training

The general approach of companies in your country to human resources is (1 = to invest little in training and employee development, 7 = to invest heavily to attract, train, and retain employees)

MEAN: 3.93

RANK	COUNTRY/ECONOMY	SCORE
1	Denmark	5.95
2	Switzerland	5.90
3	Sweden	5.80
4	Japan	5.64
5	Korea, Rep.	5.61
6	Austria	5.58
7	Singapore	5.57
8	Netherlands	5.52
9	Germany	5.50
10	Norway	5.43
11	United States	5.42
12	Belgium	5.37
13	Finland	5.32
14	Iceland	5.29
15	Ireland	5.18
16	Malaysia	5.18
17	United Kingdom	5.16
18	Luxembourg	5.15
19	Taiwan, China	5.14
20	Australia	5.05
21	South Africa	5.02
22	New Zealand	4.97
23	Israel	4.97
24	France	4.95
25	Canada	4.94
26	Puerto Rico	4.81
27	Costa Rica	4.76
28	Hong Kong SAR	4.74
29	Mauritius	4.68
30	Estonia	4.66
31	Philippines	4.57
32	Tunisia	4.56
33	India	4.56
34	Indonesia	4.52
35	Czech Republic	4.52
36	Thailand	4.44
37	Slovenia	4.44
38	Oman	4.44
39	United Arab Emirates	4.37
40	Chile	4.33
41	Lithuania	4.33
42	Barbados	4.23
43	Malta	4.23
44	Slovak Republic	4.21
45	Brazil	4.19
46	Qatar	4.18
47	Turkey	4.04
48	Kuwait	4.01
49	Latvia	3.99
50	Spain	3.97
51	Sri Lanka	3.94
52	Trinidad and Tobago	3.92
53	Portugal	3.90
54	Kenya	3.90
55	Greece	3.89
56	Panama	3.89
57	Jordan	3.89
58	Namibia	3.89
59	Bahrain	3.84
60	Croatia	3.83
61	China	3.81
62	Guatemala	3.78
63	Zimbabwe	3.77
64	Botswana	3.76
65	Mexico	3.76
66	Poland	3.74
67	Jamaica	3.73
68	El Salvador	3.72
69	Colombia	3.69
70	Honduras	3.65
71	Cyprus	3.64
72	Morocco	3.62
73	Hungary	3.61
74	Argentina	3.61
75	Nigeria	3.60
76	Saudi Arabia	3.56
77	Gambia, The	3.56
78	Macedonia, FYR	3.55
79	Italy	3.54
80	Egypt	3.54
81	Uganda	3.54
82	Vietnam	3.53
83	Romania	3.52
84	Azerbaijan	3.50
85	Peru	3.47
86	Venezuela	3.46
87	Georgia	3.40
88	Uruguay	3.38
89	Mozambique	3.37
90	Dominican Republic	3.36
91	Tanzania	3.35
92	Kazakhstan	3.34
93	Mongolia	3.32
94	Guyana	3.31
95	Russian Federation	3.30
96	Ukraine	3.25
97	Cambodia	3.19
98	Albania	3.17
99	Syria	3.17
100	Tajikistan	3.17
101	Moldova	3.16
102	Mauritania	3.13
103	Lesotho	3.13
104	Libya	3.11
105	Madagascar	3.07
106	Bosnia and Herzegovina	3.00
107	Nicaragua	2.98
108	Senegal	2.98
109	Suriname	2.95
110	Algeria	2.92
111	Armenia	2.91
112	Cameroon	2.89
113	Ecuador	2.89
114	Benin	2.85
115	Pakistan	2.85
116	Bulgaria	2.84
117	Burkina Faso	2.80
118	Paraguay	2.79
119	Ethiopia	2.68
120	Bolivia	2.67
121	Kyrgyz Republic	2.64
122	Mali	2.59
123	Bangladesh	2.57
124	Nepal	2.55
125	Zambia	2.51
126	Burundi	2.34
127	Chad	2.22

SOURCE: World Economic Forum, Executive Opinion Survey 2006, 2007

5.02 Local availability of specialized research and training services

In your country, specialized research and training services are (1 = not available, 7 = available from world-class local institutions)

RANK	COUNTRY/ECONOMY	SCORE
1	Switzerland	5.99
2	United States	5.99
3	Germany	5.98
4	Sweden	5.89
5	United Kingdom	5.87
6	Japan	5.82
7	Netherlands	5.81
8	Belgium	5.73
9	Finland	5.71
10	Canada	5.68
11	Denmark	5.65
12	France	5.59
13	Israel	5.51
14	Korea, Rep.	5.33
15	Austria	5.32
16	Australia	5.20
17	Singapore	5.16
18	Norway	5.10
19	Hong Kong SAR	5.08
20	Taiwan, China	5.05
21	Malaysia	4.99
22	Iceland	4.97
23	Ireland	4.96
24	New Zealand	4.85
25	Czech Republic	4.82
26	Tunisia	4.81
27	Estonia	4.80
28	Italy	4.78
29	Indonesia	4.74
30	Puerto Rico	4.72
31	India	4.71
32	Brazil	4.67
33	South Africa	4.64
34	Chile	4.63
35	Slovenia	4.60
36	Costa Rica	4.49
37	Portugal	4.45
38	Croatia	4.39
39	China	4.38
40	Spain	4.38
41	Poland	4.37
42	Kenya	4.35
43	Turkey	4.34
44	Luxembourg	4.29
45	Argentina	4.26
46	Senegal	4.24
47	Slovak Republic	4.21
48	Lithuania	4.19
49	Romania	4.15
50	United Arab Emirates	4.14
51	Kuwait	4.14
52	Mexico	4.13
53	Guatemala	4.10
54	Oman	4.09
55	Qatar	4.07
56	Nigeria	4.05
57	Morocco	4.00
58	Jordan	3.97
59	Jamaica	3.97
60	Hungary	3.97
61	Thailand	3.97
62	Philippines	3.94
63	Uganda	3.94
64	Latvia	3.94
65	Sri Lanka	3.93
66	Saudi Arabia	3.88
67	Panama	3.87
68	Cyprus	3.87
69	Colombia	3.79
70	Honduras	3.78
71	Uruguay	3.77
72	Vietnam	3.77
73	Greece	3.76
74	Bulgaria	3.75
75	Azerbaijan	3.74
76	Peru	3.74
77	Russian Federation	3.73
78	Barbados	3.67
79	Tanzania	3.66
80	Kazakhstan	3.63
81	Egypt	3.62
82	El Salvador	3.61
83	Ukraine	3.57
84	Trinidad and Tobago	3.53
85	Mali	3.51
86	Burkina Faso	3.47
87	Mauritius	3.47
88	Mongolia	3.46
89	Bahrain	3.43
90	Benin	3.40
91	Malta	3.36
92	Pakistan	3.34
93	Macedonia, FYR	3.33
94	Dominican Republic	3.33
95	Bosnia and Herzegovina	3.31
96	Syria	3.28
97	Nicaragua	3.28
98	Ecuador	3.26
99	Venezuela	3.24
100	Cameroon	3.24
101	Moldova	3.16
102	Algeria	3.15
103	Botswana	3.14
104	Cambodia	3.13
105	Madagascar	3.09
106	Gambia, The	3.02
107	Bolivia	2.95
108	Armenia	2.92
109	Ethiopia	2.88
110	Chad	2.87
111	Libya	2.86
112	Mozambique	2.85
113	Georgia	2.85
114	Paraguay	2.83
115	Kyrgyz Republic	2.82
116	Zambia	2.82
117	Zimbabwe	2.79
118	Tajikistan	2.62
119	Suriname	2.59
120	Nepal	2.59
121	Guyana	2.54
122	Lesotho	2.53
123	Albania	2.50
124	Mauritania	2.50
125	Bangladesh	2.43
126	Namibia	2.36
127	Burundi	2.23

MEAN: 4.00

SOURCE: World Economic Forum, Executive Opinion Survey 2006, 2007

5.03 Quality of management schools

Management or business schools in your country are (1 = limited or of poor quality, 7 = among the best in the world)

RANK	COUNTRY/ECONOMY	SCORE
1	France	6.01
2	Belgium	5.97
3	Switzerland	5.97
4	Canada	5.91
5	Spain	5.76
6	United States	5.75
7	Singapore	5.71
8	India	5.67
9	Denmark	5.63
10	United Kingdom	5.59
11	Netherlands	5.59
12	Finland	5.53
13	Sweden	5.47
14	Ireland	5.47
15	Israel	5.46
16	Australia	5.42
17	Hong Kong SAR	5.39
18	Tunisia	5.37
19	Chile	5.29
20	Iceland	5.26
21	Norway	5.26
22	South Africa	5.24
23	Malaysia	5.22
24	Austria	5.17
25	Germany	5.11
26	Korea, Rep.	5.09
27	Costa Rica	5.08
28	New Zealand	5.02
29	Taiwan, China	4.96
30	Argentina	4.94
31	Estonia	4.92
32	Indonesia	4.86
33	Thailand	4.80
34	Portugal	4.75
35	Philippines	4.74
36	Morocco	4.74
37	Qatar	4.73
38	Czech Republic	4.67
39	Puerto Rico	4.66
40	Senegal	4.64
41	Malta	4.63
42	Barbados	4.57
43	Trinidad and Tobago	4.57
44	Slovenia	4.56
45	Latvia	4.56
46	Colombia	4.51
47	Peru	4.45
48	Lithuania	4.44
49	Mexico	4.42
50	Poland	4.41
51	Uruguay	4.37
52	Italy	4.37
53	Cyprus	4.36
54	Turkey	4.34
55	Benin	4.33
56	Sri Lanka	4.31
57	Hungary	4.31
58	United Arab Emirates	4.30
59	Jamaica	4.28
60	Guatemala	4.27
61	Oman	4.25
62	Venezuela	4.24
63	El Salvador	4.16
64	Jordan	4.16
65	Brazil	4.15
66	Slovak Republic	4.15
67	Japan	4.11
68	Kuwait	4.09
69	Kenya	4.06
70	Croatia	4.01
71	Nicaragua	3.90
72	Madagascar	3.85
73	Saudi Arabia	3.82
74	Burkina Faso	3.80
75	Greece	3.79
76	Russian Federation	3.79
77	Pakistan	3.76
78	Romania	3.74
79	Gambia, The	3.72
80	Panama	3.71
81	Bulgaria	3.71
82	Ukraine	3.68
83	Zimbabwe	3.67
84	Bahrain	3.65
85	Nigeria	3.64
86	Mauritius	3.62
87	China	3.62
88	Luxembourg	3.60
89	Dominican Republic	3.59
90	Zambia	3.57
91	Macedonia, FYR	3.56
92	Kazakhstan	3.53
93	Honduras	3.52
94	Mali	3.51
95	Cameroon	3.51
96	Ecuador	3.49
97	Egypt	3.49
98	Syria	3.47
99	Algeria	3.41
100	Uganda	3.40
101	Bosnia and Herzegovina	3.40
102	Botswana	3.39
103	Suriname	3.39
104	Ethiopia	3.33
105	Guyana	3.27
106	Moldova	3.25
107	Bangladesh	3.24
108	Nepal	3.23
109	Tanzania	3.22
110	Bolivia	3.18
111	Georgia	3.12
112	Albania	3.10
113	Cambodia	3.08
114	Kyrgyz Republic	3.07
115	Azerbaijan	3.00
116	Paraguay	2.99
117	Vietnam	2.97
118	Armenia	2.93
119	Burundi	2.76
120	Mongolia	2.74
121	Mozambique	2.69
122	Lesotho	2.68
123	Libya	2.67
124	Tajikistan	2.57
125	Namibia	2.50
126	Chad	2.49
127	Mauritania	2.44

MEAN: 4.18

SOURCE: World Economic Forum, Executive Opinion Survey 2006, 2007

5.04 Company spending on R&D

Companies in your country (1 = do not spend money on research and development, 7 = spend heavily on research and development relative to international peers)

RANK	COUNTRY/ECONOMY	SCORE
1	Switzerland	6.12
2	United States	5.81
3	Japan	5.79
4	Germany	5.78
5	Sweden	5.71
6	Korea, Rep.	5.56
7	Israel	5.54
8	Denmark	5.47
9	Finland	5.31
10	Singapore	5.08
11	Malaysia	4.99
12	United Kingdom	4.95
13	Netherlands	4.91
14	Austria	4.86
15	Belgium	4.84
16	Ireland	4.82
17	France	4.78
18	Taiwan, China	4.77
19	Norway	4.62
20	Iceland	4.57
21	Canada	4.52
22	Luxembourg	4.51
23	Hong Kong SAR	4.41
24	Slovenia	4.22
25	Australia	4.21
26	South Africa	4.20
27	Indonesia	4.16
28	India	4.15
29	Czech Republic	3.99
30	Costa Rica	3.97
31	Kenya	3.91
32	China	3.90
33	Oman	3.89
34	Puerto Rico	3.86
35	Brazil	3.84
36	Tunisia	3.82
37	Estonia	3.82
38	New Zealand	3.81
39	Sri Lanka	3.78
40	Qatar	3.61
41	Poland	3.55
42	Thailand	3.55
43	Jamaica	3.51
44	Nigeria	3.50
45	Saudi Arabia	3.46
46	Croatia	3.44
47	Spain	3.42
48	Lithuania	3.42
49	Russian Federation	3.42
50	Azerbaijan	3.41
51	Slovak Republic	3.38
52	Philippines	3.36
53	United Arab Emirates	3.31
54	Portugal	3.30
55	Barbados	3.28
56	Vietnam	3.27
57	Latvia	3.27
58	Malta	3.27
59	Chile	3.26
60	Tanzania	3.25
61	Turkey	3.24
62	Morocco	3.21
63	Guatemala	3.19
64	Kazakhstan	3.18
65	Cambodia	3.18
66	Ukraine	3.16
67	Hungary	3.15
68	Mexico	3.14
69	Egypt	3.10
70	Kuwait	3.09
71	Italy	3.09
72	Pakistan	3.08
73	Peru	3.07
74	Jordan	3.06
75	Colombia	3.05
76	Trinidad and Tobago	3.02
77	Panama	3.02
78	Senegal	3.01
79	Zimbabwe	3.00
80	Cyprus	2.99
81	Mauritius	2.98
82	Venezuela	2.98
83	Greece	2.96
84	Madagascar	2.95
85	Argentina	2.91
86	Uganda	2.90
87	Romania	2.89
88	Namibia	2.86
89	Algeria	2.85
90	Suriname	2.82
91	Botswana	2.80
92	Uruguay	2.78
93	Guyana	2.77
94	Bosnia and Herzegovina	2.77
95	Mongolia	2.77
96	Burkina Faso	2.76
97	Dominican Republic	2.73
98	Honduras	2.72
99	Mali	2.72
100	Bulgaria	2.71
101	Syria	2.71
102	Benin	2.70
103	Tajikistan	2.69
104	Macedonia, FYR	2.69
105	El Salvador	2.66
106	Bahrain	2.64
107	Armenia	2.63
108	Cameroon	2.62
109	Ecuador	2.57
110	Georgia	2.51
111	Gambia, The	2.49
112	Moldova	2.48
113	Nepal	2.46
114	Kyrgyz Republic	2.46
115	Mozambique	2.43
116	Bangladesh	2.43
117	Libya	2.42
118	Nicaragua	2.38
119	Bolivia	2.35
120	Chad	2.23
121	Lesotho	2.23
122	Burundi	2.22
123	Ethiopia	2.21
124	Zambia	2.20
125	Paraguay	2.17
126	Albania	2.13
127	Mauritania	2.03

MEAN: 3.44

SOURCE: World Economic Forum, Executive Opinion Survey 2006, 2007

5.05 University-industry research collaboration

In its R&D activity, business collaboration with local universities is (1 = minimal or nonexistent, 7 = intensive and ongoing)

MEAN: 3.31

RANK	COUNTRY/ECONOMY	SCORE
1	United States	5.64
2	Switzerland	5.58
3	Sweden	5.55
4	Finland	5.48
5	Korea, Rep.	5.37
6	Germany	5.31
7	Singapore	5.28
8	Israel	5.16
9	Taiwan, China	5.10
10	Belgium	5.10
11	Denmark	5.02
12	United Kingdom	5.01
13	Netherlands	4.96
14	Japan	4.88
15	Canada	4.87
16	Malaysia	4.86
17	Norway	4.82
18	Ireland	4.82
19	Austria	4.77
20	Iceland	4.65
21	Hong Kong SAR	4.62
22	Australia	4.38
23	New Zealand	4.36
24	South Africa	4.20
25	China	4.13
26	Puerto Rico	4.10
27	Czech Republic	4.08
28	Thailand	4.07
29	Oman	3.94
30	France	3.87
31	Tunisia	3.87
32	Estonia	3.87
33	Slovenia	3.79
34	Hungary	3.75
35	Costa Rica	3.67
36	Slovak Republic	3.66
37	Croatia	3.64
38	Sri Lanka	3.61
39	Portugal	3.59
40	Luxembourg	3.59
41	Qatar	3.54
42	Chile	3.51
43	India	3.51
44	Spain	3.41
45	Brazil	3.41
46	Kenya	3.40
47	Jamaica	3.36
48	Turkey	3.32
49	Saudi Arabia	3.28
50	Lithuania	3.27
51	Colombia	3.25
52	Uganda	3.21
53	United Arab Emirates	3.21
54	Tanzania	3.21
55	Guatemala	3.20
56	Poland	3.19
57	Mexico	3.19
58	Azerbaijan	3.18
59	Russian Federation	3.17
60	Pakistan	3.17
61	Latvia	3.15
62	Indonesia	3.13
63	Ukraine	3.13
64	Nigeria	3.09
65	Philippines	3.08
66	Barbados	3.08
67	Jordan	3.05
68	Morocco	3.03
69	Kazakhstan	3.01
70	Italy	3.00
71	Kuwait	2.99
72	Trinidad and Tobago	2.96
73	Cyprus	2.95
74	Venezuela	2.90
75	Mauritius	2.90
76	Vietnam	2.90
77	Malta	2.89
78	Argentina	2.88
79	Macedonia, FYR	2.88
80	Greece	2.88
81	Panama	2.85
82	Zimbabwe	2.83
83	Egypt	2.82
84	Senegal	2.82
85	Botswana	2.81
86	Mongolia	2.79
87	Romania	2.75
88	Namibia	2.71
89	Uruguay	2.70
90	Cambodia	2.69
91	Honduras	2.69
92	Bulgaria	2.68
93	Madagascar	2.68
94	Mozambique	2.61
95	Dominican Republic	2.60
96	Suriname	2.60
97	Ecuador	2.60
98	Peru	2.58
99	Burkina Faso	2.56
100	Tajikistan	2.52
101	Armenia	2.49
102	Syria	2.47
103	Zambia	2.46
104	Bosnia and Herzegovina	2.45
105	Benin	2.44
106	Gambia, The	2.39
107	Ethiopia	2.39
108	Mali	2.37
109	Kyrgyz Republic	2.36
110	Algeria	2.34
111	Nicaragua	2.33
112	El Salvador	2.32
113	Moldova	2.31
114	Guyana	2.29
115	Georgia	2.27
116	Cameroon	2.22
117	Bahrain	2.19
118	Nepal	2.18
119	Bolivia	2.10
120	Bangladesh	2.10
121	Libya	2.09
122	Burundi	2.03
123	Lesotho	2.00
124	Mauritania	1.91
125	Paraguay	1.88
126	Chad	1.87
127	Albania	1.69

SOURCE: World Economic Forum, Executive Opinion Survey 2006, 2007

5.06 Business telephone connection charge (hard data)

One-time business telephone connection charge (US$) as a percentage of GDP per capita | 2005 or most recent year available

RANK	COUNTRY/ECONOMY	HARD DATA
1	Hong Kong SAR	0.00
1	Spain[2]	0.00
3	Switzerland	0.07
4	Iceland	0.09
5	Luxembourg	0.09
6	Qatar	0.10
7	Turkey	0.11
8	Singapore[2]	0.11
9	Greece	0.14
10	New Zealand	0.15
11	United Arab Emirates	0.15
12	United States	0.18
13	France	0.20
14	Oman	0.22
15	Germany	0.22
16	Romania	0.22
17	Belgium	0.23
18	Norway	0.23
19	El Salvador	0.24
20	Bahrain[2]	0.26
21	Malaysia	0.26
22	Israel	0.28
23	Finland[2]	0.31
24	Ireland	0.31
25	Denmark	0.33
26	Cyprus[2]	0.34
27	Korea, Rep.	0.36
28	Jamaica	0.43
29	Barbados	0.43
30	Slovak Republic	0.44
31	Australia	0.46
32	Chile	0.49
33	United Kingdom[2]	0.49
34	Tunisia[2]	0.50
35	Brazil	0.50
36	Slovenia	0.53
37	Austria	0.54
38	Peru[2]	0.54
39	Saudi Arabia	0.59
40	Taiwan, China	0.60
41	Italy	0.61
42	Portugal	0.62
43	Estonia	0.63
44	Venezuela	0.69
45	South Africa	0.77
46	Puerto Rico[2]	0.77
47	Panama	0.83
48	Costa Rica	0.84
49	Botswana[2]	0.86
50	Macedonia, FYR[2]	0.86
51	Uruguay	0.86
52	Latvia	0.89
53	Malta	0.91
54	Japan	0.94
55	Kuwait	0.95
56	Croatia	0.96
57	Argentina	1.10
58	Poland	1.16
59	Lithuania	1.20
60	Algeria[2]	1.21
61	Dominican Republic[2]	1.23
62	Bulgaria	1.26
63	Namibia[2]	1.28
64	Czech Republic	1.36
65	Mauritius	1.38
66	Guyana	1.39
67	Mexico	1.39
68	Pakistan[2]	1.52
69	Libya[2]	1.62
70	Colombia	1.94
71	Armenia	2.13
72	Ecuador	2.13
73	Mauritania	2.86
74	Thailand	3.08
75	India	3.19
76	Hungary	3.43
77	Vietnam[2]	3.46
78	Indonesia	3.54
79	Bolivia	3.70
80	Bosnia and Herzegovina	3.96
81	Suriname	4.33
82	Jordan	4.39
83	Tajikistan	4.43
84	Guatemala	4.55
85	Mozambique[2]	5.00
86	Georgia	5.21
87	Kenya	5.32
88	Honduras	5.32
89	Zambia	5.36
90	Philippines	5.49
91	Mongolia	5.53
92	Ukraine[2]	5.83
93	Senegal	5.97
94	Kazakhstan	6.36
95	Morocco	6.92
96	Nepal	7.10
97	Egypt[2]	7.12
98	Russian Federation	7.17
99	Cameroon	8.02
100	Madagascar[2]	8.07
101	Azerbaijan	8.11
102	Mali	8.76
103	Lesotho	8.78
104	Paraguay	9.42
105	Nigeria	10.17
106	Tanzania	10.54
107	Burkina Faso	11.05
108	Cambodia	13.21
109	Chad	15.45
110	Moldova	16.19
111	Sri Lanka	16.38
112	Kyrgyz Republic	17.26
113	Benin	18.90
114	Ethiopia[2]	19.77
115	Uganda[2]	20.72
116	Nicaragua	21.33
117	Bangladesh[2]	34.92
118	Burundi	51.91
n/a	Albania	n/a
n/a	Canada	n/a
n/a	China	n/a
n/a	Gambia, The	n/a
n/a	Netherlands	n/a
n/a	Sweden	n/a
n/a	Syria	n/a
n/a	Trinidad and Tobago	n/a
n/a	Zimbabwe	n/a

SOURCE: International Telecommunication Union, *World Telecommunication Indicators 2007*; International Monetary Fund, *World Economic Outlook Database* (October 2007 edition); national sources

[1] 2004 [2] 2006

5.07 Business monthly telephone subscription (hard data)

Business monthly telephone subscription to the public switched telephone network (US$) as a percentage of monthly GDP per capita | 2005 or most recent year available

RANK	COUNTRY/ECONOMY	HARD DATA
1	Puerto Rico[1]	0.11
2	United Arab Emirates	0.15
3	Luxembourg	0.33
4	Singapore[1]	0.37
5	Korea, Rep.	0.37
6	Bahrain	0.38
7	Suriname	0.43
8	Norway	0.45
9	Switzerland	0.47
10	Denmark	0.50
11	Finland[1]	0.50
12	Israel	0.58
13	France	0.60
14	Iceland	0.65
15	Hong Kong SAR	0.66
16	Greece	0.70
17	Belgium	0.70
18	Saudi Arabia	0.70
19	Germany	0.71
20	Taiwan, China	0.71
21	Qatar	0.72
22	Spain	0.73
23	Austria	0.74
24	Ireland	0.74
25	Slovenia	0.76
26	Oman	0.78
27	El Salvador	0.78
28	Algeria[1]	0.80
29	Japan	0.80
30	Cyprus[1]	0.81
31	United Kingdom[1]	0.81
32	Tunisia[1]	0.83
33	Kuwait	0.88
34	Australia	0.92
35	Canada	1.02
36	Thailand	1.10
37	Estonia	1.11
38	Costa Rica	1.17
39	United States	1.26
40	Italy	1.30
41	Portugal	1.31
42	Chile	1.36
43	Malta	1.55
44	Croatia	1.61
45	Lithuania	1.62
46	Russian Federation	1.67
47	Slovak Republic	1.83
48	Botswana[1]	1.85
49	Mauritius	1.86
50	New Zealand	1.86
51	Libya[1]	1.92
52	Latvia	2.16
53	Romania	2.19
54	Albania	2.25
55	Hungary	2.40
56	Colombia	2.41
57	Czech Republic	2.41
58	Argentina	2.65
59	Egypt[1]	2.73
60	Malaysia	2.83
61	Venezuela	2.92
62	Mexico	2.93
63	China	2.99
64	Vietnam[1]	3.18
65	Guatemala[1]	3.28
66	Ukraine[1]	3.34
67	Namibia[1]	3.57
68	Bulgaria	3.57
69	Panama	3.74
70	Uruguay	3.93
71	Dominican Republic	4.16
72	Cameroon	4.21
73	Paraguay	4.22
74	South Africa	4.23
75	Burundi	4.36
76	Georgia	4.46
77	Moldova	4.53
78	Bosnia and Herzegovina	4.76
79	Pakistan[1]	4.82
80	Ecuador	5.12
81	Indonesia	5.44
82	Honduras	5.55
83	Azerbaijan	5.68
84	Armenia	5.75
85	Barbados	5.98
86	Tajikistan	6.17
87	Macedonia, FYR[1]	6.25
88	Brazil	6.48
89	Bangladesh[1]	6.55
90	Mongolia	6.64
91	Jamaica	6.82
92	Peru[1]	7.03
93	Turkey	7.06
94	Jordan	7.34
95	Senegal	7.39
96	Bolivia	7.40
97	Kyrgyz Republic	7.60
98	India	7.66
99	Guyana	8.33
100	Mauritania	8.93
101	Nepal	9.46
102	Nigeria	9.49
103	Morocco	9.97
104	Benin	11.23
105	Chad	12.36
106	Sri Lanka	12.44
107	Burkina Faso	13.26
108	Tanzania	13.44
109	Kenya	13.88
110	Ethiopia[1]	15.06
111	Lesotho	16.71
112	Nicaragua	17.06
113	Zambia	17.15
114	Cambodia	17.17
115	Madagascar[1]	20.78
116	Uganda[1]	21.62
117	Philippines	23.72
118	Mali[1]	23.82
119	Mozambique	28.69
n/a	Gambia, The	n/a
n/a	Kazakhstan	n/a
n/a	Netherlands	n/a
n/a	Poland	n/a
n/a	Sweden	n/a
n/a	Syria	n/a
n/a	Trinidad and Tobago	n/a
n/a	Zimbabwe	n/a

SOURCE: International Telecommunication Union, *World Telecommunication Indicators 2007*; International Monetary Fund, *World Economic Outlook Database* (October 2007 edition); national sources

[1] 2006

5.08 Local supplier quality

The quality of local suppliers in your country is (1 = poor, as they are inefficient and have little technological capability, 7 = very good, as they are internationally competitive and assist in new product and process development)

RANK	COUNTRY/ECONOMY	SCORE
1	Germany	6.52
2	Austria	6.33
3	Switzerland	6.29
4	Japan	6.26
5	Sweden	6.11
6	Belgium	6.10
7	Netherlands	5.99
8	Denmark	5.91
9	Finland	5.82
10	France	5.82
11	United States	5.82
12	Canada	5.79
13	Taiwan, China	5.76
14	Norway	5.73
15	Hong Kong SAR	5.72
16	Australia	5.68
17	Korea, Rep.	5.67
18	Ireland	5.62
19	United Kingdom	5.58
20	Israel	5.55
21	New Zealand	5.51
22	Iceland	5.47
23	Puerto Rico	5.45
24	Singapore	5.44
25	Malaysia	5.42
26	Czech Republic	5.38
27	Chile	5.37
28	Italy	5.34
29	South Africa	5.29
30	Spain	5.25
31	Luxembourg	5.20
32	Slovenia	5.16
33	India	5.15
34	Estonia	5.09
35	Costa Rica	5.06
36	Kuwait	5.06
37	Tunisia	5.04
38	Thailand	5.02
39	Turkey	5.00
40	Brazil	4.97
41	Bahrain	4.96
42	United Arab Emirates	4.95
43	Lithuania	4.93
44	Portugal	4.85
45	Slovak Republic	4.81
46	Cyprus	4.77
47	Peru	4.76
48	Colombia	4.75
49	Mexico	4.71
50	Saudi Arabia	4.71
51	Guatemala	4.70
52	Indonesia	4.67
53	Malta	4.64
54	Greece	4.62
55	Latvia	4.61
56	Panama	4.58
57	Mauritius	4.55
58	Sri Lanka	4.51
59	Hungary	4.51
60	Philippines	4.49
61	Jamaica	4.46
62	Trinidad and Tobago	4.45
63	Barbados	4.45
64	Syria	4.42
65	Poland	4.40
66	Jordan	4.40
67	Kenya	4.40
68	Argentina	4.39
69	Egypt	4.39
70	Senegal	4.38
71	Croatia	4.37
72	China	4.33
73	Qatar	4.27
74	El Salvador	4.25
75	Oman	4.23
76	Bulgaria	4.17
77	Morocco	4.15
78	Ukraine	4.14
79	Pakistan	4.13
80	Benin	4.12
81	Kazakhstan	4.12
82	Uruguay	4.11
83	Namibia	4.07
84	Russian Federation	4.06
85	Honduras	4.06
86	Burkina Faso	4.06
87	Dominican Republic	4.05
88	Azerbaijan	4.05
89	Libya	4.01
90	Nigeria	4.01
91	Gambia, The	3.98
92	Romania	3.97
93	Venezuela	3.92
94	Ecuador	3.88
95	Bosnia and Herzegovina	3.83
96	Vietnam	3.82
97	Macedonia, FYR	3.80
98	Mali	3.80
99	Guyana	3.77
100	Bangladesh	3.77
101	Cameroon	3.70
102	Zimbabwe	3.70
103	Tanzania	3.66
104	Suriname	3.60
105	Mauritania	3.59
106	Madagascar	3.58
107	Botswana	3.55
108	Nicaragua	3.54
109	Paraguay	3.54
110	Cambodia	3.53
111	Armenia	3.50
112	Nepal	3.47
113	Zambia	3.47
114	Uganda	3.46
115	Tajikistan	3.43
116	Moldova	3.40
117	Algeria	3.38
118	Kyrgyz Republic	3.35
119	Ethiopia	3.31
120	Albania	3.30
121	Bolivia	3.29
122	Burundi	3.23
123	Chad	3.17
124	Mongolia	3.14
125	Mozambique	3.06
126	Georgia	2.95
127	Lesotho	2.75

MEAN: 4.52

SOURCE: World Economic Forum, Executive Opinion Survey 2006, 2007

5.09 Local supplier quantity

Local suppliers in your country are (1 = largely nonexistent, 7 = numerous and include the most important materials, components, equipment, and services)

RANK	COUNTRY/ECONOMY	SCORE
1	Germany	6.29
2	Japan	6.28
3	Austria	5.96
4	Switzerland	5.94
5	France	5.86
6	India	5.79
7	Korea, Rep.	5.75
8	Belgium	5.74
9	United States	5.73
10	Sweden	5.72
11	Hong Kong SAR	5.69
12	Kuwait	5.67
13	Canada	5.66
14	Netherlands	5.60
15	Spain	5.59
16	Malaysia	5.56
17	Czech Republic	5.52
18	Taiwan, China	5.51
19	Denmark	5.48
20	Italy	5.47
21	Brazil	5.43
22	Turkey	5.39
23	Norway	5.37
24	Chile	5.35
25	Finland	5.35
26	South Africa	5.34
27	United Kingdom	5.32
28	Iceland	5.29
29	Thailand	5.27
30	Tunisia	5.26
31	Indonesia	5.25
32	Syria	5.24
33	Australia	5.24
34	Ireland	5.21
35	China	5.20
36	Bahrain	5.13
37	Egypt	5.12
38	Slovak Republic	5.10
39	Saudi Arabia	5.08
40	Costa Rica	5.08
41	New Zealand	5.08
42	Israel	5.05
43	Portugal	5.05
44	Senegal	5.03
45	Puerto Rico	5.02
46	Peru	5.01
47	Kenya	5.00
48	Pakistan	5.00
49	Lithuania	5.00
50	Singapore	4.99
51	Jordan	4.99
52	United Arab Emirates	4.99
53	Estonia	4.91
54	Colombia	4.87
55	Malta	4.86
56	Guatemala	4.84
57	Morocco	4.84
58	Slovenia	4.81
59	Nigeria	4.81
60	Philippines	4.80
61	Panama	4.80
62	Mauritius	4.78
63	Argentina	4.74
64	Ukraine	4.73
65	Sri Lanka	4.73
66	Mexico	4.73
67	Qatar	4.72
68	Luxembourg	4.71
69	Hungary	4.69
70	Bulgaria	4.68
71	Greece	4.68
72	Burkina Faso	4.67
73	Russian Federation	4.67
74	Libya	4.65
75	Uganda	4.61
76	Cyprus	4.58
77	Poland	4.57
78	Trinidad and Tobago	4.56
79	Kazakhstan	4.55
80	Mali	4.55
81	Croatia	4.54
82	Vietnam	4.51
83	Jamaica	4.50
84	Oman	4.47
85	Azerbaijan	4.46
86	Cameroon	4.46
87	Romania	4.44
88	Dominican Republic	4.41
89	Latvia	4.36
90	El Salvador	4.35
91	Chad	4.33
92	Madagascar	4.33
93	Bangladesh	4.32
94	Honduras	4.30
95	Tanzania	4.28
96	Barbados	4.28
97	Gambia, The	4.27
98	Algeria	4.25
99	Guyana	4.24
100	Macedonia, FYR	4.24
101	Uruguay	4.21
102	Ecuador	4.18
103	Mauritania	4.16
104	Zimbabwe	4.10
105	Benin	4.06
106	Albania	3.99
107	Armenia	3.99
108	Paraguay	3.97
109	Venezuela	3.93
110	Nepal	3.92
111	Bosnia and Herzegovina	3.89
112	Burundi	3.87
113	Nicaragua	3.81
114	Ethiopia	3.81
115	Suriname	3.81
116	Moldova	3.79
117	Tajikistan	3.74
118	Cambodia	3.66
119	Mozambique	3.65
120	Kyrgyz Republic	3.64
121	Zambia	3.62
122	Namibia	3.57
123	Bolivia	3.47
124	Botswana	3.45
125	Mongolia	3.37
126	Georgia	3.21
127	Lesotho	3.00

MEAN: 4.74

SOURCE: World Economic Forum, Executive Opinion Survey 2006, 2007

5.10 Computer, communications, and other services imports (hard data)

Computer, communications, and other services as percentage of total commercial services imports | 2005 or most recent year available

RANK	COUNTRY/ECONOMY	HARD DATA
1	Azerbaijan	77.38
2	Ireland	73.00
3	Kazakhstan	71.00
4	Saudi Arabia	67.60
5	Nigeria	64.20
6	Austria	56.05
7	Croatia	54.80
8	Netherlands	54.60
9	Hungary	54.10
10	Suriname	53.72
11	Finland	51.30
12	Indonesia	51.10
13	Brazil	50.06
14	Sweden	49.60
15	Italy	46.50
16	Czech Republic	45.50
17	Spain	44.40
18	India	43.10
19	Pakistan	42.60
20	Slovak Republic	42.40
20	Slovenia	42.40
22	Macedonia, FYR	42.20
23	Malaysia	41.40
24	Romania	41.30
25	Israel	40.30
26	Poland	40.10
27	Singapore	39.40
28	Taiwan, China[1]	38.40
29	Belgium	38.29
30	Canada	37.90
30	France	37.90
32	Japan	37.80
33	Germany	37.70
34	Korea, Rep.	37.50
35	Switzerland	37.40
36	Uganda	35.20
37	Namibia[1]	35.10
38	Russian Federation	35.00
39	Denmark[1]	34.84
40	Madagascar	34.70
40	Oman	34.70
42	Portugal	33.50
43	Egypt	33.30
44	Estonia	32.70
45	Mozambique	32.20
46	Jamaica	32.10
47	Kyrgyz Republic	31.50
47	United Kingdom	31.50
49	China	30.80
50	Guyana	30.16
51	United States	30.00
52	New Zealand	29.50
53	Kenya	29.20
54	Mauritius	28.90
55	Argentina	28.74
56	Norway	27.60
57	Malta	27.05
58	Morocco	26.80
59	Latvia	25.80
60	Senegal[1]	25.60
61	Ukraine	24.90
62	Luxembourg	24.83
63	Thailand	24.80
64	Bulgaria	24.27
65	Peru	24.00
66	Iceland	23.87
67	Ethiopia	23.50
68	Hong Kong SAR[1]	23.40
69	Moldova	22.80
70	Ecuador	22.60
71	Chile	22.30
72	Botswana	22.19
73	Colombia	22.00
74	Cambodia	21.83
75	Venezuela	21.70
76	Australia	21.32
77	South Africa	21.10
78	Honduras	20.40
79	Costa Rica	20.30
80	Tunisia	20.10
81	Tajikistan	20.00
82	Albania	19.51
83	Tanzania	19.20
84	Barbados	19.16
85	Greece	18.90
85	Uruguay	18.90
87	Philippines	18.80
88	Bolivia	18.26
89	Trinidad and Tobago[1]	17.70
90	El Salvador	17.60
91	Nepal	17.30
92	Cyprus	17.02
93	Sri Lanka	16.90
94	Burundi	16.67
95	Mali	16.00
96	Lithuania	15.90
96	Nicaragua	15.90
98	Bosnia and Herzegovina	15.26
99	Panama	14.90
100	Benin[1]	14.70
101	Jordan	13.30
102	Mongolia[1]	12.80
103	Libya	11.80
104	Armenia	11.46
105	Georgia	11.40
105	Turkey	11.40
107	Bangladesh	8.39
108	Dominican Republic	6.60
109	Mexico	6.40
110	Bahrain	6.40
111	Syria	6.30
112	Guatemala	5.70
113	Paraguay	3.10
114	Gambia, The	2.20
115	Kuwait	1.80
116	Lesotho	0.02
n/a	Algeria	n/a
n/a	Burkina Faso	n/a
n/a	Cameroon	n/a
n/a	Chad	n/a
n/a	Mauritania	n/a
n/a	Puerto Rico	n/a
n/a	Qatar	n/a
n/a	United Arab Emirates	n/a
n/a	Vietnam	n/a
n/a	Zambia	n/a
n/a	Zimbabwe	n/a

SOURCE: The World Bank, *World Development Indicators 2007*
[1] 2004

Subindex B **Readiness component**

6th pillar
Government readiness

6.01 Government prioritization of ICT

Information and communication technologies (computers, Internet, etc.) are an overall priority for the government (1 = strongly disagree, 7 = strongly agree)

RANK	COUNTRY/ECONOMY	SCORE
1	Singapore	6.33
2	Malaysia	6.02
3	Denmark	6.01
4	Estonia	5.95
5	Malta	5.91
6	Korea, Rep.	5.89
7	United Arab Emirates	5.87
8	Portugal	5.84
9	Taiwan, China	5.78
10	Qatar	5.75
11	Sweden	5.67
12	Finland	5.64
13	Tunisia	5.60
14	Iceland	5.56
15	Japan	5.47
16	India	5.46
17	Hong Kong SAR	5.43
18	United States	5.42
19	Mauritius	5.41
20	Mauritania	5.38
21	United Kingdom	5.33
22	Norway	5.30
23	Jordan	5.27
24	Switzerland	5.23
25	Gambia, The	5.21
26	Israel	5.20
27	Austria	5.19
28	Thailand	5.18
29	Barbados	5.17
30	Mongolia	5.15
31	Germany	5.14
32	Netherlands	5.13
33	Bahrain	5.11
34	Canada	5.07
35	Vietnam	5.05
36	Azerbaijan	5.05
37	Luxembourg	5.05
38	Pakistan	5.03
39	Dominican Republic	5.02
40	Chile	5.00
41	Lithuania	5.00
42	Mali	4.99
43	France	4.99
44	Jamaica	4.97
45	Tajikistan	4.93
46	Senegal	4.92
47	Sri Lanka	4.92
48	Australia	4.91
49	Algeria	4.90
50	Saudi Arabia	4.90
51	Benin	4.88
52	Ireland	4.88
53	Madagascar	4.88
54	Belgium	4.85
55	Tanzania	4.84
56	Kazakhstan	4.80
57	Egypt	4.79
58	New Zealand	4.79
59	El Salvador	4.73
60	South Africa	4.71
61	Croatia	4.66
62	Puerto Rico	4.59
63	Morocco	4.58
64	Uganda	4.57
65	Slovenia	4.55
66	Oman	4.54
67	Burkina Faso	4.54
68	Botswana	4.53
69	Colombia	4.52
70	Syria	4.52
71	Spain	4.51
72	Hungary	4.50
73	Mexico	4.47
74	China	4.47
75	Turkey	4.46
76	Czech Republic	4.45
77	Costa Rica	4.45
78	Moldova	4.45
79	Uruguay	4.44
80	Albania	4.44
81	Mozambique	4.42
82	Cambodia	4.40
83	Guyana	4.39
84	Nigeria	4.37
85	Cyprus	4.37
86	Nepal	4.36
87	Ethiopia	4.35
88	Slovak Republic	4.32
89	Latvia	4.31
90	Guatemala	4.26
91	Honduras	4.25
92	Macedonia, FYR	4.25
93	Zambia	4.25
94	Greece	4.25
95	Bangladesh	4.24
96	Trinidad and Tobago	4.22
97	Kuwait	4.21
98	Russian Federation	4.20
99	Bulgaria	4.19
100	Brazil	4.18
101	Romania	4.17
102	Venezuela	4.15
103	Kenya	4.13
104	Philippines	4.12
105	Georgia	4.11
106	Armenia	4.07
107	Panama	4.00
108	Bosnia and Herzegovina	3.99
109	Libya	3.95
110	Italy	3.94
111	Kyrgyz Republic	3.91
112	Ukraine	3.90
113	Peru	3.90
114	Cameroon	3.89
115	Namibia	3.86
116	Lesotho	3.86
117	Nicaragua	3.82
118	Bolivia	3.54
119	Argentina	3.43
120	Poland	3.25
121	Burundi	3.21
122	Zimbabwe	3.11
123	Chad	3.02
124	Indonesia	3.00
125	Suriname	2.88
126	Paraguay	2.87
127	Ecuador	2.86

MEAN: 4.64

SOURCE: World Economic Forum, Executive Opinion Survey 2006, 2007

6.02 Government procurement of advanced technology products

Government purchase decisions for the procurement of advanced technology products are (1 = based solely on price, 7 = based on technical performance and innovativeness)

RANK	COUNTRY/ECONOMY	SCORE
1	Singapore	5.53
2	Korea, Rep.	5.29
3	Malaysia	5.10
4	Tunisia	5.03
5	United States	4.94
6	Sweden	4.87
7	Israel	4.80
8	Taiwan, China	4.77
9	Luxembourg	4.65
10	Germany	4.64
11	Finland	4.64
12	Switzerland	4.60
13	Denmark	4.56
14	France	4.53
15	Hong Kong SAR	4.51
16	Japan	4.49
17	United Arab Emirates	4.49
18	Qatar	4.48
19	Netherlands	4.42
20	Norway	4.36
21	Austria	4.31
22	China	4.26
23	Estonia	4.25
24	Thailand	4.17
25	Ireland	4.17
26	United Kingdom	4.16
27	Australia	4.15
28	Canada	4.15
29	Mali	4.13
30	Portugal	4.12
31	Saudi Arabia	4.12
32	Bahrain	4.08
33	Iceland	4.04
34	Mauritania	4.03
35	Vietnam	3.99
36	Oman	3.98
37	Azerbaijan	3.92
38	Jordan	3.91
39	Chile	3.88
40	Malta	3.87
41	Nigeria	3.86
42	Morocco	3.85
43	Senegal	3.85
44	Burkina Faso	3.85
45	Czech Republic	3.83
46	Benin	3.82
47	Cambodia	3.81
48	Pakistan	3.81
49	Belgium	3.80
50	New Zealand	3.79
51	South Africa	3.79
52	Madagascar	3.77
53	Sri Lanka	3.77
54	Kenya	3.77
55	Spain	3.75
56	Tanzania	3.75
57	Egypt	3.74
58	Gambia, The	3.73
59	Puerto Rico	3.72
60	Costa Rica	3.71
61	Kazakhstan	3.69
62	Lithuania	3.67
63	Mauritius	3.65
64	Barbados	3.65
65	Indonesia	3.64
66	Brazil	3.63
67	Colombia	3.62
68	Algeria	3.61
69	Jamaica	3.61
70	India	3.61
71	Tajikistan	3.59
72	Turkey	3.59
73	Uganda	3.58
74	Ukraine	3.57
75	Slovenia	3.56
76	Botswana	3.55
77	Cyprus	3.54
78	Panama	3.53
79	Croatia	3.50
80	Kuwait	3.49
81	Romania	3.48
82	Russian Federation	3.43
83	Bulgaria	3.43
84	Guatemala	3.42
85	Hungary	3.42
86	Slovak Republic	3.40
87	Honduras	3.38
88	Poland	3.37
89	El Salvador	3.36
90	Uruguay	3.35
91	Dominican Republic	3.31
92	Mexico	3.31
93	Syria	3.30
94	Latvia	3.30
95	Italy	3.26
96	Ethiopia	3.26
97	Greece	3.25
98	Trinidad and Tobago	3.25
99	Philippines	3.21
100	Mozambique	3.18
101	Cameroon	3.17
102	Namibia	3.16
103	Venezuela	3.14
104	Mongolia	3.10
105	Macedonia, FYR	3.05
106	Georgia	3.04
107	Chad	3.04
108	Guyana	3.03
109	Armenia	3.03
110	Nicaragua	3.02
111	Argentina	3.01
112	Peru	2.93
113	Lesotho	2.92
114	Libya	2.85
115	Burundi	2.83
116	Bangladesh	2.79
117	Ecuador	2.78
118	Nepal	2.68
119	Bosnia and Herzegovina	2.67
120	Zambia	2.67
121	Moldova	2.62
122	Suriname	2.59
123	Zimbabwe	2.56
124	Kyrgyz Republic	2.56
125	Paraguay	2.43
126	Bolivia	2.41
127	Albania	2.40

MEAN: 3.68

SOURCE: World Economic Forum, Executive Opinion Survey 2006, 2007

6.03 Importance of ICT to government vision of the future

The government has a clear implementation plan for utilizing information and communication technologies for improving the country's overall competitiveness (1 = strongly disagree, 7 = strongly agree)

RANK	COUNTRY/ECONOMY	SCORE
1	Singapore	6.28
2	Portugal	5.73
3	Malta	5.70
4	United Arab Emirates	5.65
5	Malaysia	5.62
6	Denmark	5.51
7	Korea, Rep.	5.50
8	Qatar	5.46
9	Estonia	5.40
10	Iceland	5.37
11	Tunisia	5.35
12	Hong Kong SAR	5.21
13	Finland	5.10
14	Taiwan, China	5.05
15	Norway	5.01
16	Sweden	4.98
17	Thailand	4.94
18	Mali	4.88
19	Mauritania	4.84
20	Chile	4.82
21	India	4.80
22	Austria	4.71
23	Jordan	4.68
24	Oman	4.68
25	Japan	4.68
26	Israel	4.65
27	Bahrain	4.64
28	United States	4.64
29	China	4.63
30	Luxembourg	4.56
31	France	4.56
32	Gambia, The	4.54
33	Burkina Faso	4.53
34	Ireland	4.51
35	Saudi Arabia	4.48
36	Egypt	4.47
37	Vietnam	4.46
38	Slovenia	4.46
39	Switzerland	4.45
40	Australia	4.43
41	Kazakhstan	4.42
42	United Kingdom	4.41
43	Dominican Republic	4.38
44	El Salvador	4.36
45	Morocco	4.32
46	Netherlands	4.31
47	Canada	4.31
48	Mauritius	4.30
49	Uganda	4.25
50	Senegal	4.24
51	New Zealand	4.24
52	Tanzania	4.23
53	Mongolia	4.21
54	Sri Lanka	4.21
55	Azerbaijan	4.20
56	Jamaica	4.19
57	Belgium	4.18
58	Barbados	4.15
59	Benin	4.15
60	Madagascar	4.14
61	Algeria	4.13
62	Mexico	4.13
63	Germany	4.12
64	Hungary	4.08
65	Pakistan	4.06
66	Ethiopia	4.06
67	Kenya	4.02
68	Nigeria	3.99
69	Spain	3.99
70	Guatemala	3.98
71	Turkey	3.98
72	Colombia	3.97
73	Lithuania	3.95
74	Cyprus	3.95
75	Brazil	3.93
76	Croatia	3.90
77	Cambodia	3.89
78	Botswana	3.87
79	Macedonia, FYR	3.86
80	Panama	3.85
81	Romania	3.82
82	Tajikistan	3.82
83	Mozambique	3.80
84	Syria	3.80
85	South Africa	3.73
86	Greece	3.73
87	Slovak Republic	3.73
88	Moldova	3.60
89	Costa Rica	3.59
90	Bulgaria	3.59
91	Philippines	3.56
92	Italy	3.55
93	Latvia	3.52
94	Uruguay	3.50
95	Albania	3.42
96	Zambia	3.40
97	Puerto Rico	3.39
98	Nicaragua	3.38
99	Kuwait	3.37
100	Honduras	3.34
101	Trinidad and Tobago	3.32
102	Peru	3.28
103	Czech Republic	3.25
104	Venezuela	3.18
105	Russian Federation	3.17
106	Bangladesh	3.14
107	Armenia	3.12
108	Poland	3.10
109	Georgia	3.09
110	Nepal	3.06
111	Libya	3.02
112	Cameroon	2.92
113	Namibia	2.91
114	Indonesia	2.89
115	Guyana	2.88
116	Ukraine	2.82
117	Bolivia	2.79
118	Chad	2.76
119	Lesotho	2.73
120	Argentina	2.68
121	Ecuador	2.66
122	Burundi	2.56
123	Kyrgyz Republic	2.53
124	Paraguay	2.47
125	Bosnia and Herzegovina	2.39
126	Suriname	2.01
127	Zimbabwe	1.97

MEAN: 4.03

SOURCE: World Economic Forum, Executive Opinion Survey 2006, 2007

6.04 E-Government Readiness Index (hard data)

The E-Government Readiness Index assesses e-government readiness based on website assessment, telecommunications infrastructure, and human resource endowment | 2007

RANK	COUNTRY/ECONOMY	HARD DATA
1	Sweden	0.92
2	Denmark	0.91
3	Norway	0.89
4	United States	0.86
5	Netherlands	0.86
6	Korea, Rep.	0.83
7	Canada	0.82
8	Australia	0.81
9	France	0.80
10	United Kingdom	0.79
11	Japan	0.77
12	Switzerland	0.76
13	Estonia	0.76
14	Luxembourg	0.75
15	Finland	0.75
16	Austria	0.74
17	Israel	0.74
18	New Zealand	0.74
19	Ireland	0.73
20	Spain	0.72
21	Iceland	0.72
22	Germany	0.71
23	Singapore	0.70
24	Belgium	0.68
25	Czech Republic	0.67
26	Slovenia	0.67
27	Italy	0.67
28	Lithuania	0.66
29	Malta	0.66
30	Hungary	0.65
31	Portugal	0.65
32	United Arab Emirates	0.63
33	Poland	0.61
34	Malaysia	0.61
35	Cyprus	0.60
36	Latvia	0.59
37	Mexico	0.59
38	Slovak Republic	0.59
39	Argentina	0.58
40	Chile	0.58
41	Ukraine	0.57
42	Bahrain	0.57
43	Bulgaria	0.57
44	Greece	0.57
45	Brazil	0.57
46	Barbados	0.57
47	Croatia	0.57
48	Uruguay	0.56
49	Jordan	0.55
50	Romania	0.54
51	Colombia	0.53
52	Qatar	0.53
53	Trinidad and Tobago	0.53
54	Peru	0.53
55	Kuwait	0.52
56	Costa Rica	0.51
57	Russian Federation	0.51
58	South Africa	0.51
59	Venezuela	0.51
60	Mauritius	0.51
61	Thailand	0.50
62	China	0.50
63	Philippines	0.50
64	El Salvador	0.50
65	Dominican Republic	0.49
66	Saudi Arabia	0.49
67	Bolivia	0.49
68	Macedonia, FYR	0.49
69	Ecuador	0.48
70	Turkey	0.48
71	Egypt	0.48
72	Kazakhstan	0.47
73	Mongolia	0.47
74	Panama	0.47
75	Oman	0.47
76	Jamaica	0.47
77	Albania	0.47
78	Paraguay	0.47
79	Azerbaijan	0.46
80	Georgia	0.46
81	Vietnam	0.46
82	Moldova	0.45
83	Bosnia and Herzegovina	0.45
84	Guyana	0.44
85	Guatemala	0.43
86	Sri Lanka	0.42
87	Kyrgyz Republic	0.42
88	Armenia	0.42
89	Indonesia	0.41
90	Honduras	0.40
91	India	0.38
92	Lesotho	0.38
93	Nicaragua	0.37
94	Botswana	0.36
95	Syria	0.36
96	Libya	0.35
97	Algeria	0.35
98	Kenya	0.35
99	Suriname	0.35
100	Tunisia	0.35
101	Namibia	0.34
102	Pakistan	0.32
103	Tajikistan	0.32
104	Uganda	0.31
105	Madagascar	0.31
106	Nigeria	0.31
107	Cambodia	0.30
108	Zimbabwe	0.30
109	Morocco	0.29
110	Bangladesh	0.29
111	Tanzania	0.29
112	Cameroon	0.29
113	Nepal	0.27
114	Mozambique	0.26
115	Senegal	0.25
116	Zambia	0.23
117	Gambia, The	0.23
118	Mauritania	0.20
119	Benin	0.19
120	Ethiopia	0.19
121	Burundi	0.18
122	Mali	0.16
123	Burkina Faso	0.15
124	Chad	0.10
n/a	Hong Kong SAR	n/a
n/a	Puerto Rico	n/a
n/a	Taiwan, China	n/a

SOURCE: United Nations, *Global E-Government Survey 2008*

Subindex C **Usage component**

7th pillar
Individual usage

7.01 Mobile telephone subscribers (hard data)

Mobile telephone subscribers per 100 inhabitants | 2006 or most recent year available

RANK	COUNTRY/ECONOMY	HARD DATA
1	Luxembourg	151.61
2	Lithuania	138.06
3	Hong Kong SAR	131.45
4	Trinidad and Tobago	126.42
5	Estonia	125.19
6	Italy[1]	123.08
7	Israel	122.74
8	Bahrain	121.71
9	Czech Republic	119.01
10	United Arab Emirates	118.51
11	United Kingdom	116.39
12	Portugal	115.95
13	Austria	112.80
14	Ireland	111.40
15	Iceland	110.58
16	Qatar	109.60
17	Singapore	109.34
18	Norway	108.57
19	Finland	107.76
20	Bulgaria	107.59
21	Denmark	107.25
22	Ukraine	106.72
23	Spain	106.39
24	Sweden	105.92
25	Jamaica[1]	105.78
26	Switzerland	102.12
27	Taiwan, China	101.97
28	Germany	101.92
29	Greece	99.62
30	Hungary	98.95
31	Croatia	98.11
32	Netherlands[1]	97.15
33	Australia	97.02
34	Poland	95.45
35	Latvia	95.13
36	Slovenia	92.56
37	Belgium	92.55
38	Cyprus	92.06
39	Slovak Republic	90.60
40	Kuwait[1]	88.57
41	New Zealand[1]	87.62
42	Malta	85.96
43	France	85.08
44	Puerto Rico	84.80
45	Korea, Rep.	83.77
46	Russian Federation[1]	83.62
47	Argentina	80.52
48	Romania	80.45
49	Japan	79.32
50	Saudi Arabia	78.05
51	United States	77.40
52	Barbados[1]	76.65
53	Chile	75.62
54	Malaysia	75.45
55	Jordan	74.40
56	Tunisia	71.88
57	South Africa[1]	71.60
58	Turkey	71.00
59	Suriname	70.80
60	Oman	69.59
61	Macedonia, FYR	69.56
62	Venezuela	69.04
63	Uruguay	66.83
64	Libya	65.81
65	Colombia	64.31
66	Ecuador	63.23
67	Thailand	63.02
68	Algeria	62.95
69	Mauritius	61.50
70	Botswana	55.68
71	Guatemala	55.60
72	El Salvador	55.03
73	Kazakhstan	52.86
74	Mexico	52.63
75	Canada[1]	52.51
76	Panama[1]	52.46
77	Morocco	52.07
78	Paraguay	51.31
79	Dominican Republic	51.05
80	Philippines	50.75
81	Albania[1]	48.89
82	Bosnia and Herzegovina	48.26
83	Brazil[1]	46.25
84	Azerbaijan	39.23
85	Georgia	38.43
86	Guyana[1]	37.46
87	China	34.83
88	Mauritania	33.57
89	Costa Rica	32.82
90	Nicaragua	32.68
91	Moldova	32.38
92	Honduras	30.44
93	Peru	29.95
94	Bolivia	28.85
95	Indonesia	28.30
96	Gambia, The	25.99
97	Sri Lanka	25.88
98	Senegal	24.99
99	Namibia[1]	24.37
100	Egypt	24.33
101	Nigeria	24.05
102	Syria	23.96
103	Pakistan	21.98
104	Mongolia[1]	21.05
105	Kenya	18.47
106	Vietnam	18.17
107	India	14.83
108	Tanzania	14.78
109	Zambia	14.02
110	Lesotho[1]	13.92
111	Cameroon[1]	13.80
112	Bangladesh	13.25
113	Benin	12.13
114	Mozambique	11.61
115	Mali	10.87
116	Armenia[1]	10.54
117	Kyrgyz Republic[1]	10.29
118	Cambodia	7.94
119	Burkina Faso	7.46
120	Uganda	6.73
121	Zimbabwe	6.36
122	Madagascar	5.47
123	Chad	4.65
124	Tajikistan[1]	4.07
125	Nepal	3.76
126	Burundi[1]	2.03
127	Ethiopia	1.09

SOURCE: International Telecommunication Union, *World Telecommunication Indicators 2007*

[1] 2005

7.02 Personal computers (hard data)

Personal computers per 100 inhabitants | 2005 or most recent year available

RANK	COUNTRY/ECONOMY	HARD DATA
1	Israel	122.52
2	Canada	87.31
3	Switzerland	86.18
4	Netherlands	85.55
5	Sweden	83.49
6	Australia	76.61
7	United Kingdom	76.52
8	United States[1]	76.22
9	Denmark	69.46
10	Singapore	68.02
11	Japan	67.45
12	Luxembourg	62.37
13	Austria	61.12
14	Germany	60.47
15	Norway	59.41
16	Hong Kong SAR	59.26
17	France	57.86
18	Taiwan, China	57.52
19	Korea, Rep.	53.19
20	Ireland	52.99
21	New Zealand	51.55
22	Finland	50.01
23	Estonia	48.91
24	Iceland	48.30
25	Slovenia	41.08
26	Belgium	37.62
27	Italy	36.99
28	Slovak Republic	35.72
29	Cyprus	33.41
30	Spain	28.11
31	Czech Republic	27.40
32	Latvia	24.53
33	Poland	23.99
34	United Arab Emirates	23.35
35	Costa Rica	23.11
36	Kuwait	22.33
37	Macedonia, FYR	22.17
38	Malaysia	21.54
39	Croatia	19.42
40	Qatar	18.64
41	Lithuania	17.98
42	Bahrain	17.62
43	Mauritius	16.87
44	Malta	16.61
45	Brazil	16.09
46	Hungary	14.90
47	Barbados	14.87
48	Chile	14.75
49	Uruguay	13.85
50	Portugal	13.40
51	Mexico	13.08
52	Romania	12.96
53	Mongolia	12.85
54	Saudi Arabia	12.82
55	Namibia	12.26
56	Russian Federation	12.13
57	Peru	10.01
58	Trinidad and Tobago	9.88
59	Armenia	9.85
60	Venezuela	9.25
61	Greece	9.17
62	Argentina	9.07
63	South Africa	8.36
64	Moldova	8.28
65	Paraguay	7.47
66	Thailand	6.86
67	Jamaica	6.75
68	Zimbabwe[2]	6.61
69	Ecuador	6.55
70	Bulgaria	6.34
71	Jordan	6.22
72	Tunisia[2]	6.22
73	Turkey	5.56
74	Bosnia and Herzegovina	5.43
75	Philippines	5.37
76	El Salvador	5.09
77	Oman	5.06
78	Botswana	4.87
79	Georgia	4.70
80	Ukraine[2]	4.61
81	Panama	4.56
82	Suriname	4.45
83	Egypt[2]	4.27
84	China	4.22
85	Syria	4.20
86	Colombia	4.15
87	Guyana	3.86
88	Nicaragua	3.77
89	Sri Lanka	3.54
90	Mauritania	2.56
91	Morocco	2.46
92	Bangladesh[2]	2.42
93	Bolivia	2.40
94	Dominican Republic	2.32
95	Azerbaijan	2.31
96	Libya	2.22
97	Senegal	2.14
98	Guatemala	2.08
99	Kyrgyz Republic	1.90
100	Albania	1.73
101	Uganda[2]	1.67
102	Honduras	1.67
103	Gambia, The	1.65
104	India	1.54
105	Indonesia	1.47
106	Kenya	1.44
107	Mozambique	1.43
108	Vietnam	1.39
109	Tajikistan	1.30
110	Cameroon	1.23
111	Zambia	1.12
112	Algeria	1.06
113	Tanzania	0.93
114	Nigeria	0.91
115	Puerto Rico	0.83
116	Burundi	0.73
117	Madagascar	0.55
118	Pakistan	0.52
119	Nepal	0.49
120	Benin	0.43
121	Mali	0.40
122	Ethiopia	0.39
123	Cambodia	0.31
124	Burkina Faso	0.24
125	Chad	0.16
126	Lesotho	0.08
n/a	Kazakhstan	n/a

SOURCE: International Telecommunication Union, *World Telecommunication Indicators 2007*

[1] 2004 [2] 2006

7.03 Broadband Internet subscribers (hard data)

Total broadband Internet subscribers per 100 inhabitants | 2006 or most recent year available

RANK	COUNTRY/ECONOMY	HARD DATA
1	Denmark	31.74
2	Netherlands	31.72
3	Iceland	29.53
4	Switzerland	29.47
5	Korea, Rep.	29.27
6	Norway	27.54
7	Finland	27.14
8	Sweden	25.87
9	Hong Kong SAR	25.24
10	Canada	23.57
11	United Kingdom	21.71
12	France	20.91
13	Israel	20.75
14	Japan	20.09
15	Luxembourg	19.80
16	Taiwan, China	19.76
17	United States	19.31
18	Australia	19.15
19	Belgium[2]	19.13
20	Singapore	18.19
21	Austria	17.41
22	Estonia	17.22
23	Germany	17.03
24	Spain	15.34
25	Italy	14.86
26	New Zealand	14.18
27	Portugal	13.85
28	Slovenia	13.41
29	Ireland	12.29
30	Barbados[2]	11.87
31	Lithuania	10.79
32	Czech Republic	10.64
33	Malta	10.44
34	Hungary	9.70
35	Romania	8.18
36	Poland	6.86
37	Chile	5.94
38	Cyprus	5.87
39	Slovak Republic	5.87
40	Qatar	5.57
41	Croatia	5.53
42	Bahrain	5.23
43	United Arab Emirates	5.17
44	Bulgaria	5.01
45	Latvia	4.78
46	Greece	4.38
47	Argentina	4.01
48	China	3.85
49	Turkey	3.74
50	Malaysia	3.48
51	Mexico	3.44
52	Uruguay	3.07
53	Puerto Rico[2]	2.99
54	Brazil[2]	2.35
55	Russian Federation	2.03
56	Venezuela	1.97
57	Macedonia, FYR	1.79
58	Mauritius	1.74
59	Peru	1.71
60	Jamaica[2]	1.70
61	Trinidad and Tobago	1.57
62	Ukraine	1.37
63	Colombia	1.36
64	Costa Rica	1.34
65	Bosnia and Herzegovina	1.02
66	Kuwait[2]	0.93
67	Saudi Arabia	0.87
68	Jordan	0.83
69	Morocco[2]	0.82
70	Dominican Republic	0.74
71	El Salvador[2]	0.61
72	Georgia	0.61
73	Vietnam	0.61
74	Algeria[2]	0.59
75	Suriname	0.59
76	Oman	0.58
77	Panama[2]	0.54
78	Moldova	0.52
79	Madagascar[1]	0.50
80	South Africa[2]	0.35
81	Nicaragua	0.34
82	Egypt	0.34
83	Guyana[2]	0.27
84	Paraguay	0.25
85	Senegal	0.24
86	Guatemala[2]	0.22
87	Kazakhstan	0.21
88	India	0.21
89	Ecuador[2]	0.20
90	Tunisia[2]	0.17
91	Thailand[2]	0.16
92	Philippines[2]	0.15
93	Sri Lanka	0.14
94	Bolivia[2]	0.12
95	Botswana[2]	0.09
96	Zimbabwe	0.08
97	Mongolia[2]	0.07
98	Armenia[2]	0.07
99	Indonesia[2]	0.05
100	Kyrgyz Republic[2]	0.05
101	Pakistan[2]	0.03
102	Syria	0.03
103	Azerbaijan[2]	0.03
104	Mauritania	0.02
105	Mali	0.02
106	Zambia	0.02
107	Burkina Faso	0.01
108	Albania[2]	0.01
109	Cambodia[2]	0.01
110	Gambia, The[2]	0.00
111	Uganda	0.00
112	Lesotho[2]	0.00
113	Benin	0.00
114	Cameroon[2]	0.00
115	Tajikistan[2]	0.00
116	Nigeria[2]	0.00
117	Ethiopia[2]	0.00
118	Bangladesh[2]	0.00
118	Burundi[2]	0.00
118	Chad[2]	0.00
118	Honduras[2]	0.00
118	Kenya[2]	0.00
118	Libya[2]	0.00
118	Mozambique[2]	0.00
118	Namibia[2]	0.00
118	Nepal[2]	0.00
118	Tanzania[2]	0.00

SOURCE: International Telecommunication Union, *World Telecommunication Indicators 2007*

[1] 2004   [2] 2005

7.04 Internet users (hard data)

Internet users per 100 inhabitants | 2006 or most recent year available

RANK	COUNTRY/ECONOMY	HARD DATA
1	Netherlands	88.87
2	New Zealand	78.77
3	Sweden	76.97
4	Australia	75.12
5	Luxembourg	72.01
6	Korea, Rep.	71.11
7	United States	69.10
8	Japan	68.27
9	Canada[1]	67.89
10	Iceland	65.30
11	Taiwan, China	63.68
12	Slovenia	63.62
13	Switzerland	60.02
14	Barbados[1]	59.48
15	Norway[1]	58.48
16	Denmark	58.23
17	Estonia	57.36
18	United Kingdom	56.03
19	Finland[1]	53.34
20	Hong Kong SAR	52.97
21	Austria	51.19
22	Italy	49.63
23	France	49.57
24	Germany	46.67
25	Latvia	46.65
26	Jamaica[1]	46.48
27	Belgium[1]	45.67
28	Malaysia	43.77
29	Spain	42.83
30	Cyprus	42.23
31	Slovak Republic	41.76
32	Singapore	39.21
33	United Arab Emirates	36.69
34	Hungary	34.75
35	Czech Republic	34.69
36	Croatia	34.60
37	Qatar	34.55
38	Ireland	34.13
39	Romania	32.36
40	Malta[1]	31.73
41	Lithuania	31.69
42	Portugal	30.47
43	Kuwait	29.53
44	Poland	28.57
45	Costa Rica	27.61
46	Chile	25.24
47	Puerto Rico	25.00
48	Israel[1]	24.43
49	Bulgaria	24.38
50	Bosnia and Herzegovina	24.28
51	Dominican Republic	22.17
52	Peru	21.49
53	Bahrain[1]	21.33
54	Guyana[1]	21.30
55	Argentina	20.91
56	Uruguay[1]	20.55
57	Morocco	19.85
58	Saudi Arabia	18.66
59	Russian Federation	18.02
60	Greece[1]	18.00
61	Moldova	17.35
62	Brazil[1]	17.24
63	Vietnam	17.21
64	Mexico[1]	16.90
65	Turkey	16.56
66	Venezuela	15.21
67	Albania	14.98
68	Mauritius	14.49
69	Colombia	14.49
70	Jordan	13.65
71	Macedonia, FYR	13.16
72	Thailand	13.07
73	Tunisia	12.68
74	Trinidad and Tobago[1]	12.48
75	Oman	12.22
76	Ukraine	12.06
77	Ecuador	11.54
78	South Africa[1]	10.75
79	China	10.35
80	Guatemala	10.22
81	Mongolia[1]	10.14
82	Azerbaijan	9.79
83	Zimbabwe	9.32
84	El Salvador[1]	9.26
85	Kazakhstan	8.42
86	Egypt	8.11
87	Benin	8.04
88	Kenya	7.89
89	Syria	7.69
90	Pakistan	7.64
91	Georgia	7.49
92	Algeria	7.38
93	Indonesia[1]	7.18
94	Suriname[1]	7.12
95	Panama	6.69
96	Bolivia	6.20
97	Armenia	5.75
98	Kyrgyz Republic	5.60
99	Philippines[1]	5.48
100	Senegal	5.45
101	India[1]	5.44
102	Honduras	4.58
103	Zambia	4.22
104	Paraguay	4.13
105	Namibia[1]	3.97
106	Libya[1]	3.96
107	Gambia, The[1]	3.82
108	Nigeria[1]	3.80
109	Botswana[1]	3.40
110	Mauritania	3.17
111	Lesotho[1]	2.87
112	Nicaragua	2.77
113	Uganda	2.51
114	Cameroon	2.23
115	Sri Lanka	2.05
116	Tanzania[1]	1.00
117	Nepal	0.90
118	Mozambique[1]	0.90
119	Burundi	0.77
120	Chad	0.60
121	Burkina Faso	0.59
122	Madagascar[1]	0.54
123	Mali	0.50
124	Cambodia[1]	0.31
125	Bangladesh	0.31
126	Tajikistan[1]	0.30
127	Ethiopia[1]	0.21

SOURCE: International Telecommunication Union, *World Telecommunication Indicators 2007*

[1] 2005

7.05 Internet bandwidth (hard data)

International Internet bandwidth (mB/s) per 10,000 inhabitants | 2006 or most recent year available

RANK	COUNTRY/ECONOMY	HARD DATA
1	Denmark[2]	349.00
2	Netherlands[2]	205.26
3	Sweden[2]	175.16
4	Jamaica[2]	155.56
5	United Kingdom[1]	130.69
6	Hong Kong SAR	129.79
7	Australia	117.65
8	Estonia	115.38
9	Belgium[1]	112.52
10	Switzerland[2]	97.90
11	Norway[2]	93.52
12	Singapore[2]	71.21
13	Germany[2]	68.45
14	Canada[2]	67.34
15	Austria[2]	66.60
16	Ireland[2]	59.97
17	Finland[2]	43.49
18	Iceland[1]	42.32
19	United States[1]	33.06
20	France[2]	33.06
21	Luxembourg[1]	32.40
22	Latvia	32.12
23	Taiwan, China[1]	31.44
24	Slovak Republic	29.07
25	Spain[2]	27.95
26	Lithuania	27.10
27	Israel[2]	25.37
28	Barbados[2]	22.22
29	Czech Republic[2]	21.77
30	United Arab Emirates	21.44
31	Italy[2]	20.62
32	Malta[1]	19.38
33	Bulgaria	17.54
34	Romania	15.03
35	Slovenia[2]	12.55
36	New Zealand[2]	11.44
37	Croatia[2]	10.37
38	Korea, Rep.	10.37
39	Japan[2]	10.35
40	Hungary	9.90
41	Portugal[2]	8.33
42	Chile[2]	7.79
43	Argentina	6.91
44	Qatar[1]	6.25
45	Turkey	6.20
46	Greece[2]	5.87
47	Bahrain[2]	5.60
48	Poland[2]	5.55
49	Colombia	5.51
50	Puerto Rico[2]	5.00
51	Uruguay[2]	4.57
52	Trinidad and Tobago[2]	3.77
53	Cyprus[1]	3.72
54	Morocco	3.61
55	Peru[2]	3.57
56	Kuwait[2]	3.27
57	Panama[2]	2.89
58	Ecuador	2.24
59	China	1.94
60	Costa Rica	1.76
61	Oman	1.70
62	Thailand	1.53
63	Brazil[2]	1.50
64	Mauritius	1.48
65	Moldova	1.35
66	Malaysia[2]	1.26
67	Tunisia	1.25
68	Egypt	1.24
69	Saudi Arabia	1.18
70	Mexico[2]	1.05
71	Senegal	1.04
72	Suriname[1]	1.03
73	Russian Federation[2]	1.00
74	Vietnam	0.83
75	Paraguay	0.79
76	Kazakhstan	0.65
77	Guatemala[2]	0.56
78	Jordan[2]	0.54
79	Venezuela[2]	0.50
80	Guyana[2]	0.48
81	Bolivia[2]	0.43
82	Bosnia and Herzegovina[2]	0.40
83	Philippines[2]	0.39
84	Kyrgyz Republic[2]	0.38
85	Azerbaijan[2]	0.36
86	Mauritania	0.28
87	India	0.24
88	Sri Lanka	0.24
89	Mali	0.22
90	El Salvador	0.22
91	Kenya	0.22
92	Libya	0.21
93	South Africa[2]	0.19
94	Namibia[2]	0.18
95	Ukraine[2]	0.18
96	Macedonia, FYR	0.17
97	Botswana	0.17
98	Burkina Faso	0.16
99	Mongolia[2]	0.13
100	Zambia	0.11
101	Cameroon[2]	0.10
102	Armenia[1]	0.09
103	Bangladesh	0.09
104	Syria	0.08
105	Georgia[2]	0.07
106	Indonesia[2]	0.07
107	Dominican Republic	0.07
108	Gambia, The[2]	0.06
109	Honduras[2]	0.06
110	Benin	0.05
111	Algeria[2]	0.05
112	Nepal	0.05
113	Pakistan[2]	0.05
114	Uganda	0.04
115	Zimbabwe	0.04
116	Albania[2]	0.04
117	Lesotho[2]	0.02
118	Madagascar	0.02
119	Cambodia[2]	0.01
120	Nigeria[2]	0.01
121	Nicaragua[2]	0.01
122	Mozambique[2]	0.01
123	Chad	0.01
124	Burundi[2]	0.01
125	Tanzania[2]	0.00
126	Tajikistan[2]	0.00
127	Ethiopia[2]	0.00

SOURCE: International Telecommunication Union, *World Telecommunication Indicators 2007*

[1] 2004   [2] 2005

Subindex C **Usage component**

8th pillar
Business usage

8.01 Prevalence of foreign technology licensing

In your country, licensing of foreign technology is (1 = uncommon, 7 = a common means of acquiring new technology)

RANK	COUNTRY/ECONOMY	SCORE
1	Singapore	5.92
2	Sweden	5.76
3	Canada	5.75
4	Indonesia	5.74
5	Taiwan, China	5.72
6	Netherlands	5.70
7	Portugal	5.67
8	Australia	5.66
9	Denmark	5.60
10	Malaysia	5.60
11	South Africa	5.60
12	Japan	5.59
13	New Zealand	5.57
14	Israel	5.57
15	United Kingdom	5.56
16	Hong Kong SAR	5.56
17	Iceland	5.55
18	Switzerland	5.54
19	United Arab Emirates	5.54
20	Germany	5.50
21	Qatar	5.48
22	India	5.48
23	United States	5.46
24	Norway	5.46
25	Bahrain	5.42
26	Belgium	5.41
27	Korea, Rep.	5.38
28	Finland	5.35
29	Thailand	5.33
30	Spain	5.31
31	Jordan	5.23
32	Puerto Rico	5.20
33	Ireland	5.19
34	Austria	5.17
35	Malta	5.17
36	Tunisia	5.13
37	Slovak Republic	5.03
38	Kuwait	5.01
39	Czech Republic	5.00
40	Chile	4.98
41	Turkey	4.96
42	Luxembourg	4.95
43	Greece	4.95
44	France	4.94
45	Croatia	4.93
46	Panama	4.86
47	Philippines	4.83
48	Kenya	4.83
49	Brazil	4.80
50	Estonia	4.78
51	Jamaica	4.75
52	Hungary	4.74
53	Trinidad and Tobago	4.73
54	Egypt	4.73
55	Mauritius	4.71
56	Italy	4.71
57	Costa Rica	4.71
58	Slovenia	4.66
59	Sri Lanka	4.65
60	Lithuania	4.63
61	Mexico	4.62
62	Dominican Republic	4.60
63	Namibia	4.58
64	Pakistan	4.55
65	Uganda	4.55
66	Cyprus	4.54
67	Venezuela	4.53
68	Saudi Arabia	4.51
69	Oman	4.49
70	Barbados	4.42
71	Morocco	4.40
72	Gambia, The	4.35
73	Zambia	4.35
74	Nigeria	4.32
75	El Salvador	4.32
76	Latvia	4.27
77	Guatemala	4.24
78	Romania	4.22
79	Botswana	4.21
80	Mauritania	4.18
81	Argentina	4.16
82	Poland	4.15
83	Azerbaijan	4.11
84	Colombia	4.09
85	Syria	4.09
86	Uruguay	4.08
87	China	4.04
88	Albania	4.02
89	Zimbabwe	4.01
90	Senegal	3.99
91	Kazakhstan	3.93
92	Tanzania	3.93
93	Honduras	3.91
94	Peru	3.91
95	Libya	3.83
96	Mozambique	3.80
97	Mali	3.71
98	Bulgaria	3.70
99	Nepal	3.68
100	Bangladesh	3.66
101	Macedonia, FYR	3.65
102	Georgia	3.59
103	Algeria	3.58
104	Mongolia	3.56
105	Russian Federation	3.54
106	Bosnia and Herzegovina	3.54
107	Benin	3.49
108	Burkina Faso	3.48
109	Cameroon	3.47
110	Ethiopia	3.45
111	Ukraine	3.38
112	Armenia	3.38
113	Ecuador	3.36
114	Lesotho	3.35
115	Cambodia	3.33
116	Tajikistan	3.30
117	Madagascar	3.22
118	Vietnam	3.13
119	Nicaragua	3.03
120	Moldova	2.98
121	Guyana	2.98
122	Kyrgyz Republic	2.96
123	Suriname	2.92
124	Paraguay	2.87
125	Burundi	2.74
126	Bolivia	2.49
127	Chad	2.45

MEAN: 4.47

SOURCE: World Economic Forum, Executive Opinion Survey 2006, 2007

8.02 Firm-level technology absorption

Companies in your country are (1 = not able to absorb new technology, 7 = aggressive in absorbing new technology)

RANK	COUNTRY/ECONOMY	SCORE
1	Iceland	6.49
2	Sweden	6.29
3	Japan	6.25
4	United States	6.11
5	Israel	6.11
6	Switzerland	6.10
7	Finland	6.08
8	Taiwan, China	6.05
9	Singapore	6.05
10	Denmark	6.02
11	Norway	6.00
12	Austria	6.00
13	Korea, Rep.	5.98
14	Germany	5.98
15	Malaysia	5.78
16	Hong Kong SAR	5.77
17	United Arab Emirates	5.72
18	Australia	5.66
19	United Kingdom	5.64
20	Puerto Rico	5.63
21	Canada	5.60
22	India	5.58
23	Ireland	5.54
24	Senegal	5.52
25	New Zealand	5.49
26	Estonia	5.48
27	Netherlands	5.45
28	France	5.39
29	Turkey	5.38
30	South Africa	5.38
31	Belgium	5.35
32	Kuwait	5.35
33	Qatar	5.30
34	Slovak Republic	5.28
35	Czech Republic	5.27
36	Luxembourg	5.25
37	Tunisia	5.24
38	Chile	5.24
39	Mauritania	5.23
40	Bahrain	5.20
41	Malta	5.18
42	Jordan	5.17
43	Portugal	5.17
44	Thailand	5.16
45	Lithuania	5.09
46	Vietnam	5.08
47	Saudi Arabia	5.04
48	Hungary	5.02
49	Panama	5.00
50	China	5.00
51	Morocco	4.98
52	Philippines	4.94
53	Jamaica	4.94
54	Brazil	4.89
55	Costa Rica	4.88
56	Kenya	4.87
57	Barbados	4.85
58	Azerbaijan	4.85
59	Guatemala	4.82
60	Spain	4.80
61	Slovenia	4.78
62	Dominican Republic	4.77
63	Sri Lanka	4.73
64	Cyprus	4.73
65	Latvia	4.71
66	Indonesia	4.70
67	Egypt	4.65
68	Pakistan	4.62
69	Madagascar	4.62
70	Trinidad and Tobago	4.61
71	Venezuela	4.59
72	Mauritius	4.59
73	Zambia	4.58
74	Kazakhstan	4.55
75	Poland	4.51
76	Gambia, The	4.49
77	Mali	4.46
78	Italy	4.45
79	Nigeria	4.44
80	Armenia	4.44
81	Benin	4.43
82	Burkina Faso	4.43
83	Romania	4.42
84	Botswana	4.42
85	El Salvador	4.41
86	Namibia	4.39
87	Mexico	4.38
88	Tanzania	4.37
89	Greece	4.37
90	Ukraine	4.37
91	Peru	4.33
92	Croatia	4.32
93	Cameroon	4.28
94	Colombia	4.23
95	Oman	4.22
96	Algeria	4.20
97	Argentina	4.18
98	Honduras	4.18
99	Uruguay	4.16
100	Cambodia	4.15
101	Russian Federation	4.15
102	Syria	4.12
103	Uganda	4.10
104	Bangladesh	4.05
105	Mongolia	3.98
106	Libya	3.92
107	Georgia	3.88
108	Moldova	3.83
109	Ecuador	3.81
110	Albania	3.79
111	Nepal	3.73
112	Burundi	3.71
113	Tajikistan	3.71
114	Guyana	3.70
115	Lesotho	3.68
116	Mozambique	3.61
117	Bulgaria	3.60
118	Zimbabwe	3.59
119	Ethiopia	3.55
120	Kyrgyz Republic	3.52
121	Suriname	3.52
122	Chad	3.51
123	Nicaragua	3.49
124	Bosnia and Herzegovina	3.46
125	Macedonia, FYR	3.38
126	Paraguay	3.35
127	Bolivia	3.20

MEAN: 4.76

SOURCE: World Economic Forum, Executive Opinion Survey 2006, 2007

8.03 Capacity for innovation

Companies obtain technology (1 = exclusively from licensing or imitating foreign companies, 7 = by conducting formal research and pioneering their own new products and processes)

RANK	COUNTRY/ECONOMY	SCORE
1	Germany	6.08
2	Sweden	5.88
3	Japan	5.85
4	Switzerland	5.80
5	Finland	5.78
6	Denmark	5.54
7	Korea, Rep.	5.50
8	France	5.50
9	United States	5.44
10	Israel	5.41
11	Austria	5.38
12	Netherlands	5.31
13	Belgium	5.12
14	United Kingdom	5.10
15	Norway	4.96
16	Taiwan, China	4.82
17	Canada	4.77
18	Luxembourg	4.72
19	Slovenia	4.70
20	Italy	4.66
21	Iceland	4.55
22	Malaysia	4.50
23	Singapore	4.50
24	Ireland	4.39
25	Czech Republic	4.27
26	Hong Kong SAR	4.24
27	New Zealand	4.23
28	Tunisia	4.05
29	Brazil	4.03
30	Australia	4.01
31	India	4.01
32	Oman	3.97
33	Portugal	3.87
34	China	3.83
35	Spain	3.82
36	Sri Lanka	3.79
37	Costa Rica	3.73
38	Hungary	3.72
39	Estonia	3.69
40	Ukraine	3.69
41	Vietnam	3.67
42	South Africa	3.66
43	Poland	3.65
44	Lithuania	3.63
45	Azerbaijan	3.63
46	Turkey	3.57
47	Croatia	3.48
48	Saudi Arabia	3.47
49	Chile	3.47
50	Indonesia	3.44
51	Puerto Rico	3.40
52	Slovak Republic	3.40
53	Russian Federation	3.40
54	Latvia	3.35
55	Thailand	3.34
56	Kenya	3.31
57	Mexico	3.30
58	Guatemala	3.18
59	Philippines	3.15
60	Malta	3.14
61	Jordan	3.13
62	Romania	3.13
63	Kazakhstan	3.11
64	Colombia	3.10
65	Nigeria	3.08
66	Peru	3.05
67	Jamaica	3.04
68	Benin	3.03
69	Cyprus	3.03
70	Pakistan	3.03
71	Armenia	3.02
72	Moldova	3.01
73	Greece	2.97
74	Uruguay	2.97
75	Barbados	2.96
76	United Arab Emirates	2.95
77	Egypt	2.95
78	Bulgaria	2.94
79	Tajikistan	2.93
80	Argentina	2.92
81	Kyrgyz Republic	2.91
82	Burkina Faso	2.91
83	Macedonia, FYR	2.90
84	Honduras	2.90
85	Morocco	2.89
86	El Salvador	2.89
87	Uganda	2.89
88	Qatar	2.86
89	Mali	2.85
90	Madagascar	2.84
91	Gambia, The	2.84
92	Senegal	2.81
93	Mauritania	2.81
94	Mauritius	2.74
95	Mongolia	2.73
96	Suriname	2.71
97	Dominican Republic	2.70
98	Georgia	2.69
99	Ecuador	2.69
100	Tanzania	2.67
101	Guyana	2.67
102	Panama	2.66
103	Ethiopia	2.61
104	Syria	2.60
105	Nicaragua	2.59
106	Kuwait	2.57
107	Botswana	2.56
108	Bosnia and Herzegovina	2.54
109	Trinidad and Tobago	2.50
110	Cambodia	2.50
111	Chad	2.50
112	Venezuela	2.50
113	Mozambique	2.48
114	Bolivia	2.47
115	Namibia	2.46
116	Paraguay	2.41
117	Cameroon	2.41
118	Zambia	2.36
119	Bangladesh	2.35
120	Burundi	2.34
121	Nepal	2.33
122	Lesotho	2.29
123	Algeria	2.28
124	Bahrain	2.22
125	Zimbabwe	2.18
126	Libya	2.17
127	Albania	1.91

MEAN: 3.45

SOURCE: World Economic Forum, Executive Opinion Survey 2006, 2007

8.04 Availability of new telephone lines

New telephone lines for your business are (1 = scarce and difficult to obtain, 7 = widely available and highly reliable)

RANK	COUNTRY/ECONOMY	SCORE
1	Switzerland	6.86
2	Finland	6.84
3	Germany	6.83
4	Denmark	6.82
5	Iceland	6.82
6	Singapore	6.82
7	Sweden	6.80
8	Japan	6.79
9	Hong Kong SAR	6.78
10	France	6.78
11	Austria	6.76
12	Norway	6.73
13	Netherlands	6.72
14	Israel	6.69
15	Canada	6.69
16	Belgium	6.64
17	United Arab Emirates	6.57
18	Jordan	6.55
19	United Kingdom	6.55
20	Chile	6.52
21	Slovak Republic	6.49
22	United States	6.45
23	Hungary	6.42
24	Estonia	6.39
25	El Salvador	6.37
26	Korea, Rep.	6.37
27	Czech Republic	6.35
28	Guatemala	6.33
29	Malta	6.32
30	Taiwan, China	6.30
31	Portugal	6.30
32	Uruguay	6.28
33	India	6.25
34	Cyprus	6.24
35	Tunisia	6.24
36	Dominican Republic	6.22
37	Egypt	6.20
38	Luxembourg	6.20
39	Australia	6.20
40	Bahrain	6.17
41	Croatia	6.16
42	Morocco	6.12
43	Malaysia	6.10
44	Thailand	6.05
45	Spain	6.04
46	Turkey	6.03
47	New Zealand	6.02
48	Lithuania	6.02
49	Colombia	6.00
50	Brazil	5.98
51	Kuwait	5.97
52	Slovenia	5.96
53	Latvia	5.94
54	Panama	5.91
55	Peru	5.89
56	Greece	5.87
57	Mauritius	5.86
58	Sri Lanka	5.78
59	Saudi Arabia	5.76
60	Mauritania	5.72
61	Mexico	5.70
62	Qatar	5.70
63	Macedonia, FYR	5.69
64	Puerto Rico	5.66
65	Vietnam	5.57
66	Senegal	5.56
67	Jamaica	5.56
68	Syria	5.54
69	Barbados	5.53
70	Italy	5.50
71	China	5.49
72	Argentina	5.48
73	Ireland	5.47
74	Philippines	5.45
75	Algeria	5.41
76	Bosnia and Herzegovina	5.33
77	Namibia	5.32
78	Pakistan	5.31
79	Mali	5.28
80	Bulgaria	5.28
81	Moldova	5.28
82	Azerbaijan	5.27
83	Uganda	5.25
84	Venezuela	5.22
85	Georgia	5.14
86	Romania	5.12
87	Gambia, The	5.11
88	Nigeria	5.06
89	Mozambique	5.06
90	Tajikistan	5.05
91	Indonesia	5.03
92	Kazakhstan	5.03
93	Tanzania	4.99
94	Russian Federation	4.99
95	Bolivia	4.97
96	Zambia	4.84
97	South Africa	4.77
98	Oman	4.70
99	Poland	4.68
100	Botswana	4.68
101	Ukraine	4.65
102	Burkina Faso	4.61
103	Ethiopia	4.57
104	Trinidad and Tobago	4.52
105	Mongolia	4.42
106	Honduras	4.40
107	Kyrgyz Republic	4.37
108	Nepal	4.32
109	Nicaragua	4.26
110	Cambodia	4.24
111	Armenia	4.23
112	Madagascar	4.21
113	Kenya	4.17
114	Cameroon	4.06
115	Ecuador	4.06
116	Burundi	3.94
117	Costa Rica	3.92
118	Paraguay	3.85
119	Chad	3.73
120	Albania	3.70
121	Lesotho	3.63
122	Libya	3.60
123	Guyana	3.44
124	Suriname	3.23
125	Bangladesh	3.00
126	Benin	2.84
127	Zimbabwe	2.21

MEAN: 5.48

SOURCE: World Economic Forum, Executive Opinion Survey 2006, 2007

8.05 Extent of business Internet use

Companies in your country use the Internet extensively for buying and selling goods, and for interacting with customers and suppliers (1= strongly disagree; 7= strongly agree)

RANK	COUNTRY/ECONOMY	SCORE
1	Korea, Rep.	6.12
2	Estonia	6.10
3	Sweden	5.96
4	United Kingdom	5.95
5	Germany	5.90
6	United States	5.87
7	Denmark	5.81
8	Switzerland	5.69
9	Japan	5.67
10	Iceland	5.64
11	Canada	5.63
12	Netherlands	5.62
13	Finland	5.60
14	Israel	5.52
15	Norway	5.52
16	Austria	5.48
17	Taiwan, China	5.45
18	Australia	5.38
19	Singapore	5.28
20	Czech Republic	5.27
21	Puerto Rico	5.20
22	Hong Kong SAR	5.18
23	France	5.09
24	Ireland	5.03
25	New Zealand	5.01
26	Belgium	4.94
27	Chile	4.85
28	Brazil	4.84
29	Malaysia	4.81
30	Luxembourg	4.76
31	Thailand	4.75
32	Malta	4.71
33	Lithuania	4.67
34	Slovenia	4.58
35	India	4.57
36	Portugal	4.50
37	Guatemala	4.46
38	Poland	4.42
39	Latvia	4.34
40	Panama	4.33
41	Jordan	4.27
42	United Arab Emirates	4.23
43	Jamaica	4.23
44	Oman	4.21
45	South Africa	4.20
46	Spain	4.20
47	Tunisia	4.18
48	Cyprus	4.18
49	Slovak Republic	4.18
50	Hungary	4.17
51	Saudi Arabia	4.17
51	Senegal	4.17
53	Russian Federation	4.11
54	Italy	4.10
55	Turkey	4.07
56	Indonesia	4.06
57	Egypt	4.05
58	Sri Lanka	4.00
59	Qatar	3.98
60	China	3.97
61	Kuwait	3.96
62	Azerbaijan	3.95
63	Honduras	3.95
64	Mexico	3.94
65	Croatia	3.90
66	Barbados	3.89
67	Philippines	3.89
68	El Salvador	3.87
69	Uruguay	3.82
70	Peru	3.78
71	Costa Rica	3.78
72	Dominican Republic	3.75
73	Argentina	3.74
74	Colombia	3.73
75	Kenya	3.71
76	Ukraine	3.70
77	Kazakhstan	3.66
78	Romania	3.65
79	Trinidad and Tobago	3.65
80	Venezuela	3.63
81	Nigeria	3.61
82	Bosnia and Herzegovina	3.61
83	Bahrain	3.57
84	Uganda	3.57
85	Pakistan	3.55
86	Gambia, The	3.53
87	Bulgaria	3.49
88	Mauritius	3.47
89	Mali	3.45
90	Tanzania	3.44
91	Zambia	3.43
92	Namibia	3.40
93	Mauritania	3.39
94	Guyana	3.37
95	Georgia	3.36
96	Tajikistan	3.35
97	Greece	3.30
98	Burkina Faso	3.29
99	Cambodia	3.29
100	Mongolia	3.23
101	Vietnam	3.18
102	Botswana	3.16
103	Nepal	3.14
104	Benin	3.14
105	Morocco	3.11
106	Ethiopia	3.08
107	Ecuador	3.08
108	Nicaragua	3.06
109	Armenia	3.05
110	Bangladesh	3.05
111	Syria	2.97
112	Suriname	2.96
113	Mozambique	2.94
114	Bolivia	2.93
115	Albania	2.92
116	Kyrgyz Republic	2.92
117	Libya	2.90
118	Madagascar	2.89
119	Moldova	2.85
120	Zimbabwe	2.77
121	Paraguay	2.74
122	Lesotho	2.71
123	Macedonia, FYR	2.62
124	Cameroon	2.58
125	Burundi	2.36
126	Algeria	2.23
127	Chad	2.22

MEAN: 4.04

SOURCE: World Economic Forum, Executive Opinion Survey 2006, 2007

Subindex C **Usage component**

9th pillar
Government usage

9.01 Government success in ICT promotion

Government programs promoting the use of ICT are (1 = not very successful, 7 = highly successful)

RANK	COUNTRY/ECONOMY	SCORE
1	Singapore	6.04
2	Tunisia	5.64
3	Malta	5.64
4	Estonia	5.57
5	Malaysia	5.56
6	United Arab Emirates	5.53
7	Korea, Rep.	5.49
8	Sweden	5.41
9	Taiwan, China	5.39
10	Denmark	5.36
11	Qatar	5.36
12	Mauritania	5.25
13	Iceland	5.21
14	Mali	5.20
15	Finland	5.16
16	Portugal	5.14
17	Hong Kong SAR	5.11
18	India	5.03
19	Gambia, The	5.02
20	Israel	5.02
21	United States	5.00
22	Jordan	5.00
23	Norway	4.95
24	Senegal	4.94
25	Bahrain	4.93
26	Austria	4.91
27	France	4.86
28	Burkina Faso	4.82
29	Luxembourg	4.79
30	Thailand	4.78
31	Madagascar	4.77
32	Switzerland	4.76
33	Azerbaijan	4.74
34	Japan	4.74
35	Saudi Arabia	4.71
36	Morocco	4.69
37	Vietnam	4.68
38	Egypt	4.68
39	Germany	4.64
40	Mauritius	4.63
41	Barbados	4.61
42	Canada	4.60
43	Netherlands	4.58
44	Benin	4.57
45	Lithuania	4.55
46	Australia	4.53
47	Algeria	4.51
48	China	4.51
49	Uganda	4.50
50	Ireland	4.50
51	Tanzania	4.50
52	Kazakhstan	4.45
53	Chile	4.45
54	United Kingdom	4.44
55	Pakistan	4.44
56	Oman	4.41
57	Mongolia	4.38
58	Jamaica	4.38
59	Sri Lanka	4.37
60	Tajikistan	4.28
61	Belgium	4.26
62	Slovenia	4.25
63	Nigeria	4.24
64	El Salvador	4.24
65	Croatia	4.18
66	Dominican Republic	4.18
67	Kenya	4.17
68	Brazil	4.16
69	Syria	4.15
70	Puerto Rico	4.12
71	Botswana	4.12
72	Turkey	4.08
73	Romania	4.07
74	Cameroon	4.07
75	Cyprus	4.06
76	Colombia	4.05
77	South Africa	4.03
78	Mozambique	4.02
79	Mexico	4.00
80	New Zealand	3.99
81	Philippines	3.97
82	Costa Rica	3.96
83	Hungary	3.95
84	Uruguay	3.93
85	Ethiopia	3.88
86	Kuwait	3.86
87	Trinidad and Tobago	3.84
88	Cambodia	3.80
89	Spain	3.80
90	Guatemala	3.80
91	Burundi	3.78
92	Macedonia, FYR	3.78
93	Moldova	3.73
94	Guyana	3.73
95	Slovak Republic	3.71
96	Bulgaria	3.69
97	Italy	3.67
98	Latvia	3.65
99	Greece	3.65
100	Nepal	3.63
101	Honduras	3.61
102	Georgia	3.59
103	Czech Republic	3.58
104	Panama	3.56
105	Libya	3.54
106	Russian Federation	3.50
107	Ukraine	3.47
108	Zambia	3.44
109	Armenia	3.40
110	Venezuela	3.39
111	Namibia	3.35
112	Lesotho	3.30
113	Peru	3.30
114	Indonesia	3.23
115	Nicaragua	3.21
116	Bangladesh	3.13
117	Bosnia and Herzegovina	3.12
118	Poland	3.04
119	Argentina	3.01
120	Chad	3.00
121	Albania	2.99
122	Kyrgyz Republic	2.94
123	Zimbabwe	2.89
124	Bolivia	2.85
125	Ecuador	2.63
126	Suriname	2.56
127	Paraguay	2.45

MEAN: 4.23

SOURCE: World Economic Forum, Executive Opinion Survey 2006, 2007

9.02 Availability of government online services

In your country, online government services such as personal tax, car registrations, passport applications, business permits, and e-procurement are (1 = not available, 7 = extensively available)

RANK	COUNTRY/ECONOMY	SCORE
1	Estonia	6.48
2	Singapore	6.31
3	Denmark	6.13
4	Sweden	5.90
5	Ireland	5.82
6	Malta	5.79
7	Iceland	5.76
8	Austria	5.72
9	Korea, Rep.	5.69
10	United States	5.69
11	Norway	5.67
12	Chile	5.64
13	Hong Kong SAR	5.63
14	United Kingdom	5.54
15	Australia	5.48
16	Canada	5.46
17	Finland	5.38
18	New Zealand	5.38
19	Malaysia	5.32
20	France	5.22
21	Switzerland	5.20
22	Taiwan, China	5.20
23	Qatar	5.17
24	Netherlands	5.15
25	United Arab Emirates	5.13
26	Portugal	5.12
27	Israel	5.09
28	Brazil	5.05
29	Thailand	4.83
30	Oman	4.81
31	Germany	4.60
32	Spain	4.58
33	Belgium	4.53
34	Lithuania	4.51
35	Slovenia	4.46
36	Tunisia	4.46
37	Dominican Republic	4.44
38	Luxembourg	4.37
39	China	4.32
40	Mexico	4.32
41	Guatemala	4.30
42	Venezuela	4.24
43	El Salvador	4.24
44	India	4.16
45	Jamaica	4.13
46	Cyprus	4.11
47	Puerto Rico	4.10
48	Hungary	4.09
49	Japan	4.08
50	Uruguay	3.99
51	Bahrain	3.98
52	Peru	3.97
53	Turkey	3.93
54	Kazakhstan	3.93
55	Panama	3.86
56	Uganda	3.81
57	Bulgaria	3.75
58	Italy	3.73
59	Argentina	3.70
60	Saudi Arabia	3.69
61	Egypt	3.65
62	South Africa	3.64
63	Colombia	3.57
64	Nigeria	3.53
65	Bolivia	3.52
66	Mauritius	3.43
67	Azerbaijan	3.43
68	Greece	3.37
69	Croatia	3.35
70	Costa Rica	3.35
71	Sri Lanka	3.34
72	Philippines	3.31
73	Romania	3.29
74	Latvia	3.28
75	Morocco	3.25
76	Mauritania	3.24
77	Honduras	3.20
78	Kenya	3.17
79	Slovak Republic	3.15
80	Ecuador	3.15
81	Ukraine	3.14
82	Gambia, The	3.10
83	Jordan	3.09
84	Czech Republic	3.07
85	Nicaragua	3.06
86	Senegal	3.03
87	Indonesia	3.01
88	Pakistan	2.95
89	Macedonia, FYR	2.89
90	Mali	2.88
91	Poland	2.87
92	Russian Federation	2.82
93	Benin	2.77
94	Botswana	2.77
95	Vietnam	2.73
96	Tanzania	2.73
97	Kuwait	2.65
98	Burkina Faso	2.65
99	Ethiopia	2.63
100	Chad	2.59
101	Zambia	2.56
102	Barbados	2.56
103	Tajikistan	2.52
104	Madagascar	2.51
105	Paraguay	2.51
106	Namibia	2.48
107	Lesotho	2.34
108	Mongolia	2.32
109	Bosnia and Herzegovina	2.31
110	Moldova	2.31
111	Algeria	2.29
112	Georgia	2.19
113	Kyrgyz Republic	2.17
114	Burundi	2.10
115	Nepal	2.07
116	Cameroon	2.05
117	Mozambique	2.02
118	Cambodia	2.01
119	Trinidad and Tobago	1.98
120	Armenia	1.86
121	Guyana	1.85
122	Albania	1.77
123	Syria	1.72
124	Zimbabwe	1.60
125	Libya	1.56
126	Bangladesh	1.51
127	Suriname	1.41

MEAN: 3.70

SOURCE: World Economic Forum, Executive Opinion Survey 2006, 2007

9.03 ICT use and government efficiency

The use of information and communication technologies by the government has improved the efficiency of government services, facilitating interaction with businesses and individuals (1 = strongly disagree, 7 = strongly agree)

RANK	COUNTRY/ECONOMY	SCORE
1	Singapore	6.14
2	Estonia	6.11
3	Denmark	5.90
4	Iceland	5.81
5	Italy	5.76
6	Malta	5.73
7	Sweden	5.72
8	Hong Kong SAR	5.70
9	Chile	5.64
10	Portugal	5.64
11	United Arab Emirates	5.64
12	Korea, Rep.	5.63
13	Malaysia	5.60
14	Taiwan, China	5.49
15	Qatar	5.48
16	Finland	5.44
17	Austria	5.43
18	Ireland	5.41
19	Norway	5.39
20	United States	5.35
21	Israel	5.25
22	Thailand	5.23
23	France	5.20
24	Canada	5.15
25	Switzerland	5.14
26	Tunisia	5.13
27	Brazil	5.11
28	Netherlands	5.04
29	Australia	4.98
30	India	4.89
31	Dominican Republic	4.85
32	Spain	4.78
33	United Kingdom	4.77
34	Mauritania	4.77
35	Germany	4.76
36	New Zealand	4.68
37	Mexico	4.66
38	China	4.62
39	Guatemala	4.60
40	Turkey	4.60
41	Luxembourg	4.57
42	Jamaica	4.53
43	Uruguay	4.51
44	Lithuania	4.51
45	El Salvador	4.49
46	Slovenia	4.49
47	Cyprus	4.47
48	Jordan	4.44
49	Bahrain	4.43
50	Azerbaijan	4.40
51	Mali	4.40
52	Oman	4.38
53	Belgium	4.37
54	Madagascar	4.35
55	Peru	4.29
56	Gambia, The	4.27
57	Kazakhstan	4.26
58	Cambodia	4.26
59	Egypt	4.23
60	Burkina Faso	4.21
61	Hungary	4.21
62	Morocco	4.18
63	Colombia	4.14
64	Pakistan	4.13
65	Japan	4.12
66	Panama	4.11
67	Uganda	4.10
68	Philippines	4.10
69	Greece	4.08
70	Saudi Arabia	4.06
71	Romania	4.06
72	Kenya	4.05
73	Nigeria	4.05
74	Sri Lanka	4.04
75	Vietnam	4.04
76	Latvia	4.04
77	Venezuela	4.02
78	Senegal	4.00
79	Slovak Republic	3.99
80	Benin	3.96
81	Tanzania	3.92
82	Croatia	3.92
83	Puerto Rico	3.88
84	Argentina	3.86
85	South Africa	3.85
86	Mauritius	3.84
87	Bolivia	3.84
88	Honduras	3.75
89	Ethiopia	3.75
90	Tajikistan	3.74
91	Ukraine	3.74
92	Algeria	3.74
93	Costa Rica	3.72
94	Nicaragua	3.66
95	Russian Federation	3.65
96	Georgia	3.65
97	Bulgaria	3.65
98	Kuwait	3.63
99	Barbados	3.57
100	Ecuador	3.49
101	Czech Republic	3.45
102	Macedonia, FYR	3.44
103	Botswana	3.41
104	Mongolia	3.41
105	Nepal	3.38
106	Mozambique	3.28
107	Poland	3.26
108	Moldova	3.22
109	Bangladesh	3.18
110	Syria	3.13
111	Cameroon	3.08
112	Chad	3.04
113	Paraguay	3.03
114	Armenia	3.02
115	Indonesia	2.97
116	Trinidad and Tobago	2.96
117	Namibia	2.90
118	Burundi	2.89
119	Kyrgyz Republic	2.89
120	Bosnia and Herzegovina	2.87
121	Lesotho	2.81
122	Guyana	2.80
123	Zambia	2.75
124	Libya	2.48
125	Suriname	2.48
126	Albania	2.44
127	Zimbabwe	2.01

MEAN: 4.22

SOURCE: World Economic Forum, Executive Opinion Survey 2006, 2007

9.04 Presence of ICT in government offices

The presence of information and communication technologies in government offices in your country is (1 = very rare, 7 = commonplace and pervasive)

RANK	COUNTRY/ECONOMY	SCORE
1	Singapore	6.41
2	Estonia	6.30
3	Korea, Rep.	6.11
4	Switzerland	5.97
5	Denmark	5.95
6	Sweden	5.90
7	Austria	5.86
8	Iceland	5.83
9	Finland	5.82
10	Hong Kong SAR	5.71
11	Norway	5.67
12	Malta	5.63
13	Taiwan, China	5.61
14	Malaysia	5.58
15	Australia	5.54
16	Netherlands	5.53
17	United Arab Emirates	5.53
18	United States	5.44
19	New Zealand	5.42
20	Germany	5.34
21	Canada	5.33
22	United Kingdom	5.32
23	Tunisia	5.30
24	Ireland	5.29
25	Chile	5.28
26	Qatar	5.26
27	Slovenia	5.25
28	Portugal	5.16
29	Lithuania	5.13
30	Luxembourg	5.11
31	Israel	5.09
32	Slovak Republic	5.09
33	Latvia	5.08
34	Croatia	5.07
35	Romania	5.05
36	Thailand	5.02
37	Japan	5.00
38	Spain	5.00
39	France	4.95
40	China	4.92
41	Azerbaijan	4.89
42	Bahrain	4.86
43	Mauritania	4.82
44	Bulgaria	4.82
45	Jordan	4.71
46	Gambia, The	4.66
47	Moldova	4.62
48	Mongolia	4.59
49	Benin	4.57
50	Hungary	4.57
51	Jamaica	4.52
52	El Salvador	4.51
53	Brazil	4.48
54	Italy	4.46
55	Albania	4.45
56	India	4.45
57	Mali	4.43
58	Senegal	4.43
59	Turkey	4.41
60	Saudi Arabia	4.40
61	South Africa	4.39
62	Vietnam	4.36
63	Oman	4.36
64	Belgium	4.34
65	Kazakhstan	4.32
66	Algeria	4.31
67	Burkina Faso	4.27
68	Mauritius	4.25
69	Morocco	4.25
70	Mexico	4.25
71	Barbados	4.25
72	Puerto Rico	4.19
73	Uruguay	4.17
74	Uganda	4.16
75	Botswana	4.14
76	Czech Republic	4.14
77	Cyprus	4.12
78	Kuwait	4.11
79	Guatemala	4.06
80	Costa Rica	4.02
81	Dominican Republic	4.02
82	Sri Lanka	3.98
83	Armenia	3.96
84	Tanzania	3.93
85	Greece	3.90
86	Georgia	3.88
87	Egypt	3.87
88	Colombia	3.84
89	Pakistan	3.82
90	Madagascar	3.76
91	Panama	3.74
92	Macedonia, FYR	3.72
93	Nigeria	3.63
94	Philippines	3.54
95	Nicaragua	3.53
96	Honduras	3.52
97	Kenya	3.52
98	Guyana	3.47
99	Ethiopia	3.47
100	Trinidad and Tobago	3.46
101	Namibia	3.44
102	Russian Federation	3.43
103	Peru	3.42
104	Ukraine	3.39
105	Tajikistan	3.36
106	Syria	3.34
107	Mozambique	3.34
108	Poland	3.29
109	Venezuela	3.26
110	Argentina	3.23
111	Bosnia and Herzegovina	3.23
112	Cameroon	3.22
113	Cambodia	3.19
114	Libya	3.05
115	Indonesia	3.02
116	Bolivia	2.99
117	Zambia	2.99
118	Nepal	2.89
119	Chad	2.88
120	Ecuador	2.86
121	Burundi	2.79
122	Kyrgyz Republic	2.77
123	Lesotho	2.72
124	Bangladesh	2.69
125	Paraguay	2.67
126	Zimbabwe	2.58
127	Suriname	2.32

MEAN: 4.34

SOURCE: World Economic Forum, Executive Opinion Survey 2006, 2007

9.05 E-Participation Index (hard data)

The E-Participation Index assesses the quality, relevance, usefulness and the willingness of government websites for providing online information and participatory tools and services to the people | 2007

RANK	COUNTRY/ECONOMY	HARD DATA
1	United States	1.00
2	Korea, Rep.	0.98
3	Denmark	0.93
3	France	0.93
5	Australia	0.89
6	New Zealand	0.80
7	Mexico	0.75
8	Estonia	0.73
9	Sweden	0.66
10	Singapore	0.64
11	Canada	0.61
11	Japan	0.61
11	Luxembourg	0.61
14	Ukraine	0.57
15	Jordan	0.55
16	Netherlands	0.52
16	Norway	0.52
16	Vietnam	0.52
19	Austria	0.48
19	China	0.48
19	Lithuania	0.48
22	Argentina	0.45
22	Brazil	0.45
24	Colombia	0.43
24	Mozambique	0.43
24	United Kingdom	0.43
27	Belgium	0.41
27	Bolivia	0.41
27	Switzerland	0.41
30	El Salvador	0.39
30	Malta	0.39
32	Costa Rica	0.36
32	Spain	0.36
34	Bahrain	0.34
34	Venezuela	0.34
36	Dominican Republic	0.32
36	Israel	0.32
36	Saudi Arabia	0.32
39	Botswana	0.30
39	Malaysia	0.30
39	Thailand	0.30
39	United Arab Emirates	0.30
43	Finland	0.27
43	Honduras	0.27
43	Mongolia	0.27
43	Philippines	0.27
47	Azerbaijan	0.25
47	Egypt	0.25
47	India	0.25
47	Ireland	0.25
47	Portugal	0.25
47	South Africa	0.25
53	Cambodia	0.23
53	Italy	0.23
53	Latvia	0.23
53	Poland	0.23
53	Slovenia	0.23
58	Burkina Faso	0.20
58	Czech Republic	0.20
58	Hungary	0.20
58	Libya	0.20
58	Oman	0.20
58	Senegal	0.20
58	Trinidad and Tobago	0.20
65	Chile	0.18
65	Qatar	0.18
67	Cameroon	0.16
67	Germany	0.16
69	Bangladesh	0.14
69	Barbados	0.14
69	Croatia	0.14
69	Kyrgyz Republic	0.14
69	Madagascar	0.14
69	Peru	0.14
69	Turkey	0.14
76	Benin	0.11
76	Ecuador	0.11
76	Jamaica	0.11
76	Mauritania	0.11
76	Mauritius	0.11
76	Panama	0.11
82	Bosnia and Herzegovina	0.09
82	Cyprus	0.09
82	Greece	0.09
82	Kazakhstan	0.09
82	Lesotho	0.09
82	Mali	0.09
82	Pakistan	0.09
82	Russian Federation	0.09
82	Uganda	0.09
91	Guyana	0.07
91	Iceland	0.07
91	Kuwait	0.07
91	Moldova	0.07
91	Nigeria	0.07
91	Paraguay	0.07
91	Slovak Republic	0.07
91	Sri Lanka	0.07
91	Uruguay	0.07
100	Armenia	0.05
100	Bulgaria	0.05
100	Burundi	0.05
100	Georgia	0.05
100	Guatemala	0.05
100	Indonesia	0.05
100	Kenya	0.05
100	Namibia	0.05
100	Romania	0.05
100	Syria	0.05
110	Albania	0.02
110	Algeria	0.02
110	Gambia, The	0.02
110	Macedonia, FYR	0.02
110	Nepal	0.02
110	Tanzania	0.02
110	Tunisia	0.02
117	Chad	0.00
117	Ethiopia	0.00
117	Morocco	0.00
117	Nicaragua	0.00
117	Suriname	0.00
117	Tajikistan	0.00
117	Zambia	0.00
117	Zimbabwe	0.00
n/a	Hong Kong SAR	n/a
n/a	Puerto Rico	n/a
n/a	Taiwan, China	n/a

SOURCE: United Nations, *Global E-Government Survey 2008*

Technical Notes and Sources

The data used in this *Report* represent the best available estimates from various national authorities, international agencies, and private sources at the time the *Report* was prepared. It is possible that some data will have been revised or updated by national sources after publication. Throughout the statistical tables in this publication, "n/a" denotes that the value is not available, or that available data are unreasonably outdated or do not come from a reliable source. The following section provides additional information and definitions for the hard data indicators that enter the composition of the Networked Readiness Index and are presented in the Data Tables section of this *Report*.

Pillar 1: Market environment

1.05 Utility patents
Number of utility patents (i.e., patents for invention) granted between January 1 and December 31, 2006, per million population | 2006
Utility patents are recorded such that the origin of the patent is determined by the first-named inventor at the time of the grant. Patents per million population are calculated by dividing the number of patents granted to a country in 2006 by that country's population in the same year.

Source: US Patent and Trademark Office (November 2007); United Nations Population Fund, *State of World Population 2006*

1.06 High-tech exports
High-technology exports as a percentage of total exports | 2005 or most recent year available
The value of high-technology exports is expressed as a percentage of the total value of goods and services exports. According to the World Bank, high-technology exports are products with high R&D intensity, as in aerospace, computers, pharmaceuticals, and scientific instruments.

Source: The World Bank, *World Development Indicators Online Database* (December 2007); national sources

1.09 Total tax rate
This variable is a combination of profit tax (% of profits), labor tax and contribution (% of profits), and other taxes (% of profits) | 2007
Source: The World Bank, *Doing Business 2008*

1.10 Time required to start a business
Number of days required to start a business | 2007
Source: The World Bank, *Doing Business 2008*

1.11 Number of procedures required to start a business
Number of procedures required to start a business | 2007
Source: The World Bank, *Doing Business 2008*

Pillar 2: Political and regulatory environment

2.08 Number of procedures to enforce a contract
Number of procedures from the moment the plaintiff files a lawsuit in court until the moment of payment | 2007
Source: The World Bank, *Doing Business 2008*

2.09 Time to enforce a contract
Number of days required to resolve a dispute | 2007
Source: The World Bank, *Doing Business 2008*

Pillar 3: Infrastructure environment

3.01 Telephone lines
Main telephone lines per 100 inhabitants | 2006 or most recent year available
A *main telephone line* is a telephone line connecting the subscriber's terminal equipment to the public switched telephone network and that has a dedicated port in the telephone exchange equipment.

Source: International Telecommunication Union, *World Telecommunication Indicators 2007*

3.02 Secure Internet servers
Secure Internet servers per 1 million inhabitants | 2006
Secure Internet servers are servers using encryption technology in Internet transactions.

Source: The World Bank, *World Development Indicators Online Database* (December 2007)

3.03 Electricity production
Per capita electricity production (kWh) | 2004 or most recent year available
Electricity production is measured at the terminals of all alternator sets in a station. In addition to hydropower, coal, oil, gas, and nuclear power generation, it covers generation by geothermal, solar, wind, and tide and wave energy as well as that from combustible renewables and waste. Production includes the output of electricity plants designed to produce electricity only, as well as that of combined heat and power plants.

Source: The World Bank, *World Development Indicators Online Database* (December 2007)

3.06 Tertiary enrollment
Gross tertiary enrollment | 2005 or most recent year available
According to the World Bank, this corresponds to the ratio of total enrollment, regardless of age, to the population of the age group that officially corresponds to the tertiary education level. Tertiary education, whether or not leading to an advanced research qualification, normally requires, as a minimum condition of admission, the successful completion of education at the secondary level.

Source: UNESCO, Institute for Statistics (June 2007); national sources

3.07 Education expenditure

Education expenditure as a percentage of GNI | 2005
This variable refers to public current operating expenditures in education, including wages and salaries and excluding capital investment in buildings and equipment.

Source: The World Bank, *World Development Indicators Online Database* (December 2007)

Pillar 4: Individual readiness

4.05 Residential telephone connection charge

One-time residential telephone connection charge (US$) as a percentage of GDP per capita | 2005 or most recent year available
This measure refers to the one-time charge involved in applying for basic telephone service for residential purposes.

Source: International Telecommunication Union, *World Telecommunication Indicators 2007*; International Monetary Fund, *World Economic Outlook Database* (October 2007 edition); national sources

4.06 Residential monthly telephone subscription

Residential monthly telephone subscription to the public switched telephone network (US$) as a percentage of monthly GDP per capita | 2005 or most recent year available
Residential monthly telephone subscription refers to the recurring fixed charge for a residential subscriber to the public switched telephone network. The charge should cover the rental of the line but not the rental of the terminal (for example, the telephone set) where the terminal equipment market is liberalized. In some cases, the rental charge includes an allowance for free or reduced-rate call units. If there are different charges for different exchange areas, the largest urban area is used.

Source: International Telecommunication Union, *World Telecommunication Indicators 2007*; International Monetary Fund, *World Economic Outlook Database* (October 2007 edition); national sources

4.07 High-speed monthly broadband subscription

High-speed monthly broadband subscription charge (US$) as a percentage of monthly GDP per capita | 2006
The International Telecommunication Union considers broadband to be any dedicated connection to the Internet of 256 kilobits per second (kb/s) or faster, in both directions. The monthly charge reflects the Internet service provider charge for one month of service. It does not include installation fees or modem rental charges if they are charged separately. Speed expressed in kb/s represents the advertised maximum theoretical download speed and not speeds guaranteed to users. High-speed monthly charge refers to a faster and typically more expensive offer available in the economy.

Source: International Telecommunication Union, *World Information Society Report 2007*; International Monetary Fund, *World Economic Outlook Database* (October 2007 edition); national sources

4.08 Lowest cost of broadband

Lowest sampled cost (US$) per 100 kb/s as a percentage of monthly income (GNI) | 2006
The lowest sampled cost in US dollars per 100 kilobits per second (kb/s) gives the most cost-effective subscription based on criteria of least cost per 100 kb/s. The International Telecommunication Union calculates this cost by dividing the monthly subscription charge in US dollars by the theoretical download speed, and then multiplying by 100. The lowest cost per 100 kb/s across all Internet services providers is used to compute the lowest sampled cost as a percentage of monthly income (GNI).

Source: International Telecommunication Union, *World Information Society Report 2007*

4.09 Cost of mobile telephone call

Cost of 3-minute local call during peak hours (US$) as a percentage of monthly GDP per capita | 2005 or most recent year available

Source: International Telecommunication Union, *World Telecommunication Indicators 2007*; International Monetary Fund, *World Economic Outlook Database* (October 2007 edition)

Pillar 5: Business readiness

5.06 Business telephone connection charge

One-time business telephone connection charge (US$) as a percentage of GDP per capita | 2005 or most recent year available
This measure refers to the one-time charge involved in applying for basic telephone service for business purposes.

Source: International Telecommunication Union, *World Telecommunication Indicators 2007*; International Monetary Fund, *World Economic Outlook Database* (October 2007 edition); national sources

5.07 Business monthly telephone subscription

Business monthly telephone subscription to the public switched telephone network (US$) as a percentage of monthly GDP per capita | 2005 or most recent year available
Business monthly telephone subscription refers to the recurring fixed charge for a business subscriber to the public switched telephone network.

Source: International Telecommunication Union, *World Telecommunication Indicators 2007*; International Monetary Fund, *World Economic Outlook Database* (October 2007 edition); national sources

5.10 Computer, communications, and other services imports

Computer, communications, and other services as percentage of total commercial services imports | 2005 or most recent year available
Computer, communications, and other services include such activities as international telecommunications; portal and courier services; computer data; news-related service transactions between residents and nonresidents; construction services; royalties and license fees; miscellaneous business, professional, and technical services; and personal, cultural, and recreational services. The total volume of computer, communications, and other services imports is divided by the total volume of commercial service imports, defined as the total service imports minus imports of government services not included elsewhere.

Source: The World Bank, *World Development Indicators Online Database* (December 2007)

Pillar 6: Government readiness

6.04 E-Government Readiness Index

The E-Government Readiness Index assesses e-government readiness based on website assessment, telecommunications infrastructure, and human resource endowment | 2007

Source: United Nations, *Global E-Government Survey 2008*. The report is available at:http://www.unpan.org/egovkb/global_reports/08report.htm

Pillar 7: Individual usage

7.01 Mobile telephone subscribers
Mobile telephone subscribers per 100 inhabitants | 2006 or most recent year available

The term *subscribers* refers to users of mobile telephones subscribing to an automatic public mobile telephone service that provides access to the public switched telephone network using cellular technology. This can include analogue and digital cellular systems but should not include noncellular systems. Subscribers to fixed wireless, public mobile data services, or radio paging services are not included.

Source: International Telecommunication Union, *World Telecommunication Indicators 2007*

7.02 Personal computers
Personal computers per 100 inhabitants | 2005 or most recent year available

According to the World Bank, *personal computers* are self-contained computers designed to be used by a single individual.

Source: International Telecommunication Union, *World Telecommunication Indicators 2007*

7.03 Broadband Internet subscribers
Total broadband Internet subscribers per 100 inhabitants | 2006 or most recent year available

The International Telecommunication Union considers broadband to be any dedicated connection to the Internet of 256 kilobits per second (kb/s) or faster, in both directions. Broadband subscribers refers to the sum of DSL, cable modem, and other broadband (for example, fiber optic, fixed wireless, apartment LANs, satellite connections) subscribers.

Source: International Telecommunication Union, *World Telecommunication Indicators 2007*

7.04 Internet users
Internet users per 100 inhabitants | 2006 or most recent year available

Internet users are people with access to the worldwide network.

Source: International Telecommunication Union, *World Telecommunication Indicators 2007*

7.05 Internet bandwidth
International Internet bandwidth (mB/s) per 10,000 inhabitants | 2006 or most recent year available

This measure shows the total capacity of international Internet bandwidth in megabits per second.

Source: International Telecommunication Union, *World Telecommunication Indicators 2007*

Pillar 9: Government usage

9.05 E-Participation Index
The E-Participation Index assesses the quality, relevance, usefulness and the willingness of government websites for providing online information and participatory tools and services to the people | 2007

Source: United Nations, *Global E-Government Survey 2008*. The report is available at: http://www.unpan.org/egovkb/global_reports/08report.htm

About the Authors

Hessa Al-Jaber

Hessa Al-Jaber is Secretary General of ictQATAR (the Supreme Council of Information and Communication in Qatar), whose main responsibilities include drafting telecommunications-related legislation and regulations as well as defining, maintaining, and implementing a national ICT vision, strategy, and master plan aimed at enabling the socioeconomic development of the nation. She brings to her role a wealth of business and academic experience in ICT development. Prior to becoming Secretary General, Dr Al-Jaber was a member of the Strategic ICT Committee responsible for shaping Qatar's national ICT strategy. Dr Al-Jaber was previously the IT adviser for Qtel and was Chair of the Computer Science Department of Qatar University; she has worked with other leading Qatari institutions, including Hamad General Hospital. Dr Al-Jaber currently sits on several boards, including the Board of Regents of Qatar University, the Board of Governors of the American School of Doha, and the newly established Qatar Financial Markets Authority. Most recently, she was the Chairperson of the World Telecommunication Development Conference 2006 held in Doha. She studied at Kuwait University before completing her Master's degree and Doctorate in Computer Science at George Washington University, Washington DC. A co-author of several publications and academic papers, Dr Al-Jaber has presented her research at conferences and symposia in the Middle East, the United States, and Korea.

Scott C. Beardsley

Scott Beardsley is a Director at McKinsey & Company's Brussels Office. Since joining the firm in 1989, he has been particularly active in helping clients around the world on a range of strategy, regulation, reputation and stakeholder management, performance transformation, and sales and marketing topics in the telecommunications, technology, and media sectors, and has recently led a variety of internal research initiatives. Over the past decade he has served many fixed and mobile telephone companies in emerging economies in the Middle East and Africa, Eastern Europe, Latin America, and Asia, in addition to numerous telecommunications firms and a leading global equipment provider in the West. He is a world leader of McKinsey's Telecommunications Practice, and formally leads McKinsey's Strategy Practice in Europe, the Middle East, and Africa. A frequent author and public speaker, he has written extensively on a variety of telecommunications, broadband, media, and strategy topics. He has co-authored chapters in several editions of the *Global Information Technology Report* series and delivered presentations on digital readiness and telecommunications sector reform, as well as the future of telecommunications regulation. Prior to joining McKinsey, Mr Beardsley was Editor and Marketing Manager at the MIT Sloan Management Review; he also worked in the strategic sales and product marketing functions for Advanced Micro Devices and Analog Devices of the semiconductor industry. He was a Henry S. Dupont III Scholar (highest honors) for outstanding academic performance at the MIT Sloan School of Management, where he graduated with an MBA in Corporate Strategy and Marketing. He holds a Bachelor of Science degree in Electrical Engineering magna cum laude from Tufts.

Ilke Bigan

Ilke Bigan is an Associate Partner at McKinsey & Company's Istanbul Office. He joined McKinsey in 1998 and worked in Turkey, Italy, Germany, the United Kingdom, Greece, and the Middle East. Mr Bigan transferred to McKinsey's Munich Office for a year in 2003. His primary industry focus is telecommunications, both mobile and integrated, where he serves clients on a wide range of topics including organization, process design, product development, pricing, and regulatory strategy. His geographical reach covers both developed and emerging markets. Mr Bigan is also a member of McKinsey & Company's Telecommunications Practice. In addition, he has developed extensive experience working with clients from the petroleum, high-tech, media, and retail sectors. He holds an MBA from the Kellogg School of Management in the United States with a concentration in Strategy and Finance, and a BA in Economics from Bilkent University in Turkey, both with high honors and distinction.

David Boyer

David Boyer is a Chief Architect in the Unified Communications Soft Clients Department at Avaya. His current responsibilities include the Avaya Presence Server and Avaya One X Communicator architecture and design. He spent more than 17 years as a researcher at AT&T, Bellcore (Telcordia), Lucent Technologies, and Avaya before moving to the Avaya CTO organization and then to the Avaya Unified Communications Division, where he served as the Avaya Presence Architect and worked with FMC systems. At Telcordia, he served as Director of the Video Networking Department and of the Wireless Networked Applications Department, where he developed middleware infrastructure, application, and technology for video object-based conferencing. At Lucent and Avaya, he worked on middleware services and applications for presence-based systems. He also developed a collaborative video environment and a supply chain exception conferencing system. Mr Boyer holds or has applied for 19 patents and has more than 40 publications to his credit. He received an R&D 100 award in 1992 and the ACM Multimedia Conference Best Paper Award in 1991 for his work on the Bellcore Personal Presence System. He holds a BS in Biomedical Engineering from Duke University and an MS in Computer Science from North Carolina State University.

Sandor Boyson

Sandor Boyson has significant expertise in technology management and supply chain management, with over 20 years of experience in strategic technology planning, systems development/management, and enterprise-wide process integration. He has served as a technology and strategy consultant to public organizations as varied as the World Bank and the US Department of Defense as well as private-sector organizations such as Kellogg Brown & Root, Allied Signal, Hughes Network Systems, and the *Chicago Tribune*. He currently serves as Co-Director, Supply Chain Management Center; and Research Professor at the Robert H. Smith School of Business at the University of Maryland, College Park. He was also the Chief Information Officer for the Business School for four years and built a comprehensive Web-based community and learning environment for the school that now serves the United States, Europe, and Asia. His research on technology and supply chain management has been highlighted in two books— *Logistics and the Extended Enterprise* (1999), which has been translated into Chinese and published by the China Machinery Press; and *In Real Time* (Praeger, 2005); as well as in numerous professional outlets. In addition to his supply chain and technology work, he has been a consultant on technology-led development to executive branch decision makers in Puerto Rico, North Carolina in the United States, Indonesia, Panama, and Gaza/West Bank. Dr Boyson has a Master of Philosophy degree from the Institute of Development Studies, the University of Sussex in the United Kingdom, and a PhD from the University of Sussex in the area of Science and Technology Studies.

Matt Bross

Matt Bross is Chief Technology Officer at BT Group, responsible for setting technology strategy and the vision and direction of innovation across BT. In his role at BT, Mr Bross is responsible for BT's Research and Venturing efforts globally. He is the leading force behind BT's multibillion pound 21st Century Network transformation, and is leading innovation for BT. He has served on the boards of many companies, providing strategic technology and business leadership. He has been a Commissioner of the Global Information Infrastructure Commission (GIIC) since December 2005, as Regional Director for Europe. GIIC is a confederation of CxO-level executives engaged in the development, deployment, operation, financing, and use of ICT services and products. Mr Bross is also a Board Member of the Alliance for Telecommunications Industry Solutions (ATIS), a United States–based body focusing on the development and promotion of technical and operations standards for the communications and related information technology industry globally. Mr Bross is the Chairman of the Board of Advisors for the Global Innovation Research Centre (GIRC), the organization that works to foster innovation in Malaysian government, industry, and education sectors. He is widely regarded as a visionary speaker on media and telecommunications issues. In recognition of this, Mr Bross was recently awarded a Stevie International Business Award for Best MIS & IT Executive.

Soumitra Dutta

Soumitra Dutta is the Roland Berger Chaired Professor of Business and Technology and Dean of External Relations at INSEAD. His current research is on technology strategy and innovation at both corporate and national policy levels. His latest books, besides this *Report*, are *The Global Information Technology Report 2006–2007: Connecting to the Networked Economy* (Palgrave, March 2007) and *The Information Society in an Enlarged Europe* (Springer, February 2006). Dr Dutta has authored seven other books and has won several awards for research and pedagogy. He is actively involved in policy development at national and European levels. He is currently a member of the Advisory Committee for ICT for the Government of Qatar and has advised other national governments on ICT policy issues. He is also the Chairman of the European Commission's Europe Innova panel on Innovation in the ICT sector. His research has been showcased in the international media and he has taught in and consulted with international corporations across the world. He is a Fellow of the World Economic Forum.

Dana Eleftheriadou

Dana Eleftheriadou is a Graduate Computer Engineer at the University of Patras in Greece and holds a Master's degree in Business Administration from the Brussels Business School. She is working in the Enterprise Directorate General of the European Commission as the Coordinator of eBSN (European eBusiness Support Network for SMEs), a network of policymakers and experts on public policies supporting the innovative use of ICT and e-business by European SMEs. Previous positions included engaging in the European Union–United States dialogue on e-commerce in addition to dealing with various e-business issues including the sectoral impact of e-business, targeted awareness activities concerning e-business, the promotion of e-business among SMEs, and benchmarking e-business policies as well as the liaison with industry and international forums, such as the Organisation for Economic Co-operation and Development (OECD), the TransAtlantic Business Dialogue (TABD), and the World Trade Organization (WTO).

Luis Enriquez

Luis Enriquez is a Principal at McKinsey & Company's Brussels Office, where he has worked primarily in areas of corporate finance, strategy, and telecommunications. He has extensive experience in telecommunications, focusing on corporate finance, strategy, operations, and regulation. Prior to joining McKinsey, Dr Enriquez also worked extensively on telecommunications liberalization and regulation issues. In 1994, he assisted the Czech Ministry of Finance in developing price regulations to support the privatization of Cesky Telecom (then SPT Telecom), and taught courses and seminars for the ministry staff and other industry stakeholders. He has participated in proceedings on liberalization and privatization in Mexico, Argentina, Poland, and other Eastern European and Latin American countries. He assisted the Chief Economist of the US Federal Communications Commission in areas including interconnection, universal service subsidies, and developing dispute-resolution mechanisms, and has worked with US incumbents and new entrants on various regulatory topics. Dr Enriquez has a BA degree in Economics from Harvard University and a PhD in Economics from the University of California at Berkeley, where he focused on the economic dynamics of interconnection among telecommunications networks.

Mehmet Güvendi
Mehmet Güvendi is a Principal at McKinsey & Company's Istanbul Office. He joined the firm in March 1999. During his career at McKinsey, he has worked in strategy, regulation, operations, and IT topics in many different sectors. In particular, he has extensive experience in regulation in the telecommunications sector, where he has helped clients in regions such as Europe, Asia, and the Middle East. Before joining McKinsey, Mr Güvendi was an IT Group Manager at Procter & Gamble Company. He worked as an IT Manager for six years in Western Europe, North America, and Turkey. He led multi-functional global process design teams for planning, and managed several major global pilot projects. Mr Güvendi also managed a data center and a multinational communications networks, and was in charge of IT systems and operations at several manufacturing sites. He is a member of the Prime Ministry Telecom Special Expertise Committee for the development of the Turkish National Five-Year Development Plan. He sits on the Advisory Council of Bilkent University Industrial Engineering Department. Mr Güvendi holds a BS degree with high honors in Industrial Engineering from Bilkent University in Turkey.

Henning Kagermann
Henning Kagermann is Chairman of the Executive Board of SAP AG and Chief Executive Officer (CEO). Together with Hasso Plattner, Co-Founder of SAP, he was Co-Chairman of the SAP Executive Board and CEO from 1998 to 2003. Following Plattner's election as Chairman of the SAP Supervisory Board in May 2003, Kagermann became sole Chairman of the SAP Executive Board and CEO. Dr Kagermann has overall responsibility for SAP's strategy and business development, and also oversees the areas of development, global communications, internal audit, and top talent management. Dr Kagermann joined SAP in 1982 and was initially responsible for product development in the areas of cost accounting and controlling. Later, he oversaw the development of all administrative solutions, including human resources, as well as industry-specific development for banking, insurance, the public sector, and health care. His duties included finance and administration as well as the management of all SAP regions. He has been a member of the SAP Executive Board since 1991. Dr Kagermann studied physics in Brunswick and Munich. He received his Doctorate in Theoretical Physics from the Technical University of Brunswick in Germany, and was promoted to Professor there in 1985. He taught physics and computer science at the Technical University of Brunswick and the University of Mannheim, both in Germany, from 1980 to1992. Dr Kagermann received an Honorary Doctorate from the University of Magdeburg in Germany, and was a Trustee of the Technical University of Munich from 2001 to 2007. He is also a member of the honorary senate of the Foundation Lindau Nobel Prizewinners Meetings.

Dr Kagermann is currently a member of the supervisory boards of Deutsche Bank AG and Münchener Rückversicherungs-Gesellschaft AG (Munich Re), as well as of Nokia.

Can Kendi
Can Kendi is an Engagement Manager at McKinsey & Company's Istanbul Office. He joined McKinsey in 2003 and has undertaken several projects, mainly in the telecommunications, banking, and petroleum sectors, serving clients in Turkey, Greece, Italy, and the Middle East on a broad range of strategic, regulatory, finance, operational, and organizational issues. Prior to joining McKinsey, Mr Kendi worked as a Construction Manager in Tepe-Turner Steiner JV in İsbank Headquarters Project, and as a Business Development Manager in Akfen Holding, covering the construction, energy, and real estate sectors. He has developed extensive experience working in Turkey, the Middle East, and Central Europe. Mr Kendi holds an MBA degree from the University of Michigan in the United States with a concentration in Corporate Strategy and Finance and an M.Sc. degree in Construction Engineering and Management from Illinois Institute of Technology in the United States, both with high distinction, as well as a BA degree in Architecture from Middle East Technical University in Turkey.

Bruno Lanvin
Bruno Lanvin is Executive Director at INSEAD, eLab, managing INSEAD's teams in Fontainebleau, Singapore, and Abu Dhabi. From 2000 to 2007, Dr Lanvin worked for the World Bank, where he was inter alia Senior Advisor for E-strategies and Regional Coordinator (Europe and Central Asia) for ICT and e-government issues. He also headed the Capacity Building Practice of the World Bank's Global ICT Department, and was Chairman of the Bank's e-Thematic Group. From June 2001 to December 2003, he was the Manager of the Information for Development Program (infoDev). In 2000, Dr Lanvin was appointed Executive Secretary of the G8 DOT Force. Until then he was Head of Electronic Commerce in the United Nations Conference on Trade and Development (UNCTAD) in Geneva and occupied various senior positions, including Chief of Cabinet of the Director General of the United Nations in New York, and Head of Strategic Planning and later Chief of the SME Trade Competitiveness Unit of UNCTAD/SITE. He was the main drafter, team leader, and editor of *Building Confidence: Electronic Commerce and Development*, published in January 2000. He co-edited the 2003 and 2004 editions of *The Global Information Technology Report* series. He holds a BA in Mathematics and Physics from the University of Valenciennes, an MBA from Ecole des Hautes Etudes Commerciales (HEC), and a PhD in Economics from the University of Paris I (La Sorbonne) in France.

Philip Lay
Philip Lay is a Co-Founder and Managing Director at TCG Advisors. With over 25 years of experience as a successful entrepreneur and executive in the IT industry, Mr Lay works closely with executive teams and boards of technology companies to address strategic challenges affecting their success in the marketplace. For the past eight years, he has also authored and published an email newsletter titled *Under the Buzz* that has a broad readership of technology executives and professionals. He is also an accomplished keynote speaker and panel moderator at national and international conferences.

About the Authors

Miguel Lucas

Miguel Lucas is a Partner at McKinsey & Company's Lisbon Office. He is a leader of the European Telecoms Practice. He joined McKinsey in Lisbon in 1989, where he worked on a variety of projects with a concentration in financial institutions, telecommunications, and transportation. In the telecommunications sector, for wireline players, his experience includes leading the redesign of SMEs strategies and of global organizational structures; supporting the design of a performance measurement system and of an objectives an incentives system for managers of a major European player; supporting the launch of a telecom data attacker; reviewing the voice and data portfolio of the retail front, leading to the launch of flat rates; and supporting the design of a strategy to manage the fixed mobile transition. For wireless players, his experience includes supporting the turnaround of two mobile players, which took in the global revision of the product offer for the residential and corporate segments as well as for the distribution channels; and leading the merge of five regional operators into a national entity at a moment when international attackers were entering the market. Mr Lucas has also been an active developer of telecom knowledge in the regulatory area—where he led projects on the new regulatory framework resulting from the European Directives—in the corporate segment, in pricing and fixed/mobile substitution. Mr Lucas holds a BA in Management from Universidade Católica Portuguesa in Portugal and an MBA from Harvard Business School.

Irene Mia

Irene Mia is Associate Director and Senior Economist with the Global Competitiveness Network at the World Economic Forum. She is also responsible for competitiveness research on Latin America and Iberia. She has written and spoken extensively on issues related to national competitiveness, serving as lead author and editor on a number of regional and topical competitiveness papers and reports; notably, she is the Co-Editor of *The Global Information Technology Report* series. Before joining the Forum, she worked at the headquarters of Sudameris Bank in Paris for a number of years, holding various positions in the international affairs and international trade divisions. Her main research interests are in the field of development, international trade, economic integration (with special reference to the Latin American region), and competitiveness. Dr Mia holds an MA in Latin American Studies from the Institute of Latin American Studies, London University, and a PhD in International Economic and Trade Law from Bocconi University in Italy.

Geoffrey Moore

Geoffrey Moore is a best-selling author, a Managing Director and Co-Founder at TCG Advisors, and a Venture Partner at Mohr-Davidow Ventures (MDV). Recognized as a leading business consultant to companies facing formidable strategic challenges, Dr Moore works with established enterprises in his role as Managing Director at TCG Advisors. He has authored *Dealing with Darwin: How Great Companies Innovate at Every Phase of Their Evolution* and four other books that are required reading at leading business schools. He also serves as an adviser to many of MDV's portfolio companies. Dr Moore, highly regarded as a keynote speaker and panel moderator, is also a Fellow of the World Economic Forum.

Ewan Morrison

Ewan Morrison joined the Cisco Executive Thought Leadership (ETL) as Editor in 2006. His responsibilities include the strategy for and development of content featuring both Cisco's senior executive team and ETL's primary research. He joined Cisco in 2001 on the editorial staff of Cisco's *iQ Magazine,* ultimately serving as Editor-in-Chief before his move to ETL. Mr Morrison has held a variety of writing and editing posts at newspapers, mainstream consumer magazines, and corporate publications over his 20-year editorial career. He received his BA in English from the University of California, Riverside.

Ng Cher Keng

Ng Cher Keng is the Director for Strategic Planning in the Infocomm Development Authority (IDA) in Singapore. The Strategic Planning Division in IDA monitors and analyzes the local and global ICT market trends and developments so as to provide inputs for policy review and decision-making. Ms Ng holds a BA degree in Economics and a Master of Public Policy from the National University of Singapore.

Ong Ling Lee

Ong Ling Lee is the Assistant Director for Strategic Planning in the Infocomm Development Authority (IDA) in Singapore. Ms Ong holds a BEng degree in Engineering from the Nanyang Technological University and an MBA from the MIT Sloan School of Management.

Carlos Osorio-Urzúa

Carlos Osorio-Urzúa is Professor of Innovation and the Director of the Master in Innovation at the Adolfo Ibáñez School of Management. He is also an Affiliate at the Berkman Center for Internet & Society at Harvard Law School, and a Research Fellow at Orkestra, the Basque Institute of Competitiveness. His current teaching and research work focus on the process of innovation and collaborative networks, and the architecture of complex systems. He has published several works in privacy and security-enhancing technologies, digital government, and the economics of information technologies. Among these, he authored, jointly with Jane Fountain, the first study about the impact of digital government in the United States, as well as the first econometric study about the economic impact of broadband in the United States with Marvin Sirbu, Sharon Gilett, and William Lehr. Dr Osorio-Urzúa has been a Visiting Scientist at MIT Media Lab and a Research Associate at the Center for International Development at Harvard University. He holds a PhD in Technology, Management and Policy and a Master in Technology and Policy from the Massachusetts Institute of Technology, a Master in Public Policy from Harvard's John F. Kennedy School of Government earned as Fulbright Scholar, and a B.Sc. in Industrial Engineering from the University of Chile.

Pamela S. Passman

Pamela Passman is Microsoft's Corporate Vice President and Deputy General Counsel, leading Microsoft's Global Corporate Affairs function. She oversees four main missions: to provide regulatory counsel to business groups and develop corporate positions on public policy issues, such as intellectual property rights, privacy, internet security and safety, international trade, accessibility, and telecommunications; to strengthen government and industry relations; to develop partnerships with governments, international organizations, nonprofits, and industry; and to oversee Microsoft's community and philanthropic investments and outreach. Ms Passman also has leadership responsibilities for Microsoft's cross-company, global corporate citizenship efforts and Microsoft Unlimited Potential, a commitment to bring the benefits of technology to the next 5 billion people. From October 1996 through April 2002, Ms Passman served in Tokyo as Associate General Counsel responsible for Microsoft's Law and Corporate Affairs groups in Japan, Korea, Taiwan, and China, including Hong Kong. Prior to joining Microsoft, she was with Covington & Burling, an international law firm based in Washington, DC. She also practiced for two years in Japan with Nagashima & Ohno and served as Special Counsel to the Office of Political and Economic Research, Executive Office of the President of Itochu Corporation. Ms Passman is a member of the Executive Committee of the Board of the Information Technology Industry Council and serves on the boards of Business for Social Responsibility, the Seattle Art Museum, and the National Bureau of Asian Research. She is a member of the Council on Foreign Relations and the Pacific Council on International Policy. Ms Passman is a graduate of Lafayette College and the University of Virginia School of Law. She was also a recipient of a one-year Thomas J. Watson Foundation grant for independent research in Japan.

Robert Pepper

Robert Pepper is Senior Managing Director, Global Advanced Technology Policy, at Cisco. He leads a team directing Cisco's global agenda for advanced technology policy in areas such as broadband, IP-enabled services, wireless, security, privacy, and ICT development. He joined Cisco in 2005 from the US Federal Communications Commission, where he served as Chief of the Office of Plans and Policy and Chief of Policy Development beginning in 1989. His focus was on telecommunications regulation, spectrum policy, and policies promoting the development of the Internet. Before joining the government, he held faculty appointments at the Universities of Pennsylvania, Iowa, and Indiana, and was a Research Affiliate at Harvard University. He serves on the Board of Directors of the US Telecommunications Training Institute (USTTI), advisory boards for Columbia University and Michigan State University, and is a Communications Program Fellow at the Aspen Institute. He is a member of the US Department of Commerce's Spectrum Management Advisory Committee and the UK Ofcom Spectrum Advisory Board. Dr Pepper received his BA and PhD from the University of Wisconsin-Madison.

Enrique J. Rueda-Sabater

Enrique J. Rueda-Sabater joined Cisco in 2006 and is currently Director, Strategy and Business Development for Emerging Markets. His role involves working on a unique "win-win" strategy: Cisco's business in emerging markets will grow inasmuch as its activities help those countries to harness the potential of IT and network connectivity for economic growth, competitiveness, and social inclusion. Before joining Cisco, Mr Rueda-Sabater spent two decades at the World Bank. His last role was as Director of Strategy and Integrated Risk Management. Earlier stages in his World Bank career included policy roles, fund-raising activities, and operational work with countries in East Asia, Africa, and the former Soviet Union. He is a Spanish national with degrees in Business and Economics. He worked for Procter & Gamble early in his career and has lectured for academic, think tank, and business audiences around the world (including on his work on Global Scenarios for 2020). He is now Vice-Chair of the nonprofit Center for Transformation and Strategic Initiatives.

Sergio Sandoval

Sergio Sandoval is an Engagement Manager at McKinsey & Company's Brussels Office. Since joining the firm in 2001, he has been serving clients in Europe, the Middle East, and Asia on strategy, regulation, and stakeholder management topics in the telecommunications, banking, and electricity sectors. He is also a member of McKinsey's Strategy Practice, where he focuses on developing knowledge around key regulatory topics. Prior to joining McKinsey, Mr Sandoval was an Advisor to the Colombian Minister of Finance on macroeconomic policy matters. Additionally, he worked as a Macroeconomic Advisor to the President of the Republic of Colombia. Mr Sandoval holds a Bachelor of Science in Economics (highest honors) and a Master of Science in Macroeconomics (highest honors) from Los Andes University in Colombia. He also holds an MBA (highest honors) from Solvay Business School in Belgium.

Ashish Sharma

Ashish Sharma is an Engagement Manager at McKinsey & Company's Singapore Office. Mr Sharma has extensively worked with multiple regulators around the globe, specifically in emerging markets in Asia and the Middle East, in revising regulation to particularly encourage the growth of broadband. He has also worked with numerous mobile, fixed, and cable operators in the areas of market strategy, operations, and network technology migration. Prior to joining McKinsey, Mr Sharma worked both in industry and consulting. He has an MBA from the Indian Institute of Management in Kolkata, and a Bachelor degree with honors in Math from the University of Delhi. He has lived and worked in countries including Singapore, India, and the United States.

Tanya Tang

Tanya Tang is an Assistant Manager at the Policy and Competition Development Group of the Infocomm Development Authority (IDA) in Singapore, which looks at policy issues arising from the rapid development of ICT technologies and markets and recommends national ICT policy frameworks for the use of ICT systems and services in Singapore. Ms Tang was previously part of the IDA's iN2015 Secretariat, which coordinated the formulation and launch of iN2015, Singapore sixth ICT master plan. She holds a BA degree in Economics from the University of Chicago and an MA degree in International Policy Studies from Stanford University.

Oleg Timchenko

Oleg Timchenko is an Associate Principal at McKinsey & Company's Kiev Office. Since joining the firm in 1999, he has worked with clients in the metals, transportation, banking, telecom, and retail industries. His recent work has been primarily in the telecommunications sector. Prior to joining McKinsey, Mr Timchenko worked with United Financial Group as an Equity Analyst. He holds an MBA degree from the Wharton School, University of Pennsylvania, where he was designated Palmer Scholar, and a BA and MA in International Economics from the Institute of International Relations, Kiev National University.

Graham Vickery

Graham Vickery is Head of the Information Economy Group in the Information, Computer and Communications Policy Division at the Organisation for Economic Co-operation and Development (OECD), covering information technology, e-business, and the ICT industry. He has authored numerous OECD publications on the information economy, technology strategies, and government policies. He holds a BA in Economics from the University of Melbourne and a PhD in Chemistry from the University of Adelaide in Australia.

Sacha Wunsch-Vincent

Sacha Wunsch-Vincent is an Economist in the Information, Computer and Communications Policy Division at the Organisation for Economic Co-operation and Development (OECD) in Paris. He has recently authored an OECD study about the role of China in the ICT industry and a series of OECD studies on digital broadband content. He holds a Master's degree in International Economics from the University of Maastricht and a PhD in Economics from the University of St Gallen in Switzerland. He was a Visiting Fellow at the Institute for International Economics, and teaches International Economics at Sciences Po in Paris and the World Bank Institute.

Partner Institutes

Albania
Institute for Contemporary Studies (ISB)
Artan Hoxha, President
Elira Jorgoni, Senior Expert and Project Manager
Denalada Kuzumi, Researcher

Algeria
Centre de Recherche en Economie Appliquée pour le Développement (CREAD)
Youcef Benabdallah, Assistant Professor
Yassine Ferfera, Director

Argentina
IAE—Universidad Austral
Marcelo Paladino, Vice Dean

Armenia
Economy and Values Research Center
Manuk Hergnyan, Chairman
Sevak Hovhannisyan, Senior Research Associate
Anna Makaryan, Research Associate

Australia
Australian Industry Group
Nicholas James, Economist
Tony Pensabene, Associate Director, Economics & Research
Heather Ridout, Chief Executive

Austria
Austrian Institute of Economic Research (WIFO)
Karl Aiginger, Director
Gerhard Schwarz, Coordinator, Survey Department

Azerbaijan
Azerbaijan Marketing Society
Fuad Aliyev, Executive Director
Ashraf Hajiyev, Project Coordinator
Saida Talibova, Consultant

Bahrain
Bahrain Competitiveness Council
Jawad Habib, Member

Bahrain Economic Development Board
Rima Al Kilani, Director, International Marketing

Bangladesh
Centre for Policy Dialogue (CPD)
Debapriya Bhattacharya, Executive Director
Khondaker Golam Moazzem, Research Fellow
Mustafizur Rahman, Research Director

Barbados
Arthur Lewis Institute for Social and Economic Studies, University of West Indies (UWI)
Andrew Downes, Director

Belgium
Vlerick Leuven Gent Management School
Lutgart Van den Berghe, Professor, Executive Director and Chairman, Competence Centre Entrepreneurship, Governance and Strategy
Harry P. Bowen, Professor of Economics and International Business
Bieke Dewulf, Associate, Competence Centre Entrepreneurship, Governance and Strategy

Benin
Micro Impacts of Macroeconomic Adjustment Policies (MIMAP) Benin
Epiphane Adjovi, Business Coordinator
Maria-Odile Attanasso, Deputy Coordinator
Fructueux Deguenonvo, Researcher

Bosnia and Herzegovina
MIT Center, School of Economics and Business in Sarajevo, University of Sarajevo
Zlatko Lagumdžija, Professor
Željko Šain, Executive Director
Jasmina Selimovic, Assistant Director

Botswana
Botswana National Productivity Centre
Dabilani Buthali, Manager, Information and Research Services Department
Thembo Lebang, Executive Director
Omphemetse David Matlhape, Research Consultant

Brazil
Fundação Dom Cabral
Marina Araújo, Research Assistant
Carlos Arruda, International Relations Director and Coordinator of the Innovation Center

Movimento Brasil Competitivo (MBC)
Jorge H. S. Lima, Project Coordinator
José Fernando Mattos, President
Claudio Leite Gastal, Director

Bulgaria
Center for Economic Development
Anelia Damianova, Senior Expert

Burkina Faso
Société d'Etudes et de Recherche Formation pour le Développement (SERF)
Abdoulaye Tarnagda, Director General

Burundi
Center of Scientific Research in Economics (CURDES), National University of Burundi
Ferdinand Bararuzunza, Professor of Economics and Dean of the Faculty of Economic and Management Sciences

Cambodia
Economic Institute of Cambodia
Sok Hach, Director
Tuy Chak Riya, Research Associate
Hang Sambopisith, Researcher

Cameroon
Comité de Compétitivité (Competitiveness Committee)
Lucien Sanzouango, Permanent Secretary

Canada
Institute for Competitiveness and Prosperity
Roger Martin, Chairman and Dean of the Rotman School of Management, University of Toronto
James Milway, Executive Director

Chad
Groupe de Recherches Alternatives et de Monitoring du Projet Pétrole-Tchad-Cameroun (GRAMP-TC)
Antoine Doudjidingao, Researcher
Gilbert Maoundonodji, Director
Celine Nénodji Mbaipeur, Programme Officer

Chile
Universidad Adolfo Ibáñez
Andres Allamand, Dean, School of Government
Catalina Mertz, Director, Institute of Political Economy
Sergio Selman, Project Coordinator

China
Institute of Economic System and Management
National Development and Reform Commission
Zhou Haichun, Deputy Director and Professor
Chen Wei, Research Fellow
Dong Ying, Professor

Colombia
National Planning Department
Orlando Gracia Fajardo, Entrepreneurial Development Director
Víctor Manuel Nieto, Advisor
Carolina Rentería Rodríguez, General Director

Croatia
National Competitiveness Council
Martina Hatlak, Research Assistant
Mira Lenardic, Secretary General

Cyprus
Cyprus College Research Center
Bambos Papageorgiou, Head of Socioeconomic and Academic Research

The Cyprus Development Bank
Maria Markidou-Georgiadou, Manager, International Banking Services Unit and Business Development

Czech Republic
CMC Graduate School of Business
Dagmar Glueckaufova, Interim President and Academic Dean
Daniela Sedlackova, Executive Assistant to the President
Veronika Stejskalova, Coordinator and Graphic Designer

Denmark
Copenhagen Business School
Department of International Economics and Management
Lars Håkanson, Head of Department
Anne Sluhan, Administrative Director

Ecuador
Escuela Superior Politécnica del Litoral (ESPOL)
Escuela de Postgrado en Administración de Empresas (ESPAE)
Virginia Lasio, Acting Director
Juan Tinoco, Project Assistant
Sara Wong, Professor

Egypt
The Egyptian Center for Economic Studies
Hanaa Kheir-El-Din, Executive Director and Director of Research

Estonia
Estonian Institute of Economic Research
Evelin Ahermaa, Head of Economic Research Sector
Marje Josing, Director

Ethiopia
African Institute of Management, Development and Governance
Tegegne Teka, General Manager

Finland
ETLA—The Research Institute of the Finnish Economy
Petri Rouvinen, Research Director
Pasi Sorjonen, Head of the Forecasting Group
Pekka Ylä-Anttila, Managing Director

France
HEC School of Management, Paris
Bertrand Moingeon, Professor, Associate Dean for Executive Education
Bernard Ramanantsoa, Professor, Dean of HEC School of Management

Gambia, The
Gambia Economic and Social Development Research Institute (GESDRI)
Makaireh A. Njie, Director

Georgia
Business Initiative for Reforms in Georgia
Giga Makharadze, Founding Member of the Board of Directors
Tamar Tchintcharauli, Executive Director
Mamuka Tsereteli, Founding Member of the Board of Directors

Germany
WHU—Otto Beisheim School of Management
Michael Frenkel, Chair, Macroeconomics and International Economics

Greece
Federation of Greek Industries
Thanasis Printsipas, Economist, Research and Analysis
Antonis Tortopidis, Coordinator, Research and Analysis

Guatemala
FUNDESA
Edgar A. Heinemann, President of the Board of Directors
Humberto Olavarría, Treasurer of the Board of Directors
Pablo Schneider, Director of the Development Initiative Centre (CIDES)

Guyana
Institute of Development Studies, University of Guyana
Karen Pratt, Research Associate
Clive Thomas, Director

Hong Kong SAR
The Hong Kong General Chamber of Commerce
David O'Rear, Chief Economist

Federation of Hong Kong Industries
Alexandra Poon, Director

Hungary
Kopint-Datorg, Economic Research
Ágnes Nagy, Project Manager
Éva Palócz, Deputy General Director

Iceland
IceTec
Eydís Arnviðardóttir, Information Manager, Innovation Centre
Hallfríður Benediktsdóttir, Information Manager, Innovation Centre
Hallgrímur Jónasson, General Director

India
Confederation of Indian Industry
Tarun Das, Chief Mentor
Ajay Khanna, Deputy Director General
Shamsher S Mehta, Director General

Indonesia
Kadin Indonesia
M.S. Hidayat, Chairman
Tulus Tambunan, Director

Ireland
Competitiveness Survey Group, Department of Economics, University College Cork
Eleanor Doyle
Niall O'Sullivan
Bernadette Power

National Competitiveness Council
Jason Cleary, Researcher
Adrian Devitt, Manager
Ronan Lyons, Economist

Israel
Manufacturers' Association of Israel (MAI)
Shraga Brosh, President
Dan Catarivas, Director, Foreign Trade and International
  Relations Division
Yehuda Segev, Managing Director

Italy
SDA Bocconi School of Management
Olga E. Annushkina, SDA Professor, Strategic and Entrepreneurial
  Management Department, SDA Bocconi School of Management
Secchi Carlo, Full Professor of Economic Policy, Bocconi University
Paola Dubini, Associate Professor, Bocconi University

Jamaica
Mona School of Business (MSB), University of the West Indies
Patricia Douce, Survey Coordinator
Michelle Tomlinson, Survey Coordinator
Neville Ying, Executive Director and Professor

Japan
Hitotsubashi University, Graduate School of International
  Corporate Strategy (ICS)
in cooperation with Keizai Doyukai
Yoko Ishikura, Professor

Jordan
Ministry of Planning & International Cooperation
Jordan National Competitiveness Team
Amjad Attar, Director

Kazakhstan
Center for Marketing and Analytical Research (CMAR)
Dias Iskakov, Director of the Competitiveness Analysis
  Department

Kenya
Institute for Development Studies, University of Nairobi
Paul Kamau, Research Fellow
Dorothy McCormick, Director and Professor
Walter Odhiambo, Research Fellow

Korea, Republic of
Graduate Institute of Management, Seoul School of Integrated
  Science and Technologies (aSSIST)
Dean Cheol Ho Shin, Professor of Strategy and International
  Business
Shin Hyo Kim, Senior Researcher
So Young Lee, Researcher

Kuwait
Economics Department, Kuwait University
Mohammad Ali Alomar, Assistant Professor
Reyadh Faras, Assistant Professor
Mohammed El-Sakka, Professor

Kyrgyz Republic
Economic Policy Institute "Bishkek Consensus"
Lola Abduhametova, Program Coordinator
Marat Tazabekov, Chairman

Latvia
Institute of Economics, Latvian Academy of Sciences, Riga
Raita Karnite, Director

Lesotho
Mohloli Chamber of Business
Refiloe Kepa, General Manager

Libya
National Economic Strategy
Omran Bukhres, Director and Professor

Monitor Group
Rajeev Singh-Molares, Director

Lithuania
Statistics Lithuania
Ona Grigiene, Head, Economical Survey Division
Algirdas Šemeta, Director General

Luxembourg
Chamber of Commerce of Luxembourg
Jean-Christophe Burkel, Attaché, Economic Department
Carlo Thelen, Member of the Managing Board

Macedonia, FYR
National Entrepreneurship and Competitiveness Council (NECC)
Dejan Janevski, Project Coordinator
Zoran Stavreski, President of the Managing Board
Saso Trajkoski, Executive Director

Madagascar
Centre of Economic Studies, University of Antananarivo
Pépé Andrianomanana, Director
Razato Raharijaona Simo, Executive Secretary

Malaysia
Institute of Strategic and International Studies (ISIS)
Mahani Zainal Abidin, Director-General
Dato' Mohamed Jawhar Hassan, Chairman and Chief Executive
  Officer
Steven C.M. Wong, Assistant Director-General

National Productivity Corporation (NPC)
Dato' Nik Zainiah Nik Abdul Rahman, Director General
Chan Kum Siew, Senior Manager

Mali
Groupe de Recherche en Economie Appliquée et Théorique
  (GREAT)
Massa Coulibaly, Coordinator

Malta
Competitive Malta—Foundation for National Competitiveness
John C. Grech, President
Margrith Lutschg-Emmenegger, Vice President
Adrian Said, Chief Coordinator

Mauritania
Centre d'Information Mauritanien pour le Développement
  Economique et Technique (CIMDET/CCIAM)
Chekroud Ould Bouhake
Aminata Niang

Mauritius
Joint Economic Council of Mauritius
Raj Makoond, Director

Board of Investment, Investmauritius
Dev Chamroo, Director, Investment Promotion
Kevin Ramkaloan, Manager, Investment Promotion

Mexico
Center for Intellectual Capital and Competitiveness
René Villarreal Arrambide, President
René Alejandro Villarreal Ramos, General Director

Instituto Mexicano Para la Competitividad (IMCO)
Roberto Newell Garcia, General Director
Juan Carlos Gonzalez Ibarguen, Analyst
Manuel J. Molano Ruiz, Consultant

Ministry of the Economy
Veronica Orendain De Los Santos, Director of Promotion,
  Office for Investment Promotion
Eduardo J. Solis Sanchez, Chief of the Office for Investment
  promotion

Moldova
Center for Strategic Territorial Development
Ruslan Codreanu, Executive Director
Andrei Smic, Program Coordinator

Mongolia
Open Society Forum (OSF)
Munkhsoyol Baatarjav, Manager of Economic Policy
Erdenejargal Perenlei, Executive Director

Morocco
Université Hassan II
Fouzi Mourji, Professor of Economics

Mozambique
EconPolicy Research Group, Lda.
Peter Coughlin, Director

Namibia
Namibian Economic Policy Research Unit (NEPRU)
Jonathan Adongo, Researcher
Mariama Deen-Swarray, Researcher
Klaus Schade, Acting Director

Nepal
Centre for Economic Development and Administration (CEDA)
Ramesh Chandra Chitrakar, Executive Director
Menaka Rajbhandari Shrestha, Researcher
Santosh Kumar Upadhyaya, Researcher

Netherlands
Erasmus Strategic Renewal Center, Erasmus University Rotterdam
Frans A. J. Van den Bosch, Professor
Henk W. Volberda, Professor

New Zealand
Business New Zealand
Marcia Dunnett, Manager, Business Services
Phil O'Reilly, Chief Executive

The New Zealand Institute
David Skilling, Chief Executive

Nigeria
Nigerian Economic Summit Group (NESG)
Felix Ogbera, Associate Director, Research
Chris Okpoko, Senior Consultant, Research

Norway
BI Norwegian School of Management
Eskil Goldeng, Researcher
Torger Reve, Professor

Oman
The International Research Foundation
Azzan Al Busaidi, Chief Executive Officer
Salem Ben Nasser Al-Ismaily, Chairman

Pakistan
Competitiveness Support Fund
Arthur Bayhan, Chief Executive Officer
Amir Jahangir, Manager, Communications

Paraguay
Centro de Análisis y Difusión de Economia Paraguaya (CADEP)
Dionisio Borda, Director
Jaime Escobar, Research Member
Fernando Masi, Research Member

Peru
Centro de Desarrollo Industrial (CDI), Sociedad Nacional de Industrias
Néstor Asto, Project Director
Luis Tenorio, Executive Director

Philippines
Makati Business Club
Alberto A. Lim, Executive Director
Michael B. Mundo, Chief Economist
Mark P. Opulencia, Deputy Director

Poland
Warsaw School of Economics
Bogdan Radomski, Associate Professor

Portugal
PROFORUM, Associação para o Desenvolvimento da Engenharia
Ilídio António de Ayala Serôdio, Vice President of the Board of Directors

Puerto Rico
Puerto Rico 2000, Inc.
Suzette M. Jimenez, President
Francisco Montalvo Fiol, Project Coordinator

Qatar
Qatari Businessmen Association (QBA)
Issa Abdul Salam Abu Issa, Secretary-General
Bassam Ramzi Massouh, General Manager
Ahmed El-Shaffee, Economist

Romania
Group of Applied Economics (GEA)
Anca Rusu, Program Coordinator
Liviu Voinea, Executive Director

Russian Federation
Bauman Innovation, Academy of National Economy under the Government of the Russian Federation
Alexei Prazdnitchnykh, Principal, Associate Professor

Stockholm School of Economics, Russia
Igor Dukeov, Research Fellow
Carl F. Fey, Associate Dean of Research

Saudi Arabia
National Competitiveness Center (NCC)
Awwad Al-Awwad, Deputy Governor for Investment
Khaldon Mahasen, Manager, Investment Performance Assessment

Senegal
Centre de Recherches Economiques Appliquées (CREA), University of Dakar
Aly Mbaye, Director

Singapore
Economic Development Board
Chua Kia Chee, Head, Research and Statistics Unit
Bernard Nee, Director, Planning

Slovak Republic
Business Alliance of Slovakia (PAS)
Robert Kicina, Executive Director

Slovenia
Institute for Economic Research, Faculty of Economics
Mateja Drnovšek
Art Kovacic
Peter Stanovnik

South Africa
Business Leadership South Africa
Michael Spicer, Chief Executive Officer

Business Unity South Africa
Jerry Vilakazi, Chief Executive Officer
Vic Van Vuuren, Chief Operating Officer

Spain
IESE Business School, International Center for Competitiveness, Anselmo Rubiralta Center for Globalization and Strategy
Eduardo Ballarín, Professor
María Luisa Blázquez, Research Associate

Sri Lanka
Institute of Policy Studies
Indika Siriwardena, Database Manager

The Ceylon Chamber of Commerce
Prema Cooray, Secretary General

Suriname
Institute for Development Oriented Studies (IDOS)
Ashok Hirschfeld
John R.P. Krishnadath, President

Sweden
Center for Strategy and Competitiveness, Stockholm School of Economics
Christian Ketels, Senior Research Fellow
Örjan Sölvell, Professor

Switzerland
University of St. Gallen
Monika Buetler, Director, Economic Department

Syria
Ministry of Economy and Trade
Amer Housni Louitfi, Minister of Economy and Trade

State Planning Commission
Talal Bakfaloni, Deputy Head of State Planning Commission

UNDP Damascus
Nuhad Dimashkiyyah, National Project Director "Towards Changing the Mindset for Competitiveness"

Taiwan, China
Council for Economic Planning and Development, Executive Yuan
Mei Yueh Ho, Chairman
J. B. Hung, Director, Economic Research Department
Chung Chung Shieh, Researcher, Economic Research Department

Tajikistan
The Center for Sociological Research "Zerkalo"
Qahramon Baqozoda, Director and Sociologist
Ol'ga Es'kina, Researcher
Alikul Isoev, Sociologist and Economist

Tanzania
Economic and Social Research Foundation
Irene Alenga, Commissioned Studies Department
Haidari Amani, Executive Director and Professor
Dennis Rweyemamu, Commissioned Studies Department

Thailand
National Economic and Social Development Board
Ampon Kittiampon, Secretary-General
Arkhom Termpittayapaisith, Deputy Secretary-General

Trinidad and Tobago
Arthur Lok Jack Graduate School of Business
Rolph Balgobin, Executive Director
Leslie-Ann Hackett, Engagement Manager, Research
Narisha Khan, Research Associate

Tunisia
Institut Arabe des Chefs d'Entreprises
Majdi Hassen, Executive Counsellor
Chekib Nouira, President

Turkey
TUSIAD Sabanci University Competitiveness Forum
A. Gunduz Ulusoy, Director and Professor
Hande Yegenoglu, Project Specialist

Uganda
Makerere Institute of Social Research, Makerere University
Robert Apunyo, Research Associate
Delius Asiimwe, Senior Research Fellow
Wilson Asiimwe, Graduate Fellow

Ukraine
CASE Ukraine, Center for Social and Economic Research
Dmytro Boyarchuk, Executive Director
Vladimir Dubrovskiy, Leading Economist

United Arab Emirates
Economic and Policy Research Unit, Zayed University
Kenneth Wilson, Director

United States
US Chamber of Commerce
Jana Cary, Senior Director, Marketing Communications
David Hirschmann, Senior Vice President
Susan Reardon, Executive Director, National Chamber Foundation

Uruguay
Universidad ORT
Isidoro Hodara, Professor

Venezuela
CONAPRI—National Council for Investment Promotion
Silvia Castillo, Consulting Manager
Giuseppe Rionero, Research Manager

Vietnam
Central Institute for Economic Management (CIEM)
Dinh Van An, President
Phan Thanh Ha, Deputy Director, Department of Macroeconomic Management
Pham Hoang Ha, Senior Researcher, Department of Macroeconomic Management

Institute for Economic Research of HCMC
Tran Du Lich, Director
Doan Nguyen Ngoc Quynh, Researcher of the Research Management and International Cooperation Department
Du Phuoc Tan, Head of the Research Management and International Cooperation Department

Zambia
Institute of Economic and Social Research (INESOR), University of Zambia
Mutumba M. Bull, Director
Patricia Funjika, Staff Development Fellow, Economics and Business Research
Inyambo Mwanawina, Assistant Director and Coordinator, Economics and Business Research

Zimbabwe
Graduate School of Management, University of Zimbabwe
A.M. Hawkins, Professor

Bolivia, Costa Rica, Dominican Republic, Ecuador, El Salvador, Honduras, Nicaragua, Panama
INCAE Business School Latin American Center for Competitiveness and Sustainable Development
Roberto Artavia, Rector
Arturo Condo, Dean
Marlene de Estrella, Director of External Relations

Latvia, Lithuania
Stockholm School of Economics in Riga
Karlis Kreslins, Associate Professor
Anders Paalzow, Rector

The World Economic Forum would like to thank Cisco Systems, Inc., for their invaluable support of this *Report*.

Cisco Systems, Inc., is the worldwide leader in networking for the Internet. Today networks are an essential part of business, education, government, and home communications, and Cisco Internet protocol–based (IP) networking solutions are the foundation of these networks. Cisco hardware, software, and service offerings are used to create Internet solutions that allow individuals, companies, and countries to increase productivity, improve customer satisfaction, and strengthen competitive advantage. The Cisco name has become synonymous with the Internet, as well as with the productivity improvements that Internet business solutions provide. At Cisco, our vision is to change the way people work, live, play, and learn. Cisco is interested in developing a deeper understanding of the relationship between information and communication technologies and organizational benefits such as innovation, improved productivity, and competitive advantage. Research projects such as *The Global Information Technology Report 2007–2008* help to identify issues and gain insight into these relationships, and apply them to improve productivity and standard of living. Cisco is deeply committed to the mission and values of the World Economic Forum, and is proud to be the sponsor of this *Report*.

Positions in the articles and papers included in this *Report* are in no way endorsed by Cisco Systems, Inc.
To view Cisco's positions on public policy matters, please visit the Government Affairs homepage:
http://www.cisco.com/gov.